entar

Religions
of the World

RELIGIONS OF

THE WORLD

John A. Hardon, S.J.

Associate Professor of Comparative Religion
at Western Michigan University

NP

THE NEWMAN PRESS · WESTMINSTER, MARYLAND · 1963

Imprimi potest: JOANNES R. CONNERY, S.I.
Praepositus Provincialis
Provinciae Chicagiensis, S.I.

April 18, 1963

Nihil obstat: JOANNES SHINNERS, S.T.D.
Censor Deputatus

Imprimitur: JOSEPHUS H. ALBERS
Episcopus Lansingensis

August 10, 1963

To the Memory of Pope John XXIII
whose charity embraced all peoples
of every nation,
and whose wisdom saw the grace of God
active in all souls of every religious
persuasion

BOOKS on comparative religion are mainly of three kinds: the informative, whose purpose is to review in more or less detail the beliefs and practices of various religious systems; the analytic, which presume on the information and go on to evaluate a number of living (or archaic) faiths according to certain normative principles; and the projective, where an author combines factual data and personal theory to anticipate what the future of man's religion may (or should) be like. Typical of the first category is the *Concise Encyclopedia of Living Faiths,* of the second, Joseph Kitagawa's *Religions of the East,* and of the third, Arnold Toynbee's *Christianity Among the Religions of the World.* Each type has its merits and limitations, and the growing output in this field suggests that among the limitations the most natural is the problem of space. There are too many religions with too much history and variety to make an adequate coverage of even the principal ones in a single volume.

The present book belongs to the first category of informative studies on the leading religions of mankind, currently practiced in the world and sufficiently known to allow some comparison of their faith and principles with those of other contemporary religious cultures.

As far as possible, the sources used were those published by representative writers within their own tradition, and always the main reliance was on the sacred books which the religions venerate as their special communication from the Deity or the sages of antiquity. In order to insure maximum accuracy and objectivity, the text of the different chapters was submitted for comment by those who have lived closely with the respective faiths, either as believers or as persons who know the religious persuasion by years of experience and study.

JOHN A. HARDON, S.J.
Western Michigan University

Contents

Religions
of the World

1. Comparative Religion in Perspective

NEVER before were there more urgent reasons to learn about the religious faith and practices of other people, beyond the universal instinct to know all we can about our fellowman in order better to know ourselves.

Translations by Western scholars of the sacred books of the East now reveal to Christians a wealth of customs and creeds that was never dreamed to exist, let alone to have flourished, from the second and third millenium before Christ. But not only the ancient religions of the Orient are coming to full light in the West. The first English translation of the Koran by an Englishman who is a Moslem was published in 1953. Previous translations, he observed, include commentary offensive to Mohammedans, "and almost all employ a style of language which Muslims at once recognize as unworthy. The Koran cannot be translated. That is the belief of the old-fashioned Sheykhs and the view of the present writer." The result is a rendition that does full justice to the Koranic text in a way not previously open to English-speaking readers.

Along with accurate versions of the sacred writings is a mounting supply of contemporary religious literature, outside the ambit of Christianity, now available in European languages. A single book like the *Poems from Iqbal* can do more to familiarize Western people with present-day Islam than a library of commentary by men whose nearest acquaintance with Mohammedanism was the writings of Averroes and Avicenna from the Middle Ages.

A rampant Communism which denies the existence of a personal God and now glories in its conquest of almost a fourth of the world's population is partly the result of ignorance on both

3

sides of the idealism of East and West. It cannot be resisted by force of arms alone but needs the cooperative strength of believers in every religious tradition, notably Christians and Moslems, whose faith is founded on a pure monotheism and who therefore understand Marxism for what it really is, a movement bent on the destruction of the inherent values of Judaeo-Christian civilization.

Among the positive elements of orthodox Confucianism now being tested to the breaking point in Red China is confidence in the basic goodness of human nature. All men alike possess the same moral powers, which direct them to the practice of virtue. "Man's nature," wrote Confucius' disciple Mencius, "is endowed with feelings that impel it toward the good. That is why I call it good. If men do what is not good, the reason does not lie in the basic stuff of which they are constituted." What a difference it would have made for the people of China, now under Communism, if the Christian West had recognized this sound optimism in the soul of a nation ground to the dust in great poverty and looking to others for help in its need.

Above the negative resistance to Communist aggression is the social evolution of the world into an ever more cohesive solidarity. Christians especially are beginning to see in rough outline a development, under the pressure of events, of a constantly narrowing international community. They know that this unification is not fortuitous but willed by the Creator, and that it should culminate in a union of minds and hearts which is held together by a common faith and a common love. To forward the progress of this movement, knowledge of what the disparate elements of the world believe in their relation to the Ultimate in indispensable, at the risk of promoting a vague humanitarianism that may do more harm than good and result in sacrificing values that have been the mainstay of every vital religion worthy of the name.

A graphic example of ineptitude in handling a grave problem is the current one of offering contraception as the best, if not unique, solution to the so-called population explosion. Many of the world's peoples resent America's promotion of contraceptives because it violates their spiritual natures. Burma, for example, is eighty-five per cent Hinayana Buddhist with high ideals of self-sacrificing charity. Its leaders are brutally frank in exposing what they consider self-interest disguised as philanthropy. "American politicians," the

Burmese are told in a Rangoon publication (*The Nation*), "are obsessed with this thing that somebody has called Asia's 'population explosion.' All that we can say is that if (the dispensing of birth control information) is the limit of American ingenuity, inventiveness and technical know-how, they are welcome to use all of it themselves."

Fifty years ago it would have been naive to talk seriously about a dialogue between Christianity and the non-Christian religions of the world. A dialogue presumes a confrontation, where two people or two cultures meet in a common effort to understand the other's viewpoint and profit from a friendly exchange of ideas. But until the present century, about the only contact between Christians and others was on a limited missionary front in Africa and the Far East, and in the cosmopolitan fields of commerce and politics, where religion is the last, or at least not the first consideration.

A great deal has happened since the turn of the century to indicate that a new era was born that would belie the phrase that East is East and West is West and never the twain shall meet. The East and West have met in the most devastating war of history and they will meet again, as one Oriental writer observed, in a conflict that may destroy one or both civilizations unless each learns to respect the other and to share what they have separately received from God.

Any response that Christians make to the non-Christian world must be predicated on the assumption that a new situation has arisen which demands intelligent appraisal and reaction. What is this new encounter with the great religions of the East, Buddhism, Hinduism, Islam, Shinto and Confucianism, to which we are supposed to respond?

In numerous ways the non-Christian cultures of Asia and Africa have entered the stream of Western thought and action to a degree unparalleled at any time in the past. Political interests of the large democracies have made information about India, China, Japan and Katanga necessary for peoples in the West, who not two generations ago were only mildly interested in what the Orientals or Africans believed or what their religion meant to them. Nationalism in many countries, only lately under colonial rule, has become the leaven for a religious renascence, where new countries are being shaped out of old colonies and the ancient faith is made the unifying element of the national structure. This in turn created tensions with minority religions, with special problems for the native Christians who are torn between fidelity to their faith and devotion to the country of their birth.

Apart from these transient factors is the universal shrinking of the earth, with speedy means of communication that practically erase distance between nations. Ideas are never sterile and religious ideas are no exception. Christians are living in the atmosphere of a world that is mainly not Christian, whose principles and institutions are daily projected into their midst to produce an encounter that is as real and potentially dynamic as the spirit of man, communicated from one mind to another and demanding a hearing.

On a lesser scale but also important is the daily meeting between Christian and Judaic cultures in all the major countries of the West, and particularly in America. To insure that the progress made in these relations be consolidated, a mutual and sympathetic knowledge of the other's religious position seems imperative, at the risk of ignoring the depth of conviction on both sides or of indulging in vague platitudes about the golden rule.

Within the Christian tradition, the ecumenical movement has stirred the embers of unitive zeal and aroused leaders in the Catholic, Protestant and Orthodox churches to reunite what was once a single community and heal what is commonly regarded as a sin before God. But Christian reunion cannot begin without previous understanding of the common heritage still retained among the churches, and of the profound differences which divide what should be the one Mystical Body of Christ.

There are grave moral problems that face all countries, particularly the less developed and more densely populated that cannot be solved apart from the ethical foundations on which the respective cultures are built. Symptomatic alleviation is possible on pragmatic grounds and without reference to the religious traditions of the people, but no lasting cure. This demands more than passing knowledge of national traditions and how they can be used to motivate a people that need above all spiritual vigor to meet the crisis of population density and the growing tension between the working and ruling classes.

Leaders in international relations are coming more and more to realize that religious factors cannot be ignored in the study of co-operative world problems. To leave aside the religious dimension on the plea of avoiding prejudice would be to fall into another prejudice and disregard an enormous proportion of the world's cultures.

Thus in an endeavor to understand the cultural values of the Orient and Occident, to bring to light their origins and foundations, to discern their full significance for the people of these two segments of humanity, the religious factor is not only present but dominant. "The metaphysical beliefs held by the men of today may have grown away from the ancestral faith; the values to which these men still hold, the standards with which they comply, spontaneously and often unconsciously, in their individual and community lives, still bear the mark of their origin, and that origin is often to be sought in religious teachings." [1]

Moreover these fundamental messages of various peoples are not reflected only in sacred writings, nor do they give rise solely to rites and beliefs. The day-to-day moral conduct of peoples everywhere is impregnated with religious implications. Intellectual systems often rest on this fund of belief. Through the centuries, it has been illustrated in literature and the arts. Legal systems, too, bear the same imprint. Daily life, no matter how secularized, whether in America or Afghanistan, still offers to the observer a reflection of prescriptions and ideals of religious origin.

Consequently the central place occupied by the religious factor cannot be overlooked if we would arrive at a real understanding of the values of all peoples. Religion, it has been said, is the key of history. It is also the key to appreciating whatever a nation produces, from the ancient monuments of the Pharaohs and inscriptions of the early Chinese kings, to the current art work of Japan or the latest novel in the United States.

For those who believe they possess the fulness of God's revelation, to know about the religious systems of the world is a means of opening their horizon and animating their zeal to communicate what they have with others who are less privileged than they. If the letters of Xavier in the sixteenth century inspired some of the ablest men of Europe to leave home and kindred and go to the Indies, nothing less may be expected of present-day Christians to sacrifice themselves for the millions untouched by the Gospel, once they have learned what the teachings of Christ would mean to those whom we patronizingly call unbelievers. As expressed by Tanaka

Kotaro, convert and chief justice of the supreme court in postwar Japan, "Christianity could be for a reborn Japan her qualification as a member of the world community of peoples, giving us for the first time in our history a sense of Japan's place and mission in the world, and providing a spiritual bond between East and West, as well as a firm basis for world peace." [2]

At the same time, knowledge of other religions offers a balance to that intemperate zeal which had much to do with creating the image of Christianity left in parts of Asia and Africa, as a mixture of colonialism, business and piety, that obscures the true religion of Jesus Christ. Mahatma Gandhi was a friend of Christians all his life; he read the Gospels and the *Imitation of Christ* regularly; and his death by an assassin's bullet was partly the result of this friendship with Christianity that some of his co-religionists resented. Yet Gandhi has written critically of those messengers of the Gospel who see nothing praiseworthy in other peoples, who seek to mold everything according to their own preconceived notions of society, and who are so far removed from reality as seriously to think that Western civilization has a kind of monopoly on culture and human intelligence.

BASIC PRINCIPLES

Any approach to comparing the religions of the world assumes certain principles of judgment, at least as a norm for classification, but more significantly in order to "make sense" of what is otherwise a maze of gods and goddesses, mythological fancies and philosophical theories, all strung together against the background of myriad details for which the average Western reader has no context and almost no point of reference.

The first thing that strikes us as we delve into the living religions of mankind is a fairly clear difference between what is properly their faith or creedal elements and the mythology that surrounds them. It has been correctly pointed out that the mythological side of man's religion belongs to the poetical part of his nature, yet it seems strangely forgotten in some quarters that a myth is the work of imagination and therefore a work of art. Unless these things are appreciated artistically they are not appreciated at all, with the result that long dissertations are written and theories spun about the origin of myths, instead of seeing them as the spontaneous and exuberant expression for certain deep but often undefined beliefs that are the true religious spirit of the people.

How clearly the natives distinguish between faith and mythology may be seen among the primitives who can be most communicative about their mythical traditions but positively silent about their inner beliefs. The same, in different measure, is true of all the great religions of the world. They have their outer shell, which admittedly for many adherents occupies most of their time and attention, and an inner core that even the crudest worshiper vaguely surmises is the heart of his religion.

This inner religious core is surprisingly theistic, in spite of bewildering mixtures of gods and heroes, where even the pantheon of India's thousands of deities centers mainly on the personal diety of preservation, Vishnu, to the extent that Hinduism can almost be summarized as Vishnuism.

Parallel with this inner religious core is another, more familiar inner structure of the main religious cultures excogitated by speculative philosophers. Since most people outside Christianity are not literate, their own faith seldom appears in print and for the most part is known only by and from those who have lived on intimate terms with this "majority mind" in Afro-Asia. All the evidence points to their faith being religious in the fundamental sense of theistic, even where a crude polytheism obscures the belief in a superior (and in that sense supreme) personal divinity. The same is not true of the litterati, whose written productivity has created the impression that what they profess (or doubt and deny) is the common possession of most non-Christians.

These philosophers are often, if not generally, a-theistic, not because they oppose the notion of a personal God but because they are indifferent to Him as eternal law-giver who must be obeyed. Thus, in its extreme form, philosophic Buddhism denies the existence of God altogether and places exclusive emphasis on the deliverance of the immortal soul from the body. Always its attitude is conditioned by an unquestioned belief in re-incarnation which it considers not as something desirable but as the supreme evil. Human life for the theorist of Buddhism is not God's greatest gift to man, but a curse that inheres in the very nature of things. Tangible matter and the body are a perpetual drag on the soul, from which the soul longs to be freed. Moreover the deathless condition which is the soul's natural habitat is not considered something we receive on trust from an external divinity, but something that can be experienced here and now, given the right method and dispositions.

An extreme emphasis on the experience of immortality, where all distinction falls away from the experiencing subject, led certain Indian philosophers of the Vedanta school to identify the human soul in this deep unity with the ultimate and impersonal source and ground of the universe. In fact, Vedanta would identify the soul with the godhead and claim that once this condition is empirically realized the whole phenomenal world is seen to be an illusion.

But Vedanta is not the religion of most Hindus, even as Zen is not the system of most Buddhists. Unless this distinction between Oriental philosophy, which tends to monism and atheism, and Oriental religion in the hearts of the masses is kept in mind, the most extravagant theories of individual (although influential) thinkers will be saddled on the less pretentious but more theistic faith of the uneducated and unphilosophical believers.

Reflecting on the datum of man's religious history, two principal positions have been taken by comparative religionists. The one sees religious culture as only another phase of the evolutionary process of development from the less to the more perfect. According to this hypothesis, monotheism is a late phenomenon of religion. The trend towards monotheism, it is held, was gradual and had preparatory stages. The first stage was what is called monarchianism. After the analogy of human society, one deity was exalted above the rest and became king of the gods. A more advanced stage was that of monolatry, where other gods were admitted to exist, but worship was limited to one.

In the evolutionary theory, the earliest attempt to introduce monotheism, in this case a solar monotheism, was that of the Egyptian Amenhotep IV, in the fourteenth century B.C. His efforts failed because of the popular pressure in favor of many gods. More impressive was the monotheism of Zarathustra about eight hundred years before the Christian era. However Zoroastrianism fell into the trap of a rigid dualism, in which all the goodness in the world comes from a good Deity and all the wickedness from an ultimate principle of evil.

Finally, by the time of the eighth century prophets of Israel, the earlier monolatry became a true monotheism, and the dualism of the Avesta was cleared away. Jewish monotheistic universalism finds its clearest expression in the work of Deutero-Isaias, from which heritage of the Hebrew religion Christianity derived its pure monotheism, and the same influence is manifest in the religion of Islam.

Needless to say there are facts in religious history to support this theory, certainly the monotheistic influence of Judaism on its contemporaries and of Christianity since the time of Christ. But that is a far cry from maintaining that the hypothesis of a primitive monotheism lacks foundation and is intrinsically improbable.

However, the real issue involved is not whether cultural anthropology has established on scientific grounds the existence of a primitive monotheism, from which later polytheisms are decadent deviations. The question is whether man's religious history is to be interpreted on *a priori* grounds of an evolutionary hypothesis, postulating a strict natural continuum from earlier to later stages, where everything that follows is explained by what precedes, and allowing for no supernatural breakthrough on the part of God as master of the universe and provident Lord of creation.

Judaeo-Christianity believes that historic religion is more than a natural phenomenon, rising on its creedal side from animism, through polytheism, to the monotheism of the Hebrews and Christians; and on its ritual side from magic and fetishism, through tabu, ancestor worship and tribal kings to propitiation of nature spirits, culminating in adoration of the one invisible God. Aside from the curious fact that most contemporary religions are not purely monotheistic, which is hard to explain on the premise of a "natural" development of human culture, the Judaeo-Christian principle of religious origins shows from provable history that God has, indeed, broken through the sequence of world events to communicate truths and establish norms which transcend the capacity of the human mind to conceive naturally or implement by its own genius. This revelation was given, already in time immemorial, to the first progenitors of man, continued through centuries of pre-Mosaic history and other centuries from Moses to the last of the prophets. It reached its highest expression in the time of Christ, in the person of Jesus of Nazareth and His apostles, and closed, as to content but not interpretation, around the end of the first century of the Christian era.

The coexistence of these two concepts of religious history, the naturalistic or continuous and the supernatural or revelational, dates back to the early period of Christianity. Always the focus was the acceptance or denial of miraculous intervention on the part of God to communicate the mysteries of faith to His people, and their responsive obligation to believe His message and follow the precepts which He laid down. In the middle of the second century, Justin the Martyr wrote an *Apology* to the Emperor Antoninus Pius, answering the Roman objection that perhaps, "the one whom we call Christ was a man born of men, and has worked what we call miracles through the art of magic, and thus appeared to be the Son of God," without valid claim. His reply was an elaborate defense of the holiness of Christ, foretold by the prophets and fulfilled during His mortal life. The argument was that no one in league with the evil spirit would be the object of ages of prophetic prediction, or have lived so closely united with God, and have been so devoted to the welfare of His fellowman.[3]

Before the end of the second century, the Roman Celsus concentrated on the resurrection of Christ which he recognized as pivotal in the new religion. The resurrection of Jesus, he said, should be equated with the stories of heroes in pagan mythology; with the story of Zamolxis who dwelt beneath the earth for three years and returned to the surface alive, of Rhamsinitus in Egypt who played at dice with Demeter in Hades and returned to the upper world with a golden napkin he received from her as a gift, or Orpheus among the Odrysians, Protesilaus in Thessaly, Hercules at Cape Taeranus, or Theseus and other like fables.

Has anyone who was really dead ever risen with a veritable body? When others relate such stories, you brand them as specious and mythical, and do you explain your own myth as beautiful and believable, telling us how he (Jesus) spoke in a loud voice when dying on the cross, how the earth shook and darkness fell, and, though unable to help himself during life, arose from the dead and showed the marks of his punishment and the place where his hands had been pierced? Who beheld all of this? A half-frantic woman, as you state, and some other one, perhaps, of those who were engaged in the same system of delusion.[4]

Origen answered the charge through a closely-reasoned analysis of the historical evidence for Christ's resurrection and the absence of any proof for the fables of mythology. Point by point, he replied to Celsus, and concluded with an appeal to logic. "I hold that a clear and unmistakable proof of the resurrection are the subsequent labors of His disciples, who devoted themselves to the teaching of a doctrine which was attended with danger to human life, a doctrine they would not have taught with such courage had they invented the resurrection of Jesus from the dead. The disciples not only prepared others to ignore death, but they were also the first to show how they despised its terrors." [5]

Before the end of the third century, another concerted challenge to the supernatural origins of a religion was made by Hierocles, provincial governor under Diocletian, who wrote a book (*Philalethes, Lover of Truth*) in which he tried to show that a first-century philosopher, Apollonius of Tyana, was as remarkable a worker of miracles and as potent an exorcist as Jesus of Nazareth. Hierocles was promptly answered by the Christian apologists of his day, notably Lactantius in the *Divine Institutes* and by Eusebius of Caesaria in a special work dedicated to that purpose.

Since the rise of Deism in the sixteenth century and up to modern times, critics of the Christian revelation have used the life of Apollonius to advance their own naturalist theory of religion. Renan placed Apollonius above Socrates and equal to Jesus as a god. Guignebert believed there was an "essential similarity of means and results" between the wonders of the man from Tyana and the miracles of Christ.

Quite apart from Apollonius, however, a common approach to religious movements is to assume that because of superficial similarities they are all essentially alike and exhibit the same tendency to apotheosize their founders, with equal lack of foundation in fact. In this scheme, Christianity is no exception.

The most striking parallels occur in the case of the notion of miraculous birth for the messiah of the movement. Scores of half-man, half-god personalities were announced to be of virgin birth, spiritual conception, or in some fashion not tainted by the normal processes associated with being born. Such accounts were given for all of the following persons before Jesus: Krishna, Buddha, Codom, Lao-tsze, Confucius, Horus, Ra, Zoroaster, Hercules, Prometheus, Mercury, Apollo, Alexander the

Great, Cyrus the Persian, and even Plato. In each instance there are accounts which contain claims to authenticity. Where does this leave the person committed to the view of biblical inerrancy? Why should one account be considered more authentic than any other, since each is vouched for by a written testimony? [6]

The difficulty with this approach is not its interlarding of fictional characters (Krishna, Mercury, Hercules and Apollo) with real persons (Confucius, Alexander and Cyrus), or even its lumping together of poetic fiction with empirical fact, but its calm ignoring of the mountain of evidence in favor of one Person who proved His claim to transcendence by verifiable phenomena and established a spiritual community whose twenty centuries of corporate existence alone argue to more than human origins.

Behind such naturalism is a principle that would not only rule out the supernatural character of Judaism and Christianity, but deny the very possibility of a divine entrance into human existence by way of special relevation. Immanuel Kant's *Religion Within the Limits of Reason Alone* and Julian Huxley's *Religion Without Revelation* illustrate the principle and, at least with Kant, had much to do with shaping it.

The same intransigence which explains all religious beginnings by purely human agencies has developed an elaborate theory on the future destiny of the world's religions, which are seen to be merging into one composite whole. It begins by assuming their essential oneness but separate inadequacy and therefore postulates a time when each will borrow from the other to form a syncretism which happily combines them all. In the words of the *Kasidah* of Haji Abdu el-Yezdi, "all Faith is false; all Faith is true. Truth is the shattered mirror strown in myriad bits; while each believes his little bit the whole to own." When all the broken chips are pieced together, then the wholeness of truth will be known.

Parallel with a naturalistic hypothesis of religious origins and final consummation is the Judaeo-Christian interpretation which recognizes that "When in former times God spoke to our forefathers, He spoke in fragmentary and varied fashion through the prophets. But in this final age He has spoken to us in the Son whom He has made heir to the whole universe." [7] Man was not left to his own resources but received communication from eternal Truth, addressing Himself to the rational creatures whom He destined to a share in His eternal beatitude.

Nor was this all. Although the public revelation, as it is technically known, closed with the death of the last apostle, the hand of the Lord is not shortened. He does not cease to enlighten by the internal light of His grace every man who comes into the world, teaching and directing the souls of the most distant Pygmies to arrive at the saving knowledge of His name.[8]

While saying this, however, and admitting that divine revelation has affected all nations or that interior illumination is open to every heart disposed to receive it, we compromise on the essential message of supernaturalism if we add with Arnold Toynbee that, "We ought to try to purge our Christianity of the traditional Christian belief; that Christianity is unique. This is not just a Western Christian belief; it is intrinsic to Christianity's uniqueness." [9] Of course Christianity should not be intolerant of persons. It must recognize the right of each man to follow his own conscience; but it cannot help being sure of its uniqueness without betraying its own nature and denying the very purpose of its existence, which is to teach men the way to salvation.

Yet there is a legitimate sense in which the Christian can be convinced of the absolute truth of his own position without belittling and much less despising other religious systems than his own. He may consider his own religion normative for others, without looking upon them as empty of content or devoid of profound insight into man's relations with God.

When Thomas Aquinas built the edifice of Medieval Scholasticism and united the corpus of Christian revelation into a marvelous synthesis, the structure he used was mainly that of a "pagan" philosopher, Aristotle, together with borrowings from Homer, Plato, Virgil, Sallust, Seneca, Horace, two great Islamic writers, Averroes, Avicenna and the Jewish sage, Moses Maimonides.

It is only speculation to surmise what would have been the course of Western religion if the Renascence and Reformation had not occurred. The Renascence revived interest in classical thought and mythology, discovering the riches of Homer and Plato, Virgil and Cicero; and the recovery of an appreciation of the glories of ancient Greece and the splendors of pagan Rome might have led to a corresponding discovery of the wisdom of China and India, as suggested by the sixteenth century labors of Matteo Ricci and Robert de Nobili. But the Renascence was quickly followed in Northern Europe by the narrowing influence of a new theology which circumscribed the native capacities of human nature. Instead of the broad tolerance of Aquinas whose veneration for Aristotle led him to speak of the Stagyrite simply as the Philosopher, "the Calvinistic doctrine of the inherent depravity of unredeemed humanity reacted against a sympathetic understanding of pagan religion." The consequences have been felt for centuries directly in the Protestant tradition and indirectly, through Jansenism, in Catholic circles.[10] Fortunately they are being neutralized on all sides by a return to the wisdom of the early Church, which distinguished in other religions the authentic spirit of God, whose Truth is not limited to one people or nation, and the aberrations caused by the weakness of man's intellect because of the Fall.

The ancient Fathers, Augustine, Jerome, and Prosper of Aquitaine said some harsh things about pagan depravity and the spectacle of a thousand gods. But they never lost sight of the "naturally Christian soul" described by Tertullian, and even defended the classical authors against their traducers, as when Gregory Nazianzen opposed the imprudent zealots who would forbid Christians to learn Greek and Roman writers.

Implicit in this attitude is a realistic optimism which steers a middle course between two extremes, neither considering those outside Judaeo-Christianity so perfect as to ignore their need of revelation nor so depraved they are given no credit for any spiritual achievement. With St. Paul, it asserts the power of the mind, even of the unregenerated, to arrive at some knowledge of God and of the moral law, "for all that may be known of God by men lies plain before their eyes; indeed God Himself has disclosed it to them. His invisible attributes, that is to say His everlasting power and deity, have been visible, ever since the world began, to the eye of reason, in the things He has made." If they fail to worship the Creator, "there is no possible defence for their conduct," if, "knowing God, they have refused to honor Him as God, or to render Him thanks." [11]

It is not the role of comparative religion to pass moral judgment, but only to describe phenomena and evaluate them according to objective norms. For the Christian these norms are remarkably broad and inclusive. They are based on the double premise that, in spite of the consequences of sin, man's spirit remains substantially intact and therefore capable of autonomous insight and volition in matters religious; and that God's grace is universal and therefore active on all men without exception, since it is His will that all should come to a knowledge of the Truth and be saved.

From this viewpoint, the study of world religions becomes more than a catalogue of numerous beliefs and rites. It is an effort to trace the cosmic dialogue between God and the human race, of His operation on the souls of men and of their response to His claims.

2. Primitive Religion

IT IS only as a concession to common usage that we may speak of primitive peoples or of a primitive religion. Strictly speaking there are no genuine primitives anywhere on earth today. Evidently we have no direct knowledge of the earliest beginnings of religion and therefore of the true chronological primitive. Our observation of present-day backward tribes does not obviate this difficulty, for such people are after all our contemporaries, with as long a history behind them as our own and the possibility of degeneration cannot be excluded. Simply to equate the backward with the actual primitive is uncritical and unwarranted.

Yet a large percentage of the peoples of the earth, about one in ten, are commonly called primitive and their religion is similarly described. They have remained from time immemorial out of general and influential contact with other peoples and as a consequence are said to possess some religious beliefs and institutions which characterized mankind nearer the beginning of human history than other, major religions like Hinduism, Judaism and Christianity.

These peoples are by no means barbarian or uncivilized. Some authors prefer to speak of them as pre-literates, since their culture commonly antedates the arrival of modern literacy. Nor again are they boorish or stupid, even though by Western standards they are uncultivated. Their religious thought is, in fact, remarkably sensitive, and often refined and intelligent. It is also highly complex, to a degree that ethnologists after more than a century of study are still struggling to clarify their complicated beliefs and ritual practices.

In order to sift the concepts in a field that bristles with technical terms and subjective interpretations, a careful distinction should be made between the known culture of peoples who formed the oldest

18

civilizations of Egypt, Sumeria and the Ancient Near East, and those whom certain evolutionary theorists project into the uncharted ages of the past. Thanks to the labors of eminent ethnologists and historians of religion, we can see more clearly that many of the ideas formerly held regarding the "pre-logical" state of man in earliest times need revision. Until a few decades ago, it was commonly said that primitive man was incapable of abstraction, and no doubt philosophical theorization was quite foreign to him. But if we turn to the Ancient Near East and study the condition in those earliest periods which we can reach through inscriptions or by linguistic methods, we find extended power of intellectual insight.

All the earliest known stages of the Egyptian, Sumerian and Semitic languages reveal that general qualities like goodness and justice allowed for extraction from the related adjectives and identification as abstract ideas by some linguistic device such as suffix, prefix, or internal vowel change. In fact such formations were known to exist before the Egyptians separated from their Semitic neighbors, at least 5000 B.C. Generalized classifications, such as "mankind, divine being, god," were equally familiar at just as remote an age.

Our concern, however, is not with these nations of whom we have extensive archaeological evidence, who were not, by any criterion, mentally sub-human. We are speaking of those familiarly called primitives but who are actually present-day peoples whose relative isolation from the major streams of culture suggests their lineage from the chronological ancestors of the human race. Their religious condition is therefore on a par with other phases of knowledge and conduct, ranging from the very undeveloped (or decadent) to a fairly advanced type of civilization.

Two levels of primitive religion are generally distinguished. The lower type has been either less directly affected by one of the major religions, or shows less speculative development. It is correspondingly more animist or fetishist, that is, more given to attributing souls to every object and believing in magic or sorcery. Allowing for numerous exceptions, the following are generally held to profess a lower pre-literate religion: the Negritos of the Philippine Islands, various tribes of Micronesia and Polynesia, the Papuans of New Guinea, the black Aruntas of Australia, the Andaman Islanders in the Bay of Bengal, the Kols and Pariahs of Central and

South India, the Pygmies and Bushmen of the Central Congo basin, the Caribs of the West Indies, and the Yahgans of the extreme south of South America.

On a higher religious plane are the Samoans and Hawaiians, the Kalmuks of Liberia, the Veddas of Ceylon, the Todas of the Nigiri Hills in South India, the Bantu of south central and southern Africa, and the Eskimos and Amerinds, or American Indians, in North and South America.

Both the lower and higher types may be further distinguished according to their origin, as traditional, syncretist, or spontaneous. The distinction is essential in order to avoid crediting the primitives with more than they deserve or deny them religious ideals that are truly their own. Traditional primitives have fairly maintained their ancestral religion with little outside influence to change the original pattern, which may have declined; they are normally isolated groups, in mountains or islands, or otherwise physically removed from neighboring cultures. Syncretists are very common, and represent an amalgam of their own culture and that of one of the higher religions. The spontaneous creations appear to be traditional primitives that reacted against their own cultural decline and produced, by way of reaction, new forms of belief and especially of ritual.

CONCEPT OF DIVINITY

Undoubtedly the most significant feature of the primitives' religion is their notion of the deity. They are remarkably monotheistic, while allowing for considerable decadence and for the influx of alien ideas. In the degree to which they have remained truly primitive, they believe in some kind of Supreme Being, more or less clearly conceived; and where the idea is obscured by polytheism or a vague nature-worship, this may be shown to have happened within comparatively recent times through a process of retrogression.

TYPICAL BELIEFS. The African continent offers the best evidence of this unsophisticated faith in one High God, who is variously named but whose existence seems to be present everywhere, even among the remotest and simplest tribes.

An outstanding example is the Ewe people who believe in God and give him a name, without being able further to describe his attributes. They call him *Mawu* or *Mahou,* and their faith in the Deity is so deeply felt that they frequently pronounce his name instinctively. When danger menaces them, they say, "Mawu, help me, I ask you." When some unexpected benefit comes their way, like finding water after several hours of marching, they pronounce a word of thanksgiving, "Mawu is good." Victims of a false accusation before a tribunal, they cry out, "Mawu knows my soul." At the moment of death, it is no longer to the spirits that they address themselves, but to the High God, "Mawu have pity on me." And to console those who grieve over a deceased relative or friend, they say, "It is Mawu who has called him."

However, if the Ewe are asked who is this Mawu, they fall back quickly into a chaos of different and strange opinions. They identify him as a Master who lives retired somewhere beyond the firmament; or equate him with the firmament itself, and call the clouds his robe and the clap of thunder the sound of his voice.

Characteristically Mawu is never represented in figure. There is neither statue nor image of him. People honor him by looking at the sky, towards the west, at the hour when the sun is setting, and confide to the setting sun the message they wish to give him. One chief is reported to have said, "If a man rises in the morning without pronouncing the name of Mawu, this man would be nothing but a beast."

Though the ordinary Ewe do not honor Mawu by any special cult or rite, one sect among them, the more wealthy tribesmen, have a form of public and private worship. They consider themselves Mawu's favorites because he has blessed them with an abundance of material goods. A curious practice is to administer a little dose of poison to oneself at the right moment, which causes some inconvenience but does not cause death. The purpose is to reanimate one's fervor for the cause of Mawu and to stimulate zeal for recruiting new devotees. There are villages which follow no other cult than that of Mawu.

Similar evidence of faith in a High God is found in Rhodesia, where the religious beliefs of the natives are reflected in their proverbs and prayers. They call the chief deity Lesa Mukulu, which means, God the Supreme Being. To express the idea of his universal goodness, they say, "Lesa, the blacksmith (creator), does not forge for one alone but for all," or that "Lesa, the tailor (creator) does not make clothes for one alone but for all." His mastery is found in such expressions as, "Lesa does not need our offerings of flower in trees; Lesa does not need our meat." They profess a divine providence by saying, "Where Lesa prepares food for you there is no smoke, he gives it to you when you least think of it."

Every element of nature and every occurrence among men, beyond the pantheon of lesser spirits, is attributed to one supreme God. "It is Lesa who stirs the forests in murmuring." When taking an oath, the same name is invoked, "May Lesa strike me dead if I lie." Prayers are addressed to him, "May Lesa preserve me in good health," as well as curses, "May Lesa punish you."

Among the Rhodesians there are some indications of syncreticism, or at least of previous contact with the Hebraic religion. They believe that Lesa is the creator of mankind, that the first parents sinned and as a result brought death into the world; and they subscribe to much of what we know were distinctively Jewish customs like the avoidance of certain types of meat, the offering of first-fruits, and concern over practically the same legal defilements as are enumerated in Leviticus.

Other African tribes have lapsed into a sort of nominalism. They may retain the name of a high God but deprive him of some of his attributes. Their idea of the origin of the world makes no provision for divine providence in the Christian sense of the word. Lesa has created the world and all that exists, but since then does not bother himself about anything. Consequently there is no question of looking to him for aid, nor of dependence on his care, nor of worshiping Lesa. From him nothing is to be expected and nothing feared. All events depend on two kinds of spirits, the *mipaji* and the *nguru.*

The *mipaji* are by nature the spirits of the dead, among whom the most powerful are the spirits of the deceased chiefs. Some of them are good and others bad, and according to their character cause sickness and death. Worship given to the spirits consists mostly of food and drink, offered on the graves of the dead, to propitiate their favor and ward off their anger. Small huts are built in and around the town to "house" the souls of the deceased. People may also communicate with the spirits through magicians, whose bases of operations are *kabbas,* filled with gruesome objects like pieces of skull, jawbones, and other parts of human skeletons. Other means of communication are persons possessed by the spirits of the chiefs, mostly women, who act as agents with the visible world. Thus, a person may be sick and begins to tremble with spasms or convulsions. This means he is struggling with the spirit, who must be calmed down, after which rapport is established with the indwelling invisible power.

In contrast, the *nguru,* though spirits, are neither gods nor men, though they also may be good or bad. Their function is to control the elements like rain, drought, famine and weather. Since they understand medicine, they point this out through possessed persons. Normally the *nguru* are located in the mountains, falls, and alongside rivers, where they live in lions, leopards, snakes and big trees. Not infrequently the natives will refuse to cut down a tree or kill a wild animal because *nguru* live in them. As with the information about medicinal herbs, they make known the place of their homes by means of possessed persons, and like the *mipaji,* they also have sacred huts built for their exclusive use, where food and drink are put for their use. Great travelers, the *nguru* go from one part of the country to the other, in answer to appropriate incantation. They enter a person, speak through him, and otherwise make their presence felt in favor of anyone who invokes their aid.

A similar mixture of vague (or sometimes fairly clear) monotheism, and a belief in lesser spirits pervades most of primitive religion. Unfortunately the first impressions left on those who observe them is that the primitives are polytheists. There is much to sustain this suspicion, although it is not accurately descriptive of their faith. Moreover, whatever vestiges of monotheism remain, they represent a dimension of thought which many primitives rarely associate with religion in the sense of worship.

The Congo and Angola regions typify this mentality. Among many tribes, there is no cult to any gods and less still to the Supreme Deity. Believing in the unique and transcendent divinity *Nzambi,* they do not allow this faith to disturb their traditional ceremonies. God exists; He excels and they let Him excel quietly. At times they call on *Nzambi's* conscience to witness. His name is used to pledge oaths. They trust in his omnipotence and in his virtue of superior domain over all things. From all appearances, it seems that this notion of the Divinity has undergone considerable regression, and that centuries ago the High God was not only recognized but worshiped.

The current practice is to cultivate the inferior deities, comparable to the kind the Romans sought to protect their private interests, families, and social undertakings. But these are scattered here and there, and unless forestalled will do injury to people and human enterprises.

REFLECTIVE ANALYSIS. Since the scientific researches of Andrew Lang and Wilhelm Schmidt, anthropologists have found that the most archiac form of culture accessible to inquiry shows definite monotheistic strains. Thus the Tasmanians, Bushmen, Andaman Islanders, Semang of the Malay Peninsula, Congo Pygmies and a few others of comparable level, including a few tribes in the New World, all share the belief in a High God. The question arises as to whether this faith is really primitive, in the sense of reaching back to primeval history, and not rather a borrowing from other peoples or even a higher stage of religious development similar to the progress which these primitives have made in material and social spheres.

There is no doubt that borrowings have taken place in Africa, and recent archeological finds indicate the antiquity of Jewish influence in widely separated areas of the continent. Numerous papyri found at Elephantine, at the first cataract of the Nile, reveal the existence of a Jewish community there from the end of the sixth century B.C. They show that this community had a temple to Yahweh. Similar discoveries, like Jewish coins from the pre-Christian era found in Natal and Zululand, confirm the opinion that the Hebrew religion had entered the culture of the African peoples and may be a partial explanation of whatever monotheism the primitives still profess.

A striking example of possible Hebraic inpact on religion in Africa is the hieratic Egyptian text variously dated from the tenth to the sixth centuries B.C. and entitled *The Instruction of Amon-Em-Opet.* Its close relation to the Book of Proverbs has evoked numerous controversies, with good evidence pointing to at least indirect dependence on the Jewish sapiential writings. Justice in dealing with others stands at the head of the moral precepts enjoined by the Egyptian king, and always in terms of pleasing or displeasing the highest deity, Aton. "Do not talk with a man falsely—the abomination of the god. . . . Do not confuse a man with a pen upon papyrus—the abomination of the god. . . . Make not for thyself weights which are deficient; they abound in grief through the will of God." [1]

Thus every aspect of a man's life, his successes and failures, is known to the supreme God and responsive to divine guidance, so there should be no room for anxious worry but only confidence in Aton's care.

Do not spend the night fearful of the morrow. At daybreak what is the morrow like? Man knows not what the morrow is like. God is always in his success, whereas man is in his failure. One thing are the words which men say, another is that which the god does. Say not, "I have no wrongdoing," nor yet strain to seek quarreling.

If a man pushes himself to seek success, in the completion of a moment he damages it. Be steadfast in thy heart, make firm thy breast. Steer not with thy tongue. If the tongue of a man be the rudder of a boat, the All-Lord is its pilot.[2]

But the same Hebraic influence cannot be argued for other primitive lands, notably in Asia, where the impact of a monotheistic culture somewhere in pre-Christian times may be ruled out. Here at least, and also to some extent in Africa, belief in a distinctive High God points to the perdurance of an archaic religion.

The general pattern, whether in Africa or elsewhere, is that this High God is supposed to live in the sky and is not clearly soul-like. He is eternal, all-knowing, and almighty without abusing his power. He acts with sovereign freedom as author of the moral law, and rewards or punishes not only in this life, with prosperity or adversity, but beyond the grave in a life after death. Unlike the gods of mythology he is asexual, although mythological influences have endowed him with human emotions and traits. Such a personage inspires believers with reverence, so that they are reluctant to name him. They do not worship him in temples or through images but invoke him in spontaneous prayer in times of special need, and may offer him first-fruits in token of adoration, and not as though he were the ghost of a dead person who receives food for his sustenance.

ANIMISM AND FETISHISM

As commonly understood, animism consists in attributing the human qualities of mind, will and passions to material objects, or to non-human living creatures. These objects, considered as animated, and endowed with a soul or *mana*, can in certain circumstances enter into direct relation with man in his personal and social activities. Since the power attributed to the objects is regarded as extraordinary or even superhuman, it is only a short step to invoke them, and establish ceremonies directed to appease or placate them and finally to treat them as gods.

In the heyday of evolutionary anthropology, all religion was said to stem originally from animism, on the theory that man began as an undeveloped anthropoid who only through countless millenia reached the higher stages of monarchianism and finally monotheism. More objective scholarship reveals that animism is less archaic than formerly thought, and appears rather as a form of religious decadence, which may coexist among modern primitives in the degree to which their truly primeval religion has retrogressed.

Thus we find the anomaly of peoples believing in one High God, whom they respect, and at the same time cultivating a host of lesser beings who inhabit the earth or fill the elements of nature. However, it is impossible to generalize, either on the degree to which monotheism is infected by animistic beliefs, or on their mutual relationship. No two primitive peoples are the same in these respects.

Animism is especially prominent among some of the Melanesians and Indonesians, the Africans of the West Coast, South American natives north-east and south-west of the Amazon, and the early North American Indians of the north-west and south-east. But even here not everything is supposed to have a soul. The Indonesians do not say that inanimate objects have a spirit; they simply believe that independent spirits live in objects of particularly noticeable shape or kind, and not even all plants have a soul.

In Melanesia, human beings and certain animals like domestic beasts may have as many as seven souls, which on analysis may turn out to be only different faculties. Most frequently, the primitives hold that a person has two souls: one belongs to the body and is connected with the blood or the breath, the other is a kind of shadow or phantom that the people usually associate with the future life.

The situation existing in Dahomey, on the coast of West Africa, may illustrate the complexities in animism. Dahomean religion has a pantheon of worshipful spirits, deified ancestors, and yet also a sky-god creator, *Mawu*. As parent of the other gods, he gave them power, holds the formulae for the creation of man and matter, and mysteriously controls human destiny.

On being questioned, most Dahomeans are not sure how many souls a man has, although they are certain it is more than one. The majority hold that many men have four souls, but women only three. Their first spirit is a kind of guardian soul which they inherit from an ancestor. You can recognize whose soul was inherited from the characteristics which reappear in the new possessor. In case of doubt, a diviner is consulted to say whose spirit has been received.

A person's second soul is strictly his own, and is often described as his voice, which more than anything seems to characterize an individual. On death, the personal spirit leaves the body, at the moment when a man becomes incapable of speaking. The third soul is a particle of the High God which exists in everyone's body. In this way the creator, or his female counterpart, sends a bit of himself to each person in order to retain control over the people he made. When a man dies, this particle reverts back to the High God or subsidiary goddess.

Not all people have a fourth soul, which can be acquired only by those who undergo special ceremonies. Once received, its function is less personal than social, and directs both the person who possesses it and others under his care, like members of his family or household, to their present and final destiny.

When a man dies, his personal soul leaves the body and starts on a journey to the land of the dead. Anticipating numerous obstacles en route, the surviving relations must prepare beforehand. Several rivers have to be crossed and boatmen paid to ferry the soul across the waters. If there are three boatmen, each receives some offering for his task, money, tobacco or special funeral ritual. Unless these oblations are made, the soul cannot cross the rivers and may venge itself on the living who neglected to help.

Even after reaching the land of the dead, where the soul meets the deceased members of its family, it deserves still further attention in ritual sacrifices at the risk of showing its displeasure by causing illness or some other misfortune on the negligent survivors. When illness strikes, a diviner is called in to ascertain how the ancestors must have been offended to bring on the calamity.

In other primitive societies, the worship of one's ancestral spirits is the central object of religious cult. Notwithstanding profession of belief in a creator god, the Bakongo of southern Congo believe that all one's benefits in this life come from the ancestral shades. The Manus of Melanesia say that each head of a family has a personal spirit from the world of the dead, that he is quite literally the ghost of his father. But in all tribes, the disembodied spirits are not believed to be permanently harmful, either because of a vague belief that souls finally cease to be, or because they are reborn, if malicious, in children who begin a new cycle of life, death and spirit existence.

The number and variety of Dahomean deities cannot be classified. Moreover the natives are notoriously uncommunicative with strangers on matters dealing with tribal customs and religious beliefs. It is known, however, that there are sky gods and earth gods, deities of iron, the hunt, and of drinking water, and among the divinities priests and priestesses with their own rites and followers.

A feature of Dahomean ritual is the worship of serpents, whose spirit manifests itself in all long, sinuous objects, such as roots of trees, the nerves of animals, and the human umbilical cord, a symbol of life and fertility. Since the serpentine spirit is unrelenting when offended, it is much feared and propitiated.

Primitive animism is often manifested in a worship which has been called fetishism. A fetish is a common object of no value in itself but which the primitive keeps and venerates because he believes it is the dwelling-place of a spirit. This can be anything: a stone, root, vase, feather, log, shell, colored cloth, animal's tooth, snake's skin, box, an old rusty sword. However the term is specially applied to those more or less crude representations, generally in wood, though sometimes in metal or clay, consecrated to various *genii* that flourish in the religions of Western Africa. The first type of fetish, therefore, is not a portrait or figure like the "idols" of Buddhism, but symbolic of a certain spirit who may be invoked in given circumstances.

Another kind of fetish is an image connected with the worship of one's ancestors. These figures surmount or enclose the remains of the dead, their skull bones, hair or other human relics; and their value depends on association with the remains. Finally a third category is destined for operations of black magic, to induce spells or diseases, or satisfy someone's vengeance.

All three types derive their power solely from the spirits to which they are related: family fetishes from the relics of the ancestors to protect the domestic family, clan or tribe; fetishes of tutelary *genii* embody the spirits whose agency is believed to be defensive against evil; and the fetishes of bewitching spirits are means of invoking malicious forces to cause people harm.

Besides fetishes, the primitive also uses amulets and talismans, although not directly because of his animistic beliefs, since a fetish is held to be animated and conscious, and intrinsically efficacious because of the spirit which inhabits it. On the other hand, an amulet, or *grigri* in African parlance, is a lifeless object carried on the person, which the people credit with secret and innate power to preserve from misfortune or prosper any undertaking. In much the same way a talisman has no consciousness of its own, yet because specially marked or ceremonially prepared, is believed to exercise magical influence on things and events, beyond the expectations of nature. Unlike amulets, talismans are not constantly worn but placed over the door of a house, or inside the home, or at the cross-roads outside the village. Their effect depends on the type and formula used in making the talisman.

Current literature on the primitives uses the term "animism" in two quite different senses, and the difference is more than semantic. Animism, as defined by the English anthropologist Tylor, is the belief in spirit beings. Their essential quality is their ethereal embodiment; they are beings without real flesh and blood. Although immaterial, they are real enough for those who believe in them. Primitive man, according to the evolutionary theory of religious origins, derived the idea of animism from the phenomenon of dreams as compared with the waking state, and from death in comparison with life. Once disembodied, the spirits of men, animals and plants were believed to be beyond the ordinary laws of nature and capable of animating (or re-animating) anything, with results that were good or bad, depending on the character of the spirit and the degree of control that people exercised over this invisible world. Animation of material or sub-human elements by disembodied rational souls was particularly important and, in some schools of ethnology, is the prototype of primitive animism. A primitive, therefore, is one who personifies inanimate phenomena by filling an empty world with the ghosts of the dead.

More commonly, however, animism in primitive culture describes the unitary way certain peoples look upon the world. "Primitive man," it is said, "has only one mode of thought, one mode of expression, one part of speech—the personal." The world appears to him neither inanimate nor empty but redundant with life. And life for him has individuality, in man and beast and plant, and in every phenomenon that confronts man—the clap of thunder, a sudden shadow, the eerie and unknown clearing in the wood, the stone which suddenly strikes him when he stumbles while on a hunting trip. In the language of existentialist philosophy, any phenomenon may at any time face him, not as "It," but as "Thou." In this confrontation, "Thou" reveals its individuality, its qualities, and its will. "Thou" is not contemplated with intellectual detachment but experienced as life confronting life, involving every faculty of man in a reciprocal relationship. Thoughts, no less than actions and feelings, are subordinated to this experience.

Fetishism thus appears as a species of animism, where the animated object is not naturally alive but has living qualities attributed to it in virtue of whatever spirit is believed now to be inside. The word "fetish" seems to have come from the Latin *facticius,* an amulet, by way of the Portuguese *feitico,* after the use of the term by Portuguese adventurers who first met with the practice in their voyages along the west coast of Africa. Fetishes are, therefore, symbolic (or real) repositories of supernormal power, and they serve the psychological function of objectifying the primitives' belief.

Significantly the representation of a human figure is not considered an effective fetish until it has passed through the hands of a medicine-man and received its power from him. What confers upon the object its extraordinary potency is solely the mysterious spell sung over it, or the wonder-working substance, like the *ngula* paint, thrust into a ventral cavity. Hence in many localities, only a small number of human or animal figurines are really fetishes. They can become such only if ritualistically consecrated for that purpose.

FORMS OF WORSHIP

With notable exceptions, the external manifestations of primitive ritual are centered in the family or tribe, or at least connected with the basic social structure of primitive society.

Heading the list of objects of worship are the ancestral tombs and the spirits of the dead. Tombs and cemeteries thus become sacred places, and veneration of the departed an act of religion. Little booths may be built where the souls of the dead come for rest; small altars are also built, on which to offer sacrifices to appease or invoke them in favor of the living.

Relics of the dead become objects of religious care, usually connected with some fetish. In some places a part of the skull itself is preserved, painted red and placed in a receptacle made of bark on which may be carved a bust of the deceased. Real statues are not unknown, for instance in Loango (Congo) and among the Melanesians in New Guinea. These are placed above the relics, in niches at the back of the public house of a village. A crude altar is often built in front of the statues for occasional offerings.

Likewise tutelary spirits of extra-human origin have their own shrines and altars. In East Africa, small huts are erected for them at the cross-roads, where the persons in special need can offer sacrifices of flour, grain or other precious commodity. After a possessed person is delivered, he is expected to build one of these huts to placate the spirit that had left him, at the risk of being re-possessed or otherwise gravely harmed.

In East Africa, in addition to the booths, a sacred enclosure is built to honor the manes (ikigabiro). It is a round place, several yards in diameter, and marked off for the exclusive purpose of sacrifice. In the center a fig tree is planted, and around fine grass is spread in the form of a bed on which the national spirit is invited to come and take his rest. Sick people may be seen sitting on this bed or even sleeping there, in hopes of being cured, and dying persons are sometimes laid in the enclosure to discover the cause of impending death.

The worship of the supreme deity among primitives is highly characteristic. No images are made of the High God and, for the most part, he is invoked only in times of crisis or special need. Too often his cultus is buried under the debris of lesser deities.

Yet, while remaining in the background and far away, veneration of the ultimate divinity is not completely forgotten, even for public worship. In the samples which follow, the name "God" is substituted for the native equivalent of the supreme deity, who stands above all as creator of men and the world.

Among the *Wa-pokomo* who inhabit the right bank of the Tana in East Africa, the priest recites a ritual prayer, after the sacrifice is offered, and the people join him in chorus.

O God, we ask You!
O Manes, we ask You!
O Ancestors, we ask You!
God, grant us peace. Grant us tranquility, And may the blessing come.
He who bewitches our village, may he die.
He who utters an evil spell against us, may he die.
He who says this village is rich, these men are numerous, he who speaks
    thus is a jealous one, may he die.
We also ask for some fish, may the fish come.
Thus eating, let us eat in peace.
This woman is ill. O God, give her health to her, and to her village, and
    to her children, and to her husband; may she get up, hurry to work,
    take care of the kitchen; may happiness return, may it come from
    the other bank, may it come from the other bank.[3]

At times, prayers are directed solely to the High God, as in the petition for one who is ill. "You are God and Master. I say to You, free this person from his sickness." More often the supreme deity is invoked together with the lesser spirits, as when going to cultivate a new piece of ground. "O God, I beg of You. I am going to cultivate this field. Very well, it is in order to have things to eat, that I may have life and health. Come, *Manes!* I till this field that the grain may spring up abundantly and that I may harvest it when it is ripe." [4]

Sacrifice among the primitives is universal. Like prayer and the offering, it is addressed to the *Manes,* the lesser spirits or to the High God. In Zanzibar, sacrifices are offered on graves by the families of the deceased. Flour and water, palm wine or beer, with some pulp or maize or sorghum are common oblations. On special occasions, small fowl, or even goats, sheep and oxen are killed and their blood allowed to drench the graves. When the fishermen of Gabon, in equatorial Africa, catch their first fish of the day, they carefully cut it open, remove its entrails, and throw them into the sea as a first-fruits offering to the spirit of the waters. A common practice, before taking any fermented drink, like palm wine or sorghum beer, is to pour a little on the ground as a libation of sacrifice.

MAGIC AND MORALITY

In order to understand the culture of the primitives, a distinction should be made between its irrational element which consists in elaborate myths and is practiced through magic, and the rational element that is truly religious and may inspire high moral conduct.

Magic is understood as the art of making use of the forces of nature by certain occult observances that have a religious appearance, or of courting the secret influences of the invisible world. Two types are found among the primitive peoples: natural and supernatural magic, which differ widely in their character and religious implications.

Natural magic is based on the theory that nature is full of many objects whose hidden, protective or curative properties can satisfy practically every need and drive away a host of evils. The problem is to find these objects. With his uncritical mind and animistic prejudice, the primitive easily turns from a valid exploitation of the physical forces of nature to a superstitious cult of the unknown, in the form of charms, philters, auguries, omens, the art of divination and respect for scores of sacred prohibitions and taboos.

Supernatural magic is a kind of anti-religion which has its own orders of worship, incantations, evocations, rites, fetishes, sacrifices, priests and meeting places. Primitives practice it along with natural magic, yet carefully distinguish the two and have different names for specialists in one and the other. The first is called by various names that correspond to the English "to treat, heal, diagnose," or "diviner" and "seer;" the second is associated with the terms "to charm, bait, bewitch, poison, prowl."

Sorcerers and sorceresses generally ply their trade as individuals, but as witches they band together in secret societies. One account tells how their members meet clandestinely in a forest, or at least at some distance from the village. The hour is near midnight. An imitation of the hoot of an owl, which is their sacred bird, is their signal call. They profess to leave their corporeal body lying asleep in their huts, and claim that the part which joins in the meeting is the spirit body, whose movements are not hindered by walls or solid obstacles, and can pass through the air with lightning speed. At their meetings they have audible converse with malevolent spirits, whom they invoke against the victims of their sorcery.

So far from identifying their religion with these practices, the primitives search out likely sorcerers or witches and after a token trial summarily put them to death. In east Africa, men and women found guilty are burned on a fire of ebony outside the village at the crossroads.

What adds to the suspicion of sorcery is the mystery that surrounds sickness and death. Three agents may be responsible: the High God, one of the lesser spirits, or a human enemy. A diviner is consulted, and if the supreme deity was the cause, the victim or his family reconcile themselves to the inevitable. If a spirit was behind the effect, he must be appeased by suitable offerings or sacrifice. But if the sickness, and particularly death, came by the magical designs of another man, he must be found and punished without delay.

Taken under suspicion of being responsible for another's death, the native may voluntarily undergo an ordeal to prove his innocence. Vegetable poison, boiling water and hot iron are common methods of testing. If the person survives, he is acquitted, and the diviner who named him may be punished.

Although the meaning of magic and sorcery is seldom distinguished in popular literature, the difference is considerable and greatly affects their respective function in primitive religion. Magic is the generic term which describes the effort to produce an effect by means that are disproportionate to the result expected, through the invocation of lesser spirits as though they were divine. When the intended purpose is to benefit or protect from harm, the magic is "white," otherwise, if the intention is to do injury, it is "black."

Yet not all black magic is sorcery. It may also be witchcraft, depending on the character of the person performing it and especially on the method employed. In sorcery the agent uses certain prescribed, esoteric rites, or pronounces certain formulas whose efficacy is built into the ritual itself. Provided the correct formula is recited or the right gestures are used, the magical effect takes place, irrespective of the character or personal qualities of the one performing the ritual. Sorcerers, therefore, are professionals whom people consult or ask to intervene in order to injure an enemy or work vengeance against a hated rival. They ply their magic as an evil art, but themselves may be quite normal and socially respectable.

Witchcraft, on the other hand, is practiced by persons who are evil by nature, so to speak. Among many primitives, witches are supposed to be born of parents who are witches themselves. The evil they do others is not the result of prescribed ritual but the spontaneous effect of a wicked person's spirit harming those whom it hates. Much of their evil trade is done at night, while they and their victims are asleep; and the clandestine meetings of witches are the strange councils of disembodied spirits (temporarily leaving the bodies while at sleep), at which prospective victims are "eaten alive," in the sense that their souls are spiritually masticated and the bodies take harm according to the malice and intent of the witches in session.

Morality in primitive peoples varies across the spectrum of tribal customs, geographical locality, contact with other cultures, and, above all, the level of religious beliefs. As they recede from truly archaic beliefs with their stress on fear of the supreme divinity, the moral practices and even principles regress. On the other hand, there are still many so-called primitives whose ethical standards and conduct are remarkably high.

Marriage is generally surrounded by elaborate ceremonies and numerous prohibitions. Near relatives may not marry, adultery is forbidden, and conjugal relations are not allowed during pregnancy, the period of nursing, and during certain times like war and hunting. Causes for divorce also exist, favoring the husband who can repudiate his wife for laziness, suspicion of magic and adultery. Cruelty to a mother-in-law gives the wife a right to divorce her husband.

Many faults condemned are proscribed by native tradition. Abusive language, poisoning, murder, and calumny are commonly forbidden and punishable by tribal or family justice. Among the Bavili there are five classes of prohibitions of which the first concerns the High God, the second refers to the use of magical divination, the third to mothers correcting their children, the fourth to observing each fourth day by abstaining from certain occupations, and the last comprises all the ceremonies and duties incumbent on women regarding their premarital and marital morality.

According to primitive casuistry, free consent is not required to commit a fault or break a taboo. Every violation, whether voluntary or not, is punishable. Some tribes distinguish between offenses against the supreme deity and against man. Such crimes as incest would be considered sins against the High God, who might punish the whole community as a result.

To free themselves from remorse and recover peace of mind, some primitives have special ceremonies called (in one locality) *ko-tahikio,* which literally means "to vomit" one's sin. Ethnologists are agreed that the *Kikuju* who practice this purification had been closed from time immemorial and until recently to Christian influences.

At appropriate times, the penitents gather together or come individually to the leader of the tribe, in the open air at some deserted corner of the village. They squat on the ground and, out loud, tell in sequence what evil things they had done, e.g., allowing a serpent to cross their path, spilling some food on the ground, having shaved the wife's head. If the fault is too personal, they may go a distance away, tell the crime to a sacred pole, and bring the wood back as equivalent to a verbal accusation.

In Tahiti the natives have a series of expiatory prayers, animated by a great spirit of humility. Concluding a solemn ceremony, the priests address the Supreme God. "Hearken, O God, to our petition with food. Here is the sacrificial pig for thee, a sacred pig, a pig without blemish. It is a pig of atonement, to set free sinful man. Here also is the fat, small eating, for thee and the gods here in thy presence, O God, accept it. This is our petition, hearken unto us." [5]

Behind these sentiments of atonement stands a religious theory which determines primitive morality and gives it meaning. Often the ethical standards are low, as in the widespread countenance of polygamy and the savage cruelty practiced on the enemy. But even then, the rudiments of a moral law are founded in religious principles and bear a direct relation to dependence on the deity.

Not the least feature of primitive religion is the wide range it covers, from wholly selfish attempts to win divine blessings for oneself or curses against an adversary, to lofty idealism. Independent of this difference, however, the attitude of the natives towards the higher powers is uniformly one of self-abasement. They recognize, often more clearly than people who profess the "higher religions," that not only their existence depends on the High God and the spirits below him, but every event in human life is affected by agencies that are above man and yet accessible to man's invocation.

As we approach the so-called "higher religions" it may be useful to compare briefly the two religious dimensions, primitive and higher, in order better to understand how precisely the one is superior to the other.

In terms of strict content of popular belief, primitives are not infrequently superior to those who are ostensibly more civilized and cultured. There is a strain of monotheism among most primitives that we sometimes look for in vain among the Hindus, Buddhists and followers of Shinto. There is also a correlation between morality and religion that other, supposedly higher, systems often do not show. Theravada Buddhism, for example, can be quite atheistic in its outlook on life and corresponding attitude towards morals; and Confucianism is also divorced, in many writings, from a professedly religious interpretation of human conduct. Whatever crudities are found among the primitives, at least their ethics are not secular but so closely tied in with the invisible world as almost to be defined in sacred and spiritual terms. Their animism is unintelligible from any other viewpoint.

On the other hand, primitive religions lack what their higher counterparts possess, namely an organized system of thought or a theological development or any one of numerous features that characterize the major living faiths of mankind. Since most primitives are not literate, they do not have sacred writings such as are common to Judaism, Christianity, Hinduism and Islam. They also do not have a written tradition for the same reason, although the oral traditions among certain tribes in Africa and elsewhere are highly developed.

Perhaps all the principal differences between the primitives and others can be reduced to the absence of literacy among the former and the consequent loss of that continuity which is typical among the higher religions. Some would say further that the illiteracy itself is indicative of a specifically lower grade of intelligence and therefore primitives do not have a reflective religion, in which the mind systematizes the tribal beliefs and consciously synthesizes its particular approach to the divine. It is impossible to generalize, however, except in the broad sense that primitism is notoriously uncritical in its faith and equally correspondingly simple in ignoring the great problems of religious philosophy.

PART ONE

Oriental

Religions

3. Hinduism

HINDUISM can better be described than defined. It is less a religion than a religious culture, and less creedal than ethical or racial, which historically identified the people living in a particular region, namely, beyond the Indus River, which runs in a south-western direction from the present State of Kashmir to the Pakistan city of Karachi. The correlative words Hindustan, Hindi, and the modernized India have the same origin.

According to its own spokesmen, Hinduism is an amorphous, many-sided faith, about which it is hard to say anything with precision in the accepted Western sense of the concept of religion. Hindus describe themselves as persons who chiefly base their beliefs on the complex system of faith and practice of at least three millenia. "If I were to define the Hindu creed," wrote Mahatma Gandhi, "I would simply say, a search after truth through non-violent means. A man may not believe in God and still call himself a Hindu. Hinduism is relentless pursuit after truth. Denial of God we have known, denial of truth we have not known." By this norm the solidarity of Hinduism is due more to the accident of geographic limitation than to any other factor. There is no founder of a church, no governing body, and no semblance of an ecclesiastical organization.

VEDIC LITERATURE

Unlike Confucianism, the Hindu religion professes to be founded on revelation, and the very names of its Scriptures, the *Vedas* and *Sruti,* mean "knowledge" and "thing heard," by communication from the god Brahman "like truth or smoke emanating from wood." Absolutely speaking the Vedas are the ideas in the Eternal Mind, while *Sruti* is the material expression of some of these divine concepts. The former are objectively inexhaustible, even as the Divine Mind is beyond limitation, whereas the latter are only as old as humanity, having first been heard by ear and later put into writing.

Vedic literature cannot be strictly classified into Scripture and tradition because of numerous overlappings, or into revelation properly so-called and human interpretation. However roughly comparable to the Scriptures is the Hindu *Sruti,* and to Tradition the *Smriti* (recollection). The composite is a bewildering maze of books and treatises that were composed over a period of fifteen hundred years, to about 600 B.C.

THE FOUR VEDAS. Historians variously date the writing of the basic Vedas between 3000 to 1500 B.C. The generally accepted estimate is that they were composed around the sixth century before Christ, and correspond to the time when Buddhism came on the scene. Buddha's life-span is commonly placed from 563 to 483 B.C.

There are four Vedas, which together form the *Samhitas* (collections), of varying length and concerned with a different aspect of faith and practice. The oldest part of the Vedas consists of songs (*mantra*) and ritual formulas that exist in three anthologies, the *Rig Veda,* the *Sama Veda,* and the *Yajur Veda.* A fourth book, *Atharva Veda* contains directives for Hindu priests and only much later obtained recognition.

The *Rig* (verse) *Veda* is the oldest document in Indian literature and consists of more than a thousand hymns arranged in ten "circles" or books. Prayers of petition and praise addressed to the gods are the dominant theme. A Hindu commentator, Yaska, writing about 500 B.C., classified the chief Vedic deities into the gods of the earth—*Agni, Soma, Yama,* and *Brihaspati;* the gods of the air—*Indra, Vayu,* the *Maruts* and *Rudra;* and the gods of the bright heaven—*Savitar, Surya, Ushas, Pushan, Vishnu, Additi* and her sons, especially *Varuna* and *Mitra.*

Western scholars are lavish in their esteem for the *Rig Veda,* describing the works of praise addressed to the gods as "miraculous in the image power of their sonority." Recited according to rigid laws of melody, they reflect an age that had behind it centuries of religious culture. Yet the religion of the *Rig Veda* is quite different from the Hinduism of later times: more simple and less speculative, concerned more with pastoral worship than with conceptions of the infinite which became characteristic of classic Hinduism, as in the *Upanishads*.

By way of exception, the tenth and last book of the *Rig Veda* includes such elevated concepts as creation and worship of the (one) Unknown God. Its composition was relatively late, about 1000 B.C., which accounts for the contrast between its evident monotheism and the crude notions of many deities in the aspects of nature occuring in the earlier books. It is addressed to *Ka* (who), or the God whom men do not know.

He who gives breath, who gives strength, whose command all the bright gods revere, whose shadow is immortality, whose shadow is death: Who is the God to whom we shall offer sacrifice?

Who through his might became the sole king of the breathing and twinkling world, who governs all this, man and beast: Who is the God to whom we shall offer sacrifice?

Through whose might these snowy mountains are, and the sea, they say, with the distant river (Rasa), of whom these regions are indeed the two arms: Who is the God to whom we shall offer sacrifice?

Through whom the awful heaven and the earth were made fast; he through whom the other was established, and the firmament; he who measured the air in the sky: Who is the God to whom we shall offer sacrifice?

Whom heaven and earth, standing firm by his will, look up to, trembling in their mind; over whom the risen sun shines forth: Who is the God to whom we shall offer sacrifice?

When the great waters went everywhere, holding the germ (Hiranyagarbha), and generating light, then there arose from them the sole breath of the gods: Who is the God to whom we shall offer sacrifice?

Who by his might looked even over the waters which held power (the germ) and generated the sacrifice (light), Who alone is God above all gods: Who is the God to whom we shall offer sacrifice?

May he not hurt us, Who is the begetter of the earth, or he, the righteous, who begot the heaven; who also begot the bright and mighty waters: Who is the God to whom we shall offer sacrifice? [1]

For the most part, the object of desire in the *Rig Veda* is the satisfaction of the common, unreflective needs of life. An apparent exception is the splendor of Varuna, before whom the people felt they should have their sins removed and forgiven. Yet even here, the escape offered is rather from punishment for past misdeeds with little realization of the inner malice of sin. A solitary peak is reached in a single passage, where the sinners plead, "Let us be thine own beloved, Varuna, and cast all these sins away like loosened fetters."

But the hymns to Varuna are few and his cultus is already overshadowed by Indra, who was the popular god. Indra could be appreciated by his followers. He could be genial and generous to them if they furnished him with soma to drink. He was anything but the god of sanctity, and often depicted in his own way as a leader in drunkenness and debauchery. There was no question of fearing such a god for the commission of sin, and other deities in the Vedic pantheon were not much higher. They were like powerful men on earth, whose favor could be assured by gifts and to whom sacrifices were considered not reparations for guilt or means of expiation, but a sort of commerce between the god and his worshiper. Men gave that the gods might give in return; it was a religious business between two parties that were not much separated even according to moral standards.

The *Sama Veda* or Veda of melodies complements the *Rig Veda* by repeating many of the verses of the latter but supplying a musical notation for the performance of sacred chant. Four sets of chants are provided, with a number of isolated tunes intended as hymnal prayers.

Unlike the preceding, the *Yajur Veda* is addressed not only to the gods but also to the cultic objects that acquire a sacred character by reason of these invocations. Some of the formulas describe what can be attained by the object in question, others urge the object to action or impel another object to come into connection with it. A number of prayers are litanies, in which a statement or invocation is followed by a repetitive petition, as in the hymn to Thought.

The divinity that rises far when man is awake and falls back into him when he is asleep, the far-traveling light of lights is Thought. May it be friendly to me in what it devises.

That thought with which the wise skilfully perform their tasks in the sacrifice and rites—an unheard of wonder within all creatures—is Thought. May it be friendly to me in what it devises.

That which is knowledge, consciousness and will, an immortal light within living creatures, without which no action can be performed: such is Thought. May it be friendly to me in what it devises.

That by which immortality encompasses all that was, is and shall be, by which the sacrifice is performed with the seven officiants is Thought. May it be friendly to me in what it devises.

In it are the verses, melodies and formulas like spokes in a car's nave; in it all the thinking of creatures is woven. Such is Thought. May it be friendly to me in what it devises.

Driving men as one drives swift steeds with the reins like a skilful charioteer; dwelling in the heart, yet moving and most rapid, such is Thought. May it be friendly to me in what it devises.[2]

Similar to the *Rig Veda* but regarded as inferior is the *Atharva Veda,* whose preoccupation with placating the devils, casting of spells, and averting harm gives an insight into the homely concerns of the Hindu religion not supplied in the earlier Vedas. Every phase of life is consecrated by religion, and charms are available for every contingency, from warding off the attack of robbers to winning the love of a husband.

Among the more exalted incantations is one in which the breath is invoked against fear.

As both the heaven and the earth do not fear, are not harmed, so, my breath, fear not.

As both the day and night do not fear, are not harmed, so, my breath, do not fear.

As both ritual and dominion do not fear, are not harmed, so, my breath, do not fear.

As both truth and untruth do not fear, are not harmed, so, my breath, do not fear.

As both what is and what is to be do not fear, are not harmed, so, my breath, do not fear.[3]

In the *Atharva Veda* the magical spells are not only "white" but also "black" or witchcraft, by which a wife may kill a hated rival or a Hindu priest destroy the noble who robs him of his cows.

THE BRAHMANAS. How long the original Vedic form of Hinduism flourished is unknown. But in time ritualism became the dominant form of religion, and gradually fell under the monopoly of the priestly caste. Elaborate prose treatises were written as commentaries or interpretations of Brahman by means of symbols and ceremonies. Two types of these commentaries (*Brahmanas*) are distinguishable: the prescriptive and the explanatory, the two forming a vast repertoire that leaves nothing to the imagination. Whether an action should be done at the right or the left, whether a jar should be in this spot or that, whether a blade of grass should be laid down pointing to the north or the northeast, whether the priest stands before or behind the fire, into how many pieces the sacrificial cake is to be divided—all this and more is treated in great detail.

Each Veda has one or more Brahmanas of commentary, with three for the Sama Veda, and eight Brahmanas all told. Closely associated with this phase of Hinduism is the rise of the *Brahmin* or priest, who came to exalt himself above the gods, for he alone possessed the secret of the sacrifice which is able to bend the will of the gods.

Woven into the Brahmanas are legends on the origin of the world, epic tales, anecdotes about the goddesses and commentaries on the songs. One of the best known is the story of the flood in which Manu, the generic name for the father of mankind, is one morning approached by a fish to warn him of a universal deluge. The fish's advice was to have Manu rear it until it became a kind of whale, and at the same time build a huge ship. "After he had reared it in this way, he took it down to the sea, and in the same year which the fish had indicated to him, he attended to the advice of the fish by preparing a ship; and when the flood had risen, he entered into the ship. The fish then swam up to him, and to its horn he tied the rope of the ship, and by that means he passed swiftly up to a distant northern mountain." [4] After the flood Manu was left alone in the world, but on offering a sacrifice of butter, milk and curds, he produced a daughter, through whom he generated the present human race.

Reacting against the ritualism of the Brahmins are works of an esoteric nature called the *Aranyakas* or "forest treatises." Hermits used to recite them outside the community in the silence of the woods, in order to penetrate more deeply into the meaning of ritual sacrifices without performing the rites themselves. Like the Brah-

manas, these commentaries are also attached to the Vedas, two
for the *Rig Veda* and one for the *Atharva Veda;* but they go beyond the Brahmanas in mystic and magical formulas. Among the
treatises is a verse composition on human sacrifice. The prospective
male victim is a Brahmin or other noble, bought at the price of a
thousand cows and a hundred cattle, who is permitted a year of
freedom, in which he can do as he wishes, except that he must remain chaste. Another Brahmin or member of the royal family performs the sacrifice, which historians assign to the post-Vedic age,
after the rise of Buddhism.[5]

THE UPANISHADS. With the Aranyakas are certain "secret
teachings" that contain in unsystematized form the fundamentals of
Hindu philosophy. Since they come at the end of the Vedic literature, they are called *Vedanta,* or "end of the Vedas." Their more
familiar title is *Upanishad,* which literally means "sit down before"
(a teacher).

If there is one master idea in the Upanishads, it is the doctrine
offered by previous sages and expanded into a means of redemption
from the burdens of life and the wearisome trials of birth, death and
reincarnation. This mystery of salvation is expressed by the equa-
tion: Atman = the Brahman, in which Brahman stands for the
transcendent yet immanent supreme divinity and Atman for that
eternal portion of Brahman which abides in every living being.
Atman is a part of Brahman as salt is part of the water in which it
dissolves.

"Place this salt in water, and then wait on me in the morning."
The son did as he was commanded.
The father said to him, "Bring me the salt, which you placed in
the water last night."
The son having looked for it, did not find it because it was dissolved.
The father said, "Take a sip from the surface of the water. How is
it?"
The son replied, "It is salt,"
"Taste it from the middle. How is it?"
The son replied, "It is salt."
"Taste it from the bottom. How is it?"
The son replied, "It is salt."
The father said, "Set it aside. Then come back to me."

He did so, saying, "It is always the same."

Then the father said, "Here also, in this body, although you do not perceive Being here, nevertheless it is there.

"That which is the finest essence—this whole world has that for its soul. That is Reality. That is Atman (Soul). That you are, Svetaketu." [6]

If the main theme of the Upanishads is that Brahman and Atman are the same, that the reality of the world outside is identical with the reality of the self within, this final secret is found only as the crowning discovery of a long and painful search. On the way towards that solution many alternative suggestions are made and rejected. But when the ultimate revelation has been fully grasped, it can only be repeated again and again in a sort of rapture. "I am Brahman," and "You are That," are the key words of the Upanishads which unlock all beatitude.

For all their subtlety, the Upanishads are still within the ambit of Vedic literature. Their fourteen principal treatises are correlated with the four Vedas, with the surprising fact that the masterful *Rig Veda* has only two Upanishad commentaries compared with seven for the cultic and magical *Yajur Veda*.

SOURCES OF POPULAR RELIGION

Vedic literature is the mainstay of Hinduism, but only a fraction of its total concept. With the rise of Buddhism the needs for a broader appeal of Hindu theory were developed into what some writers summarily call *Smriti* (tradition), but which, more familiarly, may be considered popular religion. Two types of lore are concerned: the formalistic body of *Sutras* (concise formulas) and a set of epics that for most Westerners are all they know about Hinduism.

SUTRAS. At first glance the Sutras appear to be anything but popular, and certainly they are erudite enough. But their purpose was to popularize, in the sense of extend, the scope of Vedic ideas by their application to a wide range of topics what might otherwise have been untouched by Hinduism. Six disciplines are involved, with Sutras covering each: ceremonial, phonetics, prosody, grammar, etymology and astronomy.

Among the Sutras, the first which deals with ritual (*Kalpa*) is the most important. Similar to the Confucian idea of *li*, the Hindu *Kalpa* comprehends in separate tracts the basic ceremonies in the offering of public sacrifice, the regulations for domestic devotions, and a detailed study of social behavior for people in the various castes along with aphoristic rules for different conditions and stages of life. "One should speak the truth," the Kalpa prescribes, "and speak it pleasingly. One should not speak the untruth because it is displeasing. Whatever is dependent on others is misery; whatever rests on oneself is happiness."

BHAGAVAD GITA. The greatest of Indian religious writings, *Bhagavad Gita* (Song of the Blessed One) is the best known work in Indian literature, whose influence on Hindu thought has been monumental. It has been called "India's favorite Bible," which permeates the collective religious consciousness of the people as no other single piece of Hindu writing. Gandhi memorized its contents (about 30,000 words) as an act of devotion, and found in it, as generations had before, a gospel of action, with promises of deliverance that are quite unique in the religious systems of the East.

Actually the *Gita* is only a fragment of a larger epic, the *Mahabharata*, which contains upwards of a hundred thousand couplets. The epic is a mixture of religious sentiment, warlike legends and philosophical speculation that suggests a compound of Homer, Plato and Virgil—yet fused into a remarkable synthesis. Its ultimate goal is *Bhakti*, or the prospect of complete union with the sole Being, whose names are innumerable but whose invitation to divine friendship is unmistakable.

With your thoughts all actions casting upon Me, devoted to Me,
Turning to discipline of mentality, keep your mind ever fixed on Me.
If your mind is on Me, you shall cross over all difficulties by My grace;
But if through egoism you will not heed, you shall perish.
Be Me-minded, devoted to Me; worshiping Me, revere Me;
And to Me alone shall you go; truly to you I promise it—
Because you are dear to Me.
Abandoning all other duties, go to Me as your sole refuge;
From all evils I shall rescue you: be not grieved!
This you may never tell to one not mortified, or without devotion,
To one that obeys not, or to one that murmurs against Me.
Whoever in utmost shall make known this secret to My devotees,

Will assuredly come to Me.
No one among men does anything more pleasing to Me than he,
None shall be dearer to Me on earth than he.
And whoever shall study this communion of duty between us two,
By him shall I be worshiped with knowledge: so I hold.[7]

Built into the *Gita* are two speculative systems, theism and pantheism, which the author (or compiler) does not try to resolve. Various theories have been proposed to explain the two irreconcilable strata. One is that the poem was originally theistic and professed belief in a single transcendent Deity, distinct from the universe; this was later edited to satisfy monistic philosophers in the Brahmin tradition. More likely, however, the *Gita* was first a kind of Upanishad, or philosophic meditation cast in poetic form, whose original monistic thesis of an absolute Brahman was modified in the interests of a rising cult of Krishna, the incarnation of Vishnu (cosmic and solar deity), with whom some speculators had identified Brahman.

The *Gita* is clothed in the form of a story timed on the eve of a great battle, featuring Arjuna, a reflective warrior who hesitates about entering hostilities because of the carnage in which this will result. While brooding over the death of so many people, including his loved ones, the god Krishna rebukes his scrupulosity "that leads neither to heaven nor to honor."

Krishna explains that once a person has been born into the world, it is forever and that he will never die. Souls are without beginning and without end, and the enclosure of a soul in a particular body is unimportant. Consequently there is no real slaying, for at death the soul puts off one body only to put on another, much as a man removes and puts on his clothes.

These bodies come to an end, it is declared, of the everlasting, unperishing, incomprehensible, Body-Dweller. Therefore fight.
This never is born, and never dies, nor may it after being come again to be not.
This unborn, everlasting, abiding Ancient is not slain when the body is slain.
As man lays aside worn-out garments and takes others that are new, so the Body-Dweller puts away worn out bodies and goes to others that are new.

Swords cut This not, fire burns This not, water wets This not, wind dries
This not.

Unshown is This called, unthinkable This, unalterable This, therefore
knowing it is this wise, you do well not to grieve.[8]

So much for theory. As for practice, Krishna reminds the hero
to exert himself, yet not seek reward for the work that he does.
Rewards do not belong to the Self but to the passing modes of
(bodily) nature. Krishna had advocated this teaching in his many
previous births, even as he himself works and yet is workless. Epitomized in one statement, "On action alone be your interest, never
on its fruits. Let not the fruits of action be your motive, nor be your
attachment to inaction." [9]

The highest virtue, however, is not mere stoicism, not seeking
reward, nor "holding in indifference alike pleasure and pain, gain
and loss, conquest and defeat," but meditation on Self or the indestructible Reality within. "For the man whose delight is in Self,
who finds contentment in the Self, and satisfaction only in the Self,
there is nothing for which he should work." [10]

Unfortunately man's desires betray him into ambition and blind
him to the real values of things. Hence the advice "by constraining
the senses, free yourself from this sinful one that destroys knowledge and discernment." No doubt the senses are exalted. But
"higher than the senses is the mind, higher than the mind is understanding; and higher than understanding is This," namely, knowing Self to be higher than understanding, and supporting the self by
Self.[11]

Entreated to identify himself, Krishna reveals the heart of
Hindu theology. He describes his origin by his own power, his
frequent incarnations, his right of domain over the good and wicked
in the world, his finality as the goal to which disciplined souls are
destined even to entering the divine estate.

Though unborn and unchanging of essence, and though Lord of born
beings, yet resorting to My own material nature, I come into being by
my own mysterious power.

For whenever the law fails and lawlessness uprises, then do I bring
myself to embodied birth.

To guard the righteous, to destroy evildoers, to establish the law,
I come into birth age after age.

Whoever knows my wondrous birth and actions as they truly are, goes not to rebirth on leaving the body. He comes to Me, Arjuna.

Rid of passion, fear and wrath, made of Me, taking refuge of Me, cleansed by the austerity of knowledge, many have come into My Being.[12]

While depreciating the value of action and warning against the hope of reward, Krishna recommends sacrifice to the deity, since "not even this world is for him who does not offer sacrifices. How then the next?" [13] Yet material oblations are not the peak of divine worship. "Better than sacrifice that consists of substance is the sacrifice of knowledge."

Thus the *Gita* gives recognition to two opposing schools of Hindu thought, which it calls the "speculative" and the "discipline method." By the first is meant salvation through the power of perfect knowledge, which implies passivity or withdrawal from the world and renunciation of activity. By the second is meant the contrary, the quest of emancipation by selfless performance of duty. Both methods are approved, with full credit to the "way of philosophic speculation." Nevertheless the *Gita* normally favors "disciplined activity" or "indifference in action," which, in turn leads to knowledge, and is more simple than the way of knowledge and inaction.

Towering above both methods, however, is the easiest way to salvation—the way of devotion or love of the deity. By filling his being with Krishna, and doing all his acts as a service to him, man attains that union with the Eternal which is final salvation.

Whatever be your work, your eating, your sacrifice, your gift, your mortification, make it an offering to Me.

I am indifferent to all born things; there is none that I hate, none that I love. But they that worship Me with devotion, dwell in Me and I in them.

Even though he should be an evildoer who reveres Me with devotion, he shall be deemed good, for he has the right intention.

Quickly his soul becomes righteous, and he goes to eternal peace. Be assured that no one who is devoted to Me is lost.[13]

To be sure, this highest "path of devotion" carries an implicit contradiction. The Krishna elsewhere pictured as all-provident is here said to be "indifferent to all born things," and in the very act of soliciting the highest human devotion, professes there is "none that I love." Such incompatibilities are only part of the larger unresolved issue in the *Gita,* of an authentic personalist theism paralleled by the Vedantic theory of an impersonal, world soul Absolute. But this very tension may explain the *Gita's* popularity among Hindus who see it as a reflection of their own ambivalent views of the universe.

HINDU SECTARIANISM

Two types of sectarianism are discernible in the history of Hinduism, one theological and the other mainly philosophical. The latter accounted for the rise of such heretical systems as Buddhism and Jainism, and will be examined later. On its theological side, the Hindu religion had sown the seeds of division when it failed to explain the equal dignity of Brahma, Vishnu and Siva in the sacred writings. Brahma was not a popular deity, and quite naturally the followers of Vishnu and Siva each claimed the honors of supremacy for their favorite. Out of this rivalry grew two distinct sects—Vishnuism and Sivaism, which became solidified through centuries of sectarian writings called the *Puranas* (Antiquities), extending from the first centuries of the Christian era to the twelfth.

Not the least feature of both types of sectarianism is the role played by Krishna, who had already gone through three radical developments—from warrior, to demi-god, to the equal of Brahman. In the Puranas he appears in all the lewd obscenity that has deeply (and unfortunately) colored the Western ideas of Oriental religion.

On reaching manhood, Krishna gave himself up to a life of dissipation and unbridled debauchery. He did not even respect the virtue of his sisters or his own mother. After carrying them off by force, he treated them as if they were his legitimate wives. After slaying his uncle, he carried off the maiden Rukhmani, but the legend says he had sixteen thousand wives and a prodigious number of children.

Yet within the same Puranic tradition we find Krishna not only worshiped as a god, or equated with Brahman, but he receives adoration from Brahma (the rival of Vishnu and Siva) and is praised in language that simply identifies him with the world.

"Krishna is the Soul of all souls, the Self of all selves, with whom all souls are eternally united. In reality it is Krishna who has become all things. He has become, indeed, the whole universe." [14]

Between the two sects, Vishnuism and Sivaism, the former conceives its deity as benevolent and many times incarnate through mercy for the human race. Consequently the Vishnava is primarily a devotionist. His piety is analogous to the love of a mother towards her child or of a husband for his wife. The two main incarnations of Vishnu, Rama and Krishna, symbolize the deity's concern for the weakness and needs of mankind.

Sivaism, on the other hand, venerates its god more out of fear than love. Siva is in a special manner the great god of the Himalaya mountains; inaccessible, transcendent, absorbed in divine contemplation. The Ganges River came down from the heavens because Siva bore on his matted hair the forceful impact of its falling torrents. He creates and destroys, and at times obscures by his power of illusion (*maya*), and on occasion may even be gracious to the suffering. Mythologically he is the successor of the malicious Vedic divinity, Rudra, author of sickness and death. Understandably Vishnuism is more popular and more widely diffused than Sivaism in modern India.

Besides the two main divisions numerous other sects are scattered among the millions of Hindus, and often impossible to classify because they have no ecclesiastical structure and no definable creed.

Saktism concentrates on the cult of the feminine form of the god and professes belief in the *sakti* or "divine energy." It may best be described as worship of the Mother-Goddess, Sakti, either alone or in the company of her consort, or as one of many feminine deities that arose in Hindu mythology outside the Vedic tradition. The sacred books of Saktism are the *Tantra,* written about the eighth century A.D., but reflecting theories prevalent for some three hundred years before. A thousand popular stories are told about Sakti (or her equivalents): her birth in the mountains, her youth, her courtship of Siva, and her children. Like Sivaism, the cult of the goddess on its speculative side is directed towards an identification of the individual with the Supreme Being.

Lesser sectarian groups generally follow some religious reformer, ascetic or sage, and have developed a literature of their

own. The Madhva sect preaches salvation through the immediate
and intuitive knowledge of the deity; the Vallabhas teach a variety
of divine grace; the Gosvamins are heads of monasteries and
temples; for the Kapalikas the chief acts of worship are singing and
dancing; Pasupatas seek to attain ecstasy by means of violent
practices; the Lingayats are directed by wandering monks who
reject the Veda, caste system and images; the Bhagavatas profess
an extreme form of devotionalism and interpret the eroticism of
Hindu mythology in terms of mystical love.

BASIC RELIGIOUS PRINCIPLES

Every analysis of Hindu religious principles must take into
account the two main segments of Hindu society, the popular or
undeveloped majority and the intellectual minority, which some
have aptly called the "outer" and "inner" forms of Hinduism.

OUTER HINDUISM. The ordinary Hindu believes in many gods,
out of a pantheon estimated at "thirty-three crore" or thirty-three
times ten million male and female deities. Warrant for this polytheism is found in the *Rig Veda,* which honors a profusion of gods
and prescribes sacrifices in their name. Chief among the animal
sacrifices are two possessions which the ancient Aryans most prized,
the horse and the cow. The latter is the animal most often given
divine honors in Hinduism, and no pious Hindu would ever kill
one.

Out of these deities the average Hindu chooses one as patron
god (*istadevata*) who becomes the object of special veneration. He
may have a vague idea of Brahman, but is quite satisfied to consider
his favorite the only god, who is normally Brahma, Vishnu or Siva,
or one of their incarnations like Krishna or Rama. All this is con-
formable to the Vedas which allow the worship of God under any
form and in any manner; nor is there any objection to joining the
worship of a favorite god together with other deities. Polytheism,
therefore, is the hallmark of the popular Hindu religion, unless
we call it henotheism, in which one god is preferred but others are
not excluded.

Along with the worship of the gods, Hinduism teaches transmigration of souls and obedience to caste customs. The two con-

cepts are closely related. The theory is that when a man dies his soul goes to the particular heaven of his particular god, as a reward for devotion to that deity. Later the soul returns to earth and is rejoined to another body, by transmigration from one corporeal dwelling to another. This process goes on forever, and the soul is inexorably bound to the "wheel of existence" that turns around and around, from birth to death to birth to death, in unending repetition.

Sojourns in heaven between re-incarnations are temporary and their duration depends on the virtue practiced before death. Souls are rewarded (and punished) on earth also, as may be seen from the fact that some are healthy and others sick, some wise and others ignorant. A soul is born into one of these groups according to its merits in previous bodily lives.

This doctrine is the key to understanding the caste system in Hinduism. For the Hindus believe that a person belongs to a high caste as a reward for virtue in a previous existence. Similarly demerits, or the Hindu equivalent of the consequences of sin, explain why some people belong to a low caste, like the Musahars (Mouse Eaters) or to the lowest group of Pariahs (Untouchables) who belong to no caste at all. They are at the opposite end of the Hindu caste system, ranging from the highest, the Brahmins (Priestly caste) through lower but still elevated classes like the Rakputs (King Sons) or Kshatriyas (Rulers).

Orthodox Hindus believe the castes are fixed and irrevocable, determined solely by one's conduct in a prior bodily existence. Nothing can change a man's lot during life to place him in a higher caste, but if he is faithful to caste regulations he may deserve this privilege in a future reincarnation, even to becoming a Rajput or Brahmin.

INNER HINDUISM. Parallel with this popular form of Hinduism is the religion of the educated and intellectuals. They follow the Upanishads, tolerate idols on the ground that this helps the ordinary man to pray and offer a sophisticated balance to the henotheism of the masses. Two strains in this "inner" Hinduism must be carefully distinguished: the more familiar pantheism which holds there is only one reality, Brahman, the foundation of all beings; and the less well known but widespread position which admits some kind of distinction between Brahman and the individual soul. Common to both schools are certain basic attitudes towards the deity and the prospects of escape from the "wheel of existence."

Brahman is the Absolute beyond all multiplicity, change, division or relation. It is the One Reality which is the Ground and Principle of all things. Nothing can be predicated of Brahman because all qualities or attributes would contradict the absoluteness and unicity of the Supreme Reality. Brahman *is,* but we should be limiting Its infinity if we said that Brahman is this or that. To know correctly one must resort to negation, the "not this not that" of the Upanishads. When Hindus speak of Brahman they do not refer to God as Creator, Ruler or Savior. They even affirm that Brahman is impersonal because It is rather the Godhead than God, apprehended by relation to the world as an object of devotion. They do not pray to Brahman, they meditate on It.

The descent from this impersonal unicity of Brahman to pantheism came by way of a radical concept of the universe. Hindu philosophers, in common with thinkers in all nations, held to the principle that "Out of nothing, nothing comes into existence," yet not in the sense that nothing exists without a sufficient cause, but that without a material cause nothing can be produced, even by divine power. Given this premise, they found themselves affirming that God is immanent in all of apparent creation. "Truly," they declare, "all this is Brahman." [15]

Evidently such monism which makes God impersonal and the world unreal does not correspond to the common sense notion of religion, which is the relation between a rational creature and a personal Deity. Hindu speculators recognized this and sought for a compromise between their own intellectualism and the popular religion. Their compromise in essence was to say there are two aspects to Brahman. God considered in Himself is the Absolute and Impersonal; but as manifesting Himself in creation He is Relative and Personal. There is consequently a two-fold Brahman: one that is phenomenal and another noumenal. The first is the existing, visible world; the second is the reality which underlies the world. Only the latter is absolutely real; the former is only relatively real, i.e., to us. Technically Brahma (masculine gender) is the sensibly perceptible universe, whereas Brahman (neuter gender) is the impersonal Absolute.

Texts abound in which this duality is proposed. "There are two forms of Brahman; the crude and the subtle, mortal and immortal, limited and unlimited, definite and indefinite." [16] Correspondingly there are two forms of religion, one higher and the other lower. The lower type consists in seeing Brahman in its various created forms and is expressed in the positive dictum, *asti, asti* (it is this, it is this). But the higher type consists in apprehending the Brahman Absolute in Itself, by way of a negative axiom, *neti, neti* (not this, not this).

Can these two kinds of religion be reconciled? Not really, according to the Hindu elite, except that one may be suffered to continue until the other is (if ever) discovered. The "pedagogic truth" in Hinduism's sacred books which claims that Siva or Krishna is God is not really true; neither is it true that we and the world around us really exist as distinct entities. Simple people who take the sacred books literally are mistaken, and when they assume their own individual existence they are under an illusion. Indeed they *are* an illusion. Were it otherwise, they would understand that they are the One, Infinite God who is all there was, is or ever will be.

Professing pantheism, "inner" Hinduism says to the multitude of uncultured believers that those who follow the ways of the gods receive the reward of the gods, a brief taste of heaven between successive rebirths on earth. But they will never be delivered from the "wheel of existence" with its illusory lives and deaths until they realize that only God exists and all else is illusion (*maya*). To achieve this liberation three ways are mainly proposed: by means of concentration and self control (*yoga*), through unselfish performance of duty, and by way of intense devotion or contemplative love.

Indian spirituality is perhaps best known by the practice of *yoga*, derived from the root *yuj*, to unite or yoke, which in context means union with the Absolute. Numerous stages are distinguished in the upward progress towards the supreme end of identification, by means of knowledge, with the deity: the practice of moral virtues and observances of ethical rules, bodily postures, control of internal and external senses, concentration of memory and meditation—finally terminating in total absorption (*samadhi*), "when the seer stands in his own nature."

Although the psychic element is far more important in *yoga* than the bodily, the latter is more characteristic of this method of

Hindu liberation. Its purpose is to secure the best disposition of body for the purpose of meditation. The practice begins with a simple device for deep and slow breathing.

Stopping the right nostril with the thumb, through the left nostril fill in air, according to capacity. Then without any interval, throw the air out through the right nostril, closing the left one. Again inhaling through the right nostril, eject through the left, according to capacity. Practicing this three or five times at four hours of the day, before dawn, during midday, in the evening, and at midnight, in fifteen days or a month purity of the nerves is attained.[17]

After such preliminary exercises, more complicated practices are undertaken, but not without the guidance of a professional yogin called *guru*. The meditative phase begins with fixing the mind on one object, which may be anything whatsoever, "the sphere of the navel, the lotus of the heart, the light of the brain, the tip of the nose, the tip of the tongue, and such like parts of the body"—or also God. Gradually by sheer concentration of attention the mind reaches a state of trance, where all mental activity stops and the consciousness rests in itself. The state of *samadhi* is the culmination of *yoga* and beyond it lies release. The life of the soul is not destroyed but is reduced to its "unconscious and permanent essence."

Not everyone can practice *yoga*, at least not in the sense of prolonged application of mind, disengaged from the phenomenal knowledge of the world and coming face to face with its own subsisting ground which is the Universal Spirit. Many cultured believers who take Hinduism seriously seek release from endless reincarnations by way of unselfish performance of duty, especially through works of charity and social welfare. Its full Sanskrit equivalent is *karmaphalatyaga*, which is generally shortened to *karma*. This was basically Mahatma Gandhi's philosophy of life and the motive force of his crusade against untouchability. His war on this miasma was conducted in terms of Hinduism. "I do not want to be reborn," he stated, "but if I have to be reborn I should be reborn an untouchable so that I may have their sorrows, sufferings, and the affronts leveled against them in order that I may endeavor to free myself and them from their miserable condition." [18]

Other Hindus are inspired to follow the Vedic praise of *Bhakti* or loving devotion as the means of final release. Their system, if it may be called such, may not differ radically from the more ascetical *yoga* except for a shift of emphasis on the will and emotions. It teaches the rules of love and directs the affections with varying stress on Self (*Atman*) or outside of self on that which is infinite Beauty.

Whosoever is desired by this Atman attains this Atman and to him this Atman is revealed. Whosoever is intensely loved by this Atman will become the favorite of this Atman. Thus, in order that the loved one might attain the Atman, the Lord himself intervenes. For the Lord said, "I shall direct the will of those who offer Me constant attachment and adore Me with love and I shall show them the way to reach Me." This continual remembrance is expressed by the word *Bhakti*.[19]

Theistic interpreters of the method of devoted love call it the highest expression of authentic natural mysticism, which has no desire to merge into the unconsciousness of the Absolute, but rather to be conscious of the presence of a personal God and savor Him intensely. Undoubtedly some Hindus so conceive *Bhakti* spirituality. But they are exceptions to a speculative tradition which tries to solve the antinomy between the claims of religion asking for a personal god and those of Hindu metaphysics, denying absolute transcendence to a personal being.

The object of the bhakta's devotion, therefore, is not God but *a god,* the highest he can imagine, some individual being endowed with all the attributes that belong to the divinity, a being which is said to be the Supreme Person, identified even with Brahman, yet conceived as related and internally subject to change, affirmed as transcendent while seen against a philosophical background of a centuries-old pantheism.

Nevertheless the *bhakta* wants to love and give himself to a god he can see and touch and serve, a god who is near to his devotee with the promise of liberation from the eternal cycle. Throughout the writings of Hindu mystics, there is a pathetic yearning for the incarnate god in human form, only partially satisfied by the *avataras* (descents) of Hindu mythology.

CASTE SYSTEM

It would be inadequate to say that Hindu society is nothing more than the caste system, whose foundations rest on the earliest

Vedic sources. Nevertheless, the social ethics of the Hindu religion is certainly based upon caste.

Traditionally the origin of castes goes back to the *Rig Veda,* which says that, "One fourth of the Supreme Being constitutes all beings, while three fourths of Him are immortal and stand above. With the one-fourth below, He extended on all sides into the animate and the inanimate. . . . His face became the *Brahmin.* His arms were made into the *Kshatriya.* His thighs became the *Vaisya.* From His feet the *Sudra* was born." [20]

Many historians believe this passage describes the social organization created by the Aryans after they had settled on Indian soil. As a theocracy it was ruled by divinely appointed kings (*Kshatriya*), assisted by priests and ministers who explained the code of laws (*Brahmins*), arming and trade were handled by the Vaishyas. The aborigines (*Sudras*) were reduced to slavery by the upper three classes.

Since the Sanskrit word for these categories is *varna* (color), it seems the racial element played some part in first stratifying the caste system. *Brahmins* (white) were assigned the highest duties: studying, teaching, sacrificing, assisting others with alms and gifts. *Kshatriya* (red) were also allowed study, sacrifice and almsgiving, but further privileged to use weapons and protect life and material possessions. The *Vaisya* (yellow) had privileges similar to the preceding, along with the duty to trade and tend cattle. Finally the *Sudra* (black) had the obligation of serving the other three *varnas.* In time the prohibition of inter-marriage would create new classes of people that later proliferated into the twenty-five hundred castes of Medieval India.

Other scholars prefer to add the certain fact that prior to the Aryan invasion there had been well-established religious and magical tabus, which together with occupational monopolies provided a logical basis of the caste system. The Aryans exploited the existing social divisions they found in India, and in time superimposed on them the dogma of *karma* (deed done), by which every man was told that his birth in a particular caste was the result of his previous existence, and that strict observance of the rules of his caste gave him the only hope of (possible) eventual liberation.

Already in the *Gita,* the hero is persuaded by Krishna to fight because such is his duty as a member of the ruling class. Previous arguments had appealed to the immortality of the true Self.

Look at it from the point of view of your caste duty (*svadharma*). Why hesitate? For a Kshatriya, is there anything more noble than a righteous war? Happy are the Kshatriyas to whom such a battle as this comes. It opens a door to heaven. Were you to refuse to fight, you would spurn your duty and incur disgrace and sin. Everyone will speak ill of you in the future. For a man of honor, that kind of disgrace is worse than death.[21]

Outside the pale of the four varnas are the untouchables who do not properly belong to any caste. They are the Pariahs whom Gandhi affectionately renamed the *Harijans* (people of the god Hari), and who are further divided into a great number of sub-castes.

According to traditional Hinduism, the life of the members of the upper three castes should be spent in four successive stages (*ashramas*), which are carefully regulated. First comes the "stage of the celibate" who should "abstain from wine, meat, perfumes, garlands, sweetmeats and women. He should not take acid food and should do harm to no living being. Gambling, gossip, slander and untruth are to be shunned. He should neither look at nor touch women. He should never strike anybody." [22] After studying the Vedas he is to marry and begin his life as householder, with manifold duties stressing hospitality, almsgiving, industry and fidelity to caste prescription. With the advancement of age, the faithful Hindu (alone or with his wife) should retire from active duty in order to pray, practice austerity and finally reach the state of a *Sannyasi* which is the apex of human morality.

While these prescriptions are only remotely approximated in modern times, they represent an ideal that Hindus still respect: as, for instance, in the character sketch of the Sannyasi portrayed in the law books of the castes.

Wishing neither for death nor for life, the Sannyasi should wait for the appointed time as a laborer for his wages. His feet guided by his eyes, the water he drinks strained through a cloth, his speech purified by truth, his conduct governed by reason. Let him endure insult without retaliation, let him have no enemy, knowing that his body is of no value. He should never answer anger with anger, and he should bless those who curse him. Truthful in his speech, he should find his delight in the Supreme and be indifferent to all pleasure; having no friend but himself, let him wander here upon earth in quest of true happiness.[23]

No provision is made for the special training of women, who are supposed to acquire the qualities of their caste in life as wives and mothers in the household in which they are born.

Apart from its religious justification, the caste system is a complex phenomenon which it is hard to define. However, there are certain characteristics that stand out to distinguish it from any comparable structure in other religions. Each caste may be considered a closed social group, theoretically based on heredity, so that a person belongs to the caste in which he is born. In Vedic times a non-Aryan could become a Brahmin, provided he had the qualifications. Later on the three primary castes became separated by watertight partitions, making it practically impossible to pass from one to the other.

Each caste, moreover, has an independent organization, a nominal head and council which may meet on special occasions. It has common festivals and common usages, particularly in the matter of marriage and diet. As a rule, members of a caste practice the same profession or trade; and within their groups they are liable to certain penalties, of which the most serious is expulsion from the caste.

Among the castes, only the first (Brahmins) is invested with truly religious authority, although lower groups participate in varying degrees in the ritual ceremonies. Technically the Brahmins stand at the top of the social hierarchy with corresponding privileges. Ancient tradition says that "the very birth of a Brahmin is the eternal incarnation of the Law." For centuries they were the philosophers and writers who taught the Vedas and were entrusted with all that pertains to the priesthood. They were required to meditate on the Hindu scriptures, bathe twice daily in running water, become strict vegetarians and wear the sacred thread symbolizing their caste. Without the aura of near-divinity which formerly surrounded the Brahmins, they are still the intellectual leaders of Hinduism, numbering such men as Sarvepalli Radhakrishnan and Jawaharlal Nehru.

Formerly the warrior caste, the Kshatriyas were to defend the right, protect the weak and use force when necessity required. Indian sovereigns used to be chosen from this caste and until modern times they were members of the nobility. At present only the Rajputs, a segment of this military class, survive in any number. Most of the others have entered clerical professions and represent a kind of middle class in Hindu society.

Vaisyas have the business of dealing with material goods of every description. They promoted internal and foreign trade, engaged in farming and industry, and played a major role in creating the Republic of India. Mahatma Gandhi belonged to a sub-caste of the Vaisyas, the so-called *Baniya* or grain-merchant clan.

Unlike the Pariah untouchables, the fourth and lowest caste of Sudras have never been slaves, but were free to carry on or leave their work and place of employment. Their service of the upper castes was not such that others might not perform it, but it was theirs by class privilege. Servants, shepherds, artisans, and workmen of all kind were traditionally Sudras. An interesting restriction to which they were subject was the prohibition to learn the Vedas, but with the option of studying the great epics and Puranas instead. Subdivided into hundreds of subordinate castes, they are the majority of India's population and Brahmin writers still describe the Sudras as born to labor and naturally unable to do anything better or higher.

Outside all the castes, and barred from ever becoming *sannyasis,* the untouchable Pariahs are of unknown origin, although the classic Laws of Manu state that "illicit marriages between people of different castes, marriages contrary to rule, omission of the prescribed ceremonies, these are the origin of the impure classes." Hindu theology would explain their existence in terms of *Karma* and punishment for a bad life in a previous existence. Since Gandhi's crusade in their favour, their condition has much improved, notably in greater freedom to intermarry with members of the castes and worship in temples that had formerly been closed to them. Employed as tanners, butchers, sweepers, and the like, their history includes a fair quota of Hindu "saints," since the same Laws of Manu admit that in certain cases Pariahs of the lowest and most degraded groups may obtain supreme bliss without passing through re-incarnation.

RITUAL AND WORSHIP

For most Hindus, worship and ritual are the mainstay of religion, and more important than what god they choose for patron or whether, as for many intellectuals, they accept any personal deity at all. The whole of a faithful Hindu's life is punctuated at regular intervals by rites and external practices to which he is bound if he wants to maintain the Aryan *Dharma* (Sanskrit for "law"), as the traditional Hindu way of life is called.

RITES, SACRIFICES AND OBSERVANCES. The variety and complexity of religious practices in Hinduism defy classification. Castes, sects, and philosophical schools are the main source of difference; but modern conditions in the city demand further adaptations of a ritual that was meant for rural and not urban ways of life.

Since the Brahmins are not only the highest social caste but their whole life is supposed to be controlled by ritual, their religious practices serve as models for the other castes. A survey of their customs will give a cross-section of the ritual observances throughout Hinduism.

Rising before sunrise, a Brahmin should avoid looking at any inauspicious objects or persons, like a widow or a sweeper. His right foot must touch the ground first, and once out of bed he rinses his mouth three times and winds the holy thread round his neck and over the right ear. After bowing to the sun he takes the morning ablutions, preferably in running water, and concludes with a prayer to the gods, ancestors and sages.

Then begins the morning prayer (*Pratah-sandhya*) which must be finished before sunrise. While seated on a low stool and facing the east, the Brahmin sips water and pronounces the sacred formulas (*mantras*) over the ashes he has brought with him to mark his forehead, arms, ribs and knees. Closing one nostril after the other, he exhales and inhales, repeating the consecrated *gayatri* invocation, "Let us meditate on the excellent radiance of the divine sun. May he stimulate our minds." Besides other prescriptions, the *gayatri* is repeated one hundred and eight times on a rosary counting the beads.

Following this is the offering of ghee (semi-fluid butter), curd and rice to the fire. Called *homa,* the morning sacrifice must precede the first meal, and is followed by spiritual reading with another detailed ritual. The right hand is placed successively in front of the mouth, the eyes, ears, nose, lips, top of the head, chin, forearms, navel, and the back in order to invoke the gods and attain their protection. After repeating the *gayatri,* a sacred book is briefly read.

Next comes the triple propitiation ceremony. After sipping water and facing east, the worshiper pours water from his straightened finger while the sacred thread hangs over the left shoulder. This is to propitiate the gods. He repeats the pouring, but now between the two little fingers, with thread hanging around the neck and he facing west—to propitiate the sages. Lastly he faces south, thread hanging from the right shoulder, and pours water between thumb and first finger of right hand—to propitiate the ancestors.

A final ritual is the worship of the deity, normally in a small room of the home where an image of the favorite god is reserved. Part of the ceremony is to use blessed water which the Brahmin sprinkles over the utensils of worship (bell, copper vessel, spoon, sandal-wood paste, incense, conch shell) and over the worshiper himself. Special prayers and rubrics depend on the deity who is worshiped. At the end comes a prayer asking forgiveness of sins.

For the sake of convenience, shorter rituals are provided to cover the five daily essentials: bath, morning prayer, sacrifice, reading and worship. Even where Hindus have given up the long morning ceremonies, they still daily recite the *gayatri* to the sun.

Sacrifices on a large scale, as practiced in Vedic times, are now practically reduced to oblations honoring the home and temple deities. Occasionally, however, something of the ancient custom is revived to propitiate the gods on a grand scale, as in the expiation ritual where a number of Brahmins are invited to supply by proxy the estimated two million times that a householder is supposed to recite the *gayatri* during his lifetime. The priests may take several days to complete the required quota, while pouring ghee on the fire during the recitation.

In a broad sense, sacrifice for the Hindus takes on various meanings and as such is prescriptive for every day. Reading the sacred writings is considered a sacrifice to Brahman, the offering of propitiation is sacrifice to one's ancestors, the morning *homa* satisfies for a sacrifice to the gods, feeding of animals is said to be sacrifice to the elements, and hospitality is sacrifice to human beings.

Temple worship for the Hindus is not strictly liturgical in the sense of a public ceremony. When the faithful come to a shrine, the priest alone performs the ceremonies, with no participation of the laity, who join in the ritual by reading some holy book, reciting their beads or joining in religious song. Instructions are also sometimes given.

In the innermost chamber of the temple is an image of the main god, while other shrines may surround the principal one in honor of lesser deities. The daily ritual consists in treating the image as a living person. Before dawn the god is awakened with sweet music, he is bathed, often by washing a mirror reflection, and then dressed and made ready to meet the pilgrims for the day. Meals are served him twice daily, and before sunset another light refreshment followed by changing of clothes and retirement for the night. The god Siva is usually represented by the phallic symbol, to which the same kind of ritual is given, and in some temples this image is bathed continually.

Though blood sacrifices to the male gods are rare, the goddesses, especially Kali, are often propitiated by the offering of animals beheaded by the priests, and their blood used by the people to smear on their foreheads. Private worship in the temples requires the saying of prayers and the offering of an oblation to the gods at the hands of a priest. After sacrifice, the faithful receive a small portion of their offering to the deity as a memento.

Vows are often made to the gods for obtaining some favor like the birth of a child or cure of an illness. Votaries also promise some act of mortification if their petition is heard, say, walking around the temple a certain number of times or abstaining from salt for several weeks or months.

Apart from the regular home or temple ceremonies, the Hindu religion is filled with special observances that affect every detail of a person's life. Consulting horoscopes before marriage or choice of profession is done by professional astrologers, whose decisions are highly respected even by the most educated classes.

Every day of the week carries some auspicious or inauspicious regulation. On Mondays cloth and shoes should not be bought, nor journeys eastward started, but birth and weddings are promised good fortune; Tuesdays there should be no sowing, shaving or shopping, and traveling north is discouraged; Wednesdays are lucky for the birth of a boy, but unlucky for a girl, and anything done on Wednesday will bear double fruit; Thursdays white food is recommended, but not travel southward; Friday is a good day for buying land but bad for traveling west; Saturdays are inauspicious for almost everything, except to begin a friendship, engage a servant or move into a new home; Sundays are days of fast for barren women and lepers, and ideal for travel in any direction.

Similarly certain days of the lunar month are either lucky or ominous. The eleventh day of each fortnight is the holiest and most propitious; whereas the first, fourth, ninth, and fourteenth are the opposite. On the last day of the month, the moonless day, no marriages ever take place because of the risks involved.

Together with the gods, who are invoked and worshiped, Hinduism has a myriad of demons and evil spirits against whose influence the people must be protected. For this reason amulets are worn, usually around the arm, and contain an image of a god, a piece of paper or bark on which some spell has been written, a coil of thread or a tuft of hair.

Spirits who wander are propitiated by giving them a home and due homage. They are often represented by a stone, smeared with vermilion, and surrounded by other stones. During worship, the stone is bathed, smeared with ghee, the vermilion renewed and oblations of fruit and sweetmeats offered. Particularly dangerous spirits are propitiated by bloody sacrifices, which may involve the devil-dance performed by a medium who allows himself to be temporarily possessed by the demon, to the accompaniment of furious music. Exorcisms are also practiced, and vary from physical violence to the recitation of simple prayers.

MAJOR PURIFICATIONS. Although Hinduism has no sacramental system, the term it uses for special purifications, *Samskara,* has been adapted by Christians as the standard word for "sacrament." Hindus disagree on the actual number of *samskaras,* some counting as many as forty, including the household ceremonies previously described. However, four at least are commonly recognized as primary, and coincide with the most important events of a person's life: birth, initiation, marriage and death.

Shortly after marriage a ceremony of oblation to the sun takes place, in which husband and wife pray for the conception of a son, "Faithful wife" the husband concludes, "give birth to a son who will live long and perpetuate our line." Three months later the ceremony is repeated, followed in turn by three pre-natal ordinances in the fourth, sixth and eighth months of pregnancy.

At the time of birth, the father anoints the child's tongue with a rice and barley emulsion and gives it ghee mixed with gold powder to eat, and four months later offers his offspring to the moon. Either then or on the first birthday the child is given a name, chosen by the father after invocations and according to which lamp burns more brightly before one of two tablets signed with alternate names. Touching the mouth, nose, ears and eyes of the baby, the father pronounces two prayers, whispering the name in the mother's left and the child's right ear. According to the caste, different prefixes are added, for example *sharma* (auspicious) for Brahmins and *dasa* (servant) for Sudras.

Initiation ceremonies are reserved for boys, which nowadays take place at the time of adolescence. The main features are a sacrifice of ghee; holding of water in the hands and dropping same; being touched on shoulders, navel, and heart by a religious preceptor; and having the sacred thread imposed in three strands—of cotton for Brahmin, and of hemp or wool for the lower castes. From the initiation on, the Hindu must perform the religious duties proper to his class. Many Hindus are faithful in reciting the *gayatri* prayer throughout life.

Although some changes are inevitable in modern India, the average Hindu marriage is pre-arranged by the parents of the prospective groom and bride, whose first duty is to consult a genealogy expert to make sure of a right choice. As a rule bride and groom do not meet before marriage, though an exchange of photographs is permitted.

Astrologers are further consulted about the day and time of the wedding, at which the bride's father officiates as religious minister. Sprinkling blessed water on the tied hands of the young couple, and reciting his own and their genealogies, he says to the groom, "I give you this my daughter, arrayed in clothes and ornaments, and devoted to Prajapati (Lord of the populace)." However the marriage consent is not officially given until the bride, at the request of the bridegroom, takes seven steps, to symbolize her acceptance of him as her protector, master and husband.

Consistent with their belief in re-incarnation, as the Hindus approach death they wish to make sure that no ritual purification is omitted in order to insure, if possible, final emancipation (*moksha*) and avoid return to earth for another round of bodily expiation. Just before death, the dying person is laid on the floor to escape the evil spirits who roam between heaven and earth. Formerly they were brought to die at the banks of the river Ganges.

Immediately after death the body is washed, wrapped in new cloth, and taken in procession on a stretcher, led by the person who carries the jar of fire to be used for cremation. At the funeral pyre, the body is washed or sprinkled with Ganges water, and burned at a slow fire (about three hours) into which ghee is regularly poured. Children under eighteen months, ascetics, lepers and people with certain diseases are not burned but buried. Following the funeral a ritual of purification takes place, which goes on for eight to thirty days, as a prelude for the all-important *shraddha* ceremony on which the destiny of the deceased finally depends. Differing greatly according to caste and locality, the main feature of the *shraddha* is offering and invocations of ancestors, which should be done by the deceased person's son and therefore explains why every Hindu is anxious about his fate after death until a son has been born to him.

DOMINANT PERSONALITIES

More than with most religions, Hinduism has depended on the leaders of Indian history who have shaped its religious culture. The number of lesser figures is legion, and even those who have made a substantial contribution are numerous. Certain names, however, stand out either because their influence is fully established by centuries of tradition and a dedicated following, or, in more recent times, because their ideas are considered representative of the best in Hindu thought.

Sankara (788-820) was the most noted of all Hindu commentators. Born into a Brahmin family of Malabar, Sankara early became noted for his wisdom and practice of yoga. He wandered from place to place, studying and teaching, either alone or with his disciple Padmapada. At Benares he wrote commentaries on the Brahman Sutras, the Upanishads and the Bhagavad Gita, and died in Kanchi at the age of thirty-two.

A creative thinker of the first rank, Sankara developed what has since become known as "illusionist monism," or "non-dualism" (*advaita*), according to which the world and Brahman do not really exist separately. Only the One is real; the many are illusion or *maya*.

His writings show a sincere effort to give the doctrine of the Upanishads greater unity and coherence. He does this by distinguishing two forms of knowledge, a higher and lower, or more accurately, knowledge and nescience. The higher knowledge recognizes only one reality—the Self, which is inherently unknowable because it is subject and not object of knowledge. Outside the Self, the phenomenal world is knowable, indeed, but unreal. Sankara held it is the business of philosophy to distinguish between the two spheres and give the self a sense of unity with the infinite and uniquely real Brahman.

Since ethics and religion belong to the phenomenal world they are unreal. "The knowledge of active religious duty has for its fruit transitory felicity, and that again depends on the performance of religious acts. The inquiry into Brahman, on the other hand, has for its fruit eternal bliss and does not depend on the performance of any acts." [24]

Although Sankara's commentaries were originally personal interpretations of the *Vedanta,* or "end of the Vedas" section of the Hindu sacred writings, their doctrine became so influential it is often described simply as *the* Vedanta. Its purpose is to discover the identity of the objective reality of the universe with the subjective reality of the thing-in-itself, much as Kant used the term in his philosophy.

In common with Hindu thinkers before and since, Sankara insisted on the need for redemption, which he said can come only by the knowledge of this identity between Brahman and the self. "Release," he taught, "is nothing but being Brahman. Therefore release is not something to be purified." Its meaning has "not the slightest relation to any action, except knowledge." [25] For persons qualified to obtain such knowledge life has no other significance.

If a man knows Brahman, he is one with Brahman, who is neither agent nor enjoyer. He can say, "I neither was an agent or an enjoyer at any previous time, nor am I such at the present time, nor shall I be such at any future time." [26] Taken literally this doctrine would destroy moral responsibility, but Sankara's disciples insist that such is not the case for those truly enlightened.

About three centuries after Sankara arose another famous commentator, Ramanuja (1050-1137), who used the same Vedic texts to arrive at a different philosophy of life, a "qualified non-dualism," which is still a type of monism, but with a difference. He rejected the distinction between the higher and lower knowledge, the idea of unreality in the world, and of the individual's absolute identity with Brahman. He sought to explain the Vedanta on the theory of a supreme God of grace.

We know from the sacred writings that there is a Supreme Person, whose nature is absolute bliss and goodness, who is fundamentally antagonistic to all evil, who is the cause of the origination, sustenance, and dissolution of the world, who differs in nature from all other beings, who is all-knowing, who by his mere thought and will accomplishes all his purposes; who is an ocean of kindness, as it were, for all who depend on him, whose name is the highest Brahman. [27]

Souls are delivered from the cycle of birth and rebirth by their devotion to Brahman, and they are redeemed not by merger with the One but by enjoying intercourse with him.

Yet Ramanuja did not rise entirely above a monistic conception of reality. He spoke of the "highest Brahman which is the sole cause of the entire universe," but at the same time held that, "of this Brahman, the individual selves are modes, in so far, namely, as they constitute its body." Since the true nature of these selves is obscured by ignorance, we come to understand the highest Self by a process of release not unlike that of Sankara, except that instead of knowledge the redemptive means is devotion to Brahman. [28]

In modern times, Ramakrishna (1834-1886) was the founder of the mission which bears his name and whose purpose was to spread Hinduism beyond the borders of India to other nations. Born in the Hoogly district of Bengal as Gadadhar Chatterji, Ramakrishna Paramahmsa assumed this name when he became a *sannyasin*. Though uneducated in any formal sense, he produced a powerful impression on his contemporaries because of his personal history of intense religious striving and ability to teach the Hindu way of life in simple and vivid analogies.

Ramakrishna had a series of remarkable experiences, which began with hours of a kind of mystic ecstasy in the temple of the goddess Kali, where he served as priest. For years he sought release and unity with Brahman, mainly by a passionate devotion for Krishna which he cultivated by dressing himself as a woman and expressing himself in terms as graphic as those of "Radha, my paramour."

Desiring to experiment with other religious systems, he lived for a while as a Moslem and reflected for days about the life of Jesus. He finally concluded that while all religions are alike, "for the Hindus the ancient path, the path of the Aryan *Rishis* is the best." His favorite deity was Kali.

After his death, his disciple Vivekananda (1863-1902) traveled far and wide to spread the teachings of the master. He spoke as the representative of India at the parliament of religions in Chicago in 1893, and on his return to India was received with enthusiasm as the successful protagonist of Hinduism to the Western world. Adopting certain Western methods of organization he founded a society of like-minded native Hindus and converts, whose headquarters are in Calcutta but with centers in many Indian cities and affiliates in other countries.

Ramakrishna, through Vivekananda, has been greatly responsible for the image of Hinduism prevalent in the West, and correspondingly their writings are a quarry for the Hindu estimate of alien faiths, notably the syncretist notion that while all religious cultures are good, Hinduism at its best is superior to any other religion of mankind.

Rabindranath Tagore (1861-1941), one of the great poets of the Orient, symbolized in his person and writings the genuine spirit of modern Hinduism. His religion was based on a deep love between the Supreme soul and the soul of all existing beings. "In this love," he felt, "strength and beauty, form and emotion, the limited and the unlimited have all become one." [29]

Tagore wrote a great deal on religious themes and after receiving the Nobel Prize in 1913 his influence outside India has been enormous. Perhaps no Hindu in the past century has offered the

West a better insight into the character of his religion, or, according to the Indian people, more accurately described their philosophy of life. The fact that he wrote in English and Bengali made his work readily accessible to European and American readers.

"I am no authority on Metaphysics," Tagore confessed. "In any controversial discussion regarding monism and dualism I shall remain silent." Yet he was not silent on his own conception of the Deity or of his relations with the one he called God.

I can only say from what I feel that my innermost God has a joy in expressing Himself through me. This joy, this love pervades every part of my being, suffusing my mind, my intellect, this entire universe which is so vivid before me, my infinite past and my eternal destiny. This game of life is beyond my comprehension, and yet right within myself He is intent on playing His game of love continuously.[30]

He was often asked about his religion, and tried to satisfy those who inquired, while admitting that the categories of his thought transcended the facile beliefs of the common man.

What is generally called "religion," I cannot say I have achieved within myself in a clear, deep-rooted form. But there has been in my mind a steady onward growth of something alive which I have felt on many an occasion. It is not, by any means, a particular conception— but a deep awareness, a new awakening.

What the Scriptures say, whether they are true or not, I do not know. Most of the time they profess truths that are of little use to me. In fact they are quite non-existent as far as I am concerned. Whatever I build up to perfection with my life-efforts is the ultimate truth for me.[31]

The deepest religious sense he knew was the realization of affinity with the infinite universe. "I know that just as the stars, the planets, the sun and the moon shall ever exist," so there has been in every man "a constant creative process from time immemorial." But "what will be the outcome of all this I do not know," nor did he think it necessary to inquire.[32] The essential thing was to foster communion with whatever this ultimate of existence may be, as he succinctly expressed it in a prayer which he composed on his eightieth birthday.

He is one alone and one attribute, and yet by His union with many powers creates infinite attributes fulfiling their hidden meanings. Into

Him the world is dissolved finally, who is God from the beginning of creation. May He unite us with Mind that is auspicious.[33]

If Tagore identified religion with anything objective, it was with the love of mankind, "not in the practice of established customs and rites," and still less in creedal beliefs. Its manifestation was to sympathize with all religions and never to reject any. After describing a variety of creeds, he asked himself, "which of these religions I claim for my own." His answer, when sought in his innermost heart, was that "I am not in favor of rejecting anything, for I am only complete with the inclusion of everything. I want to accept all excluding nothing, for it is I, my friend, that waits outside to meet me." [34] On this cryptic note he finished his final testament of religious faith.

Unlike Tagore in many ways, Sarvepalli Radhakrishnan is yet one with him in the conviction that the essence of all religions is the same, since, as he explained, "religion is not a creed or code but an insight into reality."

Radhakrishnan has shown himself a versatile genius, universally recognized and acclaimed for his remarkable ability as teacher, scholar, philosopher, statesman, and India's cultural ambassador throughout the East and West. His wide learning, brilliant style and absolute tolerance brought him recognition as the greatest interpreter of Indian philosophy and religion in the present century.

Radhakrishnan is credited with two major contributions to Hindu thought: his re-interpretation of the doctrine of *maya* in the Vedanta system of Sankara, and his exposition of a profound philosophy of the religion of the spirit.

According to him, *maya* has not meant to Hindus that the world is all illusion. No doubt the world of everyday events and things is not the ultimate reality, but neither is it unreality. The only *maya* he admits is the mystery of how the finite rises from out of the bosom of the infinite, while discarding the simplicist Christian theory of creation.

We know that there is the absolute reality, we know that there is the empirical world, we know that the empirical world rests on the Absolute, but the *how* of it is beyond our knowledge. The hypothesis of creation is a weak one, and it assumes that God lived alone for some time and then suddenly it occurred to him to have company when he put forth the world. The theory of manifestation is not more satisfying, for it is difficult to know how the finite can manifest the infinite.

If we say God is transformed into the world, the question arises whether it is the whole of God that is transformed or only a part. If it is the whole, then there is no God beyond the universe and we lapse into lower pantheism. If it is only a part, then it means that God is capable of being partitioned.[35]

Since none of these theories satisfies him, Radhakrishnan prefers to believe, "it is not possible to determine logically the relation between God and the world." The premise that runs through his voluminous books is the postulate that unless the mind can understand how something exists and can explain its nature, it should remain agnostic on the subject. Given the fact that "the history of philosophy in India and Europe has been one long illustration of the inability of the human mind to solve the mystery of God to the world," it follows that "a wise agnosticism is more faithful to the situation" than spurious devices for evading the problem or authoritarian creeds which pretend to give the answer.[36]

His religion of the spirit, joined to a deep religious fervor and conviction, provided him with a concept of life that some have said is the most persuasive presentation of Hinduism since the time of Sankara. It is certainly the most intelligible to Western readers, since most of Radhakrishnan's writings are in English, and his years of contact with European culture gave him the categories of thought needed to make an Oriental religion understandable in the West.

Experience, in Radhakrishnan's terms, is the soul of religion, and all the religions of history are only extensions of the experienced insight of great men into reality. Thus the Hindu religion "is not a 'founded religion'; nor does it center round any historical events. Its distinctive characteristic has been its insistence on the inward life of spirit. To know, possess, and be the spirit in this physical frame" has been the constant aim of the Hindu religious endeavor.

The Hindus look back to the Vedic period as the epoch of their founders. The Veda, the wisdom, is the accepted name for the highest spiritual truth of which the human mind is capable. It is the work of the *rishis* or the seers. The truths of the *rishis* are not evolved as the result of logical reasoning or systematic philosophy but they are the products of spiritual intuition, the *drishti* or vision. The *rishis* are not so much the authors of the truths recorded in the Vedas as the seers who were able to discern the eternal truths by raising their life-spirit to the plane of the universal spirit.[37]

However, although the Vedas are highest in value because they are deepest in insight, they are not alone in their penetration of being. Buddha, Moses, Christ and Mohammed also had visions of existence. Indeed "witnesses to the personal sense of the divine are not confined to the East." Socrates, Plato, Augustine, Dante, Wesley and numberless others testify "to the felt reality of God." The only mistake would be to equate this personal vision with its interpretation, since institutions abide, while interpretations change. "Theory, speculation, dogma, change from time to time" as the intuitions become better understood. "Their value is acquired from their adequacy to experience." [38] When religious forms dissolve and interpretations are doubted, it is an invitation to get back to experience itself and reformulate its contents in more suitable terms, which Radhakrishnan believes he has done for Hinduism and suggests may be needed for other faiths as well.

ESTIMATE OF CHRISTIANITY

The influence of Chistianity on Hinduism is recognized in the purification of certain cultic divinities, like Krishna, who was rediscovered as the dignified god of the *Gita* and thus replaced the wanton shepherd god of the later *Puranas,* mischievous and lustful as no man could ever become. And more profoundly in modern times, the result of contact with the Christian West has affected Indian thought by extroverting its predominant individualism and preoccupation with self to the point of deification as Atman. Hindu writers with no sympathy for what they call Occidental materialism admit the chief impetus to the great social conscience in Hinduism has come from the West.

Quite alone among the religious leaders of the East, the father of his country, Mahatma Gandhi has spoken and written at length about Christianity, and thereby offers a valuable insight into Hindu religious thought.

When the prime mover in India's struggle for independence was assassinated by one of his co-religionists in 1948, the assassin's motive for the crime was partly that Gandhi seemed to be compromising on Hinduism and catering to Islam. The judgment was a commentary on the prevalent Hindu spirit which looks with sympathy, if not with positive favor, on other religious systems including Christianity.

In his autobiography, he tells about his early prejudice against Christians because some missionaries he met "used to stand in a corner near the high school (at Rajkot) and hold forth, pouring abuse on Hindus and their gods. I could not endure this." Later when he heard about a convert who began to speak critically about the religion of his ancestors and their customs, "this thing created in me a dislike for Christianity." [39]

However this was only an early impression, which soon gave way to a broad tolerance that grew out of Gandhi's long experience with Moslems, Christians, Buddhists and Sikhs, and was nourished by his devotion to a sixteenth century version of the religious epic *Ramayana,* that for three hundred years has been the most popular scripture among the common people of North India. Written by Tulasi Das (1532-1623), its philosophy is a simple gospel of salvation to all people, in homely and idiomatic vernacular (not as the Vedas and *Gita* in Sanskrit) that goes straight to the heart of the average Hindu, oppressed by the prospect of perpetual rebirth and depressed by the impossibility of the unlearned ever grasping the knowledge of the Absolute demanded by the metaphysicians of Hinduism. Centered in the epic are the exploits of Rama, one of the celebrated incarnations of the deity Vishnu, to whom Gandhi was so devoted (as a Vishnuvite) that his dying words were the invocation, "O Rama! O Rama!"

Writing in his mature years, Gandhi said "I regard the Ramayana of Tulasi Das as the greatest book in all devotional literature." It was the basis of his eclectic theory of toleration that illustrates to a marked degree the peculiar genius of the Hindu people.

As a young man he often joined in community worship with Mohammedans and Christians, and read the religious classics of the different religious with no fear of being unfaithful to his own traditions. In reading their texts, he discovered that "I was equi-minded towards all these faiths although perhaps I was not then conscious of it. I do not find I ever had the slightest desire to criticize any of these religions merely because they were not my own, but read each sacred book in a spirit of reverence, and found the same fundamental morality in each." [40] At times he could not understand what he read, or was bored by the contents, as with certain parts of the Old Testament, but he asked himself, "What was the meaning of saying that the Vedas were the inspired Word of God? If they were inspired, why not also the Bible and the Koran?" [41]

As a consequence, Gandhi's theology accepted into fellowship every religious creed, which in turn made him the object of suspicion among those who were less syncretist than he. He defended his position.

In spite of my being a staunch Hindu, I find room in my faith for Christian and Islamic and Zoroastrian teaching, and therefore my Hinduism seems to some to be a conglomeration, and some have dubbed me an eclectic. Well, to call a man eclectic is to say that he has no faith, but mine is a broad faith which does not oppose Christians. It is a faith based on the broadest possible toleration. It is that broad faith that sustains me.[42]

Not only did he defend himself against the charge of eclecticism but he took issue with those for whom religion means dogma and intransigence of faith. The need of the times, he felt, is not one religion but mutual respect for the devotees of different religions. "We want to reach not the dead level, but unity in divinity," and any attempt to root out religious traditions is sacrilege. "The soul of religion is one, but is encased in a multitude of forms. The latter will persist to the end of time. Wise men will ignore the outward crust and see the same soul living under a variety of crusts." [43] What exists in nature is equally true in religion—a fundamental unity running through all the diversity. Or from another viewpoint, "for me the different religions are beautiful flowers from the same garden, or they are branches of the same majestic tree. Therefore they are equally true, though being received and interpreted through human instruments equally imperfect." [44]

Gandhi saw the issue in epistemological terms, which he derived from a theory of knowledge in which the mind always approaches truth without ever reaching absolute certitude.

We have not realized religion in its perfection, even as we have not realized God. Religion of our conception, being thus imperfect, is always subject to a process of evolution and re-interpretation. Progress towards Truth, towards God, is possible only because of such evolution. And if all faiths outlived by men are imperfect, the question of comparative merit does not arise. All faiths constitute a revelation of Truth, but all are imperfect, and liable to error. Reverence for other faiths need not blind us to their faults. We must be keenly alive to the defects of our own faith also, yet not leave it on that account, but try to overcome these defects. Looking at all religions with an equal eye, we would not only not hesitate, but would think it our duty, to blend into our faith every acceptable feature of other faiths.[45]

Going a step further, Gandhi placed the criterion of truth in religion not in objective evidence but in the autonomous mind, since "the seat of religious authority lies within." If he spoke of Vedic literature or the New Testament as revealed, it was only by an extension of language. "I cannot let the scriptural text supersede my reason." [46] Even God is subject to this relativity. "I do not regard God as a person. Truth for me is God. But you need not go into what may sound like mystic lore; you may simply worship what you find to be the Truth, for Truth is known relatively." [47] If we must speak of revelation, "I have no hesitation in regarding the Koran as revealed, as I have none regarding the Bible." Only let us not assume what is "an essentially untrue position to take, for a seeker after truth, that he alone is in absolute possession of truth." [48]

The concept of Christ in this scheme of values is not what believing Christians take Him to be. Against the backdrop of ten *avatars* for Vishnu alone, one incarnation more or less would seem to be inconsequential. But Gandhi knew that Christianity regards its founder as more than a figure like Krishna or Rama, and infinitely superior to the human *sannyasis* of Hinduism. Sometimes he praised the person of Jesus as a great moral figure and model of selfless charity. "Jesus," he admitted, "came as near to perfection as possible." And "I regard Jesus as a great teacher of humanity." [49] But that was all. There could be no question in Gandhi's mind of accepting Christ as the eternal *Son of God.*

Some of his analyses suggests that he had never understood what Christian theology means by the Trinity or the Hypostatic Union. "That Jesus is the only-begotten son of God is to me against Reason, for God cannot marry and beget children. The word son there can only be used in a figurative sense." [50] At other times he seemed to grasp the issue but his mind was preconditioned by theories of absolute determinism propounded for centuries by Upanishad interpreters, sympathy with the mythological incarnations of Vishnu and Siva, and more than passing familiarity with the rationalism of such men as Albert Schweitzer whom he did not hesitate to call "that most Christlike of all Christians." [51] Among these elements the most important was determinism, which prompted Gandhi to discount the miraculous groundwork of the Christian Gospels. There was no miracle, for example, in the story of the multiplication of loaves and fishes. "A magician can create that illusion." The same with resurrections from the dead.

I do not deny that Jesus had certain psychic powers as he was undoubtedly filled with the love of humanity. But he brought to life not people who were dead but who were believed to be dead. The laws of Nature are changeless, unchangeable, and there are no miracles in the sense of infringement or interruption of Nature's laws. But we limited beings fancy all kinds of things and impute our limitations to God. We may copy God, but not He us.[52]

Understandably, therefore, Gandhi had little patience with the efforts of Christian missionaries evangelizing the Hindus, on the principle of bringing them the message of salvation. His apodictic statement, "If I had power and could legislate, I should stop all proselytizing," [53] was consistent with the larger pattern of regarding Christianity as only a partial, even inferior, insight into religious truth. So averse was he to the whole idea of conversion that he felt people should not "even secretly pray that any one should be converted, but our inmost prayer should be that a Hindu should be a better Hindu, a Muslim a better Muslim and a Christian a better Christian." For his part, "Hinduism with its message of *ahimsa* (non-violence) is to me the most glorious religion in the world, as my wife to me is the most beautiful woman in the world." Religion is such a personal matter that "I believe there is no such thing as conversion from one faith to another" in the accepted Christian sense of the term.[54]

ERA OF CHANGE

Of all major religions in the world, Hinduism is the most closely identified with ethnic origins and, since the founding of the Republic, with specified geographical boundaries. With the emergence

of India as an independent nation, this correlation of the sacred and
secular has assumed still deeper meaning to the point where Western observers speak either of India's prospective role as a leader in
the family of nations or of Hinduism as a world force, whose religious principles have become matters of vital importance to all
peoples.

No one is more conscious than the Hindus of the new responsibility which national autonomy has created for a religious culture
that numbers one seventh of the world's population, and yet is concentrated in an area one third the size of the United States. Centuries of domination by petty overlords, Islamic rulers, and British
colonialism have produced a desire (and the need) for self-realiza-
tion that make the present generation the most critical in the four
millenia of Hindu history.

Their own writers are not agreed on all the means to be used,
but generally recognize certain factors that characterize the emerg-
ing spirit of modern Hinduism: its ready adaptation to the demands
of co-existence and even cooperation with other, non-Hindu, religions; its use of religious motivation in the interests of material
progress; its willingness to shed, no matter what the cost, a multitude of social customs and traditions that for centuries had been
part of the Hindu way of life; and its practical reversal of what
critics had assumed was inevitable policy, by erecting a political
state in which the majority are professedly Hindu believers and yet
giving freedom of belief and practice to all the citizens.

Continuing in the footsteps of Gandhi, who said "when I am
gone, he will speak my language," Jawaharlal Nehru could be severely critical of the Christians who exploited their colonial possessions. But he was also open to the influence of Christian ideals, and
wrote in his autobiography about the "many books on Catholicism
and papal encyclicals" a friend gave him to read while the future
prime minister was in prison. "Studying them," he observed, "I realized the hold it (Christianity) had on such large numbers of
people. It offered, as Islam and popular Hinduism offer, a safe
anchorage from doubt and mental conflict, an assurance of a future
life which will make up for the deficiencies of this life." [55]

Typical of this ecumenical trend is the Birla Mandir temple at
New Delhi, named after the prominent industrialist who endowed
it. Though its architecture and sculpture are in the traditional style,

the interior is symbolic of a resurgent culture that is willing to accept whatever values other religions have to offer. Besides the gods of Hinduism, there are worshiped here the chief teachers of other lands and faiths—Jesus and Mohammed, Confucius and Lao-tzu, Plato and Aristotle.

Gandhi defended himself against charges of eclecticism and Nehru, without the Mahatma's deep sense of piety, nevertheless saw in all religions and not only in Hinduism that nourishment of "inner development," without which merely "external progress" was futile and illusory. In order to achieve the former some of the latter is necessary and yet their relationship is that of means to end.

It is a commonplace that in the modern industrial West outward development has far outstripped the inner, but it does not follow, as many people in the East appear to imagine, that because we are industrially backward and our external development has been slow, therefore our inner evolution has been greater. That is one of the delusions with which we try to comfort ourselves and try to overcome our feeling of inferiority. It may be that individuals can rise above circumstance and environment and reach great inner heights. But for large groups and nations a certain measure of external development is essential before the inner evolution can take place.[56]

Nehru appealed to Gandhi's authority in directing the spiritual resources of Hinduism both as a motivating force for action to raise the physical standard of living and as goal to be attained once the "external development" is assured. "No man can live without religion," he quoted Mahatma. Religion sustains men in their efforts for temporal improvement, and offers them ideals beyond the achievement of secular ends.

Hindus themselves admit that along with the essentials of their religion, a heavy superstructure of all kinds of customs and superstitions have been piled on the principles of faith. As a result vast numbers of people accepted these customs and habits as a necessary part of religion. "The caste system, untouchability, and many other major and minor shibboleths, which New India is gradually and relentlessly determined to discard, were in the past incorporated in Hinduism." [57] They are being removed under steady pressure from the law and by systematic education.

Apologists for this renascence argue that the social organization of the Hindus is the result of unregulated growth which through historical reasons came to be stunted in its early stages; that the fragmentation of social feeling is the outstanding feature of Hindu society and based on the pseudo-religious theories of joint family and caste; that these and similar institutions of the Hindu people are not objectively connected with their religion but derive entirely from law and custom, and so are secular; and therefore that the whole structure should be re-examined and modified through national legislation.

A graphic example of the new approach is the article on Pariahs in the Constitution of India. " 'Untouchability,' " it declares "is abolished and its practice in any form is abolished. The enforcement of any disability arising out of 'Untouchability' shall be an offence punishable in accordance with law." [58]

However, the most significant feature of current Hinduism is its creation of a non-Hindu State, in which all religions are equal; where social, economic, and political aspects of life bear no relation to the faith of a citizen. The framers of the Constitution fully allow for belief in God and the acceptance of the higher laws of the universe which govern the physical world of space and time. But there is no constitutional preference in favor of Hinduism, and conversely, other religious cultures are given parity before the law. "Subject to public order, morality and health," the provision reads, "all persons are equally entitled to freedom of conscience and the right freely to profess, practice and propagate religion." [59]

At the same time cognizance is taken of the special status of Hinduism, since nothing in the Constitution should be construed as preventing the State from "providing for social welfare and reform or throwing open of Hindu religious institutions of a public character to all classes and sections of Hindus," who are defined to include Buddhists, Sikhs and Jains, as historical derivations of the parent religion. [60]

Not all Hindus are satisfied with this modified "secularity" as they call it. They feel that Hinduism should be more dominantly integrated in the juridical construct of the nation, and to this end have successfully urged that instruction in the schools be in Hindi, and that the change-over should take place within a fixed period. They further argue that severance of the social values from their religious moorings is not a Hindu but a secularist move inspired by years of indoctrination among the educated classes in the philosophy of John Stuart Mill, Herbert Spencer and other rationalist thinkers, in whose scheme religion and dogma had no place. The danger, they feel, is that some alien ideology like Marxism may come along to fill the vacuum created by divorcing the ancient religion from the institutions to which it gave life.

These and similar objections are met by Radhakrishnan and others with a redefinition of concepts that show better than anything else how fluid and, by Western standards, hard to describe is the Hindu way of life. They insist "there has been no such thing as a uniform, stationary, unalterable Hinduism, whether in point of belief or practice. Hinduism is a movement, not a position; a process, not a result; a growing tradition, not a fixed revelation. Its past history encourages us to believe that it will be found equal to any emergency that the future may throw up, whether on the field of thought or of history." [61]

Accordingly after a long winter of many centuries, they believe this is one of the creative periods of Hinduism. They see their society in a condition of unstable equilibrium, in which there is much wood that is dead and diseased that has to be cleared away. They are convinced that what seems to the orthodox like surrender of principles is only their restatement with special reference to the needs of a more complex and mobile social order.

4. Buddhism

APOLOGISTS of Buddhism describe it as the richest, broadest and most lasting of Aryan religions. Yet the name itself is of recent origin and refers to the vast system of teachings that trace their ancestry to the Indian sage, Gautama or the Buddha, who lived and died about the fifth century before the Christian era. There is even question of whether Buddhism should be called a religion and not rather a religious culture, which has permeated Asia to a point where it is impossible correctly to estimate the number of professed Buddhists in the world. Figures range from less than two hundred million, to more than five hundred million, with the lower number closer to reality.

But numerical strength is no index of the vitality of Buddhism, and still less of its impact on Oriental thought. Beginning as a heresy from Hinduism and practically exiled from the land of its birth, it has shown surprising adaptability to new situations and a remarkable power of assimilation. Though sometimes mistakenly called a world religion, it is nevertheless Asiatic in the full geographic and historic sense of the term. Every country in the Orient is deeply saturated with Buddha's philosophy. For two thousand years he has been the dominant personality in the Far East.

SACRED WRITINGS

The amorphous and often contradictory nature of modern Buddhism suggests the need for clarifying its sources and distinguishing the classic religion from its numerous, bewildering variations. Early Buddhism is in many ways part of the complex of Hinduism and received from it much of its doctrine and most of its mythology. Unlike the parent, however, it has the rare advantage of possessing a historic founder around whom later developments clustered and with whom the religion has since become identified.

Like Hinduism it has a body of sacred writings, but centered around the teachings of one man, comparable to the place of Mohammed or Confucius in their respective religions. The Buddhist scriptures, therefore, are historically associated with Buddha and have more or less authenticity according to their fidelity to his teaching.

Buddha himself left nothing in writing, but traditions about him have come down to us in two versions, Pali and Sanskrit. Pali is a literary language very similar to the vernacular spoken by Gautama. Although abandoned in India it remained the basis for the original Buddhist literature still extant in Ceylon, Burma, Thailand and Cambodia. Later writings were in Sanskrit, the ancient language of the Hindus, and in the native tongues of other nations which adopted the new religion, notably Tibetan and Chinese.

Since the Pali texts represent the earlier and more accurate tradition, scholars commonly turn to them for an understanding of primitive Buddhism. The sacred writings are extant in the form of palm-leaf books, all since the coming of Christ but reportedly based on books written in the first century of the Christian era by Buddhist monks in Ceylon who feared lest the rigors of war might destroy the oral traditions of their faith.

The Pali Canon is said to have been determined by three special councils, which met before the third century B.C. to codify and interpret the Buddhist scriptures. However the whole history of this period is shrouded in obscurity, and European scholars believe that only some fragments are thus ancient and authoritative. In its present form, the canon consists of three collections known as *Tipitaka* or the "Three Baskets." An equivalent term would be "Three Traditions," since the word "basket" means "something handed on." Their contents are *Vinaya* (Disciple), *Sutta* (Discourses), and *Abhidhamma* (Doctrinal Elaboration). Students of Buddhism are often confused by the apparent inconsistency of names. This is partly explained by the interchange of Pali and Sanskrit terms, which are quite different, yet sufficiently alike to mislead. Custom dictates that the Pali form should be used except where the Sanskrit is more familiar.

True to its monastic outlook, the Vinaya deals at length with regulations for the conduct and community life of Buddhism monks and nuns. In the first part are two hundred and twenty-seven rules which make up the *Patimokkha,* or means of self-examination used by the monks on the fast days held twice a month. The second part gives elaborate prescriptions on personal behavior. Running as a theme is the corporate ideal of monasticism, which does not ignore the laity but assumes a paternalistic attitude towards them and stresses the fact that Buddhism is essentially a movement of monastic asceticism.

The *Sutta* is our main authority for the teaching of Buddha, and deals mainly with the *Dhamma,* a fluid concept that means rule of deity or of social obligation (Hinduism); the truth, saving doctrine or simply "the way," as in early Buddhism; or, in later Buddhistic thought, any reality or essential quality which deserves to be understood. Five divisions in the Sutta correspond to different types of discourses arbitrarily put together to facilitate memorization.

Since the *Abhidhamma* collection was compiled after a major schism had occurred, two competitive forms exist. The word itself means "further" or "special" *dhamma,* so that the third Basket deals with metaphysical analysis and elucidation of the truth, way of life or reality.

Outside the Pali canon is a massive quantity of literature, often mistakenly called scripture, which defies classification and yet merits attention because it is the ordinary source of popular knowledge about Buddhism. A collection of smaller works, the *Khuddaka Nikaja* is sometimes put as an appendix to the Exposition treatise. It includes the most familiar of Buddhist writings, the "Path of Virtue" or *Dhamma pada,* an anthology of doctrine in poetic form. Also famous are the Birth Tales (*Jataka*), a gathering of stories that narrate the five hundred and fifty previous births of the Buddha. They are particularly valuable for preserving a great deal of Indian folklore, and showing the early synthesis of Buddhist speculation with primitive beliefs.

One more book, the *Questions of King Milinda,* though not technically scripture, is indispensable for a correct understanding of authentic Buddhism. A series of dialogues between a Greek King of Bactria (Milinda) in southeast Asia and a Buddhist philosopher (Nagasena) illustrates the deep Hellenist penetration following the

eastern conquest of Alexander the Great (356-323 B.C.) and helps
to explain the mutual influence of Buddhist and Western ideas.

LIFE OF BUDDHA

The environment in which Buddhism came into being was a
period of intense religious fervor and conflict. Dominant Hinduism
had encouraged the formation of schools of thought, in which questions of man's existence were debated, along with the practice of
specialized forms of worship or asceticism in keeping with the
Hindu belief in transmigration of souls. To avoid the awful prospect
of an eternity of such transmigrations, different theories were proposed: good moral deeds, ritual, and self-discipline. Depending on
the emphasis, new sects arose, each with its own leader and established customs within the ample folds of the Hindu way of life.

Buddhism was originally one of these sects. Its originator had
the personal name of Siddhartha, and the surname Gautama (both
in Sanskrit rather than Pali). He belonged to the Sakya clan of the
Kshatriya or warrior caste, who were aristocrats one rung below the
Brahmins in the social scale of India. Another name by which he
is known is Sakya-Muni (from his clan) or Bhagavat (the blessed
one). He called himself Tathagata (the one who has arrived).
Married to a woman variously named Bimba or Gopa, he had one
son, Rahula.

After some years of apparently happy married life, Gautama
renounced the world, and left his parents, wife, and child. Legendary stories expatiate for chapters on the stoic heroism of a royal
prince whom the father dramatically tries to dissuade from leaving
home and the future throne. What seems probable is that he was
reared apart from the harsher aspects of life and then was shocked
by some unexpected contact with sickness, old age and death.

In the *Jataka* tales, the introduction (from the fifth century
A.D.) anticipates the whole span of Gautama's life, going back to
his previous existences which to believers in transmigration were
naturally of great interest. It is related how the gods saw the world
in such commotion they begged the future Buddha to come into the
world and be born in central India. Strange marvels are told of his
conception, and the day of his birth great things occur: his future

wife, closest friends, the great Bo-tree where he will be enlightened, and four huge urns filled with treasure suddenly come into existence. When five days old, eight Brahmins foretell his destiny as the Buddha, on condition that he retire from the world. To prevent this, the king his father had three palaces built for him and (at the age of sixteen) gave him forty-thousand dancing girls. Yet thirteen years later, in spite of all the father's efforts, Gautama left everything to find, in his own words, "the incomparable security of a *Nirvana* free from birth" and endless reincarnation.

The same parallel versions, a barely traceable outline of a few scattered facts and volumes of embellishment by commentators centuries later, follow the rest of Gautama's life until his death around the age of eighty. It is uncertain how long he led a wandering career, perhaps for six years, in search of an answer to the mystery of human existence. At first he studied under two Hindu masters of Yoga, who taught him all they knew about philosophy but did not satisfy his needs. Then he tried further ascetical practices and meditation on his own, going to extremes like rigorous fasting almost without food, eating repulsive herbs, and repressing his natural emotions. Five ascetics watched his mortification in the hope this would give him the wisdom he sought. But when Gautama gave up the self-discipline they left him, on the grounds that by returning to the "abundant life" he would never obtain "power surpassing other men, nor the superiority of full and holy knowledge."

Finally Gautama found what he was looking for. One day, as he sat in meditation under a wide-spreading bodhi tree, the light suddenly dawned. Not everything came at once, and several weeks were required to complete the illumination. From that time on he was the Buddha, the "enlightened one." He felt himself liberated from the eternal succession of deaths and rebirths, and delivered from sensual passion and all desire. "In my emancipated self arose the knowledge of my deliverance." He realized that "there is nothing for me beyond this world. Ignorance was dispelled, knowledge welled up. Darkness disappeared, light had risen." Buddhists believe the enlightenment took place in Gautama's thirty-sixth year. They point to the exact spot where he sat under the bodhi tree, and resolved to "turn the wheel of law" by teaching others the way that he had found. Preaching this message became the guiding purpose of his life, and was carried on in systematic fashion. Most of the year he traveled from place to place, talking to all who would listen. In the company of his followers he would beg food, and depend on the generosity of those who heard him. During the rainy season he retired for about three months of quiet rest. Otherwise his day was divided between itinerant preaching in the morning and receiving visitors for discussion at night, with the afternoons reserved for private meditation.

At first the communities he founded were only for men, but later his aunt prevailed on him to allow women "to go forth from the household of life and enter the homeless state under his supervision." Gautama yielded, but laid down severe rules for the women disciples. He sadly foretold that if women had not received permission to enter, the religion he taught "would have stood fast for a thousand years," instead of five hundred years because of this concession.

Conflicting reports obscure the number of converts the Buddha made or the extent of his influence on contemporaries. He was strongly opposed by the Brahmins for teaching that gifts to the Buddhist order were of more merit than the sacrifices which Hindus practiced. Yet many high caste Indians joined the new sect in an age of rampant sectarianism. More serious were dissensions within the ranks. Devadatta, a cousin of Gautama, persecuted him through life and exploited the opposition aroused by the Buddha's refusing to practice austerities according to the ascetical customs of the day. The master triumphed over his rival by gentleness and the use of magic charms.

Shortly before death, Gautama assembled the members of his order and gave them final instructions. "Be lamps to yourselves," he bade them. "Betake yourselves to no external refuge. Hold fast to the truth as a lamp. Hold fast as a refuge to the truth. Look not for refuge to anyone besides yourselves." [1] Then he partook of a meal of boar's flesh, served by one Chunda, which produced dysentery and hastened the hour of death. A moment before he died, the "blessed one," as the narrative calls him, spoke once more to his disciples. "Behold now, brethren, I exhort you, saying, 'Decay is inherent in all component things!' Work out your salvation with diligence." To which the scribe added the comment, "This was the last word of Tathagata." [2]

In this oldest account of Buddha's demise, the writer describes in monotonous detail how "the blessed one" entered into the first stage of deep meditation. And rising out of the first stage, he passed into the second. And rising out of the second, he entered the third, and the fourth. Then five more stages, traced and retraced—until "passing out of the state between consciousness and unconsciousness, he fell into a state in which the consciousness both of sensations and of ideas has passed away." [3]

Seven days after death the body was cremated with all the honors due to a king. The ashes were carried in procession and deposited in a shrine, from which grains of the burnt remains were distributed to "eighty thousand" places where *stupas* and *dagobas* (shrines) were built for their preservation.

BASIC PRINCIPLES

It is not difficult to isolate the main features of Gautama's doctrine while admitting that what now is attributed to him personally was centuries in the making and consequently represents also the mind of his interpreters. In the *Dharma* or teaching, the master did not discard the substructure of primitive Hinduism, but rather built upon it. He seems not to have doubted the existence of gods and of evil spirits. His concern was uniquely with deliverance, as found in an ancient text assigned to him, "Just as the ocean has only one taste, the taste of salt, so has this doctrine and discipline only one flavor of emancipation." [4] And emancipation meant breaking through the chain of repeated birth and rebirth.

To obtain this liberation, the disciple must discover and put into practice what the Buddha considered the four basic truths. His work, he insisted, is not speculative but therapeutic. The truths he offered were intended as a revelation of the symptoms of a man's disease, its causes, healing, and the manner of obtaining the cure. Historians see in Gautama's tetralogy an application of the medical categories of his time, which he adapted to his own purpose.

According to tradition, Buddha first preached these "Four Noble Truths" in his inaugural sermon at Benares, the holy city of the Hindus, in the Ganges valley of northern India. They are, in sequence, that existence involves suffering, that the cause of suffering is desire and the clinging to existence, that the way to escape from suffering and existence is to be rid of these desires, and to be delivered one must follow the eightfold path mapped out by "the enlightened one." Gautama further insisted that throughout the process each one must do the work by himself. Other human beings may help, and therefore community life is useful, but in the last analysis everyone saves himself.

FIRST NOBLE TRUTH—SUFFERING. The Buddha was eloquent in describing the various kinds of human misery. In general, "birth is painful, old age is painful, sickness is painful, death is painful, sorrow, lamentation, dejection, and despair are painful. Contact with unpleasant things is painful, not getting what one wishes is painful. In short, the five-fold clinging to existence is painful," [5] which means the grasping for bodily form or shape, pleasant feeling or sensation, attractions of the will, internal fancies and mental consciousness.

Gautama was not satisfied that his followers know these sources of suffering academically, and much less have misery ignored. He bade the monks contemplate the sordidness of their life. Let them reflect on their bodies, from sole of the feet to the crown of their head, and remember all the uncleanness contained by the skin. Nor should the reflection stop there, but knowledge of pain learnt from others—the old, the sick and the dead.

Did you ever see in the world a man or a woman, eighty, ninety, or a hundred years old, frail, crooked as a gableroof, bent down, supported on a staff, with tottering steps, infirm, youth long since fled, with broken teeth, grey and scanty hair, or baldheaded, wrinkled, with blotched limbs? Has the thought never come to you that you also are subject to decay and cannot escape it?

Did you ever see in the world a man or a woman, who being sick, afflicted and grievously ill, was lifted up by some people and put to bed by others? Have you ever thought that you also are subject to disease and cannot escape it?

Did you ever see in the world the corpse of a man or a woman, one, two or three days after death, swollen up, blue-black in color, and full of corruption? Have you never thought that you also are subject to death and cannot escape it? [6]

Western commentators who read these and like passages in Buddha's teaching often call it pessimism. Although graphic with Oriental realism, he was not really preoccupied with the morbid side

of life. He felt the first truth of suffering (*dukkha*) needed no dem-
onstration, but only periodic advertence to be seen. Even the more
subtle kind of pain, arising from unsatisfied delight in bodily form
or feeling, volitional craving or pleasures of the imagination, and
the joys of the human mind are found from experience to beget
pain. He added, "whoever delights in suffering," that is, indulgence
in such delights, "will not be freed from suffering. This I say," and
thus he laid the foundation of his system.[7]

Buddha preached a religion devoid of speculation, and it is only
on this premise that his accent on suffering can be understood.
More than once he was reported flatly to refuse to discuss metaphysics. His silence on the subject was criticized by many. Yet in
spite of frequent urging, he continued his "noble silence." The reason he gave was simple: greed for views on questions of this kind
"tends not to edification." If his practical program was demanding,
he would not allow himself to be diverted from the task by indulging in needless theorizing.

A famous parable, told in his own person, perfectly illustrates
the Buddha's point of view.

It is as if a man had been wounded by an arrow thickly smeared
with poison, and his friends and kinsmen were to get a surgeon to heal
him, and he were to say, I will not have this arrow pulled out until I
know by what man I was wounded, whether he is of the warrior caste,
or a Brahmin, or of the agricultural, or the lowest caste. Or if he were
to say, I will not have this arrow pulled out until I know of what name
of family the man is; or whether he is tall or short, or of middle height;
or whether he is black or dark or yellowish; or whether he comes from
such and such a village or town or city; or until I know whether the bow
with which I was wounded was a chapa or a kodanda, or until I know
whether the bow string was of swallow-wort, or bamboo fibre, or sinew,
or hemp, or of milk-sap tree, or until I know whether the shaft was from
a wild or cultivated plant. . . . Before knowing all this, that man would
die.

Similarly, it is not on the view that the world is eternal, that it is
finite, that the body and soul are distinct, or that the Buddha exists after
death that a religious life depends. Whether these views or opposites are
held, there is still rebirth, there is old age, there is death, and grief, lamentation, suffering, sorrow, and despair. . . . I have not spoken of
these views because they do not conduce to absence of passion, that is,
to tranquillity and Nirvana.[8]

The value of seeing the Buddha's extreme practicality is that it forestalls many preconceptions about the true nature of Buddhism, at least in its primitive stages. Present-day Buddhism can be highly speculative, but this philosophical structure is mainly accretion built upon the Gautama's unique concern: how to free man, from the inside, from the dreadful sufferings to which human nature is universally heir. Historic Buddhism was a religion of intense self-effort to overcome suffering.

SECOND NOBLE TRUTH—CAUSE OF SUFFERING. Proceeding a step further, Gautama taught that the cause of suffering was thirst or desire, which leads to rebirth, accompanied by pleasure and lust, and finding its satisfaction here and there. Three kinds of thirst are the fountainhead of all pain: thirst for pleasure, for prosperity, and for continued existence.

Approaching this crucial area of Buddha's doctrine, we must distinguish between his own comparatively simple statement of the case and its philosophical development (and complication) by speculative interpreters. He had already said that the mere fact of being born under the conditions of human existence makes all of us subject to the evils of sickness, old age and death, and to the sorrow that comes, when the things which we like are taken away from us. These constitute the inevitable cycle of life and state, in a word, the problem of evil.

However, these things would not make us unhappy except for the blind thirst (tanha) in nature which drives us to demand for ourselves and the persons we love more than the universe is ready to give. We crave bodily pleasure and either do not get it, or find that it does not satisfy, or face the prospect of losing what we enjoy. The same with prosperity, and the desire for continued living is frustrated by the certainty of death.

As with the first truth on suffering so here the Buddha vigorously exposed the causal nexus between desire and pain, and viewed the connection from every possible angle. He stressed the social evils resulting from desire, reflected in the whole ambit of human relationships. "Due to sensuous cravings, kings fight with kings, princes with princes, priests with priests, citizens with citizens; the mother quarrels with the son, the son with the father; brother quarrels with brother, brother with sister, sister with brother, friend with friends." [9] Similar and worse hostilities are provoked among persons in society and within the heart of every man by the craving for prosperity and the desire for eternal life.

However, this is not the whole picture. Gautama was more than repeating a proverb, that all pain is frustrated desire. He was setting up a religious system, built out of the pieces of Hinduism which he selected to suit his plans.

The Hindu Upanishads recognized in man a permanent soul which their philosophers said passed on from one bodily home to another in a cycle of rebirth, and could only come to rest through realizing its oneness with Brahman. Buddha denied there was such a soul. What the Hindus called a soul, he considered an ever-changing appearance due to the temporary concurrence of bodily and mental elements. If there is to be deliverance from cyclic transmigration, it must be through eradicating human desires far beyond the ethical abnegation familiar in Christianity. The self-denial he advocated was literal, a denial of self-hood with its mirage of an individual and personal soul.

THIRD NOBLE TRUTH—EXTINCTION OF SUFFERING. From the outset of his preaching ministry, Buddha denied the existence of the self as a distinct reality. In the conclusion of his sermon at Benares all signs of a self are missing. Form, sensation, consciousness—none of these things are self, and it is by reflecting on this and finally realizing it that a "learned, noble hearer becomes weary" of all the causes of suffering, and by his weariness "divests himself of desire" until "there is for him no further return to this world." [10]

The founder of Buddhism postulated that life is a stream of becoming. There is nothing permanent in the empirical self. One thing is merely dependent on the other, which is called the "law of origination." Even the self is a mental construct, with no distinctive reality, which the mind mistakenly identifies with the composite of form, feeling and the rest. In a classic passage of the *Questions of King Milinda,* the antiquity of this doctrine of selflessness (*Nairatmya*) is traced to Gautama. The Buddhist sage Nagasena has come to visit the King, and introduces himself by saying, "Your majesty, I am called Nagasena. However, that is just by way of counting, a term, an appellation, a convenient designation, a mere name, this Nagasena. For there is no ego here to be found." On hearing this, the king objects.

Nagasena, if there is no ego to be found, who is it, then, furnished you priests with the priestly requisites—robes, food, bedding and medicine, the reliance of the sick? Who is it makes use of the same? Who is it keeps the precepts? Who is it applies himself to meditation? Who is it destroys life? Who is it takes what is not given him? Who is it commits immorality? Who is it tells lies? In that case there is no merit; there is no demerit; there is no one who does or causes to be done meritorious or demeritorious deeds; neither good nor evil deeds can have any fruit or result.[11]

To press his point the king asks a series of questions (forty-five by actual count), in which the subject is some part or faculty of a person and the predicate is Nagasena. "Are nails, teeth, skin, flesh, lungs, brain, sensation, perception, consciousness Nagasena?" Each time the sage's answer is, "Nay, verily, your majesty." Still not convinced, but evidently confused, the king tells him, "Nagasena is an empty sound. What Nagasena is there here? You speak a falsehood, a lie. There is no Nagasena."

Then the sage takes over. He goes through the same set of questions the king had asked him, only this time about a chariot, on which his majesty had come to the palace. "Is the axle the chariot? Are the wheels the chariot?"—on through all the physical parts of the vehicle. Finally the conclusion.

Your majesty, although I question you very closely, I fail to discover any chariot. Consequently the word chariot is a mere empty sound. What chariot is there here? Your majesty, you speak a falsehood, a lie. There is no chariot. You are the chief king in all the continent of India; of whom are you afraid that you speak a lie? Listen to me, my lords. Milinda the king here says thus, "I came in a chariot," and being requested, he fails to produce a chariot. Is it possible for me to assent to what he says?

To which the king replies that he speaks no lie. "The word 'chariot' is but a way of counting, term, appellation, convenient designation, and name for pole, axle, wheels, chariot-body, and banner-staff." Nagasena praises the royal intelligence and applies the principle first to himself and then to all human beings.

Thoroughly well do you understand a chariot. In exactly the same way, your majesty, in respect of me, Nagasena is but a way of counting, term, apellation, convenient designation, mere name for the hair of my head, hair of my body . . . brain of head, form, sensation, perception,

the predispositions, and consciousness. But in the absolute sense there is
no ego here to be found. And the priestess Vajira, your majesty, said
as follows in the presence of the Blessed One (Buddha): "Even as the
word of 'chariot' means that members join to frame a whole; so when
the groups appear to view, we use the phrase, 'a living being.' " [12]

This central teaching of the Buddha has never been minimized
by his followers. The great work that he urged to be done was "self-
naughting," as one commentator expresses it: the eradication, root
and branch, of the notion "I and mine." All suffering, according to
the master, is bound up with this concept, "I am this or that," and
to lay aside this burden is a beatitude than which there can be none
greater. Of all the delusions that men are attached to, the worst is
their belief in the constancy and reality of their "name and shape,"
of the Ego or Self. And the most dangerous aspect of this belief, on
Buddha's principles, is that the identification of Self is not with the
visible body (evidently inconstant) but with the invisible "soul"
whose perdurance throughout mortal life and after death is blithely
assumed.

Very near the core of Gautama's philosophy, therefore, is a destructive analysis of the postulated (*sammuta*) "self" or "soul" or
"being," which he did not understand in the prosaic sense of "un-
selfishness," but in the full objective meaning of the term "unself-
ness," of which the ethical idea is (or may be) only an external
symbol.

But this was not all. The goal that Buddha set before his disciples was cessation of suffering or *Nirvana* (Sanskrit for the Pali
Nibbana), which is the state achieved by the removal of ignorance
about the unreality of the Ego, and the conquest of cravings which
arise from such ignorance. It is the spiritual destiny of Buddhism.

The ambiguity of what the Buddha meant by Nirvana has given
rise to endless conflicts and sectarian divisions, some of which will
be examined in context. One difficulty is that we have no direct
access to the master's own ideas, but only as filtered through conflicting interpreters centuries after his death. It seems, however, that
he was consistent, and that just as he did not affirm a positive reality
underlying the world of change, and denied a substantial self underlying the empirical series of sensible and mental happenings, so he
at least did not assert the positive and objective character of
Nirvana.

Throughout life, all his sermons, exhortations and counselings had only one theme, Nirvana. Yet the important question for him was not, "What is Nirvana?" but, "How is Nirvana attained?" His mission was not to explain theoretically what Nirvana means, but to witness for the Nirvana which he personally experienced under the bodhi tree and conceived a towering urge to communicate. One who has achieved Nirvana, he said, "is like a deer living in a forest, who might lie down on a heap of snares, but is not caught by them."

From this point of view, theories were unimportant. Gautama was mainly interested in the ethical remaking of man, and, so his disciples explain, because he felt that metaphysical disputations would take people away from the task of individual change, he kept silent on the nature of the absolute reality and Nirvana. What mattered was the attainment of this goal, the elimination of ignorance and selfishness by the famous eightfold path of morality.

FOURTH NOBLE TRUTH—THE PATH. In common with moralists of every age, Gautama advocated a middle way between extremes, and the term "right" in his vocabulary first meant the avoidance of excess and defect. "These two extremes, O monks, are not to be practiced by one who has gone forth from the world. What are the two? That conjoined with the passions, low, vulgar, common, ignoble, and useless, and that conjoined with self-torture, painful, ignoble, and useless. Avoiding these two extremes the Tathagata (himself) has gained the knowledge of the Middle Way, which gives sight and knowledge, and tends to calm, to insight, enlightenment, Nirvana." [13]

But more specifically, the way that leads to the extinction of suffering is the holy eightfold path, namely right understanding, right mindedness, right speech, right action, right living, right effort, right attentiveness, and right concentration. Each phase of this path has a variety of subdivisions.

Right Understanding means first the acceptance of Buddha's tetralogy: the existence of suffering, its origin in desire, the extinction of desire in Nirvana, and the right method of reaching this haven of rest. It also means that a disciple believes in demerit which, in Gautama's terms, is destruction of any living being, stealing, unlawful sexual intercourse, lying, talebearing, harsh language, frivolous talk, covetousness, ill-will and wrong views. The opposite to this decalogue are meritorious actions, or, in general, the root of merit is "absence of greed, absence of anger, and absence of delusion." [14]

Right Mindedness is to preserve one's thoughts "free from lust, from ill will, and from cruelty. This is called the earthly Right Mindedness, which yields worldly fruits and brings good results." But beyond this is an "Ultramundane Right Mindedness," out of which the former arises, namely whatever thinking or reasoning the mind does by "being turned away from the world and converted to the path" leading to Nirvana.[15] In other words, the mind must not only believe in Buddha's teaching, but reflect upon it to attain the nirvanic goal.

Right Speech avoids lying, tale-bearing and the other demeritorious actions, in so far as they pertain to communication of thought. But the person who practices it also avoids harsh language. "He speaks such words as are gentle, soothing to the ear, loving, going to the heart, courteous and pleasing, and agreeable to many." [16]

Right Action abstains from the same demeritorious conduct as Right Speech, with emphasis on avoidance of unlawful sexual relations "with such persons as are still under protection of father, mother, brother, sister or relatives; with married women, female convicts and persons engaged to be married." [17] So, too, Right Living means that a person "gets his livelihood by a right way of living," which may be earthly or ultramundane Right Living, as in the case of Right Mindedness.

Right Effort included four types of exertion: the effort to avoid, to overcome, to develop, and to maintain. In the effort to avoid, "the disciple incites his mind to avoid the rising of evil, demeritorious things, that have not yet arisen; and he strives, puts forth his energy, strains his mind and struggles."

Thus when he perceives a form with the eye, a sound with the ear, an odor with the nose, a taste with the tongue, a contact with the body, or an object with the mind, he neither adheres to the whole, nor to its parts. And he strives to ward off that, through which evil and demeritorious things, greed and sorrow, would arise, if he remained with unguarded senses, and he watches over his senses, restrains his senses. Possessed of this noble control over the senses, he experiences inwardly a feeling of joy, into which no evil thing can enter.[18]

In the effort to overcome, a man does not retain any sensual or other evil thoughts that may have arisen, but "he abandons them, dispels them, destroys them, causes them to disappear." If while regarding a certain object, there arise demeritorious ideas, the disciple should "gain another and wholesome object," or "reflect on the misery of these thoughts" and on the "painful results" they produce, or "pay no attention to these thoughts," or "with teeth clenched, tongue pressed against the gums, he should with his mind restrain, suppress, and root out these thoughts," and in doing so the mind will be "inwardly settled" and composed.[19]

The effort to develop means the striving to cultivate one's enlightenment, primarily through inciting the will "to arouse meritorious conditions that have not yet arisen." [20] Whereas the effort to maintain seeks to preserve what has been thus incited, namely, to bring such ideas to maturity. For example, the disciple may keep in mind a favorable object of concentration, "as the mental image of a skeleton, of a corpse infested by worms, of a corpse riddled with holes, of a corpse swollen up." [21]

Right Attentiveness is directed to further self-mastery through the contemplation of four kinds of objects: the body, feelings, the mind and phenomena in general, each with detailed prescriptions that are found especially in the *Digha-Nikaya,* the treatise in the "Sermon Basket" of the Buddhist scriptures.

Contemplation of the Body is an elaborate process, which consists mainly in a studious attention to every part of one's own anatomy and to every bodily action a man performs.

The disciple is clearly conscious in his going and coming; clearly conscious in looking forward and backward; clearly conscious in bending and stretching any part of his body; clearly conscious in eating, drinking, chewing and tasting; clearly conscious in walking, standing, sitting, falling asleep and awaking; clearly conscious in speaking and in keeping silent.

And further, the disciple contemplates this body from the sole of the foot upward, and from the top of the hair downward, with a skin stretched over it. . . . Thus he dwells in contemplation of the body, either with regard to his own person, or to other persons, or to both.[22]

The benefit of such attention is to give mastery over delight and discontent, conquest of fear and anxiety, and endurance of "cold and heat, hunger and thirst, wind and sun, attacks by gadflies, mosquitoes and reptiles." In fact a man will be able patiently to endure "wicked and malicious speech, as well as bodily pains, though they be piercing, sharp, bitter" and even dangerous to life.[23]

Moreover certain preternatural gifts are acquired, like the magical powers, the "heavenly ear" for hearing sounds at a distance, insight into "the hearts of other beings," the remembrance of previous births, and a "heavenly eye" for beholding things appear and vanish and seeing "how things are reborn" according to their deeds in a previous life.[24]

Contemplation of the Feelings and the Mind follows the same pattern as for the body, with fixed attention on each emotion and mental state as it occurs. Here, too, the purpose is not only to be conscious of these vital functions but to grow in the realization that they are present in him, and yet that "he lives independent, unattached to anything in the world."

In the Contemplation of Phenomena, the entire foregoing process, from the first to the fourth noble truths, and from the first to the present (seventh) method of the path to Nirvana, itself becomes the object of scrutinizing attention. But now the method is more reflective, and bids the disciple "dwell with attentive mind, wisely investigating, examining and thinking over the law," so as to reach fullest perfection.

Finally in Right Concentration, after complete detachment from sensual and demeritorious things, the Buddhist adept reaches "fixation of the mind to a single object," literally, one-pointedness of mind, which results in a series of four trances, beginning with "rapture and happiness" and ending with the "state beyond pleasure and pain" which is Nirvana.

HISTORICAL DEVELOPMENT

All the evidence indicates that Buddhism was firmly established in the eastern Ganges basin by the time of Gautama's death (probably 483 B.C.). There is also a tradition, though questioned by many scholars, that in the very year the master died his disciples held a council at Rajagaha to determine the contents of the Buddhist scriptures. A hundred years later another council was reportedly held at Vesali, to condemn those who were trying to mitigate the Buddha's teaching.

As first organized, Buddhism was essentially a system of moral discipline which catered not to the masses but to a small group of ascetics who belonged to the Order. The novitiate training could be made under any monk, during which time the candidate had his hair and beard shaved, clad himself in the yellow robe and declared that he took refuge in the Buddha, in the Teaching, and in the Order. In the second stage, the assembly determined whether the candidate should be admitted. Conditions for admission included freedom from certain diseases, and a resolution to keep ten precepts, namely, abstain from destroying life, stealing, unchastity, lying, intoxicants, eating at forbidden times, dancing-music-theaters, garlands, high or large beds, and gold or silver.

During the Buddha's lifetime, monasteries were not permanent residences but places to rest for the three months' rainy season. Also in the early period, there was no corporate worship since there were no prayers or sacrifices to offer. In this sense, original or "authentic" Buddhism is accurately called atheistic, not as though the gods of Hinduism or Brahman were explicitly denied, but because nowhere in his "religion" did Gautama provide that a transcendent deity should be invoked or even that his existence should be formally acknowledged.

The high point in early Buddhist history was the reign of King Asoka (274-232 B.C.), whose empire extended from Afghanistan on the west, the Ganges on the east, China on the north, and the Madras region in the south. Converted to Buddhism at seeing the horrors of a bloody war, he spent the rest of his life consolidating the new-found religion throughout India and sending missionaries to propagate the same in Hellenistic Asia, northern Africa, Nepal, Ceylon and, so the Buddhist chroniclers say, distant parts of Europe. Historians describe him as "not so much a pious emperor as an archbishop possessed of exceptional temporal power." He tolerated and protected Hinduism and Jainism, but favored his own interpretation of Buddhism.

Asoka's influence was crucial. He extended his adopted faith into the far reaches of Asia, gave it honor along with Brahmanism as a religion of the state and left to posterity the oldest recorded inscriptions of Buddhist history. Carved on rocks and pillars of stone in various parts of India, the inscriptions are conspicuously silent about the Four Noble Truths, the Eightfold Path, and even about Nirvana. What they describe was a kind of applied Buddhist ethics, applicable to all men and not only to a handful of professional ascetics. In one inscription, carved in a small granite stone at Calcutta, he commends to his people the meditation on seven works "by the blessed Buddha," no longer extant; and urges that "the devout laity of both sexes" profit from this reflection, and not only "communities of monks and nuns."

According to the Pali canon, the third Buddhist council was held at Pataliputra (Patna), in northeastern India, during the reign of Asoka. It seems the king was disturbed by the division and corruption within the monastic orders, and ordered the meeting to promote discipline and internal unity.

In spite of the political upheavals that followed Asoka's death, Buddhism continued to flourish and received a new impetus from King Kanishka in the second century before Christ. Kanishka introduced Greek and Persian elements into Buddhist literature and art, and sponsored a fourth religious council at Kashmir, at which the Sanskrit canon of the scriptures is said to have been fixed. This fixation was demanded by the new schism that broke between two radically different concepts of Buddhism, to become known as Mahayana and Hinayana.

Kanishka promoted other changes. The relics of Buddhist saints came to be worshiped, images of Buddha were made objects of popular veneration, monasteries were opened to temporary residents and students who were taught secular subjects, and, in general, Buddhism was further transformed from an exotic cult to a religion of the many.

Until the rise of the Gupta dynasty around 320 A.D., Buddhism fairly held its own in India. But under the Guptas, Hinduism became dominant. In spite of several brilliant representatives, the Buddhist religion declined on Indian soil—partly by absorption in the Hindu tradition which made Buddha an incarnation of its god Vishnu, partly by the Moslem invasion which was intolerant of Buddhist anthropocentrism, and partly by the exportation of the valid Buddhist spirit into Tibet, Mongolia, China, Java, and Japan.

The growth and character of Buddhism outside of India are

among the most intriguing phenomena in the history of religion. Their ramifications are only now becoming better known to Western scholars, but substantially two types are easily recognized: the *Mahayana* in China, Japan, Korea, Vietnam, Tiber and Nepal; the *Hinayana* in Thailand, Burma, Ceylon, Cambodia, India, and Indonesia.

An ancient metaphor used to speak of the Buddha's teaching as a ship in which a man could cross the ocean of birth and death (*samsara*), of successive individual existences in transmigration, and safely reach the shore in Nirvana. The two main forms of Buddhism, therefore, took the names of the "Great Vehicle" or *Mahayana,* and the "Small Vehicle" or *Hinayana,* to symbolize their relative ability to carry many or few passengers across the waters of cyclic reincarnations to perfect deliverance. A sub-type, *Mantrayana,* permeates the main species, especially the "Great Vehicle," and is so named from the sacred text or spell, *Mantra,* which consecrates the Buddhist initiates and gives them access to the *Tantras* or magical formulas (hence Tantric Buddhism) that are unknown to the common people.

DOCTRINE OF THE MAHAYANA

The historical origins of *Mahayana* are shrouded in obscurity. Its own apologists claim it was started by Kanishka, in the second century B.C., when he sanctioned the addition to the canon of Sanskrit commentaries which embodied, in some systematic form, the views of a modified Buddhism that was open to all the people. Certainly Mahayana was a strong reaction against primitive positions and introduced revolutionary changes that were completely foreign to Gautama and his followers in the first two centuries of the Buddhist era.

THEISTIC GROUNDWORK. Original Buddhism had no room for a deity, and therefore no theology as a doctrine of God. While it respected the "gods" of the Indian pantheon and the "heavens" in which they dwelt, they were considered only different, happier kinds of existence and the rewards for a good *Karma*. In the teaching of Buddha there is no concept of a deity in the full sense of the word, as the principle and ruler of the world. Mahayana introduced the idea of a deity into the religion, both on a speculative level which belongs more to philosophy, and in a popular way that was more like the polytheism of the masses.

On its speculative side, Mahayana began with the postulate that the emergence of an earthly Buddha had a hidden background in eternity. Out of this Buddha came as a kind of emanation. In the *Lotus of the Good Law,* the great textbook of orthodox Mahayana, the Buddha is simply regarded as the Krishna of the later Hindu religion, that is, the embodiment of the divine. Addressing a host of lesser deities, he declares that he reached enlightenment an infinite number of ages ago, has preached the law to people in an infinite number of worlds, and, although he announces final extinction, he will himself not become extinct. The Nirvana he experienced under the bodhi tree was only a pedagogical device and not real. His conclusion is self-explanatory.

I am the Father of the world, the self-born, the healer, the protector of all being. Knowing them to be perverted, infatuated, and ignorant, I teach final rest; myself not being at rest. What reason should I have continually to manifest myself? When men become unbelieving, unwise, ignorant, careless, fond of sensual pleasures, and, from thoughtlessness, run into misfortune, then I, who know the course of the world, declare: I am so and so, and ponder: How can I incline them to enlightenment? How can they become partakers of the Buddha-laws? [25]

Ostensibly, therefore, Buddha in this classic work was the greatest of the gods and lord of the world. However, since the dominant philosophy (*Madhyamika*) in Mahayana Buddhism maintained that no positive statement can be made about the Absolute, that the ultimate reality was an "emptiness," even these passages about Buddha's divinity are subject to an orthodox, i.e., atheist, interpretation. Yet for the purposes of popular religion, he became the supreme deity, much as Krishna was for the average Hindu, although identified with the attributeless absolute of a more philosophic form of Hinduism.

COMPASSIONATE HIGHER BEINGS. Equally significant was the popular phase of Mahayana which superimposed on the primitive teaching the doctrine of the *bodhisattvas*. The name means "a *bodhi* being," or "one whose whole nature is permeated by *bodhi* (enlightenment) and, as such, appears in the ancient writings. It meant anyone who is on the point of entering on the supreme incarnation as a Buddha. That was the only meaning of the concept, until Mahayana constructed a whole religious system around it.

There are many bodhisattvas or noble persons in past ages who trod the path of the Buddha, and became eligible to attain to Buddhahood. But they stopped at the bodhisattva stage and did not take the final step out of compassion for a suffering humanity. In their love and pity they preferred to remain in a position where they could help others, and therefore postponed their elavation to the full rank of Buddha. At the end of the Buddha path lay Nirvana, where existence ceases and consequently all possibility of assistance to others. So the bodhisattvas chose to wait and continue their ministry of mercy from the heavens where they dwell in angelic glory. Periodically they came down to earth in one of a myriad of incarnations, often in answer to prayer or in fulfilment of a promise made during their mortal sojourn among men.

If bodhisattvas are a peculiar creation of Mahayana Buddhism, they are also its most distinctive feature. As a consequence, the whole center of gravity of Buddhist doctrine was shifted from preoccupation with self to the opposite extreme. Mahayanist writings, all dating from the Christian era, are filled with legends of bodhisattva generosity.

An author from the seventh century speaks of "an insatiable tendency, an enormous tendency, an uninhibited tendency, a tendency towards the good. The bodhisattva would like at every moment to create world levels as numerous as the sands of the Ganges, all filled with jewels, so as to be able to give them away." [26]

Not only are the bodhisattvas generous to an extreme, but their assistance through prayer is indispensable. They are never invoked in vain. No executioner can slay, no chains hold, no demon or monster will hurt any one who calls on their names.

IDEALS OF CHARITY. Correlative with the belief in compassionate celestial beings, remarkable changes took place in Mahayana ethics. Though Buddha had spoken of kindness, it was cold, introspective and self-centered. Now charity was commended towards man and beast, to a degree that shocks the Western mind, which may yet be edified as the spirit behind this "fantasy of Buddhist altruism." There is the story of a monk who had accumulated merit by being faithful to a vow of chastity for forty thousand years, and yet, out of charity, yielded to seduction to please a licentious woman, although by so doing he lost the merit and earned only hell. Or again, the case of a prince who met a tigress that was dying of hunger with its little ones. Immediately he wished to be devoured by it, but the tigress lacked the strength to eat him. So he gashed himself, the blood flowed, and by licking the blood the tigress recovered enough strength to consume him.

Simple folk were instructed by such parables, but the altruism was intended for even the most cultured. Mahayana writers, especially in the early (Christian) Middle Ages, make charity the principal theme of their discourses, addressed to the earthly bodhisattvas who are to imitate their heavenly patrons. There is no need to teach the bodhisattva a great number of rules, they say. There is one which includes them all. When a bodhisattva is full of compassion, he fulfils all the conditions required for Buddhahood —just as all the senses function in the person in whom life is active.

The praise of charity sometimes reaches lyrical heights, as in the Buddhist Santideva. "If the suffering of many is brought to an end by the suffering of one, the one should foster this suffering in himself by means of compassion. Have one passion only: the good of others. All who are unhappy, are unhappy from having sought their own happiness. All who are happy, are happy from having sought the happiness of others. You must exchange your well-being for the miseries of others." [27]

To be genuine, the altruism must prove itself in deeds. "It is through actions that I shall proclaim the law. What is the use of simply repeating the words? What good would an invalid get merely from reading a book on medicine?" [28] Among the most fundamental needs is to subjugate one's pride. "There is someone doing a humiliating task; why should he, when I am there? If it is pride that prevents me from taking his place, let my pride be destroyed." [29] There is also a definition of disinterestedness that leaves no room for self. "It is a desire, a need, a hunger for the happiness of others, a love which remains untainted by either personal pleasure or the hope of reward." [30]

On further analysis, the practice of kindness depends on cultivating two mental attitudes: the identification of oneself with others, and the substitution of one's own ego for that of others.

First reflect deeply on the likeness which exists between yourself and others. "Since all have the same pains and the same joys as I have, I should care for them as I care for myself." The body, despite the differences between its various members, is looked after as a single thing: it should be the same with the world in which different beings have their joys and sorrows in common.

Reflecting on the fact that you are yourself full of faults and that others are brimming over with good qualities, you will endeavor to throw off your own personality and adopt that of others.

You are interested in your various members as parts of your body: why not in men as parts of humanity? The person who wants to save himself must practice the great secret: put himself in the place of others.[31]

As commonly interpreted, there are four stages to Buddhist charity. It begins with *ahimsa* (not harming), grows into *maitri* (loving-kindness), finds expression in *dana* (giving), and reaches perfection in *karuna* (compassion). Each stage has abundant literature to illustrate its presence and qualities, and especially to exhort the monks and laity to put it into practice.

The basic moral duty laid upon every Buddhist is that of *ahimsa,* to do no injury to anyone. Familiar to Hinduism and the Jains before the time of Buddha, *ahimsa* implies the prohibition of committing any kind of wrong, whether physical or moral, to any living being. "Any act which is harmful to others," taught Sakyamuni, "is a sin." Accordingly before a man performs an action, he should ask himself whether it is harmful to others or to himself. If it is, he must not do it, "for it is an evil action whose fruit will be suffering."

Next in the hierarchy is loving-kindness, which presumes the foregoing but adds to it a certain feeling or state of mind, at once unassuming and gentle, that becomes the habitual source of practical charity. The sacred writings are filled with panegyrics of *maitri,* whose worth in things of the spirit is greater than that of all other virtues.

None of the means employed to acquire religious merit has a sixteenth part of the value of loving-kindness. Loving-kindness, which is freedom of heart, absorbs them all; it glows, it shines, it blazes forth.

In the same way, as the light of all the stars has not a sixteenth part of the value of the moonlight, but the moonlight absorbs it and glows and shines and blazes forth; in the same way none of the means employed to acquire religious merit has a sixteenth part of the value of loving-kindness.

In the same way, as at the end of the rainy season, the sun, rising into the clear and cloudless sky, banishes all the dark spaces and glows and shines and blazes forth; in the same way again, as at night's end the morning star glows and shines and blazes forth, so none of the means employed to acquire religious merit has a sixteenth part of the value of loving-kindness.[32]

However, *maitri* is not genuine unless it leads to *dana,* according to the definition that "the good man seeks his own good and that of others." All the acts of charity which history and legend attribute to Buddha have become part of the idealization of the practice of outgoing goodness. Nowhere else, perhaps, is the radical difference between Hinayana and Mahayana Buddhism more evident than in their respective attitudes towards *dana.* Among the former, for example, the practice of medicine was forbidden, whereas among the latter it is not only permitted but encouraged as a means of serving the neighbor.

The height of generosity (*dana-paramita*) is defined in terms that leave nothing to selfishness and extend equally to all animate things with no thought of profitable return.

It means helping men and animals with acts of loving-kindness; having concern for the multitude who are in error; rejoicing that the wise have achieved liberation; protecting and helping all living beings; transcending the boundaries of heaven and earth with charity as wide as a river and as large as the sea; performing acts of generosity to all living beings; feeding the hungry, giving drink to the thirsty, clothing those who are cold, refreshing those overcome by the heat, being ready to help the sick; whether it be carriages, horses, boats, equipment, or any kind of precious material or famous jewel, or loved one or son or kingdom— whatever it may be that you are asked to give, it means giving it at once.[33]

Nor is this the end. At the outer limits of charity is compassion (*karuna*), which is regarded so precious a virtue that Buddha is often simply called "The Compassionate One," and anyone who desires to attain the Nirvana he reached must follow him in the practice of pity. While both the main streams of Buddhism insist on this virtue, the Great Vehicle has developed its theory with great precision. Milarepa, the Tibetan poet and ascetical writer, made this perfectly plain. "The person who only thinks of his own salvation," he wrote in his *Spiritual Testament,* "harvests *samsara,*" that is, the ocean of birth and death or successive individual existence in transmigration. "And the one who does not distribute what he has gathered meditates in vain. He will remain without virtue." [34] Milarepa wished to show that charitable compassion includes, with emphasis, pity for the spiritual lot of others, and not only for their material needs, at the risk of not gaining the very salvation a man desires for himself. "Living beings," Buddhist sources say, "are unhappy because of their acts, because of their nature. It is impossible to make them happy by supplying them with merely material aids. The best way of helping them is to establish them in goodness." [35]

Exhortations to the same effect are found multiplied in Mahayana ethics. However they must be balanced by one factor that quite alters the first impression they may give. Invariably the ideal they portray, whether in legend or instruction, is extreme and correspondingly unreal. "It is not sufficient for a bodhisattva to be charitable, virtuous, patient and so on. He must have an 'insatiable' or 'colossal' capacity for charity, virtue and patience." [36]

By the ordinary law, a bodhisattva must not eat without giving part of his good to the needy. But this rule is too lenient for the author of *Ratnarasi,* who tells the bodhisattva to think of the bacteria in his body and say to himself, "Inside me there are eighty thousand legions of microbes. May they comfort themselves with this food! At the moment I am providing for their wants with meat; when I have attained to illumination, I shall provide them with *dharma* (something more substantial)." [37]

Should a real bodhisattva happen to be involved, he can fulfil the most fantastic vows because miraculous achievements are at his ready disposal.

The bodhisattva of the body of the law can transform himself in a twinkling into innumerable bodies and so render homage to the Buddhas of ten provinces at once. In a twinkling he can create immense riches and give them to other beings. It is by this kind of exercise the bodhisattva of the body of the law practices the perfection of the virtue of giving.[38]

Accustomed to this kind of extravaganza, the Buddhist believer can take refuge in symbolism. He correctly assumes that only a vague sort of fellowship is signified by all the imagery. And the very exponents of superhuman generosity confirmed the assumption. Not charity itself but "the thought of sacrificing all one possesses—and even the fruit of one's sacrifice—to all things, is the perfection of charity. Charity is therefore entirely of the mind." [39] So that every human action, even the most pleasant and insignificant—like eating or going to bed, washing one's hands or sitting down—gathers immense value provided the motive is to benefit "all things." Not the actions themselves, but the desire to put them into effect constitutes virtue.

POLYTHEISM AND MYTHOLOGY. Belief in the celestial bodhisattvas opened the door to an array of superhuman beings that appealed to popular piety. They were often given names with both visible and spiritual properties. Avalokitesvara, who is ruled by compassion, holds a lotus, and in his mercy helps everyone in distress; his capacity for transforming himself into any shape is inexhaustible. Manjusri excels in wisdom, holds a sword in his hand, and specializes in giving knowledge. Maitreya is a coming Buddha who represents friendliness and holds a flask with the elixir of immortality. Samantabhadra rides a white elephant and distributes magical formulas that avert all danger.

Bodhisattvas are as deserving of worship as the Buddhas, and according to some Mahayanists, more so. "From the Buddha," says one authority "arise only the disciples, but from a Bodhisattva the perfect Buddha himself is born."

With the development of celestial beings came the multiplication of mythical Buddhas. This was due mainly to the familiar Buddhist tendency to stress the spiritual and symbolic side of their founder while belittling the importance of his actual physical existence. Gradually the historical Buddha faded away, leaving the Buddha as an expression of Dharma (the ultimate void) as the only reality. In the *Diamond Sutra* occurs the famous statement in which the Buddha warns against confusing him with the man who lived on earth. "Those who saw me in physical form and followed the voice they heard, were misguided in their efforts and will never see me." [40]

It is almost impossible to classify the variety of items that Buddhism places under the single term "Dharma," not excluding the concept of Buddha as an expression of the ultimate void. Dharmas may be the sense faculties or sensations, vital power, process of being born, death, hatred, greed, blindness or delusion, perception or realization, and spiritual concentration. Dharmas are also qualities without specific properties, substances without a subject, and occurrences without a common substratum to which they can be referred. The reason why so many different, and contradictory, notions are associated with the single word "Dharma" is that Buddhism itself contains such varied (and by Western standards mutually exclusive) concepts on the meaning of life and death, the finite and infinite, the human and divine.

Without denying the historical Buddha, not only Mahayana but all forms of Buddhism see in him only the manifestation of a type, and one of a series of Buddhas who appear on earth throughout the ages. Their number grew with the passing of time—from seven, to twenty-four, to a myriad who fill the heavens. It also enabled Buddhist missionaries to prepare the way for acceptance by other religions. With the help of numerous bodhisattvas and Buddhas, polytheism, belief in demons, and other alien ideas could be readily assimilated to Buddhism. The gods and demons of other peoples were declared to be incarnations or duplicates of the Buddhist pantheon.

HINAYANA—THE LESSER VEHICLE

The expression *Hinayana,* or lesser way, was coined by the opponents of the primitive Buddhist religion which they accused of reactionary selfishness and unrealistic conservatism. It was a "lesser way" because only a small number, mainly monks and nuns, originally belonged to it and were therefore given the chance of attaining Nirvana. Since the implication chafes, the Hinayanists prefer to call themselves members of the *Theravada* or "school of the elders." Geographically they represent that form of Buddhism which prevails in Ceylon, Burma, Thailand, Laos and in general in South and Southeastern Asia. "Southern Buddhism" is a common synonym for *Hinayana,* and "Northern Buddhism" for *Mahayana,* but only broadly because of their constant mutual influence.

Hinayana professes to follow the basic principles of the Pali canon and, by this standard, may be identified with primitive Buddhism. Certainly its emphasis on the Four Noble Truths and the Eightfold Path places it nearer to the original teachings of Gautama than Mahayana whose express purpose was to reinterpret the Buddha's esoteric doctrine in order to make it universally acceptable.

Present-day Mahayanists distinguish themselves from Hinayana in five ways, which may be taken as a valid description of the latter, less popular but seemingly more authentic form of Buddhism. The Hinayanists are said to be too literal-minded, adhering to the letter rather than to the spirit of the ancient writings, and on the whole averse to change; they are scholastic, overoccupied with the analysis and classification of mental states; they are one-sidedly negative in their conception on Nirvana and the Path; they are overattached to the merely formal aspects of monasticism; and most gravely, they are spiritually individualistic.

The literal-mindedness appears in their habit of regarding intellectual formulations of doctrine as valid in the ultimate sense, as being not merely conceptual symbols of reality but constituting its fully adequate description. Buddha had spoken of the essential unreality of the so-called individual being by analyzing it into its most prominent phenomena-bodily form, perception and the rest. Hinayanists proceeded to treat each of these phenomena as ultimately real, thus actually deviating from Gautama's uncompromising nihilism. Then they equated their theory with its verbal expression and, after the oral tradition was committed to writing, refused to depart a hair's breadth from the precise wording of the "canonical" scriptures.

Ultra-conservatism, so their critics say, has kept them from understanding that, as the Buddha says in their own texts, the Dharma (or law) is simply a raft. Had the Buddhists of Burma, for instance, been able to grasp this vitally important teaching, they would never have spent ten million rupees (two million dollars) on the so-called Sixth Buddhist Council (Rangoon, 1954-1956) in order to determine whether a certain letter of the texts was a "t" or a "d." [41]

Scholastic preoccupation with mental states was based on what the Mahayana claim is an unfounded theory, that the Pali texts to which they appeal contain the direct utterance of the Buddha himself. External historical evidence shows there were centuries of speculative interpretation built into the Pali canon, and internal evidence confirms the fact. Furthermore, instead of putting these texts into practice, the Hinayana have reportedly been satisfied to study, analyze and classify. The result of this intellectualizing has been "the almost total neglect of the practice of meditation, which is so striking a feature of modern Theravada Buddhism." [42] Philosophical analysis has replaced the ancient practice of inward concentration.

A negative concept of Nirvana leads the Hinayanists to describe the goal of Buddhist ethics in terms of non-existence, and so to stress the present that the future life is implicitly denied. The same negativism affects the deity. Where Mahayana has developed a medley of gods and added the divinities of other religions to its own, Hinayana is mainly responsible for the common notion that Buddhism is a religion without God. In Zen terminology, "Buddhists understand the universe and God as one. There is no remainder in the mathematics of infinity. All life is one, therefore there cannot be God and man nor a universe and God." [43]

As a result, Hinayana does not believe in prayer, and submits to no ultimate heavenly authority. Taking Buddha literally, to "work out your own salvation," it interprets this dictum so rigidly that the negative consequence is removal of all dependence on superhuman powers. Any concession to theism is a compromise of Hinayana principles.

Overattachment to the merely formal aspects of monasticism is a common charge raised by the Mahayanists against those who claim to be treading the ancient path. No alien critic of Oriental customs is so merciless as Buddhist commentators on their own rival tradition.

Scholasticism, by exalting rational understanding above realization, inhibits both the practice of meditation and the attainment of wisdom, thereby not only depriving morality of its transcendental sanction but dispensing with the need for any ethical training other than a merely external conformity with the disciplinary precepts. Exclusively negative conceptions of *Nirvana* and the Way lead to a misinterpretation of the ideal of renunciation, "giving up the world" being regarded as synonymous with a life of idleness and inactivity. Rigid observance of the strict letter of the *Vinaya* (discipline), at least while under public surveillance, is all that is expected of the monk in most parts of the so-called Theravada world today.[44]

Spiritual individualism is the final distinguishing mark of the "lesser vehicle" type of Buddhism. Both types describe themselves by a comparison drawn from one of the ancient writings. A glow-worm, goes the simile, does not think its light would illumine the whole of Asia. Just so the disciples of Hinayana do not think they should, after winning full enlightenment, lead all beings to Nirvana. But the sun, when it has risen, radiates its light over the whole continent. Just so a Bodhisattva (in the Mahayana tradition), after he has done the practices of charity which lead to the full enlightenment of Buddhahood, leads countless persons to Nirvana.

The issue between the two systems runs deeper than the familiar difference between the active and contemplative life in Western religious thought. It implies a radical dichotomy between two contradictory moral philosophies: Mahayana admits a personal deity (or deities) and therefore allows for the concept of social justice and charity under obedience to a higher power. Hinayana denies or prescinds from any god outside and above man and so logically concerns itself only with self, which it seeks to spare the trial of continuous rebirth by Nirvana annihilation.

MONASTICISM

Buddha made monasticism an inseparable part of his creed, and the *Triratna,* or Three Jewels, which Gautama prescribed on his followers were, "I believe in the Buddha, in Dharma (law) and the Sangha (monastic order)." As originally conceived, the function of Buddhist monasticism is twofold: to provide suitable conditions for one's personal development, and to teach the law to other people.

During Gautama's lifetime, he was the head of the Order, and after his death no one has replaced him as universal superior of the brotherhood, not even a body of men or council with juridical authority to govern. However there may be, as in Burma, national heads of the Order elected by the monks. At first each school of Buddhist thought had a superior and now each monastery (*Vihara*) within the sect, but his position is only one of honor, a *primus inter pares,* and not of real jurisdiction over the monk or *Bhikshu.* The latter is to obey the rules of the order and follow the common life through voluntary self-asceticism, although he may be dismissed for grave violations.

Men are normally admitted to the Order after the age of twenty, provided they are healthy and otherwise suitable. After a novitiate during which he shaves his head (which also applies to women), he receives the monastic robes, a new name, and agrees to keep the Rules of the Order—two hundred twenty as they stand today— known as the Patimokkha, and accepted with slight modifications by all forms of Buddhism. However no vows are taken, and the monk may leave the Order upon notice when he wants to, either for a while or permanently.

Many men join the Order late in life, when their family duties are satisfied, or in middle-age, when they want to spend all or some of their remaining years in seeking the Buddhist release from suffering. In Burma, Thailand and Cambodia many boys spend part of their early years in a monastery, from several weeks to a decade or more. The purpose is to have them learn the sacred writings, and habits of discipline and morality not easily taught at home. One result of the practice is to instill a deep respect from childhood for the monastic way of life.

A certain hierarchy of advancement is provided for those who make the Sangha their career. Beginning as a novice (*Samarena*), the monk dedicates himself as *Bhikshu*. After a time he becomes an ancient (*Thera*), and if he perseveres for twenty years, a great elder or *Mahathera*. In practice the distinctions are quite nominal except for an increased reverence from the people, and within the monastery from the monks.

Begging is a common custom, following the example of Gautama who went around with a bowl in his hand asking for a donation of rice. Depending on the locality, individual poverty is often strictly interpreted, allowing for three robes, a waist cloth, begging bowl, razor, water strainer and needle. However, this depends on the relative wealth of the people in the district, and even the strictest monks often have other belongings. But the monasteries, by contrast, are wealthy land owners, in some areas owning upwards of a third of the arable land.

Begging has not only economic value, according to some of the best commentators. It also has a deep moral significance, which ascetical writers are at pains to explain. One benefit is to teach the beggar humility, and another is to make the donor accumulate the merit of self-denial.

Both have a great social value when they are understood in their proper bearings, and what is most strongly emphasized in the monk's life is this social meaning, and not necessarily its economic importance. For if it were necessary to support themselves by some other means, the monastery authorities would soon have found a way for it. But on account of its educative value begging has been selected for the monks to be the chief method of maintaining themselves physically.[45]

On certain days the monks may go out in large groups, forming a long line and walking slowly in the streets, crying "Ho." Each monk carries a bowl, in which people are to place money or rice. More often the monks go out in small companies of four or five. They wear broad-brimmed hats that permit the monk to see only a few feet ahead, and not even recognize who gives them a donation. This is done on purpose.

The donor is not to know who the beggar is, nor does the beggar observe who the donor is. The deed of charity is to be practiced altogether free from personal relationships. When the latter are present, the deed is apt to lose its spiritual sense. It is just an act of favoritism, that is, it harbors in it on one side the feeling of personal superiority and on the other the degrading consciousness of subserviency.[46]

Corresponding to their second purpose, the monasteries are to communicate their possessions. As expressed by the Buddha, "There are two kinds of gifts, the gift of material things and the gift of the law. Of these two, the gift of the law (*Dharma*) is pre-eminent." For centuries the monks have followed this counsel, yet without striving to make converts; rather their intention is to share with others the method and practices they have found useful in the attainment of spiritual enlightenment.

Until modern times, the *Bhikshus* were the ordinary schoolmasters for the children, and thus inculcated principles of morality and Buddhist ethics in their young charges. Since the secularization of the schools in many countries and, in China and North Vietnam since their appropriation by the Communists, this essential function of the monasteries is gradually removed, with comparable changes effected in the monastic life itself.

As previously seen Gautama himself admitted women to the Buddhist Order, who are called *Bhikkunis* or nuns. In the early centuries, in India, they had their own monasteries, completely subject to the men; but as their status declined they practically ceased to exist in community life and became instead lay women disciples (*Sila-Upasika*) in countries of Hinayana Buddhism. They often lead austere lives and particularly in Burma and Ceylon have been pioneers in social service fields.

It should be noted that the *Bhikshu* may be considered a monk, friar or religious—although strictly speaking none of these—but he is not a priest except in the broad sense of leading prayers and assisting with such ritual as the offering of incense or the burning of candles.

Circumstances differ, and Buddhist monasticism varies considerably in different countries. The most notable difference is found between Hinayana monasticism, mainly as just described; and the Mahayana Order in China, Japan, and Korea, along with extreme adaptations in Tibet and Outer Mongolia.

When Buddhism was first introduced into China, the Chinese were long unfavorable to the implications of monastic life and after they admitted the *Sangha* it was basically changed in the process. Japan followed the lead of China, and in both countries the monastic concept was tailored to fit the national pattern. The basic difference was the creation of the bonzes in Japan and the incorporation of ancestor worship into Chinese monasticism.

A Japanese bonze may marry, and he is often responsible for a certain quota of families (like a parish) who support a particular temple. Instead of the uniform yellow or orange robe of monks elsewhere, he wears a dark *Kimono,* covered by a short silk robe to denote his peculiar sect. On feast days the silk robes are of gorgeous color and the altar equipment of the lowliest temple is luxurious in comparison with the simple flowers and bowl of incense of the Hinayana Buddhists.

Moreover there are thousands of female bonzes in Japan. They sometimes live in separate convent temples or they share the same monastery with the men, although living in quarters of their own.

With head shaved and dressed like the monks, they perform their own religious services, engage in meditation, and do some outside activity—although less than the men. Until recently the monastic vocation was regarded as an honorable career for the daughters of the aristocracy. Their typical routine within the convent is much like that of the monk. At some convents the first chanting service begins at four-thirty, followed by breakfast, and various duties about the temple. After a second service at eleven, there is a mid-day meal, and a third service in the evening after supper. In China, Japan and Korea, the bonzes may be equally considered monks or priests, and nuns or priestesses, although the respective duties of different bonzes will vary, according to age, rank, sect and sex.

In a class by itself is the monasticism of Tibet, where religion in the eighth century became an amalgam of Buddhist magic and Tibetan demon worship. The mixture is called Lamaism from the name, *Lama* (the superior one), given to the higher Tibetan monks. Tibet was invaded by the Mongols in the thirteenth century, which marked the beginning of Lamaistic influence in Mongolia. Kiglai Khan himself was converted in 1261, and centralized the monastic system which later controlled the country. Reformed by Tsong-ka-pa (1358-1419), the monks became "the virtuous order" or *Geluppa*. Tsong's nephew was the first grand Lama and propounded the theory that all grand Lamas are divine incarnations. His fourth successor developed the idea into the present theory by specifying the god who becomes incarnate, namely, Avalokita, and in 1650 obtained from the Chinese emperor the title *Dalai Lama* (the Great Lama), by which Europeans commonly know him.

At the death of Dalai Lama, a successor would be chosen from a child born near the time of death, in whom the god is supposed to have become reincarnate. The infant chosen was taken to the monastery, garbed as a monk at the age of four and enthroned, four years later to become a full monk and assume full authority at eighteen.

Since the Communist invasions in China, Vietnam and Tibet, Buddhist monasticism has been drastically changed. Some Buddhist institutions have been allowed to function provided they cooperate. According to the "Land Reform Laws" the monks may keep as much land as they can cultivate to meet a predetermined quota of crops. Failure to meet the quota means forfeiture of land. City monasteries are required to undertake certain manufacturing industries. In Tibet, the Dalai Lama was driven into exile, and the quasi-religious administration of the country by the Lamas was abolished.

THE LAITY

In view of its heavy stress on the monastic life, Buddhism has been almost equated in the popular mind with cloistered asceticism and segregation from the world, whereas from its earliest history it has shown an awareness of the laity that compares favorably with the most laic religions of the East.

Buddha himself taught the laity as well as monks, and was mindful of the average person's mode of life in society. Furthermore, by his own wishes, the Sangha developed as a monastic institution within society, supported by it and intended as source and focus of its religious energy. Consequently the Buddhist literature often presents guidance and examples for the laity, and not only for monks, even when the latter are primarily concerned. To a great extent the *Dharma* (teachings of the Buddha, doctrine, law, norm) can be interpreted as well singularly as plurally, socially as well as metaphysically, to serve the needs of people in the world no less than of monks and nuns in the monasteries.

At the same time Buddhism has absorbed numerous social customs and beliefs from other religions and integrated them into the stream of its own tradition, with the result that what theoretically is a monastic religion has become very laicized. Every aspect of Buddhist life and thought is now open in greater or less measure to all segments of the population. Yet there are differences, mainly between the Hinayana and Mahayana forms, where the historical cleavage naturally affects the place which the laity occupy in the respective religious systems.

The classic Pali scripture texts for the guidance of lay persons have deeply influenced Buddhist practices in South Asia. In symbolic language the Buddha's counsels express what are substantially the same principles which bind the monks. They are generic enough to allow adaptation to particular circumstances and susceptible of infinite interpretations, as appears from the various commentaries. In context, Gautama is talking about a young householder, whom he instructs "to protect the six quarters," which he proceeds to identify. Parents are the eastern quarter, teachers the south, wife and children the west, friends and companions are the north, servants and work people represent the nadir, while religious teachers and monks are the zenith.

In five ways a child should minister to his parents as the eastern quarter: Once supported by them I will now be their support. I will perform duties incumbent on them. I will keep up the lineage and tradition of my family. I will make myself worthy of my heritage.

And in five ways parents thus ministered to by their child show their love for him: They restrain him from vice, they exhort him to virtue, they train him to a profession, they contract a suitable marriage for him, and in due time they hand over his inheritance.

In five ways pupils minister to their teachers as the southern quarter: by rising from their seat in salutation, by waiting upon them, by eagerness to learn, by personal service, and by attention when receiving their teaching.

And in five ways do teachers, thus ministered to love their pupil: They train him in that wherein he has been well trained. They make him hold fast that which is well held. They thoroughly instruct him in the lore of every art. They speak well of him among his friends and companions. They provide for his safety in every quarter.[47]

In like manner the wife, as western quarter, should be cared for by the husband, "by respect, by courtesy, by fidelity, by handing over authority to her, by providing her with adornment." And he in turn ought to be served by the wife "performing her duties well, by hospitality to his parents and hers, by fidelity, by watching over the goods he brings home, and by skill and industry in all that she does."

A faithful Buddhist will practice virtue towards his friends and familiars as the northern quarter by generosity, courtesy and benevolence, by treating them as he treats himself and by being as good as his word. They reciprocate by protecting him when he is off guard and on such occasions guarding his property; they become a refuge for him in danger, do not forsake him in trouble and show consideration for his family.

With regard to servants and employees, the nadir of virtuous concern, they are to be "assigned work according to their strength, supplied with food and wages, tended in their sickness, receive a share in unusual delicacies, and occasionally given vacation." The employees for their part are to love their master in five ways. "They rise before him, they lie down to rest after him, they are content with what is given to them, they do their work well, and they carry about his praise and good name." Thus is the nadir protected and made safe for both sides.

Finally the layman fulfils his duty towards religious teachers and monks by "affection in act and speech and mind, by keeping open house to them, and by supplying their temporal needs." In like manner the recluses, Brahmins and priests show their love for the layman if they "restrain him from evil, exhort him to good, love him with kindly thoughts, teach him what he has not heard, correct and purify what he has heard, and reveal to him the way to heaven." [48]

These precepts have been implemented through centuries of private morality and under the impact of two world wars in a variety of social ventures that were formerly quite undeveloped in dominantly Hinayana (Therevada) Buddhist territories. Such welfare activities as education for children, provisions of facilities in temples or other buildings for orphans and the poor, the aged, and sometimes unfortunate animals, medical dispensaries and vocational training centers, supplies for leper and refugee settlements, moral guidance for delinquents and similar projects are now advocated by political authorities and religious leaders through an appeal to the ideals of "the Compassionate One."

In contrast with the more conservative and exclusively monastic Hinayana, Northern or Mahayana Buddhism has always emphasized the role of the laity and developed a balance between them and the monks that goes back to the earliest period of Buddhist history. Especially among the Japanese, the example of prominent lay Buddhists inspired civil officials and rulers to take an active part in state affairs from religious motives. When this was com-

bined with the strong Confucian emphasis on loyalty to one's ancestors (whether in the family or society), the result was a powerful means of integrating religion with life in the world.

The name of Vimalakirti, a disciple of Buddha, is a household
word in Buddhist circles as the ideal of a layman who achieved
greater holiness than most persons attain by following the monastic
discipline. A place was reserved on the court calendar in Japan
for reading and expounding the text which tells the story of his
virtues. "Praised by all the Buddhas, revered by all the disciples
and all the gods," his memory has been kept alive as the paragon
of lay sanctity.

Though he is but a simple layman, yet observing the pure monastic
discipline; though living at home, yet never desirous of anything; though
possessing a wife and children, always exercising pure virtues; though
surrounded by his family, holding aloof from worldly pleasures; though
using the jeweled ornaments of the world, yet adorned with spiritual
splendor; though eating and drinking, yet enjoying the flavor of the
rapture of meditation; though frequently at the gambling house, yet leading the gamblers into the right path; though coming in contact with
heresy, yet never letting his true faith be impaired; though having a
profound knowledge of worldly learning, yet ever finding pleasure in
things of the spirit as taught by Buddha.[49]

Mahayana can also be speculative, but its approach to the laity
is normally through personalities rather than abstractions, and the
fame of Vimalakirti is indicative of a tendency in this type of Buddhism that has the merit of ready appeal to men of the world but
the disadvantage of being subject to their whims and secular tastes.
It was this easy adaptability that has made Northern Buddhism
more sectarian than its Southern counterpart and created divisions
and subdivisions within the Buddhist ranks which are present but
never so prevalent as in the North.

Japan is a good example of this sectarianism induced by centuries of laicization. Six sects were introduced from China between
the years 625 and 754 A.D., and these have now grown into close
to a hundred distinct bodies which are further divided into smaller
units. The Nara sects arose through their patronage of the wealthy
aristocratic classes; Tendai groups were the result of embracing the
popular Shinto deities into the Buddhist pantheon; Shingon catered

to the mystical and esoteric tastes of the people; Nicherenism offered the prospects of salvation with the minimal effort of reciting certain formulas, while Zen made certain demands in externals but allowed great liberty otherwise.

Nowhere else is the lay character of Buddhism better seen than in the Amida sect, named after Amitabha or Amitayus (Japanese, *Amida*), one of the transcendent Buddhas. It was founded by the priest Honen (1132-1212), who studied all the sects of his day and became discouraged over the difficulty of attaining true enlightenment. Then he came on a simple and effective way of universal salvation. A single passage in the sacred writings held the secret. "Whether walking or standing, sitting or lying down, only repeat the name of Amida with all your heart. Never cease the practice of it even for a moment. This is the very work which unfailingly issues in salvation, for it is in accordance with the original vow of that Buddha." Honen started a movement on the basis of Amida's vow, teaching that the mere recitation of the phrase, "adoration of the Lord of boundless light and infinite life" would give final assurance of rebirth in "the pure land" if it were accompanied by faith.

The rapid spread of Amidaism and its millions of present adherents testify to the genius of Buddhist ideology to reduce religious precepts to a minimum and yet evoke great dedication from the masses. Dubbed the "easy way" by its critics, Amidaism has the largest number of Buddhist followers in Japan and, in fact, is to be found all over the Far East even outside the ranks of Buddhism. Its doctrines could be understood by the common people, and its requirements were ultimately only an expression of confident faith in the Buddha Amida. In contrast to the intricate doctrine and practices of Tendai, Shingon, Zen and Nara, it asked little of its followers. Its teaching on "hell" and "paradise" became deeply rooted in the minds of devout people and favorite themes for children's stories. For almost a thousand years it has affected the daily life of countless Orientals, and provided them with ideals that are absent or obscured in other Buddhistic forms. Pathos, pessimism, generosity, the suicide of young lovers for the sake of a happy married life in another world, the restraint on vice and motivation to virtue because of eternal rewards and sanctions—all these reflect the power of an ostensibly monastic religion to become laicized and flourish outside the cloister.

WORSHIP AND RITUAL

Buddhist worship is extremely variegated, with the differences arising from opposing Hinayana and Mahayana traditions, from the incorporation of other religions into Buddhism, from varied national customs, and within a single country or even city, from the multiform sects that may have almost nothing in common except a vague devotion to the Buddha.

CONCEPTS OF PRAYER AND SACRIFICE. As might be expected, there is no single, consistent notion of prayer or sacrifice in Buddhism. In strict fidelity to Gautama, the Buddhists should not pray to a deity or invoke the assistance of higher powers in the spiritual world. Many Buddhists, especially the Hinayana and the majority of intellectuals, firmly adhere to this principle in theory. They pray because of the good effects which the act of prayer produces in their own mind and character. A monk in Rangoon was quoted as saying that, "Prayer and offering are not received by the Buddha in the sense that they have any effect upon him, nor in the sense of being means of procuring anything from him. Their value is subjective purely. A prayer for peace or purity is likely to bring about its own fulfilment, especially if accompanied by the thought of the Buddha as our ideal. The Buddha, indeed, is for practical purposes quite dead, but he is the ideal of what humanity might be and of what each of us ought to be. Thus prayer for the enlightened Buddhist is not supplication but mental discipline."

Parallel with this idea is a basic scepticism about the value of rites and ceremonies. Again from the vantage point of the "enlightened Buddhist," he is early told in the monastery to free himself, first from the general delusion that correct outward action will ensure a man's salvation, and then from the particular delusion that religious rites and ceremonies have intrinsic value to the attendant devotee. In a word, nothing will avail as substitute for *self-liberation*. Gautama was emphatic on this point. Buddhas only point out the way; "work out your salvation with diligence." For the educated (and orthodox) Buddhist, his religion is above all others a philosophy of individual effort, wherein no one, man or God, should stand for good or evil between a cause and its effect, whether in the practice of virtue or the attainment of Nirvana.

Perhaps as a reaction to this practical atheism, a large segment of the ordinary Buddhist faithful has gone to the opposite extreme. Not only are petitions to the Buddhas and higher beings salutary, but their mechanical repetition or even written inscription carry an efficacy that is simply magical.

A crude practice is the use of the six syllable formula, *Om manipadme hum,* which can be translated, "O Thou in whose lotus the jewel stands." Popular in Tibet and elsewhere, and addressed to the god *Avolakita,* its esoteric meaning is obscene but its power almost incalculable. These six syllables can be seen everywhere, written on walls, painted on flags, which, when they flutter in the wind, spread the force of the words about. Noted down on strips of paper, they are placed in greater or smaller cylinders, and put in rotating movement by a turning of the hand or even of a waterfall.

In the same spirit on a still broader scale, everywhere at shrines and temples people write their prayers on little pieces of paper and offer them to a god. Men pledge themselves to abstain from wine and women for definite periods of time. Some promise to give up gambling and others who are diseased promise a thank offering if cured. Lovers pray that the object of their love may come to them or that estrangement may be healed. Women pray for many things. Some are asking for a happy delivery, others are sick or troubled and seek relief. Before Yakushi, the Buddha of healing, a woman troubled with warts on her face prays for their removal within two weeks; a weary mother asks that her peevish child may cease crying at night and that her own swollen limbs may recover.

NATURE OF THE DIVINE. Beneath these contrary attitudes towards prayer lies an ambivalent notion of the divine, which perplexes the Western observer and has led more than one writer to dismiss all Buddhism as atheistic, or see in it an oriental counterpart of ritual (especially of Catholic) Christianity. It may be either, and the complexity of Buddhism lends plausibility to both concepts.

At one extreme is Zen (meditation) Buddhism, which has deeply influenced the religions of China and Japan. Historically Zen Buddhism was partially derived from Taoism as a naturalistic form of Confucianism, and currently is either pure subjectivism or pantheism, depending on the viewpoint. In Zen, there is no dualism of heaven and earth, natural and supernatural, man and God, matter and spirit, mortal and immortal, for ordinary men and Buddhas, present existence (*Samsara*) and future destiny (*Nirvana*), are all the same. "Buddhism," the Zen monks declare, "places the center of the universe in the subjectivity of individual mind, whereas other religions put it in the objectivity outside the individual mind." In reply to the question: What is the first cause of all things?, they say "Some religions answer God, Allah, Brahma, or something outside the individual. Buddhism sweeps aside your idle speculation and tells you to find the answer in your own realization." [50]

Yet the same monks who sweep aside the idle fancies about God's existence specialize in meditation beyond anything comparable in the Western world. A typical Zen monastery has a large meditation hall, whose chief adornment is a shrine or Buddha with perhaps a single spray of flowers before it. The hall itself is long and narrow, parallel on two sides with tinted paper screens, concealing entrances into the surrounding courtyards and cupboards where the monks keep their bedding. Along the walls are low platforms on which the monks sleep at night and practice their Za-zen, "to sit in meditation."

When the gong sounds for meditation, they enter the hall in procession and take their seats on the platforms facing the center of the room. The superior goes forward and prostrates himself before the shrine, while outside another monk summons any members of the community who may be late. Rising from the floor, the superior then lights a stick of incense to mark time, and as soon as he returns to his seat the meditation begins.

Thereupon two other monks, after due reverences to the Buddha, take up a flat piece of wood and begin to walk up and down in front of the two rows of meditating monks. Their duty is to keep a watchful eye on anyone who shows signs of drowsiness. If he starts dozing, one of the guards gives him a few sharp slaps across the shoulder to wake him up. When the incense stick burns out, the superior sounds a bell as a sign for relaxation. The shutters are opened, and the monks march around the hall, until another stick of incense is lighted and the next stage of meditations is made, as before. About three hours of Zen each morning, and a comparable period in the afternoon or evening are not uncommon in strict monasteries.

What is the object of their meditation?—so to concentrate attention on right posture and breathing as to relax the body, banish wandering thoughts, and thus prepare for solving the problems of human existence, after the meditation is over.

With minor differences in procedure all Buddhist meditation follows the same external pattern. Whenever the person of Buddha is brought into the exercise as something approaching real prayer, the one meditating reflects on the identity of the Buddha, the maker of the prayer, and the object of it. Thus if he would pray for a friend in need, he reflects on their common identity with the Buddha. By destroying the illusion of suffering and pain, based on the false assumption that persons are distinct and their physical experiences real, he destroys the source of unreality and frees the person (or himself) from the unreal needs.

At the other extreme to worship without invoking a personal God, many monks in the Mahayana tradition and numerous Chinese and Japanese Buddhists address themselves to a deity whose compassion is so great that simple faith in Amitabha (Amida) may even dispense with the necessity of good works. So great is the power and mercy of this Buddha that no matter what crimes a man may have committed, if he utters at death the name "Buddha Amitayus," he expiates at every utterance sins that would otherwise keep him in a cycle of births and rebirths for eighty million *Kalpas* (a period of cosmic time). While dying he will see a golden lotus flower appear like the sun and find himself born in the world of highest happiness.

TEMPLES AND SHRINES. Buddhist temples differ greatly in architecture, but the most widely admired are those of Japan. They serve all sorts of functions. Children and sometimes adults find the temple court a kind of playground; monthly or otherwise periodic fairs are held in the temple, when the whole edifice may be luminous with colored lanterns and filled with gay streamers of paper or cloth; funeral and memorial services, feast-days and anniversaries are temple affairs.

In some sects the main hall of the temple is sometimes closed. However except at night, the temple proper and at least one of its shrines are always open, to allow worshipers to enter and depart any hour of the day. The interior is seldom uniform, but normally the temple has a central shrine, with an image of one or another Buddha, before which stands an altar. This is a long and narrow table that usually has a large incense burner in the middle, two candlesticks on each side, and at either end a spray of lotus leaves carved out of wood and gilded. Worshipers may cover the altar with offerings of food, flowers and candles, or, as often happens, the image may be kept hidden and exposed to view only on festive occasions, and the votive offerings are made at one of the numerous secondary shrines.

Regular temple services vary as much as their respective creeds. Some sects have elaborate liturgical functions that include, besides chanting, rhythmic movements of sacred objects and the presentation of symbolic offerings by the celebrant (man or woman), dramatic gestures and magical incantations. Others, in the same country and city, are more reserved. Their usual sequence is a chant by the choir of monks, prayer intoned by the celebrant followed by burning of incense during another chant, a period of silent worship, chant by the monks while the celebrant walks around the shrine after appropriate bows, the sounding of a gong and reading of a poem with the chorus alternating a response, a final chant and bows (with the ringing of a gong), and recessional by the monks.

The laity are accustomed to remaining for private devotions after the liturgical ceremonies are over, after which many will go to one of the larger halls of the temple where a preaching service may be held. Most sects allow the laity to attend the solemn ritual services, although some restrict the attendance to participating monks or nuns.

In addition to temples, *pagodas* are a characteristic Buddhist edifice in China, India, Japan and Vietnam. They are often massive structures rising to more than three hundred feet, built to house relics, sacred images or, frequently, as charms to ward off evil influence of wind and water.

Among the interesting private devotions of the people are strings of beads, distinctive of each sect. In most cases they are used to count the number of formal prayers. A common type has 108 beads because, says this group, there are 108 Buddhas. In using the beads, the worshiper names all the Buddhas. Another interpretation is that 108 is twice the number of steps the Buddha took in reaching Buddhahood. One meditates on these steps, twice over, and offers the first recitation for himself but the second for the community. The Shingon sect which invests the practice with deep symbolic meaning was founded in the ninth century by the famous Japanese monk Kobo Daishi, disciple of the Chinese Buddhist Hui Kuo who is known to have borrowed from the customs of Nestorian Christian missionaries. Shingon Buddhists also celebrate sacrificial rites for the welfare of the dead.

TOWARDS THE FUTURE

In the past generation, Buddhism has been subject to more changes than any other major living faith, and there is evidence that still greater changes are due in the near future. Every aspect of Buddhism is being affected and every country in which the religion of Gautama has been established.

Where the Communists have taken over, as in China, Tibet and North Korea, monastery properties are expropriated and the monks subjected to such conditions that the heart of Buddhism—which is monastic—is being stifled out of existence. Oblivious of the leavening cultural effect of Buddhist religious, the new overlords treat the monks and nuns as social parasites and force them to engage in what is considered productive labor, on the farms and in factories. At the same time, the government is spending money to explore Buddhist sites of historic interest, and has taken steps to preserve buildings, books, and works of art that are national treasures. Its aim is to foster the impression that Communism is well disposed towards the ancient religion.

Japanese Buddhism received a new lease on life with the defeat of Japan in the second world war and the disestablishment of shrine Shinto as the state religion. Now placed on a par with Shinto as a voluntary denomination, its special appeal is to the plain, simple folk. Centuries of pacifist tradition now make Buddhism particularly attractive to those who fear rearmament and the dangers of another war. Programs of religious education and forms of worship are being stimulated by competition with Christianity, whose missionary efforts in Japan are the most extensive in the nation's history; and numerous adaptations are modeled on the ritual and customs of Christians, especially of the Protestant churches.

At the same time, grave inroads were made in the monastic solidarity of Nipponese Buddhism through the breaking up of large landed estates, and their redistribution among small peasant proprietors. The main effect was to cut off the main source of financial support, since the endowments of temples and monasteries were mostly lands.

Until recently, Westernization had little effect on the mainstream of Buddhist thought and practice. This is no longer the case. Wider familiarity with European and American literature, contact with Western peoples through the period of the war and its aftermath, and particularly the native tendency to inclusiveness, have brought into learned Buddhist circles a sympathy for Occidental ideas whose effects are bound to be farreaching.

Two kinds of Western influence are operative: a naturalistic humanism that finds in Buddha a kindred spirit, and a valid Christianity that seeks to build on the disciplinary ideals of Gautama. Humanists in the English-speaking world have been specially partial to the Buddhist idea of religion without creeds and even without a clear notion of a personal God. This attitude has been reciprocated by those in the East who are led to believe that Western progress and civilization are the fruits of an ideology that differs only in accidentals from historic Buddhism. A new impulse is thus created to follow in the old path of the *Dharma*, and even to project it into the West on a scale previously unknown in countries like America and England. Some are seriously looking forward to a renascence of Buddhist evangelism comparable to the missionary expansion from India to the rest of Asia at the beginning of the Christian era.

On the other hand, Christianity is making a lasting impression quite apart from its own evangelization. The religions of the East, but especially Buddhism, are re-evaluating their position against the background of the Christian faith whose foundations in history and theological structure are a challenge to the inquiring mind.

5. Jainism

J AINISM is a sectarian offshoot of Hinduism, whose origins are traditionally dated with the lifetime of Vardhamana Mahavira (599-527 B.C.), a contemporary of Buddha. The name itself is derived from *Jina* (conqueror), which his followers applied to Mahavira in much the same sense that Gautama's disciples called him the Buddha or "enlightened one."

Mahavira is often mentioned in the Buddhist scriptures as "the naked ascetic," and, according to his own account, he was the twenty-fourth and last of a series of prophets who expounded the true meaning of Jainism, in opposition to the Hindu Vedas and on the sole basis of logic and experience. Although confined to India, Jainism has played a major role in shaping the religious culture of the Orient, quite out of proportion to its relatively small number (a few million) adherents.

ORIGINS AND DEVELOPMENT

Like the founder of Buddhism, Mahavira was the son of a leader of one of the wealthy tribes living in the region north of the Ganges. Also like Buddha, he is supposed to have left home in the late twenties to become an ascetic, searching for a means of deliverance from the endless cycle of deaths and rebirths that has repelled Hindu malcontents at every period of Indian history.

The guiding inspiration of Mahavira's teaching was the example of his parents. His father had belonged to a religious sect strongly opposed to the idea of Vedic revelation. Sharing the common Hindu fear of rebirth, they enjoined a peculiar method of avoiding it, by committing suicide. Their purpose was not to induce violent death, but slowly to drain away vital energy by deprivation of food.

In this way the life-force was reduced to a degree of extinction which made it incapable of further transmigration. Mahavira's father converted his wife to the same faith, and in due time both underwent the form of "martyrdom" to which they were committed.

At first Mahavira was dejected by his parents' death, and for a time reacted against the ideals they taught him. Gradually he became reconciled to the underlying theory that liberation is not possible except through self-renunciation, and embarked on his quest of wisdom. He wanted none of the existing religious systems, whether Hindu or heretical, and to show his complete withdrawal from civilized life he dispensed with every convenience and worldly possession, including all clothing.

After some twelve years of meditation and mortification, Mahavira discovered full enlightenment and became a "perfected soul" (*kevalin*) or "conquerer" (*jina*). Immediately he sought to find recruits, and was remarkably successful among the mercantile classes. Thirty more years of preaching and direction were finally terminated at the age of seventy-two, by the rite of voluntary self-starvation (*sellekhana*), which is still practiced by his more devoted followers. The place of his death is localized at Pava, a village not far from modern Patna, and to this day a great center of pilgrimage for Jain devotees. Most modern scholars believe he died in 468 B.C., or sixty years later than the traditional date.

By the time of his death there were about ten thousand Jains, some of whom formed themselves into monastic communities of men and women. Surprisingly, the harsh practices required of believers seemed to attract some people, and the standing wonder is that the group has remained substantially intact for over twenty centuries.

Occasionally Jain monks have tried to spread their doctrine outside of India, but there were few converts. Like Buddhism, the Jainists have suffered a great schism. Mahavira organized an order of monks with various superiors. About 300 B.C. the superiors were reduced to two, who jointly ruled the whole community. Then came a famine in Northern India, and one head (*Bhadra-bahu*) migrated to the South with many monks and lay members of the order. Years later a remnant returned north, but in the meantime a cleavage had set in.

By the first century of our era, there were two chief branches of Jains: the "white-clad" Shvetambaras and the "sky-clad" Digambaras. The differences between them are not philosophical but natural, and to a certain extent theological. Where the "white-clad" allow their members to own property and permit clothing, the "sky-clad" insist that a true Jain should own nothing, not even clothes, and therefore encourage the practice of going naked. The "sky-clad" hold that a perfect saint goes without food, at least in anticipation of his final deliverance. They deny that salvation is possible for women, whom they call "the greatest temptation in the world" and "the cause of all sinful acts." Women are never admitted to the ranks of *arhats* (saints) and may never become nuns. Mahavira, they claim, never married and they encourage leaving one's parents regardless of their need. The Digambaras are localized mainly in South India.

The more numerous "white-clad" Jains admit women to full membership in the monastic order, as candidates for *Nirvana*. Normally monks and nuns are accepted only after their parents' death or evident independence of their children. They use images in private and public worship, and clothe them, and have often remonstrated with the southern segment for their idolatry in deifying Mahavira and other famous *jinas*.

Although Jains as a rule have little use for scripture and are, in fact, called *Nirgranthas*—people having no books—the "white-clad" adhere to a biblical canon which they say was systematized by the Council of Patali-Putra (Patna) about the end of the fourth century B.C. But even they admit that it has a traceable history and was given final shape only in the fifth century after Christ.

This canon consists of the reputed teaching of Mahavira, organized in three divisions and much of it now available in English. But the "sky-clad" repudiate the canon, claiming the main body of Jain literature was destroyed about 789 A.D. by order of the Hindu protagonist of Vedanta philosophy, Sankara, for which the northern Jains say "no evidence exists." Southern Jains admit that some books were saved in Nepal and in Mysore, the headquarters of South India, where a colossal statue of Gomtesvara, a favorite deity, is the focus of a popular pilgrimage.

THEORY AND SIGNIFICANCE

According to Jainist metaphysics, there are in the world only eternal souls (*jivas*) and eternal non-living material elements (*a-jivas*). These exist in contact, yet in such a way that man's jiva is fettered by what its own activity has gathered about it. A web of false knowledge and evil deeds has been spun into everyone's life, from which he must extricate himself by gradual freedom from gross matter, from dependence on sense perception and by breaking ultimately from all contact with the lifeless a-jivas.

Souls still struggling for release are said to be in bondage. Once they attain deliverance (*mukta*) they reach certain degrees of perfection determined by previous merit. Five classes of salvation are distinguished, ranging from the lowest *siddha* to that of the highest Lord of Jainism, exemplified by Mahavira himself.

Descriptive of the state enjoyed by the "perfect souls" to which every devout Jainist aspires are the rare qualities they possess. They can avert famine in a broad area, about eight miles radius, by a simple act of the will; they remain raised above ground whether walking, standing or sitting; they are able to face everyone simultaneously in all four directions; they can destroy all destructive impulses in persons around them; they are completely immune from all possibility of pain and disturbance; they live without food, possess mastery of all sciences and arts, and their bodies do not cast a shadow.

In addition to these, the souls in perfection acquire the attributes of perfect knowledge, power, perception and happiness; yet not all are alike, even to the extent that some retain their bodies and others do not.

There is no place for God in Jainism, which has constructed a complicated theory of *Karma* and Karmic matter. Karma is that general energy of the soul which causes its attachment to matter and its subsequent defilement, a kind of link between matter and spirit. All the effort at liberation, therefore, must be directed to controlling Karma, and all by autonomous activity. Any mediation of divine grace or forgiveness is rejected as evading the problem of sin, suffering and redemption. Each person must work out his own deliverance.

Jainist commentators speak of eight kinds of Karma, and as many as one hundred forty-eight subdivisions. Knowledge of these categories is a great help to knowing what stage in the process of deliverance has been reached, and what means have yet to be used to complete the purification.

Closely tied-in with this primary duty of "evolving and perfecting" the soul, one's own and that of others, is the idea of "non-hurting" of life (*Ahimsa*) irrespective of its distinction into higher and lower. It is sometimes called the main ethical principal of Jainism, to which even the principle of truth may be sacrificed. "Hurt no one" is a sacred mandate which enjoins love and compassion for all living beings. Jainists build asylums and rest homes for aged and diseased animals, where they are kept and fed until they die a natural death.

If a man desires salvation under these conditions, he subjects himself to innumerable hardships to be rid of the Karma already had and avoid new Karma not yet acquired. He may not kill anything, even unintentionally, and the involuntary stepping on an ant may have serious consequences for the soul. Injury with deliberation is more grave than harm caused without reflection, but both are inexorably punished by the accumulation of Karmic matter with dire consequences for the indefinite future.

Not only living things, but everything in nature must be respectfully treated. Water and fire, for example, may not be abused at the risk of increasing one's possession of Karma.

Jain writers have developed an intricate system of ethics, based on the theory of Karmic matter. One of the most influential was Umasvati Acarya, whose commentary is dated somewhere after the third century A.D., and accepted by all orthodox Jains. In context he is speaking of how to stop the flow of Karmic matter into the soul. "It is produced," he says, "by preservation, carefulness, observances, meditation, conquest of sufferings, and good conduct." Each method has its own classifications.

Thus preservation means "proper control over mind, speech and body." Carefulness requires taking "proper care in walking, speaking, eating, lifting and lying." The observances are manifold: "forgiveness, humility, straightforwardness, contentment, truth, restraint, austerities, renunciation, non-attachment, and chastity."

Subjects for meditation should be "transitoriness, unprotectedness, the cycle of life and death, loneliness," and such problems as the nature of the universe and the difficulty of attaining the right path in the practice of virtue. Right conduct, which implies all the preceding, consists of "equanimity, absolute non-injury, freedom from subtle passion and passionless conduct."

Besides these positive precepts, the faithful Jain must practice austerities which demand "fasting, eating less than one's fill, daily renunciation of delicacies, sleeping in a lonely place, and mortification of the body"—done externally. Internal austerity includes "expiation, reverence, service, study, giving up attachment to the body, and concentration," which means "confine one's thoughts to one particular object." This, in turn, demands avoidance of "wicked concentration," by keeping the mind off "delight in hurtfulness, falsehood, theft," and "preservation of objects of sense-enjoyment"; and conversely, fixes on the contemplation of "the subject matter of scripture teaching, the knowledge and conduct of people, and the nature and constitution of the universe." [1]

Not all Jainists are equally obligated. The "three jewels" of right faith, right knowledge and right conduct are not of the same value, since right conduct alone really delivers the soul from the cycle of reincarnations. To insure doing the right things and to persevere in the practice, the faithful take vows or solemn pledges. If they are laymen they take the first set of twelve pledges: never intentionally to take life, i.e., to destroy a *jiva,* never to lie nor exaggerate, never steal nor take what is not given, never be unchaste by marital infidelity or unclean thoughts, curb desire by giving away all excess at least at the end of one's life, avoid such occasions of sin as unregulated travel, limit the number of things used, guard against unnecessary evils, keep fixed periods of sinless meditation, observe special times of limitation, spend some days as a monk, and give alms to support the ascetic community.

At the approach of death, the Jain layman is urged to take the vow of "non-attachment," by which he disposes of all his possessions and refrains from taking food. One evidence of the effectiveness of the "twelve" promises is the very low rate of civil and criminal offenses committed by Jainists in India.

The eleven intermediate pledges may also be taken by the layman as an intensification of his moral life and a prelude to the life of an ascetic. Where the layman is satisfied with observing moderation, the ascetic (*arhat*) binds himself to the strictest self-denial. His five vows forbid any injury to anyone (or anything) and stealing, which amounts to using or taking nothing (even a trifle) without the owner's permission; require absolute sincerity in speech, chastity that precludes even thoughts involving sex pleasure, and renunciation of attachment for any person or thing.

Their ethical standards are considered the most glorious part of Jainism, which in one respect are very simple—based on the fundamental duty of *ahimsa* (non-injury). But in reality they are most demanding, as illustrated by the number of rules covering every phase of conduct. Cruelty alone is analyzed into nine types, each more subtle than the preceding.

Yet if Jainist ethics are specified to an extreme, Jainist philosophy is the opposite. According to Jainism, the Buddhists err in their doctrine of change and nothingness, terminating in the Nirvana; Hindus are also wrong in their theory of absolute identity of the soul with divinity. The proper attitude for the mind with respect to reality is aloofness from categorical affirmation or denial. *Anekantavada* is the principle of many-sidedness, whereby a person never positively affirms or denies anything. His judgment is always a qualified "maybe" (*Syad*).

There are seven points of view (*Nayas*) possible, say the Jainists, each more complex than the other. At the simplest is the judgment that, "Maybe it is" or "Maybe it is not," and at the most abstruse, "Maybe it is and is not, and is inexpressible." In other words, no affirmation is ever absolutely true. Everything has an infinite number of qualities, each of which can be expressed in only a limited sense. So that to be "sincere in speech" for the Jainist requires the severest self-control to keep from ever stating anything except provisionally.

Although Jainism has never been a popular religion, its influence on Hindu thought has been out of all proportion to the size. The theory of "many-sidedness" has introduced a form of religious relativism that is not typically Hindu. No doubt the ebb and flow of the cosmic process is from the universal point of view absolutely determined, and Jainism is built on this settled conviction. But from the viewpoint of the individual believer, a man has only approximate certitude. His very freedom of moral choice is only relatively true; and the life-struggle consists precisely in striving after that emancipated condition where the "perfect soul" can survey the whole of space and time and know the fulness of absolute truth. The resulting influence from an educated and highly cultured Jain society has been two-fold: scepticism about the objective superiority of any single religious system, whether Hinduism, Jainism or Christianity; and pragmatism in the moral order, on the assumption that discipline pays and self-control is effective, but neither should be bound to any absolute values, not excluding the existence of an ultimate supra-human deity.

Symbolic of the deep effect of Jainism on modern Hindu thought is the part it played in shaping the career and philosophy of Mahatma Gandhi. Born in Kathiawar, where Jainism is strong, he was much influenced by the ascetic *sadhus* whom he met in his youth, especially by the famous Jain teacher of the last century, Raichand Bhai, of whom he speaks with great veneration in his autobiography.

Gandhi was always a great absorber, not the least of Jainist principles that claimed to reform a dormant Hinduism in the sixth century B.C. He felt the same kind of reformation was needed today. The Jain monk, Becharhi Swami, helped Gandhi go to England for his studies, after administering an oath to Gandhi, that he would not touch wine, women or meat. In later life, when passive resistance became the Mahatma's main instrument for India's independence, he declared, "Many take me to be a Jain," since he followed so closely in the footsteps of Mahavira, whom he called "the incarnation of compassion and non-violence."

Thanks to the wealth and education of the Jains in India, there seems little likelihood of their absorption by the great body of Hinduism. More likely the Hindus will continue to be affected by the disciplinary ideals of a people whose religion forbids injury to any living thing, and encourages persuasion of others to follow the same path of final deliverance.

6. Confucianism

CONFUCIANISM is the whole body of religious, ethical and political doctrine which Confucius gathered together from antiquity, personally taught by word, writing and example, and passed on to his successors. It is this same body of doctrine which Mencius in the pre-Christian era consolidated into a compact system and to which Chu Hsi in the early Middle Ages gave the naturalistic interpretation that, at least in learned circles, has prevailed into the present century.

Some historians prefer to consider Confucianism neither a religion properly so-called nor a system of philosophy, but a way of life that for our two thousand years has inspired the religious sentiments of the Chinese people and given them ethnic solidarity. Having no creed, priesthood, or ecclesiastical organization, it is yet a religion in the broad sense of an expression of belief in spiritual reality and of man's ultimate attitude towards the universe. Confucianism makes no claim to an original divine revelation, and its sacred books are highly respected but, unlike the Koran of Islam or the Vedas of Hinduism, are not considered supernatural communications to chosen prophets or seers.

LIFE AND VENERATION OF CONFUCIUS

The present Latinized name, Confucius, was given to K'ung-Fu-Tze by Jesuit missionaries to China, notably Mathew Ricci, who in the late sixteenth century introduced the founder of Chinese culture to the European world. Born in 551 B.C. in what was then the feudal province of Lu and is now the province of Shantung, Confucius came of a family of the lesser nobility. His father, Kung

Shu-Liang Ho, married at the age of seventy a young girl of fifteen, and Confucius was their only known child. Orphaned by his father at the age of three, and his mother at twenty, Confucius married shortly before his mother died. While we know nothing about his wife, it is certain he had one son and at least one daughter. Though reputedly descended from the royal line, he lived in poverty. Biographers mention that his stature, over six feet in height, added to his moral prestige and earned for him the name of "giant."

From childhood he showed a great love for learning, and though poverty required that he work as a servant to support himself and his mother, he found time to cultivate his favorite studies and by the time he was twenty opened a school that attracted a large following. Tradition has it that when teaching he always faced the south and spoke from an elevation of several steps above his audience. The figure of three thousand disciples seems exaggerated, among whom he chose seventy-two special confidants; of these, ten were called the "flower of the school."

His method was to stimulate private reflection. "I teach nothing," he used to say, "to those who make no effort to understand. I cannot force expression on those who will not speak. If after I have explained one angle of a question, people are unable to find the other three, I will not repeat what I have said." Among the six liberal arts that young Chinese studied between the ages of ten and twenty, Confucius taught only writing, music and mathematics. He held it as a point of honor to discover nothing new, but only to transmit the wisdom of the ancients. "I communicate and do not invent. I have faith in antiquity and consecrate all my affection to its cause," which meant that his only aim was to give others a faithful interpretation of the past.

China in the time of Confucius was a feudal country, divided into a large number of petty states, of which something like one hundred covered the territory in the basin of the Yellow River. Over these ruled a king of the decadent dynasty of Chou, whose sovereignty was mostly nominal. Around 517 B.C. Confucius betook himself to the court at Loyang, present Honan, to better pursue his study of the ancients. This was the turning point of his life, where he discovered much of the wisdom that would later immortalize his name, especially from the writings of the Duke of

Chou, father of the first king of that country, dating from the eleventh century B.C.

From 501 to 499, he first accepted the governorship of a city, later the office of superintendent of public works and finally that of minister of justice in the principality of Lu. His administration brought on an amazing change of manners. Men were recognized for their faithfulness and sincerity, and women for their chastity and submissiveness. Merchants dealt honestly with their customers and employers with their workmen.

Confucius became the ideal of the people, but also the subject of suspicious envy. Neighboring princes began to fear that if Lu continued in this prosperous condition, it would soon gain the ascendancy and dominate the whole kingdom. To forestall this possibility, they sought to distract its prince by sending him eighty attractive dancing girls and one hundred twenty-five of the finest horses. The stratagem worked, and Confucius was forced to leave on seeing his advice wasted on a dissipated prince who neglected the people. For fourteen years he traveled from state to state in the hope of finding somewhere a ruler willing to accept his counsel.

At length in his sixty-ninth year he was able to return to Lu and spent the remaining five years of his life in meditation and writing the books that have since become attached to his name. In his last illness, he was seen walking in front of his house, cane in hand, chanting amid tears that "The highest mountain is about to fall. The roof-beam is due to collapse. The wise one will soon have to depart." He died in 478 B.C. in his seventy-fourth year, as a contemporary of Buddha who died in India shortly before at the age of eighty.

The most complete character portrait of Confucius has been left us by his disciples in *The Sayings of Confucius,* particularly in the tenth chapter, where the man's natural dignity is portrayed in full.

Among his own country folk, Confucius wore a homely look, like one who has no word to say. In the ancestral temple and at court, his speech was full, but cautious. At court he talked frankly to men of low rank, winningly to men of high rank. In the king's presence he looked intent and solemn. When bearing the sceptre, his back bent, as under too heavy a burden. He held his hands not higher than in bowing, nor lower than in giving a present. He wore an awed look, and dragged his feet, as though they were fettered.

He did not eat much. He did not talk at meals, nor speak when in bed. His stables having been burnt, the Master on his return from court said, "Is anyone hurt?" He did not ask after the horses. When summoned by the king, he walked, without waiting for his carriage. When a friend died who had no home to go to, he said, "It is for me to bury him." When a friend sent a gift, even of a carriage and horses, he did not bow. He only bowed for sacrificial meat.[1]

Relatively unknown in his lifetime, Confucius became famous from the day of his death. The prince of Lu made up for his previous neglect of the sage by erecting a temple in his honor, where at every station an oblation was to be offered. Yet the cultus remained localized for over four centuries, until in 57 B.C. when a decree enjoined the offering of sacrifices to Confucius at the Imperial University and the principal colleges of the empire.

However the veneration of Confucius still remained associated with the Duke of Chou, his master. It was only in 609 A.D. that rooms came to be built in honor of Confucius alone. The custom of building these monuments, mistakenly called temples, continued into the present century, notably at institutions of learning. No statues of idols are displayed, but only tables of inscriptions listing the names of Confucius' disciples and the principal exponents of his doctrine. Before 1912 the emperor offered sacrifices in his honor twice a year, in the spring and fall, and over the centuries imperial documents are filled with the praises of Confucius' virtue and wisdom.

After the Christian penetration into China in the sixteenth century, the problem arose of whether converts to Christianity might continue to pay their respects to Confucius, which provoked the heated controversy over the Chinese rites. By 1939 the issue had sufficiently cleared for a formal declaration in favor of converts to Catholicism, allowing them not only to retain their veneration for Confucius but show external marks to that effect, without compromising their Christian beliefs. Few statements emanating from the West describe as accurately the status of Confucianism in modern times. "It is a matter of common knowledge," the decree stated, "that some ceremonies common in the Orient, though in earlier times connected with rites of a religious character, have at the present time, owing to changes in customs and ideas in the course of centuries, no more than mere civil significance of filial respect for ancestors, of patriotic sentiment or of social amenity." Hence a different attitude should be adopted by Chinese Christians than was formerly prescribed.

Inasmuch as the Chinese Government had repeatedly and explicitly proclaimed that all are free to profess the religion they prefer, and that it is foreign to its intentions to legislate or issue decrees concerning religious matters, and that consequently ceremonies performed or ordered by the public authorities in honor of Confucius do not take place with intent to offer religious worship, but solely for the purpose of promoting and expressing the honor due to a great man, and proper regard for tradition: it is licit for Catholics to be present at commemorative functions held before a likeness or tablet of Confucius in Confucian monuments or schools.

Hence it is not to be considered illicit, particularly if these authorities should order it, to place in Catholic schools a likeness of Confucius or even a tablet inscribed in his name, or to bow before such.[2]

The declaration goes on to explain that where scandals might be feared, the right intention of Christian admirers of Confucius should be made clear; but there is no question of suspecting their integrity of faith if they manifest what formerly were considered acts of religious Confucianism, not excluding "inclinations of the head and other signs of civil respect in the presence of the dead or before their images, or even before a tablet inscribed simply with the name of the deceased."[3] They are all to be regarded as "licit and proper."

WRITTEN SOURCES

The Scriptures of Confucius are two sets of writings, not considered inspired in the ordinary sense, but all somehow associated with the memory of the great sage. They are the Five Classics, also called the texts of *King,* and the four *Shu,* which means the four books. Not all were written by Confucius, but they were at least sanctioned by his authority or, like the last of the Shu, composed by one of his disciples.

First among the King texts is a manual of divination, the *Yi King* (Book of Changes). It consists of a series of diagrams of unknown antiquity together with the more modern commentaries upon them. The diagrams now number sixty-four, but may have been originally eight. These eight are made by taking two straight lines, one continuous and the other broken in the middle, and setting them one above the other to form three lines or trigrams, varying the relative order of the two species of line in every possible manner, e.g., three unbroken lines ☰ or three broken lines ☷ ☷ or one of several combinations like ☳. To the original trigrams ancient mystical meanings were attached, typifying the heavens, body of water, fire, thunder, running water, hills or mountains and the earth. Each also represented a point of the compass.

The trigrams were further combined with one another to form hexagrams, which became instruments of magic. They are still employed for casting lots, and decisions of importance are reached by appealing to them. A common method is by reading the marks on tortoise shells or the arrangement of the stalks of the *Chi* plant, such as still grows by the traditional grave of Confucius. These natural markings direct the soothsayer to one or another of the trigrams or hexagrams, and by consulting the commentators he judges of the future.

However something more than magic was brought into the *Yi* in the twelfth century B.C. when a certain Wan, founder of a royal dynasty, was cast into prison by a rival and to pass the time wrote moral (and not magic) interpretations of the sixty-four hexagrams. His son added to the commentaries and, according to the Chinese, Confucius added still others. There can be no doubt that Confucius was deeply interested in the Yi and is reported to have spent two years studying only the first two hexagrams. In his old age he declared, "If I could be assured of enough years, I would devote fifty of them to a study of the Yi."

Many of the hexagrams have remarkably sacred interpretations, as the famous *Chien* hexagram which is an exhortation on humility. The figure consists of five broken and one unbroken lines: ☶☷. It is the fifteenth in a series and appropriately follows the *Ta Yu* hexagram that treats of abundant possessions. The commentary, here as elsewhere, consists of a short introductory statement and six explanatory ones, for each line of the figure.

Chien indicates progress and success. The superior man, being humble as it implies, will have a good issue to his undertakings.

The first line, divided, shows us the superior man who adds humility to humility. Even the great stream may be crossed with this, and there will be good fortune.

The second line, divided, shows us humility that has made itself recognized. With firm correctness there will be good fortune.

The third line, undivided, shows the superior man of acknowledged merit. He will maintain his success to the end, and have good fortune.

The fourth line, divided, shows one whose action would be in every way advantageous, stirring up the more his humility.

The fifth line, divided, shows one who, without being rich, is able to employ his neighbors. He may advantageously use the force of arms. All his movements will be profitable.

The sixth line, divided, shows us humility that has made itself recognized. The subject of it will with advantage put his hosts in motion; but he will only punish his own towns and State.[4]

According to Chinese scholars, this is "the lord of the hexagram," when a whole third line amid five others divided occupies the topmost place in the lower trigram. It is said to represent humility which is strong and yet willing to abase itself. Not all the hexagrams are equally intelligible, and some are entirely cryptic, except to the initiates who have made a lifetime study of their meaning.

A short essay following the main treatise adds reflective notes on the principal hexagrams. Thus to explain the meaning of the word *Shan*, "when we speak of Spirit we mean the subtle presence and operation of God with all things," or *"Chien* is the symbol of heaven, and hence has the appellation of father. *Khwan* is the symbol of earth, and hence has the appellation of earth." [5] Several hundred terms are defined, correlated with one another and offered as "symbols . . . emblems . . . words that suggest the idea of" a maze of items which the expert diviner discovers from examining tortoise shells or configurations of the stalks of plants.

The *Shu King* (Book of History) is a work of moral and religious narrative which traces the hand of Providence in the great events of the past, while teaching the lesson that the Heaven-god blesses only virtuous rulers with peace and prosperity. It reaches

back to the early third millenium before Christ and is therefore
China's oldest history.

Typical of the idealism of the *Book of History* is the last of
several instructions of I Yin (died about 1700 B.C.), minister of a
ruler named Thang, addressed to the people on the occasion of his
retirement from office. He compares the lot of virtuous men like
himself and the King of *Shang* with the weakness and cruelty of
oppressive monarchs like the King of Hsia (a rival prince). The
narrator remarks that I Yin was setting forth admonitions on the
subject of virtue; and then quotes the minister at length:

It is difficult to rely on Heaven; its appointments are not constant.
But if the sovereign see to it that his virtue be constant, he will preserve
his throne; if his virtue be not constant, the nine provinces will be lost
by him. The King of Hsia could not maintain the virtues of his ancestors
unchanged, but condemned the spirits and oppressed the people. Great
Heaven no longer extended its protection to him. It looked out among
the myriad regions to give its guidance to one who should receive its
favoring appointment, fondly seeking a possessor of pure virtue, whom
it might make lord of all the spirits.

Then there were I Yin and Thang, both possessed of pure virtue,
and able to satisfy the mind of Heaven. Thang received in consequence
the bright favor of Heaven, so as to become possessor of the multitudes
of the nine provinces.

It was not that Heaven had any private partiality for the lord of
Shang; it simply gave its favor to pure virtue. It was not that Shang
sought the allegiance of the lower people; the people simply turned to
pure virtue. Where the sovereign's virtue is pure, his enterprises are all
fortunate; where his virtue is wavering and uncertain, his enterprises
are all unfortunate. Good and evil do not wrongly befall men, but
Heaven sends down misery or happiness according to their conduct.[6]

I Yin concludes by exhorting the new king and his minister to
the practice of virtue, above all to humility of spirit. "Do not think
yourself so great," he tells the incoming rulers, "as to deem others
small." Their reward will be to have a place after death in the
temple of the ancestors.

In the *Shih King* or Book of Songs are collected three hundred
short lyric poems, some going into the Shang dynasty in the
eighteenth century B.C., but most belonging to the Chou period

under which Confucius lived. On first reading, the hymns appear to be mainly secular and even earthy in tone, with only rare songs of a more religious nature. But the Chinese find innumerable symbolic overtones in these odes and have written volumes of commentary on single pieces.

One of the best known and most religious, entitled *A Multitude Of Counselors But No Wisdom,* carries through the same idea developed earlier by I Yin. The author is supposed to be one of the officers of the royal court of King Yu. His purpose is to create disgust at the king's readiness to listen to anyone, wise or foolish, and as a result forfeit the help of the deity.

Heaven, that was once compassionate, is wrathful now.
Its anger lowers above this wicked world of ours.
For the king will not abate his purposes for ill designed.
Why loves he crooked ways to choose, and better counsel to refuse?
Distressed am I in heart, in mind.

The omens now are mute and dead, discerned once from the tortoise-
shell.
Counselors many among us dwell, yet nothing is accomplished.
Upon the court they pile a load of speech, yet not a deed is done.
A man may prate of going on, nor take one step along the road.
Rulers of the State, choose for patterns men of yore,
Who thought all shallow trifles less than naught,
Whose principles were calm and great.
You build a house beside the way, in vain you try to finish,
For all the travelers passing by derange your plans by what they say.[7]

Implicit in the hymn are the principles of Confucius, that wisdom abides with the ancients and those who depart from tradition are doomed. Present counselors are therefore to be measured for prudence by their agreement or discord with the teachings of the past.

The Book of Rites (*Li Ki*) in its present form dates from the first to the fourth centuries of the Christian era, but contains material from the Chou dynasty. As a code of rules on worship, social and family relations, it remains to this day the authoritative guide for good conduct among cultured Chinese. In the *Li Ki* are many of Confucius' aphorisms and several treatises by his disciples that faithfully reflect their master's teaching, including the tract *Chung-*

yung or "Doctrine of the Mean" which is assigned to a grandson of Confucius, and the "Great Learning" which describes the qualities of a political ruler who lives according to moral standards. Last in the King series is a bare set of chronicles, known as the *Annals of Spring and Autumn,* that tell the history of the state of Lu for three hundred years, up to the fifth century B.C.

Tradition has added a sixth book to the Five Classics, the *Hsiao King* on filial piety, which the Chinese attribute to Confucius but Western scholars commonly say is the product of Tsang-tze, one of his followers. Only a small part deals with the obedience and respect due to parents (to be seen later), and most of the treatise is concerned with civic virtue. Few other works of Confucian origin give a clearer insight into the comprehensive nature of filial piety among the Chinese.

At the top rung stands the filial piety of the highest ruler of state, the "son of heaven." Devotion to his parents is a lesson of virtue to the people, and "he becomes a pattern to all within the four seas." Next in line is the piety of princes of lesser states. "When their riches and nobility do not leave their persons, they are able to preserve the altars of their land and their grain, and to secure the harmony of their people and men in office." [8] Ancient commentators dwelt on the princes' duty to sacrifice to the Spirit (or spirits) presiding over the land. So long as a family ruled in a region, its chief offered these oblations. The extinction of sacrifices was an emphatic way of describing the ruin and extinction of the ruling House.

Filial piety among high ministers and great officers was to be shown in their clothing, speech and conduct. "When these three things—their robes, their words, and their conduct—are all complete as they should be, they can preserve their ancestral temples." [9] Again the accent on worship, except that for ministers and state officials their ancestral temples served the same function as the altars for feudal lords. Every grand officer had three temples or shrines, in which he sacrificed to the first chief of his family or clan, to his grandfather, and to his father. While these remained, the family remained, but once they were neglected, everything else collapsed.

Among inferior officers, the twin duties of love and reverence to their superiors were enjoined, after the manner of love for one's mother and reverence for one's father. "Not failing in this loyalty and obedience in serving those above them, they are able to preserve their emoluments and positions, and maintain their sacrifices." [10] Unlike the higher officials, the lesser gentry had only private or personal places of sacrifice. They had no right to offer oblations in the name of others.

The logic of the *Hsiao King* is not abstruse. Under the concept of filial piety is included every aspect of devotion to the originators of one's being. It begins with obedience and respect for one's parents. "Our bodies—to every hair and bit of skin—are received by us from our parents, and we must not presume to offend or injure them. This is the beginning of filial piety." Next come the heads of government and their ministers whose office corresponds in the social order to that of parents in the physical; consequently filial piety "proceeds to the service of the ruler." Finally there is Heaven or God, which the classic books of China equate, to be served by living according to one's "heaven-sent nature." And therefore filial piety "is completed by the establishment of character." [11]

An interesting sidelight on the *Hsiao King* is the admission it makes that already a thousand years before the Christian era Chinese religion had in various places fallen from its previous nobility. Ostensibly quoting Confucius, the writer says that "Anciently, the intelligent kings served their fathers with filial piety, and therefore they served Heaven with intelligence. They served their mothers with filial piety, and therefore they served Earth with discrimination. They pursued the right course with reference to their own seniors and juniors, and therefore they secured the right relation between superiors and inferiors throughout the kingdom." [12]

This nostalgic reference to the past is repeated in order to emphasize its importance; and though admittedly obscure it suggests that already during the Chou dynasty (1122-256 B.C.) unguarded preoccupation with filial piety first tended to dualize the divinity, after the analogy of parenthood, and later to lower it still further by mingling an earlier monotheism with some form of nature worship. Monotheism never disappeared, but became heavily obscured. The Chou, it should be recalled, set the pace for Chinese emperors to call themselves *T'ien Tzu* or "Son of Heaven." In this capacity they worshiped Heaven in the people's behalf at regular ceremonies, without which it was felt that the harmony between earth and heaven, i.e., man and God, would be disrupted.

In the eleventh century of our era, two of the treatises of the *Book of Rites,* namely the *Doctrine of the Mean* and the *Great Learning,* were combined with the *Analects* and the *Book of Mencius* to form the four Shu which constitute the second category of Confucian sacred writings.

The basic *Analects* were at first orally transmitted by successive generations, until put into written form at the beginning of the fourth century before Christ. However the extant text dates only from six hundred years later, although based on manuscripts written about 200 B.C. As the best known and most popular Confucian sources, the *Analects* have been translated into all the modern languages, and in twenty short chapters give an authentic picture of the main lines of historical Confucianism.

Mencius' volume of commentary, written more than a century after Confucius, stabilized the master's teaching by giving his ethics a more speculative form. More strongly even than Confucius, he stressed the natural goodness of human nature. "Benevolence, righteousness, propriety and knowledge," he thought, "are not infused into us from without. We are certainly furnished with them." [13] Like Confucius, he believed in a spirit world and accepted the current worship of ancestors, but his main interest was ethical and not professedly religious.

CONFUCIAN ETHICS

If Confucianism as a national culture is a glomeration of religion, philosophy and ritual, its characteristic feature is ethical. It was the ethical standards that Confucius borrowed from the ancients, sifted and interpreted, and passed on to his people that represent his main contribution to the religious system that now bears his name. These standards are scattered throughout the written sources but concentrated in the *Analects* which correspond to the *Memorabilia* of Xenophon or the *Symposium* of Plato in their description of Socrates. However the *Analects* are in no sense pane-gyric. They are a simple collection of aphorisms, often in dialogue form, which Confucius' disciples had memorized of their master's teaching. As the foundation of Confucianism, they offer the best primary insight into its spirit and orientation.

SUPERIOR MAN. Thematic in the *Analects* is the "superior man," *chun-tzu*, or "gentleman," whom Confucius described from numerous character angles as the prototype of human perfection. "Look at a man's acts," he advised, "watch his motives; find out what pleases him. Can the man evade you?" His personality is self-revealing in the actions he performs. Then follows an elenchus of qualities that should distinguish the man of virtue.

What is a superior man? He put words into deed first, and sorts what he says to the deed. A superior man is broad and fair; the vulgar are biased and petty.

A superior man has no likes and dislikes below Heaven. He follows right. Superior men cherish worth; the vulgar cherish dirt. Superior men trust in justice; the vulgar trust in favor.

A superior man considers what is right; the vulgar consider what will pay. Men of old were loth to speak, lest a word they could not make good should shame them. A superior man wants to be slow to speak and quick to act.

Tzu-lu asked, "What is a gentleman?" The Master said, "A man bent on shaping his mind." "Is that all?" said Tzu-lu. "On shaping his mind to give happiness to others." "And is that all?" "On shaping his mind to give happiness to the people," said the Master.

A superior man makes right his base. Done with courtesy, spoken with deference, rounded with truth, right makes a superior man. His unworthiness vexes him; to live unknown does not vex him. He fears lest his name should die when life is done. He is firm, not quarrelsome; a friend, not a partisan. He is consistent, not changeless.[14]

However in the very act of describing virtue, Confucius admitted he was painting the ideal. "A superior man," he summarized, "has nine aims: to see clearly, to understand what he hears, to be warm in manner, dignified in bearing, faithful in speech, painstaking at work, to ask when in doubt; in anger to think of difficulties; in sight of gain to remember right." On which he sadly reflected, "I have heard these words, but met no such men." [15]

One religious note in this catalogue is motivation. "A superior man holds three things in awe. He is in awe of Heaven's destiny; he is in awe of great men; he is awed by the speech of the holy." [16] In view of the heavy emphasis on precept and words, the reference to heavenly sanctions and the distinction between wisdom and goodness are significant.

MEANING OF LOVE. Parallel with the stress on fidelity to duty as a mark of virtue, Confucius pointed out the necessity of love. When a prominent person was praised before him, he admitted the man's courage and justice, or even his learning and humility, and then would ask, "But had he love?" This was the acid test of greatness, lovingkindness to others. "Love," he said, "makes a place beautiful. Who chooses not to dwell in love, has he got wisdom?"

His disciples frequently questioned him on "what is love?"— to which he gave different answers, each bearing on the single virtue of concern for others.

Fan Ch'ih asked, What is love? The Master said, "To be respectful at home, painstaking at work, faithful to all. Even among savages none of these may be dropped."

Tzu-Chang asked Confucius, What is love? "Love," said Confucius, "is to mete five things to all below heaven: modesty and bounty, truth, earnestness and kindness. Modesty escapes insult; bounty wins the many; truth gives men's trust; earnestness brings success; kindness is the key to men's work."

Fan Ch'ih asked, What is love? The Master said, "To love mankind!" He asked, What is wisdom? "To know mankind." [16]

Confucius did not speculate. His definitions are descriptions of virtue in action. Occasionally he reflected on the benefits of affection. "Loveless men cannot bear need long, they cannot bear fortune long. Loving hearts find peace in love." And while affirming that "Love can alone love others," he added, "or hate others," when spurned. On the other hand, "a heart set on fire will do no wrong," and therefore should be prized above all other virtue. "Shorn of love, is a superior man worthy of the name? Not for one moment may he sin against love, not under provocation nor in excitement, nor even when utterly opposed."

Again realistically he confessed that "were a man to give himself to love but for one day, I have seen no one whose strength would fail him. Such men there may be, but I have not seen one." [17] He offers to people the norms of morality but laments that so few, if any, live up to them.

FILIAL PIETY. The practice of filial piety is the well-spring of Confucianism and, though his disciples developed the fragmentary passages in the Analects, the principles set down by the Master became normative for all subsequent commentators.

In Confucius' theory, the family stands at the foundation of the whole political and social structure of the state. Even the sovereign can rule successfully only if he imitates the paternal relationship that should obtain in the family. In proportion as the domestic virtues of kindness, obedience to authority, respect for elders, and devotion to the memory of one's ancestors are cultivated, the civil life of the nation at large is assured.

Filial duties are divided into two classes, the material or physical and the spiritual. Under the former, Confucius listed due attention to the bodily needs of parents; caring for one's own body as a legacy received from one's ancestors; rearing children to provide for the family continuity and perpetuating the family name. Under spiritual obligations he included obedience to parental authority; respectful remonstrance with them when they fall into error; being mindful of them after death by annual sacrifices; carrying out their cherished wishes and unfulfilled plans; and winning all the success and honor that bring lustre on the family name.

It is undesirable, said Confucius, for a son to live far away from his parents during their lifetime. He cannot delegate his duties to others, and must not make it physically impossible to care for his aging parents. "While his parents are alive, a son should not go abroad to a distance. If he does go abroad, he must have a fixed place to which he goes. A father's and a mother's age must be kept in mind; with joy on the one hand and with fear on the other." [18]

Obedience is the touchstone of piety. One of his disciples asked the duty of a son, to which the Master answered in one word. "Obedience." When further asked to explain, he said, "While parents are alive, they should be served according to propriety. When dead, they should be laid to rest according to propriety, and sacrificed according to propriety." [19]

A man is called dutiful today if he just supports his parents. But we keep dogs and horses, without having reverence for them. Surely there must be something to distinguish the one support from the other. The difference is in the cheerful readiness to help. When parents have some troublesome work to be done, and their children assist them; or when the young have wine and food set before their elders, is this enough to satisfy the duties of filial piety? [20]

Devotion to one's parents does not forbid calling their attention to what is wrong. "A father and mother may be gently reproved. If they do not change, be the more humble in their regard, but persevere in your kindly reproof. Do not complain, however, if trouble follows because the correction was not taken in good part." This would be a rare exception since Confucius assumed that parents are models of virtue to their children. Thus, if for three years a son does not forsake his father's ways, he may be called dutiful, after reaching maturity.[21]

The *Analects* say little about the duties of children toward their parents after death, except recommending "careful attention to perform the funeral rites for parents, and let them be followed when long gone with the ceremonies of sacrifice. Then the virtue of the people will resume its proper excellence," should it have fallen into decay.[22] More detailed emphasis on this obligation is found in the *Doctrine of the Mean* which, though written by his grandson, faithfully reflects the mind of Confucius.

Dutiful sons, says the *Doctrine,* have always served their deceased forebears as they would have served them alive, paying homage to the departed as they would have done had they continued living among them. Nothing is better calculated to establish a stable social order than fidelity to the two-fold respect to God and to the spirits of the dead. "By the ceremonies of the ancestral temples the people sacrificed to their ancestors. He who understands the ceremonies of the sacrifices to Heaven and Earth, and the meaning of the several sacrifices to ancestors, would find the government of a kingdom as easy as to look into the palm of his hand." [23] For all his insistence on ancestor worship, however, the basic motive for

Confucius was social. Its observance was to help preserve the unity of the family, and secure political peace and social security; yet quite naturally. He never asserted that the spirits of the dead can supernaturally intervene, to bless or inhibit the welfare of those on earth, depending on whether sacrifice is offered them or not.

On the distinction between a natural and supernatural concept of ancestor worship rests the whole tension between original and, it would seem authentic, Confucianism and its popular development or aberration. Confucius and his followers stressed the value of sacrifice to ancestors because of its psychological importance. As the *Book of Rites* explained, sacrifice is at once an act of "gratitude towards our originators and a memorial of our beginnings." Ancestor worship, therefore, is merely an extension of filial piety.

DOCTRINE OF THE MEAN. Not unlike the ethical theory of Aristotle who taught that moral virtue consists in a mean (*mesotes*) suitable to our nature and fixed by reason, Confucius held to the *Doctrine of the Mean,* which is both the title of a Confucian classic and the expression of an ethical ideal. "Perfect is the virtue," the Master is quoted in the *Analects,* "which is according to the Mean. Rare for a long time has been its following among the people." [24]

In order to achieve the perfection of virtue (*jen*), we must strive after balance in our actions, by failing neither through excess nor defect. "I know how it is," Confucius explained, "that the way of the Mean is not followed. The clever exceed it, and the foolish do not come up to it. I know how the way of the Mean is not comprehended—the men of talents and ability go beyond it, and the worthless do not approach it. All men eat and drink, but few approach the more subtle flavors." In like manner only the cultured man of *jen* attains the reasonable medium between exuberance and its opposite.

He cultivates a friendship harmony with others without being weak in conviction. How courageous he is! He uses the mean of two extremes without inclining to either side. When good government exists, he carries out his fundamental principles without leaning to others. When bad government prevails, he pursues the path of reason until death without changing.[25]

Despite its similarity to the Aristotelian *mesotes,* however, the Confucian concept of the mean is less stable, and therefore, can less accurately be called a standard or fixed norm of morality. It partakes of two elements that are at most implied in Aristotle, namely, adaptation to circumstances and submission to higher powers. The superior man, *chün-tzu,* has developed an instinct for adaptability to environment and conformity to the will of Heaven.

He does what is proper to the station in which he is; he does not desire to exceed this. In a position of dignity, he does what is proper to a position of dignity. In a poor and humble position, he does what is proper to such a condition. Situated among wild tribes, he does what is proper in a position among wild tribes. In a position of sorrow and difficulty, he does what is proper in such a condition.

The superior man can find himself in no situation in which he cannot be himself. In an exalted position, he does not treat his inferiors with contumely. In a humble position he does not curry favor with superiors. He rectifies himself and asks for nothing of others, and so has no dissatisfactions. He neither murmurs against Heaven, nor grumbles against man. Thus it is that the superior man is quiet and calm, waiting for the appointments of Heaven, while the mean man treads on dangerous ground, seeking for the happenings of chance.[26]

It is difficult to reconstruct a philosophy of the Confucian doctrine of the mean without invoking the authority of the Master's great disciple Mencius (371-288 B.C.), who is considered "the Second Inspired One." More strongly than Confucius, he gave to ethics a naturalistic form, and at the same time systematized the Sage's teaching. Taking Mencius as guide, we may further analyze virtue not only as a balance between extremes but the concept of moral goodness in itself.

All men are alike endowed with the same moral nature, which is intrinsically good. This is the bedrock of orthodox Confucian ethics. "Man's nature," wrote Mencius, "is endowed with feelings which impel it toward the good. That is why I call it good. If men do what is not good, the reason does not lie in the basic stuff of which they are constituted. All men have the feeling of sympathy, shame, and dislike, reverence and respect, and recognition of right and wrong. These feelings give rise to the virtues of benevolence, righteousness, propriety and wisdom. These virtues are not infused into me from without, they are part of the essential me. Therefore it is said. 'Seek them and you will find them, neglect them and you will lose them.' Men differ from one another, some by twice as much, some by five times as much, some incalculably, simply because in different degrees they are unable fully to develop their natural powers." [27]

Accordingly the term "good" in Confucian language is that which arises spontaneously from human nature. Mencius points out that men's mouths, ears and eyes are alike and have the same responsive powers; in the same way their minds instinctively approve similar moral principles. If men deviate from this inborn approval they become less good, or evil.

But why do men deviate from this "Inner Sage"? The immediate reason is not because they abuse their free will but because of the circumstances in which they find (or place) themselves. If you want a child, Mencius taught, to speak the dialect of ch'i, you should send him to the province of Ch'i, where everything around him will conduce to his knowledge. So if you want a man to cultivate virtue, have him associate with virtuous people. A wise king who wants his subjects to be good, must provide the kind of environment in which moral goodness will flourish. Good example and a sufficiency for bodily needs are paramount; without the one the native *jen* in man's person will not be evoked and without the other it may arise but soon be stifled to extinction.

STAGES OF DEVELOPMENT. Parallel with the orthodox theory of morality evolved by Confucius and Mencius, were other systems of ethics that have had great influence in shaping the Chinese religious culture.

Within a century of Confucius' death, the social anarchy of the late Chou dynasty (350-220 B.C.) made such optimism as "natural goodness" less plausible. Hsün-Tzu (335-288 B.C.) took the opposite view, that human nature is evil. His description of man as essentially evil is one of the most graphic in religious literature.

The nature of man is evil. Whatever is good in him is the result of acquired training. Men are born with the love of gain; if this material tendency is followed, they are contentious and greedy, utterly lacking in courtesy and consideration for others. They are filled from birth with envy and hatred of others; if these passions are given rein they are violent and villainous, wholly devoid of integrity and good faith. At birth a man is endowed with the desires of the ear and eye, the love of sound and color; if he acts as they dictate he is licentious and disorderly, and has no regard for justice or moderation or the code of correct behavior.

How control these inordinate desires or stem this tide of passion? Certainly not by conforming to nature. "To accord with man's original nature and act as instinct dictates must lead to contention, rapacity, and disorder, and cause humanity to revert to a state of violence." The only remedy is instruction and discipline supplied from outside of man.

Crooked wood must be steamed and forced to conform to a straight edge, in order to be made straight. A dull blade must be ground and whetted, to make it sharp. Similarly human nature, being evil, must be acted upon by teachers and laws to be made upright, and must have *li* and justice added to it before men can be orderly. Without teachers and laws, men are selfish, malicious and unrighteous. Lacking *li* and justice they are unruly, rebellious, and disorderly.[28]

When his critics challenged Hsün Tzu to explain how the teachers acquired wisdom or rulers the prudence to pass good laws, he was unconvincing. "The sages," he answered, "were able to produce *li* and justice, and set up laws and regulations, only as a result of long thought and correct practice." These things "were produced by the acquired training of the sages, not by man's original nature." [29] This repudiation of man's innate capacity to discover truth and goodness left a void that later generations of authoritarianism and mysticism sought to fill—the one by legalists who claimed that few men are capable of altruism, and that most people can be kept in order only by laws imposed upon them by force; the other by successive waves of Buddhism and Taoism which supplied the religious elements that were lacking in Confucian thought.

Between the second century B.C. and the early Middle Ages of the Christian era, most Confucians sought to reconcile the extremes of perfect optimism and pessimism by adopting some intermediate position offered by the compromisers—generally in the direction of Confucius and Mencius. Yang Hsiung (52 B.C.–18 A.D.) believed that human nature is a composite of good and bad. Han Yü (768-824 A.D.) segregated the human race into three classes: the naturally good, who can be improved by education, the naturally bad who can only be restrained by fear of punishment; and those who are a mixture of good and evil, and capable of going in either direction. The founders of Neo-Confucianism, Ch'eng Yi (1033-1107 A.D.) and Chu Hsi (1130-1200 A.D.), revived the orthodox theory in qualified form.

Chu Hsi did more than restore Confucian optimism in ethics. He elaborated a philosophical system whose central idea is a form of dualism reminiscent of Buddhist speculation. In fact Chu Hsi had much to do with strengthening the hold of Buddhist ideas on modern Confucianism. Man's nature, he said, is his *li* or principle, which is a part of the Supreme Ultimate and the same in all men. But their *chi* or substance is different. If the latter is impure, the nature is vitiated, and hence the task of moral improvement is to recapture one's original (good) nature by getting rid of the personal adulteration. This is accomplished by reflective meditation on reality, for which Chu Hsi found ample warrant in such Confucian Scriptures as the *Great Learning*.

Those who anciently wished to exemplify illustrious virtue to the whole world, first ordered well their own states. Wishing to order well their states, they first regulated their families. Wishing to regulate their families, they first cultivated their own characters. Wishing to cultivate their characters, they first rectified their hearts. Wishing to rectify their hearts, they first made their thoughts sincere. Wishing to make their thoughts sincere, they first extended their knowledge to the utmost. This extending of their knowledge to the utmost lay in the investigation of things.[30]

In Chu Hsi the victory of Confucian optimism was made permanent. Later thinkers modified his dualism according to idealist or materialist standards, but they did not substantially change his ethical structure. For six hundred years, into the present century, his commentaries on the classics were officially approved and made mandatory reading for government examinations.

RELIGIOUS PRINCIPLES

Confucius never considered himself the founder of a new religion, and much less a kind of deity. With the exception of the very ignorant, the Chinese never made him a god but considered him only their "Foremost Teacher" and "Ultimate Sage," with no implications of divinity.

It is more than academically important to recognize that Confucianism, at its roots, is truly religious and grounded on the acceptance of a supreme, supra-mundane entity. Some would say "it is perhaps more true of Confucius than of any equally famous thinker that he divorced ethics from metaphysics." [31] And according to Max Weber, "In the sense of the absence of all metaphysics and almost all residues of religious anchorage, Confucianism is rationalist to such a far-going extent that it stands at the extreme boundary of what one might possibly call a 'religious' ethic." [32]

These opinions are impossible to square with the authentic statements of Confucius and with the evidence of almost two millenia of recorded Chinese history.

No doubt, Confucius' own teaching was secondarily religious, but only because he accepted from the ancients and bequeathed to others the worship of a Supreme Being, who from at least the twelfth century before Christ was called *Ti* or the Ruler, or more often *Sciamti* or Supreme Ruler: and from the eleventh century B.C. was known as *Ttien* or Heaven, without qualification or modified by such adjectives as August and Immense. These titles were quite interchangeable as appears from a passage in the *Book of History* where the fame of a certain king of Uen is said to have "reached even the Supreme Ruler, and the Ruler approved of his deeds. Thereupon Heaven gave a grand commission to the king of Uen." [33]

The *Analects* of Confucius show that for him, as for all the ancient Chinese, Heaven is the "only Great One," on whom everything depends, "I have heard that life and death are allotted, that wealth and honors are in Heaven's hand." [34] From Him the wise man receives his wisdom, the good man his virtue, and the philosopher his knowledge. In conflict with his enemies at K'uang,

Confucius looked to help from above. "If Heaven uphold wisdom, what can the men of K'uang do to me?" [35] More than once he recommended asking for assistance from the spiritual world. When lying ill, he accepted the prayers of his disciples, on the strength of a tradition to "pray to the spirits in heaven above and on earth below." [36]

When tempted to discouragement over his ill-success among men, he found solace in the fact that Someone at least understood.

> The Master said, "Alas, no man knows me." Tzu-King said, "Why do you say that no man knows you?" The Master said, "Never murmuring against Heaven, nor finding fault with men; bearing from the lowest, cleaving to the heights, I am known but to One, but to Heaven." [37]

On one occasion, Confucius was asked whether it is better to worship one of the lesser gods than the God of the Home. He replied, "Not at all; a sin against Heaven is past praying for," suggesting that unless the Supreme Deity is honored, no prayer is of any avail.[38]

From the dawn of the Chinese nation, the ruler used to offer to this Supreme Ruler or Heaven a sacrifice which tradition assigned to one of the southern suburbs of the capital. To this day the Chinese favor suburbs for their business transactions and celebrations, which historians trace to the immemorial custom of holding religious gathering in suburban areas.

The oblations would be made out in the open, before dawn, on a platform erected for the purpose. Only the sovereign was permitted to offer these sacrifices, of which there is historical evidence from the twentieth century before Christ. During the whole of the two millenia, the offerings were made to Heaven alone, until in 31 B.C. the Earth was associated with the heavenly Deity and the two remained coupled until modern times.

An unfortunate consequence of this coupling was to obscure the spirituality of Heaven by conceiving it as the Sky; and in time a host of lesser deities were joined in the pantheon, of whom less than a tenth had any historical foundation. For the most part they were legendary figures of the air, earth and sea.

In the fourteenth century, under the Mongols, there was a partial renascence of the ancient simplicity. Many of the divinities were suppressed, and others were made subordinate satellites of

Heaven and Earth. Even this dualism seems never to have been taken too seriously by the more educated Chinese, many of whom tolerated the dualist terminology but conceptually worshiped one highest Being, who was immaterial, personal, and knowable to the human mind, whom they called the Highest Lord. Confucius was speaking in this strain when he observed that "people serve the Supreme Ruler when they offer sacrifice to Heaven and Earth in the suburbs." [39]

The Chinese recaptured something in the past five hundred years of their original monotheism, under emperors who annually celebrated the cultus of Heaven at the winter solstice, notwithstanding the heavy inroads that Buddhism and Taoism had made among the unlettered peasants.

CUSTOM AND RITUAL

The five cardinal virtues of Confucianism may be paraphrased in English as benevolence, seen especially in sympathy; duty, reflected in the feeling of shame; wisdom, shown in the sense of right and wrong; trustworthiness, or fidelity to promises made; and propriety or good manners, manifested in deference given to all persons but especially to those of superior station or ability.

If benevolence, *jen*, is the highest of the virtues, propriety, *li*, is the most consequential because it touches the whole of a man's life—his dealings with others and relations with the spiritual world. Indeed the concept of *li* profoundly affects the very notion of society according to traditional Confucian standards.

As a nation, the Chinese never looked with favor on the legalist school which said the social order must be sustained by prescriptions from without, and by punishments for disobedience of the law. They admitted the necessity of force, but preferred the sanction of custom on all its social levels: between father and son, ruler and subject, husband and wife, elder and younger, friend and friend. Speaking to rulers, Confucius told them, "If you govern men by regulations and subdue them by punishments, they may avoid trouble but have no sense of shame. But guide them by example and rule them by manners; they will learn shame and come to be good." [40]

RITUAL PRACTICES. It is not surprising that the word *li* should have religious as well as social connotations, and that propriety in human relations should take on the meaning of ritual in matters of worship.

Among the ceremonies described in detail by the *Book of Rites,* the capping ritual is not unlike the *Bar Mitzvah* among the Jews. On reaching his twentieth year a young man was given a special name and a square cornered cap to mark the reaching of maturity.

As laid down in the same source, the recommended age for marriage was thirty for the man and twenty for the woman. Arrangements were to be made by the respective parents, after preliminary divination to ascertain the suitability of the couple for each other. Inter-family unions were discouraged, by forbidding espousals within the fifth degree of kindred. Monogamy was represented as the ideal, but divorce of the wife was allowed for any of seven causes, including infidelity and failure to bear a male offspring.

The mourning of the dead, especially of the father of a family, meant upwards of two years of marital abstinence, and Confucius sternly rebuked those who said a son might reduce the period of bereavement to one year.

In a traditional Chinese house may be found a family shrine in the main hall. Centered in the shrine are the ancestral tablets, going back five generations and including the last member of the family to die. Flanking the shrine are the names of various divinities and guardian spirits, Confucian, Buddhist or Taoist, depending on the local tradition. Elsewhere in the house are reserved other tablets of lesser deities, like the god of the bed chamber, the kitchen and the door. Oblations of food, wine, candles and incense are common; to be offered on the new and full moons or on festive occasions like the New Year, the day of Mid-Autumn and the Winter Solstice. Whenever anything of significance happens to the family—like birth, sickness, or recovery—the dead ancestors are informed because they are still concerned although unseen.

The *Li-Ki* has a memorable passage on the preparations and procedure to be followed in offering sacrifice. It illustrates the mystical element imbedded in Confucianism from the beginning and retained to the present day.

The severest vigil and purification are to be maintained and practiced in the inner self, while a looser vigil is maintained externally. During the days of the vigil, the mourner reflects on the departed, how and where he sat, how he smiled and spoke, and what were his aims and views, what he delighted in, and what he desired and enjoyed. By the third day he will perceive the meaning of such exercise.

On the day of sacrifice, when he enters the apartment (of the temple), he will seem to see (the deceased) in the place (where his tablet is). After he has moved about (to perform the ritual), and is leaving the door, he will be arrested by seeming to hear the sound of his movements, and will sigh as he hears the sound of his sighing.

Still and grave, absorbed in what he is doing, he will seem unable to sustain the burden, and in danger of letting it fall. Thus he manifests his mind and thought, and in his lost abstraction of mind seeks to commune with the dead in their spiritual state of being.[41]

Sacrifice, as an essential element of *li,* has always had a dual function in Confucianism. On the ethical side it was one of the means to integrate the kinship group, which is the strategic point for understanding the Chinese social organization. In secular terms, therefore, ancestor worship helps to cultivate family values like filial piety, kinship loyalty and continuity of the family lineage. This was no doubt the main intention of Confucius and his great disciples in promoting familial oblations. But on the spiritual level, for the common man another dimension has never been absent. The welfare of the soul of his departed relatives, and the prospect of their assistance as guardian spirits urged him to undertake sacrifice even when poverty stricken and perhaps unable to afford the expense. The hope of supernatural help and the fear of supernatural punishment, along with sympathy for the dead, have been powerful influences in stabilizing ancestral worship in the Confucian religious scheme.

This supernatural element does not mean belief in a higher than natural order of being, which in the Christian religion is the realm of divine grace. Perhaps a better term would be supramundane, in the sense of "beyond earthly" acceptance of an invisible world of reality that includes an objectively personal God, whose providence extends to mankind and on whose assistance depends the success of all human effort and action.

MUSIC AND SONG. Confucianism from ancient times attached great importance to music. The Chinese were acutely aware of the power of music over the emotions and its possibilities as a social force by refining or corrupting the listener. Comparable to the supernatural efficacy attached to ceremonial rites, they conceived of music as mysteriously contributing to the harmony of the universe or disturbing its equilibrium. In the same context where he said that "people may be made to follow, they cannot be made to understand," Confucius placed melody at the acme of effective agents over the human mind. "Education," he said, "begins with songs, is confirmed by practice of the rites, and is completed by music." [42]

In his time, he felt one of the gravest duties of the government was to forbid the lascivious airs of Chêng, and promote instead the compositions of Shao. "The Master said, 'All beautiful and noble is the music of Shao.' Therefore, choose for music the Shao and its dance, but banish the strains of Chêng, for they are wanton." Again, "when the Master was in Ch'i, he heard the Shao music, and for three months did not notice the taste of his food. 'I never imagined that music had reached such height,' he said." [43] His philosophy on the role of music in coordinating social life is epitomized in the chain sequence which begins with deceit and hypocrisy in speech, through the "misuse of words," and ends in political tyranny. "When words are misused, human relations go wrong. When human relations break down, propriety and music weaken. When propriety and music weaken, law and justice fail. And when law and justice fail them, a people can move neither hand nor foot in servitude."

Confucian interest in music and its association with ritual and social custom is based on a theory that is typically oriental. Rites and music are twin instruments for pacifying unruly desires in the individual and community. Where ritual and custom set limits to these desires according to age and social rank, music is the "crown" of propriety for harmonizing the passions, on the assumption that passions are not of themselves evil but become such only when not coordinated. The classic expression of this theory of harmony occurs in the *Book of Rites.*

Music makes for community, the rites make for distinction. When there is community, there is mutual affection; when there is distinction, there is mutual respect. When music predominates, differences lead to estrangement. It is the task of rites and music to coordinate the passions and to ornament appearances.

Music issues from within, the rites act from outside. Serenity is the result of music issuing from within, refinement is the result of the rites acting from the outside. Great music must be simple, great rites must be easy. When music is at its best there is no resentment, when rites are at their best men do not contend. It is to rites and music that this saying refers, "By bowing and giving way one could set the world in order." [44]

Confucian tradition sees music as the human counterpart of the cosmic harmony in the universe. It is man's imitation of the variety of creatures in the world, all placed in their respective spheres of action and, though all different, cooperating to a common end— as in the interplay of celestial bodies with the forces of earth. "The graces of heaven and earth cooperate. They are drummed on by thunder, stirred by wind and rain, kept in motion by the four seasons, warmed by the sun and moon, from which the innumerable transformations arise. Music is therefore the harmony of heaven and earth." [45] Its religious purpose is to duplicate within man and among men the peaceful effects of coordinated regularity.

THREE RELIGIONS OF CHINA

Although Confucianism is popularly considered the only religion of China, there are actually two other major religions among the Chinese, Buddhism and Taoism, which join the first in a strange coexistence that would be hard to find in any other country. Perhaps the best explanation is that Confucianism needed the support of alien religious elements to supply for its own deficiencies, which are numerous.

Confucius and his disciples may have differed on many things, but they were at one in stressing the seriousness of life and the grave responsibility men have to improve themselves and the world in which they live. Early in its history, Confucianism took two un-

fortunate turns which Taoism sought to correct. One was the preoccupation with duty, imposed on every man by a rigid code of
custom he had nothing to do with shaping; the other was new
exploitation of the common people by despotic rulers who would
make their subjects mere pawns in the game of politics, for their
own ambitious ends. The result was a deep pessimism that was
bound to create a reaction. A fair example of this gloomy attitude
occurs in a Taoist work called *Lieh Tzu*. Its reputed author, Yang
Chu, may never have written the book, but its spirit belongs authentically to the period when the first rival of Confucianism came
into existence, between the mid-fifth and third centuries before
Christ.

No man lives more than a hundred years, and not one in a thousand
that long. And even that one spends half his life as a helpless child or
a dim-witted dotard; of the time that remains, half is spent in sleep, or
wasted during the day. In what is left he is plagued by pain, sickness,
sorrow, bitterness, doubts, losses, worry, and fear. In ten years and
more there is hardly an hour in which he can feel at peace with himself
and the world, without being gnawed by anxiety.

Do we live for the sake of being cowed into submission by the fear
of the law and its penalties, now spurred to frenzied action by promise
of a reward or fame? Never for a moment do we taste the heavy wine
of freedom. We are as truly imprisoned as if we lay at the bottom of a
dungeon, heaped with chains. In life all creatures are different, but in
death they are all the same. They are just rotten bones. And rotten
bones are all alike; who can distinguish them? So let us make the most
of these moments of life that are ours. We have no time to be concerned
with what comes after death.[46]

This is not Taoism, but its sentiments ushered in a religious
system that sought to modify the cold if not harsh legalism inherent
in Confucian philosophy, by stressing the ideal of simplicity. Instead
of a painful struggle to conform to customs set up by the ancients,
let nature alone be the guide. Indeed all artificial institutions and
all strivings are wrong. Activity by itself is not wrong, but all strain-
ing to obtain what causes anxiety is an error. In the words of the
Taoist Bible, the *Lao Tzu,* "There is no greater misfortune than
not to know when one has enough, and no calamity more blight-
ing than the desire to get more." [47]

The early Taoists condemned the Confucians mercilessly. For one thing the Confucians were successful philosophers when Taoism arose; they were also the guiding thinkers behind the government, which by Taoist standards could only do harm. When open assault failed, the Taoists claimed that Confucius was himself a secret convert to Taoism, which he criticized only to hide his real beliefs.

In the course of time Confucianism and Taoism became reconciled, in spite of periods when Taoists were persecuted by the state religion. One of the paradoxes of Taoism is the ability to survive with all its anti-Confucian, anti-governmental and often antinomian tendencies; and even flourish as a collaborator of Confucianism to produce the national culture. Where Confucianism stressed custom and man's responsibility to society, Taoism favored the individual as a single person, and his right to call his soul his own. While Confucianism would amalgamate persons as members of a clan and subjects of the state, Taoism sought to liberate them by communing with nature (to the point of assimilation) and has inspired the best in Chinese art and literature.

The role of Buddhism in China has been much the same, except that Buddhism is a foreign import from India and entered China to offer a religious metaphysic rather than challenge the basic principles of Confucian thought.

Chinese Buddhism came into prominence, if not existence, somewhere about the first century of the Christian era. By the year 65 it was professed by a member of the imperial family, and by 165 it was accepted by the Emperor Huan Ti. By the beginning of the fourth century Chinese intellectuals were defending it as the greatest religious system created by the genius of man.

Not unlike Taoism, the Buddhist religion came to fill a void by offering balance to a rigid determinism and lack of spiritual ardor. Its impressive liturgy, monastic idealism and the answers it gave to the problems of life were spontaneously welcome. Near the center of these needs created by Confucianism was the question of human destiny. A famous naturalist, Wang Ch'ung (27-97 A.D.), called himself a Confucian, yet subscribed to a whole-hearted fatalism.

In conducting affairs men may be either talented or stupid, but when it comes to calamity or good fortune, there are some who are lucky and some unlucky. The things they do may be right or wrong, but whether they meet with reward or punishment depends on chance.

There are many persons who wish to display their loyalty (to a ruler), yet he rewards some and punishes others; there are many who wish to do him benefit, yet he trusts some and distrusts others. Those whom he rewards and trusts are not necessarily the true ones, nor are those whom he punishes and distrusts necessarily the false. It is simply that the rewarded and trusted ones are lucky, while those who are punished and distrusted are unlucky.[48]

There were two answers to this fatalistic uncertainty. Native Confucian thinkers had relied mostly on the explanation that fate was shared by members of the same family or clan, or by people who lived in the same area. This principle of joint responsibility of family or neighborhood has been woven into the fabric of Chinese government and law.

Buddhism was less simplicist. Its theory of *Karma* and transmigration of souls accounted for retribution not only in one life but through a chain of subsequent incarnations.

Illustrative of the impact and dissemination of Chinese Buddhism are the temples and monasteries it established throughout the country, and the voluminous sacred writings it produced, upwards of sixteen hundred distinct works on every phase of religious thought. In Hangchow alone, a city in East China, a survey made in the early 1930's showed there were almost a thousand Buddhist monasteries and temples for a total population of less than a quarter million. Most of the monks are drawn from poor families, although some are wealthy and well educated. Many are purchased by the monastery as children, where needy parents are willing to sell their offspring for a small fee and give their son (or daughter) an assured livelihood. Until the advent of Communism, which permits some Buddhist institutions to function, the inmates of monasteries enjoyed special imperial or government favor. This encouraged "vocations" to the monastic life. During one brief period of disfavor in North China, authentic records show that three hundred thousand monks and nuns were forcibly returned to secular life.

Although relatively few could become monks or nuns, everybody could be a lay Buddhist, and millions did. The appeal to a universal salvation, albeit delayed and not equal, satisfied the innate desire for eventual happiness; a vast array of spirits and divinities represented in exquisite figures of wood, ivory and porcelain, pleased the eye and religious emotions; and a graphic description of the fate of the wicked, through purgative states of horrible torment, answered to an instinctive sense of justice at which Confucianism only hinted, and Taoism largely ignored.

Undoubtedly many Chinese Buddhists have been ignorant people attracted by magic and naive superstitions, but this is by no means a rule. A high ethical code drew some of the best minds to accept the religion of the Buddha while remaining ostensibly faithful to the precepts of Confucianism.

It is next to impossible to distinguish clearly on the precise religious affiliation of the people in China. Some historians have coined the term Siniticism to describe the mixture of Confucian ethics, Taoist naturalism, and Buddhism mysticism, which is actually professed by the majority of Chinese. Not that all three are simultaneously verified in any one person, but all have contributed to the structure of his faith. Confucianism stands for the politico-religious side of Chinese life, the Community and the State ranking foremost in the mind of its founder. Taoism symbolizes individualism, with stress on the spiritualistic and magical aspect of national life. Buddhism is also individualistic, but insists on the vanity of all things visible and the reality of things unseen.

UNDER COMMUNISM

The origins of Communism in China may be traced to the Marxist study groups formed in the spring of 1918 at Peking University under the leadership of Li Ta-chao. A severe critic of Confucianism, he felt the people had not gone far enough in dethroning Pu Yi, the last Manchu monarch in 1911 and setting up the Chinese Republic. Writing in October, 1918, he described the Russian Revolution as a cosmic liberation. "The real victory," he said, "is not the victory of the Allies against the Germans, but the victory of the Bolshevists. Henceforth all national boundaries, all differences of classes, all barriers to freedom will be swept away." [49]

While tempted by the messianic claims of Marxism, however, Li and his followers were too Confucianist to accept the full implications of Communist ideology. In 1919 he was trying to reconcile his fervent faith in the power of the human conscience with Marxist doctrine. He repeated his belief that "the existence of a moral sense is something we must all accept," and that "the call of duty exists in the human heart." Yet there was a perceptible change, which symbolized the revolution going on in the minds of many Chinese intellectuals. The source of this moral sense should not be traced, as in Confucius or the *Doctrine of the Mean,* to any superhuman source, but can be found in the social instinct which man has developed in the course of his struggle for existence. While still not orthodox Leninism, this shift in traditional Chinese belief was only a shade removed from dialectical materialism.

Among the young students whom Li ta-chao converted to the Marxist camp was Mao Tse-tung, the Lenin of Chinese Communism and the first chairman of its Soviet Provisional Government.

Unlike Li, Mao Tse-tung had no compromise to effect with the ancient traditions. "I hated Confucius from the age of eight," he once wrote. And in *The New Democracy* he claimed that "emphasis on the honoring of Confucius and the reading of the classics, and advocacy of the old rules of propriety (*li*) and education and philosophy are part of that semi-feudal culture" which must be overthrown. "The struggle between the old and new cultures is to the death." [50]

Yet even he could not divorce himself from the past, and in outlining the future of his people stressed the distinctiveness of Communism in China, with its roots in Confucian thought. It must be admitted that "in the past China has suffered greatly by accepting foreign ideas simply because they were foreign. Chinese Communists should remember this in applying Marxism in China. We must effect a genuine synthesis between the universal truth of Marxism and the concrete practice of the Chinese revolution. Only after we have found our own national form of Marxism will it prove useful." [51]

Among the most valuable tools the revolution needed was the acceptance of authority and uniformity of thought, which Confucian ethics could be made to supply at will. Above all respect for the ancient customs has been so inculcated by centuries of Confucianism that deference to the "traditional culture" and the wisdom of "previous ages" had to become part of the Communist approach. No mere aping of European revolutionaries is to be done, but a critical sifting of what is good (by Marxist standards) from the worthless debris of China's past.

China's culture should have its own form, the national form. The long feudal period in China's history created the brilliant culture of previous ages. To make clear the process by which this traditional culture developed, to discard its feudal residue, and to absorb its democratic essence, are necessary steps for developing our new national culture and heightening our national confidence. This assimilation, however, must never be uncritical. We must carefully discriminate between those completely rotten aspects of the old culture that were linked with the feudal ruling class, and the excellent popular culture, which was more or less democratic and revolutionary in character.[52]

Other Communist leaders wrote in the same strain. They extolled the merits of Marxist principles but stressed the unique character of their Chinese implementation. More than unique, Communism in China is not only "powerful, armed with Marxist-Leninist theory," but "the heir of all the splendid traditions of the many progressive men of thought and action who have illumined the pages of Chinese history." [53]

Confucius, Mencius and other philosophers were quoted, and their ideas integrated with Marxism. Reminiscent of the age-old discussion whether the sage emperors Yao and Shun were spiritual beings, with wisdom beyond the capacity of ordinary men, "There are those who say it is not possible, by means of study and self-cultivation, to attain the qualities of such revolutionary geniuses as Marx, Engels, Lenin and Stalin. They consider Marx, Engels, Lenin and Stalin to have been mysterious beings from birth. Is this correct? I think not." Then a reminder of the Confucian tradition, "Mencius said, 'Any man can become a Yao or a Shun.' " [54]

Instead of rejecting China's Confucian ancestry, the new prophets denounced those who have failed to live up to its ideals. Those were criticized who pretended to honor the Master's teaching but were actually using it to oppress the people and further their own interests. "Of course we Communist Party members can-

not adopt such an attitude in studying the principles of Marx and
Lenin, and the excellent and useful teachings bequeathed to us
by the ancient sages of our nation. As we speak, so we must act.
We are honest and pure; we cannot deceive ourselves, the people,
or the men of old." [55] Thus the new wine of Communist dogma
was poured into the old bottles of Chinese form to create a religion
for the masses.

The use of Confucianism for ideological propaganda is nothing
strange in Chinese Communism, but the issue runs deeper. Quite
apart from the contortions to which Marxists subjected the teachings
of Confucius to serve their preconceived ends, the whole religious
background of the Chinese played into their hands. The nation
had suffered grievously through a generation of war and was being
strangled to death, as Madame Chiang Kai-Shek expressed it, by
an economic noose fashioned by Japan out of the short-sighted
policy of the Western democracies. Soviet Russia alone seemed to
be ready to cooperate with China on the basis of equality. Sun Yat-
sen, the father of the Chinese Republic and no Marxist, offered
Three Principles of the People as a legacy from Russia, namely,
"to curb the strong, support the weak, and promote justice," and
he promised the Soviet Union to "use the strength of our four
hundred millions to fight against injustice for all mankind." [55] He
found the inspiration for "this our Heaven-appointed task" in the
Analects of Confucius.

7. Taoism

Taoism, which literally means the religion of the "Way" (*Tao*), has had the most chequered career of the three main religious cultures of China. According to its own historians, it once commanded respect from the nation's leaders, until Confucianism replaced it as the guardian of the State. For a time, too, it appealed to the simple and uncultured people, but then Buddhism came along to win the allegiance of the masses. Its final and present stage is an elaborate complex of polytheism, whose priests are regarded as the most expert magicians and exorcists, yet whose philosophy has won the admiration of Western scholars.

Historians of China regard Taoism as perhaps the most characteristic of the Chinese people. In its fundamental concept, Taoism has always been a worship of nature inside and outside of man, and an attempted harmony between the two. The perfect man, in Taoist language, is not the person who obstructs nature, but who gives himself completely over to nature, thereby producing what some have called the highest ethical standards of the Chinese character, and others a repudiation of all objective law.

Since Taoism has never been independent of Confucian and Buddhist influences, it is more accurate to speak of a Taoist emphasis than of a particular set of doctrines and practices. Nevertheless certain features of faith and worship are sufficiently distinctive to qualify one out of ten native Chinese as a professed Taoist, with the other nine also deeply affected by the same philosophy of life.

ORIGINS AND DEVELOPMENT

The historical beginnings of Taoism are obscure. Its reputed founder was Li-poy-yang, which his followers changed to Lao-Tze

(Old Master) as a title of respect. His birth is assigned to 604 B.C., or fifty-three years before Confucius. If this were correct, the tradition about Confucius rebuking him "for his proud airs and many desires" should be discarded.

More significant, however, is the claim that Lao-Tze wrote the bible of Taoism, the *Tao Teh Ching* (Classic of the Way and Virtue), which modern writers normally assign to a much later date and trace to a gradual development by way of reaction or counterpoise to early Confucianism. Actually three men are held to be responsible for the rise of Taoism: the legendary compiler of the *Tao Teh Ching,* a naturalist philosopher, Yang Chu (440-366 B.C.), and the "Chinese Nietzche," Chuang Tzu, who died about 295 B.C.

Yang Chu was neither a hedonist nor a pure subjectivist, as orthodox Confucianists later dubbed him. Yet, unlike Confucius, who stressed devotion to one's ancestors and society as the ideal of human conduct, Yang was an individualist who was unwilling "to pluck out a single hair even if it might have benefited the whole world." Personal integrity and self-protection, "to live as long as possible," were the main tenets of his school.

Chuang Tzu operated on a different level. His concern was mainly speculative, to develop a theory of existence that might explain all reality. According to Chuang, the *Tao* produced all things and is, in fact, the ground of all things and in all things. He advocated man's unity with the universe as the answer to life's problems. A contemporary of Mencius, the great interpreter of Confucianism, Chuang opposed the latter for accentuating statecraft and ethics, and creating what later became the social construct of a state religion.

Still another ingredient entered the final composite of Taoism. From the late third century B.C. arose the Yin Yang theory, which held that all beings are made of two universal energies: *Yin* (dark, evil, female) and *Yang* (light, good, male), which unite in varying combinations to produce the noxious and beneficial substances of the world. The secret is to discover which have *Yin* and which *Yang,* and to use them accordingly.

Under pressure from a competitive Buddhism, the followers of *Tao* towards the end of the second century A.D. began copying Bud-

dhist methods and policy. They gradually built up a strong ecclesiastical cultus, with a ruling hierarchy, a pantheon of gods and lesser
spirits, and an elaborate ritual. By the fifth century, two Taoist
leaders, Tao Sheng and Hui Yuan, revolted against the ritualistic
Buddhism of their day and contributed to the emergence of a sect
that had much in common with the Quakers, professing belief in an
Inner Light and advocating the practice of sustained contemplation.

Hui Yuan is likewise credited with developing the Pure Land
or *Amida* sect, in which merit is gained by the simple repetition of
faith in Amida, one of the Buddhist deities worshiped by the Mahayana. This easy practice opened the prospects of a future happy
life to the Chinese coolie and the peasant, as much as to the learned
philosopher. Centuries later the cultus of Amidaism penetrated into
Japan and, along with Zen, swept away many of the older and
more formal sects.

A popular Taoist movement known as "Five-Bushel-Rice Taoism" arose some time during the second century after Christ. The
acknowledged leader was Chang Ling, a follower of Zoroastrianism, who organized his co-religionists into a well-knit society,
modelled on Mazdaism. Believers were taxed five bushels of rice,
they worshiped Tao in place of Ahura Mazda, and Chinese folk
gods instead of the Persian angels. At first the movement served
only to consolidate disparate political units in China, but later (184
A.D.) the new Taoists rebelled against the government, and eventually grew into one of the major forces that challenged Confucian
bureaucracy. In the fifth century the followers of Chang Ling and
the older Taoists merged into an amalgam that survives to the
present day.

BASIC PRINCIPLES

The spirit of Taoism is best described in the pages of Lao-Tze's
Book of Tao, which more than almost any other single work of
literature can claim to interpret the Orient and epitomize all that is
necessary to understand the Chinese religious character. It has been
called the first enunciated philosophy of camouflage in the world,
teaching the wisdom of appearing foolish, the success of appearing
to fail, the strength of weakness and the advantage of lying low,

the value of yielding to an adversary and the futility of striving for power.

CONCEPT OF TAO. Central to Lao-Tze's classic is the idea of *Tao,* a term familiar from pre-Confucian days as meaning the "way," or "method," a "course" and "order" or "norm." To Confucianists it meant the way to heaven, and therefore represented the moral ideal by which a person should guide his life.

While retaining this elementary notion, Taoism invests the term with much deeper significance. The Tao for them has become a symbol for the ineffable first principle of being, at once eternal, immaterial, and all-present, which guides the destinies of men and rules even over the gods.

> Tao is all-pervading, and its use is inexhaustible.
> Fathomless, like the fountain head of all things,
> Its sharp edges rounded off, its tangles untied,
> Its light tempered, its turmoil submerged.
> Yet crystal clear like still water it seems to remain.
> I do not know whose Son it is,
> An image of what existed before God.[1]

Nothing higher can be known than *Tao,* and no greater virtue is possible than to live according to the same. "The works of great Virtue follow alone from Tao;" yet for all its indispensability, "the thing that is called Tao is elusive, evasive." But latent in it are forms and objects, "dark and dim," and a life-force that is very true. "From the days of old till now, its manifested forms have never ceased, by which we may view the Father of All Things," whose image the phenomenal world reveals.[2]

Tao is superior to all things, and before all things. "Before the Heaven and Earth existed there was something nebulous: silent, isolated, standing alone, changing not, eternally revolving without fail, worthy to be the Mother of All Things. I do not know its name and address it as Tao. If forced to give it a name, I shall call it 'Great.'" If other things are also great, like heaven, earth, and the king, their greatness is only borrowed. "Man models himself on the earth, the earth models itself after heaven, the heaven models itself after Tao, but Tao models itself by that which is so by itself."[3]

Although great beyond compare, Tao is not really transcendent.

It is at the same time primordial matter, formative principle, the self-existing, self-acting, homogeneous, omnipresent, boundless and inscrutable, the Real One, beside which the "many" are phenomenal and unreal.

Lao-Tze's Tao was inherent in the Universal, not in the particular. What is real is the whole and not its parts. As the One, the Tao is not merely the sum total of the Many, but more. "The several parts of the carriage are not the carriage," which reminds us of the Buddhist speculations in the Hinayana tradition. While producing all things, the Tao is greater than all its products, and is also independent of them. At the same time it is in all and through all and, as some Taoists believe, it *is* all or *is becoming* all.

The Great Tao flows everywhere. Like a flood it may go left or right.

All things depend on it for their production, which it gives to them, not one refusing obedience to it. When its work is accomplished, it does not claim the name of having done it.

It clothes all things as with a garment, and makes no assumption of being their lord; it may be named in the smallest things.

Being the home of all things, yet claiming them not, it may be considered great. Because to the end it does not claim greatness, its greatness is achieved.[4]

MEANING OF VIRTUE. Correlative with *Tao* (way) is *Teh* (virtue) which derives from the former. In general terms, the whole process of morality and, indeed, all nature, depends on acquiring the One (Tao), each according to its needs. "Through possession of the One, the Heaven is made bright and pure, the earth is made firm and sure, spirits are supplied with powers, valleys are made full, all things live and grow, princes and kings get the model which they give to others. All these are the results of the One (Tao)."[5]

In Taoist language, Teh is the moral expression of the philosophic Tao. It stands as a symbol for the will (or heart) caught in a net and advancing gradually to perfection, where the net means the finite world into which Teh enters as a manifestation of the infinite Tao.

A synthesis of Taoist ethics is found in *The Three Treasures,* under which title Chinese Buddhism is also known. Lao-Tze admits that "while my Tao is great, everyone says it yet appears to be inferior to other systems of teaching." Paradoxically, "it is just its greatness that makes it seem to be inferior," because of the character of the things it calls great.

I have three treasures which I prize and hold fast: the first is Love. The second is, Never too much. The third is, Never be the first in the world.

Through Love, one has no fear; through not doing too much one has enough of reserve power; through not presuming to be the first in the world, one can develop one's talent and let it mature.

If one forsakes love (gentleness) to become bold, restraint to waste reserve power, and following behind to rush in front, he is dead.

For love is victorious even under attack, and invulnerable in defense. Heaven arms with love those it would not see destroyed.[6]

Kindness and gentleness, therefore, are the first qualities of superior virtue, coupled with humility which does not honor itself, which avoids display and is not self-seeking. Its motto is: If you wish to conquer, be conquered. "There is nothing weaker than water, but none is superior to it in overcoming the hard, for which there is no substitute. Everyone knows that weakness overcomes strength, and gentleness conquers harshness, but no one can put it into practice." [7]

This gentleness is more than a philosophic mean. It is the virtue of inactivity, the ideal of *laissez-faire,* as appears from a comparison between two devotees, the one of ordinary learning and the other of Tao. The former aims to increase his knowledge day by day, the latter "seeks from day to day to diminish his doing. He diminishes it and again diminishes it, till he arrives at doing nothing on purpose. Having arrived at this point of non-action, there is nothing which he does not do." [8]

There are strong reminiscences in Taoism of Buddha's moral ideal by canonizing the negation of appetite, while yet promising this-worldly recompense for a man's self-obscuration.

To yield is to be preserved whole. To be bent is to become straight. To be hollow is to be filled. To be tattered is to be renewed. To be in want is to possess. To have plenty is to be confused.

Therefore the Sage embraces the one thing of humility, and manifests it to all the world. He is free from self-display, and therefore he shines. He does not justify himself, and is therefore far-famed. He does not boast of himself, and therefore people give him credit. He does not pride himself, and is therefore the ruler of men. It is because he does not contend that no one in the world can contend against him.[9]

Of rewards and punishments, Taoism knows little, except in the vaguest terms. If virtue is possessed by the peaceable, since "he who argues is not a good man," and wisdom by the ignorant, since "he who knows many things is not wise"—by the same token the Sage does not accumulate for himself, "he lives for others, and grows richer as a result." He gives to other people and has greater abundance in return.

Anticipating the later stress on magic and the preternatural, the followers of Tao are promised marvelous gifts, similar to those of children. "Who is rich in virtue is like a child. No poisonous insects sting him, no wild beasts attack him, and no birds of prey pounce upon him. His bones are soft, his sinews tender, yet his grip is strong." And negatively, "he who is against Tao perishes young." [10] Centuries of interpretation have elaborated on these sanctions and invested them with graphic meaning that was quite alien to primitive Taoism.

On the walls of the famous Taoist temple at Anking, on the Yang-tze river above Nanking, are numerous inscriptions that hark back to the "Tao of Heaven," to which Lao-Tze refers only once in his sacred book. "The shelter is wide and large," one inscription reads, "dreadful, famous, clear and effective, shines upon the hearts of men. The Tao of Heaven both rewards and punishes." The presiding deity is made to say, "You must know that I am a just god who rewards and punishes." So "when you look upon the rewards of the chaste and the punishments of adulterers, you will wash your face and clean your heart. You will believe in Tao and turning your boat will reach safe harbor," by reforming a life of misdeeds.[11]

Taoist philosophy of achievement by inaction is synthesized in its code on the art of government, which bids the ruler abstain from legislating at the risk of making the people lawless. The code distinguishes between governing people by *cheng* (normal, straightforward means) and winning a war by *ch'i* (abnormal and deceitful strategy.)

Rule a kingdom by the Normal.
Fight a battle by abnormal tactics of surprise.
Win the world by doing nothing.

How do I know it is so?

Through this: the more prohibitions there are, the poorer the people
become.

The more sharp weapons there are, the more prevailing chaos in the
state.

The more skills in technique, the more cunning things are produced.

The greater the number of statutes, the greater the number of thieves
and brigands.

Therefore the Sage says: I do nothing and the people are reformed
of themselves.

I love quietude and the people are righteous of themselves.

I deal in no business and the people grow rich of themselves.

I have no desires and the people are simple and honest of themselves.[12]

Underlying what seems to be naive simplicity is a theory of
knowledge that identifies true wisdom with a mystical intuition
that eschews if it does not despise human erudition and cunning.
"The Ancients," according to Lao-Tze, "who knew how to follow
the Tao aimed not to enlighten the people, but to keep them ignorant." If there is a conflict among citizens, the reason is that they
have been taught too much. "Those who seek to rule a country by
knowledge are the nation's curse. Those who seek not to rule a
country by knowledge are the nation's blessing." Anyone who
knows these two principles, understands the Ancient Standard, "and
to know always the Ancient Standard is called the Mystic Virtue.
When the Mystic Virtue becomes clear, far-reaching, and things
revert back to their source, then and then only emerges the Grand
Harmony." [13]

PRACTICES AND PRESENT STATUS

Since the second century A.D., a segment of Taoism has been
organized as a complex of religion and magic, with a supreme
Master of Heaven at the head. Chang Tao Ling was founder of this
priestly dynasty, whose members until recently had their seat of
authority on Dragon Tiger mountain in the province of Kiang-si.
Legend had it that each successive ruler received from his predecessor a sacred sword, that was at once a symbol of his office and an
instrument of miracle.

The Celestial Master on Dragon Tiger mountain was leader

only of the "Principle One" sect, whose belief was centered in the ability of their high priest to transmit to others his own hidden powers over nature. His disciples were furnished with diplomas in the magical arts: making charms against rain, drought and devils, exorcizing evil spirits, and acting as mediums for the souls of the dead. They lived for the most part as married laymen among the people, and differed from the Taoist monks who were celibates in monastic communities, dedicated to meditation and ascetical discipline. Often in the history of China, these master sorcerers were summoned by the court to check natural calamities or divine the future prospects of war and political enterprise.

Less notorious but more important was the "Perfecting the True" sect, founded in 1280 by Chiu Chang Chun, who was invited by the emperor to reside with his disciples in the White Cloud temple near Peking. Later this temple became the center of the sect whose teaching follows Lao-Tze very closely by stressing the need for being in harmony with Nature. To become calm and simple, the sect advocates ascetical practices that are quite Manichean in their rigor. Members of the group are all priests who left their homes and adapted a strictly vegetarian diet in monasteries. The "Perfecting the True" sect is the most syncretist. It seeks to combine Taoism, Buddhism and Confucianism into one religion.

Since the beginning of the present century and up to the Communist invasion, Taoist beliefs and practices were also carried on by numerous and mostly secret societies. Among these, the principles of the "Pervading-Unity Tao" sect most closely resemble the Hegelian concept of a dialectic conflict which issues in a new cosmic state. The universe, they believe, will pass through a number of catastrophes marking the end of revolutionary changes. We are at present in the midst of the third catastrophe, but will be saved by the "Old Mother transcending Life," whose worship began already in the Ming dynasty (1368-1644). Practitioners of this cult are given to using charms, magical phrases and incantations. They also use the planchette, a small board (often symbolically designed) which is supported on casters at two points and a vertical pencil at a third point, supposed to move of itself when lightly touched by the fingers and the pencil, thereby tracing mysterious word messages.

Like the monastic groups, "Pervading-Unity Tao" also forbids the use of meat, tobacco and alcohol. Images of all religions, including the Christian, are worshiped, and the ritual indiscriminately includes prayers from Buddhist and Taoist sources.

Another sect that did excellent social work during the second World War was the "Hall of the Tao," a twentieth-century creation that came into existence as a result of new revelations from the planchette. While concentrating its worship on the ancient Taoist deity, the "Greatest One," it gave place of honor also to Confucius and the Buddha, and used symbols from Christianity and Islam in its liturgy. With a stress on the spirit of world brotherhood, works of charity have been a prominent feature of this group.

There was a secret society in Shantung, which professed to give up all private property and hold everything in common. Its communal character is a familiar pattern in pre-Communist Taoism, and its ancestry has been traced to the pre-Christian era.

After the 1911 Chinese revolution, which ended the reign of the Manchu emperors, there began a wild growth of secret Taoist inspired societies. When Mao Tse-tung proclaimed the People's Republic of China in 1949, one of his first acts was to dissolve these secret organizations. Leaders of the "Pervading-Unity Tao" were arrested, and by 1951 the survivors had practically all apostatized. The last head of the "Principal One" sect, the sixty-third Celestial Master, fled to Formosa, and with him passed out of corporate existence the most ritual (and magic) minded of the Taoist denominations.

However, Taoism is by no means defunct in China. It is more alive than ever before, and has been encouraged, if not actually promoted, by the new Communist regime. In 1957 the China Taoist Association was formed at Peking, at the closing session of a congress attended by Taoist monks and nuns from every province. Suggestive of the future course of Taoist ideology, the first head of the association was abbot of the Shengant monastery and a member of the central committee of the Chinese Communist Party. The published aims of the new federation are to unite Taoists throughout the Chinese mainland, to promote the traditions of ancient Taoism, to support the Socialist reconstruction of the country, and, unexpectedly, to assist the political authorities implement a policy of religious freedom.

8. Zoroastrianism

ZOROASTRIANISM is one of the oldest living faiths, and yet it has the smallest number of adherents. Although its ancestry is traceable to the sixth century before Christ, there are less than two hundred thousand professed Zoroastrians, only the Parsis in India and a small community in Persia (modern Iran). But their religion merits careful study because of the attention it has received in the history of Western thought, and because of the influence which many scholars believe it exercised on other religious cultures. "Christianity," according to a modern writer, "claims to be the heir of the prophets of Israel. If there is any truth in this claim, it is no less heir to the Prophet of ancient Iran, little though most Christians are aware of the fact." [1]

SACRED WRITINGS AND ZOROASTER

The chief source of our knowledge of Zoroastrianism is the *Avesta,* a term of uncertain origin but most likely meaning "text" or "wisdom." Only a fraction of the Avesta survives today. Apart from fragments, it contains three main sections. The *Yasnas* are prayers to be recited by the priests when offering sacrifice. Into the Yasna, the great liturgical text, are inserted a series of *Gathas* or hymns, seventeen in number, which are written in the first person and therefore believed to be the work of Zoroaster himself. Accordingly the Gathas are the principal, if not only, authentic source for the doctrines as actually proclaimed by the prophet.

The *Vendidad,* or Law against Demons, has been called the Parsi Leviticus. Composed of twenty-two chapters, all but the first two expound the rules to be observed in the various circumstances

187

of life, in case faults have been committed, in time of sickness, death and ceremonial uncleanness. In the first two chapters the Vendidad relates the story of creation and tells about *Yima,* the Iranian Noah.

Similar to the Gathas are the hymns of praise or *Yashts* addressed to specify deities or angels. Together with some minor pieces they form the Minor Avesta, which is a collection of prayers to be used by the laity as well as by the priests.

Parsi tradition claims that two complete copies of the Avesta were destroyed in the invasion of Alexander the Great (356-323 B.C.), and that the Avesta we have today was compiled by order of the first Sassanian king (226-240 A.D.), who reconstructed the text out of fragments that a predecessor had collected. The original language of the scriptures was Avesta, the vernacular of ancient Bactria, in eastern Persia, and closely related to the Vedic of the Hindus. They were translated into Pahlavi, spoken by the people of post-Christian Iran, but Zoroastrian commentators commonly charge that the translation is both faulty and misleading. As a result, the Pahlavi version cannot be considered reliable.

Western opinions differ on the composition and especially the date of the Iranian Bible. A favored position is to regard the older portions of the Avesta as going back to Zoroaster himself, some time within the sixth century B.C. This old Avesta suffered mutilation over the centuries until fixed into a canon under Shapur II (310-379 A.D.), or, as others believe, not until the eleventh century of our era.

At the other extreme are Iranian scholars who maintain that the whole of the ancient Avesta perished during the Alexandrian period and that the post-Christian restoration meant the composition of an entirely new book, in which a residue of the old ideas were reshaped to a new religious philosophy influenced by Gnosticism and Neoplatonism. One of the main arguments for this theory is that the Gathas constantly speak of a kingdom whose coming is awaited by the faithful, a reflection of the Jewish Messianic Kingdom which the Iranians borrowed from the Hebrews.

In the absence of Avesta manuscripts from the early patristic age, let alone before the Christian era, it is impossible to decide for certain how much of the original Zoroastrian doctrine may now be found in the Avesta, whether in its "original" language or in subsequent translations.

By the same token, we cannot recover more than the main lines of the biography of Zoroaster, though he was certainly an historical personage. His name, which probably means "golden camel," is the Greek form for Zarathustra, as always given in the Avesta. Greek and Latin writers assign him to dim antiquity. Pliny the Elder, following Aristotle, asserts that Zoroaster lived six thousand years before the Trojan War. Direct Zoroastrian tradition places him between 660 and 583 B.C., and describes him as a reformer who sought to change the religion of Bactria, in southwest Asia, which appears to have been primarily a worship of the forces of nature.

Against this primitive animism, Zoroaster proclaimed that there was one God alone, who was holy and almighty. Every man was faced with one supreme duty, to choose between truth and falsehood. By his own witness, Zoroaster chose truth and on this foundation built his message of conversion.

> I who have striven for the awakening of the soul united with
>   the Good Mind,
> And who know the rewards of the Wise Lord for our deeds,
> While I can and may, I will teach the seeking of Righteousness.
> Knowing thee as Righteousness, thee together with the Good
>   Mind,
> Shall I see thee, and see also that the most mighty Wise Lord
>   has a throne and a Discipline?
> Through this saying, with our tongue we will convert the men
>   of prey to the greatest things.[2]

All the evidence indicates that Zoroaster met with little success in his reformation. He was forced to endure rejection and contempt, and the Gathas record more than one prayer begging for success. "To what land shall I flee," he asks, "where bend my steps? I am thrust out from family and tribe; I have no favor from the village to which I belong, not from the wicked rulers of the country. How, then, O Lord, shall I obtain thy favor?" [3]

Zoroaster feels the reason for his lack of success in his poverty "in men and cattle." Therefore he turns to the Wise Lord, as a friend to a friend. He at least will vindicate him. To those who do not put his word into practice there "should be woe at the end of life." He prays to know what reward will be given to the wise, and what punishment to unbelievers, "that he may convert all men," even "the robber horde" who now seek nothing but evil.

Finally he converted a certain chieftain king, Vishtaspa, and his two ministers. When defenders of the prevailing faith aroused the neighboring tribes to attack, Zoroaster urged Vishtaspa to take up arms, and in time the new religion was firmly established. Very likely Zoroastrianism was carried from Bactria to Media, from which it spread to Persia and was accepted, it seems, by the great Achaemenian kings in the Persian Empire. There is some doubt about Cyrus the Great (558-528 B.C.), but his successor Darius (521-485 B.C.) was a devoted Zoroastrian.

Iranian tradition says that Zoroaster began his ministry at the age of thirty, converted Vishtaspa twelve years later, and was slain at seventy-seven, when the Turanians successfully attacked Balkh.

CONCEPT OF GOD

Besides the unsettled question of the historical origins of the Avesta is another unsolved problem in Zoroastrianism, namely, what was the original teaching of Zoroaster himself. The two issues are closely connected, and the most satisfactory way of handling them is simply to take the Avesta at its face value but recognize that traditional Zoroastrianism is a compound of Avestic doctrine and centuries of interpretation up to modern times.

AVESTA TEACHING. The concept of two ultimate principles, one of good and the other of evil, was not inherent to original Zoroastrianism. Its good deity was called *Ahura-Mazdah* (the God who sees all, remembers all), who is omniscient, almighty, supreme, sovereign, good and merciful. He is the creator of the ten "Immortal Holy Ones" on whom the government of the whole material world depends. He also made the angels or lesser spirits, paradise, the vault of the sky, air, fire, and water, and also man. In a passage which reminds us of the Book of Job, Zoroaster asks rhetorically who made the world.

Who was the first father of Righteousness at the birth?
Who appointed their path to sun and stars?
Who but thou is it through whom the moon waxes and wanes?

Who set the Earth in its place below, and the sky of the
clouds, that it shall not fail?
Who the waters and the plants?
Who yoked the two steeds to wind and clouds?
Who, O Wise One, is the creator of the Good Mind?
What artificer made light and darkness, what artificer sleep
and waking?
Who made morning, noon and night, to remind the wise man
of his task?
Who created Devotion, sacred with the Dominion?
Who made the son reverential in soul towards his father?
Thus I strive to recognize in thee, O Wise One, as sacred
spirit, the creator of all things.[4]

Ahura-Mazda was the creator of all things, which contradicts
the popular notion that Avestic theology is essentially dualistic because the Spirit of Evil exists independently of Ahura-Mazda. The
dualism was a later development, occasioned by Zoroaster's preoccupation with Ahura-Mazda's rival, Anro Mainyus, whose name
the Parsis simplified into Ahraman or Ahriman. In the Avesta he
appears to exist coeval with Ahura-Mazda, yet not without some
kind of dependence on the latter.

Throughout the Avesta is this constant refrain: truth and falsehood, justice and wickedness, good and evil, and the choice that all
must make between the two constitute reality. Ahura-Mazda himself, as well as his "most sacred spirit," must make this choice.
There is no doubt that Zoroaster thus divided the world of being.

In the first of two crucial texts, he describes the two primeval
Spirits who never agree. "I will speak out," he proclaims, "concerning the two Spirits of whom, at the beginning of existence, the
Holier spoke to him who is Evil. Neither our thoughts nor our
teaching, nor our wills, nor our choices, nor our words, nor our
deeds, nor our convictions, nor yet our souls agree." And his warrant for this knowledge is a revelation received, "which the Wise
Lord has told me, he who knows." [5]

In the second text, after restating the objective co-existence of
the two primal Spirits, the prophet explains how all invisible creation made a choice between the two, and how the destiny of men
depends on whom they choose to follow. This passage gives the
central doctrine of dualistic Mazdaism.

> Now at the beginning the twin Spirits have declared their nature, the better and the evil.
>
> In thought and word and deed. And between the two the wise ones choose well, not so the foolish.
>
> And when these two Spirits came together, in the beginning they established life and non-life.
>
> And that at the last the worst existence shall be for the wicked, but for the just one the Best Mind.
>
> Of these two Spirits, the evil one chose to do the worst things; but the most sacred spirit, clothed in the most steadfast heavens, joined himself unto Truth.
>
> And thus did all those who delight to please the Wise Lord by honest deeds.
>
> Between the two, the false gods did not choose rightly; for, as they deliberated, delusion overcame them so that they chose the Worst Mind.
>
> Then did they, with one accord, rush headlong unto Wrath, that they might thereby deprave the existence of mortal man.[6]

The Evil Spirit, Ahriman, does not work alone. In India, the *Devas* or Shining Ones remained lesser gods, and the *Asuras* were degraded into demons. In Zoroastrianism the opposite takes place, and the *Devas* are the enemies of the good deity. Together with the Bad Spirit they "defrauded mankind of happy life and immortality." Nomad tribes who worship them are no better than the evil gods. "All of you are the breed of Bad Mind, Evil and Pride."[7]

Like Zoroaster, all men and even the false gods, had asked to be in the service of the Wise Lord, to be his messengers and "ward off those who are hostile to you." But the Wise Lord, united with the major Entities, declared his choice—the Devotion of the righteous. It shall be his through his Dominion. At the same time he rejected the false gods with their followers. They belong to the Bad Mind—the opposite of the Good Mind, to Evil—the opposite of the Right, and Pride—opposite of Devotion. He reproached the false gods with having seduced man to evil and estranged him from the "will of the Wise Lord and the Right," thus depriving him of eternal bliss because he obeyed the spirits of evil.

Zoroaster refers to the Good and Evil spirits as twins, and he calls Ahura-Mazda the father of the first of these. Logically, then, he should have made the Wise Lord also the father of the Evil Spirit. But he seems never directly to have said so. In his view Ahura-Mazda, the supreme deity, "generated" two Spirits, one of whom chose Truth and the other chose "to do the worst things." This second Spirit, then, became evil by choice, and was not such by nature. His dualism was moral (based on freedom) rather than metaphysical (arising from nature).

The founder of Mazdaism made so much of this necessity of choice that not even Ahura-Mazda escapes it. He, too, had to make the great choice that all others are bound to, between good and evil. His relation to the Evil Spirit is clear from the passages where the "false gods" approach the supreme God in supplication, whereby they acknowledge his supremacy. However, since they had already made their decision and were deceived, their fate is fixed, and Ahura-Mazda repudiates them.

Summarily, therefore, Zoroaster recognized only one God, maker of heaven and earth and of all things. This God, in relation to the world acts through something like "faculties," which the Avesta more than once describes as being engendered by Ahura-Mazda—his sacred Spirit, Good Mind, and Right-mindedness. He is also master of the Kingdom, Wholeness, and Immortality, which are, as it were, aspects of the one highest deity.

Righteousness or Truth is the objective norm of right conduct, first chosen by God, contrasted with the Lie or Disorder, which is the standard chosen by the Evil Spirit at the beginning of existence and of all that militates against God ever since. Ahriman was not yet co-eternal with God, in the Avesta, as he became in later Zoroastrianism.

LATER DEVELOPMENT. Zoroaster never fully accounted for the origin of the Evil Spirit, beyond saying that he chose "to do the worst things." But he left the door open for his followers to a system of metaphysical dualism by stating that the sacred Spirit and the Evil Spirit are twins.

At an early date in Iranian history, the sacred Spirit became identified with God himself, that is, Ahura-Mazda. If, however, the Good Spirit and Evil Spirit are twin brothers, they must have had a common ancestor. So it came about that a dominant group of Zoroastrians concluded to a principle above Ahura-Mazda and Ahriman, which they named Infinite Time, *Zurvana Akarana,* and who thereby became the first principle from which the good and evil Spirits arise.

Soon the embarrassing passages in the Avesta, which teach monotheism, were either ignored or mistranslated, and the purely dualist position became stabilized, whereby Ahura-Mazda and Ahriman, God and the Evil Spirit, were ultimate and equally eternal principles, the one perfectly good and the other absolutely evil.

When Zoroastrianism became the state religion of Persia in 226 A.D., under the Sassanian emperors, the two views, monotheistic and dualistic, alternated; until the latter became the orthodox doctrine, probably under Khusraw I (531-578). In 650 A.D., the Persian Empire was completely overrun by Moslem armies, and after a while the Zoroastrians were fiercely persecuted. Most accepted Islam, others fled to India where, according to their chroniclers, they landed at Sanjan in 716, bringing with them their sacred fire; and a remnant was left in Persia.

The religion of these exiles and of the Persian remnant became rigid dualism, transmitted through the Pahlavi books of translation and commentary on the Avesta. Until fairly modern times, Zoroastrianism and dualism became almost synonymous terms. "I must have no doubt," their doctrinal manual read, "but that there are two first principles, one the Creator and the other the Destroyer. The Creator is Ohrmazd who is all goodness and light; and the Destroyer is the accursed Ahriman who is all wickedness and full of death, a liar and a deceiver." [8]

Each of these two principles was given a separate abode: one existing on high in the light and the other down below in the darkness. They are separated by the Void. Realizing that the Evil Spirit would attack him once he discovered Ohrmazd's existence, the good deity created the spiritual and material worlds in self-protection. Thus classical Zoroastrianism easily "solved" the origin of evil and the problem of creation. Evil is a separate principle, so that its origin has no mystery. God created because he had to, as a means of preserving himself from the machinations of his archenemy. And the Evil Spirit, for all his malice in entering the world through causing sickness, pain, and death, yet finally will also destroy himself.

Zoroastrians of the old school explained the conflict with a parable. Ahura-Mazda (Ohrmazd) is like the owner of a garden, which destructive beasts are intent on spoiling by doing harm to its fruit and trees. To save himself trouble and keep the animals at bay, the gardener devises a stratagem to capture the beasts by means of cleverly designed traps. These are so made that, without killing the victim, they weaken it through its vain struggles to escape. After being thoroughly debilitated, the beasts are released from the snares but their faculties for doing harm are put out of action.

Man is not alone in this conflict with Ahriman. His allies are the hierarchy of spirits, comparable to the angels, who in later Zoroastrianism became distinct personal beings. Among these demigods, the most powerful was Mithra, who had enjoyed a remarkable career in Roman mythology.

The human contribution to this cosmic battle with the forces of evil consists mainly in thinking good thoughts, speaking good words, doing works, reproducing oneself through children, and making the earth as fruitful as possible with new and abundant life. For just as life is the creation of Ohrmazd, so death was introduced into the world by the Spirit of evil. Understandably, therefore, Zoroastrians were never fond of asceticism, which implies mortification, whereas their concept of virtue was not to deny but to increase the vital processes.

INFLUENCE ON MANICHAEISM. Symptomatic of the extreme dualism latent in Avestic theology was the rise of Manichaeism as a Zoroastrian offshoot in the third century. Founded by Manes (215-275 A.D.), a native of Seleucia-Ctesiphon, capital of the Persian Empire, it began as a Zoroastrian sect until opposition from the monotheist party forced Manes into exile in India. When he returned, he was for a time favored by the king, but then fell from the royal favor and was put to death by being flayed alive. His Persian disciples were banished from the country. Yet Manichaeism spread to all parts of Asia, North Africa and into distant Europe. Among its most famous disciples was St. Augustine who later wrote devastating treatises against the Manichaeans.

What Manes borrowed from Zoroastrianism was its approach to the problem of evil, by postulating two eternal and ultimate principles, and two completely disparate kingdoms, that of Light (physical and moral goodness), which is governed by God, and that of Darkness (physical and moral). Satan comes forth from the darkness, invades the realms of light and declares war on God.

In Manichaean theory, man was indeed created by God with pure elements, but he was made a prisoner by Satan who plants in him the seeds of darkness. Since that time, man has become the subject of struggle between God and the evil Spirit. The only hope for man is by the practice of severe asceticism, which comprises the three seals or mortifications of the mouth, the hands, and the passions.

What Manichaeism had in common with Zoroastrianism was a preoccupation with evil and attempting to save the goodness of God by depriving Him of absolute sovereignty. It was tolerated for a while as sectarian Mazdaism, and would likely have entered the stream of Zoroastrianism tradition with no further impact on history, except that Manes absorbed enough of Christianity to make his teachings attractive far beyond the intrinsic merits of the dualistic philosophy that lay beneath.

The followers of Manes developed his main ideas to which they added Gnostic speculations, claiming, as the Gnostics did, to a special *gnosis* or divine insight. They explained the Zoroastrian dualism by saying that from the good principle there emanated, in the first place, primeval man, who was the first to enter into the struggle with evil; in the next place the Spirit of Life, who rescued primeval man from the powers of darkness; finally the World-Soul, Christ, the Son of primeval man, who restored to man the light he had lost in the conflict with darkness. They distinguished in man two souls—the soul that animates the body, and the soul of light, which is part of the World-Soul, Christ. The former is the creation of the powers of darkness, the latter is an emanation from light itself. Thus, man's soul is a battlefield on which light and darkness are at war, as they are in the universe at large. Human action depends on the outcome of the contest; there is no freedom of choice. All material things are evil and the cause of evil.

The object of the practice of religion, according to Manichaeism, was to release the particles of light which Satan had stolen from the world of Light and imprisoned in man's brain; and that Jesus, Buddha, Zoroaster, and Manes had been sent to help in the task. Unlike its parent Zoroastrianism, the Manichaean sect spread rapidly. It was established in Egypt before the end of the third century, and at Rome early in the fourth. In the later fourth century Manichaeans were numerous in North Africa, where they were combatted by Augustine, Serapion and others. Their spirit influenced such anti-social movements as the Albigenses, Bogomiles, and the Paulicians. They held their ground in China till the fourteenth century, and recent excavations in Middle Egypt uncovered several papyri books (equivalent to two-thousand pages) in the Coptic dialect containing works by Manes and his first disciples.

RETURN TO MONOTHEISM. Numerous factors contributed to a reversal of thought in Zoroastrianism, away from extreme dualistic theology and back to what appears to have been the monotheism of the original Avesta. Pressure from a militant Islam, which still brands the Zoroastrians in Persia as Guebres, from the Arabic *Kafir* (unbeliever), was perhaps the single largest element. The influence of Christianity on the Parsis in India has also been recognized.

In its present form, Parsiism can best be described as monotheism modified by a physical and moral dualism, which admits sin and physical evil, together with an ethical system based on what is believed to be a divinely revealed moral code and human free will. If anything, the monotheism of today's Parsi is more rigid and determined than in the Avesta, due to centuries of contact with Islam.

MORAL CODE AND WORSHIP

Zoroastrian morality may be summed up in the two statements professed by every believing Mazdean. "I praise good thoughts, good words, and good deeds," he says, and "I praise the sound Mazdayasnian religion which allays dissensions and which realizes brotherhood." This preoccupation with goodness is simply corollary to its identification of God with goodness to the point of questioning even His permissive responsibility of evil. Accordingly right-mindedness in Zoroastrian terms came to signify becoming like Ahura-Mazda, and the idea is still vital in the Parsi religion.

On the ethical side, however, righteousness was interpreted by borrowing from the Greeks, notably Aristotle, and calling it the "mean." Ignoring the Hellenic ancestry, Parsi apologists say the idea is all their own. "Iran has always commended the mean, and censured excess and deficiency." In the Byzantine Empire the philosophers, in India the learned, and elsewhere the specialists have in general commended the man whose argument showed subtlety, "but the Kingdom of Iran has shown approval of the truly wise," who avoided all extremes.

Since Zoroastrian ethics developed in the period when the Avesta was the basis of the Persian state religion, it acquired an aristocratic stamp that is still familiar. Some have described Parsi morality as essentially urbanity or gentlemanliness, an ethic of moderation. But this is an oversimplification.

The duties of the *Ashavan* or righteous are especially honesty and straightforwardness. He is required to observe scrupulous personal purity, which consists not only in abstinence from unnatural crimes, but in all manner of ritual performances, often relating to the sexual relations, and to all contact with ceremonially unclean persons or objects, including corpses. Charity towards the poor, hospitality to the stranger, are likewise enjoined and practiced. Among social functions, the duty of tilling the soil is exalted to the rank of a primary virtue. To cut a tree becomes a sin. The tenderest care surrounds the ox and the dog.

There is a curious mixture of sublimity and triviality in Zoroastrian ethics that is hard for the Western mind to reconcile. The ethical ideal may be seen in the marriage hymn of a believing Parsi for his daughter. Bride and groom are exhorted to seek the good pleasure of *Mazda* "in thought, word and action. Let each of you strive to excel the other in the Right, for it will be a prize for that one. Happiness shall flee from those who despise righteousness. In this way you destroy for yourselves the spiritual life." Always the stress on life as a great conflict between good and evil, in which every believer must play his role with courage and unwavering fidelity.

At the same time, this plain moral teaching is burdened with prohibitions that remind one of the Pharisees in the time of Christ. An elaborate scale of stripes has been worked out for varying kinds of fault. Ceremonial transgressions are placed on a par with moral

offenses. A typical case is the penalty of death for letting the comb-
ings of one's hair or paring of the nails to fall to the ground, unless
these are carefully buried in a hole in the ground with appropriate
ritual ceremony. Failure to carry out the prescription increases the
evil strength of the Devas or demons as much as if the hair and
nails were offered to these evil spirits.

Particularly grievous is the crime of defiling the pure elements
of earth and fire. Therefore to bury in the earth the corpse of a
dog or a man is punishable by "thousands of stripes," unless the
evildoer repents and disinters the cadaver within the end of the
second year. Negligence to carry out this precept is a sin "for which
there is no atonement, for ever and ever."

Supporting the moral obligations is an elaborate theology of the
future life. For three days after death, the soul haunts a man's home
and then takes wing for the judgment tribunal, where it presents
itself before Mithra, Sraosha and Rashnu, three lesser deities.
Merits and demerits are carefully weighed in the balance. If neither
side sinks, so that good and bad actions during life are equal, the
soul proceeds to a "place of equilibrium," where it will have nothing
to suffer except from heat and cold. Otherwise the destiny is bliss
or damnation.

Paradise, for which the Persian word is *Behesht* (the most excellent), is the home of eternal light, the lovely dwelling place of
Vohu-Manah, or Good Thought, a progeny of Ahura-Mazda, the
good God. Damnation means being hurled into infernal darkness
so thick that the hand can feel it. The Persian Dante, Arda Viraf,
in a celebrated vision waxes eloquent over the horrors of the
damned, where the soul after one day cries out, "Alas! are they
not over, the nine thousand years that are to pass before hell shall
be opened." For all its terror, then, the Mazdean hell is not eternal.
A General Resurrection will renew the entire world. After countless
years, there will be one final trial, out of which every one comes
out pure and sanctified, and all men shall thereupon enter a life
of "infinite time," in a world wherein evil has disappeared.

Parsi worship is based on a hereditary priesthood, although the
priestly right lapses if, for the third generation, a family has re-
frained from qualifying for the priesthood. Most priests belong to
the lowest order, called *Ervad*. When twenty years old, an Ervad

may become a *Mobed,* priest of a Fire-temple. One condition is to know the Yasna by heart. High priests are the *Dasturs,* whose office usually passes from father to son.

Basically a Parsi community has two ritual requirements, a Fire-temple for the living and a Tower of Silence for the dead. The most sacred Fire-temples are the *Atesh Behram,* of which there are several in India. Though simple in construction, the temples can be expensive commodities because of the combination of different fires they demand, each with an elaborate ceremonial. Sixteen fires are amalgamated in the Atesh Behram, four in temples of the second class, and an ordinary house fire in temples of the lowest grade. Faithful Parsis go often to the Fire-temple to recite their prayers before the fire, but they are not fire worshipers. They direct their worship not to the flames, but to sacred truth which the fire signifies.

The Tower of Silence (*Dakhma*) is the necessary receptacle for the bodies of the dead, on the theory that burying would defile the earth and burning would pollute the flames. Instead, the dead are laid on the floor of a circular tower, and the vultures swoop down and remove the flesh. After some days, professional corpse bearers return and throw the dried bones into a central well, since by then their power to contaminate is passed.

A private ceremony in childhood illustrates the deep religious sentiment of the modern Zoroastrians. In the initiation rite, the boy or girl (between the ages of seven and fifteen) puts on the sacred shirt, cord and cap, which are symbolic of a "second" or "new" birth. Thenceforward the shirt must always be worn, except at night.

Before investiture with the sacred shirt (*sudreh*), the young neophyte repeats the Mazdean creed.

Praised be the most righteous, the wisest, the most holy and the best Mazdayasnian Law, which is the gift of Mazda. The good, true, and perfect religion, which God has sent to this world, is that which the prophet Zoroaster has brought in here. That religion is the religion of Zoroaster, the religion of Ahura Mazda, communicated to holy Zoroaster. Righteousness is the best gift and happiness. Happiness to him who is righteous, for the sake of the best righteousness.[9]

Later the candidate joins with the priest in a solemn prayer to God, clearly recognized as superior to the Evil One.

The Omniscient God is the greatest Lord, Ahriman is the evil spirit that keeps back the advancement of the world. May that evil spirit with all his accomplices remain fallen and dejected. Omniscient Lord, I repent of all my sins. I repent of all the evil deeds that I may have entertained in my mind, of all the evil words that I may have performed. May Ahura-Mazda be praised. May Ahriman, the evil spirit, be condemned. The will of the righteous is the most praiseworthy.

This prayer, together with another Mazdean creed, are commonly repeated three or four times a day. Public worship only rarely includes a sermon or instruction; its function is exclusively to give praise to God.

The liturgy includes the daily recitation of a few verses of the Avesta, which is conveniently divided into small portions, arranged according to the date to be recited. While the priest recites the prayers, he holds in his hands the *baresman* or bundle of twigs.

Each day and every month has its patron. The principal feasts are the New Year, which has since become also the greatest holiday of Islamic Persia; the spring and fall equinoxes consecrated to Mithra; the *gahambars* at the change of one season into another; the Days of the Dead at the end of each year; the Days of the Fall and the New Moon. Normal sacrifices consist in offering bread and *myazda* which means meat but has come to be used for milk. Another sacrifice, the *haoma,* is that of an intoxicating plant, of which the stems are crushed in a mortar and the juice drained off. Offered before the fire, the drink is taken by the priest and his assistants, and at birth a child has his lips steeped in haoma, but he does not become a full Zoroastrian until the initiation ceremony.

With such a tradition, it is no wonder the Parsis have become a distinctive people at once separated from the others among whom they live, and superior to their neighbors in religious principles. In India, no community is more advanced, or has gained more from Western civilization. Their philanthropy is world famous, and pride of race has made them conscious of a heritage that some have called the highest religious result to which human reason, unaided by revelation, can attain.

9. Shinto

THE origins of Shinto are lost in the dim past of Japanese history, and over the centuries its role has been to integrate with other systems, notably Confucianism from China and Buddhism from India, to give the people of Japan the most complex religious amalgam in the Orient.

At the same time Shinto has served to consolidate the nation and became the religious expression of patriotism, where the divine right of kings, familiar in the West, was an object of faith and the emperor a descendant of the gods. "Religion and government being one," wrote a modern Shintoist, "all the heavenly functions which the sovereign undertakes and all the works that he performs as the representative of heaven are means of serving the heavenly forbear. Therefore that his line should endure as long as heaven endures is a natural consequence of the order of things." [1]

This divinization of the sovereign was shattered by the events of the second World War, which left Shinto in the emancipated position of a free religion, on a par with other religions, but also deprived the people of Japan of that religious mooring to which they had been accustomed for generations. It is not likely that the ancient traditions will be easily abandoned; and although some are already speaking of a post-Shinto era, the experience of history suggests rather a new form of syncretism that will build on the best elements of the past.

NATIVE DEITIES

Of the three contributory sources to the religion of Japan—Buddhism, Confucianism and Shinto—only the latter is indigenous to the country, and most distinctive of the religious culture of its people. While Shinto has no sacred writings in the sense of revelation, its origins are rooted in two writings that fairly describe the spirit which still prevails. *Kojiki* or *Records of Ancients Matters,* and *Nihongi* or *Chronicles of Japan* were both compiled in the early eighth century of our era, when Japanese writers were already strongly influenced by Chinese traditions.

It is difficult to distinguish the pure native traditions in these works. Many of the events described are anachronistic, and many of the legends are chosen to confirm the religious or political claims of the ruling dynasty. Nevertheless certain strains of faith and methods of worship are so close to what we know of primitive religion that they seem to be authentically Japanese.

Shinto mythology begins with the creation of the islands in the archipelago by two gods, *Izanagi* (the Male-Who-Invites), and his wife *Izanami* (the Female-Who-Invites), who were commanded by the deities to "make, consolidate, and give birth to this drifting land." Izanami died in giving birth to the god of fire (*Kagutsuchi*). Overcome with grief, her spouse went down to the nether world to see the Female-Who-Invites, and she consented to return to him on condition that he did not look at her meanwhile. But in his impatience, he looked at her and saw the corruption of her body. She was angered by this impertinence and sent infernal deities to drive him out of Hades, where Izanami was left to be the great goddess of "the land of darkness."

Returning to earth, Izanagi purified himself, and from this purification were born many gods, of whom the most famous are the sun-goddess, born as he was washing his left eye; the moon-god when he washed his right eye; and *Susa-no-wo,* a god of swift impetuosity. Then follows a tedious record of the birth and copulation of further deities with names descriptive of their attributes and earthly function, until finally *Jimmu Tenno* is born as the fifth-generation descendant of the sun-goddess *Amaterasu.* At the age of forty-five, on February 11, 667 B.C., according to official chronology, Jimmu ascended the imperial throne and thus founded the Japanese dynasty.

The concept of God is expressed by the term *Kami* which means primarily "above" or "superior" and is applied first of all to the various divinities of heaven and earth mentioned in the ancient records, as well as to their spirits which reside in the shrines where they are worshiped. So characteristic is the term that the word *Shinto* is simply the Chinese reading of two characters meaning "The Way of the Gods," the way of the *Kami,* the native spirits of Japan as distinct from the deities of Buddhism, whose introduction from China in the middle of the sixth century A.D., was the reason for coining a distinctive name.

However not only human beings but animals, plants, trees, seas and mountains and all other things which deserved to be feared or revered for the extraordinary powers they possess, are called *Kami.* Among human beings, highest in rank as a *Kami* were the successive imperial rulers; and among the forces of nature, thunder, lightning and storms.

Although *Kami* are far removed from the idea of God as an infinite personal being, they possess two essential properties which qualify them as deities: knowledge and volition, and superhuman power. These two concepts may be united either by attributing sense and will to the great elemental objects and phenomena, or by applying to human and other living beings ideas of the mighty forces on whose operation the people constantly depend. Shinto therefore has two kinds of deities, nature-gods and man-gods, of whom the first are the result of personification and the latter of deification, although apologists frequently deny the fact and insist that their religion has been purified of nature worship. Perhaps the most plausible explanation is that the religion of the masses is still permeated with veneration of nature, which the more cultured Shintoists avoid.

Both categories of deities, man and nature gods, have further subdivisions, according as they are deities of individuals, of classes, or of qualities. They are all exemplified in Shinto. The sun-goddess represents an individual object; *Kukuchi,* the god of trees, a class; and *Musubi,* the god of growth, an abstract quality. *Jemangu* is a deified individual statesman, *Koyana* represents a clan or family, and *Taji-kara no wo* is a personified human quality (hand-strength-male).

Although the ancient Japanese produced many gods, they remained only feebly characterized. In fact most of them have no characters at all. They are popularly reckoned at eighty (or eight hundred) myriads. Admitting this as a poetic exaggeration, Shinto is essentially polytheistic and numbers its known deities in the hundreds. Yet there is a constant depletion by the mere lapse of memory, along with new deities that come into notice. Different gods may be identified with one another, others split into pairs of several gods, and the same deity at different places will have different rank and qualities.

HISTORICAL DEVELOPMENT

The earliest extensive reference to the religion of the Japanese comes to us from the histories of the Chinese dynasties, about 300 A.D., in which the typical Shinto stress on purity and purification is already evident. Speaking of the Japanese, the chronicler says, "When death occurs mourning is observed for more than ten days. When the funeral ceremonies are over, all members of the family go into the water together to cleanse themselves in a bath of purification." [2]

At this early stage the main features of the Japanese religion, besides polytheism, were a strong awareness of national solidarity occasioned by the insular geography of Japan, and a ritual concern for invoking the deities in order to be freed from legal impurities. Defilement for touching a dead body was only one of many such pollutions. It called for normal purification that implied no corresponding internal change of heart. As long as the *Kami* was invoked by someone outwardly clean, and if the mode of such invocation was technically correct, the aid of the spirit's magic power would be received, no matter how evil the mind or heart of the suppliant.

Then Buddhism entered Japan, about 552 A.D., through the envoys of the Korean king, who told the Japanese emperor that their "doctrine is among all doctrines the most excellent, but it is hard to explain and to comprehend." Even Confucius, they said, had not attained to a knowledge of it. This doctrine can create religious merit and retribution without measure and without bonds, and so lead on to a full possession of the highest wisdom. "Imagine a man in possession of treasures to his heart's content, so that he might satisfy all his wishes in proportion as he used them. Thus it is with the treasure of this wonderful doctrine. Every prayer is fulfilled and nothing is wanting." [3]

The Emperor Kimmei was delighted with the new religion and fostered it zealously, but the conservative elements at court objected, saying that the worship of foreign gods would bring ruin on the nation. Their opposition was short-lived, and up to the middle of the eighth century, when Buddhism in Japan reached its climax, the Korean import permeated every phase of Japanese religious thought and worship. Buddhist monks and images came in a steady stream from Korea, and Japanese went to China to learn about Buddhist doctrines and Chinese customs. Soon Japan had absorbed the more advanced Chinese religious culture, while adapting what it received to its own preferences and past.

The climax was reached in 765 A.D. when the Empress Suiko Tenno, who was an ardent Buddhist, published an edict on the occasion of the feast of the First Fruits. Its fertility connections made the festival a distinctively Shinto rite, yet the empress passed a decree that showed how deeply Buddhism had penetrated the royal house. "My duties are first to serve the Three Treasures (Buddha, the Buddhist law, and its monasteries), next to worship the Spirits (of Shinto mythology), and finally to cherish my people." Her subjects had only to examine the sacred writings of their country to find it is proper for Shinto deities to protect and respect the teachings of Buddha.[4]

Meantime Confucianism had entered the stream of Japanese belief to reshape its ethical side. Like Buddhism, the morals of Confucius came into Japan from China by way of Korea, as early as the beginning of the fifth century. But the first sign of a decisive influence of Confucianism appeared during the reign of Prince Shotoku (572-621), who promulgated the classic "Seventeen Article Constitution" in 604 to buttress the position of the central government. Its main provisions borrow the Confucian ideal of obedience of the people towards their sovereign, and the need for harmony between rulers and subjects on every level of communal authority.

Shotoku, like the empress in the next century, paid his respects to Buddhism in the Constitution, whose Confucian norm of "the mean" was wedded to the Shinto concept of the emperor as a descendant of the gods. The norm of morality (still valid in Shinto) is the voice of custom. "How can anyone lay down a rule by which to distinguish right from wrong? For we are all, one with another, wise and foolish, like a ring which has no end. Therefore, although others give way to anger, let us on the contrary dread our own faults, and though we alone may be in the right, let us follow the multitude and act like them." [5] Such is the norm prescribed for matters of interest; but where public policy is concerned, incontestable authority is in the sovereign.

When you receive the imperial commands, fail not scrupulously to obey them. The lord is Heaven, the vassal is Earth. Heaven overspreads, and Earth upbears. When this is so, the four seasons follow their due course, and the powers of Nature obtain their efficacy. If the Earth attempted to overspread, Heaven would simply fall in ruin. Therefore is it that when the lord speaks, the vassal listens; when the superior acts, the inferior yields compliance. Consequently when you receive the imperial commands, fail not to carry them out scrupulously. Let there be a want of care in this matter, and ruin is the natural consequence.[6]

The process of amalgamation went on apace, with deep Buddhist and Confucian elements entering Japanese religious faith and worship. From Buddhism, Shinto supplied the deficiency of image-making, which made the national religion more personal and concrete, and served to fill out the scanty and vague outlines of its mythology. Above all Buddhism gave Shinto a philosophical framework on which the popular piety and state worship were able to construct a systematic religious structure, whose moral fiber was in large measure borrowed from Confucianism.

Besides the general leavening influence, the unionist tendency produced a number of real Buddhist-Shinto hybrids that have survived to the present day. *Shingon* or the True Word sect was founded by Kobo Daishi (774-835), a Japanese sage, who went to China to study Buddhism and returned to organize a pantheistic mixture which claims the universe is a dual manifestation of national and indestructible elements of a Buddha identified with the sun-goddess of Shinto.

By the middle ages, the blending of Buddhism and Shinto ceremonies became almost universal. Since most of the shrines were controlled by Buddhists, their images were worshiped as representatives of the Shinto gods, and Buddhist ritual equipment was used alongside the customary paper streamers and ropes. Although monks and nuns were not allowed to penetrate the inner sanctuary of certain Shinto shrines, like that of the sun-goddess at Ise, and individual Buddhist sects kept aloof from Shinto, by and large the two religions had combined in a fusion which still remains a general feature of Japanese religious life. Its technical name is *honji suijaku,* which means that the real basic entity (*honji*) is Buddhism, while the material and localized manifestation of religion (*suijaku*) is Shinto.

Inevitably periodic attempts were made to purify Shinto of its foreign (mostly Buddhist) accretions. Mongol invasions in 1274 and 1281 aroused a new sense of Japanese loyalty, and the successful repression of the invaders was interpreted as proof of protection by the native gods. Not long after a Shinto patriot, Kitabatake (1293-1354), wrote his *Records of the Legitimate Succession of the Divine Sovereigns,* to show the supremacy of Japan over China and India because Japan's single line of emperors was descended from the gods. About the same time were forged the *Five Classics,* which purported to have been written in distant antiquity and attempted to set forth a Shinto philosophy and ethics, ostensibly native, yet really borrowed from Buddhism and Confucianism.

"Japan is the divine country," wrote Kitabatake. "The heavenly ancestor it was who first laid its foundations, and the Sun Goddess left her descendants to reign over it for ever and ever. This is true only of our country, and nothing similar may be found in foreign lands. That is why it is called the divine country." [7] A century later, the chief figure in the "Primal Shinto" school was Yoshida Kanetomo (1435-1511), who did not try to discredit Buddhism but sought instead to shift the emphasis to Shinto while admitting the union. He explained *honji suijaku* to mean that the Japanese gods were the original substance, whereas Buddha and the *bodhisattvas* were the material, localized traces.

Yoshida depended much on the forged classics, and when these failed to meet his needs he supplied previously undiscovered sources of his own. His most famous statement has become proverbial in oriental literature. "During the reign of the Empress Suiko, the thirty-fourth sovereign, Prince Shotoku (*c.* 765 A.D.) stated in a memorial that Japan was the roots and trunk in civilization, China its branches and leaves, and India its flowers and fruit. Similarly, Buddhism is the flowers and fruit of all laws, Confucianism their branches and leaves, and Shinto their roots and trunk. Thus all foreign doctrines are offshoots of Shinto." [8]

RISE OF PURE SHINTO

The triumvirate which did most to purge Shinto of alien elements were Kamo Mabuchi (1697-1769), Motoori Norinaga (1730-1801), and Hirata Atsutane (1776-1843). By their research into Japan's classics and appropriation of what they considered best in the nation's tradition, they provided both a scraper to remove the layers of foreign, mostly Chinese and Indian, lacquer, and the key to open the Japanese treasure that lay beneath. Their combined contributions are the most significant in Shinto history and have joined to produce all the distinctive features of "the Way of the gods."

Kamo Mabuchi was the first scholar of national importance in the Shinto revival. He argued that the *Manyoshu* poetry of the eighth century, an anthology of ancient classics, had been free of foreign influences and represented a true concept of the Japanese spirit in an uncorrupted form. These compositions, he asserted, "are the natural expression of our ancient heritage; they are the voice of our divine land." Mabuchi then set about composing poetry of his own, in the *Manyosha* style, and won remarkable success. Soon other writers followed his lead and their productions inaugurated a religious crusade that went straight to the heart of the Japanese, surmounting all intellectual and class barriers. The creative participation of the people won for this movement a more widespread acceptance than volumes of learned speculation.

In his *Study of the Idea of a Nation,* Mabuchi wrote in pure Japanese and attacked Chinese thought which he calls Confucian but that more certainly was a Taoist perversion of Confucianism. His contention was that Japan had prospered under its own spiritual ideals, only to have them corrupted by the intrusions from China.

Japan in ancient days was governed in accordance with the natural laws of Heaven and earth. There was never any indulgence in such petty nationalizing as marked China, but when suddenly these teachings were transmitted here from abroad, they quickly spread, for the men of old in their simplicity took them for the truth. In Japan there had been generation after generation, extending back to the remote past, which had known prosperity, but no sooner were these Confucian teachings propagated here than in the time of Emperor Temmu (631-686) a great rebellion occurred. Later, at Nara (in central Japan), the palace, dress, and ceremonies were Chinesified, and everything took on a superficial elegance; under the surface, however, contentiousness and dishonesty became more prevalent.[9]

Mabuchi is less critical of Buddhism. He concedes that "Confucianism made men crafty" and that some people speak ill of Buddhism. But since the latter "is a teaching which makes men stupid, it does not represent a grave evil; after all, rulers do not prosper unless the people are stupid," on the Taoist principle that knowledge surely leads to greed and ambition and therefore to disorder and rejection of authority.

He rests his case on what he calls "a country of wicked-heartedness," namely, China; there no amount of profound instruction, even from a genius like Confucius, could convert the people from their evil ways. "Japan," on the contrary, "has always been a country where the people are honest." The tragedy was that a foreign import was allowed to enter the country and corrupt the minds of a naturally law-abiding nation. He appeals to the past and urges a return to the times when "we worked in accordance with the will of Heaven and earth," whose living symbol was the reigning monarch.

The emperor was the sun and the moon, and the subjects the stars. If the subjects as stars protect the sun and moon, they will not hide it as is now the case. Just as the sun, moon and stars have always been in Heaven, so our imperial sun and moon, and the stars his vassals, have existed without change from ancient days, and have ruled the world fairly. However, some knaves appeared, and as a result the emperor is diminished in power, and his subjects too have fallen off. The *Age of the Gods* is where we may gain a knowledge of this.[10]

In order to restore the original glory of Japan, let the people examine the words and thoughts of her early writers, and find there the promise which Shinto holds for the future.

Motoori Norinaga went beyond his teacher Kamo. He recognized that an enduring religious movement needs more scriptural authority than even the most elevated literature can give. His first task was to reinstate the first Japanese annals, the *Kojiki,* to their deserved place as the primeval source of the national religion. Though compiled in 712 A.D., the *Kojiki* had long been neglected owing to the greater popularity of the official chronicle, the *Nihongi.* Besides the *Kojiki* were a deplorable maze of curious legends and genealogical records of the emperors which afforded small room for reflection, coupled with anecdotes that the first Western translators prudently rendered into Latin.

But Motoori was not discouraged. He reasoned that whatever belongs to gods and goddesses is beyond human comprehension, and redirected the principles of Shinto by shifting the emphasis away from philosophy and ethics (as in Buddhism and Confucianism) to an emotional response to the deities. First he insisted on the ancient communication from the gods to the human race, in a period which he calls the Divine Age, which some had perverted to suit their own ends.

No one knows with whom these ancient traditions began, but they were handed down orally from the very earliest times and they refer to the accounts which have since been recorded in the *Kojiki* and the *Nihongi.* The accounts recorded in these two scriptures are clear and explicit and present no cause for doubt. Those who have interpreted these scriptures in a later age have contrived oracular formulae and have expounded theories which have no real basis. Some have become addicts of foreign doctrines and have no faith in the wonders of the Divine Age. Unable to understand that the truths of the world are contained in the evolution of the Divine Age, they fail to ascertain the true meaning of our ancient tradition.[11]

Not a few Japanese, he charged, presumed to interpret the Way of the Gods (*Shinto*) on the principles of a foreign religion. Denying that the sun-goddess was divine, they claim she was only "an earthly person and forebear of the nation." These are "arbitrary interpretations purposely contrived to flatter foreign ideologies."

Coming to grips with the fundamental issue of rationalism, that all things religious may be understood by the human mind, Motoori is at pains to show that man's reason is inadequate to comprehend the wondrous manifestations of the power of the gods, and mocks at the Confucian pretension that we have a rational answer to every problem. The objection was raised that, "You are obstinate in insisting that the Sun-Goddess is the sun in heaven. If this is so, perpetual darkness must have reigned everywhere before her birth."

Motoori at first sidesteps the difficulty. "I cannot understand," he tells the objector, "why you say that I am obstinate. That the Sun-Goddess is the sun in heaven is clear from the records of the *Kojiki* and the *Nihohgi*." Then he appeals to a higher principle, to the fact that divine revelation must of necessity surpass the understanding of man.

The acts of the gods cannot be measured by ordinary human reasoning. Man's intellect, however wise, has its limit. It is small, and what is beyond its confines it cannot know. The acts of the gods are straightforward. That they appear to be shallow and untrue is due to the limitation of what man can know. To the human mind, these acts appear to be remote, inaccessible, and difficult of comprehension and belief. Chinese teachings, on the other hand, were established within the reach of human intelligence; thus to the mind of the listener, they are familiar and intimate and easy of comprehension and belief. The Chinese, because they believe that the wisdom of the Sage (Confucius) was capable of comprehending all the truths of the universe and of its phenomena, pretend to the wisdom of the Sage and insist, despite their small and limited minds, that they know what their minds are really incapable of knowing.[12]

At the same time, the Chinese "refuse to believe in the inscrutability of the truth," handed down from the divinities, for this, they conclude, would be irrational. "This sounds clever, but on the contrary, it betrays the pettiness of their intelligence," which refuses to confess its limitations before the superior intellects of the gods.

Then follows one of the most cogent argumentations in all Shinto literature. Beginning with the premise that the "Way of the gods" must be above the comprehension of man, Motoori turns the table on the Confucianists and runs through a litany of purely natural phenomena that, by Confucian principles, should be explainable and yet are mysterious. By what right, then, do they question the mysteries of the gods if they cannot account for mysteries of physical nature. "Thus," Motoori concludes, "the universe and all things therein are without a single exception strange and wondrous when examined carefully. Even the Sage would be incapable of explaining these phenomena. So, one must acknowledge that human intelligence is limited and puny while the acts of the gods are illimitable and wondrous." [13]

As the most analytic spokesman for Shinto in modern times, Motoori's concept of good and evil, and their relation to the gods may be accepted as traditional. "All things in life, great and small, and their very existence in the universe, even man himself and his actions—are due to the spirits of the gods and their disposition of things." However not everything is good, but some things are evil and others a mixture of both. Whence evil in the world? "Such things," says Motoori, "are the acts of the evil deities. The evil deities are those who do all manner of evil, moved by the spirit of the deity," which appears to be a kind of fatalism. "When such evil deities flourish and are unchecked, there are times when even the protective powers of the shining deities prove inadequate." In proof of which we have the ancient writings, that "this has been true since the Divine Age" described in ancient scriptures.

The analysis proceeds to examine the most palpable of human evils, death, on which every possible theory has been concocted, but without convincing evidence. "Some foreign doctrines teach that death should not be regarded as profoundly sorrowful, while others assert that one's actions and attitude of mind in this life can modify the situation after death. So comprehensive and detailed are these explanations that people have been deluded into thinking they are true." All that we know about death is what was "fixed in the Divine Age and recorded in the *Kojiki* and *Nihongi*." They teach that death is, indeed, sorrowful, and that "the land of death is situated beneath the ground or at the bottom of the earth. It is an extremely dirty and evil land, where the dead go." [14] Before all these "pointless theories" about man's destiny were invented, people simply believed in the truth that at death they would go to the land of death, and death was cause for them to weep in sorrow. More than this is human speculation.

Hirata Atsutane completed the work of his predecessors, Kamo and Motoori. Where the latter had succeeded in making "national learning" based on Japanese antiquity a subject worthy of a scholar's attention and thereby restored the sacred writings to a place of respect, Hirata sought to make Shinto supreme in Japan as a religion and as a body of knowledge. His blend of extreme nationalism and real scholarship did much to shape the destinies of his country up to the present day.

Whereas Motoori was satisfied to show that Shinto had a rightful place alongside Buddhism and Confucian thought, Hirate insisted that there was room for nothing else. He also modified the concept of Shinto as more than just a religious faith, by extending its boundaries to include other forms of knowledge.

Instead of decrying foreign ideologies, Hirata preferred to absorb them. "All the various types of learning, including Confucianism and Buddhism, are joined in Japanese learning, just as the many rivers flow into the sea, where the waters are joined." [15] Otherwise than Kamo and Motoori, he urged the Japanese to study "all the different kinds of learning," even those of the West, "so that they can choose the good features of each and place them at the service of the nations." This was daring eclecticism, in which the people of Japan were credited with a spontaneous ability to recognize the good in alien religious systems. His self-assurance was based on the heavenly lineage of the nation. "Even in countries where our ancient traditions have not been transmitted, the peoples recognize Japan as a divine land because of the majestic effulgence that of itself emanates from our country." [16] Consequently people now everywhere refer to Japan as the Land of the Gods.

Hirata borrowed at times from Christian theological writings and integrated his findings with Shinto mythology. Books by Christians had been banned in Japan for almost two hundred years, but Hirata is known to have obtained copies of at least three written in Chinese by Catholic missionaries in Peking. In one early essay, for example, he took with slight adaptations the arguments of Mathew Ricci in favor of Christianity and used them against Confucianism in order to bolster the cause of Shinto.

Among the areas where Hirata's Christian borrowings seem to be most evident are his treatment of creation and life after death. Still imbedded in Shinto parlance, they are quite un-Shintoist in the doctrines expressed.

Writing in *Kodo Taii* (Summary of the Ancient Way), Hirata examines the origins of the word *Mi-musubi,* and concludes that while the ancient records speak of two gods who made the sun and moon, the name itself "stems from their miraculous creative power" which should rightly be attributed to a single deity, *Takami-musubi,* whom he sometimes calls *Kami-musubi,* as another aspect of the same divinity.

Takami-musubi must be credited with the creation of Heaven and earth . . . a god of incomparable power. Without doubt he resides in Heaven and reigns over the world. Despite the pellucidly clear nature of these truths, scholars whose minds have been damaged by Chinese and Indian learning—as well as people who in their ignorance display impious disbelief—do not understand that the very fact of their own birth is immediately attributable to the creative power of this god. They persist in their scepticism and declare that the ancient truths are merely legends peculiar to Japan which they refuse to believe. These truths are by no means confined to Japan. In many other countries it is believed that the seed of man and all other things owe their existence to the powers of this god.[17]

To prove his point, Hirata refers to certain Confucian writers who believed in a single, ultimate divinity; he identifies the Hindu Brahma with this creator of heaven and earth. Then most pertinently, he says that "far to the west of India are numerous other countries, and in each of them are traditions of a god of Heaven who created the heavens and earth, man and all things.[18]

So convinced was he of these discoveries, that he took issue with his teacher Motoori on the correlative doctrine of life after death. "Accounts of the afterworld," he admitted, "are so confused it is only natural that they arouse bewilderment. Even my teacher did not escape this confusion." Hirata vacillated in his own position, and is embarrassed by the legends in the old Japanese mythology, but the general outline of his teachings is nevertheless remarkably Western.

He admits that the more common belief is that the dead spirits go to *Yomi,* the foul netherworld described by Motoori. But, he argues, the spirit of man is not his body, it is of a different nature than the corpse left behind when a man dies. Hesitant about making a universal judgment, he says, "this is one reason why we know that all human souls do not go to Yomi. Since the soul is bestowed on man by the god Musubi, by nature it should return to Heaven.

However, I have not yet found positive evidence or old traditions to prove that this is true of all men." [19] He might have added that traditional Shinto belief was quite to the contrary.

Consistent with the belief in immortality and the prospect of happiness after death, Hirata chided those "self-important scholars (who) conclude that the realm of the dead does not exist, simply because they do not see it, but this is exceedingly foolish." Rather, man's lot in the "realm of the dead" is somehow conditioned by his status and condition during life on earth. "Their souls become gods, differing in the degree of excellence, virtue, and strength according to the individual." [20] Apparently, he assumed that all souls reach beatitude, and implicitly rejected the Buddhist theory of endless reincarnations and the ambiguous existence-less Nirvana.

MEIJI ERA TO THE PRESENT. Shortly after the death of Atsutane, yet without the impress of his clear insight, "Pure Shinto" was one of the factors which brought about the Restoration of 1868, when the Mikado, Emperor Meiji, ascended to effective power as offspring of the sun-goddess. The Meiji era (1868-1912) crystallized the traditional concept of a divine sovereign and at least temporarily increased the popularity of Shinto. However, the government felt constrained to distinguish between two types of Shinto: the Shinto of the shrines (*jinja,* god houses) and Shinto of the churches (*kyokai*). *Jinja* meant the buildings which the government either took over or had erected for the performance of a national ritual, while *kyokai* were the religious edifices for church services by the various (about a dozen) Shinto sects. Priests serving the *jinja* were state supported, the others depended on voluntary contributions. Sect Shinto, along with Buddhism and Christianity, was given freedom of worship and propaganda by the 1889 Constitution.

Before long the political interests of the country tended to obliterate the distinction between the two types of Shinto, and for years Christians and others were subjected to grave hardships by the duty of joining in shrine Shinto ceremonies and education, which the state insisted was not strictly religious. Catholic consciences, for example, were relieved in 1936 when Rome allowed participation in the *jinja* because it was "a mere civil expression of patriotism."

In the years immediately preceding the war and during the conflict, Shinto ideology reigned supreme. Statements were issued to reassure the people of their divine ancestry and the heavenly mandates of the emperor. Then came the humiliating defeat of Japan in 1945 and with it disappeared by official proclamation the centuries old status of the emperor's divinity and the more recent innovation of shrine Shinto.

In his New Year's message to the nation in 1946, the reigning emperor Hirohito declared, "The ties between Us and Our people have always stood upon mutual trust and affection. They do not depend upon mere legends and myths. They are not predicated upon the false conception that the emperor is divine and that the Japanese people are superior to other races and are fated to rule the world." A few weeks earlier (December 15) State Shinto and all it stood for was abolished with the incisive statement that "the perversion of Shinto theory and beliefs into militaristic and ultra-nationalist propaganda" had plunged the Japanese nation into a tragic war.

BASIC PRINCIPLES AND PRACTICES

Apart from isolated exceptions among scholars like Atsutane, the Shinto deities worshiped by the masses are called *Kami* because they cover such a large variety of entities, quite literally anything which custom or the religious fancy has divinized by the attribution of supra-human qualities. The *Kami* are universally conceived in anthropomorphic terms. They are born, get married, beget offspring, work, play and die. Without being omnipotent or all-knowing, they are gifted with extraordinary powers, though limited to their respective spheres. They have a kind of soul, called *mi-tama,* represented in the temples by a "substitute for the *mi-tama*" or *shintai,* that may be any object, like a mirror or stone, in which the divinity abides invisibly incorporated in order to enter into contact with the faithful. These objects are not mere symbols nor divine attributes but quasi-incarnations of myriad deities. Everything has its particular god, from rain to smoke, and from rice to a peasant's barn. Added to these are the ancestors, of family, clan and country, which Shinto introduced according to the Confucian faith.

Although primitive Shinto did not have a set code of morality, a rudimentary ethical principle was early developed in the concept of purity and the parallel horror of contamination, based on a mysterious relationship to the gods. The purity was mainly ritual and physical, not moral, and contamination either visible (through contact with dirt), or invisible (through contact with such impure things as blood or a cadaver). A contaminated person was displeasing to the gods and had to be cleansed to avoid *tatari* or heavenly punishment, by death, suffering or some misfortune.

This notion of an extrinsic morality, with only a vague recognition of what the Judaeo-Christian world calls the natural law concretized in the Decalogue, is still characteristic of Shinto. Western scholars point out that Shinto has hardly anything in the shape of a moral system. The *Ohoharahi,* a service in which the Mikado, by divine authority, declared to his ministers and people absolution of their offenses against the gods, makes no explicit mention of any one of the sins of the Decalogue. No doubt there are moral elements in the *Ohoharahi,* but they are scanty. Not only is there no mention of the sins commonly understood, but they are scarcely condemned even by implication. Shintoists do not deny this feature of their religion, but say that the absence of a code of ethics is proof that the natural goodness of a people does not need such artificial aids to virtuous conduct. Actually the ethical elements in Shinto are numerous, but largely inherited from Confucianism.

A stress on legal defilement was balanced by a similar emphasis on ritual purification, still considered one of the mainstays of Shinto. Three types of cleansing are dominant: through exorcism (*harai*), ablution, especially with water (*misogi*), and abstension (*imi*).

The most ancient of these rites, *harai,* is regularly done by priests. It consists of reading from a sacred text and making an offering by which the sins pass away in the course of the recitation, in a way similar to the familiar scapegoat in Mosaic legislation. After the ceremony, the expiatory gifts are thrown into the fire or the sea, or otherwise destroyed. Originally the gifts were some personal belonging of the penitent, but later on they assumed a symbolic function. A common practice is to use slips of paper on which the penitent writes his sex and the year and month of birth, then proceeds to rub his body with the paper and breathe upon it, by which his own sins pass on to the symbolic substitute (*katashiro*). When the ceremony is made in a group, all the *katashiro* are gathered together and thrown into the fire or sea.

Of the other types of cleansing, *misogi* may be done privately with water, or water and salt, to remove minor contaminations as a result of sickness, marital relations and the like. The *imi* are mainly protective practices against impurity, as keeping the body free from dirt, eating certain kinds of food cooked over the open flame and wearing of purifying garments. Priests are normally required to administer the *imi* to the people.

Shinto temples are classified in hierarchical order, at the head of which are the *jingu,* or temples, associated with a particular level of holiness. Such are the temples of Ise and Atsuta. All others are called *jinga,* which in turn are classified as "temples of State," where until recently were held the civil ceremonies of State Shinto; "provincial temples" for larger geographical areas; "city temples" for the main urban districts; and "rural (or village) temples" which are most numerous.

The principal Shinto shrine of Ise is located at Uji-Yamada, in central Japan and southeast of Kyoto. It has two temples, an interior one dedicated to the goddess of the sun, and an exterior one to the goddess of food. Founded in ancient times, the temples are periodically torn down and reconstructed, with amulets made of the wood from the old structure. Pilgrimages to Ise are a common religious event, on which a man's success or failure in life is believed to depend.

CLERGY AND FESTIVALS

In view of the close connection for centuries between Shinto worship and the secular government, it is not surprising that the clergy have in many cases not risen above the level of civil functionaries. However with the passing away of the established religion, the clergy associated with popular Shinto have come into their own, with a recognized religious status and corresponding ritual duties. Originally stratified in a kind of hierarchy, from the grand-master of the temple of Ise to the lowest *shisho* connected with the village places of worship, Shinto priests now belong principally to one of the numerous sects that had always been distinct from the government sponsored religion.

For almost a century, the state religion found its main outlet in the celebration of rites considered necessary to the deepening of national unity. In its traditional form, the main element in shrine functions was the reading by priests of ritualistic prayers (*norito*) before the altars of the gods, asking for a good harvest, peaceful family life, success in war, sufficiency of food and a long life for the emperor. These activities continue, with understandable changes, in the new era, directed as much to satisfy the religious aspirations of the people as to consolidate their sense of racial solidarity.

Upwards of fifty major religious festivals are presently celebrated in Japan. Their number and variety offer a good cross-section of the variegated nature of the Japanese religion: Shinto in its ethnic tradition and worship of the national gods, Buddhist in the metaphysical groundwork that underlies it, and Confucian in the application of religious values to private and social morality.

Early in January is celebrated the Bullfinch Exchange Feast of the Dazaifu shrine, slightly north of Nagasaki. On the evening of the festival (January 7), the people flock to the shrine precincts and in the dim light of the small bonfire they pass quickly from hand to hand small bullfinch-shaped pieces of wood. In the meantime, twelve gilt ones are passed out in the crowds by the shrine priests without exciting any suspicion. Those who finally end up with the coveted golden bullfinches are assured of special blessing from the gods.

On March 12 is held the time-honored exorcism festival of the Todaiji temple at Nara in central Japan. Twelve large torch stands are brought onto a stage. Each stand has at the top a large round iron basket in which a fire is kept burning. Young priests brandish the burning torches by drawing circles of fire and shaking off the burning pieces. The people make a rush to gather up these fragments which are believed to have special power against malicious spirits. At two in the morning begins the water-drawing ceremony, accompanied by ancient Japanese music. While priests draw water from the sacred well, other priests blow conch horns, as a harbinger of heavenly blessings on the spring.

The greatest of all festival is the *Higan,* the spring and autumn equinoxes, both of which are national holidays. At *Higan* the farmers invoke and thank the gods for good crops, which is the Shinto part of the celebration. Simultaneously the Buddhist temples throughout the country during a whole week hold special services in honor of the dead. People visit the tombs of their ancestors to do homage to the memory of their departed.

The *Gion* religious festival in mid-summer, observed at Kyoto, may justly be considered the representative celebration of modern Japan. Dating back to the ninth century, it commemorates the permission then given by the head priest of the famous Yasaka shrine to a large number of men and women to escort the decorated shrine carts as an act of prayer to the gods for protection against the pestilence then raging in the city. Typical of the *Gion* are the huge, colored floats paraded in the city to the accompaniment of music. *Yama* floats, covered with Shinto mythological figures, are carried by long poles; the *hoko* floats, rising to a height of more than a hundred feet, are hung with lanterns that for many people have lost their original significance as offerings to the gods.

A NEW ERA

When State Shinto was formally suppressed in 1945, the effect on the nation was less drastic than might have been expected. For a while the people reacted strongly against the religious system which the Japanese militarists had used to exploit their extreme nationalism and plunge the country into a disastrous war. But soon the age-old traditions began to reassert themselves, and the ancient faith found new expression, even without the government support that some felt was indispensable for the continued existence of Shinto.

Prior to the decree of suppression, sectarian Shinto was relatively unimportant, although nourished by association with the state religion. When the latter passed out of the picture, the sects came into their own to fill the vacuum thus created, and they show every promise of flourishing under the status of religious liberty guaranteed by the Constitution.

Within a month after Hirohito publicly disclaimed his divine lineage and frankly called emperor-worship a legendary myth, the previously obscure sects formed (February 3, 1946) a religious organization in which they combined with the former representatives of State Shinto. Under the title *Jinja-honcho* (Central Administration of the Jinjas), they have their headquarters at the temple of the Emperor Meiji at Tokyo, and chose for president the ex-prince Nobusuke Takutsakasa. This promptly identified the federation with the royal family.

If the *Jinja-honcho* attaches little importance to doctrinal issues beyond the acceptance of the traditional Japanese gods, it promotes a steady program of propaganda, urging the people to recover their former heritage and has undertaken a careful preparation of its priests, not only in Japan but through studies in other countries. In 1951, after the peace treaty was signed at San Francisco and Japan regained her sovereignty, the *Jinja-honcho* was authorized to participate in the temple services for the soldiers who had died in the late war. The following year it received legal recognition, according to the provisions of the law that had been passed in 1945, which meant the reinstatement of Shinto as one of the major religions of Japan.

Heading the new Shinto is the president assisted by his council, which is subdivided into functionary departments. The primary temple remains the shrine at Ise to the sun-goddess Amaterasu, ancestress of the royal family, but otherwise the temples are not mutually dependent, as they had been before the war. Their position is technically one of equality, while retaining fidelity to historic traditions. Several periodicals are published by *Jinja-honcho*, directed to "promoting the prosperity of the Shinto temples, inculcating the eternal laws of sound morality, offering of sacrificial actions in order to obtain blessings from the divinity (*Kami*), advancing a way of life under the constant influence of the same divinity, favoring of legitimate traditions and good customs, and contributing to the welfare of humanity."

Little by little the temples destroyed by the war are being rebuilt and the number of worshipers increases annually, without the government directly entering the religious scene.

To all appearances the association is growing rapidly, although accurate statistics cannot be found. In Japan it is no contradiction for one person to belong simultaneously to several religions, especially Shinto and Buddhism. Official sources place the adherents of *Jinja-honcho* at more than fifty percent of the national population with some ninety thousand *jinjas*. Other estimates divide the given number of adherents by three, while admitting the figure on the number of shrines.

What complicates the picture is the shifting religious status of the people, who may favor all three major Japanese religious, including Confucianism, and attend now one kind of function, now another, without feeling any inconsistency in the practice. As a rule Buddhism is associated with the darker and more sombre aspects of religion, and Shinto with the brighter and more joyful. So that weddings are normally under Shinto auspices, and for funerals the Buddhist services are preferred.

Yet Shinto offers the common people a hopeful outlook which Buddhism cannot supply. In referring to the death of a man, the Buddhist will say he has become a *hotoke,* a candidate for annihilation, whereas the Shintoist says the equivalent of "he has become a saint." Some years ago a Japanese scholar analyzed about ten thousand prayer-formulas used in Shinto worship. He found that almost without exception they refer to prosperity and happiness in this life, with a special concern for families and other persons, in contrast with the native individualism of the Buddhist philosophy of life.

Preoccupation with this-worldly values, however, makes Shinto an easy prey to Western secularization, of which Japanese religious leaders are deeply aware. Japan is the most highly industrialized nation in Asia; it is also the most densely populated. Despite its impressive efforts and results, demographers, both Western and Japanese, do not believe Japan can sustain an increase in population. Emigration has few available outlets. As a consequence, the moral conscience of the people has been put to a severe test by the so-called Eugenics Protection Law, legalizing abortion, sterilization and the sale of contraceptives. Japan has reported the sharpest birth decline in any nation in modern history, yet inherited new problems that Japanese spokesmen fear will take more than the ancient "Religion of the gods" to solve.

10. Sikhism

IKHISM is one of the least known living religions of the world, and yet one of the most interesting from the viewpoint of comparative history. Although practically confined to a single province of the Indian Republic, the Punjab region in the north-western part of the country, the Sikhs have made more than a proportionate contribution to the religious culture of their times. They are sometimes lightly dismissed as a hybrid of two old religions, Islam and Hinduism, made into one, as though it were really possible to fuse two such completely different concepts of life. Or again they are described as Hindus who have simply grafted Moslem monotheism on to the trunk of the ancient Vedas; that most of their other doctrines are taken directly from Hinduism, with little if any change. Sikhism, therefore, is an example of conscious syncretism and one of the few that has ever been successful.

While these estimates are correct enough descriptively, they do not take into account the radical differences which separate the followers of Nanak, the founder of Sikhism, from all their contemporaries; differences that are rooted in a wholly distinctive philosophy of man's relations with God.

ORIGINS AND DEVELOPMENT

To understand the nature of Sikhism, it is important to know the state of affairs in northern India before the birth of Nanak. The chaotic condition of the country was occasioned by the decadent state of Hinduism and by the remorseless pressure of the Moslems who invaded India and by the eleventh century practically dominated most of its northern regions.

Early in the twelfth century a Hindu reformer, Jaidev, used a

phrase that was later to become a key-word of Sikhism: he taught
that all religious ceremonial and austerity were as nothing compared with the devout repetition of God's name. This inroad of
Islam was strengthened by the Moslem teacher Kabir (died 1398),
who accepted the Hindu theory of retributive justice—Karma and
reincarnation—but as a Moslem insisted on the fact that God is a
single particular personality who should be worshiped and invoked.
Upon this basis of ethical monotheism, the founder of Sikhism
established his new religion.

Guru Nanak (1469-1539) was the son of a petty official living
some thirty miles from Lahore. He began studying Hinduism and
Islam almost from boyhood and after marrying and rearing a family
decided to become an ascetic. He prayed, fasted and meditated a
great deal, until finally he felt qualified to convey his message to
the people. His early preaching was very simple, which he summarized in the statement, "There is no Hindu, there is no Mussulman."

Unlike other ascetics, however, Nanak decided to combine his
mission with the domestic obligations of a husband and father, and
to this end advocated a way of life that allowed for the fulfilment
of family and civic duties along with the spiritual. When he died,
Moslems and Hindus vied with one another for the possession of
his body, and to this day his name is a symbol of harmony between
the two religions. A popular couplet speaks of him, "Guru Nanak,
the King of Fakirs, to the Hindu a Guru, to the Mussulman a Pir,"
in which the terms *guru* (counsellor), *fakir* (ascetic), and *pir*
(religious mentor) are indiscriminately applied to him by both
parties.

Nanak was followed by nine other Gurus, who succeeded him
on the basis of their knowledge of the master's teaching and devotion to his cause. For two centuries this succession provided Sikhism with the stability it needed to become consolidated as a religion, and gradually into a political state. A testament of the fifth
Guru, Arjun (1563-1606), illustrates how completely the Sikhs
had liberated themselves of Moslems and Hindus within a century
of their founder's death.

I do not keep the Hindu fast, nor the Muslim Ramadan.
I serve Him alone who is my refuge.

I serve the one Master, who is also Allah.
I have broken with the Hindu and the Muslim.
I will not worship with the Hindu, nor like the Muslim go to Mecca.
I shall serve Him and no other.
I will not pray to idols nor say the Muslim prayer.
I shall put my heart at the feet of the one Supreme Being.
For we are neither Hindus nor Mussulmans.[1]

After the death of Arjun, Sikhism underwent a major transformation. Conscious of the need to protect themselves by armed force against persecution from Moslems and Hindus, the Sikhs began to train in the art of self-defense and to this day are characterized by their skill in the use of arms.

Under the leadership of Guru Gobind Singh (1666-1708), the Sikhs were further developed into a military group with an inner fraternity which adopted certain customs that have become typical of their religion and (where practiced) still distinguish them externally from Hindus and Mohammedans. They were to wear the five K's: the *kes* or long hair on head and chin, the *kungha* or comb, the *kuchha* or short drawers, the *kara* or steel bracelet, and the *kirpan* or steel dagger. They were to abstain from smoking and alcoholic beverages, refrain from entering marriage with Moslems, and eat meat, if they had not done so already. After a "baptismal" ceremony, which consisted of drinking sweetened water out of a common bowl (as a mark of casteless brotherhood), they adopted the common prefix *Singh* (lion) added to their family name. Actually the Singhs originally came out of the main body of Sikhs and have since stood out in dramatic contrast to the more pacifist group which they now outnumber. The latter, called the *Nanakpanthis* (followers of Nanak) have a variety of sects and have been all but absorbed into the mainstream of Hinduism.

With the death of Gobind Singh ended the line of the Gurus. On orders from Gobind before he died, the Sikhs were henceforth to rely solely on their sacred writings (*Granth*) for spiritual guidance and solidarity. True to this injunction, they have had secular rulers only, while the Granth is literally worshiped at the Golden Temple in Amritsar.

Through the eighteenth century, the political history of the Sikhs had been a succession of wars, first of confederacy to organize the various factions against their surrounding enemies, and then of self-defense against the British. In 1849 the last Sikh ruler, Dalip Singh, surrendered to the English and as a token of submission and pledge of loyalty gave to Queen Victoria the famous Koh-i-nur diamond. When the Moslems and Hindus rebelled in 1857, the Sikhs supported the British and helped save India for the English crown. This and similar evidence of their fidelity and military prowess gave the Sikhs an ascendancy in India and elsewhere in the East out of all proportion to their numbers. They became the favorite constabulary of the British colonial authorities.

With the partition of India in 1947, the Sikhs fell upon bad times. Their home territory was divided between India and Pakistan. When Sikh landholders were driven from the Canal Colonies, this was countered with violence. Within a few days hundreds of thousands of Sikhs, and with them terrified Hindus, were on the march from Pakistan to India. By this time anti-Moslem riots had spread all over East Punjab and the refugee movement became a two-way traffic. Atrocities were committed on both sides, and by the time the transfer of population was finished, about ten million people had changed homes, and perhaps a hundred thousand fell victims to marauding bands, floods and disease.

A dark side of Sikh activities prior to the division of the country was their participation in Marxist agitation for the violent overthrow of British rule in India. During the second World War, the Communist Party of the Punjab was the most active provincial group in India. It was almost entirely Sikh, with only a handful of Moslems and Hindus connected with publicity and trade union efforts.

FAITH AND WORSHIP

Sikhs have been described as people "who believe in the ten Gurus and the Granth Sahib," namely the traditions of the early religious leaders and the doctrines of their sacred writings. This is true in an inclusive sense, although there are Sikhs who challenge the absolute authority of both doctrinal sources and want to include extraneous elements from other religious beliefs.

The concept of God is unmistakably monotheistic. In the pre-

amble to the morning prayer *Jupji,* recited at the beginning of all
ceremonial exercises and known as the *Mool Mantra,* the Sikhs
declare their faith.

> There is One God.
> He is the supreme truth.
> He, the Creator,
> Is without fear and without hate.
> He, the Omnipresent,
> Pervades the universe.
> He is not born,
> Nor does He die to be born again.
> By His grace shalt thou worship Him.

> Before time itself
> There was truth.
> When time began to run its course
> He was the truth.
> Even now, He is the truth,
> And evermore shall truth prevail.[2]

In their attitude towards God, the Sikhs emphasize the divine
unity and truth; other attributes like omnipresence, omniscience,
timelessness, and the power to destroy evil were complementary
and given stress according to religious mood.

Nanak went out of his way to accentuate human activity as a
means to salvation, in order to distinguish his teaching from the
predestination of Islam and the relative passiveness of Hinduism.
He explained the cooperative effort by using rural similes. We are
driven by the ploughman, our teacher, as a team of oxen. By the
furrows made are thus written our actions on the paper of this
earth. The beads of sweat falling from our brows are like seeds
that the ploughman sows. When harvest comes, we reap according
to our measure, "some for ourselves to keep, some to others give."
Again, if a man wishes to cultivate the fruits of salvation, let the
love of the Lord germinate in his heart. "Let thy body be as the
fallow land where in thy heart the Farmer sows his seeds of righteous action and good deeds, then with the name of God irrigate." [3]

Since God is expressly believed to be one and formless, the
Sikh religion forbids anything like the worship of idols or emblems.

"They who worship strange gods, cursed shall be their lives, cursed their habitations. Poison shall be their food—each morsel, poisoned, too, shall be their garments. In life for them is misery, in life hereafter, hell." [4]

The compilation of the Sikh scriptures, the Granth Sahib, was mainly the work of the fifth Guru Arjun and his disciple, Gurdas. This bible is known as the *Adi Granth* (first scripture) to distinguish it from the *Dasam Granth* (tenth scripture), which was compiled after the death of the last Guru.

In contents, the Sikh scriptures are a collection of the writings and sayings of the Gurus, of Hindu and Moslem ascetics (notably the Moslem Kabir), and of various bards who accompanied the Gurus on their journeys of preaching. At least five languages are used, including Punjabi, Persian, Sanskrit and certain dialects of northern India. The entire work is set to measures of classic Indian music.

Unlike any other religion of the East, Sikhism makes its scriptures the central object of worship and ritual. In all temples, copies of the Granth are placed under a canopy, with the book itself draped in cloth. When a person appears before it, he bares his head and takes off his shoes, makes obeisance by rubbing his forehead to the ground in front of the book and offers money or food on the cloth placed near the scriptures.

On important feast days, a ceremony of non-stop reading of the Granth is performed by relays of worshipers, known as the *Akhand Path*. It takes about two days and nights to complete. A more simple ceremony, which may be done privately at home, is to read through the Granth in seven days; this *Saptah Path* allows for interruptions at night and during the day.

Children born into Sikh families are given names which begin with the first letter appearing on the page at which the Granth happens to be opened. Sikh youths are baptized (taking sweetened water) with recitation of prayers in front of the Granth. Couples are married to the singing of hymns from the same book, while they walk around it four times. At death other hymns from the Granth are read aloud in the dying person's ears; and on cremation they are chanted as the flames consume the body.

Reacting against the caste system, Nanak spoke in severe language against those who discriminate among various classes. "There are ignoble among the noblest," he taught, "and pure among the despised." In recent years, however, a quasi-caste discrimination has plagued the Sikhs with the growing division between the agriculturists (*Jats*) and all others (*non-Jats*). At one time the division threatened to divide the community into two sects, almost like the Moslem divisions of *Shia* and *Sunni*. But with the partition of the country in 1947 and the legal abolition of caste privileges, the Jat-non-Jat differences are likely to disappear.

Though the Sikhs have no priesthood and all adults, of whatever status or sex, may perform religious ceremonies, there is a class of professional readers (*granthis*) and musicians (*ragis*) who operate in the larger cities where the religion is established on a more institutional basis.

Sikh tradition reacts strongly against positive injunctions on ascetical practices like the renunciation of society, celibacy and penance. In a famous passage attributed to Nanak, he says religion does not consist in a patched coat, or in a Yogi's staff, or in ashes smeared on the body; it does not consist in earrings worn, or a shaven head, or in the blowing of horns; it does not consist in wanderings to tombs or places of cremation, or sitting in Hindu attitudes of contemplation; it does not consist in going to foreign countries, or bathing at places of pilgrimage.

Above all else, prayer makes religion. The Sikh scriptures are filled with exhortations to repeat "the true name" of God and chant his praises, as a purification from sin and impious thoughts, which alone stand between the soul and its destiny. Prayer and action, therefore, are the means of salvation.

> As hands or feet besmirched with slime,
> Water washes white;
> As garments dark with grime,
> Rinsed with soap are made light;
> So when sin soils the soul
> Prayer alone shall make it white.

> Words do not the saint or sinner make.
> Action alone is written in the book of fate,
> What we sow that alone we take;
> O Nanak, be saved or for ever transmigrate.[5]

There is a clear moral code which the Sikhs are expected to follow, that goes beyond the abolition of caste, or prayer, and certainly beyond what they consider the artificial norms of cleanliness familiar to other religions. Nanak was merciless in his criticism of those who say, "This is pure, this unclean." See, he said, that in all things there is life unseen. "There are worms in wood and cowdung cakes. There is life in the corn ground into bread. There is life in the water which makes it green." How, he asks, can a person be clean when impurity is in everything he touches?

Real purity, according to Nanak, is within, and uncleanness in the will. "Impurity of the heart is greed, on tongue, untruth. Impurity of the eyes is coveting another's wealth, his wife, her comeliness. Impurity of the ears is listening to calumny." Sikhs are constantly reminded of this ideal. They are told to learn to love, "be merciful and forbear, be mild, be patient, have no lust, nor wrath, greed nor obstinacy." And the penalty for sins is pain.

One of the paradoxes of the Sikh religion is its pacifism in theory and militarism in practice, which can be explained only by a reference to history. Their resort to arms to protect what they considered sacred interests is epitomized in a Persian couplet which they invoke. "When all other means have failed, it is righteous to draw the sword." Actually the principle is partly Islamic, since the Koran is explicit about using the sword against the enemies of Allah; it is also partly anti-Islamic because the military aspect of Sikhism arose at a time when new Moslem invasions from the north threatened to destroy any people or institution which resisted their progress. However, the Sikhs themselves are concerned to return to the original teaching of their founder, who preached love and humility, and to sheathe the sword in the interests of peace.

PART TWO

Religions of Judaic Origin

11. Judaism

JUDAISM is the oldest living religion of the Western world, and historically is the parent of Christianity and Islam, which together count one half the population of the human race. The pre-Christian phase of Judaism is not our concern, both because its vital elements have remained substantially unchanged and because, paradoxically, the Jewish people have greatly changed since the coming of Christ—and our interest is in the religious cultures of the present day.

Not the least difficulty in speaking of Judaism is the question of terms. Etymologically there is no problem. The name "Jew" is derived from Judah, one of the twelve tribes of Israel. Later it came to apply to any one belonging to the Hebrew race, and finally to those who profess the religion of Judaism. The problem is whether Judaism is basically ethnic or religious, since there are many Jews who are not lineal descendants of Abraham and many others who may be so descended but do not profess the Judaic faith. Perhaps the best definition is to see Judaism as the mind and Jewry as the body of a permanent moral tradition, which has its roots in the Old Testament prophets and its hopes in a forthcoming Messias.

THE GREAT SCHISM

Historians of the Jewish people trace their origins in the Christian era to the teaching and ministry of Paul of Tarsus. They charge him with having broken the bond that formerly united the chosen race. St. Paul, they explain, urged the Jews to accept Jesus as their Messias. "Be it known to you," he told them, "that through Him forgiveness of sin is proclaimed to you, and in Him everyone who

235

believes is acquitted of all the things of which you could not be acquitted by the law of Moses." [1]

As explained by Jewish apologists, Paul used the terminology of Jeremias and Philo, and substituted circumcision of heart for circumcision of the flesh. By this formulation Paul laid the foundation for the final break of Christianity from the Jewish nation. In the company of Barnabas, he spoke out plainly. "It was necessary that the word of God should be spoken to you first, but since you reject it and judge yourselves unworthy of eternal life, we now turn to the Gentiles. For so the Lord has commanded us." [2]

In less than a generation began a series of events that not only sealed the fate of Judaism but crystallized the form it was to assume for the centuries to come. In the year 70, the Roman armies under Titus besieged Jerusalem, destroyed it, and massacred or sold into slavery its inhabitants to the number of half a million. Eusebius relates how the Christians in the city, forewarned by their Master, were saved from the final catastrophe by escaping to Pella, east of the Jordan.

Shortly after the fall of Jerusalem, the scattered remnants of the Jews founded two rabbinical schools in separate communities, one east of the Euphrates centered in ancient Babylonia or modern Iran, and the other at Jamnia, a dozen miles south of the Israeli port of Tel Aviv-Jaffa. It was at Jamnia that the rabbis held, about 100 A.D., a historic synod at which the canon of the Old Testament was redefined for the people.

The synod laid down four criteria to determine which books should be removed from the Jewish Scriptures as apocryphal. The book had to conform to the Pentateuch, namely, Genesis, Exodus, Leviticus, Numbers and Deuteronomy; it could not have been written after the time of Esdras; and it had to be written in Hebrew and in Palestine. Since certain books used by the Jews of the Diaspora (dispersion) did not meet these requirements, they were rejected. Baruch and the Epistle of Jeremias were not of Palestinian origin, Ecclesiasticus and First Maccabees were written after the time of Esdras, Tobias along with parts of Daniel and Esther were composed originally in Aramaic and also probably outside of Palestine, the Book of Judith was probably written in Aramaic, Wisdom and Second Maccabees were written in Greek. After dropping these books from the Palestinian canon, the latter was closed, and once the contents were fixed the text was also agreed upon. In their own words, the rabbis "made a fence around it."

They also provided for a new translation into Greek to replace the Septuagint, made in the third century B.C., which the Gentile Christians had appropriated and were using for apologetic purposes, for example, to prove the virginal conception of Christ from the term *parthenos* (virgin) in Isaias 7:14. The Jewish translator, Aquila, rendered it *neanis* (young woman).

Under Hadrian, the Jews were stimulated to revolt by the Messianic pretensions of Bar-Cochba, "Son of the Star." According to Cassio Dio, they rebelled because the emperor gave orders for the rebuilding of Jerusalem, with the temple of Jupiter Capitolinus to be erected on the site of the ruined temple. Early in the revolt, the Jews held Jerusalem for a time, but after a bloody war that lasted three and a half years, they were all but annihilated on the fields of Bether (135 A.D.), a few miles from Jerusalem.

Characteristic of their power of resurgence, the scattered remnant had a flourishing community in Palestine by the year 165, when Rabbi Juda I succeeded Simon II (grandson of Gameliel described in the Acts) as president of the Sanhedrin and patriarch of the West. His pioneer work on the Hebrew oral law, together with that of his confreres in Babylonia, became a kind of constitution that still unifies the religion of Israel.

SOURCES OF TRADITION

If pre-Christian Judaism is unintelligible without the Old Testament, the Jewish faith since the coming of Christ is unexplainable without the Talmud, which is the principal repository of Judaic tradition. As a collective name, Talmud literally means "instruction" and comprehends two sets of writings: the third-century Mishnah, compiled by Rabbi Juda about 215 A.D., and the fourth to sixth centuries' Gemara, which has come down in two forms, the Babylonian in Eastern Aramaic and the Palestinian in Western Aramaic.

Mishnah has a double meaning, either "study by repetition" or "second" because considered second to the Pentateuch. It is a codification of Jewish laws, *Halakoth,* from the time of the Restoration until the end of the second century. Originally oral, the laws were later reduced to written form.

From the early third century the Mishnah supplanted the numerous earlier collections and so put an end to much controversy, notably between the schools of Shammai and Hillel. Rabbi Judah was a lineal descendant of Hillel, who upheld the liberal and lenient interpretation of the law and whose followers were conciliatory in all controversies. The Mishnah, therefore, is not an original work but a redaction of earlier material and it is written in the Hebrew typical of Jewish scholars at that time.

Each of the six divisions—Seeds (laws on agriculture), Festivals and Women (marriage laws), Injuries (civil and criminal regulations), Holy Things (worship and ritual) and Purifications—is divided into two parts or Tractates, which are further subdivided into chapters, and the chapters into paragraphs or precepts.

As a sectarian law-code, the Mishnah builds on the principle of precedent, giving the sayings of learned rabbis, in quotation or paraphrase, and often only a sentence in length. No effort is made to classify the statements beyond a general assembly or similar material under a single heading.

Most of the legislation is extremely minute. Thus, "an egg laid on a festival may be eaten on the same day. So say the school of Shammai; the school of Hillel, however, say it must not. The school of Shammai say that leaven the size of an olive and browned bread the size of a date are to be removed before the Passover; but the school of Hillel say that both must be removed when the size of an olive only." [3] Then follow thirteen pages of commentary, pro and con, discussing the two opinions on the foregoing and the allied subject of burying wild game or fowl on festival days.

Among numerous prohibitions for dealing with heathen non-Israelites are several referring to the latter's religious holidays. Thus "three days before the festival of the heathen it is forbidden to have any business with them. One must not lend them anything which can be useful to them, nor borrow such from them. And the same is the case with cash money, even to pay or to receive payment is forbidden. Rabbi Jehuda, however, maintains: To receive payment is allowed, because it is a displeasure to the payees. And he was answered: Although it is now a displeasure, it pleases them in the future." [4] Again a long commentary of eleven pages evaluating the different interpretations.

Indicative of the high regard in which the Talmudic tradition was held, a Mishnah in the Treatise *Sanhedrin,* decrees that "the punishment of him who transgresses the decision of the Scribes is more rigorous than for that which is plainly written in the Scriptures." [5] The example given is that of a person who claims, against the Scribes, that the Jewish phylactery (or leather case containing vellum strips with four passages, from Exodus and Deuteronomy) should have five strips instead of four. One explanation of this "strange passage" is that some Jewish Christians were adding a fifth text, from the prologue of St. John's Gospel. [6]

However not all the Mishnah is so rabbinical. The treatise *Aboth,* on the Fathers of the Synagogue, is a collection of wise epigrams and homely counsels that are very quotable. One statement follows another with no logical correlation.

Rabbi Tarphon was in the habit of saying, "The day is short, the work is great, the workmen are slothful, the reward is rich, the Master is urgent." [7]

Rabbi Ishmail said, "Be obedient to a superior, affable to a petitioner, and friendly to all mankind." [8]

Rabbi Jannai said, "It is beyond our power to explain either the prosperity of the wicked or the afflictions of the righteous." [9]

Rabbi Jacob used to say, "This world is only a vestibule of the world to come. So prepare yourself in the vestibule to be admitted into the banquet hall." He also said, "Better is one hour of repentance and good deeds in this world than all the life of the world to come, though one hour of bliss in the future is better than a lifetime in this world." [10]

A great deal of Jewish tradition on the meaning of various aspects of religious ritual and practice prescribed by the Bible derives from the Gemara, whose lengthy interpretations form the quantitative bulk of the Talmud.

The treatise *Pesachim* (Passover) covers almost three hundred pages in a standard edition, divided into ten sections or sets of regulations: concerning the removal of leaven from the house on the eve of the Passover and the exact time when this must be accomplished; the time for eating leavened bread on the eve of the

Passover; what material is to be used for making unleavened bread and bitter herbs; articles which cause transgression of the law prohibiting leaven to be seen or found in the house of an Israelite; work which may and such as must not be performed on the day preceding the festival of Passover; the sacrifice of the Paschal Lamb; acts which supersede the due observance of the Sabbath; sacrifice of the paschal offering and what is to be done if one sacrifice is confounded with another; the roasting of the Paschal Lamb; the manner and procedure if the Paschal Lamb becomes defiled, which parts of the lamb are eaten; those obligated to eat the Paschal Sacrifice, where it is to be eaten, companies appointed to eat it, and the difference between the first and second passover; the second Passover, concerning cases where the Paschal sacrifice had become mixed; and regulations about the meal on the eve of the Passover and the four cups of wine to be drunk with the meal.

With rare exception, the Gemara expands on the Mishnah, clarifies obscurities, and offers as many as a dozen opinions on what the Mishnah states as a single prescription. According to the Mishnah, for example, the duty of eating bitter herbs on the Passover may be acquitted with lettuce, wild endive, bitter coriander, and horseradish, if fresh or dry, but not pickled or cooked in any way. On which the Gemara offers variant interpretations, including the general one that, "all herbs emitting white juice may serve to satisfy the duty of eating bitter herbs on the passover." In fact Rabbi Johann ben Berokah allowed even such as when cut should become a shade paler. "Anonymous teachers, however, say that all bitter herbs emit white juice, and become a shade paler when cut," so that any herb showing this quality may be used at the Passover meal.[11]

Commentators on the Talmud sometimes mistakenly leave the impression that no distinction is recognized between scriptural and rabbinical prescriptions, and certainly there has been enough to warrant this judgment in the case of some Jewish leaders. But the Talmud itself occasionally distinguishes between the two levels of obligation, as in the same context on the use of herbs and unleavened bread at the Paschal supper. The Hillel referred to was the contemporary of Christ, whose followers opposed the school of Shammai as the more liberal and tolerant interpreters of the Law.

Rabhina said, "Rabbi Mesharshia, the son of Rabbi Nathan told me, that so said Hillel, quoting a tradition: A man should not place the bitter herbs between unleavened cakes and eat them in that manner. Why not? Because the eating of unleavened cakes is a biblical commandment, while the eating of bitter herbs in this day is only a rabbinical ordinance. Now if the two be eaten together, the bitter herbs might destroy the taste of the cakes, and thus a rabbinical ordinance would supersede a biblical commandment. And even according to those who hold that one commandment cannot nullify another when both are fulfilled at the same time, such is only the case when both are biblical or both are rabbinical. But when one is a biblical and the other a rabbinical commandment, the rabbinical nullifies the other, and hence their joint fulfilment is not allowed." [12]

Other passages in the Talmud which place rabbinical tradition on the same level as the Bible should be read in the light of this more modest rabbinization.

The same treatise has a series of fours: types among men, temperaments, disciples and almsgivers.

There are four types of men: The ordinary one says, "What is mine is mine, and what is yours is yours." The queer one says, "What is mine is yours, and what is yours is mine." The saintly one says, "What is mine is yours, and what is yours is yours." The wicked one says, "What is mine is mine, and what is yours is mine." [13]

Occasionally the title Rabbi is omitted from a sage's name, as with Elisha ben Abuya (born about 80 A.D.). Elisha had been a Talmudic scholar but eventually turned free-thinker. More often no author of a statement is given, but only the title, "Mishnah."

Gemara is the commentary on the Mishnah, and both are now included in the Talmud, with interpretation following rabbinic tradition. Jewish authorities in Babylonia organized those laws which had developed from the close of the Mishnah down to their own times; their commentaries together with the Mishnah received the name Babylonian Talmud. It represents the final codification of Jewish law. In Palestine the law was less well organized, mostly because of the unsettled conditions under the Roman Empire. What exists, however, has the name of Jerusalem or Palestinian Talmud.

If the Mishnah is detailed, the Gemara is minute in the extreme. This is specially true of the Sabbath treatise, which discusses in a single chapter such varied items as permissible and forbidden oils and wicks for lamps on the Sabbath, legitimate balsams, whether broken vessels may be used for fuel, practical laws regarding egg-shells and whether chairs may be dragged on the Sabbath, whether a light may be extinguished on the Sabbath either for fear of accident or to afford rest for the sick.

Tosephtha is still a further element in the Talmud, literally meaning "supplement," which corresponds roughly to the Mishnah in structure, but is shorter, drawn from ancient and more recent Judaic schools, and lacks the subtlety and precision of the standard Mishnah. Some scholars claim the Tosephtha represents the Palestine Mishnah, and that our Mishnah was reedited in Babylonia. Normally verbose, a sample exception is a triad of terms. "A prophet is called by ten different names. They are: ambassador, faithful, servant, messenger, seer, watchman, man of scrutiny, dreamer, prophet, and man of God. There are ten names for the Holy Spirit, namely, proverb, metaphor, riddle, words, saying, calling, commandment, prophecy, sacred speech and vision. Joy has ten different expressions: gladness, joy, rejoicing, joyfulness, pleasure, relish, satisfaction, complacency, delight and cheer." [14]

A Talmudic eccentricity is the penchant for numbers: three, four, six, seven and ten of anything. Rabbi Nathan's Tosephtha discusses, in sequence, the meaning of three crows, charitable men, scholars, kinds of sweat, advantages of an earthen vessel—to which he adds six kinds of tears. Of charitable men, he says, "He who gives in charity may be blessed, but if he gives in the form of a loan it is still better; but he who gives one money to do business with, on the understanding that he shall pay him half the profits, is best of all." [15]

Running as a theme through the Mishnah, Gemara, and Tosephtha is the value of studying the Torah (Mosaic law), which is to be prized above wealth, honor and life itself; and the wickedness of profaning the Holy Name, for which "there is no repentence pending, and the Day of Atonement does not forgive." The precept of justice is repeated under a hundred forms, and always a respect for the wise men whose "thought concerning this world is: All that is in the world is of no importance to me, for this world is not mine. They are occupied in teaching others, and no one can see in their teaching anything wrong. Their questions are to the point and their answers according to the law." [16]

Targum is the Hebrew for "interpretation" and the name given to the Aramaic translations or paraphrases of the Old Testament, made when Hebrew had ceased to be the normal medium of speech among the Jews. They were the outcome of the explanatory oral matter which for a long time had been unofficially added to the Scripture readings in the worship of the synagogue. The Mishnah has extensive directions on how and how much of the Targum was to be given and forbade that it be written down. But this regulation very likely did not apply to private use or study, since Targumic literature seems to have existed from the first century after Christ. While the oldest extant Targums are not earlier than the fifth century, their theological content certainly goes back to Old Testament times.

Whatever else it is, the Talmud makes no pretense of being a code or catechism, laying down in summary categorical form what the Jewish obligations are. It is rather the record of a process, the actual process by means of which the Mosaic law is made clear. This explains the tensions it preserves: different views in conflict, argument advancing and receding, contradictions reconciled only by the subtlest dialectic, disparate subjects somehow unified by means of the association of religious ideas, and the succession of generations of Talmudic scholars seeking for new insights to meet new situations that are sanctioned by the old laws.

In spite of this variety and movement, however, the Talmud leaves the general impression of unbending rigidity, where the main concern is to preserve the ancient traditions. But that is only one phase of the Jewish religious literature.

Officially approved Targums were produced first in Babylon and later in Palestine, the most famous being the Targum of Onkelos on the Pentateuch, and the Targum of Jonathan on the Prophets, both of which were in use in the third century after Christ. All of the books of the Old Testament had their Targums, with the exception of Ezra, Nehemias, and Daniel, which already contained large sections in Aramaic.

What is highly significant about the Targums is the degree of freedom they show in interpreting the Bible, by way of paraphrase, circumlocution, legendary additions and rhetorical disgressions that point up the non-restrictive doctrinal content of Judaism, already in the first centuries after the "great schism." Otherwise than Christianity, its stress has not been on definite dogmatic teaching and still less on mandatory creeds. The Targums also help to explain the present status of the Jewish religion on its dogmatic side.

Midrashim are the rabbinical commentaries on the Hebrew Scriptures. Technically the singular *Midrash* refers to the general study or explanation of the Old Testament, whereas the plural *Midrashim* are free interpretations made by the ancients, which were later collected into formal commentaries on the Bible.

Etymologically the term Midrash is the Hebrew for "investigation," and refers to the Jewish method of biblical exegesis which aimed at discovering in the sacred text a meaning deeper than the literal one, not unlike the "spiritual sense" in the Christian Bible. The unexpressed basis of the Midrashim was a belief that every detail of the text is important because it is all of divine origin. Two kinds of commentaries exist: *Midrash Halacha* which deal with the derivation of the Oral Law (*Halacha*) from the Scriptures; and *Midrash Haggadah* as an exposition of the non-legal parts of the sacred text for purposes of edification.

Midrashim are not really distinct from the Talmud, but rather make it up, from the viewpoint of rabbinical exegesis. Less conspicuous in the Mishnah, the Gemara and Tosephtha portions are filled with biblical quotations around which the Talmudic commentary revolves.

Not untypical of the Midrashic method is a Gemara from the Sabbath treatise.

Rabbi Elazar Hakappur said, "A man should always pray for deliverance from poverty, although if he himself will not eventually come to poverty, his children or his grandchildren will, as it is written (Deuteronomy 15:11), 'There will not be wanting poor in the land where you dwell, therefore do I command you to open your hand to your needy and your brother.' The Hebrew term 'therefore' is *Biglal* and the school of Ishmael taught that *Biglal* is the equivalent of *Galgal,* meaning a 'wheel,' thus inferring, from that word, that poverty is like a wheel, always turning from one to the other." [17]

Not only are the Midrashim indispensable evidence of the authentic Jewish mentality, but they serve as guideposts on the Judaic attitude towards Christianity, at least obliquely by their interpretation of classic Messianic passages in the prophetic books of the Old Law.

FROM MOSES TO MOSES

Comparable to the Talmud in authority and in many respects more influential in shaping the mind of Judaism are the writings of the Rabbinic sage Moses ben (son of) Maimon, known commonly as Moses Maimonides.

It is no exaggeration to say that Maimonides stands next to the prophet Moses in the estimation of many Jews as their greatest religious leader and the man whose wisdom produced the Judaism of modern times, even as Moses had shaped the religion of Israel centuries before Christ. "From Moses unto Moses," it was said, "there was none like Moses," meaning that in the twenty-five hundred intervening years (and since), from the prophet Moses, no one has more clearly assessed the genius of his people or more accurately expressed its spirit than Maimonides.

For the Christian believer, Maimonides' importance is paramount because of his effect on St. Thomas Aquinas. While denying the assertion that without Maimonides there would have been no Aquinas, it can fairly be said that after Aristotle, the greatest non-Christian influence on the Angelic Doctor was Moses Maimonides. Writing a century before Aquinas, he brought Judaism into harmony with Aristotelian philosophy. Like St. Thomas, Maimonides placed great emphasis on reason and knowledge. Knowledge for him was man's greatest perfection, which made him like to God. He thought faith should be built on a rational foundation, and in his opinion no one excelled Aristotle in earthly knowledge. Besides natural knowledge, which should not be cultivated for itself alone, Maimonides pointed out the necessity of revelation, partly for the instruction of the people and partly to serve as a criterion for the scholar. Between faith and knowledge there is no contradiction since both are derived from God. Thus in Maimonides, St. Thomas found many positions that belonged to the Christian tradition, which had affected Moslem and Jewish thought in Spain and North Africa since the patristic age.

Born at Cordova in Spain in 1135, Maimonides received a comprehensive education from his father, a learned Talmudist. During an anti-Jewish persecution by the Moslem Alhomades (1149), his family fled into exile and settled at Fez, the capital of Morocco, where he wrote the "Letter of Consolation" to strengthen his co-religionists in their trials. He concluded with a prayer.

When misfortunes overtake us, and there is no king to order our affairs, and no adviser to guide us, and no place of safety where we can flee, and no army wherewith we may be protected, and no power even to speak, when we are deprived of every resource, and when every refuge is cut off and all our hopes are frustrated, there is no escape but to You. We call and You come to our aid, we cry and You answer, for You are our refuge.[18]

When a purist Jewish writer charged that all Jews who compromised in the least with Islam, even externally, were apostates, Maimonides defended their action as licit because under duress, but had to flee Morocco on account of the religious antagonism he aroused. After a brief stay in Palestine, he settled at Fostat (Cairo) where he became the head of a flourishing Jewish community.

In 1168 he finished his commentary on the Mishnah known as the *Luminary*. But a mind as original as his could not be satisfied with mere comment. He often boldly differed from the Talmud and especially rapped at errors and superstitions. When commenting on the Mishnah passage which enumerates those unbelievers who are excluded from a share in the world to come, Maimonides stressed that Judaism is a religion at once exclusive because it embodies a set of revealed doctrines and inclusive because others than Jews, provided they believe in these truths, have assurance of salvation. His list of thirteen articles of faith are a synthesis of the Jewish religion and to this day are a convenient standard of orthodoxy. Within a century of his death, this precis of belief was employed as a theme for synagogue poems in all countries of Jewish habitation. Altogether some ninety poetic versions are to be counted, of which the most popular is the *Yigdal,* the liturgic verse which has been the inspiration of numerous musical creations.

In prose-form the articles are a condensation of the Old Testament and Talmud, and of ten centuries of Judaic faith.

I believe with perfect faith that the Creator, praised be He, is the Creator and Guide of all creation, and that He alone has made, does make, and will make all things.

I believe with perfect faith that the Creator, praised be He, is a Unity, and that there is no unity like His in any manner, and that He alone is our God, who was, is, and will be.

I believe with perfect faith that the Creator, praised be He, is not a body, and that He is free from all attributes of a body, and that He has no form whatsoever.

I believe with perfect faith that the Creator, praised be He, is the first and the last.

I believe with perfect faith that to the Creator, praised be He, and to Him alone is it proper to pray, and that it is not proper to pray to any besides Him.

I believe with perfect faith that all the words of the prophets are true.

I believe with perfect faith that the prophecy of Moses our great teacher, may he rest in peace, was true, and that he was the father of the prophets, both those who preceded and who followed him.

I believe with perfect faith that the entire Torah now in our possession is the same that was given to Moses our teacher, may he rest in peace.

I believe with perfect faith that this Torah will never be replaced, and that there will never be another Torah from the Creator, praised be He.

I believe with perfect faith that the Creator, praised be He, knows every deed of men and all their thoughts, as it is written, "He fashions the hearts of them all and observes all their deeds" (Psalm 33:15).

I believe with perfect faith that the Creator, praised be He, rewards those who keep His commandments and punishes those that transgress His commandments.

I believe with perfect faith in the coming of the Messiah, and though he tarry I will wait daily for him.

I believe with perfect faith that there will be a revival of the dead at a time when it shall please the Creator, praised be He, and exalted be His fame for ever and ever.[19]

According to Maimonides only that person is a true Jew who recognizes the validity of these articles without analysis. Anyone who denies even one of them should have no part in the Jewish community.

Maimonides chose thirteen principles because, he said, God possesses thirteen fundamental attributes (*shalot-esreh middot*), by which the universe was created and continues under divine guidance. Consequently to question any of the articles would be, in effect, to deny God's basic attributes, through which alone the elements of the world have their being.

This elenchus of dogmas gave stability to historic Judaism as a way of life. Particularly the first five, on the existence and nature of God, helped to create modern Jewish theology. No such clear statements on the person of the Deity had been given in the Synagogue before. No doubt the divine attributes were in the Bible and Talmud, and in the rabbinical commentaries, but the average Jew was not equipped to make the necessary distinctions. Maimonides distinguished the essence from the accidentals, notably the unique character of the Torah in God's plan of communicating His truth to the world. Historically he was specially concerned to assure the eternal validity of the Judaic Law against two forces which derived from it: to insure its sufficiency in answer to the Christian claim that the Law must now be supplemented by the Gospel, and to safeguard its permanence against Islam which said the Koran replaces the writings of Moses.

About ten years after the "Luminary," Maimonides brought out his *Mishneh Torah* (Second Law) in Hebrew, a Talmudic code in fourteen parts arranged by subject matter. It consists of a classification of Jewish religious doctrines, their interpretation by the masters, and their moral and philosophical implications. Among its surprising features is the inclusion of non-Jewish authorities in support of Maimonides' judgments.

In 1190 appeared his principal Arabic treatise, the *Guide for the Perplexed,* which scholars in every tradition consider a part of world literature. Through the *Guide* not only Maimonides but Judaism entered the orbit of Christian and Islamic thought. The work of the "Egyptian Moses" was studied assiduously by Albertus Magnus and Thomas Aquinas, who quoted him often.

The purpose of the *Guide* was to achieve a working harmony between reason and revelation. Its three sections treat of the idea of God; the arguments for God's existence, His manifestations, the world of spirits, the creation of the world in time, and prophecy; and the interpretation of Ezechiel's vision, the problem of evil, the end of creation, divine providence and divine knowledge. Maimonides' aim was to achieve a synthesis of the data of Jewish revelation and the speculation of human reason found in Aristotle. With all his devotion to Aristotle, however, Maimonides was too much a believer not to differ with the man he called "the chief of philosophers" and from whom he imbibed many ideas. In so doing he became the stumbling block for generations of Jews to the present day—some of whom admire Maimonides but speak of "the unsure weapon of naive faith" with which he faced the problems of existence, whereas others see in him the great exemplar of human wisdom acknowledging its own limitations.

The cardinal issue on which Maimonides opposed Aristotle was creation. He saw that by accepting the biblical dogma of creation out of nothing every problem of God's relation to the world is solved and the basic agreement of reason and faith established. God is then sovereign ruler of the Universe which He governs according to His will, and man is bound by the law of his own contingency to obey and love his Creator. But rejecting this doctrine in favor of the Greek philosopher's theory of the eternity of the world, a host of difficulties, not to say contradictions, face the intelligent believer, of which not least is how to reconcile God's absolute dominion with the existence of a universe co-eternal with God.

If we were to accept the eternity of the universe as taught by Aristotle, that everything in the universe is the result of fixed laws, that nature does not change, and that there is nothing supernatural, we should necessarily be in opposition to the foundation of our religion, we should disbelieve all miracles and signs, and certainly reject all hopes and fears derived from Scripture, unless the miracles are also explained figuratively. The allegorists among the Mohammedans have done this, and have thereby arrived at absurd conclusions.

Accepting the creation, we find that miracles are possible, that Revelation is possible, and that every difficulty in this question is removed. Owing to the absence of all proof, we reject the theory of the eternity of the universe.[20]

Maimonides' concern to safeguard the doctrine of creation is indispensable for a proper understanding of Judaism, in view of its later development, when men like Spinoza and Einstein could profess a pantheistic philosophy of life and yet be considered worthy, even outstanding, representatives of the Jewish religious culture.

A curious position in Maimonides, on which St. Thomas opposed him, was the belief that divine Providence is limited to intelligent beings, and among these to persons who cultivate the religious spirit. "Providence," he said, "watches over every rational being according to the amount of intellect which that being possesses. Those who are perfect in their perception of God, whose mind is never separated from Him, enjoy always the influence of Providence. But those who, perfect in their knowledge of God, turn their mind sometimes away from God, enjoy the presence of Divine Providence only when they meditate on God; when their thoughts are engaged in other matters Divine Providence departs from them." [21] Needless to say, this concept of a withdrawing Providence was inconsistent with the rest of Maimonides' philosophy, as Aquinas was quick to point out.

In treating of the immortality of the soul, he quoted passages from the Bible, gave the opinions of Greek and Arabian writers, distinguished between the soul that is born in us and the intellect we later acquire, and ended by teaching that only the souls of the just are immortal. This doctrine of acquired or merited immortality became one of the most distinctive features of later Judaic thought. Moreover, when Maimonides spoke of resurrection after death, he excluded the body. "In the world-to-come, there is nothing corporeal, and no material substance; there are only souls of the righteous without bodies—like the ministering angels."

The other published writings of Maimonides, mostly Arabic, include a famous treatise on *Repentance* which illustrates his perfectly orthodox Judaism. Among those who "have no portion in the World-to-Come, but are cut off and perish" are those "who deny the Torah, the resurrection from the dead or the coming of the Redeemer," along with "Heretics and Epicureans." In Maimonides' vocabulary, there are five classes of heretics, including

the man "who says there is no God and the world has no ruler"
and the one "who says that there is a ruling power but that is is
rested in two or more persons." [22] Among the three classes of
Epicureans are those who claim that "the Creator changed one
commandment for another, and that this Torah, although of divine
origin, is now obsolete, as the Nazarenes and Moslems assert."
Thus Christians, along with pagans and Moslems, are excluded
from the way of salvation.

Jewish commentators, for all their admiration of Maimonides,
are painfully conscious of the consequences of this principle. In
theory, if he thought he had truth, every other view was false. Thus
Maimonides, with his systematic mind, thrust men out of Judaism
instead of keeping them in. They became *Minim* or heretics by
reason of the boundary of religious belief which he established.
This produced a reaction: among the plain men of Jewish faith who
could not subscribe to dogmas which human reason had carved out
of the Torah by using the tools of Hellenism; and among intellectuals who respected Maimonides as a scholar but challenged his
authority to impose dogmatic creeds.

MYSTICISM AND THE CABALA

The main stream of Judaism has always had its competing or
schismatic elements. Long before Christ there were Samaritans, the
ancient "fundamentalists," worshipers of the letter of the Pentateuch, who still survive at Nabus in West Jordan. In the eighth
century appeared the Karaites whose schism is indicated in their
Hebrew name, "Sons of the text," and the motto of their leader
Anan, "search the Scriptures." But these and like schismatic movements have practically died out, or been absorbed in the main body
of Jewry. It was otherwise with the rise of Jewish mysticism, stabilized in the Cabalistic renascence of the thirteenth century.

Literally *Cabala* means "oral tradition" and implies the tradition of the mystical schools. It was a development of tendencies
similar to Gnosticism, and reached the height of its influence in the
later Middle Ages, although Cabalism is still active today, in a
greatly modified form, as Hasidism.

It is difficult to trace the beginnings of Cabala, which is often the Hebrew equivalent for mysticism. According to the Cabalists, Moses on Mount Sinai and the prophets all received the Cabala. Actually we know that Ben Sira in the second century before Christ warned against preoccupation with "secret things," and the Jewish apocalyptic writings before and after Christ taught a good measure of Cabala. The Essenes, Alexandrian Jews, and the early rabbins who favored the Pythagorean theory of numbers were forerunners of classic Cabalism.

Two types of Jewish mysticism became early manifest: the speculative or theosophic, and the practical or theurgic. Practical mysticism stressed the wonder-working power of controlling nature through a knowledge of the names and functions of angels; speculative mysticism held that all things exist as a result of ten emanations which graduate from God to the universe and serve as mediators.

After centuries of extravagances, the two types were combined, if not fused, by the thirteenth century Spanish Jew, Moses de Leon in the *Zohar,* an esoteric commentary on the Pentateuch which became the sacred handbook of Jewish mysticism. The *Zohar* was historically a reaction against the rationalistic spirit of Maimonides. Yet in its effort to recapture "authentic Judaism" by re-emphasizing the spiritual, it went to the opposite extreme. It drew heavily on Persian and Hindu sources and seriously tried to read into the five books of Moses what the Hindu Upanishads read into the four Vedas. The result is a curious mixture of oriental stress on ecstatic union with God, and Judaic concern for the service of mankind.

On its speculative side, the most characteristic feature of classic Cabalism is the theory of the fulfilment of God. According to the Cabalists, the supreme and central mystery of religion is the Holy Union or "sacred marriage" between two aspects of the divine, the male with its creative dynamism and the female or receptive counterpart.

What is true of the deity is equally true of man. For Cabalism, neither God nor man reaches the totality of perfection except in the union of the two sexes. A layer of mythology, borrowed from Hinduism, was thus laid on the foundations of Judaism—to the effect that perfection is possible only in the married state. In fact, the Cabala was the first system in the West to develop a mystical metaphysics of the sexual act, which bears more than superficial resemblance to the later theories of Sigmund Freud (1856-1940), Austrian Jew and founder of the theory of sexual psychoanalysis.

More serious, however, than its overstress on marriage, Cabalism shifted the whole center of Judaism from God to man. Its root conception represented God as being in need of man, and depending on man for the maintenance or restoration of His divinity. Where the Pentateuch says, "Be holy as I your Lord am holy," and the trend of valid Jewish tradition teaches that God is Master of creation, the Cabala replaces the biblical theme with an esoteric but none the less emphatic pantheism, wherein the future destiny of God is bound up with the perfection of human society, mediated, as the Cabalist Isaac Luria explained, through the Jewish people.

Modern Judaism is unsympathetic with Cabalistic meanderings in the realm of numbers, or invoking the names of angels by way of incantation. Yet compromises have been made with its theory on the fulfilment of God and the need which the Deity has of man, although this has been against the main body of Judaic thought. Most Jewish writers tell the faithful to repudiate Cabalism as a form of idolatry; others are not so intransigent.

ORTHODOXY IN DOCTRINE AND RITUAL

Modern Judaism is commonly divided into three types: the Orthodox, Reform and Conservative, each professing to be truly Jewish and yet differing as much and more from the others than Catholics, Protestants and the Eastern Churches differ from one another.

Historically Orthodox Jews are the oldest, reaching back to the synagogues in Palestine and Babylonia in the first century, and theologically they are most conservative. The term "Orthodox" was first applied to them in connection with the Sanhedrin convened by Napolean. Later on Reform Jews stressed the fact that Orthodox Jews follow the Bible, Talmud and the teachings of Maimonides, whereas the Orthodox themselves insist that their religion is Judaism proper, has been for thirty centuries and is today the faith of most Jewish people throughout the world. They prefer to speak of themselves simply as Jews, without qualification, or of their tradition as Torah-True Judaism, because of their adherence to the Law of Moses as the word of God.

EXISTENCE AND NATURE OF GOD. Orthodox Jews follow the articles of Maimonides fairly closely and their theology, with minor reservations, is substantially Maimonidean. They believe in one God, creator of heaven and earth, whose providence extends to all creation. In general, theories of evolution and other hypotheses of modern science on the origin of the world are considered heretical. The stress on divine unity excludes not only all forms of polytheism but also Manichaean dualism and the Christian Trinity of persons in God. All positive attributes in God are also excluded, at least on principle, according to Maimonides' dictum that "Anything predicated of God is totally different from our attributes; no definition can comprehend both." Divine unity is also defined to exclude all mediators.

Corollary with God's existence and unity is the belief that He is without form, without family, without history. He is beyond time because He was never born and will never die, and beyond space because He is not material.

God is said to have revealed Himself in what is now the Bible, which consists of twenty-four books divided into three sections: Torah or the five books of Moses; Nebiim or the prophets; and Kethubim or sacred writings, such as the Song of Songs, Ecclesiastes and the Book of Job.

MESSIANISM AND ESCHATOLOGY. One of the fundamental beliefs of Judaism and perhaps the secret of its deathless optimism is the belief in a coming Messias. This is normally coupled among Orthodox Jews with the actual, physical liberation of Israel from persecution and humiliation, its return to its native homeland, the restoration of the house of David, the rebuilding of the temple in Jerusalem and the recognition by all nations of Israel's destiny as the chosen people. The classic Messianic text quoted in their literature is Micheas, who foretold how, "out of Sion shall go forth instruction, and the word of the Lord out of Jerusalem; and He shall judge between many peoples, and shall decide concerning mighty nations afar off." [23] In the morning service of the synagogue, the

people are reminded that the Lord "will send our Anointed at the
end of days, to redeem them that wait for the end—His salvation." [24]

Among the principles of the faith, following the sequence of
Maimonides, is the twelfth which reads, "I believe with perfect
faith in the coming of the Messias, and, though he tarry, I will
wait daily for his coming." [25] Repeatedly the formulas of invocation, for private recitation or the liturgy, contain Messianic aspirations. Three times a day in the Shmone Esreh, the people pray,
"Blessed art Thou, O Lord our God and God of our Fathers, who
rememberest the pious deeds of the patriarchs, and in love wilt
bring a redeemer to their children's children for Thy name's
sake." [26]

One aspect of the Messianic hope finds frequent expression in
prayer, the desire to see Sion reestablished, with the temple and
sacrifices as of old.

On account of our sins we were exiled from our land, and removed
far from our country, and we are unable to go up in order to appear and
prostrate ourselves before thee, and to fulfil our obligations in thy
chosen house, that great and holy temple which was called by thy name,
because of the hand that hath been stretched out against thy sanctuary.
May it be thy will, O Lord our God and God of our fathers, merciful
King, that thou mayest again in thine abundant compassion have mercy
upon us and upon thy sanctuary, and mayest speedily rebuild it and
magnify its glory.

Our Father, our King, do thou speedily make the glory of thy kingdom manifest upon us; shine forth and exalt thyself upon us in the sight
of all the living; bring our scattered ones among the nations near unto
thee, and gather our dispersed from the ends of the earth. Lead us with
exultation unto Zion thy city, and unto Jerusalem the place of thy sanctuary with everlasting joy; and there we will prepare before thee the
offerings that are obligatory for us.[27]

While the hopes of a future Messias are strong, there is no
evidence that his character ever rises above the human. No doubt
there are mystical speculations about the origin and superhuman
powers ascribed to him by the ancients, and still found in scattered
Jewish writings. But these are exceptional. The rule is to consider

the Messias a mortal human being, differing from others only in being wiser and more resplendent than they. His principal role, for the Orthodox, will be to restore the Jewish people to their godly inheritance, and through them to unite all men in allegiance to the God of Israel.

Along with Messianism is the belief in an after-life of happiness or misery, depending on one's conduct before death. However opinion varies on the precise nature of this reward and punishment. The strongest rabbinical position says that *Gehenna* will not last forever except for a limited type of sinner, e.g., adulterers and slanderers. All others will be delivered from the pains after a short time of purgation, which some fix at twelve months.

Faith in bodily resurrection is still professed by the Orthodox. It is clearly expressed in the Morning Benediction, derived from the Talmudic treatise *Berakoth*.

O my God, the soul which Thou gavest me is pure; Thou didst create it, Thou didst form it, Thou didst breathe it into me; and Thou dost keep it within me, and Thou wilt take it from me, but wilt restore it unto me hereafter. As long as the soul is within me, I will give thanks unto Thee, O Lord my God, and God of my fathers, Sovereign of all works, Lord of all souls. Blessed art Thou, O Lord, who restorest souls unto dead bodies.[28]

The principle behind this faith is simple enough. Just as the soul is believed to leave the body at death, so the soul, after having left the body in death, will return to "those that sleep in the dust" at the time of the great reawakening.

LITURGICAL SERVICES. The variety of services required or commended for practice is extensive. They are not only outward forms of piety but professions of faith that touch the essence of Judaism, whose devotion to ritual is founded on the minute prescriptions in the Pentateuch.

In the rite of circumcision, participate the father of the child, the *mohel* who performs the ritual, a *sandek* or godfather, and a congregation whenever possible. The eighth day is prescribed, even if it falls on the Sabbath. While performing the rite the *mohel* recites the essential invocation, "Blessed art Thou, O Lord our God, King of the Universe, who hast sanctified us by Thy commandments, and hast enjoined us to perform the commandment of circumcision." To which the father responds in the same words, except for the concluding phrase, ". . . and hast commanded us to make our sons enter into the covenant of Abraham our father." [29] Commentators are careful to point out that circumcision, unlike Baptism, is not a sacrament which gives the Jew his religious character. Every child born of a Jewish mother is a Jew or Jewess. However the exact nature of circumcision as a liturgical rite is disputed.

On the thirtieth day after the birth of the mother's first child, if it is a son, the ceremony of "Redemption of the First-born" takes place. The *Cohen* (descendant of the Aaronic priesthood) places his hand on the head of the child, and pronounces the following Benediction: "God make thee as Ephraim and Manasseh. The Lord bless thee and keep thee. The Lord make His face to shine upon thee, and be gracious unto thee. The Lord turn His face unto thee and give thee peace. For length of days, and years of life and peace shall they add to thee. The Lord shall guard thee from all evil. He shall guard thy soul. Amen." [30]

A Jewish boy reaches his religious maturity at the age of thirteen, when he becomes a *Bar Mitzvah,* literally, "son of command" or "man of duty." A Jewish girl becomes religiously mature at twelve. The Bar Mitzvah ceremony is performed at the synagogue on a Sabbath during morning services. For the first time the boy is given a place with the other men of the congregation in the prayers, the week's readings from the Bible and the prescribed benedictions. Readers are normally chosen from the boy's family. The Bar Mitzvah himself chants the whole chapter from the Prophets and recites all the benedictions. At the end his father publicly thanks God for delivering him from the burden of his son's sins, saying, "Blessed be He who has absolved me." In some synagogues the boy gives a sermon or homily and conducts the service for the occasion. Preparation for the Bar Mitzvah often requires four years of previous study in the reading of Hebrew and a knowledge of Jewish laws and practices.

Marriage in Hebrew is called *Kiddushin,* "sanctification," and the persons married are considered to have entered a sacred state. In strictest Orthodox practice, rarely observed today, the bride must shave her head and wear a wig in order not to be attractive to other men. More commonly she undergoes a ritual purification on the eve of the wedding. Both bride and groom come to the wedding after prescribed fasting. The groom places the ring on the forefinger of the bride's right hand and says, "Behold thou art consecrated unto me, according to the law of Moses and of Israel."

This ceremony takes place in the presence of a *Minyan,* a religious quorum of ten Jews, under a *Huppah* or canopy, which symbolizes the new home to which the groom is taking his bride. It is not valid unless the groom, in the presence of two witnesses, has agreed to the *Ketubah* (marriage contract) in which he agrees to provide for his wife and assures her of a definite minimum sum as an obligation on his estate, including a stipulation to support the wife in case of divorce. The practice was begun to protect the wife who in old Jewish law could be divorced without her consent.

Seven blessings are recited during the wedding ceremonial and after the meal. The breaking of a glass before the benediction symbolizes the destruction of the temple and the social responsibility of the new couple to share in the trials of their people.

Jewish law excommunicates polygamists. However, while commending the ideal of retaining the wife of one's youth, it does not consider marriage a contract binding unto death. When marital difficulties arise, the rabbis may grant a bill of divorce, *Get,* whose conditions differ according to circumstances but generally favor the husband since tradition considers the husband very much the master.

The *Kaddish* is recited for the first time at the fresh grave of a person just deceased. It is a holy pledge, not for the dead but of the living, in which the mourner and congregation alternate in a series of invocations of God, concluding with the prayer, "May He who maketh peace in His high places, make peace for us and for all Israel; and say ye, Amen."

Mourners are to rend their garments as a sign of their loss, which they should do standing. Seven days of mourning, *Shivah,* follow and for thirty days the hair is to be allowed to grow without cutting it. For eleven months the children are to daily recite the Kaddish over their parents, and for a year avoid places of amusement or festivity. Anniversaries of death call for a recitation of the Kaddish and prayerful meditation.

It is also customary to make mention of the souls of departed parents and relations on the Day of Atonement, and the last days of the Three Festivals, expressing sentiments that suggest suffrages for the faithful departed. Thus: "May God remember the soul of my honored mother N.N. who has gone to her repose. For that I now solemnly offer charity for her sake. In reward of this, may her soul enjoy eternal life, with the souls of Abraham, Isaac and Jacob; Sarah, Rebecca, Rachel, and Leah, and the rest of the righteous men and women that are in Paradise; and let us say, Amen." [31]

Religious practices in the home begin with the symbolic sign, *Mezuzah,* affixed to the door of every residence as a sign of trust in God and promise to walk in His ways. Inside the Mezuzah case is a parchment inscribed with passages of the Torah which emphasize the unity of God, His providence, and the resulting duty of serving Him. The pious touch the Mezuzah at "Shaddai" as they pass through the door, and recite the prayer, "May God keep my going out and my coming in, from now on and ever more."

The male in the family recites his morning prayers while wearing a shawl or *Talith,* much like the stole worn by Catholic priests, but fringed at each corner with a tassel of the same material as the talith. After prayers he puts on the *arba kanfoth* (four corners), which is a kind of fringed scapular worn all day under the outer garments, in fulfilment of the precept to "encircle ourselves with fringes." Young sons of the family also wear the scapular.

While reciting morning prayers, the Jew wears phylacteries on his forehead and left arm. Called *tefillin* (prayers) in Hebrew, the phylacteries are worn every day during morning prayers except on holidays and the Sabbath. They consist of long leather straps, made from the skin of a kosher animal and dyed black. On the straps is a small case, one for the forehead and another for the arm, in which are contained four Scripture passages from the Torah, namely, Exodus 13:1-10, 11-16; Deuteronomy 6:4-9, 11:13-21. The head phylactery is tied behind the head into a knot in the form of *yod.* On the sides of the box appears the letter *shin.* Together these letters form the word *Shaddai,* "Almighty," one of the names of God. Phylacteries are to be worn by all men from the time of their *bar mitzvah.*

The liturgical preference given to men is reflected in the morning service invocations recited by men and women together,

"Blessed art Thou, O Lord our God, King of the universe, who has not made me a heathen;" and by the men alone, "Blessed art Thou, O Lord our God, King of the universe, who hast not made me a woman"; and by the women alone, "Blessed art Thou, O Lord our God, King of the universe, who hast made me according to Thy will." [32]

SABBATH OBSERVANCES. The Jews distinguish two sets of observances on the Sabbath (rest), those at home or outside the synagogue and those in the synagogue proper. The Sabbath begins on Friday night when the woman of the house lights the traditional candles, before the *Kiddush* or ceremony of sanctification. It ends at sundown on Saturday, and is followed by a ceremony of candle, wine and spices, called *Havdalah* (separating), which marks the distinction between the day of the Lord and the six working days.

No manual labor is done on the Sabbath. An observant Jew will not travel, use the phone, write, touch money, or kindle a fire. Depending on custom and circumstances, he is to withdraw completely from business and trade interests and devote himself to family, friends and religion. The negative side, therefore, is abstention from work; but positively, the observance of the Sabbath and festival days is intended to intensify family life, give unworried minds a chance to study religious history and literature, and, above all, insure a periodic concentration on prayer and the things of the spirit.

Sabbath day services in the synagogue cover a large portion of the standard prayer manuals. Formerly all the prayers and hymns were in Hebrew, but of late even the Orthodox permit at least some recitation and chant in the vernacular, and prayer books usually have Hebrew on one side and vernacular on the opposite page.

There are, in general, five functions to the synagogue service, whether on the Sabbath or festival days: readings from the Scripture or the Talmud; prayers which may be individual or communal, invocatory or meditative; chants of different kinds; preaching a sermon or giving a commentary on some sacred text; and a variety of ritual practices that are part of Jewish tradition and correspond to the prayers and hymns, but unlike the Christian sacraments have no intrinsic sanctifying efficacy.

The most important part of the public and private prayers of the Jew is the *Shema*, which every Jewish child knows before he attends synagogue. Originally the *Shema* consisted of only one verse, Deuteronomy 6-4, which says, "Hear, O Israel, the Lord our God, the Lord is One," but the regular *Shema* in the liturgy consists of three portions: Deuteronomy 6:4-9, 11:13-21, and Numbers 15:37-41. In the first portion, the faithful are commanded to love God with their heart, soul and might; to remember all His commandments and instruct their children accordingly; to recite the words of God when retiring or rising; to bind these words on their head and arm, and inscribe them on the doorposts and city gates. In the second part is a promise of reward for keeping these laws and of punishment for transgression, with a repetition of the first part. The third section contains the law regarding the *zizit* or fringes on the *arba kanfoth* and *talith,* as a reminder to keep all the divine precepts, as a warning against the evil inclinations of the heart, and in remembrance of the deliverance from Egpt. Josephus is witness to the fact that Moses ordered the *Shema* to be recited twice a day, as a divine command.

Next in importance is the *Amida* or *Shmone Esreh,* which is a collection of blessings at the morning (*Shaharit*) afternoon (*Minhah*) and evening (*Arbit*) services, as well as of the additional, *Musaf,* service on Sabbath and holy days. Literally, the name means "eighteen," though in reality, as recited in the synagogue, there are nineteen benedictions. It is often simply called *Tefilah* (prayer), as the prayer par excellence of Judaism. There are three blessings of praise (*Shebahim*), thirteen of petition (*Bakhoshot*), and three of thanksgiving (*Hodaot*).

Ten of the nineteen benedictions are explicitly Messianic, the others by implication. "Mindful of the patriarchs' love for Thee, Thou wilt in Thy love bring a redeemer to their children's children for the sake of Thy name. . . . Look upon our affliction and fight our battle and redeem us speedily for the sake of Thy name. . . . Blow the great trumpet for our liberation, and lift a banner to gather our exiles, and gather us into one body from the four corners of the earth. . . . To Jerusalem Thy city return Thou in mercy and dwell in her midst as Thou hast spoken, and build her speedily in our days as an everlasting structure and soon establish there the throne of David. . . . The seed of David Thy servant cause Thou to sprout up, and his horn do Thou lift up through Thy victorious salvation."

Each of the benedictions has a specified name, including a short one, called *Goel* (Redeemer), which addresses God as "Lord, the Redeemer of Israel," and bids Him come to save His people. In practice, the *Amida* is first prayed silently by the congregation and then repeated by the reader aloud. Great devotion is recommended in the recitation and interruptions are to be absolutely avoided. Depending on the type of Judaism, and the ritual customs, the *Amida* has many variants, which, though not substantial, stress or deemphasize one or another aspect. Elaborate rubrics explain when which benedictions are to be said, and with what external ritual.

A dramatic part of the Sabbath (and feast day) service is taking out the Torah for reading to the congregation. Seven men are called to the leader's platform to recite the blessing, "Bless the Lord who is to be blessed . . ." to which the congregation answers. After a section is read, another blessing, until the final invocation by the minister. The Torah is kept in a receptacle called the Ark *(Aron Hakodesh),* which is placed in the wall toward which the congregation and its leader, either the *hazan* (cantor) or rabbi, turn when they pray. Steps lead up to the Ark, much as the altar steps lead up to the tabernacle in a Catholic chuch. Above the Ark are two tablets, with abbreviations of the first two words for each of the Ten Commandments, five on each tablet. An embroidered velvet curtain covers the Ark; and the *Ner Tamid* hangs before it, namely, a lamp always kept burning to signify that light from the Torah must ever illumine the world. Light also comes from two large *menorahs,* or seven-branch candelabra, whose construction is minutely described in Exodus.

The Torah used for the liturgy is written in Hebrew on a scroll of parchment, rolled on pivots made of wood, ivory or silver. This *sefer* (book) Torah is wrapped in linen, silk or velvet; with another cover placed over it, usually of velvet, and like the curtains of the Ark, decorated with Hebrew letters embroidered with gold. The *Magen David* (Shield of David), two triangles forming a star, is often part of these decorations.

FASTS AND FESTIVALS. There are twelve principal and several minor fasts and festivals in the Jewish year, some of biblical origin and others introduced since the Christian era. The Jewish calendar is based upon the moon, with each month having twenty-nine or thirty days. Although the new moon always shows that a new month has begun, the twelve lunar months do not add up to 365 days. So every few years the Jewish calendar has a leap year and a whole month is added, to catch up with the civil calendar.

The first day of each month is a half holiday, the *Rosh Hodesh* or New Moon, with several ritual blessings to be pronounced on "Seeing the New Moon," one of which is to be said seven times: "As we attempt to leap towards thee, but cannot touch thee, so may those who attempt to injure us, be unable to reach us." [33]

Several names are given to the Jewish New Year: *Rosh Hashanah* or Head of the Year, *Yom Hazikaron* or Remembrance Day, and *Yom Hadin* or Day of Judgment. Its function, therefore, is to serve as a day of recollection of the past, to judge one's conduct and ask God for mercy on the sins committed in the preceding year. A Messianic tone runs through the synagogue prayers for the feast, asking the Lord "When wilt Thou reign in Sion? Speedily, even in our days, do Thou dwell there, and for ever." Two days after the New Year is the Fast of *Gedalyah,* which recalls the murder of *Gedalyah,* governor of Jerusalem and protector of Jeremiah the prophet.

After Ten Days comes the Day of Atonement, *Yom Kippur,* on which the Jews are to make their peace with God and man. There is a strict fast from sunset to sunset, and self-affliction for sin. The faithful are reminded to make peace with man before they can approach God for pardon. They must undo every wrong, and restore anything of which they may have unlawfully deprived their fellowman. Symbolic of their struggles are the two he-goats which the ancient law prescribed for sacrifice. One was to be offered to God as representing the forces in man which are dedicated to the performance of God-given duties; the other was driven into the wilderness, a scapegoat, to carry away the sins of Israel into the unknown as a sign of expiation.

Since the Jews have no animal sacrifices today a number of substitutes have been devised, of which the nearest to the ancient practice is the *Kaporoth* (atonement) in which a fowl is killed, a rooster for a man and a hen for a woman. Such act of reparation can be made either for oneself or someone else. The prayer prescribed for a woman, atoning for herself, says, "This is my change, and is my compensation, this is my redemption. This chicken is going to be killed, while I shall be admitted and allowed a good, happy and peaceful life." [34]

The feast of Tabernacles, *Succoth,* occurs in the same month and primarily has historical associations. Lasting eight days, it recalls the trust of the ancient Israelites in God's protection, although they dwelt only in huts, whence the name *Succoth.* In Palestine this is the harvest festival, so that its second significance is gratitude to God for His goodness. The most colorful part of the week-long celebration is the closing ceremony when the whole congregation makes seven solemn circuits bearing a cluster of palm, citron, myrtle and willow, to signify the cooperative spirit which Judaism seeks to develop—the palm represents beauty and usefulness, the willow neither, the myrtle and citron each has one of these qualities. By combining these elements Judaism, as all humanity, advances the cause of civilization and finds its way to God. Closing the month of *Tishri* is one more feast, the "Rejoicing of the Law," called *Simhath Torah,* when the reading of the Torah is completed and begun anew.

Corresponding to the civil month of December is the Jewish *Kislev,* when the *Hannukah* (dedication) is celebrated to commemorate the fight for freedom which the Maccabees won over the Syrian tyrant. Recalling the story of the crude oil which burned for eight days beyond its measure, a new candle is lighted successively on each of eight days, with accompanying prayers. A month later is the fast of *Tebet,* to mourn over the siege of Jerusalem by the Babylonians.

The feast of Lots, *Purim,* occurs in the middle of the month *Adar* (corresponding to March) to commemorate the deliverance of the Jews from the Persians, under Mordechai, described in the Book of Esther. Purim is the holiday on which the Jews celebrate "a great redemption." In modern Israel, the feast is no less the hope of deliverance than the joy of a free nation. At *Tel-Aviv* the streets which carry the names of some Jewish personalities are decorated, and quotations from the *Megillah* (scroll of Esther) are appended to the street names. Purim is preceded by a day's fast.

In the following month of *Nisan* (normally April), begins the Jewish (ecclesiastical) year with its celebration of the sacred Passover, *Pesah,* "because the Lord passed over the houses of the children of Israel in Egypt when He smote the Egyptians." [35] On this festival the Jews partake of no leaven, *Hametz,* which should not even be found on the premises of their houses. They recall the hurried exodus of their ancestors, who left Egypt while having time to bake only unleavened cakes, *matzot,* for the journey. The eve of the first and second days of the Passover are *Seder* (order) nights, devoted to reading the story of the liberation from Egyptian bondage.

Numerous ritual customs dating from centuries back are prescribed: three matzots representing a division of the Jewish people, Cohen, Levi and Israel; the lamb bone symbolic of the sacrificial lamb; a roasted egg typifying hope and resurrection; parsley and radish root symbolic of spring; dipping the parsley in salt water to recall the tears shed in slavery; the sweetened sauce (*Haroseth*) whose red color represents the bricks made under Egyptian tyranny.

Fifty days after the Passover occurs the *Shabuoth,* anticipated by a "count down" called the Counting of Omer. The Shabuoth recalls the giving of the Law on Mount Sinai, when the people are reminded they accepted the charge of becoming a nation of priests and a holy nation. On the second day of the Shabuoth (as also on *Yom Kippur* and the last day of the Pesach) a memorial service is held for the dead. An ancient tradition recommends the distribution of gifts to the poor on the eve of all Jewish holy days.

Before the end of the religious year, there are two periods of fasting, during the civil months of July and August, called *Tammuz* and *Av.* They commemorate the first and second destruction of the temple of Jerusalem, and its burning to the ground. During these weeks of mourning no marriages are blessed nor other joyous festivities celebrated.

DIETARY LAWS. Few practices of the Jews are more misunderstood than the laws of *Kashruth* which they have obeyed since ancient times, and which demand of the Orthodox the greatest possible sacrifice.

As a general rule, the Torah states that the purpose of these laws is sanctification. Jewish writers over the years, notably, Maimonides, have speculated which among the regulations are major and which minor, and for both, why they are prescribed. In fact, the dietary customs of strict Judaism were the main source of tension and finally of separation from Orthodox Jewry.

There are six principal regulations, or legal restrictions, covering the Jewish diet. First is the prescription to eat only such animals as have been killed by *Shehitah,* which requires that the animal be killed instantly. A delay of even one moment makes the beast unfit for food. It must also be thoroughly drained of blood. Fish are not subject to this law. *Trephah* (torn) refers to all forbidden food, while *Kasher* (also *Kosher*) means what is "right" or permitted.

Blood is absolutely forbidden, except in the case of fish, following the prohibition in Deuteronomy that, since blood is life, "thou shalt not eat the life with the flesh." [36] Regarding cattle or beasts the law says, "Whatsoever parts the hoof, and is wholly cloven-footed, and chews the cud, among the beasts, that you may eat." Among other forbidden animals, the camel, the hare, and swine, are excluded in Scripture by name.[37] While a number of birds are traditionally considered *Kasher,* all birds of prey are forbidden. Fish that have fins and scales are permitted, but snails, lobsters, crabs and "every swarming thing that swarms upon the earth" should not be eaten.[38]

Finally all mixture of meat and milk, *Bassar Behalav,* is forbidden, although the flesh of fish is not considered meat in this combination. The Scripture source for the law is the prohibition of seething a kid in its mother's milk, which the rabbis explain contains three injunctions: not to cook meat and milk (or their products) together, not to eat such a mixture at the same meal, and not derive any benefit from such a mixture. The dietary laws even require that no dishes used for meat touch any used for dairy foods.

Orthodox commentators observe that the Jew who faithfully keeps *Kashruth* has to think of his religious and communal allegiance on the occasion of every meal, wherever his lot may be cast at the time; and on every occasion, his observance of the law is a renewed acknowledgment of his ancestry and a profession of his Jewish faith.

LIBERALISM AND REFORM

Adaptation of Judaism to prevalent conditions and liberalization of its faith and practice were familiar since the beginning of the Christian era, and before that among the Sadducees who favored Hellenizing tendencies, repudiated oral tradition and, among other doctrines, denied retribution in an after-life, resurrection of the body and the existence of angelic spirits.

The high-water mark of rationalization in the early Middle Ages occurred under Maimonides, whose principles of reform were less radical than might seem at first glance, since the basic dogmas he proposed are still professed by Orthodox Jews. More sweeping were the liberal ideas of Moses Mendelssohn (1729-1786), the German scholar who claimed that "Judaism knows nothing of a revealed religion in the sense in which it is taken by Christians. Judaism boasts of no exclusive revelation of immutable truths indispensable to salvation; of no revealed religion in the sense in which that term is usually taken." Instead of being exclusive, to the Jewish people, all its essentials are "the universal religion of mankind and not Judaism." [39] His Judaism, therefore, is a compound of theistic universalism, recognition of a historic community, and acceptance of its special way of life—but no more.

With the emergence of Jews from the European ghetto and their entrance into the mainstream of social life, the theoretical ideas of Mendelssohn and other reformers began to take practical shape along clearly divergent lines.

At one extreme remained the Orthodox who still form the majority of world Judaism. Emancipation in Europe found them unprepared. Not until near the end of the last century were seminaries and schools established to train the rising generation in the delicate task of preserving the full heritage of Judaic ideals in modern society. Samson Hirsch, Israel Hildesheimer and Meir Jung were among the pioneers in Germany, with comparable developments in England, Holland and France. In the United States they organized Yeshiva University and the Rabbinical Council of America. Yet they are the first to admit that while standing unequivocally for the principle of authority of the Torah and for Judaism as a revealed religion, Orthodox congregations, in America at least, suffer from many disabilities which their more liberal co-religionists are spared. Their great contribution to the future of Judaism was the religious faith they brought to the Zionist movement which helped create the independent state of Israel.

At the other extreme, and opposed to Orthodoxy, is Reform Judaism, also called Progressive or Liberal, which began in Germany as heir of Mendelssohn and emigrated to America through men like Isaac Wise and Kaufman Kohler, fresh from their conflict with Orthodox Jewry on the continent. There was a difference, however. Whereas the Reform movement in Europe was in most cities forced to make a tenuous peace with Conservatives so as not to break up the Jewish community, American Reformers became leaders of independent congregations, entirely free to reduce principles to action.

Two factors played heavily into their hands. The theoretical negation of the value of ritual observances found a ready echo in the general tendency of Jewish immigrants to drop all cultural obstacles in their climb to material success, and the prospect of acceptance in the American community seemed too great a blessing to count the cost, even if this meant transformation of their distinctive heritage. By 1885 the movement reached sufficient maturity to draft a strong manifesto which declared that in the Mosaic legislation "we accept as binding only its moral laws, and maintain only such ceremonies as elevate and sanctify our lives, but reject all such as are not adapted to the views and habits of modern civilization." This was revolutionary doctrine especially when coupled with the declaration that, "We reject as ideas not rooted in Judaism the beliefs both in bodily resurrection and in Gehenna and Eden, Hell and Paradise, as abodes of everlasting punishment and reward." [40]

The Pittsburgh Platform, as it came to be called, was not meant to be a creed but a set of guiding norms. But even so, for many rabbis the Reform movement had gone too far. It denied the nationhood of Israel and said that Jews were members of a religious sect, with no aspirations for the restoration of Palestine as the national home of Israel. The authority and binding power of traditional Jewish law were surrendered. Basic observances were dropped and a new liturgy was projected—all of which gave expression to existing practices.

Aroused by this break with historic Judaism a group of English-speaking rabbis decided to establish a theological seminary of their own. In opposition to the Hebrew Union College (Cincinnati) created by the Reform, they began in 1887 the Jewish Theological

Seminary (New York), with Solomon Schechter of Cambridge University as president. Within a few decades, Jewish Theological became the spiritual fountain head of the third alignment in American Jewry—Conservative Judaism.

Its basic philosophy is that Judaism is not a static, revealed religion but the growing religious culture and civilization of the Jewish people. Thus its first stress is on the evolving character of Judaism. Apologists point out that Judaism has always been dynamic, by adapting itself to new ideas and new situations. Moses, the prophets, Maimonides—each saved his people by adjusting their principles to the times. The Talmud itself is a massive reinterpretation of the Torah to meet the problems of the age.

Conservative Judaism seeks to steer a middle course between Orthodoxy and the Reform. The latter saw the practical impossibility of keeping the Jewish code under modern conditions and made the mistake of abrogating the law itself. Orthodoxy unrealistically tries to keep the structure unchanged, while denying that Judaism may ever undergo development. Conservatism believes that the best in Judaic traditions can be retained, while adjusting their application to current needs. The Jewish religion, it holds, has far more flexibility than the Orthodox would allow, and more stability than the Reform movement believes.

On the difficult question of which is more true to authentic Judaism, a prominent Jewish historian, Salo W. Baron, felt that Orthodoxy and Reform are a "deviation from historical Judaism," since both have abandoned "Judaism's self rejuvenating" vitality. Only Conservatism maintains "the general validity of Jewish law" and combines it with "the freedom of personal interpretation of the Jewish past and creed."

Reform Judaism has meantime reassessed its position. In 1937 it issued a revised platform which deserves to be quoted at length as a contrast to the image of Orthodoxy fixed in the popular mind. Recalling that only a minority follow the strict Orthodox tradition, of American Jews with somewhat higher ratios in other countries, the sentiments of the other extreme should be known, at the risk of conceiving Judaism as a monolith whose beliefs are circumscribed by the Torah or whose practices are covered by the 613 precepts set down in the Talmud.

Protesting they have no intention of setting down a fixed creed, the Reform rabbis defined Judaism as "the historical experience of the Jewish people." Its message grew out of Jewish life, indeed, but is actually universal and aims at the union and perfection of mankind under the sovereignty of God. Above all the principle of progressive development in religion must be recognized, whereby ancient ideals are consciously applied to existing cultural and social patterns.

The heart of Judaism, in Reform terms, and its main contribution to religion, is "the doctrine of the One, living God, who rules the world through law and love. In Him all existence has its creative source and mankind its ideal of conduct. Though transcending time and space, He is the indwelling Presence of the world." This last declaration aims to balance the notion of divine transcendence stressed by the Orthodox and offer scope within Judaism for disciples of Spinoza and Kant, who remain Jews while urging, as did Einstein, that "In their struggle for the ethical good, teachers of religion must have the stature to give up the doctrine of a personal God, that is, give up the source of fear and hope which in the past placed such vast power in the hands of priests." [41]

Coming to grips with the core problem of assimilation, spokesmen for the Reform rest their case on a concept of revelation which is at once natural and developmental, and not limited to Jews except by the accident of superior intellect.

God reveals Himself not only in the majesty, beauty and orderliness of nature, but also in the vision and moral striving of the human spirit. Revelation is a continuous process, confined to no one group and to no one age. Yet the people of Israel, through its prophets and sages, achieved unique insight in the realms of religious truth.

The Torah, both written and oral, enshrines Israel's evergrowing consciousness of God and the moral law. . . . Being products of historical processes, certain of its laws have lost their binding force with the passing of the conditions which called them forth. . . . Each age has the obligation to adapt the teachings of the Torah to its basic needs in consonance with the genius of Judaism.[42]

Correspondingly the hope in a personal Messias from the loins of David is modified, yet less forthrightly than half a century earlier, before the Nazi concentration camps had taken their millions of victims. When Zionism was still only a vague dream, the advocates of Reform declared, "We consider ourselves no longer a nation, but a religious community and therefore expect neither a return to Palestine, nor a sacrificial worship under the sons of Aaron, nor the restoration of any of the laws concerning the Jewish state." Now they concede that "in the rehabilitation of Palestine we behold the promise of renewed life for many of our brethren." But the real aim of Judaism is more expansive. "We regard it as our historic task to cooperate with all men in the establishment of the Kingdom of God, of universal brotherhood, justice, truth and peace on earth. This is our Messianic goal." [43]

Friendly Reform critics have said these sentiments are more notable for their adroitness in avoiding a catastrophic clash on the issue of nationalism than for lucidity, logic or forthrightness. Nevertheless they illustrate the spirit of Judaic liberalism in adapting itself not only to the pressure of alien powers which demand compromise as the price of survival, but also to dominant elements within Judaism that invite cooperation from all adherents of the Jewish faith in the interests of the common good.

Jewish writers who reflect on the vast changes that have taken place in the last generations see a religious dimension in the fact that Judaism has polarized in two centers, Israel and America. They find here the two classical foci of Jewish life—the Diaspora and the homeland. For the present they seem to be in flux, but in time are expected to prove the mysterious adaptability of Judaism to every contingency, now to its new role of a minority religion, mainly in America, and a national state in the land of the Bible.

THE CHOSEN PEOPLE

Any estimate of Judaism would be incomplete that did not take into account the belief in its own destiny as the Chosen People. Its origins are bound up with the initial covenant that God made with Abraham, as with the head of a family, so that the Jewish people ever since are conceived as the ever-growing number of descendants of the "father of all the faithful." When a convert to Judaism is received, the ritual prescribes that he be adopted into the family of Abraham; and all the liturgical prayers of the people emphasize their participation in the special blessings of a *gens electa,* with whom God first made a testament under Abraham and later widened it under Moses.

Their election by God binds the Jewish people to their part of the covenant. He led them out of slavery in Egypt, and worked marvelous signs in their favor; they are to hear His voice and remain faithful to His commandments. Time and again they failed in obedience and were punished for their infidelity, and though God will judge them by stricter standards than other nations, they will never be utterly rejected or abandoned. They will always be His people, and He will be their God.

Until modern times the nature of God's election and of Judaism as His "chosen one" was closely akin to the biblical notion that appears in the Torah and that centuries of reflection had crystallized in the Talmud. But as Judaism developed under its newly emancipated condition since the early eighteen hundreds, the concept of its status as a Chosen People was variously interpreted, depending on the religious philosophy which the interpreters professed and determined by their nearness or distance to or from the ideal set forth by Maimonides in the twelfth century. Exhorting the Yemenite Jewry to withstand persecution, he told them, "Know, you are born in this covenant and raised in this belief, that the stupendous occurrence, the truth of which is testified by the most trusty of witnesses, stands in very deed alone in the annals of mankind. For a whole people heard the word of God and saw the glory of the Divinity. From this lasting memory we must draw our power to strengthen our faith even in a period of persecution and affliction such as the present one." [44]

There are now two main approaches in Jewish thought to the idea of a covenant and to Israel's role as a chosen race among nations. One approach is naturalistic, where the version of religion without revelation is dominant and God Himself is represented as the sum of a man's highest ideals; the other is frankly revelational, admitting a divine intervention in favor of His people and through them to the rest of the world.

Sigmund Freud typifies the Jewish naturalist whose personal religious convictions were far removed from orthodoxy, and yet who maintained a passionate devotion to his people and was in-

spired to heroic efforts in the advancement of what he considered
the mission of Judaism to mankind.

Freud viewed himself as "little an adherent of the Jewish religion as of any other." He had no attraction for a Judaism that involved theological beliefs distinct from Christianity. On his seven-
tieth birthday, he wrote an address to the Society of B'nai B'rith in
which he confessed that "what bound me to Jewry was, I am
ashamed to admit, neither faith nor national pride, for I have always been an unbeliever and was brought up without any religion
though not without a respect for what are called the 'ethical' standards of human civilization." [45]

Yet in spite of his irreligion, Freud was intensely Jewish and
led most of his life in mainly Jewish society. His friends and pa-
tients were largely Jewish; his private culture, down to certain details of family sentiment, exemplified a Jewishness that friendly
biographers say was more binding than religious orthodoxy. With
all his distaste for Judaism as a faith, and for Jewish ceremonies
and customs, he acknowledged himself to be a psychological Jew.
By this he meant that he found in the perennial Jewish character,
rather than in belief, the source of his personal integrity, moral
courage, intelligence, and, above all, his defensive attitude toward
the world.

More than once he linked his own work and that of his contemporaries with the fact that he and they were Jewish. This was
the source of their moral stamina. Ethnic pride gave him the
strength to project his desire for that unhampered critical utterance
which, as he explained, is the religion not of the Jew integrated into
his own community but of the "infidel Jew," who stands on the
edge of an alien culture and perpetually arrayed against it.[46] It was
hardly coincidental, he felt, "that the first advocate of psychoanalysis was a Jew. To profess belief in this new theory called for a
certain degree of readiness to accept a position of solitary opposition, a position with which no one is more familiar than a Jew." [47]
In his image, this minority may at times shrink to a group of one,
like Moses—or himself—as the solitary opponent of organized
error.

In Freud's vocabulary, this opposition to organized error was
near the heart of what he considered the mission of the Jews as a

Chosen People. In the same address to the B'nai B'rith, after admitting his laxity on the religious side of Judaism, he made a profession of faith in those "other things" which bound him to his nation.

Plenty of other things remained over to make the attraction of Jewry and Jews irresistible—many obscure emotional forces, which were the more powerful the less they could be expressed in words, as well as a clear consciousness of inner identity, the safe privacy of a common mental construction. And beyond this there was a perception that it was to my Jewish nature alone that I owed two characteristics that had become indispensable to me in the difficult course of my life. Because I was a Jew I found myself free from many prejudices which restricted others in the use of their intellect; and as a Jew I was prepared to join the Opposition and to do without agreement with the "compact majority." [48]

He returns to the same theme in other writings, as in the short Autobiography, where he looks back at the conflict he early experienced as a medical student by reason of his race. "At an early age I was made familiar with the fate of being in the Opposition and of being put under the ban of the 'compact majority.' " [49]

In terms of the Judaic mission, therefore, Freud believed it was the role of his people, even as had been the function of the ancient prophets, to stand up for what they believed to be redemptive convictions, teaching an unlistening world the truths they needed to be delivered, in Freudian language, from their illusions. One of the paradoxes of this naturalism is that the illusion from which the "compact majority" were to be freed was that of religion. "A psychologist," Freud wrote, "strives to review the development of mankind in accord with what insight he has won from studying the mental processes of the individual during his development from childhood to manhood. In this connection the idea forces itself upon him that religion is comparable to a childhood neurosis, and he is optimistic enough to assume that mankind will overcome this neurotic phase, just as so many children grow out of their similar neuroses." [50]

Needless to say the Freudian concept of Judaism is repudiated by all believing Jews, notwithstanding Freud's own claim that "I have always had a strong feeling of solidarity with my fellow-people, and have always encouraged it in my children as well. We have all remained in the Jewish denomination." [51]

On a higher level, but still within the scope of naturalism, is another idea of the Covenant propounded with marked fervor among the Reform groups in the United States. The American Mordechai Kaplan complains that "the apologists for the doctrine of Israel's election do not take the trouble to think through to a conclusion the role of religion in human civilization." They too easily assume that "religion was supernaturally revealed truth," and then argue that when such truth was communicated only by one's own people, these people had been chosen by God. "But when one abandons the idea of supernatural revelation, what becomes of religion?" It is found to be the organized quest of a people for salvation, and on the part of the Jews it is a composite of their saints and heroes, customs and folkways, sacred literature and common symbols which have been hallowed by their relation to the Judaic search for the goal of human destiny. Yet, while the Jews are not a chosen people in the traditional sense, they have a duty to help others find a conception of God that imposes on its adherents loyalty to a universally valid code of ethics. "It is only in that sense that the Jewish religion is universal." [52]

The classic interpretation of Israel's covenant begins with the premise that God has communicated a special revelation to the Jews. They are its predestined custodians, to whom Yahweh entrusted the prophetic wisdom that He wants finally to be shared by all nations. It was a clear vision of this fact which inaugurated the neo-orthodox movement in modern Judaism, as expressed in a famous letter of Rabbi Samson Raphael Hirsch (1808-1888), one of the founders of modern Jewish orthodoxy.

Because men had eliminated God from life, nay, even from nature and found the basis of life in possessions and its aim in enjoyment, deeming life the product of the multitude of human desires, just as they looked upon nature as the product of a multitude of gods, therefore it became necessary that a people be introduced into the ranks of the nations which, through its history and life, should declare God the only creative cause of existence, fulfilment of His will the only aim of life; and which should bear the revelation of His will, rejuvenated and renewed for its sake, unto all parts of the world as the motive and incentive of its coherence.

This mission required for its carrying out a nation poor in everything upon which the rest of mankind reared the edifice of its greatness and its power; externally subordinate to the nations armed with proud reliance on self, but fortified by direct reliance on God; so that by suppression of every opposing force God might reveal Himself directly as the only Creator, Judge and Master of nature and history.[53]

Hirsch declared that "the proclaiming of these great truths was to be the chief, if not the sole, life-task of this people." Has Israel any other function, he asked, than to teach all the races of man to recognize and worship the Only-One as their God; and should not Israel's unceasing duty be to proclaim through the example of its life and teaching the universal Lord and Sovereign of creation.

The same sentiments were echoed in the greatest spiritual representative of classical Judaism in the twentieth century, the chief rabbi of Palestine, Abraham Isaac Kook (1865-1935), whose mysticism was a reaffirmation of the teaching of the prophets. All the world, he taught, is waiting for the Light of Israel radiating from Him whose name is to be praised. "This people was fashioned by God to speak of His glory; it was granted the heritage of the blessing of Abraham so that it might disseminate the knowledge of God and it was commanded to live its life apart from the nations of the world. God chose it to cleanse the whole world of all impurity and darkness; this people is endowed with a hidden treasure, with the Torah, the means by which the Heaven and the Earth were created." [54]

Too often the Light of Israel is taken for a utopian dream, or some abstract morality, or merely a pious wish and noble vision. This is a mistake. "It does not wash its hands of the material world and all its values, abandoning the flesh, and society and government to wallow in their impurity, and forsaking the forces of nature, which fell in the Fall of Man, to remain in their low estate. It is, rather, a raising of all of life" to something of its pristine vigor and integrity.[55]

Rabbi Kook was realist enough to sense what he called a grave error, which is insensitive to the distinctive unity of the Jewish spirit and imagines that the Divine stuff that characterizes Israel is like the spiritual content of other national civilizations. "This error is the source of the attempt to sever the national from the religious element of Judaism. Such division would falsify both our nationalism and our religion, for every element of thought, emotion, and idealism that is present in the Jewish people belongs to an indivisible unity, and all together make up its specific character." [56] The Zionist movement was based on these two component elements of Judaism.

In pluralist countries like the United States, the same ideals have been presented but with an accent on the need for tolerance towards the non-Jewish religions. An ardent defender of the Torah, Yehudah Halevi, "who scorned the annual task of modern rabbis and Jewish pulpiteers to bring Judaism into fictitious harmony with fictitious modern culture," is cited as authority that "Christianity and Mohammedanism are cooperating with the Jew in the task of bringing near the time of the Messiah." [57]

But the task is not an easy one. Judaism which is faithful to its mission has to keep ever conscious of its inward responsibility as the people of God and simultaneously of the outward duty to communicate the divine message to others. "Neither to become assimilated with the other nations nor yet to be isolated from them completely, but rather to live with them in constant exchange of thought and act, in order to fulfil its own mission by teaching the supremacy of God—that seems to be the historical function of Israel." [58]

Evidently the interior spirit must be deep to insure preservation of those religious principles on which Judaism is built; and at the same time the desire to share this divine treasure must be strong, if both the centripetal and centrifugal purposes of God's plan are to be active. Between the two, the more difficult to maintain is interior fidelity to the Law.

The conscious and unconscious striving towards this ideal is the meaning of all Jewish history. To perpetuate ourselves in spite of the tremendous forces making for the disintegration of the Jewish type, we need the consolidating, strengthening, vitalizing influence of the Jewish environment. Such environment is created by the life in the Law. Only there pulsates the spirit of Judaism, only thence emanates that intensive permeation with our historical ideals, which enable us to continue not only our national existence, but also our contribution to the common treasury of man.[59]

If the Jewish people are ever to make the impact on the world, for which they have been destined by the Creator, it cannot come from an amorphous compromise with the less than divine principles of the world about them. "From the colorless abode of assimilation we have no message for the world," and the sad history of opposition which they have met only re-enforces the conclusion. No doubt there is a "Jewish question," but "if we are earnest about the Jewish question, we realize that its solution lies with us. Anti-Semitism, intolerance, are Gentile problems. Ours is the task to raise Jewry to the heights of Judaism," which is religious in essence and apostolic in aim.

The strongest message of Judaism for our day is the all-embracing character of religion. Judaism must remain the single upward-surging force every day of the year, every hour of the day. It brooks no pigeonholing of religion, no reduction of its scope, no confinement of its message. Its function must be as catholic as its eschatology. Torah-true Judaism is the Judaism which insists in theory on the necessity of religion to embrace synagogue, home and life, and which provides in practice guidance for every action, addressing the bride at home, the employer at his office, the youngster in school, the judge, the priest.[60]

A new dimension has been added to the classic form of Israel based on the Torah through the writings and influence of Martin Buber, commonly recognized as the outstanding Jewish religious thinker of modern times. He was a native of Vienna, where he took his doctor's degree in 1900, and played an active part in the Zionist movement, which he had joined two years before. From 1906 onwards he devoted himself chiefly to religious studies. These led him to occupation with Hasidism, whence he derived many of his ideas, e.g., those on a kind of activist mysticism and the sanctification of daily life. From 1916 to 1924 he was editor of *Der Jude,* the principal periodical of German-speaking Jewry. In 1923 he received a call to Frankfurt University, where he lectured on Jewish theology and ethics. In 1926 he started a periodical *Die Kreatur,* with Catholic and Protestant collaborators. After the advent of Adolph Hitler he became professor at the University of Jerusalem.

Outside of Judaism, Buber is best known for his treatise *Ich und Du* (1923), in which he studies the relationship between man and things, called by him the "I-It" relationship, in contrast to the relation between persons, i.e., between man and man and between man and God, called the "I-Thou" relationship. But his contribution to the religion of his own people has been equally if not more significant.

Buber applies the existential approach to the Bible, which he sees as essentially a dialogue between "the 'I' of the speaking God and the 'Thou' of the hearing Israel." For all its variety and detail, the Bible "is really one book, for one basic theme unites all the stories and songs, sayings and prophecies, contained within it. The theme of the Bible is the encounter between a group of people and the Lord of the world in the course of history." [61] Its basic doctrine is that our life is a dialogue between the above and the below, which approximates the dialogue relation that Buber finds to be the underlying reality in human existence and becomes the very foundation of biblical faith. Unlike the realm of philosophy, however, where God is man's Eternal Thou corresponding to the human I, in the Bible God is the I, and man the Thou whom He addresses. In other words, it is God who speaks first and man responds with all the vitality of his God-inspired nature.

As might be expected from these postulates, Buber has no sympathy with the static notion of Israel as a social entity, fixed once and for all by ethnic ties and bound together by a common belief in God. Certainly this is a familiar image outside of Judaism, but it is not the actual Chosen People, "not that which the prophet who harangues the people sees assembled around him. The religious character of the people consists emphatically in that something different intended for it from what it is now, that it is destined for something different—that it should become a true people, the 'People of God.' Precisely in the religion of Israel it is impossible to make an idol of the people as a whole, for the religious attitude of the community is inherently critical and postulative. Whoever ascribes to the nation or to the community the attributes of the absolute and of self-sufficiency betrays the religion of Israel." [62]

But, then, what does it mean to become a People of God, if a common belief in God and service to His name are not the constitutive elements? It means that men have engaged in personal encounter with Yahweh, have listened to Him speak in the depths of their soul, and responded not merely with faith expressed in community worship but with affection for their fellowman who is in the image of God.

Becoming a people of God means that the attributes of God revealed to it, justice and love, are to be made effective in its own life, in the lives of its members with one another; justice materialized in the indirect mutual relationships of these individuals; love in their direct mutual relationships rooted in their personal existence. Of the two, however, love is the higher, the transcending principle. This becomes unequivocally clear from the fact that man cannot be just to God; he can, however, and should, love God. And it is the love of God which transfers itself to man. "God loves the stranger," we are told, "so you too shall love him." The man who loves God loves also him whom God loves.[63]

Accordingly what makes Israel a chosen race is not its national consciousness, even when that is rooted in the acknowledgment of the one true God. It is the divine commission to go beyond itself in spiritual philanthropy, and in the generous responsiveness of the people to this mandate. "I am setting up," Buber explained, "Hebrew humanism in opposition to that Jewish nationalism which regards Israel as a nation like unto other nations, and recognizes no task for Israel save that of preserving and asserting itself." Unlike other communities, "in the historical hour in which its tribes grew together to form a people, it became the carrier of a revelation." [64] That hallmark of Judaic identity remains unchanged to the present day.

Buber's lifelong friendship with Christians made him acutely aware that they, too, considered themselves chosen by God, with a mission not unlike that of the Jews and founded, like theirs, on God's selective communication to man. In a memorable conference to Christian missionaries he brought out "the two foci of the Jewish soul," which he identified as "first the immediate relationship to the Existent One, and second, the power of atonement in an unatoned world." On these two elements rests the ultimate division between Judaism and Christianity.

As regards the first element, the Jews believe in "the non-incarnation of God who reveals Himself to the 'flesh' and is present to it in a mutual relationship." In contrast with Christians who also profess the unity of God, "we do not unite ourselves with Him. The God in whom we believe, to whom we are pledged, does not unite with human substance on earth." But the very fact that they do not conceive themselves being united with God urges them the more ardently "to demand that the world shall be perfected under the kingship of the Mighty One."

Similarly, the Jews look upon the world as yet unredeemed and therefore that salvation is still to be accomplished. "No savior with whom a new redeemed history began has appeared to us at any definite point in history. Because we have not been stilled by anything which has happened, we are wholly directed toward the coming of that which is to come." [65]

Thus on both counts, Christians and Jews seem to be utterly divided, and how often only their division has been stressed. Nevertheless they have much in common and not the least of Buber's contributions to Judaic literature has been to clarify the relationship of these two Chosen Peoples, and to offer the hope for their fruitful cooperation. "What have you and we in common," he asks of Christians. If we take the question literally, he answers, "a book and an expectation." The book is the revealed word of God, the expectation is the advent of the Messias.

To you, the book is a forecourt; to us, it is the sanctuary. But in this place, we can dwell together, and together listen to the voice that speaks here. That means that we can work together to evoke the buried speech of that voice; together, we can redeem the imprisoned living word.

Your expectation is directed toward a second coming, ours to a coming which has not been anticipated by a first. To you the phrasing of world history is determined by one absolute midpoint, the year one; to us, it is an unbroken flow of tones following each other without a pause from their origin to their consummation. But we can wait for the advent of the One together, and there are moments when we may prepare the way before Him together.[66]

When compared pre-messianically, the destinies of Judaism and Christianity are divided. To the Christian, the Jew is the incomprehensibly obdurate man, who declines to admit what has happened; whereas to the Jew, the Christian is the incomprehensibly daring man, who affirms that the redemption has been accomplished in a world that is still unredeemed. While "this is a gulf which no human power can bridge," it should not prevent the common watch for a unity to come from God for Christians and Jews.

Buber encourages both sides to hold inviolably fast to their respective faiths, "that is to our own deepest relationship to truth," and to show a religious respect for the true faith of the other. Existentialist fashion, he concludes that "whenever we both, Christian and Jew, care more for God Himself than for our images, we are united in the feeling that our Father's house is differently constructed than all our human models take it to be." [67] While this kind of relativism is hard to reconcile with the absolutes of Christianity, it is symbolic of a heartening spirit in modern Judaism, whose ranking spokesman tells his people to "meet the world with the fulness of your being, and you shall meet God," on the premise that the world outside of Judaism also has the revelation of God.

12. Early Christianity

CHRISTIANITY is unique in the history of world religions. Its ancestry derives from almost two millenia of Judaism, whose prophets for centuries had foretold the coming of a great religious leader who would establish a new spiritual kingdom on earth; its origins are rooted in extensive historical facts, from the birth of Christ to His crucifixion and resurrection from the dead; its message centers around a core of doctrines which Christ revealed to His followers not as a philosophy of speculation nor even primarily as an ethic for self-conquest, but as mysteries whose inner essence lies beyond human reason, yet on whose acceptance would depend human salvation; its character from the beginning was social in the most comprehensive sense of that term, with a communal structure, a body of truths, rites and obligations that had for their purpose not merely the personal sanctification of those who believed, but their corporate unification and internal consolidation by the invisible Spirit of God.

MESSIANIC FULFILMENT

The great hope of the Jewish people nurtured by the prophets was the advent of a great leader whom they called "The Anointed," in Hebrew "The Messiah," whose kingdom would succeed the theocratic government of Israel and extend to all nations, races and classes of people. Membership in this kingdom carried the promise of order and peace in this world and of final beatitude in the next. The Messianic kingdom would be served by priests and teachers from all nations, dispensing an abundance of divine knowledge and a relish for things of the spirit; there would be one sacrifice, offering a clean oblation to the one true God throughout the world. Those who belonged to it were assured the remission of their sins, sanctity of life, justice among people and nations, and an outpouring of divine benediction.

According to the prophets, this kingdom would be established by the Messias who was simultaneously priest, law-giver and king, who would sacrifice himself for the redemption of his people and institute a new order of society, beginning with the Jews and then to be diffused to the ends of the earth.

What the prophets foretold in the Scriptures found reflection in the extra-canonical writings of the Hebrews, like the *Testament of the Twelve Patriarchs,* in a passage that was written two hundred years before the coming of Christ.

> Then shall the Lord raise up a new priest.
> And he shall execute a righteous judgment upon the earth for
>   a multitude of days.
> And his star shall rise in heaven as of a king,
> Lighting up the light of knowledge as the sun the day,
> And he shall be magnified in the world.
> He shall shine forth as the sun of the earth,
> And he shall remove all darkness from under heaven,
> And there shall be peace in all the earth.
> And the knowledge of the Lord shall be poured forth upon the
>   earth, as the water of the seas.
> And he shall give his majesty to his sons in truth for evermore.
> And there shall be none succeed him for all generations
>   for ever.
> And in his priesthood the Gentiles shall be multiplied in
>   knowledge upon the earth,
> And enlightened through the grace of the Lord.[1]

Time and again Jesus proclaimed himself the Messias of the prophets, but never more solemnly than when, in reply to the woman at the well, "I know that the Messias is coming," He told her, "I who speak with you am he." [2] Already when beginning His public ministry at Nazareth, He opened the scroll of Isaias and read the Messianic text, "the Spirit of the Lord is upon me, because He has anointed me," and added, "today this Scripture has been fulfilled in your hearing." [3]

From the dawn of Christianity, the apostles and first leaders of the Church were at pains to verify the origins of their faith and how radically, therefore, the Christian religion differs from the mythology of pagan Greece and Rome. They were conscious of the strength of their position in having a historic center. "We do not utter idle tales," they told their contemporaries, "in declaring that God was born in form of man."

There never was a Mithra, the Romans were reminded; and he never slew the mystic bull. There never was a Great Mother of sorrows to wail over Attis and become a true mother to the suffering daughters of humanity. For all her beauty, Isis was only the idealized product of Egyptian zoolatry. The Logos of the Stoics was a pure abstraction, and of their ideal Wise Man, Plutarch wrote, "He is nowhere on earth, nor ever has been;" whereas for Christians "the Word was made flesh and dwelt among us."

The apostles staked their whole mission on this fact. Peter, writing from prison, assured the neophytes that "we were not following fictitious tales when we made known to you the power and coming of our Lord Jesus Christ, but we had been eyewitnesses of His grandeur." [4] Reproaching the Corinthians for their factious disputes, Paul appealed to historical continuity of his teaching with that of the first followers of Christ. "I delivered to you", he said, "what I also have received." Indeed the facts of Christ's life, death, and especially resurrection are so indispensable that without them the whole Christian faith is vain and "we are of all men the most to be pitied." [5]

Under pressure from their environment which was accustomed only to Greek speculation and Roman mythology, the early Christians were tempted to compromise, as many did in the Gnostic peril that faced the nascent Church. They were strengthened to resist by the aged apostle John, whose epistles seem almost strained in their effort to vindicate the foundations of the faith. "I write of what was from the beginning, what we have heard, what we have seen with our eyes, what we have looked upon and our hands have handled: of the Word of Life." [6]

In the same vein, Ignatius of Antioch stressed the need of watchfulness, not to give ear to those who would make of Christ only one of their aeons and something less than a real historical person. Christians must beware of the Docetae who denied the reality of Christ's human actions and therefore of His redemptive life and death.

> Stop your ears when anyone speaks to you that stands apart from Jesus Christ, from David to scion and Mary's son, who was really (*alethōs*) born and ate and drank, really (*alethōs*) persecuted by Pontius Pilate, really (*alethōs*) crucified and died while heaven and earth and the underworld looked on; who also really (*alethōs*) rose from the dead, since His Father raised Him up—His Father, who will also raise us who believe in Him through Jesus Christ, apart from whom we have no real life.[7]

Throughout his seven letters, written about 107 A.D., Ignatius returns to the same theme. He repeats the term *alethōs,* "really . . . truly . . . actually" the birth, life, death and resurrection of Christ took place, and therefore the faith of Christ is solidly established.

In the sub-apostolic and early patristic age, when the vested interest of the Roman Empire reacted against "the persons commonly called, who were hated for their enormities" (Tacitus), Christian apologists spent their energies proving the validity of the Gospel narrative of Christ. "Let us leave untouched," pleaded Polycarp of Smyrna (69-155 A.D.), "the useless speculations of the masses and their false doctrines, and turn to the teaching delivered to us in the beginning." [8] Not subjective theories but factual events were considered the mainstay of the Christian religion.

COMMUNITY OF FAITH AND WORSHIP

The facts of the Gospel narrative focus on the doctrines which Christ taught as the substance of His message and a condition for becoming His disciple. He proposed His divine Sonship and said He was one with the Father. When the Jews who were scandalized at this "blasphemy" picked up stones to kill Him, "He went forth out of their hands," but without retracting the claim.[9]

In much the same way He announced the Eucharist, telling the people that unless they ate the flesh of the Son of Man and drank His blood, they would not have life in them. As a consequence many of His disciples left Him, complaining that "this is a hard saying. Who can listen to it?" Yet instead of correcting a possible false impression or qualifying the mystery of faith, He turned to the Twelve and asked them, "Do you also wish to go away?" [10]

On the subject of marriage, He raised marital union to the sacramental level and added the precept of perfect monogamy, declaring that remarriage while the first spouse is living is wrong, no matter what concessions had been given to the ancient Jews. Again His followers, and this time the apostles themselves, were shocked at the severity of doctrine. Better not marry, they told Him, than to be so bound irrevocably for life. But there was no retraction; only a restatement to the effect that virginity, too, is possible with the grace of God. [11]

He proclaimed Himself the object of divine worship and demanded of His followers complete dedication. "If anyone loves father or mother, yes, and his own life also, more than me, he is not worthy of me." [12] Correspondingly He required that men pray to Him for all their needs, since "without me you can do nothing." But "whatever you ask in my name, that I will do." [13]

Implicit in all this teaching of Christ is the fact that He is communicating divine revelation to a chosen group of men, and bidding them transmit His message to all nations to the end of time. He is not expounding a purely natural philosophy or a system of ethics founded on human genius, but giving mankind a body of truths which "he who does not believe will be condemned" for rejecting. [14]

Besides uniformity of faith, Christ taught a community of worship and ritual as substantial elements of Christianity. His followers were indeed to believe in His teaching, but they had also to receive external baptism by water in the name of the Holy Trinity. He compared the effect of baptism to a new birth and emphasized in graphic language that just as in the natural order there is no life without physical birth, so in Christianity there is no life of grace "unless a man be born again of water and the Holy Spirit." In His parting commission to the apostles, He bade them "make disciples of all nations, (by) baptizing them in the name of the Father, and of the Son, and of the Holy Spirit," thus equating the initial following of Christ with ritual baptism according to a specified formula.

The early Christians stressed the consistency of the Old and New Covenants. Jesus said He did not come to destroy the law and the prophets but to fulfil them. Consequently where the Old Law had its ceremony of initiation in the rite of circumcision, membership in the society founded by Christ was to be effected uniquely through the sacrament of regeneration, which is the door of the Church and the basic external sign of every true Christian.

If baptism was the means for entering the kingdom of God on earth, the Eucharist became the normal condition for remaining in that kingdom. "He who eats my flesh and drinks my blood has life everlasting, and I will raise him up on the last day." No other mystery of faith more clearly identified Christianity as a visible society. "Take care," Ignatius of Antioch wrote to the Philadelphians, "to partake of one Eucharist; for one is the flesh of our Lord Jesus Christ, one the cup to unite us with His blood, and one altar, just as there is one bishop." [15]

In order to make the Eucharist a permanent institution and perpetuate the fruits of the Cross, Christ at the Last Supper gave His followers the power and duty to do what He had done, "in commemoration of me." When He ordained His chosen twelve, He was instituting those through whom the graces of the redemption were to flow from the Redeemer to the whole of mankind.

When pronouncing the words of his first consecration, Jesus spoke of "my blood of the New Covenant," to underscore the continuity between the two Laws and the perfection of the Christian over the Jewish dispensation. Among other early apologists, Justin the martyr argued from the Christian Eucharist to a fulfilment of the Messianic prophecies. The clean oblation foretold by Malachy, he said, is "the bread of the Eucharist and the chalice of the Eucharist." The ministry of Christ was to be open to all people, and not limited to the descendants of one family; it was to serve the welfare of all nations, and not only the sons of Abraham; it was to end the multiplicity of sacrifices among the Jews in favor of the one oblation of the Lamb of God offering Himself to the heavenly Father. This would give the Church of Christ a unity and universality that no other religion had ever enjoyed.

For the sins committed after baptism, Christ gave the Church power of remission that would further consolidate His Church as a society with tangible obligations on its members. Appearing to the Twelve the night of His resurrection, He told them, "As the

Father has sent me, I also send you." And breathing on them in a gesture symbolic of the transmission of power, He said, "Receive ·the Holy Spirit; whose sins you shall forgive, they are forgiven them; and whose sins you shall retain, they are retained." [16]

KINGDOM AND AUTHORITY

The historical work of Christ during His visible stay on earth has a variety of aspects that range through the whole gamut of God's revelation of His nature and love for mankind, and of man's duty towards Him in order to return to God. Yet the master idea of Christ's mesage is epitomized in a single word that was most frequently on His lips, the *Basileia* of the evangelists, or the kingdom. All that he taught was somehow identified with the kingdom, from the opening of His public life when He began to preach repentance, "for the kingdom of heaven is at hand," to His dying profession before Pilate that "my kingdom is not of this world, my kingdom is not from here." Christ is reported to have used the word "Church" only twice in describing the society He founded. He spoke of His kingdom in almost every chapter of the Gospels, so that whatever concept they give us of the Church must be looked for in this notion of the kingdom.

Yet immediately a problem arises. The clear impression left by the evangelists is that Christ spoke of two kinds of kingdom, an earthly and a heavenly one. When He compared it to a grain of mustard seed that a man cast into his garden, and it grew and became a large tree, He was referring to an earthly kingdom that grows and develops in membership and influence. Or again, when He said that the kingdom is like a net cast into the sea and gathering in fish of every kind, the good and bad, which are later sorted out and the bad thrown away, this cannot mean the kingdom after death. The parable illustrates what will happen at the end of the world when the angels are sent to separate the wicked from the just and will cast the former into hell. On the other hand, Jesus also spoke of a kingdom that is not of this world, or a joy that awaits those who are poor in spirit, of the reward He will give on the last day to those who during life had fed the hungry and clothed the naked in His name.

These two kingdoms are mutually dependent. The heavenly kingdom is the goal and terminus of the earthly society, and the latter a means and condition for attaining the heavenly. It would be stressing the obvious to say that Christ preached the doctrine of a celestial kingdom that will never end and that God has in store for those who love Him. Even Mohammed, who did not accept the divinity of Christ and recognized Him only as a messenger of Allah, spoke of the "rich rewards for those who believe (in Jesus) and performed the works of virtue." They are promised after death a paradise "that is watered by rivers, and whose food and shade are perpetual." [17] What is less obvious is that Christ also founded an earthly society that would carry on His mission until the end of time.

Whenever a new society is being formed, the first stage calls for a "getting together" to lay plans for the prospective organization. This is true whether the original impulse to unite for a common purpose is something mutual or comes from a single individual who does the organizing. In the origins of Christianity this impulse came from Jesus of Nazareth.

John and Andrew, the disciples of John the Baptist, were first invited by Christ to "come and see" where He lived, to learn more about this man whom the Baptist had pointed out as the Lamb of God. Later on they were called to "Come follow me, and I will make you fishers of men." At once they left their nets and followed Jesus.

Meantime, Andrew found his brother Simon and said to him, "We have found the Messias." Jesus invited him by changing his name to Cephas, the Rock. Philip was invited with a simple, "Follow me," and passed the word on to his brother Nathaniel, who responded by professing his faith in Christ as "the Son of God and the King of Israel." Matthew describes his vocation while sitting in the tax-collector's office. On hearing these words, "Follow me," he arose and immediately followed the Master. In rapid succession six others were called to join the apostles until the full complement of twelve was filled, in imitation, we may suppose, of the leaders of the twelve tribes of Israel.

They were all from Galilee, as suggested by the remark on Pentecost Sunday, "are not all these men who are speaking Galileans?" Their culture and ancestry were thoroughly Jewish. Even their names were Hebrew and Aramaic derivatives. Nathaniel, "the gift of God"; John, "Yahweh is gracious"; Thomas, "the twin"; Matthew, "gift of Yahweh." The two apparent exceptions, Andrew and Philip, likely had Jewish names beside the Greek ones. In a word, everything about the inner circle of Christ's original company was Jewish, in fulfilment of God's promise that in the seed of Abraham all nations would be blessed, beginning with the Messias and the first ambassadors of His kingdom.

Throughout the public life of Christ, the apostles were His constant, chosen companions. Over thirty times in the Gospels they are simply identified as "the Twelve." When the Master preached to the multitudes, they were with Him, and not just part of the crowd but near Him to receive the message that was intended only for them. When He worked His miracles, it seemed primarily for their benefit, from the first of His signs at Cana where He manifested His glory "and His disciples believed in Him," to His resurrection from the dead when He was most solicitous that all the apostles should be convinced, including the doubting Thomas who was favored with a special visitation. At the Last Supper, the apostles alone were chosen to share in the Savior's final testimony before the passion, and to partake for the first time of the blood of the new and eternal covenant. At the ascension, they received the mandate to go into the whole world and preach the gospel to every creature.

All the extant forms of Christianity consider themselves descended from the apostles and equally recite in the Nicene Creed, "I believe in . . . the apostolic Church." They reflect on the teaching of St. Paul to tell the Ephesians, "you are no longer strangers and foreigners, but you are citizens with the saints and members of God's household: you are built upon the foundation of the apostles and prophets with Christ Jesus Himself as the chief cornerstone."

But while commonly recognizing their apostolic ancestry, Christians are not agreed on the transmission of Christ's authority through the apostles or even on the fact that such transmission had ever taken place. Catholics believe the Church's apostolicity was climaxed in the person of St. Peter, the "Prince of the Apostles," and continues unbroken in the visible headship of Peter's successor, the bishop of Rome. Eastern Orthodox prefer to invest the whole Church with apostolic authority, in such a way that every Christian shares the right to interpret the meaning of faith, and collectively the Mystical Body is the teaching and ruling organ of all the faithful. Protestants will have the Spirit of Christ in the heart of each believer guide him on the road to heaven, where no human person and no institution but only the Savior has the power to determine man's relationship with God.

PETRINE PRIMACY. According to Catholic tradition, Christ had the option of choosing any one of a number of structures for His Church. He might have made it a democracy, or an oligarchy, or an aristocracy. But then He would have established a different Church from the existing one, because the structure He chose was monarchial. From the opening scenes of His public life, it is pointed out, He selected one man to become the visible head of the Christian community.

At the first meeting with the Master at Capharnaum, Jesus looked upon Peter and told him that his name would be changed from Simon to Cephas (Rock) as a foreshadowing of his future leadership. Gradually He accustomed the jealous apostles to Peter's singular position among them. Even among the three who were nearest to the Savior, the sequence was always Peter, James and John; notwithstanding the fact that John was *par excellence* the beloved disciple.

Peter was regularly preferred for special instructions and admonitions; he was trained above the others in humility, patience and trust in God; his faith was declared essential, in order to strengthen the others; he was recognized as the spokesman for the other apostles, not for any personal traits or natural gifts, but because the Lord had chosen him for leadership from the moment he was called to the apostolate.

Two events in the life of Christ stand out as the guarantee that Peter was intended to carry on the work of His Master with an authority that was shared by no other apostle. The first event took place in the midst of the public ministry and is recorded by the three synoptics, but especially by St. Matthew; the second occurred after the resurrection and is described only by the St. John.

Shortly after the second miraculous feeding of the multitude, Jesus took His disciples to the neighborhood of Caesarea Philippi, on the extreme borders of the land of Israel. Secluded from the crowds of followers, in a territory that was now pagan, He put His apostles to the test, in order to clarify once and for all His position in their regard and determine their role in the work He had in store for them. He asked them, "Who do men say the Son of Man is?" They answered, "Some say, John the Baptist; and others Elias; and others Jeremias, or one of the prophets." When He asked them again, "But who do you say that I am?" Simon Peter answered, "Thou art the Christ, the Son of the Living God." Jesus then declared,

Blessed art thou, Simon Bar-Jona, for flesh and blood has not revealed this to thee, but my Father in heaven. And I say to thee, thou art Peter, and upon this rock I will build my Church, and the gates of hell shall not prevail against it. And I will give thee the keys of the kingdom of heaven; and whatever thou shalt bind on earth, shall be bound in heaven, and whatever thou shalt loose on earth shall be loosed in heaven.[18]

Set in paraphrase, the essential words of Christ, "Thou art Peter, and upon this rock I will build my Church," would read: I shall make you the foundation of the spiritual edifice I intend to build. Therefore what the foundation is to the building, its source of unity, strength and stability, you are going to be that in the Church which I am about to found. And since the unified strength and stability of any society derive from ultimate authority, I shall give you and your successors all the authority you will need to preserve my Church from harm, for all time, by confirming your judgment on earth with divine ratification in heaven.

This promise must be taken in conjunction with its actual conferral after the resurrection. In spite of Peter's denial of his Master, and the fact that humanly speaking he was anything but the rock on which to build an institution that could resist the powers of hell, Christ was faithful to what He had said a year before. Calling Peter aside on the shores of the sea of Tiberius, Jesus asked him, "Simon, son of John, do you love me more than these?" When Peter answered in the affirmative, Christ told him, "Feed my lambs." Then a second time, "Do you love me?" and the same answer, with the same commission. Finally a third time, to which Peter protested, "Lord, you know all things; you know that I love you," and the closing injunction, "Feed my sheep."

When Christ gave Peter the authority to govern the infant Church, His action was determined by the character of the society He was founding: a permanent institution with a body of religious truths to be kept unchanged as the instrument of salvation, whose members were to be united by the profession of a common faith and practice of a mutual love.

Knowing the need for external ultimate authority in any stable society, Christ desired nothing less for His Church. Accordingly Peter was only the first in the line of visible heads of the Church who, like Peter, would consolidate under Christ the institution whose basic principles were determined by the Savior before He returned to the Father.

By Catholic standards, such was the substantial judgment of believing Christians for ten centuries in the East and fifteen centuries in the West, and is still a cardinal dogma of Christianity. In the words of the first Vatican Council, it is "according to the institution of Christ our Lord Himself, that is, by divine law, that St. Peter has perpetual successors in the primacy over the whole Church," and, indeed, "the Roman Pontiff is the successor of St. Peter in the same primacy." [19]

SOBORNOST, KOINONIA, AND CONCILIARITY. The Churches in the Eastern Orthodox tradition find their ultimate authority in something less defined than the Roman primacy. For want of a better word, the English "conciliarity" has been coined to translate something of what the Russians mean by *sobornost* or the Greeks by *koinonia*. As explained by a contemporary Orthodox theologian, "conciliarity of government," or the mystical union of the faithful through love, is the true notion of the Church's authority.

While there is no official teaching of the Eastern Churches on the nature of *sobornost,* it is easily found in the stream of Orthodox history and frequently discussed in contemporary writings on the subject.

The classic idea of *koinonia* grew out of historical circumstances. For centuries the Church was faced with a series of theological crises, raised by those who denied the divinity of Christ, His consubstantiality with the Father, and the necessity of supernatural grace for salvation. With notable exception the crises were resolved, though under papal mandate or approval, mainly through conciliar action whether local, synodal, provincial or ecumenical. If there were many instances when the Popes intervened without the use of a council, the dominant impression in the East was that conciliar rule and teaching should be identified with the ordinary mode of governing the Church.

After the final breach with Rome in the eleventh century, the theory took hold that the first seven ecumenical councils are the final authority for instruction and government of the Church. Pronouncements from these assemblies, 325 to 787 A.D., are normative for the Christian faith and discipline.

Still held by many conservative Orthodox thinkers, the conciliar idea of Church authority has been modified in modern times to include a broader concept of the Church as basically Catholic in essence, yet not subject to Rome or any single visible head. All believers are joined in a mysterious bond of unity, which gives them collectively what is present only *in germine* in each individual. Sharing what each one has gives the body a new power that its separate members possess only inherently. Together they teach and govern, whereas individually they are only cells of the cosmic whole. In the last analysis, therefore, the government of the Church belongs to the body of the entire Church; so that even the decrees of a general council become valid only when universally approved by the faithful.

A variant explanation that has found wide acceptance in the United States and English-speaking countries begins with the postulate that the Bible and sacred Tradition are valid sources of the Church's doctrinal and governmental mind. The hierarchy has the privilege of applying these sources to contingent situations, since it has been so commissioned by Christ, but not speaking in its own name. Bishops are only delegates of the people and their external voice or mouthpiece for making explicit what resides implicitly in the hearts of all believers. They, and not the bishops, are the "court of last appeal" in matters of faith and morals.

Yet not the bishops alone nor the people of any territory alone enjoy this magisterial power. In the Orthodox view, each local church, headed by its bishop, is the Church of God, enjoying His gifts and forming not merely a part of the Body of Christ, but the whole of His Body in its sacramental reality. Yet no single church can live in isolation from the rest. Unity of origin and faith links the disparate churches together, so that the life of one passes on to the others by means of the episcopacy.

This concept of church authority is sometimes identified with a mysterious *sensus fidelium,* or "believers' consciousness," that varies with different interpreters but fundamentally precludes anything like obedience to visible, moral power vested in the papacy or episcopacy.

The life of the Church is a miracle which cannot be subordinated to external law. The Church recognizes or does not recognize a given ecclesiastical assembly representing itself as a council: this is the simple historical fact.

There are not and there cannot be external organs or methods of testifying to the internal evidence of the Church; this must be admitted frankly and resolutely. Anyone who is troubled by this lack of external evidence for ecclesiastical truth does not believe in the Church and does not truly know it. . . . The ecclesiastical fetishism which seeks an oracle speaking in the name of the Holy Spirit and which finds it in the person of a supreme hierarch, or in the episcopal order and its assemblies—this fetishism is a terrible symptom of half-faith.[20]

In other words, in the Orthodox Church the final guardian of the purity of dogma is the Church itself, the Church people, and not any episcopal assembly. Eastern theologians who make the bishops representatives of the faithful may not require universal acceptance by the Church to validate episcopal decrees, but even they allow the people to call the bishops to task for what they teach and even depose their prelates when the Spirit of God so directs them.

SCRIPTURE AND THE SPIRIT. In the Protestant tradition, ecclesiastical authority vested in the Pope or bishops or council assemblies was replaced by the inspired word of God as found in the

Scriptures, and by the indwelling Spirit which enlightens every man who comes into this world.

The groundwork on its theoretical side was laid by the Reformers who appealed against the Catholic position by arguing that where Baptism has been received there is no further need for ordination or consecration, or their correlative claims to a specially conferred juridical power from God. "Whoever has undergone Baptism," wrote Luther, "may boast that he has been consecrated priest, bishop, and pope, although it does not beseem everyone to exercise these offices. For since we are all priests alike, no man may put himself forward, or take upon himself without our consent and election, to do that which we all alike have power to do. If a thing is common to all, no man may take it upon himself without the wish and command of the community." [21]

Protestantism begins with the premise that Jesus Christ was a historical figure, and that therefore the paramount question for theology is posed by the historical gap between God's advent in the world two thousand years ago, and the sources of religious authenticity today. Catholic bodies, it is explained, fill the gap between Jesus Christ and the modern Christian by the authority of the Church and what it calls its *magisterium,* namely the official teaching body of the Church whose spokesman is the Pope. This position is said to be based on the supposition that Jesus Christ transferred His authority to the apostles and their ecclesiastically certified successors, the Bishops under the Roman Pontiff.

For its part, Protestantism in a sense admits that Christ conferred authority upon the apostles, but it believes that the apostles were unique. Their authority cannot be handed down to others.

On the crucial Petrine text in St. Matthew's Gospel, the growing Protestant stance is to concede that Christ's words, "You are Peter, and upon this Rock I will build my Church," refer to Peter himself and not merely to his faith. "When Jesus says that he will build his *ekklesia* upon this rock, he really means the person of Simon. Upon this disciple, who in the lifetime of Jesus possessed the specific advantages and the specific weaknesses of which the Gospels speak, upon him who was then their spokesman, their representative in good as well as in bad, and in this sense was the rock of the group of disciples—upon him is to be founded the Church, which after the death of Jesus will continue his work upon earth." [22] However, with Peter as with the other apostles, they received authority only for themselves, not authority to be passed on to their successors.

What, then, is the basis for the continuity of Christians today with the authoritative Jesus Christ? The written words of the Bible are the authority, conserving concretely the message of the Savior, and assured constant illumination from the same Savior's Spirit indwelling in the hearts of the faithful. Both facets are important. Implicit in the scriptural testimony is the promise that when the apostles, through their written record, remind the Church of God's presence in Jesus Christ, God will be present by the spirit of Christ. In the graphic words of the Reformers, the exterior spirit of the biblical clinker is re-ignited by the Holy Spirit to make it glow again interiorly in those who believe.

Among the Protestants who clarified these concepts, Kierkegaard was outstanding with his insistence that the authority of God does not require a person to be what he called "a disciple at second hand." Jesus Christ Himself lives again in the spirit of man through the equilibrium of the apostolic word and the invisible divine Spirit. What becomes in that process of the rebel in every man, of that part of man's nature which resents any imposition on its freedom? It does not submit, Kierkegaard would say, as though to a way of life alien to itself. It rather finds the basis of its rebellion, the true ground of its strivings which before were only a chaotic stream of ill-directed desires.

Accordingly faith itself takes on a different meaning than found in the Catholic Church. "Christians do not claim to have the truth. They are claimed by it." And Christian realities are spiritual, personal, historical things; they are not susceptible of dogmatic, in the sense of definitive and irreversible, verbal expression. Truths of faith are called possibilities, they are never necessities. In fact, any compulsion is a contradiction of faith.

The highest truths are the truths which are spiritually discerned, and spiritual discernment, as the Bible says, always takes place in freedom. Christian authority is always consistent with assurance, never with certainty. A quest for certainty in the Christian life is an expression of bad faith. It is the antimony of trust. The corollary of this is that the truth of the Christian faith does not inhere in propositions. Its propositions are always invocations. The proper response to an invocation is not, "I consent intellectually" or "I believe it to be true." It is *sursum corda,* a lifting up of the heart in willing response.[23]

In this estimate of faith, authority may seem to reside in human institutions or personalities, but its true presence is only in God. When a Christian submits in obedience to a higher power, he makes sure that his pledge is to no one less than God. Churches and synodical conferences may propose to him what to believe and how to act, but they can never impose upon him to follow their directives. He is ultimately responsible only to the Spirit within him, whom Christ promised to send and by whom the believer is taught all that he needs.

13. Roman Catholicism

Not the least difficulty in writing about Catholicism is the problem of isolating the subject. The history of the Catholic Church is so closely woven into Christian civilization that the one cannot be told fairly without the other, and to do justice by the Church would mean to retell the story of Christianity. Moreover not only Catholics claim the first millenium of Christian history as their own. The Orthodox and Protestants might therefore resent having all the centuries from Christ to Photius and Caerularius, or to Luther and Calvin, called Catholic instead of simply Christian.

Practically speaking, however, there is no choice except to treat the first thousand years in the East and fifteen hundred in the West under Roman Catholicism. The characteristic features of the latter today are imbedded in the Church's life before the Eastern Schism and the Reformation; Catholicism makes the claim of continuing these features and retaining them substantially unchanged through all the vicissitudes of time; and, most importantly, the institution of the papacy is a historical phenomenon that reaches back to the early centuries to give Christianity that cohesion which even the sharpest critics of Catholicism are willing to admit while they deplore, in Harnack's phrase, the lot of those who "have subjected their souls to the despotic orders of the Roman papal King." [1]

APOSTOLIC TIMES

The amount of authentic Christian literature from the first century after Christ's ascension is more extensive than most people who are not specialists suppose. Besides the Gospels, written between 50 A.D. for the Aramaic Matthew and 100 A.D. for St. John, we have the fourteen letters of St. Paul, seven Catholic epistles, the Book of Revelations or Apocalypse and the Acts of the Apostles which Chrysostom called the "Gospel of the Holy Spirit," and Harnack "the manifestation in history of the power of the Spirit of Jesus in the apostles." Outside the New Testament are the *Didache*, written about the year 90 as a manual on the liturgy and Christian morals; the letter of Pope Clement I to the Corinthians (98 A.D.), the epistle of Barnabas of the same date, Polycarp's letter to the Philippians and the remarkable collection of seven epistles which St. Ignatius of Antioch wrote to seven churches while on his way to martyrdom in Rome (107 A.D.).

The first and strongest impression left us by these writings is the devotion of the early Christians to the person of Jesus. He dominates their thoughts, determines their ritual customs, inspires their daily practices and so completely enters every phase of their lives it is no wonder they were soon given the simple title of "Christians," as followers of one whom they called the Messias and on whom all their religion was centered.

According to Tacitus, the name was already current among the populace in Rome at the time of the Neronean persecution (A.D. 64) and soon became the official Roman designation for members of the new Church.[2] During times of persecution the confession or denial of this name was crucial, as reported by Pliny the Younger, proconsul of Bithynia in Asia Minor (A.D. 112). He described to the Emperor Trajan the method he used to ferret out the Christians.

A placard was put up, without any signature, accusing a large number of persons by name. Those who denied they were, or had ever been, Christians, who repeated after me an invocation to the gods, and offered adoration, with wine and frankincense, to your image, which I had ordered brought for that purpose, together with those of the gods, and who finally cursed Christ—none of which acts, it is said, those who are really Christians can be forced to perform—these I thought proper to discharge.[3]

It is impossible to read a single letter of St. Paul without feeling that for him Christianity was Christ. He speaks of himself as "the servant of Jesus Christ," and of those to whom he is writing "called to be Jesus Christ's." His preoccupation with the Savior makes him say, "if any man does not love the Lord Jesus Christ, let him be anathema." In closing salutations, he writes, "My love is with you all in Christ Jesus." When necessary, he vindicates his authority, that he is an apostle, "sent not from men nor by man, but by Jesus Christ." In his suffering, he rejoices that "I bear the marks of the Lord Jesus Christ in my body," and in humility he prays, "God forbid that I should glory save in the cross of our Lord Jesus Christ." [4]

Paul's exhortations were not so much to virtue as to the following of Christ. "Have this mind in you which was also in Christ Jesus." His reproaches are less against vice than against those who "seek their own interests, not those of Jesus Christ." His great hope is to be dissolved, and to be with Christ. By comparison with this treasure, "I count everything loss because of the excellent knowledge of Jesus Christ my Lord. For His sake I have suffered the loss of all things." And in the apostrophe which summarizes his gospel, he sets the master idea that he learned from the Savior and that Christians in all times, and not only the converts in ancient Rome, have needed to remain loyal to the faith.

Who shall separate us from the love of Christ? Shall tribulations, or distress, or persecution, or hunger, or nakedness, or danger, or the sword. Even as it is written, "For Thy sake we are put to death all the day long. We are regarded as sheep for the slaughter." But in all these things we overcome because of Him who has loved us. For I am sure that neither death, nor life, nor angels, nor principalities, nor things present, nor things to come, nor powers, nor heights, nor depth, nor any other creature will be able to separate us from the love of God, which is in Christ Jesus our Lord.[5]

Correlative with this dedication to the person of the Savior, early Christianity appears from the first as communal in character and under perceptible authority.

Shortly after the ascension of Christ, while the disciples in the company of Mary were awaiting the Holy Spirit, Peter stood up in the midst of the brethren and announced that another apostle should be chosen to replace the traitor Judas. He laid down the conditions of election, "of these men who have been with us from the time the Lord Jesus moved among us, from John's baptism till the day He was taken from us, of these one must become a witness with us of the resurrection." [6] Two candidates were put forward, Joseph called Barsabbas, and Matthias. After the assembly had asked the Lord to show "which of these two Thou hast chosen," lots were drawn and the choice fell upon Matthias, who was immediately numbered with the eleven apostles. Commenting on this first act of Peter's primacy, St. John Chrysostom remarked how spontaneously he was accepted as the shepherd of Christ's flock and the leader of the apostolic college.

When the Master commissioned His disciples to preach the Gospel, He also gave them power to work miracles in His name, to cast out demons, to heal the sick and even to raise the dead. These signs and wonders are part of the logic of revelation. If God demands faith in revealed mysteries, He makes them acceptable by integrating what exceeds human power in the realm of knowledge with phenomena that surpass human agency in the order of visible reality. Since the latter is certainly from God, the former must also come from Him. Consequently just as Christ went about simultaneously preaching His doctrine and confirming it with prodigies, so the apostles (beginning with Simon Peter) started the Christian catechesis with teaching what they had learned from Jesus and making His new-found society credible with signs and wonders that followed.

Soon after Pentecost Sunday, as Peter and John were going into the temple to pray, they met a certain man who was lame from his mother's womb. Instead of giving him the alms he begged, Peter gazed upon him and said, "Silver and gold I have none, but what I have I give thee. In the name of Jesus Christ of Nazareth, arise and walk." Immediately the man's feet and ankles became strong and "leaping up he began to walk." [7]

Illustrative of the ecclesiastical structure of Christianity in apostolic times, the authors of the New Testament outside the Gospels repeatedly speak of the Church (*ekklesia*) to describe the community of Christ's followers, as distinct from the synagogue of the Jews. The latter meant simply an existing religious gathering of people, the former the assembly of people called together by God. Also, where the term occurs in only two contexts in the Gospels, both in Matthew,[8] it is used over one hundred times in the Acts, Epistles, and Book of Revelation.

As the number of gentile converts increased, the ethnic nature of Christianity became correspondingly less Jewish. Members of the Palestinian Church who lived according to the pharisaic rule watched the development with regret and made every effort to keep the Church within the limits of Judaism. Its estrangement from Jewry, they believed, could be prevented or mitigated only when all the churches and their members agreed to observe the Mosaic law. The conflict which arose from this attitude provoked the most serious crisis in apostolic Christianity and was finally settled by the first ecumenical gathering of the Church, in which Peter presided and gave the decisive judgment. Once he declared that "We believe we are saved through the grace of the Lord Jesus, just as we are," and without the burden of the Mosaic code, "the whole meeting quieted down," and listened while Paul, the apostle of the Gentiles, and James, the venerable leader of the Judaeo-Christians, expressed their agreement.[9]

QUMRAN AND PRIMITIVE CHRISTIANITY

Since the discovery of the Dead Sea Scriptures from 1947 onwards, it is impossible to speak of Christian origins without taking stock of what some have called the most significant documents outside the Bible bearing on the foundations of Christianity.

Over sixty manuscripts and innumerable fragments have been excavated at the site of the ancient Qumran Community, located close to the Dead Sea in Palestine. The principal texts include a set of rules for the monastic community, namely *The Manual of Discipline,* A *Zadokite Document* (discovered earlier at Cairo) and a *Formulary of Blessings;* two collections of hymns, for the initiants and a psalm of thanksgiving; several commentaries, on the Books of Michaeas, Nahum and Habakkuk; a long oration of Moses which was a paraphrase of the Law; an epic on *The War of the Sons of Light and the Sons of Darkness;* and a manual for the future congregation of Israel, the so-called Messianic Banquet. Conservative scholarship holds that the scrolls were composed at various dates between 170 B.C. and 68 A.D.

The burning question on which a library is fast developing is the relation of this documentation to Christian beginnings. Some extremists have claimed that we have in these documents the rude clay of which the Christian Church was later molded, with the implication that the latter is not really unique but merely continuous with its Judaic predecessor among the ascetics at Qumran. Nothing could be further from the facts. There is in the Dead Sea scrolls no trace of any of the cardinal theological concepts of Christianity— the incarnation of the Son of God, original sin, redemption through the cross and the life of divine grace, the sacramental system or the universality of the Gospel *kerygma.*

On the other hand, there are numerous affinities which balanced scholarship has unearthed and which cast abundant light on the meaning of the Christian faith. The scrolls furnish a picture of the religious and cultural climate in which John the Baptist conducted his mission and in which Jesus of Nazareth was initially reared. They portray in vivid but authentic colors the spiritual environment whose language the Precursor and the Savior spoke, whose idea they used to teach their message of salvation, and whose sympathetic attitude they employed as the seedbed of the New Testament. They give the lie to over a century of rationalist criticism of the New Testament, that the ideals of the Gospels (notably St. John), and of the Pauline Epistles could not have come from Judaic sources but must have been imported from elsewhere, from Hellenism or from Gnostic lucubrations.

Among the affinities between the thought and language of the scrolls and that of the New Testament, the most prominent touches on the communal nature of the Qumran sect and the Christian community. The Qumran group had a variety of inspectors who were overseers and whose duty it was to admit new members, pass judgment on those in probation, direct the interests of the community and, when necessary, dismiss those who failed to live up to prescribed regulations. This spiritual leader is called "teacher" or "right-teacher." In the Gospel according to St. John, Jesus is hailed as the teacher sent by God, appointed by the Father to bring the light of truth to all nations.

In the *Manual of Discipline,* the community is promised to become a veritable "temple of God, a true holy of holies," provided it abides by the community regulations. This is more than superficially like the words of St. Paul to the Corinthians, "Do you not know that you are the temple of God and that the Spirit of God dwells in you? If anyone destroys the temple of God, him will God destroy; for holy is the temple of God, and this temple you are." [10]

Members of the Qumran body styled themselves "the elect" or "the elect of God," with an accent that is familiar in the writings of St. Paul, who spoke of himself as an apostle of Jesus Christ, "according to the faith of God's elect," and in St. Peter who said he was an apostle of Jesus Christ "to the elect who are sojourners of the dispersion." [11] In both sources, the Qumran and Christian, the faithful declared that they stand in the eternal congregation of God, hold direct converse with Him, and "share the lot of the holy beings." They enjoyed a community of goods, practiced obedience to superiors, and were told to abstain from divorce with the right to remarry. Thus in the *Zadokite Document* we read, "One of the traps is fornication, by marrying two women at the same time, even though the principle of creation is, male and female He created them." [12] And in Mark we read, 'Because of the hardness of your heart he (Moses) wrote you that precept (allowing a bill of divorce to put away one's wife). But from the beginning of creation God made them male and female." [13] Some commentators have been so struck by the similarity they rushed to conclude that the *Zadokite Document* is Judaeo-Christian.

Comparable to the Christian emphasis on the struggle between light and darkness is the theme of the Qumran manuscripts that speak at length of the two spirits, the Prince of Light and the Angel of Darkness, with constant opposition between them. While the idea is a commonplace of ancient Iranian and later Jewish thought, it suggests a development that became part of the structure of Christianity. It should be noted, however, that the New Testament subjected this doctrine to an essential change by contraposing the Angel of Darkness not with an Angel of Light but with Christ or the Holy Spirit, with never a suspicion that the two were equally matched.

Even more striking is the parallel between the meal of the Palestinian monastery and the Lord's Supper. There was no transformation of the elements in the Dead Sea documents, but otherwise the two ceremonies were quite similar. Speaking of communal duties, the Qumran members were told that "when they prepare the table to eat and wine to drink, the priest must be the first to extend his hand to bless the first portions of the bread. And if wine is being drunk, the priest must be the first to extend his hand to bless the first portion of the bread and wine." [14] So, too, in describing the Messianic banquet, "When they gather around the table to eat or to drink wine, and the common board has been spread and the wine mixed, no one is to stretch out his hand for the first portion of bread and wine before the priest. For it is he who is to bless the first portion of bread and wine, and the first to stretch out his hand to the bread. After that the Messias of Israel will place his hands on the bread." [15]

In spite of these and similar analogies, the early Church was aeons removed from the Judaic community which some have identified with the Essenes and others, with more caution, describe as the Dead Sea Covenanters. The Jewish ascetics were legalistic in the extreme, attached to externals, and at the opposite pole to the injunctions of Christ for internal faith, purity of heart and detachment from the things of this world. Their observance of the Sabbath was more demanding, if possible, than the burdens laid down by the Pharisees. They were a closed sect, socially, psychologically and even physically; and forbidden association with others at the risk of being excommunicated for consorting with outsiders. Their whole thought and practice was steeped in the Old Testament, with no hint of a new communication from on High, and combined with a rigid determinism that comes closer to the predestination passages in the Koran than to anything found in the New Testament.

Future research may reveal new correlations between Qumran and the Church of the Apostles, at least in heightening the spiritual idealism of the Jewish people at the time of Christ. It will also show that, while Christianity appealed to the best in human nature and made demands on generosity beyond anything hitherto suspected in Judaism, its inspiration did not come from the Law or the Prophets alone but from a new dispensation which fulfilled and superseded the old.

FATHERS AND EARLY COUNCILS

From earliest times, the title *Pater* (Father) was applied to bishops of the Church as witnesses to the Christian tradition. But from the close of the fourth century it was used in a more restricted

sense of a more or less clearly defined group of ecclesiastical writers
of the past whose authority on doctrinal matters carried special
weight. St. Basil (330-379) and St. Gregory of Nazianzen (329-
389) are among the first to prove the orthodoxy of their teaching
by appealing to the agreement of the Fathers, technically the
consensus Patrum, in support of their position.

By the end of the fifth century the term "Father" was also applied to teachers who were not bishops, like St. Jerome (342-420),
and even the layman, St. Prosper of Aquitaine (390-463). According to the commonly accepted teaching, the Fathers were characterized by orthodoxy of doctrine, holiness of life, approval by
the Church and antiquity. The patristic period is generally held
to close with St. Isidore of Seville (560-636) in the West, and St.
John Damascene (675-749) in the East.

The significance of the Fathers in the history of Catholicism
lies in their witness to the apostolic tradition, of which they were
the faithful transmitters and their deference to the Church as final
interpreter of Christian revelation. Quantitatively their testimony
is monumental (upwards of four hundred volumes in the Migne
edition), and qualitatively their function has been that of reservoirs
from which subsequent generations may safely draw on the deposit
of faith. Even popes and general councils, while standing above
the Fathers as final judges, depended on their wisdom and insight
to define the Church's mind.

For seven hundred years, the patristic teaching, periodically
stabilized by ecumenical councils, was the mainstay of Christianity.
Yet the Fathers were not self-made but created by a series of crises
which threatened the Church at every turn in her history.

In the second and third centuries arose the peril of Gnosticism,
a complex religious movement which denied the historical validity
of the Gospels. Essentially a claim to the possession of "higher
knowledge," independently of the stream of apostolic tradition,
Gnosticism already plagued the Church before 100 A.D. Among
the reasons which led St. John to write his Gospel was the refutation
of the Gnostic Cerinthus and the Nicolaites. At the turn of the
century, Ignatius of Antioch stressed the reality of Christ's earthly
life, death and resurrection against the Gnostic perversion of these
facts.

However this was only a prelude to the inundation that broke over the Church in the middle of the second century. The last survivors of the apostolic age felt they were faced with a new and powerful enemy that came out into the open. Now that the apostles were gone, Oriental zealots began to preach and organize religious sects. Other factors were also operative, like the rapid growth of the Church and her penetration into the world of philosophy and letters, where the simple faith of the people was exposed to Hellenic speculation and an attempt to engraft Asiatic fancies on the body of Christian revelation. '

Christ, they said, was not the Deity in human form but only an aeon, or intermediary, who was apparently endowed with human nature. Accordingly salvation was not to be obtained through the merits of Christ, but through the *Gnosis* or superior knowledge which was manifested in Him and discovered by the Gnostics. Christ, therefore, was not really born, nor did He actually live and die or rise from the grave. The events described in the Gospels were not historically but only symbolically true. Spiritual insight, possessed by the Gnostics, and not the reported words and deeds of Christ demonstratable by history, furnished Christianity with the religious truths of salvation.

The sequence of Fathers who combated Gnosticism reads like a roster of the Christian writers before the Edict of Constantine, but the outstanding among them was St. Ireneus (130-200), Bishop of Lyons, who forms in thought and action an important link between the East and West. His chief work, *Against the Heresies,* is a detailed exposé of Gnosticism.

Ireneus was the first great Catholic theologian. Unlike the Fathers in the East, he opposed Gnosticism not by setting up a rival Christian speculation, but by emphasizing the traditional elements in the Church, notably the papacy, the episcopate, the canon of Scripture and religious tradition. At every point in his writing he is conscious of the chasm that separates the Oriental concept of God and religion, inherited from the Hindus and Parsis, from the Christian message preached by Christ and handed down by His disciples. Christians have only one God, infinite Creator of all things; their revelation comes from this same Deity, especially in the person of Jesus of Nazareth, "Savior, King and God." Their faith is founded on His preaching and on the teaching of His Church, whose seed has been sown to the ends of the earth; and preserved by the bishops "who were instituted by the apostles," as the apostles were by Christ.

To discover Christian truth, therefore, and sift it from error, we have only to see what the bishops have taught since the time of Christ.

But as it would take too long to transcribe here the successions of bishops of all the churches, we will consider the greatest and ancient, known by all, founded and established by the two glorious apostles, Peter and Paul. We will show that the tradition which it received from the apostles and the faith it has preached to men have come down to us through the succession of bishops. We will thus confound those who, in whatever way, through self-satisfaction, vain-glory, blindness or error, gather in a way other than they should.

For with this Church, on account of its preeminent authority, every church must be in agreement, that is, the faithful everywhere, among whom the tradition of the apostles has been continuously preserved by those everywhere.[16]

Even before the Gnostic danger had passed, another problem arose, in the form of Arianism, which denied the uniquely divine nature of Jesus Christ. Its author was Arius (256-336), a priest of Alexandria, who in 318 began to teach that there were not three distinct persons in God, coeternal and equal in all things, but only one person, the Father. The Son is only a creature, made out of nothing like other created beings. He may be called God, but only by an extension of language, as the first and greatest person chosen to be divine intermediary in the creation and redemption of the world.

Boldly anti-trinitarian, Arianism struck at the foundations of Christianity by reducing the Incarnation to a figure of speech. If the Logos, the Word of God, was created and not divine, God did not become man nor redeem the world and all the consequent mysteries are dissolved. In Arianism we see the first major challenge of the non-Christian world to the premises of the Christian faith. Philo among the Jewish Hellenists and Plotinus among the Neo-Platonists contributed the theory of an agglomerate of ideas as the first mediator between God and the world; Gnosticism furnished the notion of aeons or lesser deities, so familiar in Zoroastrian and Hindu thought.

The Council of Nicea was convoked in 325 to meet this challenge. Since the signature texts are defective, the exact number of prelates who attended this first ecumenical gathering is not known. However, at least two hundred and twenty bishops, mostly from the East, but also from Africa, Spain, Gaul and Italy, signed the creed which affirmed the divinity of Christ. "We believe," the formula read, "in one God, the Father Almighty, Creator of all things visible and invisible. And in one Lord Jesus Christ, the Son of God, the only-begotten of the Father, that is, of the substance of the Father; God from God, light from light, true God from true God; begotten, not created, consubstantial (*homo-ousion*) with the Father." [17]

The soul of the council was St. Athanasius (296-373), Bishop of Alexandria, whose resolute character and theological clarity were the main obstacle to the triumph of Arianism in the East.

About thirty years after Nicea, some Arian bishops began to teach that the Holy Spirit is also not divine. Called *Pneumatomachi* (enemies of the Spirit), they were answered by St. Basil and the two Gregories, of Nyssa and Nazianzen, and condemned in 381 by the second general council at Constantinople, which reaffirmed the Nicene Creed and clearly defined the divinity of the Holy Spirit. The present Nicene Creed, used at Mass in the Catholic Church on feast days, dates from this council. The interpolation *Filioque,* "and the Son," was added, to its dogmatic formula to express a Double Procession of the Holy Spirit, in the next century and has since become a symbol of tension between Roman Catholicism and Eastern Orthodoxy.

Closely connected with Arianism was the theory of Nestorius (died 451), a Syrian monk who preached against the expression *Theotokos* (Mother of God), applied to the Blessed Virgin. The principal defender of Mary's honor was St. Cyril of Alexandria (died 444), whose efforts were crowned with success at the Council of Ephesus (431).

During the next century and a half, the Church underwent the interior trial of purification at the hands of Pelagius and his followers, who claimed that a man does not need supernatural grace to be saved.

Pelagius was a lay monk, born in England about 354, who came to Rome at the end of the fourth century. Having heard a bishop quote St. Augustine with relation to chastity, "Grant what You command, O Lord, and command what You will," he attacked the doctrine on the ground that the whole moral law was imperilled. If a man were not responsible for his good and evil deeds, there was nothing to restrain him from indulgence in sin. He was moreover so alarmed by the low morality of the day that he felt it could only be reformed by concentrating on man's personal responsibility for his actions. Together with his disciple Celestius, he began teaching that the only real grace we possess is free will, which alone, without any elevation or assistance from God, can lead us to heaven.

St. Jerome wrote that the world woke up one day and found itself Pelagian. He and Augustine spent themselves vindicating the traditional doctrine that free will is indeed a gift of nature, but in addition we need supernatural light and strength and, above all, infusion of sanctifying grace in order to be saved.

So numerous were the Church's pronouncements in defense of the supernatural life that by the end of the fifth century a catalogue had to be made for easy reference. Known as the *Indiculus* (short index), it re-stated the teaching of Christ, "without me you can do nothing," and closed every avenue of escape for a naturalistic interpretation of man's relations with God. "No one," it declared, "not even the person who has been renewed by the grace of baptism, has sufficient strength to overcome the snares of the devil, and conquer the passions of the flesh, unless he obtains help from God each day to persevere in a good life." [18]

One more trial plagued the Church before the end of the patristic age. Under suasion from Manichaean tendencies, inherited from the Zoroastrians, and pressure from Islam, certain Christian emperors in the East opposed the use of images in divine worship. One of their reasons was that icons are a grave obstacle to the conversion of Moslems and Jews, who outlaw sacred images on principle.

St. John Damascene, chief representative of the Christians to the Caliph, became protagonist for the believers against the Iconoclasts (image breakers) and wrote three discourses on the subject. He barely escaped martyrdom for his zeal. The second Council of Nicea (787), and the last accepted by the Eastern Orthodox, settled the issue on dogmatic grounds, but left untouched the crucial problem that three centuries later led to the separation of the East from Rome.

Caesaro-papism, or the theory of absolute control of the Church by a civil ruler, showed itself with increasing clarity during the iconoclast struggle. Started by the intervention of the State in religious matters, the conflict encountered less and less resistance in the Greek Church, especially among the secular clergy, while it was viewed by the Popes with growing apprehension. The unity achieved by Imperial decree in 787 and again in 843 proved artificial, and with the restoration of the Empire by the Franks and the development of the temporal power of the Popes, the ground was ready for the final separation between the Church of Rome and the state-dominated Church of the Byzantine Empire.

CHURCH AND STATE RELATIONS

With the disintegration of Charlemagne's empire in the tenth century and the inroads of the Northmen, Magyars and Saracens, political and moral values fell into decay and the Church herself was deeply affected by the return to "semi-barbarism." When feudalism emerged as a reaction to the crisis, ecclesiastical authority came under the sway of feudal lords and princes.

A reforming tendency inside the Church had started as a monastic movement in France (Cluny) and in Germany (Lorraine). After the deposition in 1046 of the anti-pope, Sylvester III (created by a Roman political party), a series of high-minded pontiffs ascended the papal throne, culminating in the pontificate of Gregory VII (1073-1085), who had served as secretary and adviser to his five predecessors.

The two principal objects of Gregory's reform were clerical celibacy and lay investiture, with the prior importance attached to the second as a contributing cause of the first. By controlling the elections of bishops, lay princes had been able to name their own creatures or relatives and even to sell bishoprics to the highest bidder. And after a bishop's consecration, they further assumed the power of "vesting" the prelate ostensibly with temporal assets like property and buildings but actually (as symbolized in the ring and pastoral staff used for investiture) by claiming also to give him ecclesiastical jurisdiction in the diocese. As a result, bishops considered themselves quite independent of the pope. Simony, incontinence and clerical abuses remained unchecked and were fostered by the political overlords.

A year after his election, Gregory held a synod in Rome, which renewed old legislation against simony and violations of celibacy. This was followed by another synod against the custom of lay investiture, with the result that at Worms in 1076 the Emperor Henry IV forced the bishops to repudiate the authority of the pope. Gregory thereupon excommunicated two German archbishops and the emperor, and then absolved Henry's subjects from all their allegiance—the first recorded papal deposition of a civil monarch.

Henry made his submission and was absolved at Canossa in 1077; but as soon as he had regained power, he renewed the opposition and was again deposed and excommunicated. But this time, the pope went beyond the first sentence. Not only was Henry dethroned but the royal power was granted by the pope to the Duke Rudolf of Suabia. In concluding the sentence, Gregory prayed that Henry "be confounded until he makes penance in order that his soul be safe at the day of the Lord."

This time the king retaliated by marching into Italy with an army, seizing Rome and setting up an antipope, Clement III. Gregory received protection from the Normans but had to retire to Salerno, where he passed away in 1085 as the greatest reformer in the history of the papacy. His last words were, "I have loved justice and hated iniquity, therefore I die in exile." Victor III, who succeeded him, excommunicated Clement III and continued the policy of Gregory, which even non-Catholic writers admit was the salvation of the Roman primacy.

The most controversial figure in the history of Church and State relations was Pope Boniface VIII (1234-1303), and his Bull, *Unam Sanctam*, issued in 1302, was the high point of the controversy.

In order to appreciate the full import of Pope Boniface's legislation, we should recall the circumstances under which it was enacted. Political rivalry among the Hapsburgs prevented the coronation of a Western Emperor for half a century in the late 1200's, with the result that during this time the Roman Pontiffs became the acknowledged visible heads of Catholic Christianity to a degree unparalleled in papal history. When Boniface VIII, a professional jurist, ascended the throne of Peter, he decided to embody in a general enactment the legal position of the Roman See, as it had crystallized during the thirteenth century. His instrument was the Bull, *Unam Sanctam,* which subsequently became part of the Church's Canon Law.

The immediate occasion of the Bull was a long and heated conflict between the pope and the king of France, Philip IV, called "The Fair." Philip insisted on deriving his authority in the tradition of Charlemagne and was reluctant to admit any principle of subordination to the papacy in secular matters. When the king imposed a heavy taxation on the French clergy without previous agreement with Rome, Boniface took this as an infringement of ecclesiastical rights and after protracted study of the principles involved, published the document that was to sum up the plenitude of papal power over all the Christian community, including France and her king. Some have wrongly considered the *Unam Sanctam* an angry rejoinder of the pope, composed in a fit of revenge. Actually it was the deliberate pronouncement of a synod, headed by the pope, in which there were (besides others) thirty-nine French archbishops and bishops. Nor is it a document which the Holy See has ever retracted. In fact it was solemnly confirmed by the Fifth Lateran Council in 1513; and the very point in its teaching to which exception has been taken, is reaffirmed in the Syllabus of Errors of Pius IX.

After declaring there is only one Holy, Catholic and Apostolic Church, over which Christ placed only one head, "not two heads as if it were a monster," Boniface explained the relation of the secular power to the spiritual. "We are taught by the words of the Gospel that in this Church and in its power there are two swords, namely, a spiritual and a temporal. It is necessary that one sword should be under the other, and that temporal authority be subjected to the spiritual. For, the truth bearing witness, the spiritual power should instruct the temporal power and judge it, if it be not good. Hence We declare, affirm, and define and pronounce that it is altogether necessary for the salvation of every creature to be subject to the Roman Pontiff." [19]

At the outset we must distinguish between defined doctrine and ordinary papal teaching. Only the final sentence was solemnly defined and clearly represents traditional Catholic dogma on the Church's necessity for salvation.

But how are we to understand the preceding statements on the subordination of State to Church. We cannot interpret Boniface to mean that the whole sphere of temporal jurisdiction is directly subject to the Church; an injustice against which he protested shortly after the Bull was published. Followers of Philip the Fair inserted into the document the spurious phrase, "We wish you (the king) to know that you hold your kingdom from Us," adding that anyone who denied the proposition was a heretic. In a solemn consistory, Boniface denounced the forgery. "For forty years We have studied law, and We know that there are two powers appointed by God. Who should, then, or can, believe that We entertain, or have entertained, such stupid absurdity? We declare that in no way do We wish to usurp the jurisdiction of the king. And yet, neither the king nor any one else of the faithful can deny that he is subject to Us where a question of sin is involved (*ratione peccati*)." [20]

The pope's phrase "*ratione peccati*," has since become the Church's norm to judge when and to what extent she may use her spiritual power to intervene in the secular affairs of State. She may do so when, in her judgment, an otherwise temporal affair (like civil legislation) affects the religious interests of the faithful by placing unwarranted burden on their conscience, exposing them to sin or otherwise conflicting with that spiritual welfare over which the Church believes she alone has ultimate jurisdiction by the mandate of her Founder.

THE MIDDLE AGES

The period from the beginning of the twelfth to the end of the fifteenth century, spanning about four hundred years of European culture, has been called the Middle Ages. Once viewed as a sterile interlude between the age of barbarism and modern times, it has come to be regarded as one of the most creative and fruitful periods in the word's history. For the historian of Catholicism it has special interest as the age which approached most nearly the ideal of Christendom as a religious unity.

Superficially it might seem that the source of this unity was an external agency, namely, the despotic control by an absolute papacy. Actually it was the fruit of interior solidarity of faith, which ten centuries of conflict had purified and that, in spite of sporadic upheavals, remained substantially intact until the dawn of the Reformation. The papacy was created by the faith, not vice versa; and as long as Christians believed substantially the same truths, Western Christianity remained one.

At the heart of the medieval faith was a conviction that the Church was a visible society, guided invisibly by its divine Founder but visibly directed by the successors of Peter in the apostolic see. Saints and mystics, scholars and the ordinary faithful commonly recognized this principle.

According to Paul Sabatier, Francis of Assisi (1181-1226) had been "expected, desired, longed for and prepared for by the sigh of Christian humanity. He drew from the Gospel a new spirit, a new soul, he vivified these by humility, love and submission." Yet his message and program were simple: to follow Christ in perfect poverty. Stirred by the words of the Master, "Do not possess gold nor silver," he gave away all that he had and soon gathered around him a group of like-minded companions.

True to the spirit of his age, Francis went to Rome to secure approval for his project. He had three audiences with Innocent III, whose pontificate is said to climax the medieval papacy. In the first he told the *poverello* to "go and pray God to manifest His will; when we know it we shall be able to answer you in all security." In the second he listened to Francis address him as "Holy Father" and tell the parable of the king, the poor woman and her children, personifying Christ, himself and the begging mendicants whom he wished to organize. Finally after the third interview Innocent verbally approved the Franciscan Rule. As he explained, he saw in this humble man, who asked only the authority to live by the Gospel, one who would redress the great Church of God and put it back into equilibrium.

It was no coincidence that among the provisions of the rule was this short one on Orthodoxy. "Let the Brethren on pain of being expelled from the fraternity behave themselves always as good Catholics; let them follow the usage and doctrine of the Roman Church." [21]

Excited by the reformers of the epoch, some Christians professed contempt for the sacraments administered by incontinent or simoniacal priests. Some refused to assist at Mass celebrated by them; others trod under foot the sacred species they had consecrated. One of these people approached Francis, who answered his questions with candor. "The hands of this priest may be such as you know, I know nothing about it. But even if they be so they cannot change the virtue of the sacraments. By these hands God bestows on His people a multitude of graces. I kiss those hands in honor of the benefits they dispense and of Him whose sacraments they are." [22] Francis himself was not a priest, but he knew the distinction on which the Catholic doctrine of the sacraments rests: that their efficacy is not dependent on the sanctity of the one who ministers them.

The greatest theological light of his day, St. Thomas Aquinas (1225-1274) professed the same faith. His *Summa Theologiae* has been compared to a great cathedral, built of the elements that twelve centuries of Christian wisdom had accumulated but never synthesized. "He combined, without confusing philosophy and theology, State and Church, civic and Christian virtues, natural and divine law, Christ and culture." [23] He also believed the Church of Christ was a divine creation, solid as a house built on massive foundations.

The principal foundation is Christ Himself, for other foundation no man can lay but that which is Christ Jesus. Secondary foundations are the apostles and apostolic teaching; hence the Church is called apostolic. Its strength is signified by Peter, or Rock, who is its crown. A building is strong when it can never be overthrown though it may be shaken. The Church can never be brought down. Indeed it grows under persecution, and those who attack it are destroyed.

Only the Church of Peter, to whose lot fell Italy when the disciples were sent out to preach, has always stood fast in the faith. While the faith has disappeared or has partly decayed in other regions, the Church of Peter still flourishes in the faith and free from heresy. This is not to be wondered at, for our Lord said to Peter, "I have prayed for you that your faith fail not, and you, when you are converted, confirm your brethren." [24]

St. Thomas was no idle theorist. He singled out for special mention the dangers to the Church from within in her unholy churchmen. He could recall that John XII (955-964) was elected Bishop of Rome at the age of eighteen and in less than a decade proved so unworthy that a synod, ordered by the emperor, tried and deposed him on charges of sacrilege, simony, perjury, murder and incest; that Benedict IX (1032-1048) was driven out of Rome because of his wicked life.

Although the popes, as a class, have been men of high integrity, there were tragic exceptions. And what even Aquinas had not experienced, came to pass within a century of his death, when the low morality of Catholic prelates and the weakness of several Pontiffs brought on the Western Schism (1378-1417), of which de Maistre asked, "What human institution could have withstood the ordeal?"

The schism broke over the harsh methods that Urban VI (1318-1389) used to try to reform the college of cardinals. Though Urban had been validly elected, the malcontents proceeded to choose one of their own number, Clement VII, as antipope, and until the Council of Constance settled the dispute by electing Martin V, there were three lines of rival claimants: the Roman started by Urban VI, the French under Clement VII, and the Pisan begun by Alexander V in an effort to solve the previous rupture.

Theologians, canonists and saints were divided in their allegiance, St. Catherine of Siena recognizing Urban VI and St. Vincent Ferrer Clement VII. True, the Great Schism was not schismatic in the ordinary sense because all parties upheld the supremacy of the Holy See. The problem was: which of the two or three claimants was legitimate pope? In spite of this trial, the Church grew in strength and vitality. Gregorovius, an impartial observer, remarked that the Schism "raised the papacy from decadence to a new eminence, and showed the world once again how the mystical faith of the people endows the pontiffs with powers that can rise to glory even when apparently dead." [25]

A dramatic proof of this mystical faith was the conduct of St.

Catherine of Siena (1333-1380), Dominican tertiary and contemplative. Her extant correspondence with Gregory XI and his successor Urban VI reveals the spirit of Catholicism that acknowledges the Vicar of Christ while mercilessly rebuking his human failings.

Addressing Gregory as "sweet Christ on earth, on behalf of Christ in heaven" she censures his self-love which condoned the three vices then plaguing the Bride of Christ: impurity, avarice and swollen pride. "Human wretchedness!" she exclaims. "Blind is the sick man who does not know his own need, and blind the shepherd physician, who has regard to nothing but his own advantage. Such men do as Christ says: for if one blind man guide the other, both fall into the ditch. Sick man and physician fall into hell." In another letter, she begs his pardon for her boldness, explaining it was "the great love which I bear your salvation, and my great grief when I see the contrary, that makes me speak so." Then she adds, "Take care that I do not have to complain about you to Jesus crucified. There is no one else I can complain to, for you have no superior on earth." [26]

Catherine was equally explicit with Urban VI, at once recognizing his supreme authority and his human failings. "You are father and lord of the universal body of the Christian religion; we are all under the wings of your holiness. As to authority, you can do everything, but as to seeing, you can do no more than one man." [27]

It would be naive to assume that papal authority was uncontested during the Middle Ages. A theory of conciliarism, which claimed that a general council was above the pope, had been current in France since the thirteenth century. It reached its climax in the fifteenth, at the Council of Constance (sixteenth ecumenical) that put an end to the Western Schism by electing Martin V.

Among its published decrees were statements that contradicted papal supremacy and personal infallibility. Speaking of itself, the council declared that "it holds authority immediately from Christ, and all persons, of whatever authority, even the pope himself, are bound to obey the council in all that regards the faith, the healing of schism, and the reformation of the Church of God in her head and members. Anyone who disobeys this or any other general council, even the pope himself, shall, unless they repent, suffer the punishment they deserve." [28]

In approving the Council of Constance, Martin V excluded these sentiments from his approbation, and the restriction was accepted by the Church. Under his successor, Eugenius IV, the Council of Florence (1438-1445) removed the last vestige of doubt by solemnly proclaiming "that the holy, Apostolic See and the Roman Pontiff have the primacy over the whole world, and that the Roman Pontiff is the successor of St. Peter, the Prince of the Apostles, and the true vicar of Christ, the head of the whole Church, father and teacher of all Christians." [29]

Florence came at the end of a great schism in the West and was convoked to heal the centuries-old schism in the East. Among its most celebrated members were the Greek Emperor, John VIII Palaeologus, and Joseph, Patriarch of Constantinople. A decree of union between the East and West, based on the Roman primacy and beginning with the words "*Laetentur Coeli*" (may the heavens rejoice), was signed by all but one of the Eastern delegates. Political pressure in the East prevented the union from taking permanent effect.

There is something pathetic about the Council of Florence in trying, unsuccessfully, to heal the Eastern Schism and yet taking no cognizance of the still greater rift in Christendom about to take place in the next generation.

By the close of the Middle Ages, the Church had become involved in a turmoil of change. The rise of the modern secular State created a new rival to the Church's authority and a strong competitor for allegiance from citizens who were also Catholic Christians. Contact with the culture of the Islamic East, inspired by the Crusades, opened new horizons of knowledge that were a challenge to European and, by association, to Catholic forms of thought. Discovery of the Greek and Roman classics stimulated research in the ancient languages, and produced a critical attitude towards the Scriptures and a desire to have the inspired word of God, in or from the original.

The same sort of conflict appeared on the social and religious planes. Invention of printing multiplied the diffusion of ideas by geometric proportion, and where before 1440 men like Waldo, Aquinas and Huss could affect only a small number in restricted areas, by the end of the fifteenth century dynamic concepts and personalities had influence on numberless thousands in all parts of the Christian world. For the Church this was an opportunity and a threat, depending on whose ideas became prevalent and whether the new instrument was used to support or question ecclesiastical authority.

An accurate calculation shows that ninety saints and blessed from the fifteenth century were raised to the honors of the altar, men and women whose virtues during life were so outstanding they merited to be called heroic. At the same time, the contrast with the immortality and avarice in high places, including high churchmen, was so startling that the very term "Reformation" was coined to describe the reform of the Church "in head and members" demanded on all sides. It is symptomatic of the age that one of the purest flowers of Christian sanctity, St. Joan of Arc (1412-1431), was burned to death through the connivance of a corrupt ecclesiastical court. Her words, under trial, when asked to recant, "Let all the things I have said and done be reported to Rome, to our Holy Father, the Pope, to whom, after God, I refer them," only emphasize the struggle that men had to remain faithful to their Church under grave provocation." [30]

In one of the most remarkable documents of religious history, Adrian VI (1522-1523), the last non-Italian pope of modern times, held nothing back in describing the state of affairs on the eve of the Reformation, which he called a persecution.

We frankly acknowledge that God permits this persecution of the Church on account of the sins of men, and especially of prelates and clergy. Of a surety the Lord's arm is not shortened that He cannot save us, but our sins separate us from Him, so that He does not hear. Holy Scripture declares aloud that the sins of the people are the outcome of the sins of the priesthood. We know well that for many years things deserving of abhorrence have gathered around the Holy See; sacred things have been misused, ordinances transgressed, so that in everything there has been a change for the worse. Thus it is not surprising that the malady has crept down from the head to the members, from the Popes to the hierarchy.

We shall use all diligence to reform before all things the Roman Curia, whence, perhaps, all these evils have had their origin. Thus healing will begin at the source of sickness. We deem this to be all the more our duty, as the whole world is longing for reform.[31]

Adrian has been blamed for Teutonic bluntness in making this open confession of sins. But he was too clear-sighted a theologian not to distinguish between admission of moral guilt and acceptance of divinely-instituted authority. The latter he professed with courage and humility. "We desire," he said, "to wield our power not as seeking dominion or means for enriching our kindred, but in order to restore to Christ's bride, the Church, her former beauty, to give help to the oppressed, to uplift men of virtue and learning and, above all, to do all that beseems a good shepherd and successor of the blessed Peter." [32]

All the evidence shows that the original intention of the Reformers was to reform the Church and not to separate from papal authority which they at first recognized as the bulwark of Christian unity. Among the extant writings of Martin Luther is a sermon he preached in 1516 on the feast of St. Peter in Chains. It would have done credit to Adrian himself as a testimony to the papacy. "If Christ had not entrusted all power to one man," he told the audience, "the Church would not have been perfect because there would have been no order, and each one would have been able to say he was led by the Holy Spirit." Since the invisible head of the faithful desires that "all may be assembled in one unity, Christ wills that His power be exercised by one man, to whom also He has committed it. He has made this power so strong that He permits all the forces of hell to be let loose against it without injury." [33] Clearly, as a Catholic, Luther had no misgivings about Church authority or whether a Reformation of morals was possible without a revolution of doctrine.

REFORMATION TO MODERN TIMES

The immediate effect of the Reformation on Roman Catholicism was theological. The Protestant emphasis on the Bible and rejection of the Roman primacy stimulated theologians to investigate more closely the sources of revelation in Scripture and Tradition, and establish the grounds for a rational apologetic in support of the Catholic claims. The first need was met by developing a system of positive theology, whereby the truths professed by Catholic Christianity were shown to be found in the deposit of faith.

The Jesuits, led by St. Robert Bellarmine (1542-1621), became the main expositors of this system, as they also laid the groundwork for fundamental theology, which proves from history and philosophy the credibility of the Christian religion.

Speculative theology also began a new era, occasioned by the challenges of Protestanism on almost every portion of the Catholic Church. During the twenty years of the Council of Trent (1545-1565), the combined intelligence of Roman Catholicism concentrated its efforts on so defining the nature of grace and justification, the Sacrifice of the Mass and the priesthood, the sacramental system and ecclesiastical authority, that insights were gained on which post-Tridentine writers have built an imposing theological structure.

But the fruits of the Counter-Reformation were more than theological. Since the Council of Trent, the Catholic Church has entered on a new phase of existence. The dogmatic bases were not changed, but their implications broadened; the very need of defending her claim to autonomy made the Church more than ever conscious of her corporate character; and the loss of large segments of membership (or practical disappearance under political pressure in England and Scandinavia), was made up by a new devotedness among those who remained faithful to the Church of Rome. "We must put aside all judgment of our own," wrote St. Ignatius Loyola (1491-1556), "and keep the mind ever ready and prompt to obey in all things the true Spouse of Christ, our Lord, our holy Mother, the hierarchical Church." [34]

This was no pious rhetoric. Catholics throughout Europe rallied to the defense of their common Mother and, as in England and Ireland, laid down their lives in her cause. "I am a Catholic man and a priest," Edmund Campion told the judge who condemned him. "In that faith have I lived and in that faith I intend to die."

The trials of purification during the sixteenth century were a blessing in disguise. Though at a terrible price, the Church bought a lease on her spiritual life that had no counterpart in previous history. There was a growth in the personal sanctity of her leaders and people, an expansion of zeal in missionary enterprise, a development of religious education, a deepening sense of solidarity among the laity, and a rising influence of Catholic principles on the world at large.

Holiness is an elusive concept. The title "saint" has been applied to such varied individuals as Savonarola, John Wesley, and Mahatma Gandhi. In the Catholic Church, however, only those are called saints who were either martyrs or who during life practiced the moral virtues over a long period of time, under severe trial and temptation, and to a degree that clearly exceeds the native capacity of the human will. All the virtues were comprehended, but especially charity, fortitude and temperance, including chastity. Several thousand men and women, in every walk of life, have been raised to the honors of the altar (saints and blessed) in the past four hundred years, almost seven hundred since Pius XI, as a living witness to the Church's capacity for uniting the soul with God.

Coupled with the miraculous sanctity of a small number has been a raising of demands on the conscience of all Catholics in modern times that were practically unknown in the "ages of faith." In pluralistic societies, the pressures from an alien environment, the tendency to moral conformity, the urge to follow prevalent standards in marriage, business and the professions, the example of well-meaning persons whose religious principles are foreign to the Catholic way of life, have placed clergy and laity in the dilemma of choosing between compromise or often near-heroism in remaining true to their own convictions. Mere respectability is swept along with the stream; only a strong faith and more than normal courage have been able to withstand the tide. Yet the Church has grown, from an estimated world membership of a hundred million at the turn of the century to over half a billion in the sixties.

Foreign missions outside Europe were few and sporadic until the sixteenth century. The Counter Reformation brought a rebirth of missionary zeal, comparable only to the evangelization in apostolic or early medieval times. Some have called it an effort to counteract the losses in north-western Europe. More accurately it was a spontaneous result of the change of interior life among the Catholic peoples who had for so long taken their faith for granted. A letter of St. Francis Xavier, written from Cochin to Rome in 1543, illustrates the spirit of the Gospel to which he could appeal and be heard by so many volunteers they had to be restrained from following him to the Indies.

There is now in these parts a very large number who have only one reason for not becoming Christian, and that is because there is no one to make them Christians. It often comes to my mind to go around to all the universities of Europe, and especially that of Paris, crying out everywhere like a madman, and saying to all learned men there whose learning is so much greater than their charity, "What a multitude of souls is through your fault shut out of heaven and falling into hell." [35]

Missionary enthusiasm has continued unabated through the centuries, in spite of obstacles from rapacious or near-sighted political rulers, indifference or savage reprisal among the natives, domestic and foreign wars, and all the inclemencies of learning a strange tongue and living in an atmosphere devoid of Christian principles and customs. A current annual increase of more than one million Catholics in the Far East, where Communism has become dominant, indicates the established character of the Church's missions.

Since the liberation of Christianity under Constantine, the Church had conducted an immense variety of schools and institutions in every branch of learning. In the Middle Ages, a home of study was attached to the monasteries, convents and cathedral chapters scattered throughout Europe. Chantry endowments were normally associated with giving free instructions to the children of the surrounding country-side. After some two thousand chantries were suppressed in England during the sixteenth century, there was no English grammar school for the next two hundred years which had not previously been a chantry. Universities were spread over the continent and in Great Britain, always by the initiative and under the protection of the Holy See.

If anything, Catholic education has been intensified in modern times, and in countries like the United States, where freedom of religion is enjoyed, it has reached a scope and degree of intensity unknown in previous history. Catholic education in Catholic schools for Catholic youth was the ideal proposed by Pius XI, where "all the teaching and the whole organization of the school, its teachers, syllabus, and textbooks in every branch are regulated by the Christian spirit."

In many countries, e.g., England, France, Scotland, Canada, and the Netherlands, the State contributes to the support of church-affiliated institutions, on the principle that "the school plays a vital part in the child's attitudes and sense of values. If the school gives little place to religious teaching, then the child quite naturally assumes that religion is not an integral part of his mental development." [36] The judgment on the need for religion-centered education, originally professed by the Church, is now shared by many educators in the western world.

Cultivating a sense of unity among widely scattered peoples is a difficult process, and one contributing factor to the breakdown of solidarity in the sixteenth century was that so little was done to make the faithful conscious of their common heritage and their bond of union under the See of Rome. A great deal has happened since then. The very option that Catholics were forced to make, between acceptance or rejection of the pope, resulted in strengthening the ties of membership in the Catholic Church.

But that was only the beginning. The modern world has become smaller than ever before. Mass media for the exchange of ideas and rapid transportation have made neighbors of once-distant nations and joined whole continents closer than formerly were towns of the same province. All of this has affected the Catholic Church whose inner structure is already based on a principle of inter-relationship that no other body enjoys. Where in the Middle Ages the pope was for most people only a distant figure, he is now as near (or nearer) to the average Catholic anywhere on the globe as the local parish priest; papal statements and attitudes become in a few hours the common property of all nations. The happenings and misfortunes of Catholic people in once remote places in Asia or Africa are made known to their co-religionists in America overnight.

The sense of fellowship thus created between church leaders and the laity, and among the laity themselves is a matter of experience, and heightens the faith-accepted idea that Catholics are more than members of a juridical society, that they belong to a mystical organization whose principle of unity is the Spirit of God.

Bound in with the foregoing and rising out of the Church's sense of mission, is the influence which Catholicism exercises in modern times beyond anything previously known. The Catholic Church believes itself to be in full possession of revealed truth, and divinely qualified to interpret and transmit this revelation to its own members and, indeed, to the whole world. Among the crucial areas on which it believes the human mind is naturally incapable of complete and accurate knowledge is the moral law, involving such basic responsibilities as the precepts of the Decalogue.

With the growing secularization of Western society, the call for enlightening the people, once Christian in their religious duties to God and neighbor, has increased enormously. On one side the grave need, and on the other the Church's felt duty to answer the need, have given Catholicism a role to play in "teaching the nations" that some of its worst critics are willing to respect.

It is not only papal encyclicals on the social order, like *Rerum Novarum* of Leo XIII or *Mater et Magistra* of John XXIII, but the whole gamut of natural religion founded on belief in a personal God, that passes from the Church into every phase of human society. At the first Vatican Council, when atheism and rationalism were scored as denials of man's nature and insults to God, principles were set forth that have penetrated wherever the faithful live and affect those with whom they come into contact. An issue like artificial contraception, for example, has been raised as a moral problem mainly because of the Church's stand on the intrinsic dignity of womanhood and the sacred character of sex relations in marriage.

At the opening of the Second Vatican Council, Pope John XXIII stressed a new dimension in the Church's outreach to the world at large. Where previous ecumenical councils had been convoked to stem the rise of some error or clarify a disputed area of revealed doctrine, this one was met for a different purpose. "Nowadays," the Pope said, "the spouse of Christ prefers to make use of the medicine of mercy rather than that of severity. She considers that she meets the needs of the present day by demonstrating the validity of her teaching rather than by condemnations." Behind this attitude is the conviction that no other way is more effective to promote unity among Christians and, indeed, among all men than the practice of charity, particularly of that supernatural love which seeks to communicate to others the graces it has received from God.

Such is the aim of the Second Vatican Ecumenical Council, which, while bringing together the Church's best energies and striving to have men welcome more favorably the good tidings of salvation, prepares, as it were, and consolidates the path toward that unity of mankind which is required as a necessary foundation in order that the earthly city may be brought to the resemblance of that heavenly city where truth reigns, charity is the law, and whose extent is eternity.[37]

Active participation of Protestant and Orthodox delegates at the Second Vatican Council has made history. It also demonstrated the new spirit which people in every communion sense has entered the Christian world.

MEANING OF CATHOLICISM

The term "Catholic" was first applied to the Church by Ignatius of Antioch in his letter to the Smyrneans, to whom he said that "wherever the bishop appears, let the congregation be present; just as wherever Jesus Christ is, there is the Catholic Church." [38] No doubt Ignatius used the adjective to distinguish the universal Church from particular churches in different countries. Yet the emphasis he placed on unity of doctrine suggests that already at the beginning of the second century the word "Catholic" had something of the connotation it soon acquired, of an institution that claimed to remain true to the teachings of its Founder in contrast with other Christian systems and modes of thought.

Along with the profession of fidelity there developed the idea of universality, which the early apologists were quick to exploit in their defense of Christianity. "There is not one single race of men, whether barbarians, or Greeks, or whatever they may be called, among whom prayers and giving of thanks (the Eucharist) are not offered through the name of the crucified Jesus." [39] Thus wrote Justin the Martyr around 150 A.D. But the classic expositor of what "Catholic" means was St. Ireneus, Bishop of Lyons, writing at the end of the second century in his controversy with the Gnostics.

Though scattered throughout the whole world (*kath' olēs tēs oikoumenēs*) to the ends of the earth, the Church received from the Apostles this teaching and this faith. . . . The Church carefully guards this faith, as though it dwelt in a single house; this doctrine it believes as though it had one soul and heart; this creed it teaches and communicates as if it possessed one mouth.

Although there are many different languages in the world, there is one and the same power of tradition. The churches founded in Germany teach no different doctrine from those in Ireland or the surrounding Celtic countries; those in the East, or those in Egypt, do not differ from those in North Africa. Just as the sun, the creature of God, is one and the same in the whole world, so also is the preaching of the truth, the light that shines everywhere and illumines all men who wish to come to a knowledge of the truth.

Different doctrines are not taught by more cultured and able among the leading churches, nor is tradition diminished by those who are weak in controversy. For, since there is one and the same faith, it is neither added to by the effective speaker nor diminished by the one less skilled.[40]

Here is the essence of Catholicism as its adherents understand their faith: a universality pervading all nations and languages, races and social structures.

Yet, even as they identify catholicity with universality, Catholics believe their religion is more than a broadly diffused form of Christianity. They see their Church as an extension of the Incarnation and view it as participating in the twofold nature of Christ, who was at once true man and the Son of the living God. According to one view, therefore, the visible phase as a juridical institution is stressed—corresponding to the humanity of Jesus; and according to another aspect are emphasized the internal qualities of a spiritual entity whose cohesive force is the invisible grace of God—comparable to Christ's divinity.

JURIDICAL SOCIETY. The clearest exponent of the Church as a visible institution was St. Robert Bellarmine, contemporary of Luther, Calvin, and the early Reformers. To meet their challenge of a new concept of Christianity as a purely invisible society composed of all the believers, or all the just, or all the predestined, he described the Catholic Church as "the assembly of men, bound together by the profession of the same Christian faith, and by the communion of the same sacraments, under the rule of rightful pastors, and in particular of the one Vicar of Christ on earth, the Roman Pontiff." [41] The purpose of this definition was mainly functional, to determine who are members of the Catholic Church and who are not. To make sure his meaning was not misunderstood, Bellarmine added: "the Church is an assembly of men, as visible and palpable as the gathering of the Roman people, or the King-dom of France, or the Republic of Venice." [42]

Each of three different elements set down the conditions for membership in this juridical body. Since profession of faith is the first requisite, only those who accept all that the Church infallibly proposes for belief actually belong to the Catholic Church. They may not be aware of the whole corpus of required doctrine, or may be subjectively mistaken in their understanding of what is taught, but they accept whatever is part of the Church's official teaching.

Behind this condition for Church affiliation is the premise that God came to earth in the person of Jesus Christ to teach people the way to salvation—how to live in this world in order to attain heaven in the next. If this is true, it is argued, then Christ would not have left the door of salvation opened for His own times only. He wanted His saving teachings to remain available to mankind until the end of time. Yet this availability would have been less than sterile if He had not provided a living authority to explain and interpret His doctrine as found in the Gospels. Is divorce with re-marriage moral? Was Christ born of a virgin and did He rise in bodily form after death? Does the Church in her priests have the power of forgiving sins, and will impenitent sinners be punished eternally in hell? Without a sure court of appeal, Catholicism says, moral and theological disintegration seem inevitable. It was there-fore to avert such disintegration that Christ established the Church to be His authoritative interpreter on earth, to be His one com-pletely competent spokesman for adjudicating between truth and error on life and death matters.

Sharing in the same sacraments is also necessary for Catholic membership, on the postulate that those who belong to the Church must be united not only by profession of the same faith but in the manifestation of the same forms of divine worship. The Sacrifice of the Mass in particular is considered the mainstay of ritual solidarity, wherein the same High Priest who offered Himself on the Cross for the Redemption of the world offers Himself in an unbloody manner every time the Eucharistic oblation is repeated.

Up to this point, all Christians participate in some of these conditions, and a few (among the Orthodox and Episcopalians) subscribe to practically everything. But the third element, obedience to the Roman Pontiff as Vicar of Christ, is uniquely Catholic. It explains why the term "Roman" is commonly added to "Catholic Church" in popular terminology.

In accepting papal authority, the Catholic Church understands that the Roman Pontiff has more than just the highest office of inspection as a kind of superintendent or director. He is believed to have received from Christ the full and supreme power of juris-diction over the universal Church, not only in matters of faith and morals, but also in things relating to the discipline and government of the Church throughout the world. Consequently, the pope is held to possess not merely the principal part but the fulness of this supreme power. His authority is not merely occasional or delegated, but ordinary and immediate over each and all the churches and over all the pastors of the faithful.

In Bellarmine's ecclesiology, the external phase was emphasized to bring out the Church's visibility and sense perceptibility. It is a definite society, he explained, not of angels or spirits but of men. It must then be bound together by external and visible signs, so that those who belong to it can recognize one another as members and thereby share in their common and distinctive possessions.

SACRAMENTAL AGENT. There is another, more profound con-cept of the Church, which the late Pius XII traced to the writings of St. Paul and the early Fathers. "If we would define and describe the true Church of Jesus Christ," he said, "which is the one, holy, Catholic, apostolic Roman Church—we shall find nothing more noble, more sublime, or more divine than the expression 'the Mystical Body of Jesus Christ.' " [43]

The term "mystical" has a variety of meanings in theological parlance, but when applied to the Church it describes the mysteri-ous presence of Christ which Catholics believe is the Incarnation extended into history and destined to be consummated in heaven after the last day. Once the word "mystical" is seen to be the same as "sacramental," the full import of how Catholicism understands itself becomes clearer. In a broad sense anything spiritual conveyed through bodily means partakes of the nature of a sacrament. There are seven sacraments properly so-called in the Catholic Church, containing the grace they signify and conferring that grace from the rite itself (*ex opere operato*) on those who place no obstacle in the way. However, by analogy the Church itself may be considered sacramental, and the two concepts together afford the deepest insight into the meaning of Catholic Christianity.

As explained by St. Thomas, who borrowed his ideas from the patristic tradition, the body with which St. Paul identified the Church is a living entity, and like every organism requires suitable means to enter into life, to grow and mature according to its nature. Similarly Christ has provided for His Mystical Body by endowing it with the sacraments, to give its members access to powerful channels of grace, from birth to death, and to provide for the social needs of the society He founded.

Leading this sacramental series is baptism, called the door of the Church because it is the only way a person can become an actual member of the Catholic Church. At the Council of Florence, which sought the reunion of the Eastern Orthodox, "holy Baptism" was said to "hold the first place among all the sacraments because it is the door of the spiritual life. By it we are made members of Christ and of His Body the Church. And since through the first man death has come to all men, unless we are reborn of water and the Holy Spirit we cannot enter into the kingdom of heaven." [44]

Having entered the Church, a Catholic is held by divine law to give profession of his belief in Christ, at no matter what cost and under penalty of eternal loss of his soul. When explaining this injunction, Canon Law refers to the precept of Christ: "Everyone who acknowledges me before men, him will the Son of Man also acknowledge before the angels of God. But whoever disowns me before men will be disowned before the angels of God." Since the precept is universal and may at times require extraordinary courage to fulfil, the faithful receive the sacrament of Confirmation by which they are given additional strength to protect and defend the Church, their Mother, and the faith she has given them.

Confirmation, therefore, has a double aspect: to safeguard not only one's own faith but also to defend the Church from whom the faith was received. Its function is not only negative, to shelter the faith and the Church, but openly to defend both against the forces of opposition.

Likewise, in the sacrament of Penance or Confession, the benefit is considered both individual and social. Here the Church is seen as providing a salutary remedy for those who have fallen into sin, and at the same time removing from other members of the Mystical Body the danger of contagion—besides giving them an incentive and example for the practice of virtue. As sin is removed from one cell of the Body, the rest of the Church profits accordingly, much as the removal of a diseased organ or limb benefits the whole person. What happens is not merely the checking of bad influence, in this case the effects of sin, but the transmission of new vitality in the form of grace from one part of the Church's body to all the others.

The Eucharist is pre-eminently the sacrament of Catholicism. It is a dramatic symbol of the unity of the Church, about whch St. Augustine and other ancients wrote their homilies, and illustrated in the liturgical prayers of the Mass, like the oration from the *Didache,* dated in the first century of the Christian era: "As this broken Bread was scattered over the hills and then, when gathered together became one mass, so may Your Church be gathered from the ends of the earth into Your Kingdom. For Yours is the glory and the power through Jesus Christ for evermore." [45]

Moreover in the Eucharist Catholics believe they receive the very Author of grace and the Head of the Mystical Body, and through Him an increase of charity towards God and of love for others for the sake of God. Thus the Eucharist is an aliment of the Church, wherein Christ nourishes Christ, Head to members, and they in turn become more unified with one another through Him.

In a category by itself is the Sacrifice of the Mass, which the popes down the centuries have said is the central act of worship in the Church, and the main single source of grace for mankind, benefiting people in the Church and out of it, whether in the friendship of God or estranged from Him by sin.

The Eucharist is not only a sacrament but also a sacrifice. As a sacrament it has effect upon living beings, where life is required to make a sacrament effective. But as a sacrifice it is effective on others besides the living, for whom it is offered, who are not actually but only potentially living in grace. Consequently, as long as they are properly disposed, the Mass will obtain grace for such people in virtue of that true

Sacrifice (of the Cross) from which all grace is poured into us. So that grave sins are deleted in these sinners by the Mass, not as a proximate cause but insofar as the Mass infallibly obtains for them the grace of sorrow for their sins.[46]

Extreme Unction is the sacrament of passage from the Mystical Body on earth to the Mystical Body in heaven. Where the other sacraments help the faithful to remain steadfast during life, anointing with the *oleum infirmorum* gives the promise of strength to resist the evil spirit at the hour of death. There are two effects proper to this sacrament and both are related to the Mystical Body. Its main purpose is to remove the vestiges of sin and strengthen the soul in its departure from this world, thus facilitating its entrance into the Church Triumphant, which is the Mystical Body in heavenly consummation. An important secondary effect, however, is to remove the guilt and punishment due to sin, whether grave or venial, thus restoring (if need be) life to a dead member of the Church and making possible, besides accelerating, his admission to celestial glory.

Two sacraments of the Church are conceived as providing directly for the social needs of the Mystical Body. In Matrimony the husband and wife are ministers of grace to each other. Since they are not only man and woman but also belong to a supernatural society, the procreation of children for them means more than just conserving the human race and providing for its orderly development; it means the duty of preserving and increasing membership of the Mystical Body. All the laws that nature has implanted in the two sexes to insure the welfare of mankind are sublimated by grace in the faithful for the common benefit of the Church. Where natural instinct makes the two sexes mutually attractive, grace provides for a similar attraction on a higher level, so that children will be not only physically brought into the world but also spiritually reborn in Baptism, educated and nurtured into vital cells of the Body of Christ.

It is this concept of Matrimony that makes the Catholic Church so adamant in its stand on divorce and contraception. Marriage between Christians is indissoluble because it should reflect that most perfect union which exists between Christ and the Church which is perpetual. One of the most frequent causes of estrangement from the Church of his Baptism and his deepest loyalties on the part of a Catholic is a marriage attempted after a divorce. He is reminded that "the whole of eternity is gambled against the fascination of human companionship," that men are ultimately made not for earthly happiness but for heavenly joy. "Hence, if there is loneliness and a longing for companionship, let these be looked upon not as a warrant to contravene divine law, but as a challenge to Christian fortitude." [47]

The same with contraception. "Since the conjugal act is destined primarily by nature for the begetting of children, those who in exercising it deliberately frustrate its natural power and purpose sin against nature and commit a deed which is shameful and intrinsically vicious." [48] If this applies to all married persons, it is specially pertinent to Catholics who would thus frustrate not only the natural function of sexual intercourse but the connatural way in which Christ intends His Church to increase and multiply in the supernatural order.

By the sacrament of Ordination the Church is provided with the means of nourishing the life of the faithful through the Mass and the sacraments and, in a true sense, with the juridical power to govern by legitimate authority and proclaim the word of God. Except for the sacraments of Baptism and Matrimony, which do not require ordination to be administered, all the others depend on the power of priestly orders.

Here is a crucial difference between Catholic and other forms of Christianity. In Catholic thought, the priestly powers communicated by Christ through the apostles and their successors are intimately bound up with the power of jurisdiction. In practical terms, the authority which the pope and bishops exercise in the Church derives from their ordination and consecration. No doubt a single person, say a bishop-elect, may be invested with jurisdictional powers before his consecration. But considering the Church a a whole, the power of jurisdiction requires the power of orders necessarily and absolutely. If there were no power of orders at all, there could be no ecclesiastical authority in the accepted Catholic meaning of that term.

Viewed in this light, the Catholic Church's claim to apostolic lineage is more than a simple assertion of fidelity to the teaching of the apostles. It is a claim to historical continuity from Christ, through the apostles, to all the members of the hierarchy and from them to all priests: that when Christ ordained the first ministers of the Gospel, He gave them delegated power to communicate to others what they had received, in literal and direct succession until the end of time.

However, the Catholic Church professes to more than having a sacramental system, from Baptism to Holy Orders. It claims to be itself the great Sacrament of the New Law. The logic behind this profession stems from the general principle that although God can perform by His own power all that is effected by created natures, nevertheless in the counsels of His providence He has preferred to help men by the instrumentality of other men's work; so also He makes use of human aid for that which lies beyond the limits of nature, for the salvation and sanctification of souls.

It is assumed that the divine mission committed to Him by His Father was not to end with Christ's death but continue after his ascension through the Church which He founded. Consequently as Catholics view their Church, it is undoubtedly spiritual if we consider the chief purpose of the Church, which is to make men holy, and the immediate cause of holiness, which is supernatural grace in its various forms. But as regards the persons who constitute the Body of Christ and the means which lead to these spiritual gifts, the Church is external and its very external elements are the instruments for communicating the internal life of God to souls.

This fusion of visible and invisible elements is not coincidental; it is causally interdependent. Comparable to what occurs in one area of the Church's operation in the sacramental system is perennially taking place in the Church as a whole. External unity among the members and stability in doctrine and discipline are the sign of a deeper solidarity which comes from the animating Spirit of God. Conversely, doctrine and discipline, and the juridical forms which govern the faithful carry the assurance of an invisible efficacy which for Catholics as far transcends the material instruments used as the raising of Lazarus exceeded the sound of Christ's voice or the conversion of the Mediterranean world was beyond the capacity of a dozen Jews.

The Body of Christ is said to be mystical, then, because it is sacramental, not only in the functional sense of an external action signifying the conferral of interior grace, but on the cosmic level of a visible entity whose Body, in all its amplitude, is a manifestation of God's presence on earth, begun at the Incarnation and extended into human history. Those who benefit from this communication are first of all the actual members of the Mystical Body, who receive these gifts as by a special privilege. But also outside the Body, whoever is eventually saved is told to credit his salvation to the instrumentality of the Church, whose invisible Head is the fountain of all life and holiness; and of whose fulness anyone who is sanctified must have received.

Although the main lines of this concept of Catholicism are clear enough, its full implication is open to wide development, as Pope Paul told the Second Vatican Council. "It is necessary," he said, "to elucidate the teaching regarding the different components of the visible and Mystical Body, the pilgrim, militant Church on earth, that is, priests, religious, the faithful, and also the separated brethren who are also called to adhere to it more fully and completely." [49]

For the first time since the Reformation, the term "separated brethren" has taken on a new and profound meaning, in which the Catholic Church sees other Christians as related to herself spiritually by the three-fold bond of baptism, faith and devotion to the persons of Jesus Christ.

14. Islam

To most Christians, Mohammedanism is only a vague religious movement that somehow gave rise to the Crusades and that presently affects the culture and political aspirations of certain people in North Africa, the Near East and Pakistan. Actually Mohammedanism is the most powerful force among the living religions outside of Christianity, and to many observers its greatest competitor for the spiritual domination of the world.

The correct name of Mohammedanism is Islam, which Mohammed himself adopted as a description of the faith he proclaimed. Grammatically Islam is the infinitive of a verb that means to resign, submit, or surrender, by implication oneself or one's person to God. Those who profess it are called Muslims, of which the Western form is Moslems, meaning "believers" who offered themselves to God, as distinct from Kafirs or Mushriks, "the rejectors" of the divine message of salvation. Moslems dislike the word Mohammedan because it suggests the worship of Mohammed, even as the term Christian implies the worship of Jesus Christ.

HISTORICAL ORIGINS

A balanced study of Islamic origins must take into account the religious and ethnic conditions in Arabia before the rise of Mohammed. In ancient times Arabia remained quite outside the threshold of the great civilizations. Its inhabitants never really bowed to a foreign master. The tribal and political divisions of the people combined with the rough terrain to foil attempted conquests by alien powers.

While the early history of the Arab race is veiled in obscurity,

339

historical tradition agrees in assigning Ishmael, the son of Abraham by Agar, as one of the important early ancestors of the race. In any case, the Semitic people who formed the permanent population of Arabia were joined several centuries before Mohammed by colonies of immigrants, chiefly Jews but also Christians, who settled among the native population. Thus three religious currents ran through pre-Islamic Arabia: the native Arabian, the Jewish and the Christian.

Idolatry combined with elements of Biblical tradition to form the religion of the native Arab. Derived from a primitive form of animism, it consisted largely in the worship of the heavenly bodies. Though he seems to have believed in one God, the early Arab found little difficulty combining his weak monotheism with adoration of the fixed stars and planets, or at least with offering sacrifice to the angels who were believed to dwell in these stellar bodies. The title "goddesses" or "daughters of God" was given not only to the intelligences but to their images as well, which the Arabs looked upon as either animated by the spirits or graced by their presence with the power of special protection.

Mohammed, the founder of Islam, was born into this environment at Mecca, about 600 miles south of Jerusalem, some time between 570 and 580 of the Christian era. His father, *Abd Allâh,* died on a journey to Medina, before Mohammed was born; the mother, *Aminah bint Wahb,* died ten years later. The young *Muhammad* (as spelled in Arabic) was first brought up by his paternal grandfather, and after the latter's death by his uncle *Abû Tâlib.* Except for a pathetic reference in the Koran to his hardships as an orphan, most of the early life of Mohammed before his vocation is either legendary or difficult to verify.

It is certain that he engaged in the caravan trade, became commercial agent to a widow *Khadija,* married her and had children, of whom four daughters survived. What pious tradition suggests, that he showed prophetic insight already in his youth, should be set aside. More important and surely authentic is the series of conflicts to which Mohammed was subject and which deeply affected his later experiences. His orphaned background deprived him of external care and security, and encouraged a sense of dependence on the preternatural; the evidence of idolatry among the Arabs contrasted strongly with the monotheistic religion of the immigrant Jews and, mostly Nestorian, Christians; his deep sensibility responded as by instinct to the social injustice he saw all around him at Mecca, with its extremes of wealth and poverty, and its underworld of slaves, thieves and vagabonds.

When he finally emerged about the age of forty (610-612 A.D.) as the prophet of a new revelation, the immediate object of reform and castigation was the prosperity-sodden Mecca, whose inhabitants he faced with the message of repentance because the judgment of God was at hand.

Mohammed's message to the Meccans was simple and forthright. He proclaimed the existence of one only absolute Lord and Creator, whose name Allah was known but almost buried in the Arabic pantheon. This God was sole master of mankind, whose final judgment would be a terrible vengeance on the ungodly. Man's only hope before the Deity was a blind abandonment (Islam) to the divine will, and a life of prayer and resistance to one's sinful inclinations.

But the leading people of Mecca would not listen. Religious leaders were too entrenched in their polytheism and the wealthy merchants in secular affairs to take Mohammed seriously. Gradually he made some converts, beginning with his wife, and mostly among the slaves and foreigners. Opposition arose when the impact of his ideas became more evident. Occasionally there were riots and always a hidden persecution in the form of social boycott.

For ten years Mohammed struggled to make a headway with only minimal success until the autumn of 622, when he fled secretly from Mecca, escaped his pursuers, and established himself at Medina, about two hundred miles north. The city had been suffering from a fratricidal war, and feared lest its weakness be exploited by the Jewish tribes under municipal control. So the people invited Mohammed to come to Medina as arbitrator and peace-maker.

This migration of Mohammed and his followers is known as the *hijrah* (departure) and marks the year *one* of the Moslem era. Moslem years are counted A.H., or after the *hijrah*. The flight to Medina changed not only the scene but the actor and the drama in Islamic history. In Mecca the prophet had been simply a religious leader, concerned for the social morals of his people and zealous to share his revealed convictions; at Medina he suddenly became a political and military figure, whose new role is clearly indicated by a sudden transition in the Koran.

Three important battles, provoked by Mohammed, mark the period of a slow conquest of Mecca, finally accomplished in 630. An attempted raid on a Meccan caravan was first repulsed by armed soldiers, who were then roundly defeated by the Moslems at Badr (624). The following year in a pitched battle at Uhud, the Meccans won a partial victory which they did not follow up. In the Battle of the Ditch (627), Mohammed successfully resisted a siege of Medina by digging large trenches before the unprotected entrances to the city. Three years later he determined to attack his native city with an army of ten thousand men. He took possession without a struggle, broke down the pagan idols of the Kaaba, rebuilt the sacred temple and into its foundation set the same black stone which Arabian animists had kissed for centuries as part of their pilgrimage ritual. Probably a meteorite, the stone came to be worshiped by the Semitic tribesmen as "of heavenly" origin. Islam's tradition explains the present black color of the stone as a result of contact with the sins and impurity of the pagan world.

For a moment his Medinian companions feared that Mohammed would leave them now in favor of Mecca, but they were promptly reassured. Within a few months after his entrance into Mecca, he broke the final resistance of the Bedouin tribes at the battle of Hunajn and returned to Medina to establish that city as the political capital of a new Moslem state. Here he received delegates from the Arabian chieftains who vowed their submission, and from here sent out his last miltary expeditions, including one against the Byzantine power which failed indeed but foreshadowed the vast expansion of the Islamic empire of the future.

From Medina, in 631, the prophet issued his definitive norms excluding idolaters from the pilgrimage which had become entirely Islamized, and in 632 Mohammed made the pilgrimage himself for the first and last time. An estimated forty thousand people made the journey with him. It was a pilgrimage of farewell. His mission was complete: paganism had been crushed, the new faith was solidly established, and a young generation of ardent followers was ready to carry the prophet's message to the far reaches of Asia and Northern Africa. Scholars dispute as to whether Mohammed personally ambitioned this conquest. There is not a syllable in the Koran suggesting a mission of Islam outside of Arabia, or of a conscious universalism such as we find in the New Testament. Yet expansion was inevitable—given the Moslem abomination of pagan idolatry, the claim to superseding Judaism and Christianity, the charge of polytheism against the Christian dogma of the Trinity, and Mohammed's insistence on a zealous prosecution of the enemies of Allah.

On his return to Medina after the pilgrimage, Mohammed was seized by a violent fever which caused his death at the age of sixty-three, in the eleventh year of the *Hijrah* and the year 632 (June 8) of the Christian era.

THE KORAN

The Bible of Islam is the Koran or *Qur'an*. It consists of those revelations which Mohammed claimed to have received from Allah, yet not directly but through the mediation of the angel Gabriel. According to Islamic tradition, the book is not a new creation but exists in archetype in heaven, fixed in the very essence of God and delivered piecemeal to the prophet. The word Koran means "recitation," and suggests its primary function of being recited during religious ceremonies.

Mohammed memorized his own utterances and taught his followers to do the same, but no single disciple knew the whole Koranic revelation. When the prophet died, the oracles were found on scattered bits of leather, ribs of palm leaf, and even on stones. These were gathered together, put into a chest and entrusted to the keeping of Haphsa, one of Mohammed's wives. During the reign of the first Caliph, Abu Bekr, a hurried edition of the Koran was made by Zaid of Medina, Mohammed's secretary, relying on oral tradition and scattered writings. But variant texts soon appeared, which alarmed the prophet's followers and prompted the third Caliph, Othman, to order all variants burned and have a canonical edition published by Zaid and three members of the Koraish tribe. Thus the text of the Koran was finally settled within thirty years of Mohammed's death, and in its present form is universally accepted by Moslems as authentic.

In English translation, the Koran is a book of some two-hundred thousand words, divided into one hundred fourteen chapters, called Surahs, arranged roughly in descending order of length, with some of the final chapters as short as a single paragraph. Surahs are further divided into verses, totalling about six thousand, and numbered as in the Christian Bible.

The Surahs are not numbered in the manuscripts, but are headed by titles taken from a particular matter treated, a person mentioned, or generally from the first significant words. Typical titles are: Women, Abraham, Mary, the Angels, Divorce, Small Kindnesses, and the Disbelievers.

Moslems universally recognize the language of the Koran as elegant in the extreme. "The Koran," they say, "cannot be translated." Nothing can duplicate "that inimitable symphony, the very sounds of which move men to tears and ecstasy." It is admittedly the standard of the Arabic tongue, and as the book itself teaches, beyond the capacity of any human pen. This, they claim, is a permanent miracle, greater than raising the dead and alone sufficient to convince the world of its divine original.

No satisfactory theory explains either the time or sequence of the purported revelations. Most likely the shortest Surahs were the earliest, and references to current events within the text may indicate when some of the statements were made.

Heading many of the Surahs is the declaration, "Revealed at Al-Madinah" or "Revealed at Mecca"; where no place is given, the locale of revelation is uncertain. Also at the beginning of each chapter, with the exception of the ninth, occurs the phrase, "In the name of Allah, the Beneficent, the Merciful."

Only the most uncritical Moslem holds that the Koran is wholly original. Mohammed wove into his discourse large quantities of tribal tradition, popular sayings, legends beloved by the people, and much that he had gathered from his contact with the Jews and Christians, although the latter was mainly apocryphal, and the Jewish was more rabbinical interpretation than Old Testament content.

DOCTRINE AND WORSHIP IN THE KORAN

Islam is a glomeration of sects and traditions that bewilder the Western mind. Yet after thirteen centuries, the followers of Mohammed are somehow united and their unity traceable to a common devotion to the Koran. It is the duty of every Moslem, man, woman, or child, to read the Koran and understand it according to his capacity. There runs through the book a consistent body of doctrine and of practical obligations which has remained in all ages the inspiration of the Muslim religion.

Unexpectedly, the famous *Shahada* or profession of faith, "There is but one God, and Mohammed is the Apostle of God," nowhere occurs as such in the Koran. The nearest equivalent, often called the Islamic Credo, is found in the Surah of Women: "You who believe, believe in God and His apostle, and the Book which He revealed to His apostle, and the Book which he revealed to those before him. Whoever denies God and His angels and His books and His apostle and the day of judgment has strayed far away from the truth." [1]

While the Koran itself is central, three other sources of Islamic doctrine and practice are recognized by orthodox Moslems: tradition or *Qunnah*, community agreement or *igmah*, and the principle of analogy called *gijas*.

Tradition as a source of revelation is co-equal with the Koran in binding power and authority. It consists of all the sayings, explicit or implicit, of Mohammed, which he did not personally set down in the Koran.

Consensus of believers is more difficult to define and has occasioned endless dispute and schism. But in theory it means that whenever a sizeable portion of the Moslem faithful agrees on some cardinal issue of doctrine or ritual, this becomes part of the creedal structure of Islam.

The method of analogy finds special application in the field of morals and conduct, where a new situation is evaluated by comparison with a similar one in the past. Understandably the principle of *gijas* lends itself to arbitrary interpretation and, in fact, has been the cause of grave tension and conflict in Moslem jurisprudence.

GOD. The Arabic word for God is Allah, an abbreviation for *al-ilah*, "the God," to distinguish the supreme Deity from the numerous lesser divinities that were worshiped in Arabia in Mohammed's time. Koranic attributes of God are rich and varied. He is

called the Hearer, Seer, Bestower, Reckoner, Pardoner, Keeper and
Guide; and the epithets applied to Him have been gathered together
into the ninety-nine "most beautiful names of God."

Among the most impressive descriptions of the Deity is the eloquent Throne-verse in the second Surah:

God, there is no god but He—the Living, the Self-subsisting, Eternal.
No slumber can seize Him nor sleep. His are all things in the heavens
and on earth. Who is there can intercede in His presence except as He
permits? He knows what appears to His creatures as before and after or
behind them. Nor shall they compass any of His knowledge except as He
will. His throne extends over the heavens and the earth, and He feels
no fatigue in guarding and preserving them, for He is the Most High,
the Supreme in glory.[2]

In the Koran the essential element of true belief is an uncompromising monotheism. Mohammed rejected the legends of contemporary Arabs that Allah had daughters who were goddesses,
and on the same grounds opposed the worship of Christianity as
based on human invention. Loving faith requires *ikhlas,* or surrender of oneself completely to God alone, and the basic error is *shirk,*
when companions are ascribed to the Creator and creatures are
worshiped as God. This is the one monstrous sin: "God forgives not
that partners should be set up with Him. But He forgives everything
else, to whom He pleases. To set up partners with God is to devise a
most heinous sin." [3]

God's unity, therefore, is absolute, and allows no filiation,
which would be an outrage, or even association in the making or
government of the world. He is complete Master of the universe
and by His will determines all things, whether good or bad. He has
predestined mankind according to eternal decrees, yet Koranic
teaching does not clearly reduce man's lot to a crude fatalism,
which some Moslem interpreters have since found in their scriptures.

There are two strains of thought on human liberty in the Koran.
When speaking speculatively, man's absolute dependence and even
induction into sin by God are taught for "Allah sends astray whom
He wills, and whom He wills He guides." [4] But when the context is
moral exhortation, the existence of freedom and the need for making a right choice are emphasized. In the first verse of the Koran,

these two elements are combined, at once recognizing Allah as Lord of the universe and invoking His mercy against the day of judgment for sins ostensibly committed by an abuse of free will.

In the name of the One God, the Compassionate One, the Merciful.

Praise be to God, the Lord of the Universe—the Compassionate One, the Merciful.

The Ruler on the Day of Judgment.

You do we worship, and from you do we seek aid.

Guide us into the straight path—the path of those to whom you have shown mercy.

Not to those who have incurred your anger, nor those who go astray.[5]

God is not only one and inimitable, but He is also the primal and unique cause of everything outside Himself. Although some passages obscurely suggest the pre-existence of matter co-extensively with God, elsewhere the Koran is perfectly clear on creation out of nothing. "The Originator of the heavens and the earth! When He decrees a thing, He says to it only: Be! and it is." [6] And again, "Lo! Your Lord is Allah who created the heavens and the earth in six days, then He established Himself upon the throne, directing all things." [7]

With regard to the divine moral attributes, there is confusion of thought which later gave rise to such contrary Islamic theologies as the pantheism of the Persian Sufis and the orthodoxy of a modern Koranic commentator who says "the attributes of God are so different from anything we know in our present world that we have to be content with understanding that the only fit word by which we can name Him is 'He.' (Yet) the pantheist places the wrong accent when he says that everything is He. The truth is better expressed when we say that everything is 'His.' " [8] Often the Koran presents God as a magnified Arab chief or Sheikh, who is ready to forgive, who desires the salvation of men, and sends them prophets and the Book to guide them. Elsewhere He appears to act arbitrarily and through caprice. "He forgives whom He wills and He punishes whom He wills." [9]

CHRIST AND MARY. Consistent with denying any filiation in God, Christ appears in the Koran as only a messenger of Allah,

His servant and prophet, but nothing more. The Blessed Virgin, therefore, although respectfully treated is only the Mother of Jesus. She is called Maryam, and the name occurs thirty-four times in the Koran, always referring to the Mother of Christ, except in three passages where she seems to be identified with Mariam, the sister of Moses and Aaron. Her virtue is of a high character, which many commentators interpret as absolute sinlessness from birth and even conception. According to Abu Huraira, Mohammed had said, "No child comes into this world without being at the time of his birth touched by Satan, and because of this touch the child utters a cry. Mary and her Son have been exempted from this touch." [10]

The privilege of the virgin birth of Christ is unique in the history of mankind. Appearing to Mary at the Annunciation, the angels spoke to her in words reminiscent of the Gospel of St. Luke. "O Mary," they said, "truly God has chosen you and purified you, and chosen you above the women of all nations. God gives you glad tidings of a word from Him. His name will be Christ Jesus, the Son of Mary, held in honor in this world and in the hereafter." When Mary objected, "How shall I have a son, when no man has touched me?" one of the angels assures her, "Even so, God created what He willed. When He has decreed a plan, He merely says to it, 'Be,' and it is. Your Lord says, It is easy for me. And it will take place that We may make of him a revelation for mankind and a mercy from Us, and it is a thing ordained." Whereupon "she conceived the child, and withdrew him to a far place." [11]

After His birth, when Mary brought the infant to her people they rebuked her for infamy. She referred them to the new-born babe for an explanation. "How can we speak to one who is in the cradle?" they asked. Whereupon the child spoke in defense of His mother, "Behold I am the servant of Allah. He has given me the Scripture, has made me a prophet." [12] To which Mohammed was careful to add, "It was not befitting the majesty of God that He should take unto Himself a son"—thus exalting Christ to the dignity of a prophet like Moses but insisting that He was only a man.

God performed miracles to confirm the teaching and mission of Christ, who also gathered to His company a number of apostles. "When Jesus perceived unbelief" among the Jews to whom He was preaching, He inquired, "Who are my helpers in the cause of

Allah? The disciples replied, 'We will be Allah's helpers. We believe in Allah, and do you bear witness that we have surrendered unto Him.' " [13] After finishing His mission, Jesus returned to Allah who spoke in uncompromising terms against those who should reject the Christian message. "I should punish them with a violent punishment in this world and in the next, and they shall have no aid. But as for those who believe and do good works, He will repay them their wages in full." [14]

The religion of Jesus, like that of Moses, was at first equated with his own revelation. Later on, however, when Mohammed tried and failed to reconcile the three communities, he reversed his earlier approval of Christianity. Although Jesus resembled Mohammed by receiving the Scriptures, being declared a prophet and confirmed by signs, later Surahs declare the Christians unbelievers and fit only to burn after the day of judgment. "Allah! There is no God save Him, the Alive, the Eternal. He has revealed unto you (Mohammed) the Scripture with truth, confirming that which went before it, even as He revealed the Torah and the Gospel previously as a guide to mankind. . . . He it is who revealed to you (Mohammed) the Scriptures which are clear revelations. . . . Those who reject this faith, neither their possessions nor their progeny will avail them against Allah. They are but fuel for the fire. Say to those who disbelieve: You shall be overcome and gathered into hell, an evil resting place." [15] Centuries of Mohammedan history testify to the seriousness of this anathema.

Following the doctrine of the Docetists, the Koran denies that Christ was slain by the Jews. Yet God will punish the Jews rejecting Mohammed, slandering Mary's virginity and claiming to have crucified Jesus. "Allah has set a seal upon them because of their disbelief, and of their speaking against Mary a terrible calumny, and because of their saying, 'We slew the Messiah, Jesus son of Mary, Allah's messenger.' They did not slay nor crucify him, but so it appeared to them. For Allah took him up unto Himself." [16] Inconsistently, however, in another passage the Koran explicitly affirms Christ's death and resurrection, as in the prophetic statement of the Christ Child shortly after His birth, when He miraculously announced, "Peace on me the day I was born, and the day I died, and the day on which I shall be raised alive." [17]

Woven into the Koran as a Christological theme is the repeated
denial that God could have a son and therefore that Jesus could
be one with Allah. "Jesus in Allah's eyes is in the same position as
Adam. He created him of dust, and then said to him, 'Be,' and he
is." This is the truth from the Lord, and "whosoever disputes with
you concerning him, we will summon our sons, and your sons, and
our women and your women, and we will pray humbly and solemnly
invoke the curse of Allah upon those who lie." [18] In one eloquent
passage, Mohammed consigns all Trinitarian Christians to eternal
doom.

They surely disbelieve who say, "Behold, Allah is the Messiah, son
of Mary." The Messiah himself said, "Children of Israel, worship Allah,
my Lord and your God." Whoever ascribes partners unto Allah, for him
Allah has forbidden Paradise. His abode is the Fire. For evildoers there
will be no relief.

They surely disbelieve who say, "Behold Allah is the third of three,"
when there is no god save the One God. If they desist not from so saying, a painful doom will fall on those who disbelieve.

The Messiah, son of Mary, was no other than a messenger. Many
were the messengers that passed away before him. See how God makes
his signs clear to them (the Christians); yet see how they are deluded
away from the truth.[19]

This studied reduction of Christ to the status of mere man is
part of a larger Koranic message, that Moses and Christ and
Mohammed are equally prophets of Allah, except that Mohammed
is the last of the prophetic line. Moslems are told that "Mohammed
is not the father of any man among you, but he is the messenger
of Allah and the Seal of the Prophets." [20] When a document is
sealed, it is complete, and there can be no further addition. Mohammed therefore closes the long line of prophets. God's teaching
will always be continuous, but there has been and there will be no
prophet after Mohammed. As Moses prepared the way for Christ,
so Christ was the precursor of Mohammed. This is not an arbitrary
matter. In Islamic tradition it is a decree full of knowledge and
wisdom and irrevocable with the immutability of Allah Himself.

Less familiar than the denial of Christ's divinity, is the positive
concept of the Trinity suggested by the Koran and further elabo-

rated by its commentators. According to Mohammed, on the day
of resurrection God will ask Christ the following question, "Jesus,
son of Mary, did you say to mankind: Take me and your mother
for two gods beside Allah?"—to which Christ will give the answer,
"Be glorified! It was not mine to utter that to which I had no right.
If I used to say it, then You knew it. You know what is on my
mind. Behold, You only are the knower of things hidden." [21]

Mohammed was adamant in denying the Trinity. "Believe in
God and His messengers," he told the people, "and do not say,
three. Cease, it is better for you. Allah is only one God. Far is it
from His transcendent majesty that He should have a son. His is all
that is in the heavens and all that is in the earth. And Allah is sufficient as defender. The Christ will never scorn to be a slave unto
Allah, nor will the favored angels. Whoever scorns His service
and is proud, all such will He assemble unto Him (and) will punish
them with a painful doom." [22]

Yet the Koranic conception of the Trinity is a bizarre notion
that is hard to find anywhere in contemporary religious literature.
Mohammed quite literally believed that Christians professed a divine triad of Allah, Jesus of Nazareth and Mary. He is clear in
asserting that the Messias was not divine, and equally (though less
forthrightly) clear that the Holy Spirit is not God but only a special,
mysterious power issuing from Him, or, perhaps an angel, whom
commentators identify with the Angel Gabriel who spoke to
Mohammed.

Islamic exegetes confirm this judgment in their interpretation
of the term, "Three," of the fourth Surah. Some say bluntly that
the three in question are "Allah and Jesus and his Mother." Others
are more precise and more crude. Allah, Christ and Mary are three
gods and the Messias is the child, "in the flesh" (walad' Ullah) of
Allah from Mary. Still others repeat the same Islamic tradition but
prudently add that this may not be the explanation which Christians accept, since according to them, "Three means that God is
three persons, the Father, the Son and the Holy Spirit. They understand by Father the essence, by the Son the knowledge, and by the
Holy Spirit the life" of Allah. While still erroneous, the latter at
least offers an alternative to the traditional Mohammedan concept
of the Trinity which was condemned as blasphemous.

ANGELS. For a religion as notoriously earth-bound as Islam, the spiritual world is remarkably prominent. Some thirty Surahs speak of the angels, and another dozen of the *jinn* who are created like men but of fire instead of earth. In the imagery of the Koran, angels appear to be messengers of God: to bear up His throne, descend to earth with His decrees, record men's actions, receive their souls when they die, witness for or against them at the last judgment, and stand guard over the gates of hell.

Besides the angels, there are devils, whom the Koran represents not as fallen spirits but rebellious *jinn,* also called *shaitans* who lead men astray, oppose the prophets, and try to overhear what goes on in heaven but are driven away by shooting stars. They teach people sorcery and will finally go to hell along with wicked men on the day of final resurrection.

REVELATION AND PROPHETS. Next to unity of God, the doctrine of the prophets or apostles is the central dogma of the Koran. God has at all times and to all peoples, including the *jinn,* sent His messengers to preach the unity of Allah and warn men of the judgment to come. Most of them were rejected and as a consequence brought divine punishment on the nations that refused to listen. Among the more prominent mentioned in the Koran are Adam, Noah and Abraham, Moses and Jesus the son of Mary. Unlike his predecessors, Mohammed is God's apostle to all mankind and not only to one people or time. While only implicit in the Koran, this broad universalism later on became a cardinal principle of Islam.

All told, twenty-eight prophets are named, including four obscure Arabians and eighteen Old Testament figures. Their doctrine is entirely consistent, except that each succeeding apostle adds to and clarifies the preceding, until Mohammed in the Koran not only confirms earlier Scriptures, but, as the final revelation, clears up all uncertainties and is the repository of perfect truth. In fact, Mohammed's coming was foretold by Jesus under the name of *Ahmad,* which the Jews and Christians seek to conceal by misquoting the Bible and even wilfully perverting its meaning.

ESCHATOLOGY. The last day is always present to the author of the Koran, almost to the point of obsession. It will be a cataclysmic event to come suddenly at a time known only to God. Some of the most beautiful poetry in Koranic literature deals with this theme. Whole Surahs are devoted to the same, as the eighty-second, entitled "The Cleaving," revealed at Mecca and referrable either to the judgment at death or to the final day of reckoning.

> In the name of God, most Gracious and most Merciful
> When the heaven is cleft asunder.
> When the stars are scattered abroad.
> When the seas are allowed to burst forth.
> And the graves are overturned.
> Then shall each soul know what it has sent before it
>   and what has been left behind.
> O man! What has seduced you from your most
>   beautiful Lord?
> Who created you, fashioned you in due proportion,
>   and gave you a first balance.
> Into whatever form He will, He puts you together.
> Yet, men reject right and judgment.
> But over you are appointed angels to protect you, kind
>   and honorable, writing down your deeds. They
>   know and understand all that you do.
> As for the righteous, they will be in delight.
> And the wicked will be in the fire, which they will enter
>   on the day of judgment, and will not be absent
>   thence.
> Who will explain to you what the day of judgment is;
>   again who will tell you what the day of judgment
>   is!
> A day when no soul shall have power to keep
>   another, for the command on that day will be
>   wholly with God.[23]

While modified in minor details, Koranic eschatology has remained substantially unchanged in modern Islam. After death, when the body is buried, each person is judged by two angels, Munkar and Nakir, on his faith and good works. Unbelievers and Moslem sinners will suffer "the torments of the grave," whereas prophets and martyrs enter heaven immediately. Ambiguity on the resurrection has produced two opposing theories: either that the soul dies and later rises with the body, or that it continues to live and will later be re-embodied.

Preludes of the general judgment include universal discord among nations, the appearance of a mysterious "beast of earth" and the coming of Antichrist. Jesus will return to earth, only to be slain. At the first sound of the trumpet, the world will come to an end, at the second the dead will rise and assemble on the plain of judgment. God will appear between angels, and Mohammed will intercede for the souls. Each man's guardian spirit will bear witness to his record, weighed in the balance, and his book will be placed in his right hand, if blessed, otherwise in the left. The souls will then start crossing a bridge as narrow as the blade of a knife, spanning the fires of hell, into which the wicked fall but the good, with help received from the prophet, will safely enter Paradise.

Hell is described as a valley of smoke, where the damned suffer eternal hunger, burning and chains. They are fed with boiling water and the fruit of the cursed *zaggum,* resembling the heads of demons and like molten brass in the belly. Words fail to convey the horrors implied in such dire predictions as "The word of the Lord has been fulfilled, 'Verily I shall fill hell with the *jinn* and mankind together,'" or the observation, "One day we shall ask hell, 'Are you filled to the full?' It will answer, 'Are there any more to come?'" [24]

Paradise, on the other hand, is a haven of gardens and meadows, flowing with brooks of water and streams of honey, milk and wine. Spreading lotus trees cast their cooling shade. The blessed, attired in rich garments and jewels, recline on silken divans covered with cushions and tapestry. They eat and drink to satiety, and never feel any pain. For companions they have dark-eyed maidens and wives of recurring virginity. Their only spiritual joy is a mysterious presence of God.

PRAYER. Ritual prayer, *salah,* was first prescribed by the Koran and further defined by the earliest tradition or *sunnah.* All Moslems are obligated to its prescriptions, once they reach puberty and as long as they are in good health. The aged, infirm, travelers and others are excused only as long as it is impossible to fulfil the ritual demands.

The rite consists of a series of seven movements or postures, joined to appropriate recitations, collectively termed a "bowing" *rakah,* and each *salah* is made up of a fixed number of bows. In sequence the *rakah* begins with the recitation of the phrase, "God is most great," while the hands are open on each side of the face; then the recitation of the *fatihah*, or opening *surah* of the Koran, and another passage or passages while standing upright; bowing from the hips; straightening up; falling on the knees and a first prostration with face to the ground; sitting back on the haunches; and a second prostration with face to the ground.

Only the first *rakah* in the day requires the opening salutation. Second and subsequent rites begin with the recitation of the first Koranic *surah,* and at the end of each pair of *rakahs* and the conclusion of the day the worshiper recites the *Shahada,* "There is but one Allah, Mohammed is Allah's apostle" together with ritual salutations. Then he sits up and with upraised finger makes his private prayers.

Set times for prayer are at daybreak (two rakahs), noon (four rakahs), mid-afternoon (four rakahs), after sunset (three rakahs), and in the early part of night (four rakahs). Prayers may be said in private or, preferably, together with the congregation in a mosque. When said publicly the worshipers stand in rows behind the prayer-leader, *imam,* all facing in the direction, *quibla,* of the sacred mosque at Mecca, marked by a niche in the wall of the mosque. Private recitation should be on clean ground or on a rug, in the direction of Mecca. Additional prayers, especially at night, are recommended but not prescribed.

Fridays at noon is held the main ritual service of the week, and consists of a formal address in two parts: invocations of the prophet, Moslem leaders, and the political ruler of the state; and a sermon delivered by a preacher. Similar major functions are held on the two principal feast days of the year: the day of the Breaking of the Fast after the fast of Ramadan, and the feast of the Sacrifice at the Pilgrimage.

Hours of prayer are announced by a caller, *muezzin,* from the minaret of the mosque, following the formula, "God is most great, God is most great. I bear witness that there is no god except the One God. I bear witness that Mohammed is the prophet of God. Come to prayer. Come to the Good. Prayer is better than sleep. God is most great. God is most great. There is no god but the One God."

Elaborate provisions require cleansing before prayer, whether in public or private, as prescribed in the Koran, "When you rise up to prayer, wash your faces, and your hands, and arms to the elbows, and wipe your heads and your feet to the ankles." Another, "greater ablution" must be performed after major pollutions. The purification should be done with water if available, otherwise with clean sand. Curiously the rite of circumcision, though generally binding on Moslems, is not prescribed in the Koran.

LEGAL ALMSGIVING. Two forms of ritual donation are mentioned in the Koran: freewill offerings and mandatory contribution. The latter, *zakah,* is gravely prescriptive as an outward sign of piety and a means of salvation. In juridical theory, the *zakah* is exacted on grain, fruits, livestock, silver, gold and merchandise, and amounts to about one-fortieth of the annual revenues. Though not called a tax, it is required of all who, whether voluntarily or otherwise, enter the brotherhood of Islam. As stated in the Koran, the beneficiaries of these alms are the poor, the needy, those employed in collection, persons engaged in propagating religion, slaves and prisoners, insoluble debtors, fighters for the faith and travelers.

In Moslem countries the *zakah* becomes formal taxation and applies as well to those outside the fold. Free-will offerings are also encouraged beyond the call of duty, notably in favor of religious enterprises not directly under control of the State.

FASTING. In its earliest form, fasting was prescribed by Mohammed at Medina in the same form and on the same day as for the Jews. Moslem commentators observe that until a mitigation was revealed, Moslems used to fast completely from the evening meal of one day until the evening meal of the next, and if they fell asleep before they had taken their meal, they had considered it their duty to abstain, with the result that men fainted and came near to death. Intercourse with their wives had been similarly restricted.

Given the revelation, however, which was occasioned by estrangement from the Jews and the growth of Islamic autonomy, the former fast became optional and the ninth lunar month each year, called *Ramadan,* was made a period of strict observance. It affects all Moslems in sound health who have reached maturity. The old, the sick, travelers, and women in certain conditions are exempt. But the exemption lasts only as long as the disability, and the fast must be made up later on. Breaking the fast is punishable by fines of expiation, of different quantity, depending on the gravity of the sin. The fast consists in complete abstention from food and drink, tobacco and perfumes, and sexual intercourse, from sunrise to sunset of each day of Ramadan. There are no prohibitions for the nights. Other fasts, of greater or less intensity, are also part of Islamic custom, for example, to expiate certain offences.

PILGRIMAGE TO MECCA. Much as fasting is the result of contact with the Jews, so the pilgrimage (*Hajj*) to Mecca became part of the Moslem religion through relations with the pagans. Indeed the pilgrim ritual has been largely taken over from pre-Islamic paganism, but now directed to the worship of a single deity.

At least once in a lifetime every Moslem is expected to go on a pilgrimage to the sacred mosque at Mecca, in the twelfth month of the lunar year. Physical strength for the journey and the necessary financial means are assumed to make the precept strictly binding.

The immediate object of the pilgrimage is to kiss the famous Black Stone that Arabian polytheists had worshiped for centuries before Mohammed came on the scene. Other ritual ceremonies are stoning of the pillars which represent the devil in the vicinity of Mina, offering sacrifices of sheep and camels on the way back from Mina, visiting the mosque and going seven times around the *Kaaba* (former pagan animist shrine), running between two small elevations outside the sanctuary (*Safa* and *Marwa*), and visiting the prophet's mosque at Medina. Essential to the pilgrimage are the afternoon services held at the hill of Arafa, about twelve miles east of Mecca.

Elaborate ritual purifications are required before entering the territory of Mecca. Men shave their heads, discard their ordinary clothing and put on two plain unsewn sheets, leaving face and head uncovered. Women keep their head covered. No fasting is prescribed, but the use of perfumes and sexual relations are forbidden.

The most telling effect of the pilgrimage has been to consolidate

the Moslem community and give the pilgrim a new sense of belonging to the elect. The title he acquires, *Hajji,* on returning home
adds to his prestige and assurance of final salvation.

HOLY WAR. Not the least embarrassing provisions of the Koran
for Moslem commentators are those advocating a Holy War, *Jihad,*
against pagans, Jews and Christians. Yet these prescriptions are
historically most significant to explain the propagation of Islam for
upwards of a thousand years. Three passages are classic and deserve to be quoted in full.

First is a duty stated in general terms, in the same context with
pilgrimages and fasting. Its language recalls the situation that
Mohammed faced in his conflict with the recalcitrant Meccans who
resisted his revelations.

Fight in the way of Allah against those who fight against you, but
do not transgress limits, for Allah loves not transgressors. Slay them
whenever you find them and drive them from whence they have expelled you, for tumult and oppression are worse than slaughter. Fight
them on until sedition is no more and allegiance is rendered to God
alone. But if they desist, then make no aggression except against evildoers.[25]

The foregoing was not merely directive but prescriptive, and not
only for the early period of Moslem origins but for all its subsequent history. Yet it does not so directly touch the grave issue of
ordering the sword for the extension and not only for the preservation of Islam. Two other passages do so overtly and have for centuries been understood to refer to Jews and Christians, besides the
pagan polytheists.

When the Sacred Months (of truce) are over, kill those who ascribe
partners to God, wheresoever you find them. Seize them, encompass
them, and ambush them. Then if they repent and observe the prayer,
and pay the alms, let them go their way.

Fight against those who believe not in Allah, nor in the last day, who
prohibit not what God and His prophet have forbidden, and who refuse
allegiance to the True Faith—until they pay the tribute readily after
being brought low. The Jews say, "Ezra is the son of Allah," and the
Christians say, "Christ is the son of Allah;" that is their saying with

their mouth. They imitate the saying of those who disbelieved of old. Allah Himself fights against them. How perverse they are![26]

This duty of waging a Holy War against unbelievers is a collective obligation, not an individual one. According to Islamic tradition, the world is divided into subjugated zones and regions not yet under Moslem control. To conquer the latter is an apostolic venture and those who die in the cause are not dead. "They are living. With their Lord they have provision, rejoicing because of that which Allah has bestowed upon them of His bounty."

While it is impossible to find a complete consensus of Moslem opinion on the subject, modern Islamic commentators fairly agree on certain general facts and interpretations about the Holy War. Next to their attitude toward women, they feel that Moslems have been most misinterpreted in their attitude toward the use of force.

Apologists for the more liberal view, who are in the majority, admit that the Koran teaches the *jihad*, but they insist this should be balanced by other verses where toleration is proclaimed.

There is no compulsion in religion. The right direction is henceforth distinct from error.

For each one We have appointed a divine law and traced out a way. Had Allah willed, He could have made you one community. But that He may try you by that which He has given you (He has made you as you are), wherefore press forward in good works. Unto Allah you will all return, and He will then tell you concerning that wherein you disagree.

Say: O disbelievers! I worship not that which you worship; nor do you worship that which I worship. And I shall not worship that which you worship, nor will you worship that which I worship. Unto you your religion, and unto me my religion.[27]

When reflecting on their record in history, Moslems admit to the widespread use of force, but make the countercharge that every religion at some stages in its career has been used by its professors to mask aggressions and Islam is no exception. They make three basic denials in this area: that Islam's record of intolerance is greater than that of other major religions, that Western histories have been fair to Islam in their accounts of its use of force, and that blots on their history are due to the principles of their faith.

ECCLESIOLOGY. According to an edict promulgated by Mohammed at Medina, the concept of the Islamic community is carefully defined. He substituted faith for the bond of tribal unity, and thus made believers a family of equals under the direct supervision of Allah.

In this organizational theory, the teaching authority is immediately centered in God but channeled through the Koran. Consequently Islam has no provision for divinely authorized institutions either to guard the deposit of faith, or apply its teaching to existential situations; still less has it the right to define infallibly on matters of doctrine or morals. There are only interpreters of the divine *magisterium,* the learned *Ulama,* who are laymen without clerical orders or special privileges of caste. Yet the *Ulama* have acquired quasi-clerical status by reason of the respect they enjoy as custodians of the law. Often in practice, if not in theory, their casuistic solutions become the accepted standard of Islamic morality.

The ministry reflects a similar condition. There is no organized priesthood, as there are no sacraments to administer. An oriental nomism, where the religious basis of conduct derives from external observance of law, has become so inveterate in classic Islam that the internal forum or conscience of believers is practically ignored in questions of moral judgment.

In place of a sacerdotal hierarchy, orthodox Islam has ever looked to the political sovereign for the direction of Moslem affairs, not excluding impositon of sanctions for breach of Koranic precepts and interpreting these precepts by civil decree.

MARRIAGE, DIVORCE AND POLYGAMY. In the long years of its history, Islam has undergone many changes in its attitude on sex and marriage, notably emancipating women in such countries as India and Pakistan and recognizing the impracticality of polygamy on a large scale in modern society. Yet basically the principles enunciated in the Koran still remain in effect and, as more than one historian has pointed out, most clearly distinguish Moslem culture from its Christian counterpart.

The Koran is extremely detailed on the subject of women's modesty or, more accurately, of their complete subservience and obscuration. They are bidden always to "lower their gaze" and "not display their beauty" except to husbands, fathers and a restricted clientele of relatives and friends. Covering their faces with a veil was a practical carrying out of this injunction.

A father has the right to give a virgin daughter in marriage to whomsoever he pleases. In all marriages the formal contracting parties are not the bride and groom but their fathers or other responsible male relatives. Indeed the marriage of a woman without the intervention of a qualified male relative is invalid, and where no such relative exists, his office is filled by the *gadi*. Moslem men may marry a Christian or Jewish woman but Moslem women do not enjoy the same liberty.

First marriages do not debar a man from further unions, since polygamy is legal. Also outside the married state, a husband may cohabit with an unlimited number of concubines. Their children have the same status as those of wedded wives. Mohammed formally approved polygamy. He had several wives—nine according to one tradition, and fourteen according to another. But for his followers he limited the number to four, as stated in the Koran. "Marry of the women who seem good to you, two, or three, or four." Tradition has therefore set the limit for ordinary believers to four wives, but authorizes Caliphs and Sultans, as successors of the prophet, to have nine.

Concubinage seems not to be anywhere directly sanctioned in the Koran, and the stringent Koranic laws against adultery intimate that the custom developed after Mohammed. In any case, polygamy is a costly luxury, so that only the rich can afford to practice it. For one thing, the legitimate wives cannot live together; each must have a separate apartment and domestics. Men of moderate means usually have only one wife.

Divorce by the husband's repudiation of his wife is a privilege granted in the Koran. No intervention of any judicial authority is necessary, nor any assignment of reasons or justification; but a "certificate of divorce" must be given the wife. However the husband must wait four months before actually dismissing his spouse, meantime not cohabiting with her. After a first repudiation the wife may not remarry for at least three months, during which time she may be taken back without a further contract. The same holds after a second repudiation. But a third repudiation is irrevocable, unless the woman has in the meantime married and been divorced by another man. An ancient custom allows a triple repudiation to be made at one and the same time, with corresponding effects on its irrevocability.

A woman's right to divorce her husband is highly restricted. She cannot repudiate her partner by declaration. One option is to reach an agreement with him that the marriage should be dissolved on payment of compensation, which usually means the return of her dowry. Some Moslem jurists claim that compensation is void if the reason for dissolving the marriage is cruelty by her husband. Another way open for the wife is to appeal to the courts for annulment, *faskh,* on such grounds as a husband's incurable disease or failure to support. Anticipating difficulties, Moslem women nowadays often insert a clause in the marriage contract, laying down certain stipulations which, when broken, obligate the husband to grant his wife a divorce or annulment. For centuries the stipulation that a husband should not marry another wife was held to be invalid, since it contradicted the Koran. But more recently such contracts have been considered binding.

ISLAMIC ASCETICISM

Mohammedanism as a religious culture is not naturally ascetical. Its condemnation of celibacy, absence of a priesthood with spiritual functions, sanction of divorce and polygamy, and, with emphasis, a liaison with the political and military power to exploit its aims, argue to a religion that is nothing if not this-worldly and material minded. Add to this a strong legalism and concern with external forms, and one has what seems the antithesis of asceticism and the interior life.

Yet this very preoccupation with secular values produced a reaction within a century of the *Hijra.* Popular preachers and ascetics arose who were at once depressed by the materialism so prevalent in Islam and attracted by the ideals of Christian solitaries, Gnostic and Neo-Platonist philosophers, and Oriental *sannyasis.* Among these elements, the function of Christianity was paramount. Often operating through filtered and heterodox channels, the principles of Islamic ascetism are mainly of Christian ancestry, whether present by implication in the Koran, or later explicitated by the followers of Mohammed.

Already in the time of the prophet, two of his companions, Abu Darr and Hudajfah, were known for their condemnation of Moslem rulers as sinners and for their detailed precepts on the spiritual life. Some of their disciples became public preachers, others preferred retirement. In general the dominant feature of this first phase was a fear of God's punishments, based on the Koranic threats of an imminent last judgment.

Rising out of this tradition was the earliest figure in Moslem spirituality, al-Hasan of Basra (643-728), an eloquent preacher on the interior life. By the second century of the *Hijra* appeared the name of Sufist, etymologically connected with the wearing of undyed garments of wool (*suf*). Ascetically the concept of fear became clarified into a notion of love for God, expressed in the famous verses of the woman ascetic Rabia al-Adawiya (died 801):

> I love Thee with two loves, love of my happiness,
> And perfect love, to love Thee as Thy due.
> My selfish love is that I do nothing
> But I think of Thee, excluding all beside;
> But that purest love, which is Thy due,
> Is that the veils which hide Thee fall, and I gaze on Thee,
> No praise to me in either this or that,
> No, Thine the praise for both that love and this.[28]

During the third century of the Moslem era, Sufism took on those popular features which made it suspect to religious leaders. Though firmly based on the Koran, their simplicist appeal to the rank and file and their reaction against the impersonal teachings of the orthodox, brought the Sufis into conflict with authorities. Some attempts were made to silence them, and when these failed, an example was made of their most prominent member, Mansur al-Hallaj, who was crucified at Bagdad in 922 for claiming he was God. However, repression proved futile, and the Sufite spirit entered Moslem tradition so deeply that scholars believe it has actually determined the type of Islam known at the present day.

Soon the Sufi leaders organized into congregations and instead of a bare recitation of the Koran introduced liturgical ceremonies,

the singing of litanies and other practices frowned upon by orthodox theologians. The issue between the two was deeper than appeared on the surface. It concerned the ultimacy of Islamic religion: whether, as the orthodox said, there is only one way to know
God, by means of rational dialectic (*ilm*) upon the Koran, or, as
the Sufis maintained, by direct and personal experience (*marifa*),
culminating in periodic union and absorption into God.

Among other tensions which developed was the unheard-of
praise of celibacy. "Marry those among you," is the clear directive
of the Koran. Yet Christians for centuries had praised the virginal
state. Gradually the influence was felt. Where in the third century
A.H. practically all *Sufis* were married, by the fifth we find one of
their great exponents declaring, "It is the unanimous opinion of
the leaders of this doctrine that the best and most distinguished
Sufis are the unmarried, if their hearts are unstained and their
minds free from sin and lust." [29]

Parallel with a stress on celibacy was the respect which Sufi
disciples paid their masters during life and the worship they gave
them after death. Nothing could be more alien to ancient Islam
than to have saints and intercessors with God. Yet again popular
Sufism prevailed. "Know," says the same early authority, "that the
principle and foundation of Sufism and knowledge of God rests on
Saintship." The highpoint of Moslem hagiology was reached in
the development of an elaborate hierarchy of demiurges, culminating in the *Qutb,* whose function is to superintend the universe, under Allah, as the Pole of the universe.

The revolution in Islamic thought which Sufism provoked was
finally crystallized in the life and writing of al-Ghazali (1058-
1111), whom historians rank with Augustine in religious insight
and Moslems venerate as a saint. Ghazali broke the stronghold of
the sceptic philosophers and hairsplitting theologians and reintroduced a wholesome respect for the word of God in the Koran and
in the traditions of the Moslem faithful. He did not disdain philosophy, but sought to place it at the service of the faith, and above
all, to make it intelligible to the people. His re-emphasis on hell
and the need of fear brought a welcome balance to the rationalism
of men like Avicenna (980-1037), and the near pantheism of
many Sufis,

What Ghazali did not foresee, however, was that once Sufism became orthodox, and private communion with God was a valid source of religious knowledge, not only Islamic theology but Islam itself was in danger of being submerged. Moslem leaders, the Ulama or "learned," took strong measures to meet the challenge. They gained control of education, largely through institutions of theological study (*madrasas*) with official status, salaried teachers, and a prestige that by the thirteenth century practically solidified orthodoxy in the upper classes of Moslem society.

But Sufism remained alive, in the aspirations of millions of believers and in countless traditions which have become co-essentials of the Koranic creed.

RELIGIOUS FRATERNITIES

Not the least impress of Sufism on Islamic culture is the development of what correspond to religious orders or congregations in the Christian tradition. Their general characteristics are pliability in religious beliefs, ranging from pantheism to close imitations of Christianity and, with notable exceptions, a tendency towards extremism in practice and ritual.

Typical of a conservative order are the *Qadiri,* whose members are distinguished for their piety, philanthropy and aversion to fanaticism. One of their customary prayers, to be recited a hundred times daily is, "I ask pardon of the mighty God. Glorified be God. May God bless our Master Mohammed and his household and his Companions. There is no God but Allah." Founded in the eleventh century by the jurist Gilani, credited with having forty-nine children, its members are divided into provincial congregations, with headquarters in Baghdad.

An offshoot of the Qadiri, however, is definitely fanatical. Organized by Gilani's nephew, the *Rifaiya* indulge in extreme self-mortification and thaumaturgical exercises such as glass eating, fire-walking and playing with serpents. They are found in Turkey, Syria and Egypt.

The *Mawlawyya* were founded by the Persian mystic poet, Jami, whose pantheistic effusions left no room for individual personality. "The universe," he taught, "is the outward visible expression of the Real, and the Real is the inner unseen reality of the Universe. The Universe before it was evolved to outward view was identical with the Real, and the Real after this evaluation is identical with the Universe." Jani's followers are best known for their dervish dancing. While singing their liturgical chants they gyrate in continuous circles to the sound of accompanying music. In the old Ottoman Empire, their chief had the privilege of buckling the sword on the new Sultan when he assumed office.

Among the syncretist groups, the outstanding are the *Bektashis,* fully established in the fifteenth century as a strange mixture of Islam, Gnosticism and Christianity. They honor Ali, cousin of Mohammed and husband of Fatimah his daughter, Mohammed, and Allah as a kind of Trinity. In place of the traditional Moslem ceremony, they have a sort of communion service of bread, wine and cheese. They also confess their sins to the superior, who gives them absolution. Women participate in the ceremonies without veils. Those who take a vow of chastity wear pendants on their ears as a sign of this dedication. They acquired notoriety through their association with the Janissaries, Christian youths taken captive and brought up as leading Moslem soldiers, whom the *Bektashis* indoctrinated and exploited in the promotion of Islam. They are centered in the Balkans, especially Albania, and Egypt.

One of the most recent orders, the *Sunusiya,* was organized by the Algerian, Mohammed Ali al-Sunusi (died 1859). Deeply religious and bent on converting the surrounding people from paganism, Sunusi carried on a life-long propaganda in Egypt and Syria to the point of establishing a quasi-state that took active part in both World Wars on the side of Turkey in the first and of England in the second. They contributed heavily to the growth of Pan-Islamism in North Africa and Asia Minor.

NON-CONFORMISTS

In the absence of ecclesiastical authority or infallible doctrine, dissident factions in Islam were inevitable, and began within a few years of Mohammed's death. While the number and variety of Moslem sectarians are beyond calculation, three principal heterodox movements may be clearly distinguished. Others are either subsidiary to these or qualify in spirit under the main classes.

The *Mutazilites* (dissidents) are often described as Rationalists or Freethinkers who abandoned faith in Mohammed and the Koran and constructed a religion of reason in their place, after the fashion of Ernest Renan and David Strauss in their Lives of Christ. Actually their position is more complex, and for Western readers far more significant in view of the contact they effected with classic Greek philosophy.

Mutazilism began at the end of the first century A.H. as an opposition movement to two extremists, the ethical laxists (*Murjites*) who were willing to barter moral principle for the sake of political gain, and the pragmatists (*Kharjites*) who claimed that religion must be propagated in season and out of season, if need be at the cost of life itself. Well intentioned but radical, the Mutazilites flourished for centuries until they began to force Moslem doctrines into the mold of Greek concepts and derive their theology speculatively from Greek metaphysics instead of the Koran. They passed out of corporate existence as a sect but left in Islamic tradition a worship of reason and a suspicion of Koranic faith that cultured Moslems the world over consider their special possession.

Comparable to the golden age in Christian scholastic theology, which produced Peter Lombard, Albertus Magnus, Bonaventure and Thomas Aquinas, the Arabs had Avicenna, Avempace and Averroes, all in the eleventh and twelfth centuries, whose works in religious philosophy are among the glories of Islamic civilization. Yet the master ideas of these men were alien to Moslem orthodoxy, and advanced such extreme views as the existence of only one soul in all men (Averroes), and the principle of pure potentiality independent of God (Avicenna). It is said that Avicenna knew the Koran by heart at the age of ten, and other Moslem philosophers were also, if less fervently, attached to their faith. But the solvent of rationalism which they inherited from the Mutazilites and passed on to their followers has permanently entered the religion of Islam.

Best known representative of this Moslem deism is Omar Khayyam (died 1123), philosopher and freethinker, whose *Rubaiyat* in Fitzgerald's eloquent translation symbolizes the pessimism of a culture that has lost its hold on revelation. Omar tells of listening to doctor and saint, and hearing great argument on the purpose of life, but sadly concludes, "With them the seed of wisdom did sow, and with mine own hand wrought to make it grow; and this was all

the Harvest that I reaped—'I came like water, and like wind I go' "
Or again, "I sent my Soul through the Invisible some letter of that
after-life to spell; and by and by my Soul returned to me, and
answered, 'I myself am Heaven and Hell.' "

Unlike the Mutazilites, who were mainly theorists, the *Shiahs*
came into being as a group of faithful who disapproved the election
of Abu Bakr, Omar, and Othman as caliphs to succeed Mohammed. They maintained that Ali, the prophet's cousin, and his line
were legitimate successors. Gradually political reasons were colored
by doctrinal and ritual differences to solidify the breach between
the Shiahs, "partisans" of Ali, and the Sunnis, followers of the
Sunna or "tradition." Drawing on all sorts of old oriental beliefs,
Babylonian, Persian and Indian, the Shiahs finally welded two unheard-of ideas which traditionists to this day abhor. Following the
ancient Babylonian theory of Inner Light and the more recent
Christian Gnosticism, they held that their leaders, the Imams, had
incarnated in them the Divine Light which descended through
successive generations of prophets from the time of Adam.

Among the Shiahs, therefore, the Iman is at once pope and emperor, gifted with sinlessness and infallibility. But more seriously,
Mohammed is regularly credited with divine or near-divine prerogatives, which has deeply influenced the whole of Islamic thought.
A European scholar (Abraham Kuyper) examined some two thousand prayer formulas in use by Moslems throughout the world, and
discovered that in most of them Mohammed had usurped the place
of Allah or God, being addressed three to five times in a single invocation.

The Shiahs differ greatly among themselves, ranging from the
moderate Zaidis, who in the tenth century founded the state (now
the country) of Yemen, to the extremist Ismailis, sometimes called
the "Assassins," found in India and elsewhere. Shiahs favor temporary marriage, and because of their compromises with Christianity
have found acceptance among certain Western peoples as esoteric
cults, like the Bahais, who originated in Persia and have a sizeable
following in the United States.

Besides Mutazilite nationalism and Shiah gnosticism, periodic
strains of Moslem puritanism seek to reinstate the spirit of former
days, and bring the people back to Allah and His prophet. Among

the most recent and currently effective are the Wahhabis founded in the eighteenth century by Mohammed Wahhab (1691-1787) who castigated his contemporaries for their luxury and for their worship of Mohammed and neglect of God. Originally fanatical in preaching and propaganda, they created enemies on all sides, notably among the Turks. For a time they held Mecca and Medina, where they removed from the mosques all that they held was the accretion of later superstition. Although much restricted, the Wahhabis have lately risen with new strength as protagonists of the "Arab idea" in Islam. Their efforts to purify religion and restore its pristine monotheism now constitute one of the outstanding features of modern Islam. Even politically they have regained an Arabian empire under the leadership of Abd al-Aziz, founder of the new kingdom of Saudi Arabia.

RELATIONS WITH CHRISTIANITY

From the first beginnings of Islamic expansion, Christianity in the East found itself weak to resist the Mohammedan tide. There was a proliferation of Christian sects, universal dissatisfaction with Byzantium and sympathy with the innovators among the Arab Christians and schismatics chafing under the Greek emperors.

After the first period of conquest, we find numerous anecdotes describing the peace if not cordiality existing between Moslems and their Christians subjects. The father of St. John Damascene (674-749) was the chief representative (*Logothere*) of the Christians to the Caliph. But there were also acts of violence and humiliating conditions laid on the Christians—the payment of tribute and grave restrictions on freedom. Many Christians apostatized, often following the example of prelates whose position was secure if they catered to the religious prejudice of the civil rulers.

The West labored under the strangest notions about Islam, which some merely dismissed as another Eastern heresy and others looked upon as the vowed enemy of Christianity. Things became worse when the Moors invaded Spain (711) and occupied the coasts of Italy and France, and especially when the Turks made pilgrimages to the Holy Land impossible or extremely risky. Under papal exhortation and the preaching of men like Peter the Hermit and Bernard of Clairvaux, a series of Crusades was launched that lasted from 1096 to 1270, but finally Palestine was lost to the Saracens.

After numerous trials the kings of Spain succeeded in driving the Moors out of the Iberian peninsula (1492). Sicily was delivered by Norman princes in the twelfth century, but Moslem pirates continued to ravage the Mediterranean area for centuries, thus giving rise to the several religious orders destined for the redemption of Christian captives, like the Trinitarians (1198) and Mercedarians (1220). The founding of military orders, e.g., the Templars and Hospitallers (Knights of St. John), belongs to the same era.

In Central Europe, Islam was not fully checked until late in the seventeenth century, under the Polish leader Sobieski (1683), more than a century after the Popes waged a tireless Mediterranean campaign that ended in the victory of Lepanto (1570) under Pope Pius V.

The apostolate to the Moslems by the Eastern Christians was sporadic and only minimally effective. Pioneers in the West to undertake a methodical study of the Moorish religion included the abbot of Cluny, Peter the Venerable, and the Franciscan Raymond Lull. Franciscans and Dominicans began organizing schools to prepare missionaries to the Moslems, and the Council of Vienna (1312) ordered the creation of schools of Arabic in the larger universities. St. Thomas Aquinas wrote the *Contra Gentiles* to answer Moslem arguments on the grounds of natural reason, and his treatise on Averroes challenged the latter's claim that what is true in philosophy may be false in theology, and vice versa. Prospects of converting the Moors was a leading motive in the mind of Ignatius of Loyola when he organized the Society of Jesus.

In the last century, Cardinal Lavigerie established the White Fathers expressly to work among the Mohammedans. Parallel enterprises have been going on for years in North Africa, Syria, India, and the Near East, but after hard experience the missiological method has changed, or rather became stabilized to a long range evangelization of charity, patience and study, preparing the Moslem people for the Gospel and disposing them to accept what, by their standards, is only a prelude to the religion of Mohammed.

The more seriously Mohammedans take the Koran and live up to its precepts, the stronger becomes their unqualified belief in one personal God which they share with the Christian world; and correspondingly, the further they depart from the tradition or *sunna* of their ancestors, the more easily they compromise with polytheism or, in modern times, with Marxism.

On the other hand, the same Koran teaches them "take not the Jews or Christians for friends. They are but one another's friends. If any of you takes them for his friends he is surely one of them. Allah does not guide evildoers." [30] Uncompromisingly the Moslem is told "the Religion before God is Islam. If anyone desires a religion other than Islam, never will it be accepted of him. And in the hereafter he will be in the ranks of those who have lost all spiritual good." [31] With Oriental realism, the *sunna* tells him, "He who has denied a verse of the Koran, it is allowed to behead him." [32]

The one hopeful solution is a changing climate in Moslem circles towards the followers of "the son of Mary." Conscious of the threat of Red domination, spokesmen for their people are telling Christians, "It is a prime duty of our two monotheistic faiths to establish real and abiding friendship, not only among their own adherents, but also between themselves and the followers of the other faith as well. We should collaborate as believers in the one God in defending the world against the menaces of atheism and materialism." [33]

In the same spirit of tolerance, commentators on the Koran are reinterpreting its harsh passages in a way that leaves room for Christian influence if not for Christianization. "The Muslim does not claim," they explain, "to have a religion peculiar to himself. Islam is not a sect or an ethnic religion. In its view all Religion is one, for the Truth is one. It was the religion preached by all the earlier prophets. It was the truth taught by all the inspirited Books. In essence it amounts to a consciousness of the Will and Plan of God and a joyful submission to that Will and Plan." [34] If these sentiments appear strange against the background of more than a thousand years of Koranic intransigence, they suggest that not only new Moslem nations are coming into existence but also a new Islam.

THE NEW ISLAM

Since Mohammedanism from its origins has always been closely tied in with the State, its spirit and religious outlook at any given point in history can be accurately judged by the political structure of the countries that are dominantly Islamic.

Modern Islam in its church-state dimension is being shaped by the heavy impact of Western thought and institutions, whose influence is commonly dated from the beginning of the nineteenth century, after the invasion of Egypt by Napolean in 1798. Moslem religious leaders for long resisted this Westernization. Their historical traditions had little interest outside the Islamic world, and their educational traditions were mostly confined to the Koranic sciences and supporting disciplines. Civil and political leaders, on the other hand, were more than sympathetic with European technology and such phases of Western thought and culture as promised a competitive equality with the nations of Europe.

As a result two conflicting tendencies are visible in the recent development of Mohammedan countries: a passive resistance to the influx of Western ideas and institutions, along with a reactionary Islamic renascence; and a ready ambition to adopt everything feasible from European sources, provided the adaptation can be grafted on the existing culture. While it would be an oversimplification to say that the first tendency has been directed largely by religious fervor and the second by hard-headed realism, these have been the principal motivating forces behind a tension that it may take generations to resolve.

SECULAR-STATE EXPERIMENT. Turkey is the best example of Moslem experimentation in which the secular impulse has overridden the religious to create a novel situation, quite unlike anything else in the Islamic world. Since the early nineteenth century, Turkey had reacted with political sensitivity to the ferment of Western ideas, most of which came from France and, specifically, from the ideals of the French Revolution.

At the close of the First World War, Turkey was on the verge of destruction when its destinies were taken in hand by a single individual who changed the course of its history. Mustafa Kemal

Ataturk, first president of the Turkish Republic, was born in 1882 at Salonika, at that time part of the Ottoman Empire. In 1915, Mustafa Kemal commanded the Turkish Army at Gallipoli. Four years later, following the defeat of the Central Powers (including Turkey), he organized the armies of liberation in Anatolia, and commanded the campaign which resulted in the achievement of Turkish independence.

In 1920, Ataturk took the lead in the establishment of the First Grand National Assembly, in Ankara, which in 1924 abolished the Sultanate and was the forerunner of the present Republic. To do this he had the Sultan's son, and heir-apparent to the caliphate, 'Abd-al-Majid, banished from the country, on the principle that a supreme religious leader recognized as such by the entire Moslem world, even against his will could become a focal point for reactionary ambitions. Indignation over this move was great, particularly among the Indian Mohammedans who had set their hopes for protection against British imperialism on the newly resurgent Turkish Republic. Moreover, all efforts to re-establish the caliphate in other countries necessarily miscarried, because conditions for it were nowhere so promising as in Turkey.

But Ataturk was not to be checked; he crushed a series of revolts and finally stopped active resistance by having the rebels deported to eastern Thracia. He continued the secularization of the government with far-reaching laws. The ministry for pious endowments (*Evkaf*) was dissolved in 1924 and joined with the ministry of education; in the following year all the dervish orders were forbidden, and all monasteries dissolved. In the early thirties even the number of mosques was severely limited, of which only one was to be allowed within a circumference of every five hundred meters; the number of preachers to be paid by the government was reduced to three hundred, and they were obligated to provide practical instruction on things like agriculture, in addition to preaching on religious topics.

Some of the most famous mosques were turned into museums or railroad depots, and the religious law (*Shari 'ah*) was replaced by a purely civil code, even as regards domestic relations. One result was the end of polygamy, and another that family names, hitherto unknown in Turkey, were introduced by a law of July 2,

1934. Turkish women were now given equal legal rights with men, and soon obtained the active and passive right of election. Such details as substituting the hat for the fez (that previously supplanted the turban) and other items of European custom were symbolic of the radical changes made.

The new Turkish Constitution professedly found its inspiration in the ideals of Western democracy. Its basic principle became sovereignty of the people, and the republican form of government was declared inviolable. All citizens were held to be equal before the law, and special privileges were abolished. Inviolability of person and freedom of conscience, thought, speech, press, assembly, association, travel, labor and contract were formally stated to be "the natural rights of citizens." This meant that "the life, property, honor, and home of each and all are inviolable," and correlatively that, "no one may be molested on account of his religion, sect, ritual or philosophy." To insure these and similar provisions, primary education was made obligatory and given gratuitously in the government schools.

All phases of life were affected by the new regime, to a degree that the Turkish Revolution has been considered the most complete in the twentieth century, not only because its effects were so widespread but because the ideas on which it was based were, from the Moslem viewpoint, so revolutionary. Spokesmen for the nation repeatedly declared that their Constitution guaranteed all liberties, yet on the theory of a completely secularized society, which had no responsibilities to Koranic principles.

The intention was not only to adapt the people externally to Western customs, but to impregnate them with the spirit of Europe. To achieve this goal the Arabic forms of writing had to be discarded. A new law abolished first the Arabic kind of numerals and then also the script. Schools were built everywhere in the country for people of all ages to learn the new script, which was naturalized in a surprisingly short time. Soon after, the long-established custom of teaching Arabic and Persian, which had been considered necessary for understanding Turkish literature, was eliminated from the lycees. Use of Arabic type for printing Turkish books was prohibited, with the result that innumerable productions of Istanbul printing presses were exported to Egypt, Persia and India.

With the suppression of so many aspects of Turkish culture, however, the new government had the foresight to preserve, as far as possible, the genuine religious values of the people. Formerly the Koran could be read only in Arabic, which limited its accessibility; a Turkish translation appeared for the first time in 1931, and published with a Turkish commentary. Within months, excerpts from this translation were publicly recited in the mosques. Religious freedom even made possible some conversions to Christianity, which according to old Islamic law would have been punished by death.

The guiding genius behind this revolution was Mustafa Kemal, on whom the National Assembly bestowed the title *Ataturk*, i.e., Father of the Turks, as "the expression of the gratitude and veneration of the nation for the greatest son." A born statesman and ardent nationalist, he was not troubled with theological or cultural sensitivities. From the Moslem point of view, within Turkey and outside, the changes he effected were widely criticized.

What made his critics so hostile was the reduction of Islam from the status of a religiously sanctioned system to the position of a private and inferior religious opinion. It was unthinkable to them that this could be reconciled with the innate theocratic character of Mohammedanism. Students of Islamic history observed that the problem of Islam and of Turkey's Islamic past was not being solved, but forcibly eliminated. It could not but reappear.

Their predictions were verified to the extent that a "palace revolution" in 1960 ended the late regime, ostensibly in opposition to restrictive laws and civil decrees but really in answer to a deep-felt need for closer identification between the ancient religious culture of the people, who are almost one-hundred per cent Moslem, and the political structure of the country. It is assured that the Second Turkish Republic will be more sympathetic with these aspirations.

CONSTITUTIONAL ISLAMIC NATION. At the other end of the spectrum is another Moslem country which came into existence in recent years, but whose origins were quite the opposite from those in Turkey. Pakistan, now a republic, was founded in 1947, when Great Britain withdrew from the Indo-Pakistan subcontinent. Its name, coined by Moslem graduates of Cambridge University, is in-terpreted as "Land of the Pure," in which P stands for the Punjab and A for the Afghan regions, K for Kashmir, I for Islam, S for Sind, and "tan" for the last syllable of Baluchistan. In Urdu, the Hindustani language as spoken by Moslems, *pak* means spiritual purity and *stan* means the land. Thus in the very title of their coun-try the founders of Pakistan implied devotion to religious ideals.

The Islamic beginnings of Pakistan are traceable to the first Moslem invasion from Arabia in 712 A.D., which conquered most of the Indus valley, although the main incursions came from the north and started in the eleventh century. Under successive domina-tion by the Moghuls, the East India Company, and the English, the country grew in size and prosperity, but mostly in its fidelity to the teachings of the Prophet. When India began urging her inde-pendence, Indian Moslems cooperated with the Hindus in the move-ment. But as autonomy drew nearer, the Mohammedans felt that independence would only mean changing British masters for Hindu ones. They were convinced that the two cultures, a monotheistic Islam and polytheistic Hinduism, could never coalesce; that only a separate country would enable the Moslems to develop their own cultural and religious heritage and only a separate nation could assure them freedom from religious persecution.

While an All Indian Moslem League was founded as early as 1906, the first serious efforts to establish a distinct nation came much later, due in large measure to the ideas of one man, Mo-hammed Iqbal (1873-1938), the poet-philosopher who is vener-ated as the Father of the country. His writings played a decisive role in crystallizing the twin spirit of Islamic India: that the true basis of nationhood is far less the animal ties of blood than a harmony of religious ideals, and that Islam should form a federa-tion of nations linked by the same internal beliefs.

Iqbal's devotion to Islam was almost a passion. His prose and poetical compositions breathe a love of the Koran and dedication to its teachings that no other Moslem leader in modern times has shown. For the people of Pakistan he is the philosophical light and almost absolute standard on the cardinal issue of Islam's relation to the modern world. And for all Moslems he has given a re-inter-pretation of Islam and a program for realizing a true synthesis of

Mohammedanism and Western culture. His manual on *The Recon-struction of Religious Thought in Islam* is a profound study of the problems which the followers of Mohammed must be willing to face and solve if they are to remain faithful to his memory.

Otherwise than his contemporaries, Iqbal approached the Islamic predicament as a philosopher who was deeply attached to his people's religion; and he handled the issue not from any pre-conceived notions but on the strength of years of experience at Western universities and of contact with the best (and the worst) of Western civilization. He could therefore speak with authority about the inherent values of Islam and the deficiencies of other cultural traditions.

His main contribution to shaping the Mohammedan mind was to convince the people to open their souls to the message of their own faith, and their own past as a community; and at the same time to close their eyes to the teachings of others, since the Western world had little to teach them which Islam did not know. He asked him-self, "What, shall I tell you then, is a Moslem's life?" and answered his own question.

> Ecstasy's summit joined with profoundest thought!
> Even its setting flames like a rising sun;
> Single its hue, yet manifold age by age.
> Neither with these times sharing their scorn of virtue,
> Nor with times past their bondage to myth and magic,
> Firm in eternal verity's bedrock standing.[35]

He exploited what he considered the profoundest difference between the Moslem and European thought. "Through all the West-ern *politeia,* religion withers to the roots; for the white man, ties of blood and race are all he knows of brotherhood." Even a Brahmin, converted to Christianity, "ascends no higher in life's scale," by Western norms, "because the creed of the Messiah has numbered him with its recruits." [36] Preoccupation with material things, Iqbal taught, had blinded the West to the only true bond of unity, which is a common religious faith.

When the people of Pakistan framed their first Constitution, they incorporated these principles into its laws, from the first article of the Preamble to the most detailed provisions. "Pakistan," it was decreed, "shall be a Federal Republic to be known as the Islamic Republic of Pakistan." [37] And on the international plane, "The State shall endeavor to strengthen the bonds of unity among Muslim countries." [38] Both aspects of the Islamic faith were amply provided for.

Steps shall be taken to enable Muslims of Pakistan, individually and collectively, to order their lives in accordance with the Holy Quran and Sunnah.

The state shall endeavor, as respects the Muslims of Pakistan: to provide facilities whereby they may be enabled to understand the meaning of life according to the Holy Quran and Sunnah; to make the teaching of the Holy Quran compulsory; to promote unity and the observance of Islamic moral standards; and to secure the proper organization of *zakat* (almsgiving), *wakfs* (sacred foundations) and mosques.[39]

Implementing this general intent, the State was further concerned to protect the interests of Islam by forbidding "the consumption of alcoholic liquor, otherwise than for medicinal and, in case of non-Muslims, religious purposes," and at the same time recognized that in certain cases polygamy is necessary.[40]

Along with such explicit legislation in the spirit of Iqbal, the Constitution provided for the welfare of those outside the Mohammedan fold, recognizing that "all citizens are equal before the law and are entitled to equal protection of law," and supporting this general provision with a variety of specific guarantees.

Subject to law, public order and morality: every citizen has the right to profess, practice and propagate any religion; and every religious denomination and every sect thereof has the right to establish, maintain, and manage its religious institutions.

No person shall be compelled to pay any special tax the proceeds of which are to be spent on the propagation or maintenance of any religion other than his own.[41]

The freer and more relaxed aspect of Pakistan was also visible in the generous effort to safeguard the religious convictions of children who attend the private and (Moslem directed) public schools. Thus "no person attending any educational institution shall be required to receive religious instruction or take part in any religious ceremony, or attend religious worship if such institution, ceremony or worship relates to a religion other than his own." [42]

Similar privileges were conceded to every religious community or denomination to establish and conduct schools of its own and, most significantly, "in respect of any religious institution, there shall be no discrimination against any community in the granting of exception or concession in relation to taxation," which theoretically placed Hindus and Christians on a par with Moslems in the critical area of tax exemption.[43]

Pakistan, therefore, was founded on a vastly different political theory than Turkey. In fact its foundations were less political than spiritual, with so many articles of the Constitution dealing with the subject of religion that the prominent impression was religious. True to the inspiration of Iqbal the rights of Mohammedans, who constitute almost nine-tenths of the population, were amply protected; and according to the same ideals were even promoted by juridical sanction. Yet, realistically, the minority Hindus and Christians were not ignored, either on paper or in actual practice, which compares favorably with the Arabic-speaking Moslem countries, and the discrimination against non-Islamic religions in some of the newly founded nations of Africa.

There is a tendency also to stress the ideology which Islam has in common with Western and not with Asian culture, which contrasts strongly with the studied effort to emphasize the Oriental in other rising nations of the East. But the number of conflicting forces in Pakistan had the same general effect as in Turkey, except from other quarters. Where Turkey was professedly a secular state seeking a compromise with the Moslem traditions of its people, Pakistan was founded as a Moslem nation trying to work its way in modern society. The fear of revolution in the late fifties led to a change of political structure and a revision of the Constitution, with corresponding reforms in law and education that illustrate the unsolved problem of Islam: how to retain its ancient heritage while adapting itself to modern needs.

Symbolic of the adaptation, the second Constitution of Pakistan began by simply declaring that "the State of Pakistan shall be a Republic under the name of the Republic of Pakistan." [44] Yet the Preamble provided for Mohammedan ideals by stating that "the principles of democracy, freedom, equality, tolerance and social justice, as enunciated by Islam, should be fully observed in Pakistan," and "the Muslims of Pakistan should be enabled, individually and collectively, to order their lives in accordance with the teachings and requirements of Islam." [45]

A new concept in modern Islamic jurisprudence was the formation in Pakistan of an Advisory Board of Islamic Ideology. As the name implies, its function would be advisory and not mandatory, mainly "to make recommendations to the Central Government and the Provincial Governments as to means of enabling and encouraging the Muslims of Pakistan to order their lives in all respects with the principles and concepts of Islam." [46]

ORTHODOXY AND ADJUSTMENT. More than any other religious culture, Islam is at the crossroads of its history. The situations in Turkey and Pakistan are only symptomatic of a deeper tension within the body of Mohammedanism, between orthodoxy and rationalism. All the available evidence suggests that orthodoxy is not only still in possession but promises to make a resurgence that may have lasting effects on the future of Asia and Africa, and corresponding influence on the major religions of the world.

An all-Moslem Colloquium, held at Lahore (Pakistan), clearly emphasizes this dominant trend. Delegates from every Mohammedan country were present, including representatives from Soviet Russia and Communist China. The subjects they treated show the wide range of new situations by which Islam is confronted: Islamic culture and its meaning, the Islamic concept of the State, the challenge of modern ideas and social values; the scope of legislation and the social structure of Islam, Mohammedan attitude towards other faiths and potential contribution to international peace, Islam's influence on Western history and civilization.

The guiding theme at Lahore was remarkably orthodox. Occasional outbursts against opinions considered doctrinally dangerous heightened the fact that the prevailing spirit is how to adjust positions and principles, believed undebatable and unassailable, to a rapidly changing non-Moslem world. A rare note was struck with the regret that "such a beautiful expression of human tragedy" as the Crucifixion "is not reflected in the Holy Koran," implying that Islam offered no answer to the problem of pain and no substitute for the inspiration of the Cross.

Yet the most severe test of Islamic faith comes not from its contact with the traditional West, whether Christian or secular, but from its relations with a rampant Marxism. Upwards of fifty million Moslems are directly under Communist control, and subject to all the pressures that a hostile government exercises against a socio-religious system which, by Marxist standards, is a feudal tool for reactionaries. And more serious still, the Marxist appeal to humanitarian motives is a temptation to dedicated Moslems who are highly critical of the laissez faire individualism that has characterized so much of Western social policy in the past two centuries.

Moslems have the principles of resistance to Marxism built into their religion, even when they see, as did Iqbal, the shortcomings of a society whose sins deserve the divine judgment. In a powerful verse-essay, *Lenin before God,* Iqbal pictures the revolutionary standing before Allah and asking: Of what mortal race art Thou the God? Is it of those creatures formed of dust beneath these heavens?

Europe's pale cheeks are Asia's pantheon, and Europe's pantheon her glittering metals. A blaze of art and science lights the West with darkness that no Fountain of Life dispels; in high-reared grace, in glory and in grandeur, the towering Bank out-tops the cathedral roof; what they call commerce is a game of dice: for one profit, for millions swooping death. There science, philosophy, scholarship, government, preach man's equality and drink men's blood; naked debauch; and want, and unemployment. Denied celestial grace a nation goes no further than electricity or steam.

Omnipotent, righteous, Thou. But bitter the hours, bitter the laborer's chained hours in Thy world. When shall this galley of gold's dominion founder? Thy world, Thy day of wrath, Lord, stands and waits.[47]

Put into the mouth of Lenin, these thoughts are not the passing fancy of a social visionary. They express the mind of numerous Moslems who know their own faith, know the West, and await the "day of wrath" which their Prophet foretold would befall those who fail to share their wealth "for love of God, with their kinsfolk, and the orphans, and the needy, and the wayfarer, and with those who ask." [48] There is some fatalism in this attitude, but also a great deal of truth.

15. Eastern Orthodoxy

ASTERN Orthodox writers justly complain that for over a thousand years Christianity has been identified with Europe. In the eyes of Asiatic and African people, Christendom is a Western religion and its culture equated with the civilization of Western Europe. Yet almost one-fourth of all contemporary Christians do not belong to the West but call themselves Eastern and their religious position Orthodoxy.

Geographically the Eastern Oriental Churches form a vast triangle, whose base is twelve thousand miles long, reaching across the Russo-Siberian plain from Petzamo in the West on the Arctic Ocean, to Alaska in the East where the Indians were evangelized by Russian missionaries in the last century. The western side of the triangle cuts through Finland, Estonia and Latvia, goes south towards Galicia and the Carpathian mountains, divides Yugoslavia in half, touches Albania on the Adriatic Sea and reaches the southern apex of the triangle in Egypt. On its eastern side, it passes across Palestine and reaches all the way to Japan and Korea. The great majority of Eastern Christians now live within this area, with substantial numbers in other countries, including the United States, as descendants of immigrants from the original Orthodox triangle.

It seems that historically the term "Orthodox" was coined to distinguish Christians who believed in the Council of Chalcedon (451), which defined Christ's divinity against the Monophysites. Originally the word was used to describe the Eastern Churches, in communion with Constantinople, who were orthodox or "right-believing," as against the heterodox, "wrong-believing," separated bodies like the Nestorians and Jacobites. Recently, however, the latter and also the Copts in Egypt have taken to adding "Orthodox" to their names.

In modern parlance, the Orthodox are those Christians who separated from Rome in the eleventh century through the great Eastern Schism, and whose distinctive liturgical feature is the Byzantine rite and doctrinal basis the acceptance of the first seven ecumenical councils, up to the second Council of Nicea in 787.

ORIGINS OF THE SCHISM

There are two views on the origin of the Eastern Schism, the Western and the Oriental, and their very divergence is symbolic of the difference in religious posture between Orthodoxy and Catholicism. According to the Latin version, it was not heresy but political issues that led the Greek Church to separate from Rome. The patriarchs of Constantinople had gradually acquired a dominant influence in the Byzantine Empire, by comparison with the patriarchate of Jerusalem, which was never of great importance, and of Alexandria and Antioch whose prestige had been all but lost because of heretical innovations. Moreover, they had fallen under the control of Islam in the seventh century.

Constantinople, therefore, became the official Church, and its dominance slowly developed into a disregard of Rome. Several schisms racked the capital between the fourth and seventh centuries, either because of administrative differences or as the result of the Eastern emperors' patronizing doctrinal error. This was aggravated by the invasion of the barbarians in the West, the independent growth of each church under the nominal tutelage of Constantinople, and especially by the establishment of the Holy Roman Empire of the West at the opening of the ninth century.

Then came the unfortunate conflict between Photius (810-895), Patriarch of Constantinople, and Pope (St.) Nicholas I. The latter decreed to excommunicate Photius, while admitting he was "a man of great virtue and world-wide knowledge," unless he gave up his see to St. Ignatius, the rightful occupant. Ignatius had been driven out by the emperor Michael III for refusing communion to Bardas Caesar, the emperor's uncle, who was living in notorious incest with his daughter-in-law, Eudokia.

Instead of yielding to the pope, Photius proceeded to condemn Nicholas on five charges, all but one of which arose from legitimate differences between Greek and Latin discipline. He urged these Latin "heresies": fasting on Saturdays in Lent, beginning Lent on Ash Wednesday instead of Monday, disapproval of a married clergy, objection to confirmation administered by a priest, and insertion of the *Filioque* (and from the Son) in the Creed. The last objection has made theological history and marked the beginning of Eastern accusations of heresy against the See of Rome. When Michael III died in 867, Photius fell from power and later retired to a monastery at Armeniaki where he died.

With mutual confidence between Rome and Constantinople thus shaken, the formal breach less than two hundred years later took place almost without opposition. Michael Caerularius, patriarch of Constantinople, suddenly attacked Pope (St.) Leo IX on charges of doctrinal innovation, regarding clerical celibacy, fast on Saturdays as well as Fridays, the use of unleavened bread in the Eucharist, and the *Filioque* in the Nicene Creed.

Personally ambitious, Caerularius defied pope and emperor, and struck Leo IX's name from the diptychs, or commemoration in the Liturgy. When negotiations broke down, the legates sent from Rome solemnly excommunicated Caerularius in the Church of St. Sophia on July 16, 1054. As the Liturgy was about to begin, the Roman Cardinals Humbert and Frederick and Archbishop Peter of Amalfi passed through the congregation, entered the sanctuary and laid Pope Leo's document of excommunication on the altar. "May God see to it and pass judgment," they pronounced, and departed.

The Greek version is quite different. Orthodox writers admit the foregoing facts but say they are not enough to explain the separation. No doubt the immediate cause for the first cleavage, under Photius, was due to his appointment to the See of Constantinople. But the real origins of the schism lay in the great political conflict that occurred at the beginning of the century, when in the year 800 Charlemagne restored the Western Roman Empire. In the eyes of the Greeks the pope was guilty of a grave insult to the East when he agreed to crown a barbarian like Charlemagne emperor of the West. Perforce the Byzantine ruler had to bow to the inevitable and recognize his imperial rival in Rome, but the Greeks strongly resented the pope's action. Two competitive political powers came into being, and their respective close associations with the ecclesiastical authorities drew the patriarchs of Rome and Constantinople into the vortex.

Photius precipitated the earlier crisis by calling the West heretical; the Latins retorted by producing a similar list of Eastern heresies. In a short while, the original charges grew into a formidable indictment that covered more than fifty topics. Differences in custom and teaching which had been treated as legitimate expressions of religious diversity suddenly became outrages and ground for mutual incrimination.

Even the dramatic excommunication of Caerularius was not definitive. No one at that time had any idea that this was the beginning of a schism which would last for many centuries. It took two hundred years for the tension to become hardened into formal separation, due to the coming of the Crusaders.

If the Crusades are stripped of their romantic elements, they are revealed as mass exploitations of the Eastern Christians under the guise of a Holy War. The worst evil was that Crusaders used military aggression to advance Christianity, and believed the sword can more effectively serve the Gospel than preaching the word of God. They countenanced the idea that robbery, murder and rapine are permitted, if the victim has erroneous beliefs.

At the outset of the Crusades, the East was alarmed. It had lived in peaceful co-existence with the Moslems, and under their rule, for half a millenium. It was surprised, even irritated, at the sudden burst of zeal against the infidel generated by the Christian West. These fears developed into hostility when Eastern Christians came under the rule of the Crusaders. Heedless of the warnings and exhortations of Rome, they pillaged and oppressed, trying to convert the Orthodox to Latinism, confiscating church buildings, imprisoning the clergy, and treating them as though they professed a wholly foreign religion.

The sack of Constantinople, say the Orthodox historians, dealt the final blow to brotherly relations between these two branches of the Christian Communion. It was an occasion of plunder seldom equalled for horror in world history. The riches of its churches were unsurpassed in the whole world. Soldiers and Latin clergy vied with each other in their attempts to seize some part of these riches for themselves; even the precious Holy Altar of St. Sophia was polluted, broken in pieces and sold.

This day, April 3, 1204, marks the end of the fellowship between Eastern and Western Christians, which means that the split was brought about, not by quarrelsome theologians or ambitious prelates, but by the greed and lust of those who had embarked upon a war of aggression and conquest.

The two explanations have this in common: they both admit the historical events that finally caused the break were not basically dogmatic, and the severance of Constantinople from Rome was not due to irreconcilable positions in theology but to external factors in which personalities and emotions played the major role.

HISTORICAL DEVELOPMENT

Eastern Orthodox history from the beginning of the thirteenth century is the story of trial and conflict with the civil powers that have no parallel in Western Christianity.

Russia was the first to suffer oppression at the hands of the Mongolian tribesmen, called Tartars because of their ferocity, "the detestable race of Satan, rushing forth like demons loosed from Tartarus." [1] The Mongols under their great leader, Genghis Khan, swept across China, Bokhara, Georgia and Persia. They captured the principal cities of Central Asia and after three devastating campaigns (1237-1241) conquered Russia and for the next two and a half centuries kept her in submission, at first abject, then relaxed, but always sufficient to keep the Russian people from exercising religious liberty beyond the measure determined by the political rulers.

Nevertheless the Mongols showed marked respect for certain Orthodox prelates, notably those of Kiev, whom they exempted from taxation. Alternately Russians and Greeks were appointed by the government to the key ecclesiastical posts and one churchman, Theognost (1325-1352), decided to fix his residence at Moscow, which by then had become a leading national center. Due to the courageous support given by the abbot Sergius of Radonezh (1314-

1392), the Russians defeated the Tartars at the battle of Kulikovo Pole, September 8, 1380. The resulting relaxation of control by the Mongols inaugurated the first period of Russia's spiritual renewal. Religious houses were founded all over the country, learning was revived and ikon painting reached its golden age. Over fifty monasteries were founded by the disciples of Sergius during his lifetime.

Ivan III, surnamed the Great (1462-1505), succeeded in so strongly welding the nation under his rule that the final liberation of the country from the Mongols was achieved without bloodshed. The obvious balance of power so favored Moscow that the Tartars were unwilling to oppose the Russians. Periodic attacks from Mongolian nomads continued until the absorption of the Crimea in 1783, but from 1479 (when Moscow's rival, Novgorod, was subdued) Russia became independent of the Mongols.

Yet almost simultaneously two new subjugations to the State took sudden effect, one in Russia under the Tsars, as Ivan III and his successors came to be called, and the other in Asia Minor under the Moslems.

The Russian Church's domination by the Tsars was occasioned by a split in the ranks of the churchmen, one party called "the Possessors" and the other "Non-Possessors." Those who were nicknamed Possessors emphasized unity in preaching and worship, beauty and dignity in ritual service and favored possession of material property by the monasteries and convents. Non-Possessors, on the other hand, were more concerned with freedom in religious practice and taught that God is most pleased with a simple, contrite heart, even in the absence of an elaborate Liturgy. They were the scholars and mystics, who upheld evangelical poverty and maintained that monks should support themselves by the labor of their hands.

As long as the two parties were equally divided and influential, religion prospered. But early in the sixteenth century a crisis arose which tipped the scales in favor of the Possessors. Tsar Basil III had no children by his first wife and wanted to marry another woman. He was opposed by the Metropolitan, Varlaam (1511-1521), a Non-Possessor, but supported by the Possessing prelates whose leader, Daniel, was put into Varlaam's place as Metropolitan and Basil had his second marriage blessed by the Church. The offspring of this union was Ivan the Terrible (1533-1584), the most despotic ruler in Russia until the Communist Revolution in the twentieth century.

This marked the turning point in Russia's religious history. For years the Possessors had upheld the political autocracy and allowed the State to take a leading role in the government of the Church. They preached the doctrine that the Tsars should be loved and obeyed as fathers, no matter how harsh or oppressive their rule. Now, with Basil's support, they avenged themselves on the Non-Possessors, whose leaders were imprisoned and their monasteries closed. At a time when the country most needed the saving influence of men who could withstand political tyrants, the leadership of Church and State fell into the hands of a single party. With periodic exceptions, this continued into modern times.

In the southern portion of Orthodoxy, Constantinople fell to the Moslems after the city had been largely depopulated by civil war and the ravages of plague. With only 10,000 men, the emperor Constantine IX (1449-1453) defended his capital against a powerful army of more than 150,000 Mohammedans. A renegade, Urban, aided the Turks to break through the wall and on May 29, 1453, the Eucharist was celebrated for the last time in the *Hagia Sophia*. The Islamic soldiers poured into the city, pillaging its treasures and destroying its people, including the emperor and patriarch. According to legend, the Eucharistic liturgy at St. Sophia's was not completed when Constantinople fell, and the Eastern Christians still believe the temple will one day be restored to Christian worship, when the divine service interrupted by the Moslems will again be sung in the Cathedral of Holy Wisdom.

It is impossible to read the story of the Orthodox Church under Turkish rule without admiration and pity. True to Mohammed's teaching about Christians being "People of the Book," the Turks tolerated the Orthodox while enslaving them according to the most advanced Oriental standards of despotism.

Allowed to survive and practice their religion, the Eastern Christians suffered under a thousand disabilities. They were obliged to pay tribute, wear a distinctive garb, and conform to a list of humiliating regulations. In practicing their religion, external profession had to be curtailed to the minimum set by the ruling monarch or ruling magistrate. For long periods they were forbidden to use crosses on their churches or ring bells on feast days.

Worse still, the Moslem policy appears to have been one of slow annihilation. New churches were not to be built, the systematic training of the clergy was severely restricted, higher education made impossible, and the schooling of children reduced to a few rudimentary facts. Bribery and treachery wreaked havoc with the clergy; the Sultan had to be provided with Christian slaves.

Every five years, Christian boys between eight and fifteen were inspected by the Moslem overlords. Those who were strongest and most intelligent were chosen, taken from their parents, converted to Islam and impressed into the Sultan's service. Most of them were drafted into a special army corps, the Janissaries, and used for centuries as the main instrument of oppression at home and of conquest abroad.

For administrative purposes, the Orthodox Church under the Moslems was made into a *Rum Millet* (Roman nation) with the patriarch of Constantinople at the head and all other church officials under him. He was completely subject to the Sultan, yet given civil jurisdiction over his own people within the Turkish Empire. Before the Moslem ruler, he was responsible for the conduct of the Orthodox who could approach the government only through him.

As might be expected, the result was a mixture of political and religious power that tended to secularize the Church or, if the patriarch resisted, to oppress the Christian believers. A climax was reached in the eighteenth century when the churches of Rumania, Bulgaria and Serbia came under the Turkish sway, and with it the patriarchate of Constantinople was extended from Asia Minor into the heart of Europe.

Historians of the Orthodox Church graphically describe the price their leaders had to pay for maintaining some semblance of religious authority over the people.

The patriarch received his *berat,* or confirmation of spiritual and secular authority, from an infidel source. He could be removed and, often more than once, reinstated at the Sultan's will, with consequent loss of dignity and the temptation to cater to the Moslem prince for the sake of recognition and prestige. There were notable exceptions, where some patriarchs suffered prison and death rather than compromise on religion. But the over all picture is depressing. Out of one hundred fifty-nine patriarchs in Constantinople from the fifteenth to the twentieth centuries, the Moslems on one hundred and five occasions drove the prelates from their see. There were twenty-seven abdications, often involuntary; six patriarchs suffered violent deaths, and only twenty-one died natural deaths while in office. In one short span, from 1625 to 1700, Constantinople had fifty patriarchs, or an average of a year and a half for each.

Since nominees for patriarch were promoted by a party, those who financed his promotion later expected to be reimbursed, at the expense of the suffragan sees subject to the Metropolitan. They in turn taxed the clergy, who obtained the necessary funds from the people. And behind this whole mechanism stood the power of Islam, which dominated Orthodoxy in Asia Minor until the opening of the twentieth century.

The current oppression of Orthodoxy in Soviet Russia and allied countries is unparalleled in religious history. After half a century of tension, conflict and compromise, the future is still uncertain, but the broad lines of contact between the Russian Church and the Soviet State fall into four distinct periods: from the October Revolution in 1917 to the revolt within the Church in 1922, from the revolt to the outbreak of the second World War in 1939, during the war years, and after the war to the present day.

In the first phase, following the Communist seizure of power, Orthodox churchmen reacted strongly against the wave of persecution waged against the Church by Lenin and Uritskii. Exactly a year after the Revolution got under way, the Moscow Patriarch, Tikhon, issued a ringing message to the Council of People's Commissars, in which he summarized twelve months of Soviet rule: a country running with blood in which "no one feels himself in safety; all live in fear of search, plunder, dispossession, arrest, shooting." He charged the government with inhuman armies against defenseless citizens, of ruthless execution of bishops, priests, monks and nuns "not guilty of anything, but simply on the wholesale accusation of some sort of vague, indefinite 'counter-revolution.' "

"Where," he asked, "was freedom of preaching in church?

Already many bold preachers have paid with the blood of martyrdom." He closed with a powerful indictment.

It is not our work to judge the earthly power; all power permitted
by God would draw upon itself our blessing, if it truly showed itself to
be "God's servant," for the good of those under it.

Now, then, to you, who use power for persecuting your neighbors
and for wiping out the innocent, we extend our word of admonition.
Celebrate the anniversary of your taking power by releasing the imprisoned, by stopping bloodshed, violence, havoc, restriction of the faith.
Turn not to destruction, but to organizing order and legality, give to the
people their wished-for and deserved respite from fratricidal strife.
Otherwise all righteous blood shed by you will cry out against you, and
with the sword will you perish who have taken up the sword.[2]

Tikhon paid for his criticism by being placed under house
arrest, although the Soviets took no other action against him. He
further issued a solemn decree excommunicating those who attacked Christians and profaned church buildings, but he soon discovered that such a weapon was useless. The new masters of Russia
assaulted not the Church, but God, and the threat of divine punishment only aroused worse anti-religious fervor.

In August 1922, Tikhon was arrested and kept in prison until
June of the next year, at which time he published a retraction,
declaring his loyalty to the Soviet government and his regret for
opposing the confiscation of the sacred vessels. Till his death in
1925, Tikhon was acceptable to the Church and State, although
some Christians were shocked by his act of repentance.

A more intransigent position was shown in the manifesto composed by a group of Russian churchmen who were exiled to the
concentration camps on Solovetski Island. With calm dignity they
explained that they had no political grievance against the Soviet
State, that their only concern was over the teaching of materialism
by the Communist Party which controlled the government.

The Church recognizes the existence of the spiritual principle; Communism denies it. The Church believes in the living God, Creator of the
world, Guide of its life; Communism does not admit His existence. The
Church believes in the steadfast principles of morality, justice and law;
Communism looks upon them as the conditional results of class struggle,

and values moral questions only from the standpoint of their usefulness. The Church instills the feeling that humility elevates man's soul; Communism abases man through pride.[3]

Meantime a major revolt within the Orthodox Church shook its government to the foundation and split the leaders into opposing factions: Tikhon and the monastic, celibate prelates and clergy on one side, and the "white" married clergy, on the other. The monastic bishops were charged by their confreres with reactionary measures against the State, with ultra-conservative positions in worship and polity and, above all, with intransigence regarding Communism. The Living Church movement, as the progressives styled themselves, met in congress to depose Tikhon, decree that married priests might become bishops and widowed priests might remarry, and issue an appeal to the people, saying that capitalism was the highest form of godlessness.

The reform clergy soon split into dissenting parties, but the effect of their State-encouraged opposition to the bishops (all monastics) was to inflame the masses against their ecclesiastical leaders and weaken the Church's stand against Communism.

In spite of internal weakness, however, the conservative element rallied around their new leader, the Metropolitan Sergius, who was first imprisoned by the Soviets, then made his peace with the government and released. He was allowed to register the Orthodox Church in 1927, for the first time in five years, on the theory that since physical extermination was impossible legal control by the State was better policy. Soon after, on April 8, 1929, a revised law on religion was published by Stalin. Every form of religious propaganda became a civil offense. In addition, Article 17 of the Constitution forbade every kind of philanthropic and educational activity under Church authority.

"Religious unions (parishes)," the law read, "are forbidden: to establish mutual aid funds, cooperative and productive unions, and in general to use the property at their disposal for any other purpose than the satisfying of religious needs; to give material aid to their members, to organize either special meetings for children, youth or women, for prayer and other purposes, or general meetings, groups, circles, departments, biblical or literary, handwork for labor, religious study and the like, and also to organize excursions and children's play-grounds; to open libraries, reading rooms, to organize sanatoria and medical aid. Only such books as are necessary for the performance of services are permitted in the Church building and houses of prayer." [4] These prohibitions were reinstated in Article 124 of the 1936 Constitution and still remain effectively unchanged.

This new legislation marked a radical change in the Church's status. It was now faced with a crusade of anti-religion, while allowed under government supervision to conduct religious services for the people. An unequal competition opened between the inarticulate Church and the Soviet program of indoctrination, which centered on the public schools.

The war years, 1939-1945, proved a boon to the Orthodox Church. With the outbreak of hostilities the antireligious campaign was softened to a low key; churchmen published statements of support of the government against the Nazi aggressor; and even the State promoted friendlier relations with ecclesiastical authorities. A climax was reached in 1943, when the Patriarchate of Moscow was re-established, after a lapse of two hundred years. Tsar Peter the Great had abolished the patriarchate in 1721 on the grounds that many Russians thought the patriarch was equal or superior to the emperor. A "holy governing synod," modeled on the German Lutheran synods, replaced the patriarchate. Reestablishing this office was a master-stroke of strategy to win the support of the Church for Soviet political needs.

At the Sobor (congress) which followed Sergius's death, the metropolitan Alexii was chosen patriarch in 1944. Next February at his investure, the Sobor issued a warm message of approval of the government, praying God "to increase the strength, health and years of life of our beloved Leader of the Soviet State, Joseph Vissarionovich Stalin." [5] After the defeat of Germany, Alexii published a statement to the effect that, "the most important thing the Russian Orthodox Church did in wartime was to demonstrate to the whole world its complete unity with its government." [6]

Since the war, the condition of the Orthodox Church in Russia has been precarious, in spite of ostensible growth. Honors and benefits have been conferred on dutiful churchmen by the Soviet government, and a *modus vivendi* marked out that gives the ap-

pearance of progress. But all the evidence points to a radical decline in religion among the people, due mostly to the steady pressure of Marxist teaching in the schools and control of available
media of communication.

A recent survey made by the government showed there is still
a widespread religious survival among the peasantry, partly explained by the concentration of women on the farms and of atheist
propaganda in the cities. "Precise data on the sex ratio among the
Orthodox do not exist. However, on the basis of various facts available to researchers in this field, it may be stated that about 75 to
80 per cent of all the faithful are women." [7]

This poses a new problem for the Church, to save itself and
survive the Communist State by strengthening the religion of its
women and, as far as possible, using their services in the interests
of the faith. Aware of this fact, the government is more than ever
stressing the need of teaching atheism in the homes. "The most
effective form of antireligious propaganda is systematic individual
work with the faithful within their homes, particularly with the
mothers. Since religion is most widespread among women, attention
must be directed chiefly to antireligious work among them. Women
must be drawn into public affairs as active participants. This is the
most important condition for liberating them from the narcotic of
religion," and through them the next generation. [8]

SOURCES OF FAITH

It is not easy to specify the doctrinal principles of Eastern
Orthodoxy. The very name, Orthodox, designates both "correct
doctrine" and "correct worship." In Slavonic, Orthodoxy is rendered by the work *Pravoslavie,* which means "true glory," so that
when a Russian, Serb, or Bulgarian calls himself Orthodox he proclaims his belonging to a community which praises and glorifies
God in the right way.

Consequently for the Orthodox the Church's purpose is mainly
to worship God, and to teach its members how to glorify Him in
the right spirit. This de-emphasis of doctrine affects the importance
given to different types of doctrinal positions, whether they belong
to dogma, theologumena, or theological opinion. In the absence of

an infallible defining authority, there is considerable overlapping of dogmatic teaching among churchmen, and numerous areas of uncertainty not found in Roman Catholicism. Dogmas are universally binding among the Orthodox, as emanating directly from divine revelation; theologumena are traditionally held doctrines hallowed by the authority of ancient and respected Church teachers; theological opinions are the vast body of disputed theories and explanations that scholars have devised over the centuries.

Until the seventeenth century, the Orthodox accepted the same books of the Old and New Testaments as are found in the Catholic canon. Then Cyril Lukaris (1572-1638), patriarch of Constantinople, followed the Protestant pattern and denied the inspired character of the so-called deutero-canonical books of the Old Testament, namely, Tobias, Judith, Wisdom, Ecclesiasticus, Baruch, and the two books of Maccabees. This innovation was at first resisted, but closer relations with Calvinism confirmed many, if not most, Orthodox theologians in reducing the Old Testament canon to its Protestant form.

While the concept of biblical inspiration differs among the authors, a common notion is to consider it "an immediate movement and instruction of the sacred writers by the Holy Spirit. As a result, they are not only preserved from error but positively receive a revelation of God's truth, though without violence to their natural faculties. The biographers therefore become organs for transmitting divine revelation, while retaining all their native powers and activities." [9] So exalted is this type of inspiration that the sacred authors are said to have received and communicated divine truths even as the man Christ understood and expressed revelation by means of the Word which assumed His human nature.

Tradition as distinct from Scripture is a valid source of Christian doctrine in Orthodoxy. In general "sacred tradition is that form of preserving and propagating revelation whereby the faithful and worshipers of God, by word and example transmit one to the other, the predecessors to those who follow them, the doctrine of faith, law of God, the sacraments and sacred rites." [10] The significant feature of this concept is the esssential part played by the faithful in forming and conserving tradition.

However, in spreading doctrinal tradition among all the faithful, the Orthodox recognize certain monuments of special import which differ in dogmatic value according to their greater or less respect among the people.

Highest in dignity are the Creeds: the Nicene, the Athanasian and the Symbol of St. Gregory Thaumaturgus (213-270). In the Nicene they do not include the *Filioque,* which declares the procession of the Holy Spirit from the Son. The Athanasian Creed, known as the *Quicumque* (Whosoever), from its opening words, differs from other summaries of faith in embodying anathemas against those who deny the Trinity, Incarnation and other doctrinal essentials. Though dating from the time of St. Ambrose, it was not recognized as a standard of faith in the Eastern Church until the seventeenth century, when it began to appear in the Greek *Horologium* (liturgical manual) and in Russian service books. Surprisingly the Apostles' Creed lacks "ecumenical authority" among the Eastern Orthodox.[11]

Gregory Thaumaturgus' Creed is entirely Trinitarian, and has no reference to Christology. It owes more to tradition than to the Bible, and practically typifies the character of Eastern religious thought.

One God, Father of the living Word, of subsistent wisdom, eternal power and likeness. Perfect source of the perfect One, Father of the only-begotten Son. One Lord, one alone from the only One, God of God, likeness and image of the Deity, active Word, wisdom comprehending the structure of the universe, and effective virtue of every creature. True Son of true God, Invisible of invisible, Immortal of immortal, Eternal of eternal.

And one Holy Spirit, having substance from God, and who appeared to men through the Son. Image of the Son, perfect of the perfect, life which is the cause of the living, holy well-spring, sanctity which dispenses sanctity, in whom God the Father is manifested, who is above all and in all things, and God the Son who is through all things.

Perfect Trinity, undivided and unseparated in glory and eternity and reign. Nothing created nor subservient nor introduced in the Trinity, as though it were absent before and had later come in. In like manner, the Father was never without the Son nor the Son without the Spirit; but always the same unalterable and unchangeable Trinity.[12]

Second in authority to the Creeds are the first seven general councils: two of Nicea, 325, 787; three of Constantinople, 381,

553, 681; Ephesus, 431; and Chalcedon, 451. The eighth council, of Constantinople in 869-870, deposed Photius as patriarch and by Orthodox standards marked the beginning of Western Christianity apart from the Eastern Church. All the future general Councils recognized by Rome, from First Lateran in 1123 to Second Vatican in 1962, have been held in the West, and are not accepted by the Orthodox.

The first seven councils dealt almost exclusively with the Trinity, the divinity of Christ, the divine maternity of the Blessed Virgin and the veneration of sacred images. As a result, doctrinal principles in Orthodoxy show little of the dogmatic development found in the West, through the clarifications and definitions of such major conclaves as the Council of Trent (1545-1563) or First Vatican (1869).

The Fathers of the Church most respected and followed by the Orthodox are Athanasius, the three Cappadocians (Basil, Gregory Nazianzen and Nyssa), Pseudo-Dionysius, Maximus the Confessor, Leo and Gregory the Great. It is of more than passing interest that two Roman Pontiffs are among the highest patristic authorities in the Eastern Church.

Below the Fathers but still within the concept of tradition are the symbolic books, described as "professions of faith of particular churches in recent times, especially those composed against Catholics and Protestants," or "professions of faith by certain enlightened persons in the churches, succinctly and clearly written to teach the faithful all or some of the doctrines contained in the Creeds." [13]

Among the more famous symbolic authorities are the *Confessions* of Gennadius (died 471), of Peter Mogila (1597-1646) and of Dositheus (1640-1707), and the *Catechism* of Philaret (1553-1646); Gennadius, however, is not acknowledged by many theologians. Mogila was a Wallachian theologian whose comprehensive survey of the Greek Orthodox Church was formally approved by the foremost patriarchs in 1643, re-approved by the Synod of Jerusalem in 1672, and is now a primary witness of Eastern Orthodoxy. Dositheus, as Patriarch of Jerusalem, wrote strenuously against Calvin and Bellarmine, and was a prime mover in combating Western influences in Orthodox theology.

Theodore Romanov Philaret, the Patriarch of Moscow, founded

the Romanov dynasty. Under his cousin, Theodore I, the last Tsar of the Runik family, he fought against the Swedes and was later banished to a monastery. After his son Michael was elected Tsar, he became patriarch (1619) and until his death remained virtual ruler of Russia. A zealous reformer, he established a seminary in each diocese, promoted the study of theology and composed his famous *Catechism*.

Other writings of lesser authority are sometimes called symbolic, but their value varies and practically depends on the following they have in contemporary circles. Thus a man like Vladimir Solovieff (1853-1900) is highly regarded by the Orthodox, but his later entrance into the Catholic Church naturally colors the acceptability of his doctrines.

DOCTRINAL VARIATIONS

Consistent with the undefined nature of dogmatic sources, there is considerable fluidity among Orthodox teachers on many points of doctrine that have become defined dogmas in Roman Catholicism.

According to Eastern thought, nothing which has no direct bearing on divine worship should be made a matter of absolute belief. Confessions of faith for the Orthodox are mainly a part of doxology or liturgy. At most, dogmas safeguard the beatific vision of God and the Incarnation, and are enshrined in the Creeds and dogmatic pronouncements of the first seven councils. Catholicism has a doctrinal system which includes the nature of man, the constitution of the Church, the primacy, sin, grace and the ways of salvation. All these are "problems" for Eastern Christians, in the sphere governed by Theologumena. Even such basic issues as the concept of the supernatural and the real presence in the Eucharist are open to discussion and controversy in Orthodox theology.

Nevertheless, beyond the Trinitarian and Christological teaching of the early councils are many areas of substantial agreement among the Orthodox. These form their "deposit of faith," about which, however, opinions may vary.

SUPERNATURAL LIFE. Until very recent times, the influence of Protestant theology on Orthodoxy was notable but sporadic. Since the nineteenth century, the effect has been more profound and shows itself especially in the median position between Catholicism and Protestantism that Eastern churchmen have adopted on the subject of man's elevation to the supernatural order.

Current writings indicate that many Orthodox theologians do not admit a strict elevation of man to a supernatural destiny. They variously describe this elevation as suprasensible, transcendent, what is above the common mode of action of the forces of nature, or above the natural capacity of man. While apparently subtle, their concept allows for an exigency or demand for the beatific vision, which goes beyond mere tendency or desire.

The issue became crucial for the Orthodox through their frequent relations with the continental Reformation and since the sixteenth century has given rise to opposing parties within the Eastern churches. About 1400 A.D. translations of Latin works, including St. Thomas, made Catholic writings available to the Orthodox and divided them into Latinizers and Anti-Latins, Palamites and Anti-Palamites (generally Latinizers). With the advent of the Reformation, the lines were further sharpened. Cyril Lukaris, Greek patriarch, was ardently pro-Calvinist; his *Confessio* is a thoroughly Reformed interpretation of the Greek Orthodox faith and allows for no supernatural elevation in the Catholic sense.

Twentieth-century ideas are in a state of flux, with perhaps the majority favoring the Catholic position, without clearly distinguishing between grace as absolutely gratuitous and in no sense due to any creature, and grace as an exalted sublimation of human nature.

PROCESSION OF THE SON. Historically the principal divergence from Catholicism is on the procession of the Third Person of the Trinity. Symbolized in the term, *Filioque,* it has been the main object of Orthodox theological writing for centuries. Two attitudes are discernible: that the procession of the Holy Spirit from the Father alone is a dogma, and therefore the Latin *Filioque* is heresy; or that the procession from the Father is a dogma which the Roman Church admits, so that procession from the Son is only a theological opinion which may be professed by the Orthodox.

Historically the problem goes back to the insertion of the words *Filioque* in the Nicene Creed, begun in Spain in the sixth century and later adopted by the whole West as the official expression of the revealed truth that the Holy Spirit proceeds at once from the Father and the Son, as from one principle. Photius and after him the Orthodox objected to what they called either a heretical tampering with the Creed, or an unjustified exercise of papal authority approving the insertion without an ecumenical council.

Since the turn of the century, Orthodox sentiment has been in the direction of considering the *Filioque* more irenically. In 1907 the Moscow Synodal Commission published a statement declaring that the *Filioque* had not been the cause of separation of the Churches; that the theory of Photius on the procession of the Spirit from the Father alone was a theological opinion and not a dogma; that the true meaning of the Greek Fathers who said the Holy Spirit proceeds *from* the Father *through* the Son corresponds to the Latin formula.

The Synod suggested that the two formulas concur essentially: the co-ordinating version (*Filioque*) and the subordinating (*per Filium*), since they both attest that Father and Son are the one Principle of the Holy Spirit. They also complement each other. While the former stresses the unicity and indivisibility of the Principle, the latter emphasizes that the Father is Prime Principle, while the Son as "God from God" is a Derived Principle, since with His essence He also receives from the Father the power of spirating the Holy Spirit.

More recently a leading theologian, Sergius Bulgakov, gave a critical judgment on the whole question. "The controversy about the Holy Spirit has been conducted in an atmosphere lacking in love and actuated by the spirit of schism; it has been therefore a pointless dispute." [14] Current writers ask themselves: if the controversy was so futile, why has it persisted for so long? They answer that the issue is not doctrinal but moral. A grave breach of mutual trust was committed by changing the Nicene Creed; all other factors are minor or irrelevant.

CONCEPT OF THE CHURCH. Orthodox ecclesiologists believe their concept of the Church is a balanced mean between the Reformation idea of an essentially invisible society and the Catholic definition of the Church as a visible, hierarchical institution. Within the Orthodox system, however, two quite different notions prevail: the traditional and conservative, which is perfectly consistent with

Orthodox professions of faith; and the liberal concept especially prevalent among the Slavophils.

Representative of the conservative theorists is Philaretus (Gumilevsky), who describes the Church of Christ as "the assembly of believers in Christ, instituted by the Lord and united by the divine word, sacraments and the hierarchy under the influence of the Holy Spirit, to lead people to eternal salvation." [15] This earthly society is united with the heavenly, the angels and saints, in one and the same Church of Christ. A heavy stress on the unitive character of the dual society is a feature of Orthodox ecclesiology. It is unlike the Protestant notion by its recognition of a hierarchy, and similar to the Catholic in conceiving the Church as visible in bodily structure and invisible as regards its soul.

Within the conservative camp, however, are different schools of thought, one in the direction of Rome and the other of the Reformation. Macarius Bulgakov defines the Church in terms reminiscent of Bellarmine, except for including the word "Orthodox" and excluding the Roman Pontiff. "The Church," he says, "is the orthodox society of the believers and the baptized in Jesus Christ, founded immediately by Him and through the holy apostles, and animated by Him; which is directed visibly through spiritual pastors, and by means of a teaching authority, the administration of sacred rites and a ruling body; and at the same time is led invisibly to eternal life through the most efficacious grace of the Holy Spirit." [16] Theophylact Gorskii, on the other hand, gives an almost Lutheran definition, calling the Church "the assembly of true believers and saints, rightly called together by the preaching of the divine word to attain eternal life through the great goodness of God. Only those really belong to the Church who possess the true faith, by which they are united with Christ the Head. Hence they are called members of the Body of Christ, so that the wicked, the unbelieving and hypocrites are certainly excluded from membership." [17] This differs only in detail from the classic Protestant Church of the believers and the predestined.

Slavophil ecclesiology antedates Alexius Khomjakov (1804-1860), but his theory on the Church has deeply affected Orthodox thought and found expression in the unity movements now current in the Eastern Churches. He began by conceiving the Church in its broadest possible extension, including the Mystical Body of Christ in its triple form of militant, suffering and triumphant. Then he explained that only the Eastern Orthodox Church is the true Church. Western Churches, namely Catholicism and Protestantism, do not differ essentially as sects outside the true fold of Christ. The Catholic Church fell into rationalism in the ninth century, when it introduced the *Filioque*, Protestants when they embraced private interpretation of the Scriptures. In Khomjakov's vocabulary, the Church is "a living principle," or "the Church is the universal life of love and unity, along with organic and living solidarity." [18]

Not the least value of this expansive notion of the Church has been the function it served those who sought a rapprochement with contemporary Marxism. It also gave men like Nicholas Berdyaev (1874-1948) the principles required for adapting religion to the demands of the modern mind. This "spiritual Christianity," it is felt, has no need of doctrinal definitions, bourgeois morality, and set worship.

In the absence of an ultimate juridical authority to pass judgment on the relative value of these concepts, it is difficult to know which ideas are prevalent. Certainly those most closely approximating the standard manuals of doctrine are also nearest to Catholicism, in which the Church is not so spiritualized as to include almost anyone who calls himself a Christian even though he disbelieves what the first seven councils made mandatory on all the faithful.

Although the Eastern Orthodox generally admit that the Church is a visible institution, they say that Christ alone is the head, since a visible head would be irreconcilable with the doctrine of the Mystical Body. One body can have only one head, not two, as found in Catholicism. Christ, they teach, so reserves to Himself the whole life and government of the Church that no vicar can take His place. Ministers in the Church can assist in the activity of the Head, but they cannot share in it; otherwise Christ's function would suffer encroachment and the Church which is divine would become subject to a human person.

No mortal man, they argue, can be head of the Church. He cannot exert influence over the scattered peoples of the earth; his action would supplant that of Christ and introduce into an indefectible society the fallibility and weakness of a human being. Most importantly, if the Church were to have a human head, it would cease to be celestial and become as one of the many secular kingdoms of earth.

The dominant principle in Orthodoxy is that Church authority is diffused among its members, and not as in the West, isolated in a definite source. This was strikingly illustrated in an exchange of letters between Pius IX and the Patriarchs of the East. In 1848 a reply of the Orthodox prelates, signed by thirty-one bishops and three patriarchs, informed Rome that "the Pope is greatly mistaken in supposing that we consider the ecclesiastical hierarchy to be the guardian of dogma. The case is quite different. The unvarying constancy and the unerring truth of Christian dogma does not depend upon any of the hierarchical orders; it is guarded by the totality of the people of God, which is the body of Christ." [19]

This answer reflects the common attitude of Orthodox towards the primacy and infallibility of the Roman See. "Does any one in the Church," they ask, "possess of himself infallibility in his judgment of dogma? No, he does not; every member of the Church is liable to error, or rather to the introduction of his own personal limitations in his dogmatic studies." According to this view, neither the hierarchy nor the councils are organs of doctrinal inerrancy. "Only the Church in its identity with itself can testify to the truth. It is the Church which agrees or not, with the council. There are not, and there cannot be, external forms established beforehand for the testimony of the Church about itself." [20]

Such corporate authority, however, is compatible with a hierarchical structure. Bishops and clergy have clearly defined functions in the ministry and norms of orthodoxy to maintain in their teaching. Councils on a local or provincial basis may be called, but when dealing with matters of conscience their decisions must have the approval of the whole community to take juridical effect, and even then there is no claim to infallibility.

SACRAMENTAL SYSTEM. Orthodox churchmen recognize seven sacraments, and stress the fact so solemnly they charge anyone who diminishes the number with trifling with Christian revelation. As one writer expressed it, "There are as many sacred mysteries or sacraments among the Greeks as among the Latins, namely, seven. And no one in either Church has ever called this into question." [21]

The exceptional Orthodox who departs from this norm is considered outside the stream of Eastern tradition.

Nevertheless occasional doubts arise. Thus a prominent theologian in Europe, Jerome Tarasij, suggested that other rites should be added to the sacramental system, for example, entrance into monastic life, solemn blessing of water and funeral ceremonies; but matrimony could well be dropped because there was nothing spiritual about it.[22] Tarasij has since been supported by at least one metropolitan, Antonij Chrapovickij, whose diocesan catechism allowed considerable freedom on the subject. His comment that the Church has never defined the number of the sacraments is correct from the Orthodox viewpoint, although few would doubt that the number is seven.

Eastern commentators repeatedly say that the sacraments are not mere symbols or pure signs of grace, received independently of the rite and only occasioned by its administration. They use terms like "effect grace," or "give grace," and describe the sacraments as instruments, organs or means of divine sanctification.

Yet again there are sporadic dissenting voices. The same Tarasij explicitly teaches that the causality of the sacraments does not depend on special external rites but on union with the whole Church. In the same way, the "matter" and "form" of the sacraments, which in Latin terminology stand for the material rite and the ritual words, have never been clearly defined among the Orthodox and therefore variations appear among different churches. But in general there is a remarkable consistency between Eastern and Western beliefs and practices with regard to the sacraments.

The Orthodox always place baptism in the first place among the sacraments, and recognize its institution by Christ or, as some prefer, "by the words and actions of the Lord." Pure and natural water is required along with the Trinitarian formula and a triple immersion, using the words, "The servant of God (name) is baptized in the name of the Father, the Son and the Holy Spirit." Symbolically this signifies the death of the sinner, and his redemption and resurrection as a Christian.

The ordinary minister of baptism is a bishop or priest, but in case of necessity even a lay person (man or woman) may baptize. Some Orthodox canonists question the validity of a baptism performed by laymen, unless the latter are Orthodox and have the

intention of conferring the true sacrament. Very like Catholic doctrine, the effects of baptism are said to be remission of sin, imprint-
ing of a character, entering the fold of Christ, and receiving a title
to heavenly glory. Consequently, with rare exception the necessity
of baptism for salvation is taken for granted, and therefore children
are normally baptized in infancy.

Confirmation, or holy chrismation, follows immediately after
baptism. Although the priest confers the sacrament, the holy oil or
chrism must have been blessed by a gathering of bishops of a self-
governing church presided over by their senior. While anointing
the various parts of the body, actually the whole body, the priest
recites the formula, "The seal of the gift of the Holy Spirit." However, the Orthodox do not believe that an indelible character is im-
printed; and only two sins can efface it, heresy and schism. As a
consequence, confirmation is the regular way that converts to
Orthodoxy (or fallen-aways) are received into the Church.

Orthodox theologians stress that chrismation is not a renewal
of baptismal vows, but a kind of lay ordination, by which the laymen obtain special graces to participate in the life of the Christian
community and receive the other sacraments. One important consequence of confirming infants is that from childhood they are considered full-fledged members of the Church, with all the rights and
privileges of adults, including the reception of Holy Communion.

Confession of sins is an ancient practice among the Orthodox,
which they base on three considerations: that people are normally
responsible for their actions and can have their conscience trained,
that their responsibility is a corporate affair that requires corporate
means to cultivate and may not be left to each individual indiscriminately, and that sincere reconciliation with men secures divine
forgiveness with a consequent removal of guilt.

A familiar custom is to have the penitent first visit his relatives
and close friends before going to the priest. He asks their pardon,
with or without specifying how he may have offended them. They
answer, "God forgives you." Behind the practice is the centuries-
old tradition of confessing one's sins publicly, which has now been
largely abandoned, although early in the present century a certain
John of Cronstadt revived in Russia the practice of public confessions.

Instead of kneeling before the priest, the penitent stands facing

East, as a symbol that the confessor is not absolving in his own name but as a witness of the Christian community. At least this is the custom among many Orthodox churchmen. After the penitent tells his sins, he may be asked a few questions and then hears a brief exhortation.

O Lord God of the salvation of Your servants, merciful, gracious and longsuffering. You offer repentance for evil and will not the death of a sinner but rather that he should be converted and live. Forgive now, O Lord, this Your servant (by name). Grant him the assurance of repentance, pardon, and remission of his sins, and absolve him from all his offences, voluntary and involuntary. Reconcile and unite him to Your holy Church through Jesus Christ our Lord, with whom be power and glory ascribed to You, now and for ever, even unto ages of ages. Amen.[23]

After this prayer follows the absolution, of which there are two main forms, one common to Russia and the other to the Greek Orthodox Churches. The Russian formula appears to have been influenced by Catholic divines in the seventeenth century. It is expressly indicative, i.e., the priest declares he is forgiving the sins in the name of God. "May our Lord and God Jesus Christ, through the grace and compassion of His exceeding love, forgive you, my son (here follows the Christian name), all your transgressions, and I, an unworthy priest, by the power that is given to me by Him, forgive and absolve you from all your sins in the name of the Father, and of the Son and of the Holy Spirit, Amen." [24]

The Greek version is more deprecative, i.e., the priest declares that God forgives the penitent. "May God, who pardoned David through the prophet Nathan when he confessed his sins; who received Peter bewailing the denial, the harlot weeping at His feet, and who took back the publican and prodigal; may the same God, through me a sinner, pardon you everything in this world, and cause you to stand uncondemned before His awful tribunal." [25]

After absolution the penitent is seldom required to say or perform a penance prescribed by the confessor. Its function is said to be only a subjective one, to strengthen the will of the penitent against future lapses or act as a salutary remedy for bad habits. Many Orthodox theologians do not consider satisfaction for sins necessary for the remission of punishment incurred, on the theory that Christ perfectly satisfied for our sins, so that the absolution of the priest delivers us from all penalty both eternal and temporal.

The frequency of confession differs. Four times a year is a common practice, although in the Russian Church no one may receive the Eucharist unless he has first confessed his sins. Other Eastern Churches have no set rules and may even prescribe confession only when grave sins have been committed. The same with faculties to hear confessions: some bishops restrict the privilege to a select group of priests, others allow all priests under their jurisdiction to absolve anyone who comes to them.

Holy Orders are almost, but not quite the same as in the Catholic Church. The Orthodox distinguish (as do Catholics) between major and minor orders, but they do not consider any of the minor, as well as the subdiaconate, sacraments; only the episcopate, priesthood and diaconate are called sacraments, the rest are merely sacramentals. However even the subdiaconate is regarded sufficient to make the law of continence binding; so that subdeacons, as well as deacons and priests, are traditionally forbidden to marry or to contract a second marriage if their first wife dies.

In the ceremony of ordination, the actual conferral of orders is quite simple, although the surrounding liturgy is very elaborate. Essentially the sacrament is conferred by the imposition of hands (in the Byzantine ceremonial only the right hand) by the bishop on the ordinand; this is the same for all three major orders. The form of ordination is also practically the same for bishop, priest and deacon, except for a single phrase. "The grace of God, that always strengthens the weak and fills things that are empty, advances the most devout subdeacon N.N. to be deacon. Let us therefore pray for him that the grace of the Holy Spirit may come upon him." [26]

There follows a long prayer with biblical allusions to the deacon St. Stephen, while the bishop continues to hold his hand on the subject's head. The deacon is then vested in the sanctuary and given a horarion or stole decorated with crosses and placed over the shoulders. In the ordination of priests the same formula is used, except for the words, "the most devout deacon N.N. to be priest," and for bishops, "appoints the most devout elect N.N. to be Metropolitan of the most holy Metropolis N." A priest receives the vestments and sacred vessels, the bishop is given a miter and insignia of his office.

In the Russian Church a theory prevails that ordained clerics lose their sacerdotal character when they ask for reduction to the lay state or the same is imposed on them for a grave crime. The result is that reordinations to the priesthood and reconsecrations to the episcopate are not rare in the history of the Russian Orthodox Church.

The sacrament of matrimony is called the Crowning in the Eastern Churches. Its purpose is to bestow the Church's blessing upon husband and wife, and assist them to remain faithful to each other and their respective duties until death. Husband and wife wear crowns during the ceremony, and in some places for a week afterwards. Marriage vows are pronounced during the Eucharistic Liturgy, with appropriate readings from the Gospel of St. John about the marriage feast at Cana and from St. Paul's classic epistle to the Ephesians, that "a husband is head of the wife, just as Christ is head of the Church."

Although in the marriage formula words are used to suggest a permanent union, and this is still considered the ideal, divorce with the right to remarry is commonly recognized among the Eastern Orthodox. A few dogmatists still hold that only adultery gives the privilege of a perfect divorce, but canonists and the normal practice extend this condition to a broad variety of causes. A divorce law promulgated in Russia after the Communist Revolution typifies the general attitude of the Church, which juridically reserves to itself the right to dissolve the marriage bond.

Among other grounds for dissolving marriage, besides antecedent physical impotence, are abandonment of the Orthodox faith by either party, adultery whether of one or both parties, voluntary mutilation which makes marital relations impossible, grave disease like syphilis, prolonged absence of one partner for two or three years, physical violence or injury to the spouse or children or threat of death, incurable mental illness, malicious neglect of duty proved before an ecclesiastical tribunal. In practice the two most common grounds urged before the Church are prolonged absence and malicious neglect, with the dissolution taking automatic effect after a specified time and previous adjudication by Church authorities.

Provisions are made for marriage ceremonies following a divorce. They are much different from the Crowning at a first nuptials, and contain a clearly penitential note to emphasize that those who enter on a second union have failed to preserve the purity of their first intention. A salutary prayer is read over the couple by the priest. "O Lord Jesus Christ, cleanse the iniquities of Your servants because, being unable to bear the heat and burden of the day and the hot desires of the flesh, they are now entering into the bond of their second marriage, as You did render lawful by Your chosen vessel the Apostle Paul, saying for the sake of us humble sinners, 'It is better to marry in the Lord than to burn.' " [27]

The penitential ritual is used both for divorcees remarrying, and for those who were widowed. However no permission is given to deacons and priests to marry more than once, and they are required to espouse a virgin. If they contract a second marriage, they must give up the active work of the priestly ministry and may continue to function in some subordinate position.

There is an Orthodox equivalent of the Catholic sacrament of extreme (or "final") unction called "Holy Unction," to distinguish it from the idea of a final anointing in grave sickness or at the time of death. Holy unction has a broader significance, since it is administered in cases of bodily and mental illness, even when there is no danger of death, and may be received by anyone seeking spiritual renewal and purification.

Generally the priest is invited to the sick person's home and administers the unction there, but recently the practice has arisen of offering the benefit of the *Euchelaion* to everyone who presents himself at the church during certain seasons, as in Lent, or who visits some place of pilgrimage. In a few localities anointing becomes a special preparation for Holy Communion.

There are seven lessons or readings which deal with the healing ministry of Christ, each followed by an anointing, whose original form was, "Holy Father, Physician of bodies and souls, You sent Your only-begotten Son our Lord Jesus Christ to cure every ill and to deliver us from death. Heal also this Your servant N.N. of the sickness which afflicts his body and enliven him through the grace of Your Christ." [28] This formula has since undergone many additions and changes, including invocations of the Blessed Virgin and Saints Cosmas and Damian. Seven priests are recommended to perform the unction, although one is sufficient in case of necessity. A brush is used to anoint the various parts of the body: the forehead, chin, cheeks, hands, nostrils and chest. However the practice is not uniform among the churches. Each priest performs the same ritual with an amalgam of olive oil which, at least in Russia, is mixed with wine, in memory of the Good Samaritan.

SAINTS AND FAITHFUL DEPARTED. Among the saints, the Orthodox reserve a special place for the Blessed Virgin. "Warm veneration of the *Theotokos* (Mother of God)," writes one of their theologians, "is the soul of Orthodox piety." [29] Priests and people invoke her name constantly in liturgical and private prayers; they love her not only as the Mother of Christ but as the spiritual mother of all men. Her ikons are worshiped everywhere, and the majority of Orthodox prayers and hymns are addressed to Mary under a variety of titles and with a profusion of feast days that has no counterpart in the rest of the Christian world.

In their theological reflection on this Marian piety, Eastern writers are quite technical, distinguishing between the kind of worship offered to God and to His Mother. "We worship our Lady, the Virgin-Mother of God, with hyperdulia, but not as God; as the Mother of God, but not with latria. God forbid, that would be blasphemy. For God only do we worship with latria and make our intercession with Him for sins committed after baptism, and by her we hope for remission from Him." [30]

Underlying the devotion to Mary is a profound veneration for the saints, who are considered bound to the faithful on earth by ties of grace and through a common bond in Christ. This was brought out forcefully at the Evanston Assembly of the World Council of Churches, at which the Orthodox delegates took issue with the prevalent opinion that the Church is only a community of wayfarers en route to their destiny.

It is misleading to describe the Church simply as "the pilgrim people of God" and forget that the Church Triumphant and Church Militant are but one Body. It is precisely in this unity that the Christian Hope is grounded. The Church is the great Communion of Saints. We upon earth live and strive in communion with the glorious "cloud of witnesses" revealed through the ages and are strengthened by the intercessions of the *Theotokos* and the Saints with whom we join in adoration of Christ our Redeemer.[31]

The Russian Catechism explains how the faithful who belong to the Church Militant on earth, in offering their prayers to God, call at the same time to their aid the saints who belong to the Church in heaven. Since the saints stand on the highest steps of the approach to God, "by their prayers and intercessions they purify, strengthen, and offer before God the prayers of the faithful living upon earth, and by the will of God work graciously and beneficently upon them, either by invisible virtue, or by distinct apparitions and in divers others ways." [32]

Recognizing that their devotion to Mary and the saints is a major obstacle to the acceptance of Orthodoxy by the Protestants, Eastern churchmen have gone to great lengths in clarifying what to them is an essential part of Christianity. "The Orthodox Church asks nothing of the saints except the acting as ambassadors towards God for us and the supplicating for all things needful—not even of the Holy *Theotokos* herself. Inasmuch as of her own power she can do nothing except act as an ambassador, we ask nothing of her except that, and to plead with her Son and her God for us." [33]

It comes somewhat as a surprise that the Immaculate Conception should not be admitted. Actually the Orthodox had always venerated Mary's absolute sinlessness, but since the definition by Pius IX spokesmen for the Eastern Churches have denied the doctrine, at any rate in Catholic terms. Anthimos VIII of Constantinople officially declared against it in 1895. The more common Orthodox opinion is that Mary was freed from original sin at the Annunciation.

The subject of an intermediary state between earth and heaven has been controverted among the Orthodox for centuries. They offer the Holy Sacrifice for the faithful departed and pray for the dead, but their theologians insist they do not accept the Catholic doctrine of purgatory. A measured statement about the condition of the dead occurs in the highly respected Confession of Kritopoulos.

The Church teaches that their punishment is not material, nor in their members, nor by fire nor any other material thing, but by the pain and sorrow of conscience which come to them from the remembrance of those things which in the world they did in violation of reason and against sanctity. Therefore we pray for the departed by name for each. As often as the Lord's Supper is celebrated, no matter on what day, they are remembered in common. For all who have compiled the prayers of that Sacrament, Basil the Great, Gregory the Theologian and John Chrysostom, make mention of them who are fallen asleep. It is not for us to fix the time of their purification.[34]

Other writers further speculate on the lot of the souls in purgation, but their main difference from the accepted Catholic position is a denial of the name, "purgatory," and the existence of a purgatorial fire. The latter is common teaching in Catholic theology, but at the reunion Councils of Lyons (1274) and Florence (1438-1445), out of consideration for the separated Greeks the official declarations speak only of purifying punishments (*poenae purgatoriae*), not of purifying fire.

CHURCH AUTHORITY AND MONASTICISM

The most characteristic feature of the Eastern Churches is their constitutional organization as a visible society. Many Orthodox agree that the Church is essentially hierarchical; they admit that bishops are the successors of the Apostles and visible heads of particular churches; and they invest the universal Church (including the faithful) with supreme transitory authority during an ecumenical council. But in the absence of a permanent, divinely instituted visible head, endowed with immediate jurisdiction over each diocese, they have developed a system of government known as autocephalism.

SELF-GOVERNMENT. Literally autocephalous means "self-headed" and was used in the early Church to describe bishops who were under no superior authority in their metropolitan area. Eventually the term came to describe the whole juridical structure of Eastern Orthodoxy, which may be compared to the United Nations in contrast to a monarchy such as the Catholic Church. In theory there may be as many autocephalous churches as there are dioceses or bishops, because the Orthodox recognizes no ultimate primate, and individual bishops by equal right succeed the first Apostles. But in practice there are as many autocephalous churches as distinct political units or racial bodies speaking the same language, even though not united politically.

The interior government of each autocephaly is synodal or collegial, since a monarchical form of jurisdiction is excluded not only from the universal Church but also from each autocephaly. Instead the supreme authority is vested in a college or synod. The principle holds good even in autocephali presided over by a patriarch or exarch (lower metropolitan primate), where the real governing power is a synod of bishops together with the primate. Without the synod, the latter can do little or nothing of his own accord.

Yet even the synod is only partially authoritative, because the supreme jurisdiction governing each autocephaly is twofold: the Church and State. In the territory where the synod is located, the civil government has extensive power, comparable to the rights of ecclesiastical superiors in the Catholic Church.

In defense of the synodal system, Orthodox writers appeal to Sacred Scripture, which shows that the Apostles settled controversies and treated questions of moment by means of synods. Collegial government, they add, is also more in conformity with fraternal charity. The dogmatic foundation for this system is found in the text of the Byzantine Nicene Creed. In the Slavonic version of the Creed, the word *Katholike* is translated *subornaiia,* which etymologically means synodal or conciliar. Orthodox theologians say that the ancient translators by this version wished to show that the true Church of Christ is recognized by its collegial character.

At the convention of all Patriarchal Churches held in Moscow in 1927, the assembly declared that the term *sobornost* must be understood of the conciliar form of the Church. It means "conciliarity," and stands for the joint possession by all the members of the Church of all its gifts and properties. Thus the prerogatives of ultimate authority and infallibility belong to the whole ecclesiastical community. *Sobornost,* from the Russian *sobor,* "assembly," has no exact English equivalent, but generally denotes the quality needed for charitable collaboration, with stress on the cooperation of the people. It is a feature of their Church, say the Russians, in contrast with the emphasis on authority in Roman Catholicism and the individualism of the Protestant communions.

Theoretically national autocephalism precludes anything like a real primacy of jurisdiction on the part of any prelate. Even the Ecumenical Patriarch of Constantinople has only a primacy of honor and precedence, but not of ultimate authority. In practice, however, the autocephalous churches do acknowledge a kind of primacy of jurisdiction, whether to their local prelate or the metropolitan or the patriarch. Yet the acknowledgment fluctuates and differs with the regions and the degree of autonomy from State control.

Mutual relations between the autocephali vary. On principle they enjoy equal rights, like politically independent nations. They call each other sister churches, and are urged to practice fraternal love and ecclesiastical unity, which they manifest in several ways. When a new prelate is elected, he informs each autocephaly of his appointment. The prelates of each autocephaly inscribe each other's names in the diptych and make a commemoration during the Sacred Liturgy. Those admitted into communion by one auto-cephaly should be accepted by the others; those excommunicated by one are to be ostracized by all. Doctrinal or disciplinary decisions should be communicated to all the Orthodox churches; and in the same spirit correspondence on problems and methods of procedure is encouraged, and when a council is convoked, each auto-cephalous body is to be represented.

A midway theory of government, between autocephalous and monarchical, was strongly advocated in Orthodox circles until modern times, and has recently found favor among Eastern theologians. The idea is basically an ecclesiastical oligarchy, founded on the notion that the Apostles were of equal authority but they gave supreme jurisdiction not to one of their number but to a number of prelates equal in power. Two forms have been advocated, the pentarchy and tetrarchy, each within the limits of authentic Orthodox ecclesiology.

According to the pentarchical theory, supreme authority in the Church would be ascribed to five mutually independent Patriarchs, equal in authority and simultaneously governing the universal Church, namely Rome, Constantinople, Alexandria, Antioch and Jerusalem. Just as the body is ruled by five senses, so God is said to have willed His Church to be directed by five Patriarchs, among whom is included the Roman Pontiff.

Theologians who exclude the pope from the universal Church on account of schism and heresy logically adopted the tetrarchical theory, which consigns the supreme jurisdiction of the Church to the four Oriental Patriarchs, minus the pope, whose primacy of honor passed from Rome to Constantinople with the change of empire at the time of Charlemagne.

MONASTIC LIFE. Monasticism is an essential feature of Eastern Orthodoxy. Yet its concept is quite different from the religious life in the West, where a great variety of rules and apostolic needs has produced a corresponding variety of communities dedicated to following the Christian counsels. Harnack once remarked that an

Orthodox monastery is the most perfect relic of the fourth century left in the world. Its spirit and ideals are still those which St. Benedict found and developed in Europe, but which the Orthodox have inherited from St. Basil and retained practically unchanged.

With rare exception, Orthodox monks do not engage in teaching, preaching, or the ministry. That is the concern of the bishops and secular (white) clergy, as distinct from the black clergy in monasteries, who are only a small fraction of the total monastic population. Practically all of them follow the Rule of St. Basil; the monastery on Mt. Sinai and some others in Lebanon and on the Red Sea prefer the Rule of St. Anthony the Hermit.

Each monastery (*laura*) is independent of all the rest, with no ultimate superior like a provincial or general; although most lauras are under the jurisdiction of the local Metropolitan or even the Patriarch. However daughter monasteries (*kellia*) are subject to the abbot of their parent laura. The abbot (*Hegumenos*) is elected by his own monks, approved by the Metropolitan, enthroned in a special ceremony and governs for life in cenobitic monasteries.

Of the thousand or more Orthodox monasteries scattered throughout Europe and Asia, the most famous is the monastic republic on the Holy Mountain, Athos, at the northernmost of the three peninsulas that jut from the Chalcis in Greece. There are twenty monasteries on the mountain, eleven following the cenobitic rule and nine the idiorrhythmic.[35] The word cenobite is derived from the Greek *koinos* (common) and *bios* (life); idiorrhythmic comes from *idios* (one's own) and *rhythmos* (fashion or mode).

The cenobitic rule insists on perfect obedience to the abbot, elected for life by monks who have been in religion at least six years. He is spiritual master of the community, but has the assistance of others in external administration. Monks receive property, clothing and food from the abbot; they eat their meals in common.

Idiorrhythmic monasteries first appeared in the fifteenth century and are directed by two annually changed trustees, elected from the ten or fifteen senior monks, whose decisions they enforce. A spiritual father (*pneumatikos*) has charge of the interior life of the monks. Individual members retain their property, eat meals in their own cells, which may be two or three rooms, and are left to their own judgment on matters of austerity. The cenobites consider the idiorrhythmic rule lax; but they are answered that personal initiative in the spiritual life is not stifled under the broader discipline. Actually the cenobitic are more austere and cater to a more hardy type of ascetic.

Before entering one of the monasteries on Athos, a man "from the world" visits several and chooses one, at which he presents his application. He must be at least eighteen, a member in good standing of the Orthodox Church and entering without coercion. After about three years of probation, he has the option of remaining a "beginner" without vows, or seeking advancement by taking the four vows of stability, obedience, poverty and chastity. In token of his new status, he receives a first name identical in initial with the rejected Christian name. The new name is that of a deceased saint, who serves as an inspiration; the surname is that of the monastery. Religious on this level are called "monks of the little habit." Those who seek greater perfection may do so after years of experience, to become "monks of the great habit," with duties of more prayer, stricter fasting, and more severe discipline.

The monks on Mount Athos are generally called from bed at eleven at night for an hour's private prayer, and later in the small hours for Matins and the chanting of communal hymns. There are two meals a day, with household duties interrupted by regular community prayers. Supper and Compline are between six and seven. Monks are to occupy the stalls assigned to them, and are regularly checked by the abbot to note any absentees.

Two characteristic practices in Orthodox monasteries are keeping the liturgical vigils and fasts. There are more than fifty vigils a year, which call for continuous services throughout the evening, night and following morning. Fasting varies between the cenobitic and idiorrhythmic rule. One meal without oil is taken about noon in the *coenobia* on Mondays, Wednesdays and Fridays throughout the year; and two meals on other days. No meat is served, but fish is allowed. The idiorrhythmic rule requires abstinence from cheese, butter and meat on Wednesdays and Fridays, with a stricter diet during the season of Lent, which begins on Quinquagesima Sunday, and on certain fast days before the great feasts of the year.

The general principles of Orthodox monasticism apply equally to men and women, except that before the Russian revolution "unenclosed" nuns were practically unknown. But now they engage in active works of mercy among the sick and indigent. The same change has affected some monasteries of men, who were pressured by the government and public opinion to undertake teaching in schools, conducting agricultural colleges, preaching missions and otherwise becoming involved in secular affairs. However, the number of monks and nuns who have made the turn over is fractional, and one of the major tensions they experience is the conflict of ancient ideals with the increased demands, often under severe sanction from civil authorities, to abandon what the Fathers of Eastern monasticism call the "angelic life" of separation from the world and contemplation of God.

LITURGY AND WORSHIP

The liturgy and ritual of the Eastern Churches are the product of a long process of development reaching back to the early centuries, and find their roots in the traditional doctrine of the Eucharist. Although their writers avoid the term "transubstantiation," they commonly believe in a very real presence of Christ in the Eucharist. In fact their ecumenical efforts with the Protestants often reach an impasse in the unequivocal insistence on a complete change taking place at the consecration of the elements at Mass.

We believe that the substance (*ousian*) of bread and wine remain no longer, but the very Body and Blood of the Lord, under the form and figures of bread and wine, that is under the accidents (*sumbebêkosin*). Also that under every part or smallest bit of the bread and wine there is not a part of the Lord's Body, but the entire whole Lord Christ according to His substance: that is with the soul and divinity as He is perfect God and perfect Man.

So that though there be many Eucharists celebrated in the world at one and the same hour, there are not many Christs, or many bodies of Christ, but one and the same Christ is present in all and every Church of the faithful, and there is one Body and Blood. Not that the Body of the Lord which is in heaven descends upon the altar; but because that Bread which is laid on the altar, and there offered in every Church, is by consecration changed and transubstantiated and made one and the same with that which is in heaven.[36]

When modern Orthodox theologians balk at the word "transubstantiation," their objections may be generally reduced to an unwillingness to accept the Latinized version decreed by the Council of Trent. They prefer the Greek *metousiôsis* or "transelementa-tion," but the concept behind the term is practically the same.

THE EPIKLESIS. A more serious problem concerns the moment at which the Eucharistic change takes place. With the doubtful exception of the Nestorian Christians, all the Eastern liturgies con-tain the words of institution in the Holy Sacrifice, "This is my Body," and "This is the chalice of my Blood." But they consider these words either nonessential or inadequate, on the score that an-other prayer, the Epiklesis or invocation of the Holy Spirit, is neces-sary. In the Orthodox liturgy, the Epiklesis is that ritual prayer in which God the Father is asked to send down the Holy Spirit and to effect the Eucharistic conversion, changing the sacred gifts by His divine power.

In the Liturgy of St. John Chrysostom, after the words of insti-tution, the priest recites the prayer, "We offer You this reasonable and unbloody sacrifice, and we pray You, beg You, and implore You to send down Your Holy Spirit on us and on these present gifts; and to make this bread the precious Body of Your Christ, and what is in this chalice the precious Blood of Your Christ, changing them by Your Holy Spirit." [37] Similar prayers are found in the other Eastern liturgies.

Three schools of thought exist among the Orthodox on the Epiklesis. One group attributes the consecration to the words of institution and the Epiklesis taken together; another says the Epik-lesis fructifies what is only seminally expressed in the previous for-mula; and a third holds that the entire consecratory power is in the Epiklesis. In the last theory, the words of institution are taken as a mere historical narrative. The trend in recent years has been away from the intransigence previously shown on the subject towards an acceptance of the Catholic doctrine which identifies the form of consecration with Christ's words instituting the Sacrament.

STRUCTURE OF THE LITURGY. Orthodox writers summarize the differences between Western and Eastern celebrations of the Eu-charistic Liturgy by saying that the Eucharist for an Orthodox Christian is not so much a sudden intervention of the divine from above, as a gradual revelation of the divine presence which is always here but remains hidden because of the sinfulness of men. A mystical union of the soul with God, through the operation of the Holy Spirit, also typifies the Eastern approach to the Liturgy.

Special emphasis is placed on the Eucharistic Sacrifice as a re-enactment of the whole life span of Christ, in which priest, deacon and the laity have essential roles to play. The service itself is divided into three parts, corresponding to three phases in the life of the Savior. In the *Prothesis* or preparation, the infancy and hidden life of Christ are commemorated; the *Synaxis* or assembly, which in Catholic terms is the Mass of the Catechumens, reminds the faithful of the teaching and healing ministry of the Redeemer; while the third part, the *Anaphora* or offering of the gifts, properly speaking the Liturgy of the Faithful, recalls the final events of the Gospel narrative: the Last Supper, the Cross, Resurrection, Ascension and descent of the Holy Spirit.

Among other functions during the Prothesis, the round loaf of leavened bread is cut into particles, placed on the diskos and repeatedly incensed; litanies are recited for various causes like peace, the Church, bishop, civil rulers, and fruits of the earth; and a series of antiphons is sung by the choir and ministers.

In the Mass of the Catechumens, the Trisagion is sung daily, invoking "Holy God, holy strong One, holy immortal One, have mercy on us," three times, followed by the *Gloria Patri* and then again, "Holy Immortal One, have mercy on us," and finally the whole invocation, "Holy God." While the choir sings, the priest is reciting other prayers; a reader sings the Epistle, and the deacon the Gospel, after incensation. When the deacon announces, "All catechumens go out; not one catechumen shall stay," the Synaxis is over.

Although the Anaphora is strictly speaking the Canon of the Mass, the Mass of the Faithful begins with the invitation to the faithful to "pray to the Lord in peace," along with other prayers and the famous *Cherubikon* when the choir sings, "Let us, who mystically represent the Cherubim, and who sing to the life-giving Trinity the thrice-holy hymn, put away all earthly cares so as to receive the King of all things escorted by the army of angels." At the word, "King," the Great Entrance takes place, which is the dramatic moment of the Orthodox Liturgy. The royal doors are opened and after prayers and incensation a solemn procession goes through the church, carrying the elements to be consecrated.

The sequence of prayers from the Creed to Communion is not unlike that familiar to Catholics of the Latin rite, but the external ceremonies are quite different. Choir and priest alternate more frequently, the doors separating celebrant from people are closed and shut several times, special litanies are said, a little hot water is added to the consecrated chalice, and the consecration takes place behind the *Ikonostasis* or screen which divides the sanctuary from the nave. It is pierced by three doors, the central or Royal Door admitting to the altar, and those on the right and left corresponding to the sacristy and place of preparation of the elements for Mass.

Holy Communion is received by priest, deacon and people under both species. However in administering to the sick or from the tabernacle, the consecrated Host is dipped into unconsecrated wine. Practice differs, but the Orthodox laity receive the Eucharist only rarely; one custom is four times a year on the major feasts. In the liturgy of St. John Chrysostom, the priest takes with a spoon part of the Host which is in the chalice, soaked in the consecrated wine, and gives it to the communicant, saying, "The servant of God, N.N., receives the holy and precious Body and Blood of Jesus Christ, Lord, God and Savior, for the forgiveness of his sins and for life everlasting."

The final part of the Liturgy includes a short litany with the singers, a prayer to the image of Christ, consuming the remnants of the consecrated elements, blessing and distribution to the people of the unconsecrated bread and concluding orations. At the end the doors are again shut to separate the celebrants from the congregation.

RITES AND OFFICES. Besides the Eucharistic Liturgy and the sacraments, Orthodox prayer books contain more than forty other rites and sacred blessings, covering every need and phase of human life. In all these ceremonies the stress is on the Church, which the people believe has power to sanctify and purify all life, both matter and spirit, and that whenever a benediction is received the blessing comes through the assembly from the Holy Spirit who animates the body of His faithful.

The Divine Office is held in high respect, although its full recitation and chant are limited to religious communities. Unlike the Roman Breviary, it is not combined into a single set of books but various parts must be drawn from different sources. Consisting essentially of the Psalms, it also contains numerous hymns, prayers, litanies and antiphons. Secular priests say as much as devotion and time allow, because the complete office (in at least one rite) is said to take eight hours to complete.

Prayers to the Virgin are featured in the office, addressing her, "Honored above the Cherubim, bearing the incarnate Word, Mother of God, we praise you. Hail, cause of our joy; hail, end of the curse of Adam; hail, throne of the King; hail, bearer of Him who bears all things. Spouse and Virgin, hail." An evening hymn that dates from at least the third century, the *Phos hilaron* (Kindly Light), was Newman's inspiration for the prayer he wrote shortly before his conversion. "Kindly Light of the Father's glory, blessed and holy Jesus Christ, now that we see the setting sun and light the evening lamps, again we worship God, the Father, Son and Holy Spirit. At all times it is right to praise You, Son of God and Life-giver, and so the whole world shall always tell Your glory."

Current services of the Orthodox Church follow a complex system of cycles, of which the first is the seven days of the week. Sunday is dedicated to the Resurrection, Monday to the angels, Tuesday to John the Baptist and the prophets, Wednesday and Friday in honor of Christ's Passion, Thursday is in honor of the apostles, St. Nicholas and all the saints, and Saturday commemorates all the faithful departed, especially the martyrs. Another cycle is based on the eight musical modes, each with its own set of hymns. A new mode is introduced on Saturday night and dominates the offices of the Church for the rest of the week. After eight weeks the cycle is repeated.

The annual cycle is the most comprehensive, with each day commemorating its own saints and some important event in biblical or Christian history. A special book, the *Typicon*, gives the rules and rubrics for conducting services and choosing prayers and hymns for each day. For two periods of the year the liturgical tempo changes. Lenten services are unusually long and penitential, calling for kneeling and prostration; whereas Easter is celebrated with signs of joy and festivity. The Royal Doors are not closed for seven days, and no one kneels during the six weeks following Easter Sunday. To care for all these liturgical needs, the Church provides a variety of books, in addition to the Missals and books of the Divine Office. Besides the *Typicon* at least seven are commonly used: the *Horologion* covers the unchangeable parts of the services and serves as a scaffolding for the rest of public worship, the *Octoekhos* incorporates the eight modes of musical chant, the *Menaia* (in twelve volumes) gives the hymns for daily commemoration, the *Triodion* and *Pentikostarion* serve the Lenten and Easter seasons, the *Litourgion* and *Euchologion* are used for conducting Easter worship. Manuals of prayers are also designed for the laity, and may include daily Bible lessons for private recitation.

Orthodox liturgical worship is designed to inspire by appealing to all the senses: the eyes by beholding the sacred painting of ikons, the ears by hearing the songs, the incense surrounds the worshiper with aromatic fumes, the palate is served by tasting both species of the Eucharist and the sacred bread (*antidôron*), the body joins in prayer by means of symbolic gestures. More than in any other branch of Christendom, Orthodox liturgy stresses the element of mystery and sense of community in public worship, based on the principle that religion is primarily a raising of the mind and will to God and that communal prayer is most pleasing to the Trinity, which itself is a social concept of the Divinity.

HETERODOX EASTERN CHURCHES

Although the Orthodox Christians represent by far the majority membership in the Eastern Churches not in communion with Rome, two other groups, the Monophysites and Nestorians, are also called Eastern and follow much of the Oriental ritual but their theology is heterodox by traditional Christian standards.

The Monophysites, from the Greek *monos* (one) and *phusis* (nature), hold, in general, that Christ had only a divine nature, as opposed to the orthodox teaching that He was true God and perfect man.

The essentials of Monophysite doctrine go back to Apollinaris of Laodicea (*c.* 310-390), for whom the man Christ had no human spirit, which was replaced by the divine Logos. But the real foundations of Monophysitism were laid by Eutyches (c. 374-454), archimandrite of a monastery at Constantinople, who said he was only repeating the doctrine of St. Cyril of Alexandria. His opposition to Nestorianism led Eutyches to the other extreme of claiming that the manhood of Christ was transformed into or absorbed by the divine nature. On this theory the redemption of the world by the passion and death of Christ became theologically impossible.

While there is some question of how unorthodox Eutyches was personally, the doctrine attached to his name and developed by his followers was condemned by the Council of Chalcedon in 451. In the classic form of Eutychian Monophysitism, the two natures of Christ are considered mixed or blended to produce a composite who is not properly God nor really man, but one and the other simultaneously, much as a drop of water dissolves in wine or as the elements of hydrogen and oxygen combine to make water.

A dominant type of Monophysitism was started by Julian of Halicarnassus (died after 518), who so spiritualized the man Christ as to make Him incorruptible and immortal from the moment of incarnation. Dubbed the Phantasiasts, Julian's followers were like the earlier Docetists, for whom the humanity and sufferings of Christ were only apparent and not real.

The Julianists were opposed by Severus, patriarch of Antioch (c. 464-538), who rejected Eutychianism and ostensibly professed that Christ was both God and man. Yet he and his disciples were not orthodox because they accused the Council of Chalcedon of Nestorianism, refused to accept the Church's terminology to describe the Incarnation, and explained the union of the two natures of Christ by analogies and in language that openly favored Monophysitism.

The adversaries of Chalcedon were soon divided into opposing sects and later formed churches which catered to their respective beliefs. They finally consolidated into three principal bodies: the Copts and Abyssinians; the Syrian Jacobites, named after their leader, Jacob Baradaeus (c. 500-578), and the Armenians. All three bodies still exist and accept the Fathers of the Church prior to Chalcedon, but they differ among themselves, partly in doctrine and mainly in liturgical practice.

Coptic Christians number about a million and are concentrated in Egypt. Their liturgy is derived from that of St. Mark, and a characteristic custom is the five great fasts: of Nineve before Lent (14 days), Lent (55 days), Advent (28 days), before the Ascension (9 days), and before the Assumption of the Virgin (15 days). In 1948 the Monophysites of Abyssinia became independent of the Egyptian Copts, and today the Ethiopian Church counts the majority of that country's sixteen million population.

Syrian Jacobites number less than half a million, and follow the Antiochean liturgy of St. James. One of their customs is to make the sign of the cross with one finger, to express belief in the one nature of Christ. However the term "Jacobites" is also used to describe the Monophysite Christians in Egypt.

Unlike the Copts and Jacobites, the Armenians were not represented at Chalcedon, but around the year 500 for political reasons they repudiated the council and formed a church which has a current membership of three million. The Armenians never entered into full communion with religious bodies that are professedly Monophysite.

Present-day Monophysites are closer to the mitigated variety of Severus than the radical form of Eutychianism. Their churchmen consistently oppose the latter as heresy, and in their creedal formulas approximate the wording if not the full doctrine of traditional Christianity.

Nestorianism was a fifth century heresy which held there were two distinct persons in the incarnate Christ, one human and the other divine, as against the orthodox teaching that Christ was a divine person who assumed a human nature.

Its name was taken from Nestorius (died *c.* 451), a native of Germanicia in Syria. As a monk in Antioch he came under the influence of that school of exegesis, with its emphasis on the literal instead of the spiritual or merely typical sense of Scripture. A powerful speaker, he became bishop of Constantinople in 428, but in the same year gave offense by his preaching against the expression then popular in the city, of *Theotokos* (Mother of God), as applied to Mary. When his chaplain, Anastasius, forbade the use of the term as savoring of heresy, Nestorius supported him, but soon came into conflict with St. Cyril of Alexandria and the Egyptian monks.

Both sides appealed in 430 to Pope Celestine I who sustained Cyril and threatened Nestorius with excommunication. When he refused to submit, an ecumenical council was summoned at Ephesus through the intervention of the emperor Theodosius II (431). Nestorius was promptly condemned and told to retract. Complications arose when John, the Patriarch of Antioch, led forty bishops to side with Nestorius. However, on arrival of the papal legates from Rome, 198 prelates upheld the first condemnation, deposed Nestorius, and repudiated the rebel council of John of Antioch. After two years of negotiation, a "creed of union" was adopted by the dissenters and in 435 Nestorius himself was forced into exile where he died not long afterwards.

The theology of Nestorianism can best be understood as a reaction to Apollinarianism, which separated the two natures in Christ to the point of denying His humanity. While properly insisting against Apollinarius that Christ had a perfect human nature, Nestorius could not conceive a complete existing nature that was not also a person, namely, an autonomous subject of existence and its own activity. Consequently, though he admitted that in Christ there was a divine person, he claimed there was also a human personality.

Postulating two separate persons in Christ, when Nestorius came to describe their union, he could not have them joined ontologically (in their being) or hypostatically (constituting one person), but only morally or psychologically. They would be united only by a perfect agreement of the two wills in Christ, and by a harmonious communication of their respective activities. This harmony of wills (*eudoxia*) and the communion of action to which it gives rise, are what forms the composite personality (*henosis*) of Christ.

In the Nestorian system, therefore, we cannot speak of a true communication of idioms, i.e., that while the two natures of Christ are distinct, the attributes of one may be predicated of the other in view of their union in the one person of Christ. Accordingly it could not be said that God was born, that He was crucified or died; Mary is not the Mother of God, except in the broad sense of giving birth to a man whose human personality was conjoined to the Word of God.

Nestorianism did not disappear with the Council of Ephesus. Twenty years later the Council of Chalcedon (451), which condemned Eutyches for confounding the two natures in Christ, also took issue with Nestorius. In the next century, the II Council of Constantinople (553) again rejected the Nestorian theory while extolling the orthodoxy of Cyril of Alexandria.

Through the efforts of Ibas, Bishop of Ephesus from 435, and Barsumas, Bishop of Nisibis from 457, Nestorianism was developed into a rounded theology and transported to Persia and Asia Minor where a small but influential sect was founded. The Nestorian Church survives to the present day under the name of Assyrian Christians.

Among other divergences from the Eastern Orthodox, the Nestorian Church has dropped a number of the sacraments. Confirmation was at first identified with baptism and then omitted altogether; the sacrament of penance has gone out of use except in the rare case of reconciliation of an apostate; holy unction has also practically disappeared. An unusual fact about the Nestorian celebration of the Eucharist is that their original liturgical books had omitted the words of institution; and, in spite of efforts by certain missionaries of the Anglican Church to have books printed which include the words of Christ at the Last Supper, some Nestorian priests still omit the formula of consecration.

A studied comparison of the orthodox and heterodox Oriental bodies would further reveal the cleavage that separates these two segments of Christianity. It would also show how much the majority of Eastern Churches have in common with one whom they call the "Mother Church of the West."

16. Protestantism

THERE is a legitimate sense in which Protestantism refers to all Christian movements, other than the Roman Catholic Church, that share the heritage of Western Christianity. Even the Churches of Eastern Orthodoxy have been called "Protestant," because they place the seat of ecclesiastical authority outside the papacy and within the believing community.

But these are extensions of a term which has historical rootage. Protestantism as a type of the Christian religion stems from the Reformation, and especially from the work of Luther and Calvin. Four hundred years have changed many things in Protestantism, but they have not effaced the spirit and theological emphases first created by the Reformers in the sixteenth century. Indeed every effort at renewal within Protestant ranks has been based on the principles of the Reformation, whose importance in religious history can scarcely be exaggerated. It marked a turning point in Western civilization and developed a form of religion that is baffling in its complexity, and yet so influential there is no part of Christianity whose life has not been affected by the faith and polity of Protestantism.

HISTORICAL ORIGINS

The great Luther monument at Worms, unveiled in 1868, includes a number of statues of men who are popularly considered heralds of the Reformation. Luther's central figure is encircled by statues of Savonarola, Huss, Wyclif, Reuchlin and Peter Waldo. By implication these men were precursors of the principal doctrines of Luther and of Protestantism, whereas their contribution was definitely minor and often tenuous, with only the single thread of unity that all had somehow come into conflict with the papacy.

More recent historians admit the disparity of ways which led the Reformers away from Rome, and consider it superfluous to find any forerunners of the original Luther whose genius alone, they feel, produced the Reformation and laid the foundations of Protestantism. However, one exception is admitted, namely, the influence of contemporary Nominalism, particularly in the form in which it was taught by William of Ockham (1300-1349). "I am a member of Ockham's school," Luther boasted. Time and again he referred to the debt he owed the fourteenth century philosopher for the ideas he used in his contest with Rome. Ockham's teaching was so much that of the schools through which Luther passed that the latter simply described him as "Magister meus." [1]

Ockham questioned the power of reason to prove the existence of God, the immortality of the soul, and human freedom. He held that these truths can be known with certainty only through faith. A proposition may be true in philosophy and false in theology. The ultimate cause of the eternal law he placed in the divine will. Absolutely speaking, an unworthy person might be found worthy of heaven if God so willed it. According to his theory of acceptation, everything depends on the will of God; and no supernatural virtue is necessary in the justified. Repression of reason and opposition to ecclesiastical authority were characteristic of Ockham. His political theories played an important part in the development of the conciliar movement, which placed a general council above the pope; and his radical separation of the Church from the world became tinder for the reforming zeal of Luther who looked with horror at the immorality of churchmen in high places and decided the only remedy was to sever relations with this "Babylon of iniquity."

Yet Ockham's influence on Luther must not be overstated. Too often the Reformation is conceived as only the end of a long line of lesser reforms, from the Lollards in England, through the Hussites and Waldenses on the continent, to the final conflagration. There were preludes, of course, of a practical type, as with Wyclif, and more theoretical ones, as in Ockham. But no precursors explain the changes which the Reformers introduced into Christian thought, or the revolutionary positions they adopted in theology.

The birthday of Protestantism is commonly dated October 31, 1517, when Martin Luther nailed his ninety-five theses to the church door of the castle at Wittenberg. Within ten years, every major difference from the parent Roman Catholicism had been stated by Luther, and whatever subsequent development took place only built on the foundations he laid with a clarity and vigor that prompted his friend Melanchthon to say that "Luther is a miracle among men. What he says and writes grips the heart and leaves a marvelous deep impression behind."

His basic principle was an appeal to conscience, personally enlightened by the Spirit, against what he called the accretions of the Roman Church. Standing before the Diet of Worms in 1521, and charged by the Empire with promoting heresy, Luther replied in a statement that has become famous. The imperial judges asked him for a plain reply to this accusation. In a word, was he prepared to recant or not?

Your Imperial Majesty and Your Lordships demand a simple answer. Here it is, plain and unvarnished. Unless I am convicted of error by the testimony of Scripture or—since I put no trust in the unsupported authority of Pope or of councils, since it is plain that they have often erred and often contradicted themselves—by manifest reasoning I stand convicted by the Scriptures to which I have appealed, and my conscience is taken captive by God's word. I cannot and will not recant anything, for to act against our conscience is neither safe for us, nor open to us. On this I take my stand. I can do no other. God help me. Amen.[2]

During the next twenty-five years, until his death in 1546, Luther elaborated this theory of conscience to include the whole construct of the Reformation. The conscience, he taught, is bound up with the word of God in the Scriptures. Therefore, instead of popes and councils, Scripture alone (*sola Scriptura*) became the source of religious knowledge. By the time of the Formula of Concord (1577), this had been canonized into an article of faith, that "Holy Scripture alone is acknowledged as the only judge, norm, and rule, according to which, as by the only touchstone, all doctrines are to be examined and judged, as to whether they are godly or ungodly, true or false." [3] Language could not be clearer on the Scriptures as the fountainhead of all doctrine and the only standard of Christian belief.

However, Scriptures themselves need an interpreter. Since ecclesiastical authority was ruled out, the alternative was the indwelling Spirit of God. Both the antecedent question of which books of the Bible are inspired, and the problem of determining what a given passage means, are subject not to the whims of a human institution (like the Church) but to the ever-present divine light in the soul. If this idea was thematic in Luther, it was systematized by John Calvin in his *Institutes of the Christian Religion,* first published in 1536, to become the greatest single legacy of the Reformation and the *Summa Theologica* of Protestantism.

Accordingly, the principle that by the Spirit alone (*solo Spiritu*) do we understand the Scriptures was axiomatic. "The testimony of the Spirit is more excellent than all reason. For as God alone is a fit witness of Himself in His Word, so also the Word will not find acceptance in men's hearts before it is sealed by the inward testimony of the Spirit." So that "those whom the Holy Spirit has inwardly taught truly rest upon Scripture," and "the certainty it deserves with us, it attains by the testimony of the Spirit. For even if it wins reverence for itself by its own majesty, it seriously affects us only when it is sealed upon our hearts through the Spirit. Therefore, illumined by His power, we believe neither by our own nor by any one else's judgment that Scripture is from God," or that a given meaning attached to a biblical text is divinely true. "But above human judgment we affirm with utter certainty, just as if we were gazing upon the majesty of God Himself, that it has flowed to us from the very mouth of God." [4]

Among the verities that Luther and Calvin were convinced the Spirit had taught them by the ministry of the Word was the complete depravity of human nature since the fall, and consequently that whatever good we do or hope we have of heaven come only from grace (*sola gratia*) and not at all from the effort or good works of man.

Basic to the Reformation theology of grace was the principle that original justice was due to human nature by a strict right of essence. "Original justice," wrote Luther, "was part of man's nature." [5] As a result, when Adam fell and lost the righteousness he possessed, his nature became essentially corrupt and his faculties were intrinsically vitiated. Nothing in the literature of historic Protestantism is more emphatically asserted against the "scholastic innovators" who misinterpreted revelation and the teaching of St. Augustine.

"See what follows," urged Luther, "if you maintain that original righteousness was not a part of nature but a sort of superfluous or superadded gift. When you declare that righteousness was not a part of the essence of man, does it not also follow that sin, which took its place, is not part of the essence of man either?" [6] If this were so, "there was no purpose in sending Christ the Redeemer," whose unique function was to win the grace we need to supply for our complete helplessness and inability to do any good. If, then, we are saved all the credit belongs to God and none to us; grace alone accounts for man's salvation and not in any sense the works of man, whose corruption is capable of nothing but sin and whose freedom, in Luther's phrase is "only an empty phrase." To God alone the glory, therefore, and to His grace the thanks.

One final element belongs to the foundations of Reformation thought, the doctrine that by faith alone (*sola fide*) are we saved, namely, by an absolute trust in God's mercy that in spite of our sinfulness the merits of His Son will hide our sins and spare us from the hell fire that we justly deserve. In the words of the Augsburg Confession (1530), "Our works cannot reconcile us to God or merit remission of sins and grace and justification. This we obtain only by faith, when we believe that we are received into grace on account of Christ." And to make sure there is no mistaking this trust for the dogmatic faith of Catholics, who made acceptance of revealed truths the first requisite for salvation, "Men are warned that the word *faith* does not signify the knowledge of an event—the devils and impious men have that—but it signifies a faith which believes not in an event merely, but also in the effect of an event, namely this article, the remission of sins, i.e., that we have, through Christ, grace, righteousness, and remission of sins." [7]

Thus we have the full complement of principles on which the structure of classic Protestantism was built, likened to the pillars of a massive building: the interior conscience instead of external authority, the Scriptures rather than ecclesiastical tradition, the interior Spirit supplying for the pope and councils, divine grace making up for the innate deficiency of will, and confident trust relying on the promise of the Savior, "because consciences cannot be quieted by any good works, but by faith alone, when they believe assuredly that they have a God who is propitiated for the sake of Christ." [8]

In the four centuries since these concepts were propounded,

they have undergone much development and seen applications that Luther and Calvin never suspected, but their original spirit has not been lost. This spirit has remained fairly constant, and still serves to unite what is externally the most fragmented form of Christianity in existence, whose very beginnings were marked by cleavage and division. For although it is true that Luther was the first of the Protestant Reformers, the churches of the Reformation really had four beginnings: under Luther, Calvin, Henry VIII and the Anabaptists, all within a generation of that Eve of All Saints in Wittenberg. Each prototype has since grown into a multitude of churches and denominations that, in spite of mergers and overlappings, still retain characteristic elements that are traceable to their respective ancestry, along with the common features that first marked the origins of Protestantism.

LUTHERAN AND EVANGELICAL CHURCHES

The religious crisis which Luther and his followers precipitated in Germany occasioned a series of conferences which became landmarks in the history of Protestantism. Summoned by Charles V to the Diet of Worms, Luther refused to submit and was condemned as an outlaw, but taken by the Elector of Saxony into protective custody. Eight years later, at the Diet of Speyer (1529), the Lutheran princes refused to agree that Catholic worship should be free everywhere and the new religion be allowed only in places where it already had some followers. Their "protest" at Speyer became symbolic of the whole movement and gave the name by which the Churches of the Reformation have since become known. When the Diet of Speyer proved inoperative, the Emperor called the Diet of Augsburg (1530) to effect a reconciliation between the Catholics and Reformers. While this attempt failed, a compromise was reached among the factions in the Protestant camp and the agreement was stabilized in the Confession of Augsburg, for which Melanchthon wrote an Apology after the creedal statement was challenged by the Catholics. Both documents are now doctrinal standards in Churches of the Lutheran tradition.

Luther's productivity was phenomenal. There are four Weimar editions of his writings, amounting to eighty-three volumes. The current English translation will run to fifty-five volumes in octavo.

His two catechisms, a larger and smaller, were originally intended "for the improperly indoctrinated Roman clergy who had joined the evangelicals and to the teachers of the parochial schools." They have since been recognized as the most unique of his writings and the most influential, in marked contrast with the polemic tracts he was forced to compose to meet the steady opposition toward leaders of the Reformation.

After Luther's death, the area of conflict widened between his own evangelical disciples and the followers of Calvin and Zwingli. Questions of sin and grace, justification and free will, the ministry and the Lord's Supper, baptism and predestination divided the different groups, even among the Lutherans, who were partially reconciled by the Formula of Concord, which is the last of their fundamental confessions of faith.

By the middle of the seventeenth century, Lutheranism had been established not only in Germany and Central Europe, but in Denmark, where the Church was organized in 1536 with the king as ruling prelate, in Sweden, East Prussia, Iceland, Hungary, Silesia, Poland, and Transylvania. The first Lutherans to make a permanent settlement in America came from Holland to the Dutch New Netherlands (Manhattan) in 1623. Their estimated world membership is eighty million.

DOCTRINE AND WORSHIP. Justification by faith alone lies at the heart of Lutheranism, which strenuously opposes any kind of synergism (Greek *syn*, "with," and *ergon*, "work"), that in the act of conversion the human will can cooperate with the Holy Spirit and God's grace. Its emphasis is always on God's sole activity in the process of salvation.

According to the Augsburg Confession, man has some freedom of the will in matters which do not concern salvation. But in things spiritual, no freedom is left to the natural man, who "cannot work the inward motions, such as the fear of God, trust in God, chastity, patience and the like." [8] Everything in the moral order is the fruit of grace alone. Modern Lutheran manuals of theology are equally intransigent. "One of the consequences of the hereditary corruption is the loss of free will in spiritual matters." And "if by free will is meant the ability to will or desire what is spiritually good . . . we deny that since the Fall man has a free will." [9]

Unlike the Reformed Churches, however, Lutheran bodies abstain from examining too closely into the mystery of predestination which is painfully raised by the denial of freedom in contact with grace. They concentrate on the confidence we should have in God's mercy and the gratitude we owe Him for His promised redemption. In the Evangelical tradition, therefore, God has done everything for us; we have only to trust and give Him thanks. He has already forgiven us; we need only accept His benefit with appreciation. He has already come to us in the person of the Savior; so that nothing can separate us from this treasury of goodness.

Lutheran Churches retain in large measure the pre-Reformation idea of the Atonement as something objective, and not merely personal to each individual. One modification, however, is that they do not consider the sufferings of Christ a satisfaction for sin but a punishment which Christ underwent vicariously on our behalf. This concept of the Atonement is a prominent feature of Lutheran preaching and liturgical hymns.

No area of Lutheran theology more clearly distinguishes it from others, notably the Calvinist, than the doctrine of the Eucharist. Lutherans repudiate any idea of the presence of Christ in the Eucharist in a purely spiritual manner. They hold that He is present in a bodily way, and the communicants partake physically of His body and blood, along with the visible elements. "The body and blood of Christ are received with the bread and wine, not only spiritually by faith, but also orally, in a supernatural and celestial way, because of the sacramental union. He who eats this bread eats the body of Christ." [10] Unlike the Catholic belief, there is no transubstantiation but a kind of impanation (in-breadness) in which Christ's presence exists alongside the substance and accidents of bread and wine, the union between elements and Christ being called sacramental. In the Formula of Concord, the body and blood are said to be present "in, with and under" the bread and wine. Technically the doctrine is known as *consubstantiation*.

Behind this theory is the application of a principle of Christology, adapted from the teaching of Chalcedon, that the two natures in Christ are not commingled or confused, yet are inseparably united. The Reformed Churches maintained that after the Ascension Christ's human nature was on the right hand of the heavenly Father, and therefore only His divinity was really present in the

Eucharist, together with a virtual (but not bodily) presence of His humanity. Lutherans objected that such separation is impossible, so that wherever Christ is present, He is there both as God and man, hence also in the Eucharist.

Upholding the ancient faith that Christ is true God and man, Lutherans made the miracle of the Incarnation central in their tradition and the focus of all their teaching. It was, particularly, concern to preserve such fundamental doctrines as the divinity of Christ that has led Lutheran Churches the world over to promote Christian day schools and, at great sacrifice, build an impressive system of religion-centered education. When civil pressures threatened the parochial schools, they were quick to defend their educational policy.

Whereas the Word of God, our rule of life, enjoins upon all Christian parents the duty of bringing up their children in the nurture and admonition of the Lord; therefore all Christians who educate their children in schools are in duty bound to entrust their children to such schools only as secure the education of children in the nurture and admonition of the Lord, while at the same time it is with us self-understood that we are willing to make good citizens of our children, to the utmost of our ability.[11]

In the development of Lutheran forms of worship, the basic structure was the Roman Catholic Mass, "purged of non-evangelical elements and adapted for the ordinary worshiper." Among the major changes, the most important was the removal of sacrificial prayers from the Canon of the Mass. Luther himself carried out this reform. His idea was to give expression to the doctrine of the Eucharistic Presence without the concept of sacrifice.

The normal sequence of the Canon is the Preface, Sanctus, Words of Institution, Lord's Prayer, Pax Domini, Agnus Dei, and distribution of Holy Communion. In giving the elements to the faithful, the minister says, "Take, eat; this is the true body (blood) of our Lord and Savior Jesus Christ, given into death for (shed for the remission of) your sins. May this strengthen and preserve you in the true faith unto life everlasting."

Another change was to make the sermon an essential part of the Eucharistic service. The word of God, in the sense of the word that is preached, remains to this day a prominent feature of Lutheranism. Orders of worship prescribe the sermon after the Nicene Creed and before the Offertory.

Another innovation that has since become part of most other Protestant churches was the singing of hymns by the congregation during the Communion service. As early as 1526 Luther composed his German Mass (*Deutsche Messe*), in which the *Credo* and *Agnus Dei* were replaced by German hymns so that the whole congregation could sing together. He also replaced the Latin Introit by a hymn in the vernacular and added a prescriptive hymn after the Epistle in place of the Gradual. Luther's love of music was proverbial, and faithful to his memory the churches have made religious songs almost coextensive with divine worship.

Among the authors in common use are Saints Ambrose, Bede, and Bernard of Clairvaux, the Dominican Savonarola, non-Lutheran Reformers like John Huss and the two Wesleys, and more recent writers like John Keble and William Cullen Bryant. Most of the composers are Protestant, but a few Catholics (Palestrina, Gounod and Tallis) are included in standard hymnals. Typical of the robust virility and authentic evangelical theology of the hymns is the well-known masterpiece of Luther, *Ein' feste Burg ist unser Gott.*

A mighty Fortress is our God, a trusty Shield and Weapon;
He helps us free from every need that hath us now overtaken.
    The old evil Foe now means deadly woe;
Deep guile and great might are his arms in fight; on earth is not
        his equal.
    With might of ours can naught be done, soon were our loss
        effected;
But for us fights the Valiant One, whom God Himself elected.
    Ask you, who is this? Jesus Christ it is, of Sabbath Lord,
And there's none other God; He holds the field forever.
    Though devils all the world should fill, all eager to devour us,
We tremble not, we fear no ill, they shall not overpower us.
    This world's prince may still scowl fierce as he will, he can
        harm us none,
He's judged; the deed is done; one little word can fell him.[12]

Customs differ greatly in different countries. In Germany, for instance, the liturgical heritage of Lutheranism has been much reduced; in the United States it is growing at a pace so rapid that concern has been expressed over the "ritualistic movement," comparable to the High and Low Church types in Anglicanism. Lutheran bodies closer to the Reformation spirit have altars, altar candles, vestments, and an order of worship which are remarkably Roman Catholic in external form.

RECENT DEVELOPMENTS. All the principal Lutheran Churches of Reformation times were established institutions following the norm of the Augsburg Treaty of 1555, *cujus regio, ejus religio,* which meant that civil rulers determined the religious affiliation of their subjects. To this day, Lutheranism is the state religion of Norway, Sweden, Denmark and Finland. In Germany the Lutheran Churches continued to be established bodies until the Weimar Constitution of 1919, when Church and State were declared separated throughout the country.

In Scandinavia, the national bodies are supported financially by the civil authorities and administered by a ministry of ecclesiastical affairs, which is a joint Ministry of Church and Education in Norway and Sweden. Except for assistant pastors, bishops and clergy are appointed by the Crown, and Parliament acts as the Church's highest legislative body, in spite of the fact that members of Parliament need not belong to the Lutheran Church.

The European trend has been in the direction of emancipating the Church from political control, and giving it independence in purely spiritual matters. Sweden has a national Church Assembly that can vote on ecclesiastical issues, present recommendations to Parliament, and exercise a kind of veto; but the legal competence of the assembly is naturally limited as long as the Church is officially established. In the United States the congregation is the basic unit of Lutheran church government, with no semblance of the close tie-in with civil powers as in Europe.

During the nineteenth century, two competing theological trends in Lutheranism struggled for mastery in Europe, with heavy overtones in America. In 1821, Friedrich Schleiermacher (1768-1834) published his *Christian Faith* which dates an epoch in the history of modern theology. While rationalists and supernaturalists carried on their fight in schools of divinity, Schleiermacher took the ground from under their contention by removing its main premise. The Christian faith, he claimed, does not consist in any kind of doctrinal propositions. It is a condition of devout feeling and, like all other internal experience, simply an object to be described.

Against the supernaturalists Schleiermacher maintained that Christianity is not something to be received on authority from without, but an inward state of our own self-consciousness. Against the rationalists he said religion is not a product of rational thinking, but an emotion of the heart, a feeling which occurs independently of the mind.

The net result of this emphasis on subjective experience was to usher Low Church mentality into Lutheran circles, with an undervaluation of the sacraments and a new stress on revivalism. There was a correlative downgrading of church authority and the development of an ecclesiastical structure built along Free Church and Congregational lines.

In the opposite direction, Lutheran confessionalism reacted against the liberal tendencies of the Enlightenment and the "religion of feeling" to inaugurate what can only be called a Lutheran Renascence. Since the beginning of the present century, interest in Luther's theology and Reformation thought has become the dominant characteristic of the Evangelical Churches. German and Swedish scholars have been the mainstay of the movement, but supported by Danish and Flemish theologians.

One effect of this renascence has been the discovery in Reformation sources of doctrinal principles that lay hidden for centuries, principles that are being exploited in the current drive for Christian unity. The *Una Sancta* movement brings together priests, ministers, theologians and laymen to discuss the prospects of uniting Catholic and Evangelical Christianity. *Die Sammlung* (The Gathering) is a more advanced group of Lutheran pastors which sees in Roman Catholicism a balance that Lutherans desire to reach the fulness of their own Reformation ideals.

In a declaration of principles, *Die Sammlung* calls upon Catholics and Lutherans alike to re-examine their respective positions to find out whether a corporate reunion is possible, without compromise of doctrinal convictions. Under title of the League for Evangelical-Catholic Reunion, the leaders of the movement bear witness to the fact that Christ founded only one Church, which exists in the realm of the visible and is always present, and that according to Scripture and universal Christian belief visible unity is inherent in the nature of the true Church.

The League considers the present division of Christians against the will of Christ. "It is a sin and scandal." Without seeking to blur or level off confessional differences that exist within the Evangelical Church, *Die Sammlung* believes that these contrasts can be overcome only if it should first enter into Catholic unity. Its duty is to strive for the gathering together and the formation of an Evangelical church community united with the Roman Catholic Church.

Corporate reunion with the Catholic Church is commanded because the Catholic Church is the closest to Evangelical Christendom historically, geographically, and spiritually, in comparison with the Churches of the East. It is also commanded because the essential Catholic content of Revelation is already explicitly and visibly transmitted in Sacred Scripture as confirmed in great measure by Evangelical exegetes of modern times, and this content is preserved and defended by the Catholic Church. In it is also found subordination to the authoritative rule of the Apostles and of the Bishops, established by them. From this flows a duty insufficiently comprehended by the Reformation.

Evangelical Christendom must learn that the Bishops, having at their head the possessor of the Petrine Office, make decisions with the authority of the Holy Ghost, which are binding in conscience for the individual Christian.[13]

If sentiments like these are comparatively rare, the spirit behind them is becoming more deeply felt in Lutheran writers and churchmen on both sides of the Atlantic. They are impelled, they say, by the will of God, by Evangelical responsibility for Catholic unity, and a concern to save the Church of Christ from the assaults of Communism.

An interesting sidelight of the *Sammlung* approach has been the restoration of community religious life in the Lutheran Churches. While still on a microscopic scale, the idea has taken hold in Germany and the States and shows signs of further development. The Sisters of St. Mary on the continent were founded in 1944 at Darmstadt. One of their main concerns is to pray for the unity of Christendom. Members wear a religious habit of austere gray, and they all pledge to live according to the three evangelical counsels of poverty, chastity and obedience. After a year's probation, the novitiate lasts from four to five years. The Sisters maintain a continuous vigil of prayer, holding services in a chapel, and engage in works of charity by caring for children, helping the sick, imprisoned and delinquent. They also do catechetical work.

In America a similar organization was started by a group of men who call themselves the Congregation of the Servants of Christ. The articles of incorporation set forth that "the rule, life and worship of the Congregation shall be in agreement with the Augsburg Confession."

CALVINIST AND REFORMED TRADITION

Reformed Protestantism stems from the teachings of John Calvin, synthesized in his massive *Institutes of the Christian Religion,* and for that reason often simply called Calvinism. Its doctrinal position has been stabilized in the Reformed Churches of Europe and America, and the Presbyterian bodies in France, England and the United States. Baptists have also been deeply influenced by Calvinism.

Similar to the symbolic writings of the Lutherans, there are Reformed confessional documents, but they have never played a major role in the Churches' life and policy. The main reason is that the Scriptures hold a towering position in Calvinism, with everything else, including "articles of faith," relegated to second place. Yet the importance of doctrinal standards should not be minimized; it is only that they are relatively less binding than their Evangelical counterparts.

In Switzerland the most important confessional statements are the two Helvetic Confessions of 1536 and 1566, and the *Consensus Tigurinus* of 1549. Where the Confessions are strongly Zwinglian, the *Consensus* is a compromise document drawn up by Calvin. A feature of all three is the doctrine of the Eucharist, which oscillates between the pure symbolism of Zwingli (1484-1531) and the Calvinist theory that Christ is present in Holy Communion "for all who truly believe."

In France the composition of Calvin, *Confessio Gallicana,* first drafted in 1559 at a general synod of St. Germain, is still the confessional document of the French Reformed Church. Predestination is lucidly expounded in a long article and the Eucharist is said to be received by the communicant *spirituellement.* Germany produced a parallel statement of faith in the Heidelberg Catechism of 1563, a practical and edifying work with a moderate Eucharistic and Christological doctrine. In order to avoid offending the Lutherans, there is no express mention of Predestination, but a strongly anti-Catholic tone pervades the document. The Heidelberg Catechism has become popular also in Switzerland, Hungary and Poland. In 1566 the Netherlands adopted their *Confession Belgica,* approved by a synod held at Antwerp, as the last continental document of this type compiled during the Reformation.

The Reformed faith was recognized as the national religion by the Scottish Parliament in 1560, and in the same year published the *Confessio Scoticana,* which is mildly Calvinist, with an almost Lutheran doctrine of the Eucharist and the doctrine on Predestination expressed in ambivalent terms.

However the most significant statement of Calvinist teaching is not a *Confessio* but a set of Canons formulated (1619) by the Synod of Dortrecht (Dort) in the Dutch Reformed Church. The document arose out of a heated controversy on the question of Predestination. Most ministers and theologians in Holland held the doctrine in its full severity. God had from eternity arbitrarily chosen some persons for heaven and predestined others to damnation, irrespective of their faith or good works and dependent solely on the inscrutable will of God.

A less absolute tendency was advocated by the Arminian party, named after Jacob Arminius (1560-1609), professor at Leyden. Under adverse pressure from the orthodox clergy, they submitted a Remonstrance to the government in which they stated five theses that favored Catholic teaching on grace and became the subject of a celebrated controversy. God's predestination, they stated, rests upon His foreknowledge that certain people will persevere to the end; Christ died for all men, although only believers share in His merits; divine grace is not irresistible and it is possible for a person once in grace to lose the friendship of God.

In view of its importance, the synod invited Reformed representatives from other countries, including delegates from England. In its one hundred and thirty-seventh session, the Arminians were declared heretics and a detailed statement of orthodox Calvinism was compiled. It said in substance that the election of the predestined depends solely on God, Christ died only for the predestined, grace cannot be resisted, and those who have received irresistible grace cannot subsequently fall away.

The Westminster Confession was formulated in 1646, to

become the standard of doctrine for Presbyterian Churches in the British Isles and America. A critical passage in the American version was changed with regard to the papacy. From an originally polemic statement, the present text reads, "the claim of any man to be the vicar of Christ and the head of the Church is unscriptural, without warrant in fact, and is a usurpation dishonoring to the Lord Jesus Christ." [14]

DISTINCTIVE FEATURES. The guiding motif of Churches in the Reformed tradition is the affirmation of God's sovereign majesty. Every phase of doctrine, worship and church policy is affected by this stress. Where Lutheranism might be described as anthropological, because its central doctrine is man's salvation, Calvinism is theocentric in that its governing principle is the service and glory due to God from His creatures.

Confessional standards repeatedly speak of the Glory of God which is man's universal purpose in existence. Thus the Genevan Catechism begins with the statement that "God has created us, and put us into this world in order that He might be glorified by us," and the first response of the Shorter Westminster Catechism reads, "Man's chief end is to glorify God."

Consistent with this accent, the distance between God and man is brought out in the strongest terms. In the Westminster Catechism, it is said "the distance between God and the creature is so great that although reasonable creatures do owe obedience unto Him as their Creator, yet they could never have any fruition of Him, as their blessedness and reward, but by some voluntary condescension of God's part, which He hath been pleased to express by way of covenant." [15]

Predestination and Election are organically connected with this notion of sovereignty. Since man's salvation is due entirely to God and man contributes nothing, all the praise is due to the Creator, even when He condemns the damned to eternal sufferings.

Unexpectedly the Reformed doctrine on grace has not paralyzed human activity. If anything it stimulates action, though of a particular kind. Predestination serves the function of an ethical motive, on the assumption that those who reflect on this mystery are all chosen to heavenly glory. Armed with the conviction that they are predestined, believers can afford to rejoice at their happy lot and go about life's affairs with a nonchalance that might scandalize less hardy Christians.

The whole complex of Reformed mentality on this subject is illustrated in Karl Barth, the Swiss theologian, whose commentary on the Lord's Prayer is a witness to the abiding Calvinist tradition in modern times. In the fifth petition of the Our Father are two suppositions that seem irreconcilable with orthodox Calvinism. For when we ask God to forgive us our trespasses, we imply that in some sense our sins are not yet remitted and that our prayers will contribute to this remission. When we add, "as we forgive those who trespass against us," the implication is that our own practice of merciful charity somehow determines the degree of mercy that God will bestow on us.

But Barth will have none of either. We pray, "forgive us our trespasses," and with good reason, because our lives are continuously sinful. Can our prayer for mercy avail us to obtain pardon? Not at all. "Neither man's offense, nor man himself as a sinner can be exculpated. Man is unpardonable. He has no right whatsoever to ask for a remission of his debt." [16]

Perhaps, Barth suggests, we place some kind of condition when we pray that shows God's forgiveness is somehow determined by ourselves. "No, the phrase: as we forgive those who trespass against us, is only a necessary sign to make us understand the pardon of God." When He forgives us, we become conscious of His mercy and confident of salvation. This confidence "necessarily opens wide our hearts, our feelings and our judgment with regard to our fellowmen." Some people mistakenly suppose the words, "as we forgive," are an appeal for the practice of charity. They are wrong. "This is not an exhortation, 'Come, be merciful,' but a simple statement of fact: 'When you receive forgiveness from God, you become capable of forgiveness to others.' " [17] In other words, prayer is essentially an expression of gratitude for graces received, not a petition to obtain them, and for the elect who are sure of their destiny this gratitude can well pour itself out in deeds of generosity.

Reformed teaching on the sacraments is distinctive. God is not bound by the sacramental instruments of grace, and, in any case, they are effectual only to the elect. They are "holy signs and seals of the covenant of grace," whose efficacy somehow depends "upon the work of the Spirit, and the word of institution, which contains, together with a precept authorizing the use thereof, a promise of benefit to worthy receivers." [18]

Baptism does not remit sin, but signifies becoming "ingrafted into Christ," and though it does not effect regeneration, yet infant baptism is retained. The Eucharistic doctrine has been the focus of controversy with Evangelical Protestantism since Reformation times and, like the Calvinist position on Predestination, has been much modified through tension. Present-day Reformed theology steers a middle course between the purely symbolic conception of Zwingli, who limited the sacrament to a commemorative meal and a confession of faith in Christ, and the Lutheran idea of a bodily presence and oral participation. Christ is in the Eucharist, they say, really but not bodily; and only the believers partake of Him. Familiar terms are "dynamic presence" and "virtual presence," whereby the communicant receives "the sacrificial virtue or effects of the death of Christ on the Cross."

Most characteristic of Reformed Protestantism is its unitary concept of the governing ministry. There is only one type of authority, the presbytery, but four kinds of office: pastors, teachers, elders and deacons. Presbyteries are usually organized on a geographical basis, but some exist to care for separate language groups or racial minorities. Although there are two grades of jurisdiction technically higher than the presbytery, the latter is the principal ruling body. Presbyteries consist of clerical and lay representatives within a given district, with power to receive and issue appeals or complaints, examine and license candidates for the ministry, resolve questions of doctrine and discipline, unite and divide congregations and, in general, care for whatever pertains to the spiritual welfare of the churches within the presbytery. It is more than coincidental that the only layman among the major Reformers in the sixteenth century, John Calvin, should have developed a form of polity that gives the laity equal share with the clergy in church government. This idea was soon borrowed by other religious bodies and is now practically universal in Protestantism.

FREE CHURCH MOVEMENT

The basic idea behind the Free Church Movement is nonconformity with established Protestant religions, which took different forms in different countries. On the continent the Anabaptists,

Mennonites, and Brethren; in England the Separatists, including Quakers, Baptists and Congregationalists—professed the Free Church principle of dissociating from the doctrines, polity and discipline of the dominant Protestant body in their respective territory.

Continental Free Churchism began with the Anabaptists, the "rebaptizers" who refused to allow their children to be baptized and instituted the baptism of adult believers. They argued that the Reformers were unfaithful to their own tenet of *sola Scriptura* by allowing children to be baptized, since the Bible knows only the baptism of adults. Gradually the Protestant theory of private interpretation led to a cluster of other Anabaptist beliefs and practices which have remained in possession to modern times.

One of the earliest non-conformists was Thomas Munzer (1490-1525) and the Zwickau prophets who appeared at Wittenberg in 1521. Munzer favored the Peasants' Revolt (1525) and taught a doctrine of the Inner Light which reappeared later among the English Quakers. The Swiss Brethren reintroduced believer's baptism as a condition for church membership at Zurich in 1525, along with non-resistance and rejection of Christian participation in civil government. Soon these views spread throughout Switzerland and into Germany.

Communities that found asylum in Moravia, and led by Jacob Hutter (died 1536), founded settlements based on the idea of common property. After many wanderings and trials, the Hutterites became established in Central Europe or migrated to America. A group of Anabaptists in Munster attempted to form a Kingdom of the Saints, whose left-wing segment advocated polygamy. The idea was later revived among the American Mormons or Latter-Day Saints, under the reputed revelations of Joseph Smith (1805-1844). After the Munster episode, the Mennonites were reorganized in Holland and Friesland by Menno Simons (1496-1561), who first left the Catholic Church, joined the Anabaptists, and then founded his own denomination on the twin principle of independent church organization and no common doctrine.

The Anabaptists were vigorously denounced by Luther, Zwingli and Calvin, who encouraged their suppression by force of arms. Their influence on the English Separatists (Baptists, Congregationalists, and Quakers) places them in lineal relationship to the Free Church movement in Anglo-Saxon countries.

John Smyth (1570-1612), exiled Anglican minister, started

the Baptists at Amsterdam in 1609, when he instituted the baptism of conscious believers as the basis of fellowship in a gathered church. Many Baptists were associated with the more radical spiritual and political movements in England in the seventeenth century. They were pioneers in pleas for freedom of conscience and religious liberty. John Bunyan (1628-1688), author of *The Pilgrim's Progress,* was an outstanding figure among them, not only because of his writings but because he advocated a Church community which should include Baptists and paedo-baptists (those who baptized infants).

Most of the Baptist population of the world (about ninety percent) is in the United States, divided into more than twenty bodies and following a modified Calvinism, tinged with Lutheran and Zwinglian elements. Since the stress is on baptism of believers, the attitude towards this sacrament is characteristic of Baptist theology as a whole. Baptism does not bring about the remission of sins or provide salvation. It is a symbol and "only a symbol of the blessed truths upon which remission of sins, salvation, and eternal life depend." There is nothing that comes after faith that is essential to salvation. With rare exception, baptism by immersion is considered essential.

In spite of their variety and individualism, most Baptists have remained strongly attached to the truths of evangelical Christianity. The popular evangelist, Billy Graham, became a Southern Baptist early in youth. Their worship is mainly in the Reformed tradition, and their church organization an American type of independency. Majority rule prevails in Baptist polity, "in accordance with the law of Christ." So that, "the will of the majority having been expressed, it becomes the minority to submit." [19]

Congregationalism is that form of church structure which rests on the independence and autonomy of each local church. It professes to represent the principle of democracy in Church government, said to have been the original type of organization founded by Christ and recognizing only Him as its head. Since all the members of the Church are Christians, they are all equally priests unto God. He is in their midst, wherever two or three are gathered in His name; their thoughts and actions are led by His spirit and, with no authoritarian laws to bind them, they are nevertheless united in Christ with the Church Universal.

The beginnings of Congregationalism are commonly dated from the founding, in 1581, of a church in Norwich, England, by Robert Browne, a Separatist Anglican minister. Browne was demoted from the ministry for teaching "seditious doctrines," notably that the basis of church membership was not submission to episcopal authority but acceptance of a covenant, to which a group of people gave their mutual consent. Pressure from the government forced Browne's followers to move to Holland, and then to America, where, as the Mayflower Pilgrims, they landed at Plymouth, Massachusetts, in 1620.

A few years later they were joined by a group of immigrant Puritans, with whom they signed a compact in 1629, and from whom they inherited a strong Calvinist creedalism that lasted almost two centuries. The Salem trials for witchcraft belong to the early period of New England Congregationalism. By 1730, however, the churches had become quite thoroughly secularized. This induced a reaction, called the Great Awakening, ushered in by Jonathan Edwards (1703-1758), pastor at Northampton, Massachusetts, who was consumed by the sovereignty of God, the fateful brevity of life and its eternal issues.

For more than two centuries, American Congregationalists were mainly concerned with higher education. Harvard was founded in 1636, Yale in 1701, to prepare students for the ministry. At present fifty-one colleges and universities in the United States have professedly Congregationalist affiliations. With expansion, however, came internal tension over doctrinal issues. Two conflicting tendencies threatened to dissolve Congregationalism. By the middle of the last century, about two thousand churches, originally Congregationalist, became Presbyterian; they were looking for a more authoritative and dogmatic church polity. And during the same period a smaller, but even more influential, group of liberals seceded to form the American Unitarian Association.

The current history of Congregationalism has been largely a story of mergers and unitive movements. In 1925, the Protestant Evangelical Church joined the Congregationalists. Six years later the Christian Churches merged to form the Congregational Christian denomination, and in 1957, the Evangelical and Reformed entered into organic union to produce the United Church of Christ, leaving only a segment of less than a hundred thousand Congregationalists still dedicated to the full import of their doctrine of local church autonomy.

Congregationalism has given a major impulse to the ecumenical movement. The constitutional basis of the World Council of Churches as "fellowship of churches" whose function is to "offer counsel and provide opportunity of united action" among its constituents, is a paraphrase of Congregational principles expanded to global proportions.

Quakers are the most distinctive form of Free Church ideology extant in English-speaking countries. More accurately known as the Society of Friends, the Quakers were organized as a separate Christian group in England in 1668, when George Fox (1624-1691) drew up his *Rule for the Management of Meetings.* They soon engaged in missionary work and in 1682 William Penn founded Pennsylvania on a Quaker basis.

The religious tenets of the Friends center around the idea of the Inner Light, first professed by George Fox and since become their focal doctrine. No Quaker has improved on the description of this Light given by Fox, and all Quakers subscribe to his definition.

The Lord hath opened to me by His invisible power how that every man was enlightened by the divine Light of Christ; and I saw it shine through all; and that they that believed in it came out of condemnation and came to the Light of Life, and became the children of it; but they that hated it, and did not believe in it, were condemned by it, though they made a profession of Christ. This I saw in the pure openings of the Light, without the help of any man, neither did I then know where to find it in the Scriptures, though afterwards, searching in the Scriptures, I found it. For I saw in that light and Spirit which was before the Scripture was given forth, and which led the holy men of God to give them forth, that all must come to that Spirit—if they would know God or Christ or the Scriptures aright—which they that gave them forth were led and taught by.[20]

According to the theory of the Light, its possession consists mainly in the sense of the Divine, and the direct working of God in the soul, by which a man is freed from sin, joined to Christ, and enabled to perform good works. From the paramount importance given to the Inner Light derives the Quaker rejection of the sacraments, the ministry, and all set forms of worship. Their meetings are ideally held in bare rooms and begin in silence, in "holy expectation before the Lord" until some member of the congregation feels inspired to speak.

Church organization is democratic, ranging from Preparative Meetings which consist of single congregations, to Yearly Meetings that comprise a whole country (as in England) or the Five Years' Meeting that forms one of several Quaker denominations in the United States.

The Quaker refusal to give military service and take oaths involved them in frequent conflict with civil authorities, more in Great Britain than America, and since the early nineteenth century the Friends have pioneered in promoting legislation in favor of conscientious objectors to war. Their devotion to social and educational work, as well as their high standards of personal integrity, have won popular support to their side and helped in the advancement of such humane movements as the elimination of slavery.

ANGLICAN HERITAGE

When the Tudor sovereigns in the sixteenth century decided to measure their strength against the Papacy, they found many elements in Great Britain to encourage their efforts. Criticism of ecclesiastical wealth, sporadic risings of antipapalism, remnants of the spirit of Lollardy which John Wyclif (1329-1384) initiated, merchants casting hungry glances at monastic property, religious dissatisfaction encouraged by the Renascence revolt against Scholasticism—all these were in the air when Henry VIII tried unsuccessfully to secure a divorce from his wife, Catherine of Aragon.

The historical origins of Anglicanism covered a period of thirty-six years, from 1527, when Henry VIII first proposed his divorce to ecclesiastical authorities, to 1563, when his daughter, Queen Elizabeth, promulgated the Thirty-nine Articles of the English Church. Between these dates the religious character of England completely changed.

Under pressure from Henry, the higher clergy disavowed the pope's spiritual jurisdiction in a famous "Abjuration of Papal Supremacy." At the Convocation of Canterbury in 1534, in reply to the question, "Whether the Roman Pontiff has any greater jurisdiction bestowed on him by God in the Holy Scriptures in this realm of England, than any other foreign (*externus*) bishop," they voted: Noes 34, Doubtful 1, Ayes 4. In the same year, the Convocation of York "unanimously and concordantly, with no dissentient," affirmed the same.[21]

During the minority of Henry's son, Edward VI, the Book of Common Prayer was published in two editions (1549 and 1552), first along Lutheran and then Calvinist lines. A new Ordinal was issued (1550-1552) following a Lutheran pattern, in which every mention of a priesthood offering sacrifice was carefully omitted from the ordination ritual. However the complete rupture with Catholicism did not come until 1563, when the Elizabethan Parliament made the Articles of Religion obligatory on all citizens under heavy penalties.

The main credit for establishing the English Church should be given to Queen Elizabeth (1533-1603) who inherited a religious problem at her accession and tried to solve it according to political expediency. When she became queen in 1558, the country as a whole was still predominantly Catholic, though with strong Calvinist undercurrents. Elizabeth disliked Catholics because they denied her legitimacy and spiritual supremacy, and the Calvinists because they abolished the episcopacy which she considered essential for the welfare of kings. Penal legislation was consistently directed against both elements. Among other laws, two Acts of 1593 were sweeping condemnations "of seditious sectaries and disloyal persons" who obstinately refused to attend Anglican church services, to be "committed to prison" and there to remain until they conform "according to Her Majesty's laws and statutes." [22]

After a century of controversy against Catholics and Puritans, the English Church settled down from 1689 to a period of quiet. The Methodist departure in the eighteenth century and the Oxford movement in the nineteenth marked the critical stages in a new Anglicanism, whose main features are still rooted in the Reformation but whose present status in the English-speaking world is in the nature of a compromise between historical Protestantism and the Catholic Church.

Episcopalianism, as the English Church is known in America, was brought to the colonies in 1607 by a group of English settlers who founded what is now Jamestown, Virginia. The Episcopalians officially left the parent Church at the time of the American Revolution, and proceeded to revise their juridical structure in a way compatible with a non-established denomination. They adopted the name Protestant Episcopal Church, which has been the subject of much discussion but emphasizes the unique character of American Episcopalianism: a democratic church united in spirit with the Anglican Communion throughout the world and committed to a policy of cooperation with other Protestant bodies, irrespective of their doctrinal traditions.

DOCTRINE AND WORSHIP. Although the Thirty-nine Articles are still included in manuals of instruction, they are not considered representative of what many Anglicans believe. Commentaries on the Articles range from extreme Reformed positions to an almost Roman Catholic interpretation, depending on the author and the tradition within which he is writing.

More typical of present-day Anglicanism are the broad principles enunciated at the General Convention of the Protestant Episcopal Church held at Chicago in 1886. In a revised form the Articles were approved two years later by the Lambeth Conference, the periodic assembly of Anglican bishops held at Lambeth Palace under the presidency of the Archbishop of Canterbury. The Lambeth Quadrilateral states the Anglican viewpoint on the essentials of religion. Its text has remained unchanged and serves as basis for reunion overtures with other Christian bodies.

We believe that all who have been duly baptized with water in the name of the Father, and of the Son, and of the Holy Ghost, are members of the Holy Catholic Church;

That in all things of human ordering or human choice relating to modes of worship and discipline, or to traditional customs, this Church is ready, in the spirit of love and humility, to forego all preferences of her own;

That this Church does not seek to absorb other communions, but rather, cooperating with them on the basis of a common faith and order, to discountenance schism, to heal the wounds of the body of Christ, and to promote the charity which is the chief of Christian graces and the visible manifestation of Christ to the world.[23]

However, conscious that union among Christians is possible "only by the principles of unity exemplified by the undivided Catholic Church during the first ages of its existence," the Quadrilateral isolates the four essentials of "this sacred deposit," which at once describes the substance of Anglicanism and the foundation for solidarity among the separated Churches.

The Holy Scriptures of the Old and New Testaments, as the revealed Word of God.

The Nicene Creed, as the sufficient statement of the Christian faith.

The two sacraments, Baptism and the Supper of the Lord, ministered with unfailing use of Christ's words of institution, and of the elements ordained by Him.

The Historic Episcopate, locally adapted in the methods of its administration to the varying needs of the nations and peoples called of God into the unity of His Church.[24]

Equally representative of the wide range of Anglican belief is the Book of Common Prayer, which historians believe has been the single most cohesive force in the English Church. The formula that the law of prayer is the law of belief expresses a fundamental norm of the Anglican Communion in modern times. Its liturgical life sets the standard for the Church's doctrine, and the past few generations have seen a number of far-reaching changes of emphasis. Today the liturgy is the keystone of harmony within the Churches derived from the English Reformation.

There are two main forms of the Book of Common Prayer, the revision made in England (1928) and the editions used in various countries, like the United States, where the Churches are juridically independent of Canterbury. The English revision was made over the protests of Parliament that refused to approve the moderately Anglo-Catholic version which the bishops submitted for government approval; it was therefore published without formal authority from the Crown. Different Prayer Books are substantially the same. All have set orders for Morning and Evening Prayer, for the administration of the Lord's Supper, baptism, and such "ordinances" as matrimony, visiting the sick and "making, ordaining and consecrating bishops, priests and deacons." Numerous Collects, Epistles and Gospels are offered for prayer on Sundays and Feast Days; they are drawn largely from the Roman Missal or other Catholic formularies. The complete Psalter is part of the Prayer Book, along with a Catechism, forms of prayer to be used in families, and the Articles of Religion.

Typical of the changes going on in Anglicanism, when the American Prayer Book was revised in 1928, most of the alterations affected the ultra-Protestant edition of 1552 and were a partial return to the more Catholic one of 1549. In the Offertory, Cranmer was by-passed in the direction of giving the Eucharist a definitely sacrificial tone. Answering to the demand for post-biblical saints to the liturgy, a new Proper was included, corresponding to the *Proprium Sanctorum* of the Roman Missal. Requiem Masses for the Dead were made legal, and prayers for the faithful departed were formally sanctioned. Since 1928, the Church at every Eucharistic liturgy has been remembering the souls of deceased persons, and beseeching God to grant them continual growth in His love. In the same way, extreme unction was at least partially restored as a sacrament of healing.

After three centuries of suppression in the Established Church, religious life was brought back in the middle nineteenth century, and today there are over one hundred Anglican religious communities of men and women in all parts of the world. While growing in size and influence, the communities are still in a fluid state. The most serious problem is ambiguity on the concept of religious life within Anglicanism. At the Lambeth Conference in 1958, the assembly declared how greatly it valued "the special form of vocation evident in Religious Orders and Communities" and hoped that "this form of vocation may find its expression in a wide range of ecclesiastical tradition." Yet the basic issue remained unsolved. The fourteenth of the Articles of Religion states that "voluntary works besides, over and above God's commandments, which they call works of supererogation, cannot be taught without arrogance and impiety." Newman had difficulty with this article when setting up his community at Littlemore. The tension has yet to be resolved.

Some years ago, the Archbishop of Canterbury, Geoffrey Fisher, appointed a commission to study and report on the differences between Catholic and Protestant traditions within the Anglican Church, their causes and possible solution. Among other significant judgments which the commission reached was its estimate of the Papacy.

It is one of the most remarkable facts in Christian history that the Papacy of the sixteenth century first cleansed itself of its vile and most notorious Renascence scandals, and then itself directed and impelled the cleansing of the Renascence Church.

The easy way in which the Reformers, almost from the first, simply wrote off the Papacy even as a possibility, illustrates clearly the extent to which they ignored from the outset both the New Testament doctrine of the Universal Church as an inherent part of the Gospel, and the inherence of the Divine-human society in the here-and-now of history.

If such an institution as the Universal Church is to exist, as more than a sentiment and an ideal, then some such central institution would seem to be more than just a convenience. It is at least a pragmatic necessity, as is shown by the obvious temptation of the modern ecumenical movement to try to provide a substitute for it.[25]

Sentiments like these are not uncommon in Anglican circles. They accentuate the middle-ground which the English Church and its derivatives occupy, between the individualism of the Protestant tradition and the visible unity of Catholicism under the Roman Pontiff.

METHODISM

The founder of Methodism, John Wesley (1703-1791), was an ordained priest of the Church of England who until the day of his death insisted he did not want to sever connection with the Church in which he was reared. Yet even before he died, the principles he elaborated and the stress in church policy he advocated led him to organize a distinct denomination, whose current membership in the world compares favorably with Anglicanism and, in the United States, is about three times the size of the Protestant Episcopal Church.

It is not easy to describe Methodism in doctrinal terms because Wesley himself stressed the minimal importance of belief, in the sense of confessional doctrine, and described his followers in a passage that has since become classic.

The distinguishing marks of a Methodist are not his opinions of any sort. His assenting to this or that scheme of religion, his embracing any particular set of notions, his espousing the judgment of one man or of another are all quite wide of the point. Whosoever, therefore, imagines that a Methodist is a man of such or such an opinion is grossly ignorant of the whole affair; he mistakes the truth totally.

We believe indeed that "all scripture is given by inspiration of God"; and herein we are distinguished from Jews, Turks, and infidels. We believe the written word of God to be the only rule both of faith and practice; and herein we are fundamentally distinguished from those of the Roman Church. We believe Christ to be the eternal, the supreme God; and herein we are distinguished from the Socinians and Arians. But as to all opinions which do not strike at the root of Christianity, we think and let think.[26]

Among the "opinions which do not strike at the root of Christianity," and on which his followers were free to dissent, were the character of the priesthood and the episcopate, the nature of Christ's presence in the Eucharist, and the role of the sacraments in the life of the Church.

But if Methodism allows considerable range in matters of doctrine, there is one element of its faith which not only distinguishes Methodists from their Anglican forebears but from orthodox Protestantism in general. This is their teaching on sanctification, which so closely resembles the Catholic doctrine on grace that some have called Wesley a "papist in disguise."

In his sermons and writings, Wesley constantly opposed the Calvinist theory of predestination. Even when he affirmed that God is the source of all human good, and that grace does not depend on any power or merit in man, he labored to show the untenability of any view that restricted salvation to the few who are elected by the unsearchable decrees of an arbitrary God. "The grace of God," he wrote, "whence cometh our salvation, is free in all, and free for all." [27]

When he revised the Thirty-nine Articles of the Anglican creed and sent them to America as a doctrinal basis for the new Methodist Episcopal Church, he eliminated the most extremely Calvinistic passages of Article nine, deleted the qualifying adverb *necessarily* from Article twelve, which says that good works "spring out necessarily of a true and lively faith," and entirely dropped Article seventeen, with its unqualified statement of predestinarianism.

Wesley's concern was mainly with the salvation of all men. He was convinced that Christ came to seek and save that which was lost, and the Church is commissioned to preach the Gospel of redemption. But if predestinarianism is true, Christ's advent was in vain and the whole task of evangelism a sham, because there is no need (or possibility) of saving the unsavable. Multitudes are beyond the love of God and nothing can be done to help them. He considered this a repudiation of the central truth of Christianity.

Methodism has since developed a well-integrated system of sanctification that rests on the prior belief that salvation is more than justification in the sense of removal (or hiding) of sin. It is a vital process that God intends to have grow with the passage of time and develop through man's cooperation. "Sanctification," according to the *Methodist Discipline,* "is that renewal of our fallen nature by the Holy Ghost, received through faith in Jesus Christ, whose blood of atonement cleanseth from all sin; whereby we are not only delivered from the guilt of sin, but are washed from its pollution, saved from its power, and are enabled, through grace, to love with all our hearts and to walk in His holy commandments blameless." [28]

Parallel with the Methodist teaching on sanctification is an emphasis on the Witness of the Spirit, who bears testimony to those who are reborn to God after a life of sin. By this witness is understood an inward impression on the soul, whereby the Spirit of God is believed immediately and directly to testify that a person is a child of God, that his sins are blotted out and that he is on the road to salvation.

This doctrine has inspired much of Methodist hymnology, composed by John Wesley's brother, Charles, in which the joyous experience of personal salvation is the dominant theme.

> No longer am I now afraid;
> Thy promise must take place.
> Perfect Thy strength in weakness made,
> Sufficient is Thy grace.
> Confident now of faith's increase,
> I all its fruits shall prove:
> Substantial joy, and settled peace,
> And everlasting love.
> Lord, I believe and rest secure
> In confidence divine
> Thy promise stands for ever sure,
> And all Thou art is mine.[29]

Correlative with a stress on religion as personal experience has been the Methodist conviction that Christianity is essentially social. "Solitary religion," declared Wesley, "is not to be found" in the Gospel. " 'Holy solitaries' is a phrase no more consistent with the Gospel than holy adulterers. The Gospel of Christ knows no religion but social; no holiness, but social holiness." [30] This has deeply influenced Methodist thought and action, and stimulated what has since become a new religious dimension in the Western world. Wesley's followers were introduced into a fellowship in which moral, economic, and racial issues became an integral part of living the faith; Methodists became pioneers of the "Social Gospel" which has characterized so much of American (and Anglo-Saxon) Protestantism in modern times.

A typical area of Methodist social evangelism is the temperance movement. In the spirit of John Wesley, who forbade anyone even to touch "that liquid fire," Methodists have been leaders in opposing the sale and consumption of alcoholic beverages. "Our Church," they state, "reasserts its long-established conviction that intoxicating liquor cannot be legalized without sin." And "to be true to itself the Church must be militant in opposition to the liquor traffic," as evidenced in the Methodist promotion of what became the American Volstead Act. "Adequate relief can come only through total abstinence for the individual, and effective prohibition for the state." [31] Ministers are forbidden to indulge, and may be penalized for proved breach of their abstinence pledge.

Methodism has affected the religious thinking of many denominations outside its own immediate family. The Holiness movement stems from Wesley's doctrine on sanctification from which certain Methodist churches felt the general stream of his followers had departed. The result was a score of religious bodies, like the Nazarenes, Churches of God and Holiness Churches, which are juridically distinct but united in professing a number of basic tenets of Protestant perfectionism.

Besides justification, they hold, there is a "second blessing" in which a person feels himself closely united with God. This is an emotional experience produced in the heart by the direct action of the Holy Spirit. Although instantaneous, the "second blessing" may require years of preparation. As a group, Holiness bodies claim that the teachings and practices of the larger denominations have departed from the true faith and compromised with modernism. The favorite method of preaching is popular revivals, which used to be the regular mode of Methodist evangelism in colonial America. Most of the churches profess, without always stressing, the imminent second coming of Christ which is to inaugurate a millenium of earthly peace and happiness before the last day.

The extreme left wing of the Holiness movement developed into the Pentecostal Churches. They are similar to the Holiness churches in admitting the fundamentalist principles of Christ's divinity, inerrancy of the Bible, the Virgin Birth and Resurrection, Christ's atonement and the early second coming. There is also an emphasis on sanctification as a separate work of grace which follows justification, but with an added feature that characterizes the Pentecostals and accounts for their distinctive name. When the Holy Spirit comes to perfect a soul, His advent is not merely invisible; it manifests itself by an external outpouring of spiritual gifts, not unlike those bestowed on the Apostles at the first Pentecost, especially glossolalia or "speaking in foreign tongues, even as the Holy Spirit prompted them to speak." [32]

ECUMENICAL MOVEMENT

A new spirit has entered the body of American and world Protestantism. For the first time since the Reformation leaders in every denomination are deeply concerned about their cleavage in doctrine, worship and practice, and are seriously trying to heal what they brand the "sin of disunity."

Protestant writers have taken the term "ecumenical," long used to describe the general councils of the Catholic Church, and invested it with a new connotation. They speak of the ecumenical movement as the search for a world-wide unity "from the Church as men have conceived it, to the Church as God wants it to be."

Reunion efforts began on the international level, under stimulus of the need for coordinating the Protestant foreign missions. How could pagans be asked to believe that Christianity is true unless the missionaries themselves witnessed to the truth by professing the same message of the Gospel? The idea was first broached at Edinburgh, Scotland, in 1910, and by 1921 the International Missionary Council was formed at London to become the chief organ of liaison for Protestant evangelism.

According to its constitution, the "sole purpose of the International Missionary Council is to further the effective proclamation to all men of the Gospel of Jesus Christ as Lord and Savior." Its function is not to command but to advise, by furnishing information, studying policy and strategy, "as an agency through which all the forces of world-wide missions can think and act together."

Though historically first, federating Protestant missions was only a logical outcome of reunion labors at home, one in the field of doctrine and worship, called *Faith and Order,* and another to deal with social and economic problems, under the title *Life and Work.* At the charter meeting of *Faith and Order* in Lausanne, Switzerland (1927), the leading spirit was Bishop Brent, an Episcopalian, who frankly told the delegates from seventy denominations that "in our hearts most of us are devotees of the cult of the incomplete—sectarianism. The Christ in one Church often categorically denies the Christ in a neighboring Church. It would be ludicrous were it not tragic." Two years before representatives from thirty-three countries met at Stockholm for the opening congress of *Life and Work* to face the problems of social morality that are insoluble for a divided Christianity.

By 1948 the two movements had sufficiently matured to fuse at Amsterdam into the World Council of Churches, which has since met regularly in formal assemblies. As expressed by the Secretary General, who asked himself what is the purpose of the Council, "Our name gives us the clue to the answer. We are a Council of Churches, not the Council of the one undivided Church. Our name indicates our weakness and our shame before God. Our plurality is a deep anomaly. Our Council represents therefore an emergency solution—a stage on the road." [33]

As a stage on the road, the World Council has done more in the short years of its existence to make Protestants unity-conscious than any other movement in the past four centuries. Even adding the forty years of preparation, its achievements are monumental. Presently combining about two hundred Protestant and Orthodox Churches in fifty nations, its membership covers most of the Christians who date from the Reformation.

The Council opened its third assembly at New Delhi by integrating with the International Missionary Council, which represents non-Catholic missionary groups in forty countries. By this historic action the three basic strands of the ecumenical movement were united: doctrine and worship through *Faith and Order,* social service in *Life and Work,* and evangelism under the International Missionary Council.

From its headquarters in Geneva the World Council has given Protestantism a new sense of solidarity. In spite of their divisions, they feel that God has not left them without some tokens of unity.

In our separateness we have attested the operation of the one Christ across all boundaries that divide us. We have heard the voice of the one Good Shepherd in the testimony of communions other than our own. We have experienced the power of the Name of Christ in their prayers. We have acknowledged the love of Christ to which they have borne witness in word and deed. In the fellowship of the ecumenical movement we have come together in a way which forbids us, in spite of all stresses, to break away from one another. Thus we have been led to see that the reality of Christ is more comprehensive than the limitations of our confessional traditions, and have confessed in faith our oneness in Christ.[34]

At the same time the Churches recognize how widely they are separated, not only in accidentals but in essentials of the Christian faith. They confess that their divisions are contrary to the will of Christ, and they pray God "to shorten the days of our separation and to guide us by His Spirit into fulness of unity."

But the obstacles that stand in the way are humanly speaking insurmountable. In a study of the non-theological and cultural factors in church divisions prepared for the World Council, no less than thirty areas of conflicting interest were analyzed: national antagonisms, distrust of the unfamiliar, historic isolation, political pressures, institutional pride, race, indifference, property ownership, doctored history, love of status quo, personal ambition—all were exposed to view and scrutinized.

Yet the doctrinal issues are admittedly deeper, and involve differences of understanding on almost every major element of the Christian faith. The very concepts of the Church and of the unity the Churches seek are in dispute. "If we were agreed on the nature of the Church's one-ness," observed the chairman of the *Faith and*

Order Commission, "our struggle between each other would be over." [35]

Two principal opinions prevail in the ecumenical movement on what should be done about this cleavage. There is first the theoretical position which represents the traditional Reformation concept of man, the fall and the Church of Christ. According to this opinion, the disunity among the churches is certainly sinful, but unavoidable, in view of man's depraved nature. Thus, "we may think of the Church as we are able to think of the individual believer, who may be said at one and the same time to be both a justified man and a sinner (*simul justus et peccator*)." [36] The Evangelical theory of man's justification is also the speculative basis for the Church's simultaneous unity and disunity. In the same way that individual believers are and ever remain sinners, although justified by God, in Christ who alone is *just;* so the Churches are divided among themselves, while they are somehow united because of Jesus Christ their Founder, who is *one.*

Disunity, therefore, is no less inevitable in the Churches than sin in the individual Christian. They cannot help being divided, no more than he can help committing sin. After all, the members of the Church are human beings, suffering from the common effect of Adam's fall which destroyed man's intrinsic power to do any spiritual good. If any unity is to be found in the Church, it can only be something extrinsic, a kind of appropriation, where the unity of Jesus Christ is imputed to the Society which He founded.

Is there any hope of unifying the dismembered bodies of Christendom on these principles? Not from man's side. The only hope is that through prayer and patient waiting for the Spirit, God may see fit to unify the Churches in a way similar to the way He justifies sinners: by permeating them with His grace to the extent of removing the subjective conflicts that separate the denominations, and enabling them to live with one another in amicable charity.

A far different attitude towards Christian disunity does not prejudge the case on principle but, while assuming the need of prayer and divine help, insists on the corresponding need of human cooperation. The former theory was cited by the Secretary General of the World Council of Churches, who realized that on this point rests the whole success or failure of the ecumenical movement. There are many, he said, who think that the present relationship of the Churches in the World Council is the limit of all that can be hoped for. "The danger of this is that the World Council can thus become a narcotic instead of a stimulant. We must react against this temptation of accepting the present established disorder of our ecclesiastical world simply because it has been made to look less shocking" as it has been provided with an ecumenical façade.[37]

The sanguine element in the World Council looks to find the way that leads beyond co-existence or even cooperation, "to a true unity which will make it clear to the whole world that as there can only be one Body of Christ, so there is only one Body which is the Church of His people." [38]

In the past years, however, new and unexpected elements have appeared on the ecumenical scene. The admission of Russians and other non-Protestant bodies has greatly increased the strength of Orthodoxy in the World Council of Churches. No doubt the ecumenical movement was never intended to be exclusively Protestant. But until recently a large majority of the Council of Churches has been Protestant, and probably a majority has preferred it this way. It is now evident that Christian reunion must be built on a wider base than could ever be provided by the Churches stemming from the Reformation. The entrance of several Pentecostal Churches reinforces the point, and illustrates what certain promoters of a limited ecumenism had disavowed: that the hopes of a united Christianity cannot be realized without the combined effort of the whole Christian world.

More importantly, Protestant ecumenism has revealed a kindred desire for unity in the Roman Catholic Church. The shadow of Rome hovered over the first beginnings of the World Council. In 1919 when the founders were canvassing for member churches, they called on Benedict XV and invited his assistance, which he courteously declined. In 1937 at the opening service of the Edinburgh conference on Faith and Order, the Archbishop of York declared that "we deeply lament the absence from this collaboration of the great Church of Rome—the Church which more than any other has known how to speak to the nations so that the nations hear." [38] In 1948 at the first assembly in Amsterdam, one of the principal topics was on "The Roman Catholic Church and the Ecumenical Movement." At New Delhi, in 1961, there were official observers from the Vatican, whose presence was not only welcome but showed what no amount of argument could prove, that the pope and Catholics generally are deeply impressed with the unitive spirit of Protestantism and ready to do all in their power to advance the cause of true Christian unity.

It was more than symbolic, as the head of the Council of Churches declared, that the two world assemblies of New Dehli and Second Vatican should have met within less than a year of each other. He felt "it would undoubtedly mean much for Christendom and for the world, if it became clear in the decisions of both, that these councils do not meet against each other and that each does not seek its own advantage, but seeks only to serve the Lord Jesus Christ." [39] The deliberations at New Dehli and the decrees of Second Vatican give every promise that the hopes of reuniting a separated Christianity are brighter now than they have ever been since the Reformation.

SPIRIT OF PROTESTANTISM

If it is difficult to analyze the essence of any religious faith, it is doubly hard with Protestantism, which is more a movement than a system and consequently not subject to easy classification. Yet visible as a theme in Protestant faith and practice is a respect for the person of Christ that may baffle other Christians whose theology is more consistent and who therefore tend to overlook the attachment to the Savior bequeathed by the Reformation to its followers.

The focus on Christ appears in all the great Protestant writings since the sixteenth century and, before Luther and Calvin, reaches into the *devotio moderna* of the late Middle Ages and the Brethren of the Common Life. Under the topic of prayer, Calvin pointedly stated the place that Christ should occupy in the life of a believing Christian. Alone and of himself, a man lacks everything necessary for salvation. If he is to be saved, this can only be from resources furnished him by God in the person of Jesus Christ.

In Christ, the Lord offers all happiness in place of our misery, all wealth in place of our neediness. In him He opens to us the heavenly treasures that our whole faith may contemplate His beloved Son, our whole expectation depend upon him, and our whole hope cleave to and rest in him. This is that secret and hidden philosophy which cannot be wrested from syllogisms. But they whose eyes God has opened surely learn it by heart, that in his light they may see light.[40]

So uniquely was Christ interpreted as the object of devotion that the first commandment of the decalogue, "Thou shalt have no other gods besides me," was taken to exclude every other mediation of grace; and all claims to the contrary were summarily dismissed as idolatry.

On this principle the Mass was removed from liturgical worship as a human invention which derogates from the one sacrifice of the Savior on Calvary; priestly ministration of the sacraments, veneration of the saints and the Blessed Virgin, the use of sacramentals and relics, in a word, the very notion of the Church itself as a divine creation through which the grace of Christ flows to a fallen human race, were re-interpreted in the light of what some have called the two words that best synthesize the Protestant spirit, *Kurios Christos,* "Christ is the Lord," meaning that He alone is directly the agent of man's salvation, with no one and nothing else besides.

The Lordship of Jesus Christ in the economy of redemption has been imbedded in the principal confessions of Protestantism under various aspects depending on the denominational emphasis. Among Lutherans the stress is on the merciful Savior in whom sinners may implicitly trust that their sins are not imputed because of the merits of Christ; in the Reformed tradition it is Christ the Lord of creation and sovereign master of human destiny; for the Anglicans He is the object of liturgical worship and for Methodists the motive for works of zeal and social welfare; and in the Free Churches only Christ's authority is recognized in ecclesiastical polity, to the exclusion of synods, bishops, and even of mandatory creeds.

Subscription to this principle was dramatically illustrated when the Evangelical Church in Germany came into conflict with the totalitarian pretensions of National Socialism. Faltering for a while under the impact of the new tyranny, church leaders soon rallied to make a solemn affirmation that Jesus Christ is the one Word of God whom men have to trust and obey, all other claims to allegiance to the contrary notwithstanding. Under title of the Barmen Declaration, they stated their position as Christians and Protestants.

"I am the way, the truth, and the life. No man cometh unto the Father but by me" (John 16:6).

Jesus Christ, as He is attested to us in Holy Scripture, is the one Word of God, whom we have to hear and whom we have to trust and obey in life and in death.

We condemn the false doctrine that the Church can and must recognize as God's revelation other events and powers, forms and truths, apart from and alongside this one Word of God.[41]

Commenting on the Barmen statement, Karl Barth saw in it more than a protest against the Nazi overlords. It was a stand against all the heterodox movements within Protestantism "which for more than two hundred years had slowly prepared the devastation of the Church. The protest was without doubt directed against Schleiermacher and Ritschl. The protest was directed against the basic tendencies of the whole eighteenth and nineteenth centuries and therefore against the hallowed traditions of all other Churches as well." [42] At its best, then, Protestantism asserts against all who teach otherwise that Christ is the only way, truth and life, and that all other claimants are false.

Parallel with its Christocentrism among Protestants in the biblical tradition is the same principle from another perspective among Protestants who philosophize about their distinctive contribution to the Christian way of life. Again the first commandment is invoked, this time not to exclude other mediators than Christ but other objects of loyalty than God. Paul Tillich has developed the idea in what he calls "the Protestant principle." It is the insistence that no partial allegiance may take the place of an ultimate object of loyalty. Nothing that is manmade, or less than God, may be respected and honored as though it were divine.

What makes Protestantism Protestant is the fact that it transcends its own religious and confessional character, that it cannot be identified wholly with any of its particular historical forms.

Protestantism has a principle that stands beyond all its realizations. It is the critical and dynamic source of all Protestant realizations, but it is not identical with any of them. It cannot be confined by a definition. It is not exhausted by any historical religion; it is not identical with the structure of the Reformation or of early Christianity or even with a religious form at all. It transcends them as it transcends any cultural form.

On the other hand, it can appear in all of them; it is a living, moving, restless power in them; and this is what it is supposed to be in a special way in historical Protestantism.

The Protestant principle, in name derived from the protest of the "protestants" against decisions of the Catholic majority, contains the divine and human protest against any absolute claim made for a relative reality, even if this claim is made by a Protestant church. The Protestant principle is the judge of every religious and cultural reality, including the religion and culture which calls itself "Protestant." [43]

Tillich further explains that the Protestant principle is "the guardian against all the attempts of the finite and conditioned to usurp the place of the unconditional in thinking and acting. It is the prophetic judgment against religious pride, ecclesiastical arrogance, and secular self-sufficiency and their destructive consequences." [44]

Others than Tillich have spelled out the persons and agencies in modern times against which authentic Protestantism lodges its protest whenever something less than God assumes divine prerogatives. Social and political entities, industrial combines and philosophical systems, ecclesiastical bodies in the Catholic and Protestant tradition are all guilty in varying degrees of obscuring "the chasm between the human and the divine, which the prophets of Israel had understood so well," to pretend there were persons "in control of God's redemptive powers and purposes; and were in possession of the 'keys of heaven.' " [45]

Consistent with this protest against divinization is the idea that Protestantism itself should reflect on its own character and always see it as a church of sinners. "The Reformation," it is stated, "was not completed in the sixteenth century; it is never completed. We may for the sake of comfort try to transform Protestantism into a closed system; but it breaks out again. It has no 'infallible' voice to silence other voices in decrees that are 'irreformable.' Protestantism cannot be static." [46]

There is more to this claim than admission of human frailty or ignorance, more even than a confession of human guilt. It is the positive assertion that a Christian may turn his judgment upon the Church; that he must allow for reformation not merely *in* the Church but *of* the Church, to the extent of changing not only its policies but doctrines, and looking to the future for greater changes still. By this standard, the Church is indeed reformed but always in need of further reformation, *Ecclesia reformata sed semper reformanda,* not merely in externals but, if necessary, in the very constitution of its being. To question such necessity is to fall victim to the illusion that a human creation can, in any part of its nature, be above improvement or intrinsic change.

If the Church is always a human institution, the Protestant will treat the religious group to which he belongs accordingly. He will go beyond it for his commitment in a way that the Catholic or Eastern Orthodox would not do. They believe the Church possesses the Spirit of God and speaks to its members in His name; the Protestant considers the Spirit as somehow outside the Church, not unlike the theory of imputed justification of Christ's merits to a man who still remains a sinner. The institutional Church is not literally animated by the Spirit of God to be equated, as Catholics and Orthodox believe, with the Mystical Body of Christ. It rather waits for the Spirit and lives in *ad hoc* dependence on His mercy. It is not, as Reinhold Niebuhr correctly observed, an extension of the Incarnation in the Catholic sense of these terms.

Accordingly the whole history of the Church is the history of the reformation of the Church by the Spirit. Always the Christian must accept the fact that God is leading forward His Church and changing it, that the Church may never "settle down in a revelation which it treats as if it were its own property." Instead it is constantly on the watch to receive the new order which the Spirit brings. "The Church of Jesus Christ in history is at once the congregation of sinners and the new creation, for although it continues to live and work within the brokenness and estrangement of this world and to share in its divisions, the Church belongs to the new age and the new creation. As such the Church is summoned to perpetual renewal, to put off the old life, and by the renewal of its mind to be conformed to Christ, looking beyond its historical forms to the full unveiling of its new being in the coming Lord." [47]

Here, perhaps, we come nearest to the essence of Protestantism, which sees itself in a constant process of renewal, so that all its affiliations with visible ecclesiastical structures, its adoption of various liturgical forms, and even the acceptance of certain confessional creeds are tentative. Only the Spirit of God is adhered to absolutely, and everything else with reservation.

17. Old Catholic Churches

THE origins of the Old Catholic movement go back to Reformation times, and its theological principles derive from a Calvinist theory of grace. As a historical phenomenon the movement is sometimes described almost exclusively in terms of national aspirations which came into conflict with Rome. This is correct enough as a partial explanation, but fundamentally the issue was not a tension between groups of zealous Catholics in Belgium or the Low Countries striving to rise above their environment and inhibited by papal authority; it was mainly a clash of two opposing theologies of man's relations with God, the Catholic, which holds that human nature has been elevated to a higher than natural order, and the Jansenist, which claimed that such elevation never took place, so that when Adam fell he lost for himself and posterity not the gifts added to nature but something essential to nature itself.

Although full-blooded Jansenism began with Jansenius himself, its antecedents were much earlier. They are traceable to Michael Baius (1513-1589), contemporary of Luther and Calvin and chancellor at the University of Louvain. Shortly after his appointment to Louvain, he announced his twofold intention to free dogma from the foreign elements that Scholasticism had introduced and that constituted the sole obstacle to the conversion of Protestants; and then to study the Catholic doctrine on grace in its true sources, not the anathemas of the popes but in the Bible and the writings of the early Fathers, especially of St. Augustine.

According to Baius, when man came from the hand of God he possessed perfect righteousness, which theology has called sanctifying grace but which is really a native human possession because it was Adam's by right of nature. So far, Baius was teaching straight Calvinism. But then he added a clarification. Calvin implicitly denied that grace can be resisted, but he never fully explained what this meant. Taking Calvin's principles, Baius postulated two kinds of love that necessarily attract the will: a vicious love and the love of charity, on the prior assumption that our will has been ruined by concupiscence and therefore capable of nothing but evil in the spiritual life. Charity does not rule in sinners, so that all their words and actions are sinful; in the predestined charity reigns, and they will be saved, but only because of irresistible divine action, and not for any merit or cooperation with grace on their part.

Baius was condemned by the Holy See and submitted formally, although his later writings show that he never actually gave up his opinions. His influence might have stopped with his death, except for Jacques Janson, his successor at Louvain, who discovered and encouraged one of his students, Cornelius Jansenius (1585-1638), to carry on the work of the former chancellor.

Jansenius' master work, the *Augustinus,* was not published until two years after his death. It was a bold defense of Baianism that profoundly stirred the theological world within months of its first appearance. In 1653 five propositions summarizing Jansenism and culled from the *Augustinus* were condemned by Innocent X for heresy. Meanwhile the Jansenist cause became identified with opposition to papal authority and the Gallican theory that national churches are independent of Rome. As a result, Jansenists refused to accept the condemnation of their leader and protested that the five censured statements were certainly erroneous, but they had never been taught by Jansenius.

Three years later Alexander VII published a Constitution in which he solemnly defined that his predecessor's condemnation was valid in fact and by law. "We declare and define," the document read, "that the five propositions were taken from the book of the aforementioned Cornelius Jansenius, Bishop of Ypres, whose title is *Augustinus,* and that they were condemned in the sense intended by the same Cornelius." [1]

Still the tension continued, until nine years later when Alexander composed a formula of submission to his own and predecessor's Constitutions, to be taken under oath, as a condition for ordination to the priesthood and consecration to the episcopate.

In spite of repeated censures, Jansenism not only continued in existence but spread to other countries. Under pressure from Louis

XIV, Jansenius' great disciple, Antoine Arnauld (1612-1694), took refuge in Holland, where his followers were supported by the sympathetic Calvinist government. When Spain lost control of the Netherlands, the Dutch Catholics had come under the administration of a vicar apostolic at Utrecht. Since 1688 this office was held by a Jansenist bishop, Peter Codde (1648-1710), who was deposed by Clement XI in 1702. During the resulting schism, Codde obeyed the papal injunction to the extent of not exercising his episcopal functions.

After Codde's death, the schismatic party found another Jansenist prelate, Dominique Varlet, who befriended their cause and in 1724 consecrated the former vicar general, Cornelius Steenhoven, bishop of the new movement. Three others were consecrated by Varlet, but only the last, Peter Meindaerts, consecrated his own successor. Fearing that an episcopate which depended on a single place might be lost, Meindaerts consecrated Jerome de Bock bishop of Haarlem in 1742, and John Byevelt for the see of Deventer in 1758. All parties to the action were excommunicated by the pope, but until the present day the Church of Utrecht has continued in existence on the grounds of its possession of episcopal dignity.

In the early nineteenth century, the Dutch government would not recognize the titles of the bishops as "of" Utrecht, Haarlem, and Deventer, but only "at" those cities. At the same time Leo XII sent a nuncio to bring about a concordat with the civil authorities and, if possible, reconcile the Old Catholic Churches with Rome. In 1827, the nuncio, Monsignor Capaccini, invited the Archbishop of Utrecht (John van Santen) to a conference, which turned out to be the last formal attempt at a reconciliation.

Van Santen asked why the pope should attach so much importance to signing the Constitution drafted by Alexander VII as an affirmation that Jansenius actually taught the doctrines attributed to him. The nuncio answered he could not believe the prelate would defend his own opinion against the wisdom of the Church. There is a record of van Santen's reply.

I do not wish to set my judgment above that of others. I only ask, let the Five Propositions be shown me in Jansen's book, stated in the sense in which they were condemned—that is, not in the sense in which anything similar is found in St. Augustine, for the Pope never professed to condemn St. Augustine.

Am I to understand that His Holiness asks that I should call God to witness that I do believe what I do not believe, what the Pope knows that I do not believe, what Almighty God knows that I do not believe? Is Catholic unity to be maintained by perjury.[2]

Since the negotiations broke down, the Old Catholics in Holland continued under the jurisdiction of the three original sees, of Utrecht, Haarlem and Deventer, with episcopal succession continuing in unbroken line into the twentieth century. Meantime another protest movement arose on the continent, after the definition of papal infallibility by the Vatican Council in 1870.

Although the bishops of the Catholic world subscribed to the definition, the acceptance was not universal among the lower clergy in certain areas of Germany, Switzerland and Austria-Hungary. The churches under their care seceded from Rome and joined hands with the Jansenist groups in Holland. Three names stand out among the German segment: John Döllinger, Joseph Reinkens and Franz Reusch.

John Döllinger (1799-1890) was a prominent church historian and theologian, and author of numerous books on the Eucharist, the Reformation and comparative religion. After his excommunication in 1871 he became a leader of the critics of the Vatican Council, but more concerned with reuniting the separated Christian Churches than with advancing the Old Catholic cause. More dedicated to the movement was Reinkens (1821-1896), also a church historian, who had himself consecrated first bishop of the German branch of the Old Catholic Church in 1873 with his see at Bonn. The principal organizer was the Scripture scholar Reusch (1825-1900), who took a leading part in setting up the Reunion Conferences that were later held at Bonn. But when the Old Catholics abolished clerical celibacy in 1878, Reusch objected and retired into lay communion.

All the continental Old Catholics received their episcopal succession from the Church of Utrecht. Two years after Reinkens' elevation, the first Swiss bishop, Eduard Herzog, was consecrated and given headquarters at Berne. Owing to the opposition of the government, bishops were not consecrated for the Austrian communities until much later. A bishop of Warnsdorf (Bohemia) was consecrated in 1924 and of Vienna in 1925. In 1939 the three bishoprics of Bonn, Warnsdorf and Vienna were united into one Church.

The most significant event among the Old Catholics in the past century was the series of international conferences held at Bonn in 1874 and 1875 under the presidency of John Döllinger. Their purpose was to foster reunion between the Churches which had retained the faith and order of historic Christianity. Their direction was in the hands of the newly formed branch of the Old Catholics, though Döllinger never formally joined them.

Two main interests occupied the conferences: to clarify the basic position of the Old Catholic Churches, and arrive at some agreement between the Old Catholics on the one hand and the Eastern Orthodox and Anglicans on the other. The fundamental statement of belief had to wait fifteen years, but the principles of reunion were broadly agreed upon in a series of declarations that have more than historic value because they paved the way for similar ventures in the ecumenical movement of the present century.

Outstanding among the fourteen articles of unanimous agreement with the Anglicans were the acceptance of the Protestant canon of the Old Testament, denial of real merit before God for good works performed, rejection of "works of supererogation" in the practice of the counsels, belief that five of the seven sacraments are the fruit of later theological speculation, acknowledgment of the unbroken apostolic succession in the English Church, denial of the Immaculate Conception and that the Eucharistic celebration is a "repetition or renewal" of the sacrifice of Calvary.

Concord with the Orthodox centered around the procession of the Holy Spirit in the Trinity, which included the admission that "the Holy Spirit does not issue out of the Son, because in the Godhead there is only one beginning." The Anglicans did not universally accept this compromise with the Orthodox. Among others, Edward Pusey of Oxford Movement fame was quite intransigent in his opposition to any tampering with the Western tradition on the *Filioque* in the Nicene Creed.

When the Declaration of Utrecht was drafted in 1889, the Old

Catholics settled on eight principal doctrines which, they said, characterize their concept of Christianity. Most important were the rejection of the Roman primacy and the acceptance of the Council of Trent in its dogmatic decisions "only so far as they are in harmony with the teaching of the primitive Church."

As now constituted, the Old Catholic Churches include not only the Jansenist bodies of Holland and the groups that refused to accept the decrees of the first Vatican Council but a number of national churches in the Slavonic tradition that came into existence since the late 1800's. Minor groups were organized among the Czechs and Yugoslavs, but the largest contingent was formed among the Poles in the United States. Their bond of union with the Old Catholics was a common grievance against the Roman primacy.

The Polish National Church had two independent beginnings within two years. In 1895 the Chicago priest, Antoni Kozlowski, organized an independent parish and two years later was consecrated bishop by the Old Catholic prelate, Herzog, at Berne in Switzerland. Before his death in 1907, Kozlowski had established more than twenty parishes scattered from New Jersey to Manitoba.

In 1897 another Catholic priest, Francis Hodur, followed the same course at Scranton, Pennsylvania. He also went to Europe to have himself consecrated, receiving episcopal orders from the archbishop of Utrecht in 1907. During the interim, the two national groups had merged with Hodur at the head. Until his death in 1953, Francis Hodur developed the Polish National Church into a dominant partner of the Old Catholic family, with a communicant membership exceeding that of all the other affiliates combined.

Typical doctrinal positions of the Polish nationals are their concepts of original sin and the sacraments. "We do not teach," their Catechism states, "original sin as in the Roman Catholic Church—that it comes down to us from the origin of the human race, and that we inherit it through Adam." The Eucharist is said to contain "the mystical Body and Blood of Christ under the forms of bread and wine," and in the ritual the stress is on the Eucharist as spiritual food rather than sacrifice.

In 1946 the Polish National Church joined with the Church of England and the American Episcopalians, on the basis of the Bonn agreement which the Anglicans had made with the Old Catholics about fifteen years earlier. The foundation of their intercommunion rested on three cardinal points, that have since played a major role in deepening the bond between two ostensibly different religious bodies.

Each Communion recognizes the catholicity and independence of the other, and maintains its own.

Each Communion agrees to admit members of the other Communion to participation in the Sacraments.

Intercommunion does not require from either Communion the acceptance of all doctrinal opinion, sacramental devotion, or liturgical practice characteristic of the other, but implies that each believes the other to hold all the essentials of the Christian Faith.[3]

The Anglican communions in England and America accepted the Poles as associate members. Each group then appointed a Joint Intercommunion Committee to meet from time to time for discussing mutual problems and needs. After their first meeting the delegates reported that "the two Churches are dealing with a situation which has never before existed. Their separation is not due to schism. They are in fact two National Churches which, maintaining the doctrine and fellowship that have come down to them from the Apostles, find themselves in the same territory through the accident of immigration combined with the barrier of language." [4] At the Lambeth Conference in 1948, this achievement of full intercommunion was noted "with satisfaction and approval." Besides clarifying the nature and spirit of the Old Catholic movement, this merger also sheds light on the ecclesiastical structure of the Churches which stem from the English Reformation.

Quoted References

HE references follow the numerical sequence in the text, with complete bibliographical information and credit lines (where needed) to the respective publishers. In quoting from the sacred writings of the various religions, the text used was based on standard translations which were carefully collated, so that the version given may differ verbally, though not substantially, from the original text.

The two most extensive translations consulted were those in the *Harvard Oriental Series,* and the Oxford *Sacred Books of the East,* to both of whose publishers the author is deeply grateful for permission to quote and paraphrase.

A full complement of titles on the religions of the world would fill another sizeable volume. Yet if the works cited in the text are combined with the select bibliography which follows, a representative library on world religions is offered to the reader.

REFERENCES FOR CHAPTER 1. COMPARATIVE RELIGION IN PERSPECTIVE

1. Luther H. Evans (Unesco Director General), *Culture and Religious Values.* Address delivered at Vienna, September 6, 1958.
2. *Sources of Japanese Tradition,* New York, 1958, pp. 890-891.
3. Justin the Martyr, "Apologia I," *Patrologia Graeca* (Migne), 6, 374.
4. Origen, "Contra Celsum," *Ibid.,* 11, 886.
5. *Ibid.,* 887.
6. Donald A. Wells, *God, Man and the Thinker: Philosophies of Religion,* New York, 1962, p. 228.
7. *Hebrews* I, 1-2.
8. St. Thomas has suggested that in case of necessity God would "reveal by internal inspiration what he has to believe," to the "good pagan" who followed the dictates of conscience in doing good and avoiding evil (De Veritate, XIV, 11). Some theo-

475

logians have extended the idea to say that every dying person has a supreme moral test on which his destiny depends. At that moment infidels receive a special revelation. This theory is perhaps tenable, provided a possible exception to the ordinary course of Providence is not stated as an absolute and universal law.

9. Arnold Toynbee, *Christianity Among the Religions of the World,* New York, 1957, pp. 95-96.

10. E. O. James, *Comparative Religion,* London, 1961, p. 15.

11. *Romans* I, 19-21.

REFERENCES FOR CHAPTER 2. PRIMITIVE RELIGION

1. *Ancient Near Eastern Texts,* James B. Pritchard, editor, Princeton University Press, 1955, p. 423.
2. *Ibid.*
3. F. Wurtz, *Zietschrift fur Afrikanische Sprachen,* Vol. I, p. 324.
4. *Nika-English Dictionary,* n.d., p. 284.
5. E. S. Craiqhill Handy, *Polynesian Religion,* Honolulu, 1927, p. 197.

REFERENCES FOR CHAPTER 3. HINDUISM

1. *Rig Veda,* X, 121.
2. *Yajur Veda,* XXXIV, 1-6.
3. *Atharva Veda,* II, 15.
4. "Cata-Patha Brahmana," *Sacred Books of the East,* vol. IX, pp. 61-62.
5. Arthur B. Keith, *The Religion and Philosophy of the Veda and Upanishads,* 1925, p. 347.
6. *Chandogya Upanishad,* VI, 13, 1-3.
7. *Bhagavad Gita,* XVIII, 57-58, 65-70.
8. *Ibid.,* II, 18-25.
9. *Ibid.,* II, 47.
10. *Ibid.,* III, 17.
11. *Ibid.,* III, 41-43.
12. *Ibid.,* IV, 6-10.
13. *Ibid.,* IX, 27, 29-31.
14. *Srimad Bhagavatam,* Book X, chap. 4.
15. *Chhandogya Upanishad,* III, 14, 1.
16. *Brhad Upanishad,* II, 2, 1.
17. Vivekananda, *Raja-Yoga,* p. 21.
18. Louis Fischer, *The Life of Mahatma Gandhi,* New York, 1950, p. 144.
19. Vivekananda, *Bhakti Yoga.*
20. *Rig Veda,* X, 90.
21. *Bhagavad Gita,* II, 31-34.
22. *Manu Smrti,* XI, 177-180.
23. *Ibid.,* VI, 45-49.
24. *Vedanta Sutras* (Commentary), I, 1.
25. *Ibid.,* I, 1, 4.
26. *Ibid.,* IV, 1, 13.
27. *Vedanta Sutras,* (Commentary), I, 2, 12.
28. *Ibid.*
29. *A Tagore Testament,* New York, 1954, p. 67.
30. *Ibid.,* p. 9.
31. *Ibid.,* p. 10.
32. *Ibid.,* pp. 10-11.
33. *Ibid.,* p. 107.
34. *Ibid.,* p. 42.
35. Sarvepalli Radhakrishnan, *The Hindu Way of Life,* London, p. 67.
36. *Ibid.,* pp. 67-69.
37. *A Source Book in Indian Philosophy,* Princeton, 1957, pp. 615-616.
38. *Ibid.,* p. 616.

39. Mahatma K. Gandhi, *Autobiography*, Ahmedabad, 1948, pp. 49-50.
40. Mahatma K. Gandhi, *Christian Missions, Their Place in India*, Ahmedabad, 1941, pp. 5-6.
41. *Ibid.*, pp. 24-25.
42. Mahatma K. Gandhi, *Young India*, Dec. 22, 1927.
43. *Ibid.*, Sept. 25, 1925.
44. *Harijan*, Jan. 30, 1937.
45. *Christian Missions*, p. 3.
46. *Harijan*, Dec. 5, 1936.
47. *Ibid.*, May 25, 1935.
48. *Young India*, Sept. 25, 1925; *Harijan*, Jan. 16, 1937.
49. *Harijan*, Apr. 17, 1937.
50. *Ibid.*, Mar. 6, 1937.
51. *Ibid.*, Jan. 25, 1935.
52. *Ibid.*, Apr. 17, 1937.
53. *Ibid.*, May 11, 1935.
54. *Ibid.*, Sept. 28, 1935.
55. Jawaharlal Nehru, *Autobiography*, London, 1953, pp. 376-377.
56. *Ibid.*, p. 379.
57. Vijaya Lakshmi Pandit, *The Evolution of India*, London, 1958, pp. 7-8.
58. Article 17.
59. Article 25, Par. 1.
60. *Ibid.*, Par. 2.
61. *The Hindu Way of Life*, pp. 129-130.

REFERENCES FOR CHAPTER 4. BUDDHISM

1. *Maha-Parinibbana Sutta* (Book of the Great Decease), II, 33.
2. *Ibid.*, VI, 10.
3. *Ibid.*, VI, 11.
4. *Chullavagga*, IX, 1, 4.
5. *Dhammapada*, XXII.
6. *Anguttara-Nikaya*, III, 35.
7. *Sutta-Nipata*, XXI, 3.
8. *Majjhima-Nikaya*, 63.
9. *Mahavagga*, I, 6, 38-46.
10. *Milindapanha*, II, 1.
11. *Ibid.*, 13.
12. *Ibid.*
13. *Samyutta-Nikaya*, LVI.
14. *Majjhima-Nikaya*, 9.
15. *Ibid.*, 117.
16. *Anguttara-Nikaya*, X, 176.
17. *Ibid.*
18. *Ibid.*, IV, 13-14.
19. *Majjhima-Nikaya*, 20.
20. *Anguttara-Nikaya*, IV, 13-14.
21. *Ibid.*
22. *Digha-Nikaya*, XXII.
23. *Majjhima-Nikaya*, 119.
24. *Ibid.*
25. *Lotus of the Good Law*, XV.
26. *Mahayana-Sutra-Lamkara*, XVI, 16.
27. *Bodhicaryavatra*, VIII.
28. *Ibid.*, V.
29. *Ibid.*, VII.
30. Santideva, *Siksasamuccaya* (C. Bendall edit.), p. 212.
31. *Bodhicaryavatra*, VIII.
32. *Itivuttaka*, 27.
33. *Lieou tou tsi King* (translated in *Cinq cents contes et apologetiques*, I, 2-3).
34. Milarepa, *Spiritual Testament* (J. Bacot transl.), Paris, p. 285.
35. *Samdhinirmocana Sutra*, IX, 17.
36. *Mahayana-Sutra-Lamkara*, XVI.
37. A similar expedient is the practice of offering one's corpse to be devoured by dogs after death.
38. *Mahaprajnaparamitasatra*, I, 20.
39. *Bodhicaryavatra*, V.
40. *Vajracchedika Prajnaparamita*, XXVI.
41. Bhikshu Sangharakshita, *A Survey of Buddhism*, Bangalore, 1959, p. 232.
42. *Ibid.*, p. 235.
43. Nyogen Senzaki, *Buddhism and Zen*, New York, 1953, p. 10.
44. Sangharakshita, *op. cit.*, pp. 238-239.

45. Daisetz T. Suzuki, *The Training of the Zen Buddhist Monk*, p. 17.
46. *Ibid.*
47. *Digha-Nikaya*, III, 3.
48. *Ibid.*
49. Hokei Idumi, "Vimalakirti's Discourse," *The Eastern Buddhist*, III, 2, pp. 138-139.
50. Senzaki, *op. cit.*, p. 11.

REFERENCE FOR CHAPTER 5. JAINISM

1. *Tattvarthadhigama Sutra*, IX, 2-36.

REFERENCES FOR CHAPTER 6. CONFUCIANISM

1. *Analects of Confucius*, X, 1-2, 5, 8, 15.
2. Decree of the Congregation for the Propagation of the Faith (December 8, 1939). Complete English text in Malcolm Hay, *Failure in the Far East*, Philadelphia, 1957, pp. 190-192.
3. *Ibid.*
4. *Yi King*, I, 15.
5. *Ibid.*, Appendix V, 6: 10, 10: 14.
6. *Shuh King* (Books of Shang), IV, 6: 1-2.
7. *Shih King* (Songs for the Lesser Festivals), II.
8. *Hsiao King*, III.
9. *Ibid.*, IV.
10. *Ibid.*, V.
11. *Ibid.*, I.
12. *Ibid.*, VII.
13. *Book of Mencius*, VI, 1, 6.
14. *Analects*, II, 13-14; III, 10-11; IV, 16, 22, 24; XIV, 45; XV, 17-21, 36.
15. *Ibid.*, XVI.
16. *Ibid.*, XII, 22; XIII, 19; XVII, 6.
17. *Ibid.*, IV, 5-6.
18. *Ibid.*, IV, 19, 21.
19. *Ibid.*, II, 5.
20. *Ibid.*, II, 7-8.
21. *Ibid.*, IV, 18.
22. *Ibid.*, I, 11.
23. *The Doctrine of the Mean*, XIX.
24. *Analects*, VI, 27.
25. *The Doctrine of the Mean*, IV, X.
26. *Ibid.*, XIV.
27. *Mencius*, VI, 1, 6.
28. Homer H. Dubs, *The Works of Hsüntze*, London, 1928, pp. 301-304.
29. *Ibid.*, p. 305.
30. James Legge, *The Chinese Classics*, vol. I, Oxford, 1893, pp. 357-358.
31. H. G. Creel, *Chinese Thought*, Chicago, 1953, p. 38.
32. H. H. Gerth & C. W. Mills, *From Max Weber: Essays in Sociology*, New York, 1946, p. 293.
33. *Book of History*, IV, 94.
34. *Analects*, XII, 5.
35. *Ibid.*, IX, 5.
36. *Ibid.*, VII, 34.
37. *Ibid.*, XIV, 37.
38. *Ibid.*, III, 13.
39. *Doctrine of the Mean*, XIX.
40. *Analects*, II, 3.
41. *Li-Ki*, XIV, 5-7.
42. *Analects*, VIII, 8.
43. *Analects*, III, 25; VII, 13; XV, 10.
44. *Sacred Books of the East*, London, 1926, vol. XXVIII, pp. 98 f.
45. *Ibid.*, pp. 103 f.
46. *Lieh Tzu*, VII, 1, 2.
47. *Lao Tzu*, chap. 46.
48. Wang Ch'ung, *Lun-yü*, XIII, 38.
49. *Hsin Ch'ing-nien*, vol. 5, num. 5.
50. Mao Tse-tung, *China's New Democracy*, New York, 1945, p. 48.
51. *Ibid.*, p. 61.
52. *Ibid.*, pp. 61-2.

53. Liu Shao-chi, *How To Be A Good Communist,* Peking, 1951, p. 83.
54. *Ibid.,* p. 16.

55. Sun Yat-sen, *The Three Principles of the People,* Shanghai, 1929, pp. 17, 88.

REFERENCES FOR CHAPTER 7. TAOISM

1. *Tao Teh Ching,* I, 4.
2. *Ibid.,* I, 21.
3. *Ibid.,* I, 25.
4. *Ibid.,* I, 34.
5. *Ibid.,* II, 39.
6. *Ibid.,* II, 67.
7. *Ibid.,* II, 78.

8. *Ibid.,* II, 48.
9. *Ibid.,* II, 22.
10. *Ibid.,* II, 55.
11. *Passim* in J. Shryock, *The Temples of Anking,* Paris, 1931.
12. *Tao Teh Ching,* LVII.
13. *Ibid.,* LXV.

REFERENCES FOR CHAPTER 8. ZOROASTRIANISM

1. R. C. Zaehner, *Living Faiths* (Zoroastrianism), 1959, p. 209.
2. *Yasna,* XXVIII, 4.
3. *Yasna,* XLVI, 1.
4. *Yasna,* XLIV, 3-7.
5. *Yasna,* XLV, 2-3.

6. *Yasna,* XXXIII, 3-6.
7. *Yasna,* XXXII, 3.
8. *The Teachings of the Magi* (R. C. Zaehner), 1956, pp. 22-23.
9. *The Treasure of the Magi* (J. H. Moulton), 1917, p. 162.

REFERENCES FOR CHAPTER 9. SHINTO

1. Takasu Yoshijiro, *Shinron Kowa,* Tokyo, 1941, p. 20.
2. Tsunoda and Goodrich, *Japan in the Chinese Dynastic Histories,* Pasadena, 1951, p. 11.
3. *Nihongi* (W. G. Aston transl.), II, p. 66.
4. *Shoku Nihongi,* Edict 38.
5. *Nihongi,* article X.
6. *Ibid.,* Article III.
7. *Jinno shoto-ki,* Tokyo, 1927, p. 1.
8. Quoted in Kiyowara Sadao, *Shinto-shi,* Tokyo, 1932, p. 237.
9. *Monumenta Nipponica,* II, pp. 165-

192.
10. *Ibid.*
11. *Motoori Norinaga Zenshu,* VI, pp. 3-6.
12. *Ibid.*
13. *Ibid.*
14. *Ibid.*
15. *Hirata Atsutane Zenshu,* I, pp. 6-7.
16. *Ibid.*
17. *Ibid.,* p. 27.
18. *Ibid.,* p. 28.
19. *Ibid.,* 27-28.
20. *Ibid.*

REFERENCES FOR CHAPTER 10. SIKHISM

1. Khushwant Singh, *The Sikhs,* London, 1953, p. 27.
2. *Ibid.,* p. 188.
3. *Ibid.,* p. 36.

4. *Ibid.,* p. 37 ("Amar Das," III Guru).
5. *Ibid.,* p. 42.

REFERENCES FOR CHAPTER 11. JUDAISM

1. *Acts* XIII, 38-39.
2. *Acts* XIII, 46-47.
3. Treatise *Betzah* (Yom Tob), chap. I, Mishna I.
4. Treatise *Abuda Zara,* chap. I, Mishna II.
5. Treatise *Sanhedrin,* chap. X, Mishnah IV.
6. *Babylonian Talmud,* New York, 1916, vol. 8, p. 256.
7. Treatise *Aboth,* chap. II, Mishna XVI.
8. *Ibid.,* chap. III, Mishna XIII.
9. *Ibid.,* chap. IV, Mishna XVII.
10. *Ibid.,* Mishna XIX-XX.
11. *Ibid.,* chap. V, Mishna XV.
12. Treatise *Pesachim,* chap. II, Gemara **VII.**
13. *Ibid.,* chap. X, Gemarara III.
14. *Ibid.,* "*Tosephtha—Aboth* of Rabbi Nathan."
15. *Ibid.*
16. Treatise *Derech Eretz-Zuta,* chap. I.
17. Treatise *Sabbath,* chap. XXII, Gemara VI.
18. Jacob S. Minkin, *The World of Moses Maimonides,* New York, Thomas Yoseloff, 1957, p. 27.
19. Moses Maimonides, Commentary on Mishna *Sanhedrin* X, 1.
20. Maimonides, *The Guide for the Perplexed,* Part II, chap. 25.
21. *Ibid.,* III, 51.
22. *Repentance,* 3.
23. *Micheas* IV, 1-13.
24. *Daily Prayers,* New York, Hebrew Pub. Co., p. 17.
25. *Ibid.,* p. 167.
26. *Ibid.,* p. 419.
27. *Ibid.,* pp. 567-569.
28. *Ibid.,* p. 21.
29. *Ibid.,* p. 173.
30. *Ibid.,* p. 181.
31. *Ibid.,* p. 703.
32. *Ibid.,* p. 21.
33. *Ibid.,* p. 529.
34. *Ibid.,* p. 641.
35. *Exodus* XII, 27.
36. *Deuteronomy* XII, 23.
37. *Ibid.,* XIV, 7-8.
38. *Leviticus* XI, 41.
39. Moses Mendelssohn, *Jerusalem,* London, 1838, pp. 89, 102.
40. David Philipson, *The Reform Movement in Judaism,* 1931, pp. 355-7.
41. Albert Einstein, *Out of My Later Years,* New York, 1950, pp. 28-29.
42. *Judaism,* "Symposium on the Orthodox, Reform and Conservative View," 1944, pp. 39-40.
43. *Ibid.,* p. 40.
44. Moses Maimonides (Letter to the Jews of Yemen), in *A Treasury of Jewish Letters* (F. Kobler, edit.), Philadelphia, 1954, Vol. I, p. 185.
45. Sigmund Freud, *Complete Psychological Works,* London, 1959, Vol. XX, p. 273.
46. Sigmund Freud, *Collected Papers,* London, 1950, Vol. V, p. 244.
47. *Ibid.,* p. 174.
48. *Complete Psychological Works,* XX, pp. 273-274.
49. Sigmund Freud, *An Autobiographical Study,* London, 1950, pp. 14-15.
50. Sigmund Freud, *The Future of An Illusion,* New York, 1957, pp. 95-96.
51. Sigmund Freud, *Complete Psychological Works,* London, 1961, Vol. XIX, p. 291.
52. Mordecai M. Kaplan, *The Future of the American Jew,* New York, 1948, pp. 219-220.
53. Samson Raphael Hirsch, *The Nineteen Letters of Ben Uziel,* New York, 1942 (Seventh Letter).
54. Abraham Isaac Kook, "The Re-

birth of Israel," in Arthur Hertzberg, *The Zionist Idea*, New York, 1959, p. 424.
55. *Ibid.*
56. *Ibid.*, p. 425.
57. Leo Jung, "Judaism in the Solution of the Jewish Question," *Symposium*, p. 19.
58. M. Auerbach, "Survey of Jewish History," *Jewish Library*, II Edition, First Series, p. 323.
59. Leo Jung, *loc. cit.*

60. *Ibid.*, pp. 19-20.
61. Martin Buber, *Israel and the World*, New York, 1948, p. 89.
62. Martin Buber, *At the Turning*, New York, 1952, p. 36.
63. *Ibid.*, pp. 36-37.
64. *The Writings of Martin Buber* (Will Herberg, edit.), New York, 1958, p. 296.
65. *Ibid.*, p. 275.
66. *Ibid.*
67. *Ibid.*, p. 276.

REFERENCES FOR CHAPTER 12. EARLY CHRISTIANITY

1. *Testament of Levi*, XVIII, 2-5, 8-9.
2. *John* IV, 25-26.
3. *Luke* IV, 18, 21.
4. II *Peter*, I, 16.
5. I *Corinthians*, XV, 3, 19.
6. I *John*, I, 1.
7. St. Ignatius of Antioch, *Epistle to the Trallians*, 9-10.
8. *II Epistle to the Philippians*, 7.
9. *John*, X, 30-39.
10. *John*, VI, 48-70.
11. *Matthew*, XIX, 3-12.
12. *Matthew*, X, 37.
13. *John*, XV, 5; XIV, 13.
14. *Mark*, XVI, 16.
15. St. Ignatius of Antioch, *Letter to the Philadelphians*, 4.

16. *John*, XX, 21-23.
17. *Koran*, Surah, V, 82-85.
18. *Matthew*, XVI, 17-19.
19. *Enchiridion Symbolorum*, 1825.
20. Nicolas Zernov, *The Church of the Eastern Christians*, London, 1942, p. 55.
21. Martin Luther, *Werke* (Weimar), XI, pp. 405-415.
22. Oscar Cullman, *Peter, Disciple-Apostle-Martyr*, New York, World Publishing, 1961, p. 207.
23. Carl Michalson, "Authority," in *Handbook of Christian Theology*, New York, 1962, pp. 27-28.

REFERENCES FOR CHAPTER 13. ROMAN CATHOLICISM

1. Adolph Harnack, *Das Wesen des Christentums*, Leipzig, 1933, p. 164.
2. Tacitus, *Annales*, XV, 44.
3. Pliny the Younger, *Letters*, 96, 5.
4. I *Corinthians*, XVI, 22; Galatians I, VI, 14, 17.
5. *Romans*, VIII, 35-39.
6. *Acts*, I, 21-22.
7. *Acts*, III, 6-8.
8. *Matthew*, XVI, 18; XVIII, 17.
9. *Acts*, XV, 7-11, 16-19.

10. I *Corinthians*, III, 16-17.
11. I *Peter*, I, 1.
12. *Zadokite Document*, 5.
13. Mark X, 4-6.
14. *Manual of Discipline for the Future Congregation of Israel*, ad finem.
15. *Ibid.*
16. St. Ireneus, *Adversus Haereses*, III, 3, 1-2.
17. *Enchiridion Symbolorum*, 54.
18. *Ibid.*, 132.

19. *Ibid.*, 469.
20. H. Finke, *Aus den Tagen Bonifaz VIII*, Munster, 1902, p. 156.
21. Abbé Englebert, *St. Francis of Assisi*, London, pp. 95-96.
22. Lecoy de la Marche, *L'esprit de nos Aieux*, Paris, p. 40.
23. H. Richard Niebuhr, *Christ and Culture*, New York, 1956, p. 130.
24. St. Thomas, *Expositio Symboli Apostolorum*, Art. 8.
25. Ferdinand Gregorovius, *Storia della Citta di Roma nel Medio Evo*, 1943, vol. XII, p. 249.
26. *Letters of St. Catherine of Siena*, New York, 1927, pp. 119, 235.
27. *Ibid.*, p. 261.
28. Mansi, vol. XXVII, col. 585, 590.
29. *Enchiridion*, 694.
30. J. Quicherat (ed.), *Proces de Condemnation et de Rehabilitation de Jeanne d'Arc*, vol. I, p. 445.
31. Ludwig Pastor, *The History of the Popes*, vol. IX, pp. 134-135.
32. *Ibid.*, p. 135.
33. Martin Luther, *Werke* (Weimar), I, p. 69.
34. *Spiritual Exercises*, First Rule for Thinking with the Church.
35. *Letters of St. Francis Xavier*, London, 1888, p. 10.
36. *Religious Education in the Schools of Canada*, 1953, p. 3.
37. John XXIII, *Osservatore Romano*, October 12, 1962.
38. St. Ignatius of Antioch, *Epistle to the Smyrneans*, 8.
39. St. Justin, *Dialogue with Trypho*, 117.
40. St. Ireneus, *Adversus Haereses*, I, 10, 2.
41. St. Robert Bellarmine, *De Ecclesia Militante*, 10.
42. *Ibid.*, 2.
43. Pius XII, *Mystici Corporis*, 17.
44. *Enchiridion*, 696.
45. *Didache* (Teaching of the Twelve Apostles), IX, 4.
46. Pius XII, *Mediator Dei*.
47. Richard Cardinal Cushing, *The Christian and the Community*, 1960, p. 15.
48. Pius XI, *Casti Connubii*, 54.
49. Paul VI, *Osservatore Romano*, September 30, 1963.

REFERENCES FOR CHAPTER 14. ISLAM

1. Surah IV, 136.
2. Surah II, 255.
3. Surah IV, 48.
4. Surah LXXIV, 31.
5. Surah I, 1.
6. Surah II, 117.
7. Surah X, 4.
8. Abdullah Yusuf Ali, *The Holy Qur-an*, New York, 1946, vol. I, p. 103.
9. Surah III, 129.
10. El-Bokhari, *Les Traditions Mussulmanes*, Paris, 1914, vol. III, pp. 278-279.
11. Surah III, 42-47, XIX, 19-22.
12. Surah XIX, 29-31.
13. Surah III, 49-52.
14. Surah III, 56-57.
15. Surah III, 3, 10, 12.
16. Surah IV, 155-158.
17. Surah XIX, 33.
18. Surah III, 59-61.
19. Surah V, 72-75.
20. Surah XXXIII, 40.
21. Surah V, 116.
22. Surah IV, 171-173.
23. Surah LXXXIV.
24. Surah XI, 119; L, 30.
25. Surah II, 190-193.
26. Surah IX, 5, 29-30.
27. Surah II, 256; V, 48; CIX, 1-6.
28. R. A. Nicholson, *Literary History of the Arabs*, Cambridge, 1930, p. 234.

29. Al-Hujwiri, *Kashf al-Mahjub*, Translated by R. A. Nicholson, n.d., p. 363.
30. Surah V, 51.
31. Surah III, 19, 85.
32. Ibn Madja, *Sunan, Hudub,* Bab. 2.
33. Statement of Moslem observers to the World Council of Churches, (Abdullah Igram, Dean Hekim, M. Yousef Sharwarbi), 1954, private printing.
34. Abdullah Yusuf Ali, *The Holy Qur-an,* New York, 1946, vol. I, p. 145.
35. *Poems from Iqbal,* "The Way of Islam," London, 1955, p. 65.
36. *Ibid.*
37. *Constitution of Pakistan,* Part I, art. 1 (1).
38. *Ibid.,* Part III, art. 24.
39. *Ibid.,* art. 25 (1-2).
40. *Ibid.,* art. 28.
41. *Ibid.,* Part II, art. 18, 21.
42. *Ibid.,* art. 5, 13 (1).
43. *Ibid.,* art. 13 (4-5).
44. *Constitution of the Republic of Pakistan,* Part I, art. 1 (1).
45. *Ibid.,* Preamble.
46. *Ibid.,* Part X, art. 204 (la).
47. Iqbal, *op. cit.,* pp. 42-43.
48. Surah II, 177.

REFERENCES FOR CHAPTER 15. EASTERN ORTHODOXY

1. Matthew Paris, I, p. 312.
2. *Deianiia Sviashchennago Sobora,* III, p. 83.
3. Nicholas Zernov, *The Russians and Their Church,* London, S.P.C.K., 1945, p. 163.
4. N. Orleanski, *Zakon o Religiozniykh Ob'edineniiakh,* pp. 6-12.
5. *Izvestiia,* February 4, 1945.
6. *Izvestiia,* May 12, 1945.
7. *Soviet Review,* July, 1961, p. 48.
8. *Ibid.,* p. 55.
9. M. Malinovsky, *Pravoslavonoe Dsogmateskoe Bogoslovie,* 1910, p. 77.
10. *Catechismus Philaret,* Proemium.
11. August Hahn, *Bibliothek der Symbole und Glaubensregeln der alten Kirche,* Breslau, 1897, 253.
12. St. Gregory Thaumaturgus, "Expositio Fidei," *Bibliothek der Symbole* (Hahn), Breslau, 1897, p. 253.
13. Silvester Malevansky, *Opit Pravoslavvago Dogmatecheskaro Bogosloviya,* 1884, p. 62.
14. Sergius Bulgakov, *The Comforter,* Paris, 1937, p. 184.
15. Philaretus Gumilevsky, *Pravoslavnoe Dogmateskoe Bogoslovie,* Petersburg, 1882, II, p. 221.
16. Macarius Bulgakov, *Orthodox Dogmatic Theology,* Petrograd, 1883, II, p. 235.
17. Theophylact Gorskii, *Dogmas of the Orthodox Eastern Church,* Moscow, 1831, pp. 269-270.
18. Alexius Khomjakov, *L'Eglise latine et le protestantisme au point de vue de l'Eglise d'Orient,* Lausanne, 1872, p. 228.
19. N. Birbeck, *Russia and the English Church,* London, 1895, p. 94.
20. S. Bulgakov, *The Orthodox Church,* London, 1935, pp. 67, 88-89.
21. Arcudius, *De Concordia Ecclesiae Occidentalis et Orientalis,* Paris, p. 5.
22. Jerome Tarasij, *Perelom v Drevnerooskom Bogoslovie,* Warsaw, 1927, pp. 178-184.
23. Nicholas Zernov, *The Church of the Eastern Christians,* London, 1942, p. 45.
24. I. Goar, *Euchologium Gracorum,* Venice, p. 542.

25. *Ibid.*
26. Sylvester Lebedinskii, *Classic Compendium of Theology,* Moscow, 1805, p. 523.
27. Zernov, *op. cit.,* pp. 49-50.
28. I Goar, *Euchologium,* Rome, pp. 181-204.
29. S. Bulgakov, *The Orthodox Church,* London, 1935, p. 137.
30. *Patriarch's Answer to Nonjurors,* London, 1718, p. 53.
31. "Declaration of the Orthodox Delegates Concerning the Main Theme of the Assembly," August 25, 1954, Private Printing.

32. *Longer Russian Catechism,* Moscow, p. 78.
33. *The Confession of Metrophanes Kritopoulos,* Athens, p. 345.
34. *Ibid.,* p. 353.
35. Sydney Loch, *Athos: The Holy Mountain,* London, 1957, pp. 244-248.
36. "The Confession of Dositheus" (Translated in *The Relations of the Anglican Churches with the Eastern-Orthodox,* London, 1921, p. 144).
37. F. Brightman, *Eastern Liturgies,* Oxford, pp. 386-387.

REFERENCES FOR CHAPTER 16. PROTESTANTISM

1. H. Wrampelmeyer, *Tagebuch über Dr. Martin Luther,* Halle, 1885, p. 165.
2. Luther, *Opera Latina,* VI, 8.
3. *Formula of Concord,* "De Compendiaria Regula atque Norma," 3.
4. Calvin, *Institutes of the Christian Religion,* I, 7, 4-5.
5. Luther, *Commentary on Genesis,* III, 7.
6. *Ibid.*
7. *The Augsburg Confession,* 20.
8. *Ibid.,* 18.
9. Francis Pieper, *Christian Dogmatics.* St. Louis, 1950, I, p. 555.
10. Arthur C. Piepkorn, *What the Symbolical Books of the Lutheran Church Have to Say about Worship and the Sacraments,* St. Louis, 1952, p. 30.
11. Resolution of Missouri Synod (1890), *A Century of Grace,* St. Louis, 1947, p. 207.
12. *Lutheran Hymnal,* St. Louis, p. 262.
13. *Declaration of Principles of the League for Evangelical-Catholic Reunion,* VI.
14. *Confession of Faith, Presbyterian Church U.S.A.,* XXV, 6.
15. *Ibid.,* VII, 1.

16. Karl Barth, *La Priere, d'apres les Catechismes de la Reformation,* Neuchatel (Switzerland), 1949, p. 49.
17. *Ibid.,* p. 51.
18. *Presbyterian Confession of Faith,* XXVII, 3.
19. *Baptist Church Manual,* Nashville, 1955, p. 102.
20. George Fox, *Journal,* Cambridge University Press, 1952, p. 33.
21. *Documents of the Christian Church* (H. Bettenson edit.), 1947, pp. 323-324.
22. *Statutes of the Realm,* IV, 2, pp. 841-843.
23. James T. Addison, *The Episcopal Church,* New York, 1951, p. 273.
24. *Ibid.,* p. 274.
25. *The Examiner,* December 16, 1961.
26. John Wesley, "The Character of a Methodist," *Works,* London, Vol. VIII, p. 31.
27. John Wesley, "Free Grace," *Works,* Vol. VII, p. 373.
28. *Methodist Discipline,* num. 86.
29. *Wesley's Prayers and Praises* (J. Alan Kay edit.), London, Epworth Press, 1958, p. 79.
30. Wesley, *Works,* Vol. I, p. xxii.
31. *Methodist Discipline,* num. 2022.

32. *Acts,* II, 4.
33. *The First Assembly of the World Council of Churches, the Official Report,* New York, 1949, p. 28.
34. *Report on the Main Theme of the Second Assembly,* Geneva, 1954, p. 15.
35. *Introducing the Faith and Order Report* (Evanston), August 17, 1954.
36. *Report on Faith and Order* (Evanston), 1954, p. 3.
37. Visser 't Hooft, *The Third World Conference on Faith and Order,* London, 1953, p. 130.
38. *The Second World Council on Faith and Order,* London, 1938, p. 20.
39. Visser 't Hooft, "The Calling of the World Council of Churches," *The Ecumenical Review,* January, 1962, pp. 222-223.
40. Calvin, *Institutes,* III, 20, 1.
41. *Theological Declaration of the Synod of Barmen,* May 31, 1934.
42. Karl Barth, *Church Dogmatics,* Edinburgh, 1957, vol. II, 1, p. 173.
43. Paul Tillich, *The Protestant Era,* Chicago, 1948, pp. 162-163.
44. *Ibid.,* p. 163.
45. Reinhold Niebuhr, *Our Dependence Is Upon God* (Address at the Evanston Assembly of the World Council of Churches, 1954), Document 15-A, p. 3.
46. J. T. McNeill, *The Protestant Credo* (Vergilius Ferm, editor), New York, p. 116.
47. *The Third World Conference on Faith and Order* (Oliver S. Tomkins, editor), London, 1953, p. 20.

REFERENCES FOR CHAPTER 17. OLD CATHOLIC CHURCHES

1. Constitution, *Ad Sacram Beati Petri Cathedram,* Oct. 16, 1656.
2. J. M. Neale, *History of the So-Called Jansenist Church of Holland,* pp. 363-364.
3. Theodore Andrews, *The Polish National Church,* London, 1953, p. 90.
4. *Ibid.,* p. 91. Also Lambeth (1949) Resolution 67-b.

Note: With grateful acknowledgment, the following bibliography gives complete publishers' data on the principal sources quoted and consulted by the author.

Bibliography

T HERE is an immense literature on every aspect of the living
religions of the world. The following titles are selected as
most representative on the basis of scholarship and suitability
for all classes of readers, including those who already have a good
foundation in comparative religious culture. Except for standard
source material, most of the books are recent publications or re-
editions which contain more extensive bibliographies for those who
wish to carry their studies further into specialized areas. *Titles
marked with an asterisk are available in paperback form.* Dates of
publication refer to the latest cloth-cover edition, but all the titles
are either in print or easily accessible in libraries.

No effort was made to include foreign titles, both because many
of the books have been translated into English and because the
literature in other languages tends to be highly specialized. There
are two definitive works which offer complete and up to date bibliographies in all the Indo-European languages: Maxime Gorce and
Raoul Mortier, *Histoire Generale des Religions,* Aristide Quillet,
Paris, 1947, in four volumes; and Kurt Galling, *Die Religionen in
Geschichte und Gegenwart,* Mohr, Tubingen, 1956, in seven volumes.

The brief annotations for each title are not evaluative but merely
descriptive of the contents. In the nature of things, the field of
comparative religion gives the authors wide scope for interpretation
according to their own religious persuasion or philosophy of life.
For this reason strictly interpretative writings, which are numerous,
have been omitted.

Among the higher religions, those professing monotheism are
more readily treated as distinct cultural entities, whereas other religions, notably those of the Far East, tend to overlap and flow one

into the other. This is reflected in their respective literatures, which are either distinctive or coalescent and more generalized.

SOURCES AND SACRED WRITINGS

Robert O. Ballou, *The Bible of the World,* New York, Viking, 1939. Handbook of 1400 pages with a wide selection of texts from the sacred books of eight living faiths. Abridged form as *The Portable World Bible.**

A. C. Bouquet, *Sacred Books of the World,* Baltimore, Penguin, 1960. Selections arranged to show the development of religious thought.*

Lewis Browne, *The World's Great Scriptures,* New York, Macmillan, 1946. Anthology of the sacred writings of Babylonia, Egypt, India, China, Judaism, Christianity and Islam.*

William T. De Bary, *Introduction to Oriental Civilizations,* Columbia University Press, 1958 to 1960. New series of textual selections from previously unpublished writings, in three volumes, one each for the religions of China, India and Japan.

C. R. Lanman (editor), *Harvard Oriental Series,* Harvard University Press, 1895 to the present. Forty-three volumes of texts, mainly of Hindu and Buddhist sacred literature, with commentaries.

Max Muller (editor), *Sacred Books of the East,* Oxford, Clarendon, 1879-1910. Translation in fifty volumes of the sacred non-Christian books which have shaped the religion of Asia. General index in separate volume. Complements the texts in the Harvard Oriental Series.

GENERAL SURVEYS

A. C. Bouquet, *Comparative Religion,* London (Baltimore), Penguin, 1956. Readable survey covering history, thought and practice of principal faiths.*

Mircea Eliade, *Patterns in Comparative Religion,* New York, Sheed and Ward, 1958. Encyclopedic review of ancient and modern religions, classified according to basic patterns that underlie all the faiths of mankind.

Robert E. Hume, *The World's Living Religions,* New York, Scribner's, 1959. Revision of an older work useful as reference, giving salient facts and stimulating judgments challenged by others.

E. O. James, *Comparative Religion,* New York, Barnes and Noble, 1961. Compact analysis of the dominant issues in world religion: monism and monotheism, sin and atonement, worship and prayer. Christian appraisal.*

Joseph M. Kitagawa, *Religions of the East,* Philadelphia, Westminster, 1960. Study of Chinese religion, Hinduism, Buddhism and Islam against the background of the Christian concept of the Church.

Hendrick Kraemar, *World Cultures and World Religions,* Philadelphia, Westminster, 1960. Examination of the new status of non-Christian religions in their impact on Christianity.

Benson Y. Landis, *World Religions,* New York, Dutton, 1957. Brief sketches of the principal beliefs of living religions. Statistical data.

John B. Noss, *Man's Religions,* New York, Macmillan, 1961. Quotes freely from sacred writings and primary sources. Stress on Indian religions and Protestantism.

Huston Smith, *The Religions of Man,* New York, Harper, 1958. Emphasis on religious experience explained in terms of the cultural history of the West.*

Joachim Wach, *The Comparative Study of Religions,* edited by Joseph M. Kitagawa, Columbia University Press, 1958. By the author of the standard *Sociology of Religion,* with attention to Christian and non-Christian types of religious experience.*

R. C. Zaehner, *The Concise Encyclopedia of Living Faiths,* New York, Hawthorn, 1959. Fifteen contributors on as many major religions, each a specialist in his field. Summary section interprets religion in terms of Jung's depth psychology and Hegelian idealism.

PRIMITIVE RELIGIONS

James G. Frazer, *The Golden Bough: A Study in Magic and Religion,* New York, Macmillan, 1935. Originally in twelve volumes, and later abridged to one, the *Golden Bough* seeks to prove the linear evolution of religion from magic and of Christianity from ancient mythologies.*

William J. Goode, *Religion Among the Primitives,* Glencoe, Ill., Free Press, 1951. Sociological critique of current theories on the origin of religion. Functional approach.

E. O. James, *Prehistoric Religion,* New York, Praeger, 1957. Factual study of earliest religious cultures: burial rituals, birth, fertility, food supply and the ancient sky religion.

Robert H. Lowie, *Primitive Religion,* New York, Liveright, 1952. Analysis of Crow, Ekoi, Bukaua, and Polynesian religions. Evaluaation of animism, magic and collectivist theories on religious origins.*

Bronislaw Malinowski, *Magic, Science and Religion,* New York, Doubleday, 1960. Functionalist theory on the origins of religion, following in the tradition of Frazer.*

Paul Radin, *Primitive Religion,* New York, Dover, 1957. Reconstruction of the beliefs and religious experiences of aboriginal peoples. Highly critical of other theories. Evolutionary hypothesis of religion from animism.*

William Schmidt, *The Origin and Growth of Religion,* New York, Dial, 1935. One volume edition of the ten volume work, *Der Ursprung der Gottesidee,* challenging animist theories on the origin of religion. The most archaic cultures are shown to have a high-god pattern, with animism as a decadent development.

Edward B. Taylor, *Religion in Primitive Culture,* New York, Harper, 1958. Classic exposition of the theory that animism is the primitive culture of mankind. Sees Christianity evolving towards the age of reason without dogma.*

NON-CHRISTIAN RELIGIONS

Sydney Cave, *Living Religions of the East,* London, Duckworth, 1952. Compact and highly informative review of Hinduism, Zoroastrianism, Buddhism, the religions of China and Japan, and Islam.

Sydney Cave, *Christianity and Some Living Religions of the East,* London, Duckworth, 1944. Objective analysis of the basic principles of the main Oriental religions compared with Christianity as the fulfilment of man's religious needs.

Jacques-Albert Cuttat, *The Encounter of Religions,* New York, Desclee, 1960. Catholic evaluation of Hinduism, Buddhism and Islam, based on primary sources and directed to a deeper appreciation of Eastern religious culture.

C. N. E. Eliot, *Hinduism and Buddhism,* New York, Barnes and Noble, 1954. Three volume historical study of early Indian religion, Buddhism within and outside India, mutual influence of Eastern and Western religions, and present-day Hinduism.

Stephen Neill, *Christian Faith and Other Faiths,* London, Oxford University Press, 1961. Sympathetic Christian approach to the "coming dialogue" between Christianity and the other living faiths, notably Judaism, Islam, Hinduism and Buddhism.

George C. Ring, *Religions of the Far East,* Milwaukee, Bruce, 1950.

Historical and evaluative study of the religions of China, Japan and India; also of Buddhism and Islam. Gives a Christian explanation of trends and tenets.

Arnold Toynbee, *Christianity Among the Religions of the World,* New York, Scribner's, 1957. Defends the thesis that Christians should recognize all the higher religions, especially Hinduism, Buddhism and Islam, as "revelations of what is true and right," since they also come from God."

INDIA

Sri U. Acarya, *Tattvardhadhigama Sutra* (Sacred Books of the Jainas, II), Arrah, India; Central Jaina Publishing House, 1920. English version of some of the earliest Jain sacred literature.

A. L. Basham, *The Wonder That Was India,* New York, Evergreen, 1959. Widely read history of India, with special reference to cultural developments before the coming of the Moslems. Section on calendar, mathematics, logic and alphabet.*

Surendra N. Dasgupta, *History of Indian Philosophy,* Cambridge University Press, 1922-1955. Five volume study of the main streams of Indian thought over the centuries. Sacred texts and commentaries analyzed. Entire volume on Indian pluralism.

J. M. Dechanet, *Christian Yoga,* New York, Harper, 1959. Theory and practice of those features of Indian Yoga which the author feels can be profitably used by Christians to improve their moral life and prayer.

Mahatma K. Gandhi, *Autobiography,* Ahmedabad, 1948. Full length self appraisal of the leading figure in modern Hinduism.

Mahatma K. Gandhi, *Christian Missions, Their Place in India,* Ahmedabad, 1941. Forthright exposition of the Mahatma's critical attitude towards Christian missionary efforts.

Homer A. Jack, *The Gandhi Reader,* Indiana University Press, 1956. Twenty chapters of full-text statements by and about Gandhi on a wide range of topics, including Hinduism, Communism and Christianity.

Solange Lemâitre, *Hinduism,* New York, Hawthorn, 1959. Volume in the Twentieth Century Encyclopedia of Catholicism. Traces Hindu tradition from earliest times to the present; quotations from primary sources.

Kenneth W. Morgan, *The Religion of the Hindus,* New York, Ronald, 1953. Hindu faith and practice explained for Western readers by six

Hindu scholars. Also has glossary and extension, *Selections from Hindu Sacred Writings* (130 pages), by a leading Sanskrit scholar.

Jawaharlal Nehru, *Autobiography,* London, 1953. Revealing study by the first prime minister of the Republic of India. Indispensable for a correct understanding of modern Hinduism.

Swami Prabhavananda and Christopher Isherwood, *Bhagavad-Gita,* New York, Harper, 1959. An interpretative translation of one of the major sacred writings of Hinduism. The most recent critical version is *The Bhagavadgita,* with an introductory essay, Sanskrit text, English translation and notes, by S. Radhakrishnan, New York, Harper, 1948.*

Swami Prabhavananda and Frederick Manchester, *The Upanishads,* Hollywood, Vedanta Press, 1957. Free translation of selected texts from the main philosophical scriptures of Hinduism. The standard work on the subject is *The Religion and Philosophy of the Veda and Upanishads,* in two volumes, by Arthur B. Keith, in the Harvard Oriental Series.*

Sarvepalli Radhakrishnan, *A Hindu View of Life,* New York, Macmillan, 1949. Often reprinted summary of Hindu belief by a native scholar who is well versed in Western thought.*

Sarvepalli Radhakrishnan, *A Source Book in Indian Philosophy,* Princeton University Press, 1957. Carefully selected texts covering the Vedic and Epic Periods, Orthodox and Heterodox Systems, and Contemporary Thought. Thirty pages of bibliography.

Louis Renou, *Hinduism,* New York, Braziller, 1961. After a comprehensive introduction, the leading texts of Hindu scripture and tradition are extensively quoted, correlated and explained.

Vincent A. Smith, *The Oxford Student's History of India,* Oxford University Press, 1951. Fifteen editions of a standard source, beginning with Ancient India and including the latest events. Religious orientation of contents.

Paul Thomas, *Epics, Myths and Legends of India,* Bombay, Taraporevala, 1949. Comprehensive survey of the sacred lore of the Hindus, Buddhists and Jains of India. Authoritative with 268 half-tone illustrations.

Ernest E. Wood, *The Glorious Presence,* London, Rider, 1952. Study of Vedanta and its relation to modern thought.

F. Zacharias, *Studies of Hinduism,* Alwaye (India), J.M. Press, 1945-1950. Five-volume appraisal by a Catholic scholar, based on primary sources.

Heinrich R. Zimmer, *Philosophies of India* (Edited by Joseph Campbell), New York, Pantheon, 1953. Scholarly commentary on Hindu, Jain, Buddhist and related systems.*

CHINA

Wing-tsit Chan, *Religious Trends in Modern China,* Columbia University Press, 1953. Up to date descriptive study.*

H. G. Creel, *Chinese Thought from Confucius to Mao Tse-Tung,* University of Chicago Press, 1953. Compact analysis, using first-hand sources.*

H. G. Creel, *Confucius: The Man and the Myth,* New York, Day, 1949. Critical yet sympathetic treatment, based on scholarly investigation.

John K. Fairbank, *Chinese Thought and Institutions,* University of Chicago Press, 1957. Gathering of studies by scholars on the inner meaning of China's culture, with special attention to its religion.

E. R. Hughes, *Chinese Philosophy in Classical Times,* London, Dent, 1942. Edited studies in Everyman's Library of the traditional and heterodox philosophical systems.

Joseph Needham and Wang Ling, *Science and Civilization in China,* Cambridge University Press, 1954. Definitive study in three volumes of Chinese scientific, cultural and religious history. Maps, illustrations and copious reference sources.

Leo Sherley-Price, *Confucius and Christ,* New York, Philosophical Library, 1951. Balanced appraisal of Confucian thought and organization in the light of Christian theology.

Benjamin I. Schwartz, *Chinese Communism and the Rise of Mao,* Harvard University Press, 1951. Informative essays on the sources of Communist thought in China.

W. E. Soothill, *The Three Religions of China,* Oxford University Press, 1951. Surveys of Confucianism, Taoism and Buddhism; comparative ideas about the Deity, world, soul, morality and ritual.

Arthur Waley, *The Analects of Confucius,* London, Allen and Unwin, 1938. English translation, with critical discussion of Confucian terminology.*

James R. Ware, *The Sayings of Confucius,* New York, New American Library, 1961. Selections from the writings of Confucius, numbered and classified.*

Liu Wu-Chi, *A Short History of Confucian Philosophy,* London, Penguin, 1955. Systematic account of Confucianism as developed by Chinese thinkers from Confucius to modern times.*

Y. C. Yang, *China's Religious Heritage,* Nashville, Abingdon, 1943. Interpretation of Chinese religion from a Christian viewpoint.

JAPAN

Masaharu Anesaki, *History of Japanese Religion,* London, 1930. Basic study by a Japanese scholar. Special attention to moral life and social customs.

C. R. Boxer, *The Christian Century in Japan,* Cambridge University Press, 1951. Documented and readable study of the century (1549-1650) when Japan first received a concentrated Christian influence.

William K. Bunce, *Religions in Japan,* Tokyo, Tuttle, 1955. Reliable and up to date account of the background and present status of Buddhism, Shinto and Christianity in Japan.*

D. C. Holtom, *The National Faith of Japan,* London, Kegan Paul, 1937. Standard authority on Shinto, dealing extensively with state and sect Shinto.

Francis J. Horner, *Case History of Japan,* New York, Sheed and Ward, 1948. Evaluation of the religious, educational, social and political impact of various cultures (Buddhist, Shinto, Confucian and Christian) on the past history and present status of Japan.

Johannes Laures, *The Catholic Church in Japan,* Tokyo, Tuttle, 1954. Scholarly and literary account of the progress of Catholicism from its earliest beginnings to the present day.

Carl Michalson, *Japanese Contributions to Christian Theology,* Philadelphia, Westminster, 1960. Sympathetic treatment of the religious insights furnished by the Japanese to Christian thought, mainly in Protestantism.

J. B. Pratt, *The Pilgrimage of Buddhism and a Buddhist Pilgrim,* New York, Macmillan, 1928. Survey of Buddhist movement from India to Japan. Should be read together with *Japanese Buddhism,* by Charles Eliot, which is the most authoritative study in English (London, Arnold, 1935).

George B. Sansom, *A History of Japan,* Stanford University Press, 1958, 1961. Illuminating treatment of the development of Japanese religion. First two volumes cover the periods from ancient times to 1334, and to 1615; third volume will carry the history to the present.

P. Wheeler, *Sacred Scriptures of the Japanese,* New York, Abelard, 1952. Scholarly textual compilation of sacred writings, chronologically arranged, setting forth the main currents of Japanese religious culture. With 120 pages of reference notes.

BUDDHISM

E. A. Burtt, *The Teachings of the Compassionate Buddha,* New York, New American Library, 1961. Early discourses, the Dhammapada, and later basic writings, edited with commentary.*

Edward Conze (editor), *Buddhist Texts Through the Ages,* New York, Philosophical Library, 1953. Concise and scholarly selection of texts from a broad range of Buddhist thought and history. Also the same author's *Buddhist Scriptures* (an abridgment), Baltimore, Penguin, 1960.*

Charles Eliot, *Hinduism and Buddhism,* New York, Barnes and Noble, 1954. Highly respected three-volume comparative study.

Henri de Lubac, *Aspects of Buddhism,* New York, Sheed and Ward, 1953. Sympathetic comparison of Christian and Buddhist charity, and the differences between Christ and Buddha. Complete bibliography of Buddhist writings available in English.

Richard A. Gard, *Buddhism,* New York, Braziller, 1961. Synthesis of Buddhist history and thought, supported by extensive quotations.

Dwight Goddard, *A Buddhist Bible,* New York, Dutton, 1952. Anthology of texts from Pali, Sanskrit, Chinese, Tibetan and modern sources. Many not available elsewhere in English.

Christmas Humphreys, *Buddhism,* London, Penguin, 1955. The history, development, and present-day teaching of the various schools of Buddhism. Author an Englishman who founded the Buddhist Society, London.*

Kenneth W. Morgan (editor), *The Path of the Buddha: Buddhism Interpreted by Buddhists,* New York, 1956. Eleven essays by representative scholars, including a section on the "Unity and Diversity of Buddhism."

T. R. V. Murti, *The Central Philosophy of Buddhism,* London, Allen and Unwin, 1955. Hindu reconstructs the philosophical core of Buddha's teaching by examining the various schools in India.

Robert L. Slater, *Paradox and Nirvana,* University of Chicago Press, 1951. Study of religious ultimates with special reference to Burmese Buddhism.

Daisetz T. Suzuki, *The Training of the Zen Buddhist Monk,* Kyoto, Eastern Buddhist Society, 1934. Factual explanation of the life and practices of Zen Buddhism.

Daisetz T. Suzuki, *Essays in Zen Buddhism,* New York, Harper, 1948 to 1958. Volumes in three series giving an interpretative, theological and historical review of Zen. Official textbooks included in contents.*

MINOR RELIGIONS OF THE EAST

J. C. Archer, *Sikhs in Relation to Hindus, Moslems, Christians and Ahmadiyyas,* Princeton University Press, 1946. Comparative study from a historical and doctrinal point of view. Centered on Sikhs in India and Pakistan.

Witter Bynner, *Lao-Tzu* (Way of Life According to Lao-Tzu), New York, Day, 1944. Biographical sketch and anthology of poetical works of the founder of Taoism. Companion version by R. B. Blakney, *The Way of Life: Lao Tzu,* New York, New American Library, 1957. The latter has the poetical selections also in paraphrase.*

M. M. Dawson, *Ethical Religion of Zoroaster,* New York, Macmillan, 1931. Defends the title of Zoroastrianism as the oldest or at least the most accurate code of ethics. Summary analysis of moral theory.

J. Duchesne-Guillemin, *The Western Response to Zoroaster,* Oxford University Press, 1958. Critical explanation of teaching and its challenge to Western thought.

J. Duchesne-Guillemin, *The Hymns of Zarathustra,* London, Murray, 1952. Modern scholarly translation of the traditional hymns attributed to the founder of Zoroastrianism. Christian appraisal of the latter and its limitations.

E. E. Herzfeld, *Zoroaster and His World,* Princeton University Press, 1947. Technical study in two volumes of the history, literature and principles of Zoroastrianism.

Chimanlal J. Shah, *Jainism in North India,* London, Longmans, 1932. Documented study of Jainism from 800 B.C. to 526 A.D. Definitive work.

Jagdish C. Jain, *Life in Ancient India As Depicted in the Jain Canons,* Bombay, New Book Co., 1947. Survey of history and religion of early India as reflected in the Jain sacred writings. To be read in connection with *Outlines of Jainism,* by J. L. Jaini, Cambridge University Press, 1940.

Khushwant Singh, *The Sikhs,* London, Allen and Unwin, 1953. Descriptive work by a prominent Sikh scholar, tracing history and teaching, practice and worship of his people. An appendix of selections from the Sikh founder.

JUDAISM

William F. Albright, *From the Stone Age to Christianity,* New York, Doubleday, 1957. Modern classic on the historical process of religion before Jewish times, under the Mosaic covenant, and into Christian times.*

American Jewish Year Book, New York, American Jewish Committee. Annual publication with timely information on American and world Judaism; status in various countries, statistics, current events, organizations, activities.

Leo Baeck, *The Essence of Judaism,* New York, Schocken, 1948. Gives the point of view of "Progressive Judaism." Guide to Rabbinical quotations and other sources.

Salo W. Baron, *A Social and Religious History of the Jews,* Columbia University Press, 1952-1958. Present standard work in eight volumes, with extensive bibliographies, notes, and references to comparative literature.

A. Cohen, *Everyman's Talmud,* New York, Dutton, 1949. An introductory volume for the general reader.*

Isidore Epstein, *The Faith of Judaism: An Interpretation for Our Times,* London, Soncino, 1954. Presentation of the Orthodox position. Companion volume by the same author, *The Jewish Way of Life,* London, Pardes, 1946.

L. Finkelstein, *The Jews: Their History, Culture and Religion,* New York, Harper, 1955. Cross-section of Jewish thought, in two volumes, with more than thirty authors contributing.

Judah Goldin, *Living Talmud,* New York, New American Library, 1960. New translation of one of the treatises of the Talmud, with an introductory essay.*

J. Gottman, *The Philosophy of Judaism,* New York, Meridian, 1960. Systematic analysis of Jewish thought.

Arthur Hertzberg, *Judaism,* New York, Braziller, 1961. Depicts the unity of the Jewish spirit throughout the ages as a religious way of life, expressed in the words of its classic authorities.

A. J. Heschel, *Man Is Not Alone: A Philosophy of Religion,* New York, Farrar-Strauss, 1955. Represents the mystical "neo-Hasidic" trend in modern Judaism.

Midrash Rabbah (edited by H. F. Friedman and M. Simon), London, Soncino, 1939. Ten-volume collection of the ancient Jewish scriptural exegesis directed to discovery in the sacred text of meanings deeper than the literal.

G. F. Moore, *Judaism in the First Centuries of the Christian Era,* Harvard University Press, 1954. Standard three-volume work often reprinted, which should be read in conjunction with J. Bonsirven's

Le Judaisme Palestinien au Temps de Jesus Christ (two volumes), Paris, Beauchesne, 1934.

L. I. Newman, *The Hasidic Anthology,* New York, Bloch, 1934. Valuable collection from the Jewish mystical writers, rarely accessible to English readers.

Talmud (Isidore Epstein editor), London, Soncino, 1935-1948. The Babylonian Talmud in thirty-four volumes plus an index volume. Glossary, notes and introductory explanations.

The Universal Jewish Encyclopedia (Isaac Landman editor), New York, Universal Jewish Encyclopedia, 1939-1944. Ten-volume work, with reading guide and index. Should be consulted along with the older *Jewish Encyclopedia,* New York, Funk, 1916. The latter is more scholarly and fully documented.

Zohar, translated by H. Sperling and M. Simon, London, Soncino, 1931-1934. English version in five volumes of the fundamental book of Jewish Cabbalism, which is the basic source of medieval Judaic mysticism.

ISLAM

Abudullah Yusuf Ali, *The Holy Qur-an,* New York, Murray, 1946. Critical two volume edition of the Koran, in smooth translation, along with the Arabic text and extensive (verse for verse) commentary. Also one-volume form.

Tor Andrae, *Mohammed: The Man and His Faith,* London, Allen and Unwin, 1936. Widely recognized study of the life and character of the founder of Islam by a Western scholar.*

T. W. Arnold and A. Guillaume (editors), *Legacy of Islam,* Oxford, Clarendon, 1931. Documented objective essays on Hispanic Islam, Crusades, Art, Mysticism, Philosophy and Theology, Law and Science, Architecture and Medicine.

A. J. Arberry, *Revelation and Reason in Islam,* New York, Macmillan, 1957. Penetrating analysis of the tension and conflict between faith and reason in Islamic theology.

Carl Brockelmann, *History of the Islamic Peoples,* New York, Putnam, 1947. Narrative type survey of Mohammedan history, with stress on the tie-in between Islamic religion and political movements.

Kenneth Cragg, *The Call of the Minaret,* New York, Oxford University Press, 1956. Answers the question: What are the implications of Islam for the Christian? Sympathetic study of Moslem worship and belief.

Encyclopedia of Islam, Leyden, Brill, 1954 to present. International edition in the process of composition, with text available in English, French and German. Complements the four volume edition, 1913-1938, as a dictionary of Islamic biography, ethnology and geography. Religious history emphasized.

A. A. Fyzee, *Outlines of Mohammedan Law,* Oxford University Press, 1949. Systematic presentation of Islamic laws on marriage, property, social life.

H. A. R. Gibb, *Mohammedanism,* Oxford University Press, 1953. Compact analysis of the history, religious movements, sectarian divisions, and Islamic relations with Christianity.*

H. A. R. Gibb and H. Bowen, *Islamic Society and the West,* Oxford University Press, 1950, 1957. Projected multi-volume study of the impact of western civilization on Moslem culture in the Near East. First volume in two parts covers Islamic society in the eighteenth century.

R. Levy, *Social Structure of Islam,* Cambridge University Press, 1957. Treats grades of society, status of women and children, jurisprudence, moral customs, religious and secular law, military organization and cosmology. Exceptional bibliography.

Kenneth W. Morgan, *Islam—The Straight Path: Islam Interpreted by Muslims,* New York, Ronald, 1958. Essays on Islamic history, faith and culture by scholars from Egypt, Iran, Turkey, Pakistan, China and Indonesia.

Shorter Encyclopedia of Islam (edited by H. A. R. Gibb and J. H. Kramers), Leyden, Brill, 1953. Condensed version of the larger encyclopedia, in about 700 pages.

Wilfred Cantwell Smith, *Islam in Modern History,* Princeton University Press, 1957. Study of the Moslems "in the turmoil of the modern world," with separate sections on Arabia, Turkey, Islamic Reformation, Pakistan and India.

W. Montgomery Watt, *Islam and the Integration of Society,* Northwestern University Press, 1961. Scholarly appraisal of the social implications and impact of Mohammedan principles, as seen in history and projected into contemporary life.

ROMAN CATHOLICISM

Karl Adam, *The Spirit of Catholicism,* New York, Doubleday, 1962. Forceful presentation of the inner vitality of the Catholic Church, its structure and relation to other religious bodies.*

George Brantl, *Catholicism,* New York, Braziller, 1961. Concise analysis of Catholic thought and ideals, woven into the context of the Church's fundamental teachings as illustrated in representative writings.*

A Catholic Dictionary, edited by Donald Attwater, New York, Macmillan, 1958. Standard lexicon of Catholic terms, names, and personalities.*

Celestin Charlier, *The Christian Approach to the Bible,* Westminster, Md., Newman, 1959. Up to date manual on the meaning and use of the Scriptures in Catholic thought and piety.

The Church Teaches, St. Louis, Herder, 1960. Classified collection of documents of the Church in English translation, covering all the major fields of theology, from the nature of God to eschatology.

Henri Daniel-Rops, *Jesus and His Times,* New York, Doubleday, 1960. Scholarly yet easily readable life of Christ, written in modern idiom and with special advertence to present-day Scripture thought.*

Philip Hughes, *History of the Church,* London, Sheed and Ward, 1947 to present. Three volumes to date cover: Christian origins to the Reformation. Lists, indexes and extensive bibliographies. Also by the same author, *A Popular History of the Catholic Church* (including modern times) in one volume, New York, Doubleday, 1962.*

Leo XIII, *The Church Speaks to the Modern World,* New York, Doubleday, 1961. Social teachings of Leo XIII, in lengthy quotations from encyclical letters, introduced and summarized along with the text.*

National Catholic Almanac, Paterson, N. J., St. Anthony Guild. Annual publication summarizing basic Catholic teaching and customs, with up to date information on events and personalities.

Joseph Pohle and Arthur Preuss, *Dogmatic Theology,* St. Louis, Herder, 1948. Treatises in Catholic dogma. Twelve volumes covering major fields: God and Trinity, Christology, Mariology, Grace and Sacraments, Eschatology.

Matthias Scheeben, *The Mysteries of Christianity,* St. Louis, Herder, 1946. Profound study of the implications and expansion of the principal mysteries of Catholicism. Dogmatic logic combined with affective piety.

Frank J. Sheed, *Theology and Sanity,* New York, Sheed and Ward, 1960. Compact explanation of the principal doctrines of the Catholic faith, examined in their dogmatic content and relevance to moral life.

George D. Smith, *The Teaching of the Catholic Church,* New York, Macmillan, 1960. Two volume summary of Catholic doctrine by recognized theologians, arranged in separate treatises, annotated, with marginal guides.

St. Thomas Aquinas, *Selected Writings* (M. C. D.'Arcy, editor), London, Dent, 1939. Also *Philosophical Texts* (Thomas Gilby editor), Oxford University Press, 1951; and *Theological Texts* (Ibid.), 1955.* The *Summa Theologica* of St. Thomas is available in English in three volumes, New York, Benziger, 1948; and the *Summa contra Gentiles* in paperback, New York, Doubleday, 1956.

Twentieth Century Encyclopedia of Catholicism (Henri Daniel-Rops editor), New York, Hawthorn, 1958 to the present. Projected 150 title set of volumes on a wide range of subjects. Last volume in series an index and guide to the set. Translation from the French.

N. G. M. Van Doornik, S. Jelsma and A. Van de Lisdonk, *A Handbook of the Catholic Faith* (The Triptych of the Kingdom), New York, Doubleday, 1962. Comprehensive summary of the main teachings of Catholicism, with theological analysis and moral implications.*

EASTERN ORTHODOXY

Donald Attwater, *The Christian Churches of the East,* Milwaukee, Bruce, 1961. Two volumes, treating in sequence the Churches in Communion with Rome, and the Churches not in Communion with Rome. Doctrine, ritual and practice described in a historical setting.

Francis Dvornik, *The Photian Schism,* Cambridge University Press, 1938. Definitive work from the Catholic standpoint of the origins of the Eastern Schism. Based on manuscript sources and challenges prevalent notions.

Clement C. Englert, *Catholics and Orthodox—Can They unite?,* New York, Paulist, 1961. Informative study of Orthodox teachings and practices, with a realistic appraisal of the differences and similarities between Rome and Eastern Orthodoxy.*

G. P. Fedotov, *A Treasury of Russian Spirituality,* New York, Sheed and Ward, 1948. Anthology with introductory essays of writings by and about prominent spiritual leaders of Russia up to modern times: Theodosius, Sergius, Nilus, Avvakum, Tychon, Seraphim, "The Pilgrim," John of Cronstadt and Yelchaninov.

R. M. French, *The Eastern Orthodox Church,* London, Hutchinson, 1951. Historical survey from Constantine to modern Russia; and topical analysis of Orthodox worship, monasticism, laity and current problems.

Frank Gavin, *Some Aspects of Contemporary Greek Orthodox Thought,*

London, Society for the Promotion of Christian Knowledge, 1936. Orthodox dogmas analyzed from primary sources: the nature of God, Redemption, Grace, the Church and sacramental system.

P. Hammond, *The Waters of Marah,* London, Rockliff, 1956. Appraisal of the present state of the Greek Orthodox Church, against a historical background.

Archdale A. King, *The Rites of Eastern Christendom,* Vatican, Tipografia Poliglotta Vaticana, 1947. Two volume study of the ritual, text and variations among all the rites of the Eastern Churches. Standard source book.

Sydney Loch, *Athos: The Holy Mountain,* London, Lutterworth, 1957. Narrative description of the life and customs of the Orthodox monasteries on Mount Athos, drawn from personal experience.

The Orthodox Liturgy, London, Society for the Promotion of Christian Knowledge, 1954. Text of the liturgy in use by the Church of Russia, together with rubrical directions to the faithful.

Orthodox Spirituality, London, Society for the Promotion of Christian Knowledge, 1946. Written by a monk of the Eastern Church. Penetrating analysis of Orthodox asceticism and mysticism, also compared with Western traditions.

S. Runciman, *The Eastern Schism,* Oxford University Press, 1955. Traces the remote and proximate causes of the breach with Rome. Should be read in conjunction with Rene Guerdan's *Byzantium, Its Triumphs and Tragedy,* London, Allen and Unwin, 1956.

Nicolas Zernov, *Eastern Christendom,* London, Weidenfeld and Nicolson, 1961. Comprehensive treatment of the origins and development of Eastern Orthodoxy by a writer familiar with Western thought. Primary sources used. A smaller work by the same author which treats of the unity prospects with Western Christianity is *The Church of the Eastern Christians,* London, Society for the Promotion of Christian Knowledge, 1942.

Nicolas Zernov, *The Russians and Their Church,* London, Society for the Promotion of Christian Knowledge, 1945. Historical survey from the origins of Russian Christianity to the Church's present status under Communism.

PROTESTANTISM

Karl Barth, *Church Dogmatics,* Edinburgh, Clark, 1949 to present. English translation of Barth's ten volume German work, representing the most influential Protestant writing of the century. Summarized in *Dogmatics in Outline,* New York, Harper, 1960.*

G. K. A. Bell, *Documents on Christian Unity,* Oxford University Press, 1924, 1930, 1948. Three series of collected statements illustrating the ecumenical movement. Include Protestant, Catholic and Orthodox sources.

Herbert Butterfield, *Christianity and History,* New York, Scribner, 1950. Interpretation of historical events and movements in the light of traditional Christian principles.*

John Calvin, *Institutes of the Christian Religion,* Philadelphia, Westminster, 1961. Latest, two volume edition of Calvin's classic work, critically edited and copiously annotated.

J. Leslie Dunstan, *Protestantism,* New York, Braziller, 1961. Closely woven texts of the Protestant tradition, quoted and explained to show the spirit of the Reformation and its perduring influence to modern times.*

Adolph Harnack, *What Is Christianity?,* New York, Harper, 1960. Analysis of the origins and development of Christianity by a dominant figure in modern liberal Protestantism. Should be read with Rudolf Bultmann's *Kerygma and Myth* (same), which follows in Harnack's tradition.

William Hordern, *A Layman's Guide to Protestant Theology,* New York, Macmillan, 1957. Series of essays on modern Protestant theologians, with stress on the American scene.

Winthrop S. Hudson, *American Protestantism,* University of Chicago Press, 1961. Historian's survey of the distinctive features of Protestantism in the United States, from colonial times to the present.

Kenneth S. Latourette, *The Twentieth Century in Europe,* New York, Harper, 1961. Objective, thoroughly documented history of the Roman Catholic, Protestant and Eastern Churches in Europe since the turn of the century. Complement to the author's seven-volume work, *A History of the Expansion of Christianity,* New York, Harper, 1937-1945.

Martin Luther, *Works,* St. Louis, Concordia, 1959 to present. The projected fifty-three volume English translation of Luther's writings, edited by Jaroslav Pelikan, will cover most of his published works. Many will be available in English for the first time.

Robert McAfee Brown, *The Spirit of Protestantism,* New York, Oxford University Press, 1961. Clear and incisive examination of the inner spirit of Protestantism: misunderstandings, catholicity, varieties, affirmations, basic problems and unsolved dilemmas.

Martin E. Marty, *A Short History of Christianity,* New York, Meridian, 1959. Concise review of Christian history from the Protestant viewpoint.*

Einar Molland, *Christendom,* New York, Philosophical Library, 1959. Succinct analysis of the doctrines, constitutional forms and ways of worship of the Christian Churches, especially of those in the Protestant tradition.

Religion in American Life (James W. Smith and A. Leland Jamison editors), New York, Vail-Ballou (Princeton University Press), 1961. Four volume comprehensive review of the impact of religion on American culture. Final volume in two books is a critical bibliography of religion in American life, listing and briefly annotating several thousand titles.

R. Rouse and S. C. Neill, *A History of the Ecumenical Movement,* London, Society for the Promotion of Christian Knowledge, 1954. Definitive study of the efforts to promote Christian unity over the centuries. Exhaustive bibliography, and documented sources.

Paul Tillich, *The Protestant Era,* University of Chicago Press, 1959. Provocative exposition of the thesis that Protestantism needs a new spiritual and social reformation, with the passing of the Protestant era in its historical age.*

Cornelius Van Til, *The New Modernism,* London, Clarke, 1946. Statement of conservative Protestant theology in criticism of liberal movements in Europe and America.

World Christian Handbook (H. Wakelin Coxill and Kenneth Grubb editors), London, World Dominion Press, 1962. Issued every five years as the most comprehensive statistical report on world Protestantism available. Every denomination in every country is fully treated; names and addresses of all Protestant church agencies in the world.

Year Book of American Churches, New York, National Council of Churches. Annual publication which gives statistical and other information on all the Protestant Churches in the United States, along with summary data on other American religious bodies.

OLD CATHOLIC CHURCH MOVEMENT

Nigel Abercrombie, *The Origins of Jansenism,* Oxford, Clarendon, 1936. Studies background and development of Jansenism. Treatment historical and theological.

Theodore Andrews, *The Polish National Church,* London, Society for the Promotion of Christian Knowledge, 1953. Documented study of the origins and growth of the schism under Francis Hodur, which produced the Polish National Church in America and Europe.

Emile Caillet, *The Clue to Pascal,* London, S.C.M. Press, 1944. Sympathetic appraisal of Pascal's role in the history of Jansenism.

Ronald A. Knox, *Enthusiasm,* Oxford, Clarendon, 1957. Comprehensive study, based on first-hand material, of various enthusiast movements in the history of Christianity, with special emphasis on Jansenism and allied developments in the Old Catholic tradition.

C. B. Moss, *The Old Catholic Movement,* London, Society for the Promotion of Christian Knowledge, 1949. Origins and history of the Old Catholic Churches described from the latter's standpoint, with references and quotations from otherwise unavailable sources.

Index

Two forms of index are combined in the following list of terms: the *analytic* type which briefly indicates the meaning of words, or significance of persons and writings, and the *topical* kind that simply indicates on what page the term occurs.

In order to facilitate the use of the index for reference purposes, an effort was made to further classify certain leading ideas, like God and morality, and locate where they appear in the treatment of various religions.

Finally, each of the living faiths is individually indexed under many sub-headings, and thus offers a handy summary of the religion in question.

A NOTE ON THE TYPE

IN WHICH THIS BOOK IS SET

This book is set in Times Roman, a Linotype face created by Stanley Morrison, world-famous typographical authority. It was designed for the London *Times,* which demanded a type face that should be clear and legible, precise but not mechanical, having a high letter but not condensed, of a "color" suitable for any paper or printing process, with character but not with annoying characteristics. The clear, open characters of Times Roman are the secret of its clear printing on any paper, whether it be on the coarsest of newsprint or the finest coated paper. This book was composed and printed by the Wickersham Printing Company of Lancaster, Pa., and bound by Moore and Company of Baltimore. Typography and design are by Howard N. King.